Published by Seymour Books

Authors' website
johnandcelialee.org.uk

ISBN-13 978-1-51722-060-0

Also available as a Kindle ebook
ISBN-13 978-1-84396-350-9

A CIP catalogue record for this
book is available from the British Library

Cover illustration
Portrait of HRH Prince Edward The Duke of Kent (1996)
by Barbara Kaczmarowska Hamilton.
Copyright © Barbara Kaczmarowska Hamilton.

Cover design
Alex Croft

Pre-press production
eBook Versions
127 Old Gloucester Street
London WC1N 3AX
www.ebookversions.com

Photographic credits

The author acknowledges the following copyright holders of the photographs appearing in this work on the pages identified below:

Office of HRH The Duke of Kent, St. James's Palace, London: Nos. 9, 26, 133, 142, 143.

Office of HRH The Duchess of Kent, St. James's Palace, London, granted June 3, 2015: No. 27.

AELTC Wimbledon Tennis Championships, courtesy of Wimbledon Museum. Copyright holders:
Billie Weiss: Nos. 76, 78, 79.
Florian Eisele: No. 64.
Jon Buckle: Nos. 65, 77.
Matthias Hangst: Nos. 66, 67, 68, 72, 73.
Micky White: Nos. 62, 63.
Neal Simpson: No. 75.
Neil Tingle: Nos. 70, 74.
Tommy Hindley, Professional Sport: No. 71.

Aidis Trust: Nos. 42, 43, 44.

Alex Croft: No. 108.

Anglo Jordanian Society, Hampar Narguizian, professional photographer: Nos. 102, 103, 104.

Anmer Social Club, copyright holders: Mr Peter Harris, Nos. 15, 16, 122, 123. Mr Roger Haverson, former Chairman: Nos. 10, 11, 12, 13, 14, 124, 126, 127.

BCS, The Chartered Institute For IT: Nos. 49, 50.

British-German Association: Nos. 51, 52, 53.

British Racing Drivers Club, copyright courtesy of Mr Stuart Pringle: Nos. 85, 86, 87.

Sir Richard Buckley, former Private Secretary to HRH The Duke of Kent: Nos. 27A, 27B and 27C.

Civil Service Motoring Association, courtesy of Cotswold Motoring Museum and CSMA archives: Nos. 30, 83, 84.

Commonwealth War Graves Commission with the kind co-operation of Mr Andrew Fetherston, Archivist and Records Manager: Nos. 144 to 157 (inclusive).

Cranfield University: Nos. 39, 40.

Damon de Laszlo DL: Nos. 28, 29.

de Laszlo Foundation: Nos. 1, 2, 4, 7, 8 encompassing Counter Nos. 5928, 5931, 4117, 5957, 5952, 5957, 5952.
No. 3, encompassing Counter No. 6171, copyright with the permission of the Archbishop of Canterbury and the Church Commissione.
No. 5, encompassing Counter No. 2599, Geoffrey Shakerley @ de Laszlo Foundation.
No. 6, encompassing Counter No. 7827, Jacqueline Hyde @ de Laszlo Foundation.

Duke of Edinburgh's Commonwealth Study Group, Nos. 96, 97, copyright Mr Dhruv M. Sawhney, Chairman, Tenth Commonwealth Study Conference.

Duke of York's Royal Military School: No. 137.
Freemasons: No. 54.

Honourable Artillery Company: No. 135, (published HAC Journal Vol. 44 number 364, June 1967); No. 136, (published HAC Journal Vol. 84 number 472, Spring 2007), courtesy of Miss Justine Taylor,

Kandahar Ski Club, copyright Nick Morgan: Nos. 81, 82.

P G Wodehouse Society, copyright holders Camilla Cazalet: No. 94; Sir Edward Cazalet, No. 95.

Poland and the Polish Hearth Club, copyright holders:
Andrezej Morawicz: No. 98, 109.
Andy Hannath, professional photographer: No. 119.
Barbara Kaczmarowska Hamilton: Nos. 111, 113, 115.
Christopher Malski, Commercial Photographer: Nos. 99, 112.
Henryka Wozniczka, photographer: No. 117.
Lady Belhaven & Stenton: Nos. 100, 101, 110, 116.
Tatiana Roshupkina: 114.

Royal Air Force Charitable Trust, courtesy of Air Commdore (Retired), Tim Winstanley, Director, Royal Air Force Charitable Trust: Nos. 132, 134.

Royal College OF Surgeons, Mr John Carr, photographer, Communications Department, Nos. 22, 23, 24, 25.

Royal Institute of Australia: Nos. 34, 35, 36, 37.

Royal National Lifeboat Institution, copyright holders:
Mr Nathan Williams: No. 90.
Captain Edward McGee: No. 91.
Mrs Marie McGee: No. 92.

Ski Club of Great Britain, copyright Mike Truelove photographer, No. 80.

Stroke Association: No. 17.

The Communications And Public Service Lifeboat Fund, copyright by kind permission of Royal National Lifeboat Institution: No. 93.

The Edge Foundation: Nos. 45, 46, 47.

This book is dedicated to people
everywhere who are carrying out charity and
voluntary work, and helping others.

HRH
THE DUKE OF KENT

A Life of Service

Celia Lee & John Lee

Seymour Books

Contents

Copyright & Credits
Photographic Credits

Foreword by Damon de Laszlo   1
Introduction   3
Author's Note   9

Chapter 1:
His Royal Highness Prince Edward The Duke of Kent   13

Chapter 2: Health Service Charities   27
King Edward VII'S Sister Agnes Hospital
Leukaemia & Lymphoma Research
Stroke Association
Institute of Occupational & Environmental
Medicine, University of Birmingham
Chest Heart & Stroke Scotland
Restore Burn and Wound Research
Myalgic Encephalomyelitis Association (ME)
Watling Hospital Charitable Trust
Watling and District Nursing Home
The Royal College of Surgeons of England
The Royal Society of Medicine

Chapter 3: British Overseas Trade Board   **64**
later **British Trade International**

Chapter 4: Education   **81**
The Honourable Society of Lincoln's Inn
The Royal Society
The Royal Institution of Great Britain and Royal Institution of Australia (RiAus)
Royal Geographical Society
University of Surrey and Postgraduate Medical School
Cranfield University
Cambridge University Scientific Society
London Metropolitan University

Chapter 5: Youth Education,
Work, Disadvantaged and Disabled People   **121**
Aidis Trust
Endeavour Training
Edge Foundation

Chapter 6: Professions, Business, and Engineering   **133**
Part 1: Professions and Business
Association of Men of Kent and Kentish Men
The Institute of Export (IOE) International Trade
BCS, The Chartered Institute For IT
Chartered Management Institute (CMI)
Part 2: Engineering
The Institution of Engineering and Technology (IET)
The Institution of Mechanical Engineers
Royal Academy of Engineering
Engineering Council

Chapter 7: Civic Duties and Religious Trusts   **148**
Borough of King's Lynn and West Norfolk
The Henley Society
British-German Association
Dresden Trust
Canterbury Cathedral

Chapter 8: The Freemasons' Charities   **169**
    Part 1: Who are the Freemasons?
    Part 2: The Great Work of the Freemasons' Grand Charity
    Part 3: Royal Masonic Trust for Girls and Boys
    Part 4: Royal Masonic Benevolent Institution
    Part 5: Masonic Samaritan Fund
    Part 6: Grants made to other charities
    Part 7: Disaster relief grants

Chapter 9: Prince Edward's Music
Patronages and his taste in music   **186**
Royal Choral Society
Trinity Laban Conservatoire of Music and Dance
London Philharmonic Orchestra
King's Lynn Festival and Centre for Arts
South Bank Centre
International Musicians Seminar Prussia Cove
Wigmore Hall
Opera North
Hanover Band
European Union Baroque Orchestra
Mendelssohn Society
Royal Opera House

Chapter 10: Wimbledon Tennis Championships   **219**
    Part 1: Introduction and Brief History
    Part 2: All England Lawn Tennis & Croquet Club
    Part 3: A New Millennium
    Part 4: Wimbledon Tennis Finals Winners, Year 2013

Chapter 11: Sport   **261**
Ski Club of Great Britain
Kandahar Ski Club
Army Winter Sports Association
Civil Service Motoring Association
Institute of Advanced Motoring Trust
incorporating the Automobile Association Motoring Trust
British Racing Drivers' Club
Band of Brothers Cricket Club
Kent County Cricket Club

**Chapter 12: Royal National Lifeboat Institution and
The Communications and Public Service Lifeboat Fund**   **280**
    Part 1: The RNLI – Who they are and what they do
    Part 2: The modern-day RNLI
    Part 3: International Development
    Part 4: The Communications & Public
    Service Lifeboat Fund

Chapter 13: Art, Drama, Literature, and Photography   **323**
The Catalogue Raisonné of Works by Philip de László
P G Wodehouse Society (UK)
The Noël Coward Society
The Royal Photographic Society of Great Britain

**Chapter 14: Commonwealth and
International Organisations and Overseas Visits**   **338**

    Part 1: The Duke of Edinburgh's Commonwealth
        Study Conferences and CSCLeaders
    Part 2: The Special Relationship with Poland
        Anglo-Jordanian Society
        Visit to Uganda 2012
        Visit to Ascension Island 2012
        Visit to the Falkland Islands 2012

Chapter 15: Worshipful Companies and Guilds   **391**

Worshipful Company of Mercers
Worshipful Company of Salters
Worshipful Company of Clothworkers
The Worshipful Society of Apothecaries of London
Worshipful Company of Engineers
The British Menswear Guild

Chapter 16: London Clubs   **402**

The Travellers Club
Boodle's Club
Buck's Club
Cavalry and Guards Club
The 'In & Out' Naval & Military Club
The Turf Club
The Army & Navy ('The Rag') Club
Polish Hearth Club (Ognisko Polskie)

Chapter 17: Country Pursuits   **427**

The Tree Council
Sir Peter Scott Commemorative Expedition
Anmer Social Club

Royal West Norfolk Golf Club
The Norfolk Club
The Royal & Ancient Golf Club of St. Andrews
Keighley & Worth Valley Railway Preservation Society

Chapter 18: The Royal Air Force and their Charities   449
RAF Leuchars
Guild of Air Pilots & Air Navigators
Royal Aeronautical Society
RAF Club
RAF Benevolent Fund
RAF Charitable Trust

Chapter 19: Military and Related Organisations   **459**
Honourable Artillery Company
The Duke of York's Royal Military School
Royal United Services Institute for
Defence and Security Studies (RUSI) and RUSI International
Wellington College
The Scout Association
The Tank Museum
Imperial War Museums
The Society for Army Historical Research
Combined Cavalry Old Comrades Association
The Gallantry Medallists' League
Bletchley Park Trust
National Army Museum
The Chelsea Pensioners Appeal, The Royal Hospital Chelsea

Chapter 20: Commonwealth War Graves Commission   **509**

Chapter 21: Prince Edward's Military Career   532

The Royal Scots Greys
The Scots Guards
Scots Guards Colonel's Fund
Scots Guards Regimental Association
The Royal Regiment of Fusiliers
The Devonshire & Dorset Regiment
The Lorne Scots (Peel, Dufferin and Halton) Regiment

Sources & Acknowledgements   552

About the authors   562

Foreword by
Damon de Laszlo

It is a great honour to have been invited to write a foreword to this all-encompassing book about His Royal Highness Prince Edward, Duke of Kent, describing the enormous contribution that he has made to our life and times.

Experiencing at first hand his support for the British Engineering Industry, when in 1992 the Duke opened the Munich Electronica Trade Fair, as Chairman of ECIF (the Electronic Components Industry Federation), I showed him round the British stands. His genuine interest and words of encouragement greatly boosted the morale of all the exhibitors.

More recently His Royal Highness agreed to be Patron of my wife Sandra's Catalogue Raisonné of the Works of my grandfather Philip de László. The artist painted the Duke's parents and many other members of his family, as well as Archbishop Cosmo Gordon Lang, who christened the baby Prince Edward in November 1935. We have enjoyed his keen eye and understanding of fine art and it gives us great pleasure to see the images of the paintings in Chapter 1 of the book.

I am sure our appreciation of the Duke's support and enthusiasm is shared by all the charities with which he is involved and hope this book *A Life of Service* will be an inspiration to others to emulate his dedication to good causes.

Byron's Chambers,
Albany, Piccadilly,
London, W1.

INTRODUCTION

HRH Prince Edward The Duke of Kent
A Life Of Service

His Royal Highness Prince Edward The Duke of Kent KG GCMG GCVO ADC(P), is an Aide-de-camp to Her Majesty Queen Elizabeth II, and that is signified by the post-nominal letters ADC(P). Being ADC to the Queen means Prince Edward is a senior officer of the military, appointed to act as the honorary military attendant to the monarch and as such has performed royal duties on the Queen's behalf for over 50 years. Prince Edward has represented the Queen during the independence celebrations in the former British colonies of Sierra Leone, Uganda, Guyana, Gambia, and most recently Ghana for the 50th Independence Anniversary Celebration. He has also acted as Counsellor of State during the periods of the Queen's absence abroad, meaning the Queen delegates certain state functions and powers to him when she is not in the UK or is unavailable for other reasons. In such circumstances, Prince Edward would preside over Privy Council meetings, sign state documents or receive the credentials of new ambassadors to the United Kingdom of Great Britain and Northern Ireland. [1]

Several other honours have been bestowed upon Prince Edward: Knight of the Garter (KG); Grand Cross of St. Michael and St. George (GCMG); and Grand Cross of the (Royal) Victorian Order (GCVO). When Prince Edward was invested and installed as a Knight of the Garter in June 1986, it was rather a nostalgic occasion. He wore his late father's, Prince George's, robes which had been kept since 1923.

Approaching his 80th birthday on October 9, 2015, and long after most people have retired, Prince Edward continues to lead a very busy life of service as Patron or President of charities and organisations which, combined, number over one hundred. His life is one of dedication to duty, and he works hard every day, enjoying only one month's holidays each year in August.

It would have been impossible to include in the book all Prince Edward's duties over the past sixty years, since he joined the army in 1955, and so a sample has been selected for the purpose of this book.

3

Each individual charity or organisation takes centre stage and within it Prince Edward's role is explained. The thinking behind the presentation of the book in this way has been to encourage readers (if they have not done so already) to consider adopting a charity and to contribute to a worthy cause, since charities are largely dependant for their survival upon individual donations.

By way of introduction, there now follows a short summary of each of the 21 chapters of the book.

Chapter 1, explains who Prince Edward is and his position in the British Royal family as a first cousin to Queen Elizabeth II.

Good health and how to achieve it is a topic of discussion on television, radio, and in the newspapers almost daily. Of particular concern is the ageing population and how to care for them and **Chapter 2** is therefore dedicated to health charities.

Cancer is now predicted to afflict one in every two persons. Strokes are present not just in the elderly but much younger people and even children.

The chapter covers Prince Edward's health charities: King Edward VII's Hospital Sister Agnes; Leukaemia And Lymphoma Research Trust; the Stroke Association; The Institute of Occupational and Environmental Medicine; Chest Heart & Stroke Scotland; Restore Burn And Wound Research; the Myalgic Encephalomyelitis Association (ME); Watling Hospital Charitable Trust Watling and District Nursing Home; the Royal College of Surgeons of England; and the Royal Society of Medicine.

One of Prince Edward's major roles for many years was that of representing British trade overseas. He was Vice-Chairman of the British Overseas Trade Board, later International Trade and Investment. This position, discussed in **Chapter 3**, saw Prince Edward travel abroad to represent the British Government in fostering good trading relations with foreign countries and their companies.

Maintaining the education of children and young adults who attend university, and who may study for trades, often continuing into their 20s and even 30s, is of paramount importance as the United Kingdom competes economically with other countries in relation to its position in the world. Featured in **Chapter 4** are the educational establishments: The Honourable Society of Lincoln's Inn; The Royal Society; The Royal Institution of Great Britain and the Royal Institution of Australia; the Royal Geographical Society; the University of Surrey and Postgraduate Medical School; Cranfield University; Cambridge University Scientific Society (SciSoc); and London Metropolitan University.

In **Chapter 5**, three charities are discussed that cater for children, young people and adults who are disadvantaged in some way.

By being able to just blink or move a finger, a severely disabled person can now use modern computers and software to communicate both in speech and in writing. They can learn on-line, work from home, and can shop and make contact with services, friends, family, and support networks. These facilities have been brought about by the Aidis Trust.

Endeavour Training is a national youth and education charity, working with the young, aged 8 to 16 years. Their purpose is to provide developmental opportunities for children and young people.

Edge Foundation campaigns to raise the status of technical, practical and vocational education. They sponsor WorldSkills and the Skills Show to showcase vocational excellence and they also sponsor an Association of Colleges Beacon Award for excellence in practical learning in colleges.

A variety of business and engineering companies are featured in **Chapter 6**.

The Association of Men of Kent and Kentish Men which also has more than equal numbers of women members, promotes a pride in their historic county, educational activities in youth, and possesses a host of other important objectives, not least in sport.

Kent County Show is primarily an agricultural show, presenting farm produce, livestock, and demonstrations of traditional skills.

The Institute of Export represents and supports the interests of everyone involved in importing, exporting, and international trade. They offer a world-renowned suite of qualifications and training.

The objectives of BCS, The Chartered Institute for Information Technology are to promote the study and practice of computing and to advance knowledge and education therein for the benefit of the public.

The Royal Academy of Engineering brings together the country's most eminent engineers from all disciplines to promote excellence in the science, art and practice of engineering.

The Engineering Council is the regulatory body for the engineeerng profession. Prince Edward is on the Advisory Panel of the Mountbatten Medal Award, and he is an Honorary Fellow of the Chartered Management Institute; the Institution of Engineering and Technology; and the Institution of Mechanical Engineers.

Prince Edward's civic duties discussed in **Chapter 7**, are somewhat varied and includes his being High Steward of the Borough Council of King's Lynn & West Norfolk.

The Henley Society arrange visits, lectures, and events for members to enjoy historic and interesting places. They also work to ensure that the highest standards are applied to the future developments of buildings in their town.

The British-German Association exists to promote and strengthen friendship and understanding between Britain and Germany.

The decision was taken in 1985, to rebuild the beautiful, Protestant, Lutheran, Church of our Lady, the Frauenkirche, in Dresden that was destroyed during a Second World War bombing raid, and a Dresden Trust was set up to raise the funds.

Canterbury Cathedral (at time of writing) still needs to raise £7.4 million to provide a Welcome Centre that will offer improved learning, hospitality, and public space. New visitors, including children and families, will be able to join the journey as a programme of outreach to schools and communities unfolds.

Chapter 8 explores the great work of the Freemasons, including education and housing and grants to other charities and worthy causes. With their customary kindness they immediately donated £50,000 to the Red Cross to help the people whose lives have been devastated by the Nepal earthquake of April 25, 2015.

Prince Edward is a lover of music and **Chapter 9** discusses several musical organisations, including the London Philharmonic Orchestra, Trinity Laban

5

Conservatoire of Music and Dance, and the renowned British cellist, Steven Isserlis, who performs at the International Musicians Seminar Prussia Cove, and a host of others.

Chapter 10 is dedicated to the Wimbledon Lawn Tennis Championship finals where Prince Edward has given out the prizes to the winners and runners up for many years. Along with his wife Katherine the Duchess of Kent, he has met dozens of famous international tennis players that have included Britain's Virginia Wade, Scotland's Andy Murray, and the US female tennis stars, Venus and Serena Williams. One of Prince Edward's favourite past times is skiing, and he likes cars (**Chapter 11**). Luckily he is Patron of the Ski Club of Great Britain, the Kandahar Ski Club, the Army Winter Sports Association, the Civil Service Motoring Association, the Institute of Advanced Motoring Trust, incorporating the Automobile Association Motoring Trust, and President-in-Chief of the British Racing Drivers' Club.

Chapter 12 is dedicated to the Royal National Lifeboat Institution. The RNLI saves hundreds of lives on our shores and on the high seas every year in the UK, the Republic of Ireland, and the Channel Islands. Their efforts to assist those overseas involves their International Development programme, whereby they offer assistance in the form of training, and they sell modern, reliable lifeboats to other countries.

Chapter 13 deals with both the intellectual side of life and entertainment, looking, for instance, at art in the collection of paintings portrayed in the The Catalogue Raisonné of Works by Philip de László; the humour and novels of P G Wodehouse as enshrined in the P G Wodehouse Society UK, which provides some light relief when Prince Edward visits in his role of Patron and joins in their festivities; and the plays and songs of Noël Coward, kept alive by the Noel Coward Society, encapsulating warm memories of Coward's friendship with Prince Edward's parents.

Prince Edward is a keen amateur photographer and is an Honorary Member of The Royal Photographic Society of Great Britain.

Chapter 14 marks a return to business, with Part I detailing the Duke of Edinburgh's Commonwealth Study Conferences. Part II explores the Kents' special relationship with Poland, and The Anglo-Jordanian Society, and details the visits Prince Edward made in 2012 to Uganda, Ascension Island, and the Falkland Islands as an example of his official duties.

Chapter 15 provides a brief historical tour of the ancient Worshipful companies located in London, covering such institutions as the Worshipful Companies of Mercers, Salters, Clothworkers, Apothecaries, Engineers, and the British Menswear Guild.

Chapter 16 allows the reader a peek inside the London clubs of which Prince Edward is a member: Boodle's, Buck's, The In & Out, The Travellers Club, The Turf Club, The Army and Navy Club ("the Rag"), the Cavalry and Guards Club, and the Polish Hearth Club (Ognisko Polskie). They each have a unique history and are of cultural and historical significance.

Chapter 17 takes the reader on a stroll amongst charities and clubs situated in or connected with the countryside.

The Tree Council charity is of the utmost importance as trees provide the oxygen we breathe and some of the foods we eat. They also provide shelter, medicine, and tools. Beyond their utilitarian value, trees bring an atmosphere of peace and serenity to our gardens, streets, parks and woodlands, and provide habitats for birds and other creatures.

Prince Edward is a steam train enthusiast. Keighley & Worth Valley Railway Preservation Society is situated in historic Bronte country in Yorkshire. Older style railway carriages and steam trains are very much a serious study and of interest to many people today. As these older, sturdily constructed trains still run perfectly, they are used to transport local people about their normal business and are also a big tourist attraction.

Anmer Social Club on the Queen's Sandringham Estate in Norfolk was the local club of Prince Edward and the Duchess Katherine when they first got married and lived in Anmer Hall. The Club is still thriving today with musical entertainment and bowls matches. The local craft of lacemaking dating to the middle of the 16th century continues to flourish.

Sir Peter Markham Scott carried out an expedition to the beautiful Pitcairn Islands in 1973. Reports were compiled of the geological make up of Henderson Island and the rare specimens uncovered there.

Several golf clubs that are set in beautiful surroundings, are presented to the reader: Royal West Norfolk Golf Club, of which Prince Edward is Patron; Norfolk Club of which he is an Honorary Life Member, and The Royal And Ancient Golf Club of St. Andrews in Scotland, of which he is an Honorary Member.

Prince Edward is a Royal Honorary Air Chief Marshal in the Royal Air Force and holds a number of titles therein, as discussed in **Chapter 18**. The RAF Benevolent Fund has the duty of providing welfare support to the serving members of the RAF. The Royal Air Force Charitable Trust crucially includes the RAF families of charities as potential beneficiaries.

RAF Leuchars of which Prince Edward is an Honorary Air Commodore is primarily responsible for maintaining a Quick Reaction Alert capability, providing crews and aircraft at high states of readiness 24 hours a day, 365 days a year, to police Northern UK airspace and to intercept unidentified aircraft.

The Guild of Air Pilots and Air Navigators exists to bring all pilots and navigators together and is concerned with the technical aspect of flying.

The Royal Aeronautical Society has 63 branches worldwide. Its objectives include the support and maintenance of high professional standards in aerospace disciplines.

Chapter 19 is dedicated to military and related organisations, including educational establishments.

The Duke of York's Royal Military School, of which Prince Edward is Patron, is a state boarding school for pupils whose parents are serving or have served in any branch of the United Kingdom armed forces.

Prince Edward is President of Wellington College, which is a leading, co-educational public school. For many years, Wellington was a college for the sons of military families. Only a minority of the children now have military connections. The first girls were admitted into the Sixth Form during the 1970s.

The stated aim of The Scout Association, of which Prince Edward is President, is to "promote the development of young people in achieving their full physical, intellectual, social and spiritual potential, as individuals, as responsible citizens and as members of their local, national and international communities". A programme is provided to help achieve this aim for young people from the age of six to 25.

The Imperial War Museums, where Prince Edward is President of the Board of Trustees, and The Chelsea Pensioners Appeal of which he is Royal Vice-Patron, are discussed along with other of his patronages: Combined Cavalry Old Comrades Association, the National Army Museum, the Tank Museum, the Honourable Artillery Company, The Society for Army Historical Research, Royal United Services Institute for Defence and Security Studies, the Gallantry Medallists League, and Bletchley Park Trust.

Chapter 20 discusses The Commonwealth War Graves Commission, of which Prince Edward has been the President since February 1970, the fourth in an unbroken line of royal princes to hold that post since its foundation in 1917. With his close personal links to the British Army, and a profound interest in military history, Prince Edward invests a huge amount of time advancing the work of the CWGC and boosting the morale of its workers around the world. Combining this work with his many other overseas duties, he seems to have been conscious of leaving as small a carbon footprint as possible, long before this concept became of general concern.

Chapter 21 reminds us that Prince Edward was a professional soldier in the British Army for 21 years, serving as a regimental officer in the Royal Scots Greys (later the Royal Scots Dragoon Guards) and in some important staff roles. Upon his retirement he was made an Honorary Field Marshal and continues to represent the Army every year at a number of functions, most notably around the Armistice events each November.

He retains his close association with the army as Deputy Colonel-in-Chief of the Royal Scots Dragoon Guards; Colonel of the Scots Guards (and Patron of their Regimental Association); Colonel-in-Chief of the Royal Regiment of Fusiliers; Colonel-in-Chief of the Devonshire and Dorset Regiment; and Colonel-in-Chief of Canada's The Lorne Scots (Peel, Dufferin and Halton) Regiment.

Endnote to Introduction

[1] There are other categories of aides-de-camp to the Queen. Most are serving military, naval, and air officers, usually of colonel or brigadier rank or equivalent. There are also specific posts for very senior officers, such as First and Principal Naval Aide-de-Camp, Flag Aide-de-Camp, Aide-de-Camp General, and Air Aide-de-Camp each with its own specific entitlement to post-nominal letters. [Source: Mr Nicholas Marden, Private Secretary to His Royal Highness The Duke Of Kent].

Author's Note

I researched and wrote Chapters 1–19 of this book. I also carried out much of the research for Chapters 20-21, written by my husband, John Lee.

The book is a study of the public work of His Royal Highness Prince Edward The Duke of Kent KG GCMG GCVO (P). It is not, therefore, a biography, and it is the first time in the history of the monarchy that such a study has been undertaken.

As a senior member of the royal family, Prince Edward carries out an immense amount of charity and educational work, to which no form of remuneration is attached. One of the reasons Prince Edward often undertakes trips of a most complicated and event-crowded nature is to minimize the expenses involved. The Duke and Duchess of Kent do, of course, jointly receive a parliamentary annuity from the Civil List of £236,000 per annum, for the upkeep of their household and their share of public duties.

The book has a triple purpose: the first is to explain to readers the nature of the charities and to say something of how they operate and the service they provide to humanity; the second is to provide some understanding of Prince Edward's role as patron or president or other involvement with the charities; the third and most important aspect of the study is to encourage readers to adopt one or more charities and to contribute to them.

One aspect of the royal family in general that the author has become aware of is that the number of their members available to undertake charity work has diminished over the years. Queen Victoria and Prince Albert had nine children; King Edward VII and Queen Alexander had six children [1]; King George V and Queen Mary also had six children. [2] The traditional line of large royal families was, however, broken when Edward, The Prince of Wales, who was for a short time King Edward VIII, failed to marry young and produce children. He reigned for only 326 days and then, in 1936, age 43 years, he abdicated and married Mrs Wallace Simpson, who was aged 41 and appeared to be past childbearing age.

King Edward's abdication meant that his brother Prince Albert, who took the name of George at his coronation, became King George VI. George was already married to the former Lady Elizabeth Bowes Lyon, (April 26, 1923), and they had only two children, the Princess Elizabeth, born April 21, 1926, who in 1952 became

Queen Elizabeth II, and Princess Margaret, born August 21, 1930.

Queen Elizabeth II married (1947) Philip Mountbatten, Prince of Greece and Denmark. The Queen and Prince Philip, who was given the title His Royal Highness The Duke of Edinburgh after their marriage, had four children: Charles, Prince of Wales, Princess Anne, The Princess Royal, Prince Andrew, 8th Duke of York, and Prince Edward, 1st Earl of Wessex.

Due to the breakdown of the marriage of Charles, The Prince of Wales and his wife Diana, Princess of Wales, they had only two children, the Princes William and Harry. William has married only recently in 2011, Miss Catherine Middleton. Their first child, Prince George, was born to the Duke and Duchess of Cambridge, July 22, 2013, and their second child, Princess Charlotte was born on May 2, 2015. It will be about 18 years before Prince George can carry out royal engagements, including charity work and 20 before his sister Princess Charlotte can do likewise.

As Prince Harry has not yet married it will be many years before his children will carry out official engagements.

In the meantime, vast numbers of charities and like organisations continue to come into being. The numbers increase yearly, and many of them would be pleased to have a member of the royal family as their patron or president. As we shall see in the chapters in this book the role of that person in relation to the charities discussed therein is quite crucial to them.

Prince Edward carries out significant numbers of engagements yearly; in 2011, he fulfilled 160; in 2012, 148; and in 2013, 137, and it was in the spring of that year that he suffered a mild stroke and was hospitalised. That the numbers of his charities have diminished slightly does not mean that there is less to do.

Given the amount of charity work being undertaken by Prince Edward and other members of the royal family, and with the increase in the number of charities, it would seem that to slim down the monarchy would be a mistake. Since the register of charities was established in the 1960s the numbers of charities have increased at an average of 2,500 per year. In 2010, 4,448 new general charities were registered, and in 2012, the number was 4,200. [3]

It would therefore seem advisable that all the descendants of Her Majesty the Queen and Prince Philip are given the title of His or Her Royal Highness, as it is a compliment to any charity or organisation who are inviting them to become their patron or president if they hold a royal title.

The involvement of a royal patron in any charity or organisation is an uplifting experience. It provides those who work hard to raise funds for worthy causes with a sense of pride and self-worth to have a royal patron who visits them. The royal patron arriving to open the new wing of a care home for the elderly or to participate in an event at a hospital, like the opening of a new wing, is an important experience, and one which many people look back on with pride for the rest of their lives.

The royal family work hard to sustain their charities but we need more of them, not fewer. Titles that have been discontinued may need to be restored. The monarchy is one of Britain's finest assets. No board of directors of a flourishing commercial company would diminish the size of their organisation, they would invest further and expand. It does not make sense, therefore, that our popular monarchy should be decreased in size by the removal of the royal title from their descendants.

In 2010 overseas tourists spent more than £500 million visiting attractions associated with the royal family, according to the British tourism agency. Buckingham Palace, and its inhabitants, is one of the biggest tourist attractions in the world and in the same year, 413,000 people visited the interior of Buckingham Palace, the highest number in sixteen years, and the second highest since 1993. Of the 30 million tourists to Britain in 2009, 5.8 million visited a castle, 5 million went to an historic house, and 6.4 million saw a religious monument. The top most popular attractions were the Tower of London, The National Maritime Museum, the Victoria and Albert Museum, Windsor Castle, and Buckingham Palace.

The authors would take this opportunity to pay tribute to Prince Edward's staff in the offices of St. James's Palace, London. We found them to be most helpful. Our experience there was one of cheerfulness and kindness, and their welcome with cups of hot coffee and biscuits was greatly appreciated when we visited on a cold morning. This book could not have been written without their co-operation.

All the proceeds of this book, which is being published to celebrate Prince Edward's 80th birthday on 9th October 2015, will be donated to his charities.

Celia Lee
September, 2015

Endnotes to Author's Note

[1] Their eldest son Prince Albert Victor The Duke of Clarence and heir apparent died of 'flu on January 14, 1892.

[2] Their youngest son Prince John, died of epilepsy, aged 13, on January 18, 1919.

[3] Figures have been taken from the NCVO UK Civil Society Almanac for the years 2012 and 2015.

*1. HRH Princess Marina of Greece and
Denmark, 1934, later HRH 1st Duchess of Kent.*

CHAPTER 1

HIS ROYAL HIGHNESS PRINCE EDWARD

THE DUKE OF KENT KG GCMG GCVO ADC(P)

On October 9, 1935, Princess Marina the 1st Duchess of Kent, went into labour earlier than expected with her first child. The Kents were then living at their first home, 3 Belgrave Square, London. Downstairs the Fleet Street 'pressmen', as they were referred to in those days, today's journalists, eagerly awaiting news, were assembled in a ground floor room. Shortly before midnight Princess Marina's husband, Prince George, the 1st Duke of Kent, informed them somewhat cheerfully that "hot coffee will be served presently." He then indicated that they might be there for the night, saying: "Someone will be on duty just after six [am] who will get you some breakfast. I do hope it'll be over soon. I don't think I could stand much more of this."

In the event breakfast would not be required for, upon returning to his wife's bedside, at 15 minutes past midnight, Princess Marina gave birth to a baby boy. Prince George who had insisted upon being present throughout, witnessed his infant son coming into the world, which was rare, if not unheard of, for a father in the 1930s.

The new baby was named Edward George Nicholas Paul Patrick. He had been given the first name Edward after George's elder brother, Prince Edward, (referred to in the family as David, and later King Edward VIII), as the brothers were very

13

*2. HRH Prince George 1st Duke of Kent, 1934,
at the time of his marriage to Princess Marina.*

close. Prince Edward was the grandson of the monarch, his surname was Windsor, and he was a first cousin to the Princesses Elizabeth and Margaret. When the nanny wheeled baby Prince Edward out into Belgrave Square there were crowds waiting to see him. [1]

Prince George The Duke of Kent was the fourth son of King George V and Queen Mary, and was, at that time, fourth in line to the throne. The new Prince Edward's mother, the former Princess Marina of Greece and Denmark was the daughter of Prince Nicholas of Greece and Denmark and the Grand Duchess Elena Vladimirovna of Russia.

Prince Edward, or "Eddie" as the new baby would become affectionately known, was christened in St. George's Chapel, Buckingham Palace, on November 20. The celebrant was The Most Reverend Archbishop of Canterbury, Dr Cosmo Gordon Lang GCVO PC. The Duke of Connaught, who was a brother to the late King Edward VII, was the baby's godfather though, being unable to attend, his son, Prince Arthur of Connaught stood proxy. Prince Edward's godparents were King George V and Queen Mary; Prince Nicholas of Greece and Denmark (Princess Marina's father); his namesake Edward, Prince of Wales, (later The Duke of Windsor); Princess Mary, The Princess Royal (daughter to the King and Queen); and Princess Louise the Duchess of Argyll, who was a daughter to Queen Victoria and Prince Albert.

In 1936 a second child was born to the Kents on Christmas Day, December 25, named Princess Alexandra who, in 1963, married the Honourable Sir Angus Ogilvy. On July 4, 1942, Prince Michael was born. In 1978 he married the former Baroness Marie-Christine von Reibnitz, Princess Michael of Kent.

The title "The Duke of Kent" dates back to the 11th century, when King William I conferred it upon his half-brother, Bishop Odo. It was discontinued and

3. Dr Cosmo Gordon Lang,
1st Baron Lang of Lambeth GCVO PC,
Archbishop of Canterbury, 1937.

at the end of the 18th century, when it was given to Queen Victoria's father, also named Edward but was again discontinued. The title was revived again, when, in 1934, Prince George married Princess Marina, at which time King George V bestowed upon his son the prestigious title of the 1st Duke of Kent.

Soon after Prince Edward was born a crisis took place in the monarchy. His grandfather, King George V, died in January 1936, and his eldest son and heir apparent, succeeded to the throne as King Edward VIII. By December of that year, however, to the dismay of the Royal Family, the British Parliament, and the country at large, the new King abdicated to marry the twice-divorced American, Mrs Wallis Simpson. The late King's second son, Prince Albert, (Bertie), who was married to Lady Elizabeth Bowes Lyon, became King, taking the title King George VI, and his wife became Queen Consort.

A further crisis was to develop in the young Prince Edward's life with the death of his father at the early age of 39 years. Prince George was an experienced pilot, having flown 60,000 miles on active service with the Royal Air Force. After lunch on Tuesday August 25, 1942, Prince George and fourteen fellow officers set out on active service to fly to 'the frozen north', as Prince George referred to his proposed destination of Reykjavik, Iceland, where they were going to inspect RAF bases. Just after 1 pm the pilot began take-off in a Sunderland flying-boat over the calm waters of the Cromarty Firth at Invergordon, Scotland. The remote Scottish landscape was hilly, and rugged. Because of the calmness of the waters, take off without a tail wind took longer than usual and visibility was poor because of low cloud and mist. All that is officially known is that about thirty minutes into the flight the 'plane lost altitude and crashed into a remote hillside. Two-and-a-half thousand gallons of aviation fuel exploded into a fireball. The flames, leaping up into the sky could be seen for miles around. Fourteen of the fifteen crewmembers on board, including Prince George, died instantly. There was one survivor, Flight Lieutenant Andrew

4. HRH Prince Arthur,
Field Marshal The Duke of Connaught
and Strathearn.

Jack, who was the rear gunner in the 'plane's gun turret, and though badly burnt, he was thrown clear. An elderly doctor, Dr Kennedy, who lived nearby at Dunbeath, and two special police constables, went to the scene and identified the Duke's body. Having been thrown clear, Prince George had suffered a deep gash to his head, but he was still fully clothed in his flying suit and had escaped being burnt. His identity bracelet was inscribed: 'His Royal Highness The Duke of Kent, Coppins House, Iver, Buckinghamshire'. [2] There is no truth in subsequent rumours that the Duke was at the controls of the 'plane and may have caused the accident.

Princess Marina the Duchess of Kent was left a war-widow in the middle of the Second World War (1939-45), at which time she was Commandant of the Women's Royal Naval Service (WRNS). Prince Edward and his siblings were left fatherless, Prince Michael having been christened only two weeks earlier. At the tender age of six years and 10 months, Prince Edward succeeded to the title of the 2nd Duke of Kent. Consequently he was very reliant upon his mother's guidance throughout his early life, and Princess Marina, as she preferred to be known, did a splendid job of bringing up her children on her own. Prince Edward says: "My mother's motto was always that honour, dedication to duty, discipline, and good manners, were of the utmost importance in life." [3] After a short break, duty was all important and Princess Marina continued with her work for the WRNS, until the time of her death in August 1968.

The year after Prince Edward's birth, he had moved with his parents to live at Coppins House at Iver in Buckinghamshire, which belonged to Prince George, his aunt Toria having left it to him in her will in 1936. Set in picturesque countryside on Bangors Road South, the house enjoyed extensive grounds, and had once housed Princess Victoria's model farm. Though not a great house by aristocratic standards of the day, it was a happy family home. Prince George put his artistic and interior designing talents to work, sweeping away the old Victorian facade, and had the

5. The Duchess of Argyll,
née Princess Louise Caroline
Alberta, 1915

5. Prince Nicholas of Greece
and Denmark, 1934.

house decorated in delicate colour schemes with pale pine panelling, and brightly coloured fabrics. The only reminder of the Victorian/Edwardian era was a large bust of King Edward VII that dominated the hallway. There was a dining room that seated fourteen, and two sitting rooms. Prince George and Princess Marina were both musical, a talent they passed on to their son Prince Edward, hence the large music room (see Chapter 9). Prince George would play his Ilbeck baby grand piano or his Steinway. The music room doors opened onto a lovely garden, where he would sit and listen to jazz records whilst Princess Marina, who was very artistic, would sit at her easel painting pictures. Henry 'Chips' Channon, the famous diarist, was a great friend of the family and he and his wife, the brewing heiress Lady Honor Guinness, were frequent visitors. 'Chips' lived at No.5 Belgrave Square, London, next door to the Kent's London home. It was here that the friendship between the two families was struck up and 'Chips' liked to write about what he found there in his diaries.

To return to the 'plane crash, on that bleak afternoon in August 1942, on a lonely Scottish hillside, all that family happiness was shattered forever. At Prince George's death the house became the property of his elder son Prince Edward in his will. His father obviously did not anticipate dying young and had left all his money to Prince Edward invested in a Trust Fund. It meant that his mother was left in genteel poverty. Though Princess Marina was only 37 years old, she never remarried, and was very brave and dedicated her life to her children and her royal duties. As a member of the royal family, with many duties to carry out, Prince Edward would learn his role by his mother's side.

At age eight years, Prince Edward began his education at Ludgrove School, a preparatory boarding school for boys in Wokingham, Berkshire. In 1948 he entered Eton College, near Windsor in the County of Berkshire, and thence to a Baccca-

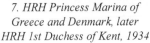

7. *HRH Princess Marina of*
Greece and Denmark, later
HRH 1st Duchess of Kent, 1934

8. *Prince George,*
1st Duke of Kent, 1935.

laureate School, Le Rosey, near Rolle in Switzerland, in 1951.

At age just 16 years, Prince Edward went on his first royal overseas tour. Princess Marina was President of the National Association for the Prevention of Tuberculosis in England and was invited by their Anti-Tuberculosis Association to open a new clinic in Singapore. Other engagements were added until it became a full-blown Far Eastern tour. Princess Marina would visit the Wrens in Singapore and the 1st Battalion, The Queen's Own Royal West Kent Regiment, of which she was Colonel-in-Chief, in Malaya. There would be other official engagements in Singapore, Malaya, Sarawak, North Borneo (now Sabah), Brunei, and Hong Kong.

Prince Edward accompanied his mother and it was as an ideal opportunity for him to learn some of the duties he would later perform as a senior member of the royal family. The entourage included Mr (later Sir) Philip Hay, Princess Marina's Private Secretary since 1948, and Lady Rachel Davidson who was her lady-in-waiting. John Spencer, Viscount Althorp, (later 8th Earl of Althorp) aged 28, who had been equerry to King George VI and lately also to the new Queen Elizabeth II, was seconded to accompany Princess Marina on the trip. Travelling on the same 'plane, the Sunderland flying boat Atalanta, which had taken Princess Elizabeth and Prince Philip to Kenya in February just prior to the death of the King, the party left on Saturday, September 27, 1952, on a five-week tour.

It would be three days before they would reach Singapore. They flew south and east to Rome, stopping off at Cyprus and Colombo. At Bahrain they were received by Sheik Sulman bin Hamed al-Khalifah at his palace in Manama. At Ceylon (now Sri Lanka) the Kents were welcomed by Prime Minister Senanayke that marked the beginning of a 24-hour visit.

As their 'plane approached Singapore, six Vampire jet fighters flew out to

9. HRH Princess Marina,
1st Duchess of Kent, as
Commandant of the WRNS.

10. Anmer Hall on the Queen's Sandringham
estate, Norfolk, first home of their Royal
Highnesses Prince Edward and Katherine The
Duke and Duchess of Kent.

escort it into Kallang Airport. Princess Marina and Prince Edward were the first royal visitors to arrive there in just under 25 years, and they were announced with a 21-gun salute and the reception committee included a guard of honour. Waiting to receive the royal party were John Fearns Nicholl, the Governor of Singapore, and Malcolm MacDonald, Commissioner-General for the United Kingdom in South-East Asia, and the party were driven to Government House. The route was lined by thousands of cheering, flag-waving school children.

Princess Marina visited the Royal Naval base, the Admiralty Asian School, the University of Singapore, and the British Military Hospital, and opened the anti-tuberculosis clinic that had been the original reason for the visit. There were further visits to hospitals, barracks, and an RAF station. A ball at Government House in her honour provided some light relief from royal duties. Possessing a relaxed and cheerful manner, Princess Marina was quite beautiful with a tall, elegant figure and lovely clothes. Walking about amongst the crowds, she smiled and shook hands wherever she went.

On October 5, they flew to Kuala Lumpur where Princess Marina stayed in the King's House whilst Prince Edward stayed with the High Commissioner. They drove through terrain which was subject to terrorist activity, to visit the headquarters of the Queen's Own West Kent Regiment at Kuala Kubu Bharu, forty miles from Kuala Lumpur. Princess Marina carried out an inspection and Prince Edward practised on the rifle range. At Malacca they visited a rubber plantation and feasted on local food.

On their return journey they were in Singapore for Prince Edward's 17th birthday on October 9. The Governor celebrated with a dinner at which Shui Pi Nan Shan soup was served, the name meaning May you Live as Long as the Southern Mountain, followed by eggs that were a thousand years old, and almond chicken. There was a Malay birthday cake and a present of a kris dagger which he was to use to cut it. Whilst waving the dagger around in Malay style, he accidentally touched

11. Church of St Mary   *12. The 15th-century spire*
The Virgin, Anmer, Norfolk.   *of St Mary's Church Anmer.*

his mother near the eye, and blood poured down her face and dress. But Princes Marina had nursing experience during the Second World War and would not have been alarmed by blood. Having been a helper at Iver and Denham Cottage Hospital, she was later a nursing auxiliary nurse at University College Hospital, London, working under the name of Nurse Kay. The dagger wound was very minor and, with a sticking plaster over it and a change of dress, she returned to the party.

On October 14, the Kents attended two garden parties and a youth rally and made some other visits. They flew from Singapore to Sarawak, one of the two Malaysian states of Borneo, where they were met by a barge that took them to the palace that was the former home of the Brooke family Rajahs who ceded the territory to the Crown after the Second World War. They received a warm welcome, attended garden parties and were given presents. A Dyak tribesman showed the Princess a piece of hair he wore on his belt and told her it came from the severed head of a Japanese officer.

In North Borneo Princess Marina carried out the official openings of Marina Barracks, the new Duchess of Kent Hospital, and the new police headquarters.

Arriving in Brunei the royals were carried through the streets in a state litter, rather like a sedan chair, to the Sultan's palace where they were treated to curry and champagne. Inside a canopied dais they listened to a speech by the Sultan Omar Ali Saifuddin.

At the oil town of Seria Princess Marina opened an oil well that was named after her and she had a bottle of champagne smashed against the drill as though she were christening a ship.

The royal party returned to Singapore for a weekend and then went to Hong Kong for a five-day visit, where they found it in the process of post-war regeneration. Princess Marina laid foundation stones, attended dinners, and made visits, and carried out an inspection.

The party left Hong Kong on November 9, and when they arrived at Heathrow a tremendous welcome awaited them. They were met by the Queen, Prince Philip, the Queen Mother, Princess Margaret, and Princess Alexandra. The trip was viewed by the British people, the royal family, and the politicians as a great success. On November 16 a lunch was given in Princess Marina's honour at the Mansion House, London, hosted by Oliver Lyttelton (later Viscount Chandos) who was Secretary of State for the Colonies. It was attended by the Conservative Prime Minister Winston Churchill, the former Labour Prime Minister Clement Attlee, and the High Commissioners for Australia, South Africa, Pakistan and Southern Rhodesia.

Lyttelton proposed the toast to Princess Marina and she replied with her usual modesty emphasising the 'affection which peoples of all races throughout the Commonwealth feel towards the Queen.'

Princess Marina had carried out 69 official engagements and the success of the tour meant that she would again be called upon to go abroad and represent the Queen. On her next tour, to Canada in 1954, she took her daughter, the 17-year-old Princess Alexandra, with her.

Prince Edward entered the Royal Military Academy, Sandhurst, in 1953. During his time there he won the Sir James Moncrieff Grierson prize for French and qualified as an interpreter of French. Prince Edward's knowledge of languages meant that he was particularly adept to the requirements of the Commonwealth War Graves Commission and other overseas travel to countries promoting British business.

It was whilst he was serving with his regiment in Yorkshire that Prince Edward met and fell in love with the lovely Miss Katharine Worsley. But they were soon separated by her tour of the USA. Katharine was the youngest child and only daughter of Sir William and Lady Worsley. They were married on June 8, 1961, at The Cathedral and Metropolitical Church of St. Peter in York. More commonly

13. Sunset on the pond after which Anmer may have been named.

known as York Minster, it was an unusual diversion as all the other royal weddings had taken place in royal chapels. Katharine then became Her Royal Highness The 2nd Duchess of Kent.

Sir Richard Buckley KCVO, who was Prince Edward's Private Secretary for 28 years (1961-1989) remembers the Duchess as a 'fairy tale bride', the Duke was 'devoted to his children' and 'christenings at Windsor Castle were joyous occasions.' [4]

The Kents have three children: George, the Earl of St Andrews, born June 1962, who is married to the former Miss Sylvana Palma Tomaselli; Lady Helen Windsor, born April 1964, who was lately a well-known fashion model, and who married Mr Timothy Taylor; and Lord Nicholas Windsor, born July 1970, who married the former Princess Paola Doimi de Lupis de Frankopan.

Having lived most of their married life in army accommodation, when Prince Edward retired from the army, he and his wife Katharine and the children went to live at York House, in the grounds of St. James's Palace. The palace was a Roman Catholic monastery until the time of King Henry VIII. [5] The complex of buildings adjoins the main road on one side and the Mall on the other and there are no gardens to act as a buffer against traffic, and the Kents found it rather noisy. The Queen granted them a well-deserved grace and favour home, Wren House, in the grounds adjoining Kensington Palace.

Prince Edward's sporting interests include skiing and tennis, and in the past flying, and he is an enthusiastic amateur photographer. At Eton he participated in rowing, which he enjoyed. He likes horse riding and attends the Royal Ascot horse racing event held in Berkshire each year. Ascot is closely associated with the British Royal Family, having been founded in 1711 by Queen Anne, and is located just six miles from Windsor Castle. Prince Edward is President of the All England Lawn Tennis and Croquet Club and gives out the prizes for tennis each year at Wimbledon. He is President-in-Chief of the British Racing Drivers' Club, and is involved in several other sporting organisations.

14. Winter scene at the Anmer Social Club.

Sir Richard Buckley knows his former employer well. While Prince Edward is in constant attendance at State Banquets and at the Cenotaph, he is not on the Civil List. He therefore paid Sir Richard's salary out of his own purse. Sir Richard admires the Duke greatly, and will not see him harmed in any way. 'We act for our principals' is his motto!

Sir Richard says that when they first met the Duke was 26 years old, and Sir Richard was in his early 30s. Sir Richard was a career naval officer and had been teaching a course for lieutenants on Motor Torpedo Boats and submarines at Dartmouth College over a two-year period. Then one day he received a welcome telephone call asking him to take up the appointment as Prince Edward's Private Secretary. He remarked to the authors: 'I was going from teaching young men of the Duke's age to working for one!'

Sir Richard emphasised that the royals are different from other people. Their whole background is one of duty and they are carefully prepared for their role in public life. The Duke he says, is aware of this, but, for him, 'being different is not being better.' He is an under-rated royal and has never been self-promoting. 'He sees his role as to support the monarch.' [6]

A recent instance of how easily and quickly Prince Edward can rise to the occasion was when, in June 2013, His Royal Highness Prince Philip The Duke of Edinburgh was hospitalised for several weeks. As the Queen's Aide-de-Camp, Prince Edward, who is a Field Marshal in the British Army, and Regimental Colonel of the Scots Guards (the Queen being Colonel-in-Chief), was called upon to take Prince Philip's place during trooping the colour on Saturday June 15, which marked the Queen's official 87th birthday. Wearing the scarlet tunic and bearskin of the Scots Guards, Prince Edward accompanied Her Majesty, who wore a stunning, royal blue summer coat and hat, and together they rode in a vintage glass coach to Horse Guards Parade. There, by the Queen's side, Prince Edward took the salute in brilliant sunshine. The Queen and the royal family then assembled on the balcony of Buckingham Palace to watch the fly past by the Royal Air Force. They were joined by Prince Edward and Katherine the Duchess of Kent, looking very lovely and wearing a soft white coat and hat trimmed with a lavender flower.

Of Prince Edward's development from youth into manhood, Sir Richard Buckley observed: 'Look at him at King George VI's funeral. A new image was emerging.' He had been a bit wild with cars as a youth, and 'he would have to grow out of a certain image in the press of the day.' [7] Prince Edward has 'an excellent memory', and a 'great ability to balance his formality with his informality', which comes out well in his role as Grand Master of the Freemasons. 'He has a great sense of humour, and a sense of the ridiculous. He is never rude, or cross, and has never been known to raise his voice.' The former Labour MP, the late Lord George Brown, once wrote a letter criticising one particular instance of Sir Richard's work. 'Prince Edward wrote a formal reply saying that his Private Secretary was "doing his duty".' For Prince Edward, 'loyalty is a two-way street.' [8]

Speaking of him as a former employer, Sir Richard said that Prince Edward 'writes well, and speaks well. Nor is he daunted by large crowds. His command of English is excellent. He was always good at English, French, and Literature. He is

*15. HRH The Duke of Kent presenting the Anmer Social Club
end-of-season prizes for the gentlement's darts competition, circa 1970s.*

very well read, and good at paperwork, handling it quickly and efficiently. He takes decisions firmly and sees everything through. His punctuality is legendary.' [9] As authors of this book we had personal experience of Prince Edward's punctuality. When we lunched with him in 2007 at The In & Out Army and Navy Club at St. James's, he walked in through the front door of the club on the dot of 1.00pm as arranged.

For him, says Sir Richard, it is 'expectation and an obligation – another two-way street.' [10] But Prince Edward is not blinkered in this regard. 'He is aware that overseas visits are very complicated affairs, and that timings can be a problem and on occasion flexibility is needed.' Sir Richard recalled one Commonwealth War Graves Commission visit to France that included 'a stop at a French farmhouse for lunch.' The lunch had been a lengthy affair. 'Officials began to mutter about an aeroplane being kept waiting and about the need to hurry up. Anyone else would have politely skipped desert.' Prince Edward 'quietly said 'No!'. Madame had clearly spent some hours baking the tarte on offer and he intended to eat it and enjoy it', commenting further to Sir Richard that 'the lady would have spent two weeks preparing this special dessert.' [11] It was at moments like this that the authors were mindful of the unique training Prince Edward had received by his mother in relation to the pains-taking efforts women put into baking and cooking, and which she became acutely aware of during her work of many years with the WRNS, especially when she travelled around the country during the Second World War visiting workplaces and kitchens that were experiencing food shortages.

Prince Edward would show consideration on other occasions. Once Sir Richard was due to meet him at RAF Northolt for an overseas visit. The 'traffic was awful' and Sir Richard to his intense regret drove up 'ten minutes late'. Far from being annoyed, this humane Royal Duke simply said: 'I knew you would come'. [12]

Prince Edward's confidence grew over the years. His wife the Duchess Katherine, who was aged 82 on February 22, 2015, has been a good influence over him, with her charming ways and gentle, genuine personality. Describing Katharine as being 'very much a modern duchess and a big fan of Pink Floyd' the English rock band of the 60s, Sir Richard says she was 'a wonderful Duchess and wife.' (She is herself a fine musician). Breaking the ice at formal events and overseas visits, Katharine 'would often make it easier for her husband to fit in. The Duke is very devoted to his wife, and admires her greatly. He is very supportive of the extensive charity works she still carries out today.' [13]

Prince Edward often took up duties once carried out by his parents. One may also assume that the work undertaken by his late father had some influence over him and doubtless was spoken of to him by his mother. When Prince Edward became involved in business and industry and the British Overseas Trade Board, he was to some degree following in his father's footsteps. Prince George had become a Civil Servant, taking up a job at the Home Office as a Factory Inspector on April 12, 1932. He took an interest in working men and his aim was to encourage employers to provide better working conditions for their employees in the factories.

Prince George's duties had included: spot checks on factories without giving the employer prior warning; seeing to the necessity for placing safety guards on machinery; the problems involved of loading and unloading ships at the London docks which processes were prone to accidents; the newly discovered health problems caused by breathing in asbestos dust; the principles of factory ventilation and lights; problems relating to the different branches of the engineering and woodworking industries; and the building industry which had recently amended its code of safety regulations. [14] These are all types of issues that Prince Edward would take up after he left the Army.

Taken together, the influence over Prince Edward by both his parents would shape him into a responsible, caring, diligent, and hard-working member of the royal family who would always put his country and its people first.

16. HRH The Duke of Kent presenting more Anmer Social Club
end-of-season prizes for the gentlemen's darts competition, circa 1970s.

Endnotes to Chapter 1

[1] Hugo Vickers, author of several royal biographies.

[2] Details in part taken from authors' interviews with HRH The Duke of Kent.

[3] Author's interview with HRH The Duke of Kent.

[4] Interview with Sir Richard Buckley KCVO, February 23, 2008.

[5] Interview with Mr Nicholas Adamson LVO, OBE, Private Secretary to HRH The Duke of Kent, (1993-2011).

[6] Interview with Sir Richard Buckley KCVO, February 23, 2008.

[7] Ibid.

[8] Ibid.

[9] Ibid.

[10] Ibid.

[11] Ibid.

[12] Ibid.

[13] Ibid.

[14] Report of Sir Malcolm Delevingne, Permanent Under-Secretary of State to Sir Herbert Samuel, Home Secretary (August 26, 1931-October 1, 1932).

CHAPTER 2

HEALTH SERVICE CHARITIES

In the modern age, good health and how to achieve and maintain it is a very important topical subject and is discussed on television, radio, and in the newspapers almost daily. The National Health Service (NHS), founded in the United Kingdom in 1948, was, and still is, considered the jewel in the crown of progress in standards of health amongst the British people and is admired abroad.

Much of the concern today is of an ageing population, with so many people expected to live to 90 years of age and beyond, due to better food, improvements in medical science and health care, improved quality in living conditions, and the diminishing poverty of earlier years.

Prince Edward who, it will be recalled is now in his 80th year, is still in full-time employment and is concerned with the issues relating to the health of the nation, not least the ageing population. Prince Edward had learnt a good deal about the subject from his mother Princess Marina who was Patron of the Elizabeth Garrett Anderson Hospital and the Chest and Heart Association.

The health care organisations of which Prince Edward is patron or otherwise involved are discussed in this chapter and are as follows: President of King Edward VII's Hospital Sister Agnes, 1969, and President of their Council, January 1, 1973; Patron of Leukaemia & Lymphoma Research, June 1, 1972; President of The Stroke Association, December 1, 1977; Patron of the Institute of Occupational and Environmental Medicine, University of Birmingham, June 1, 1984; President of Chest Heart & Stroke Scotland, September 30, 1990; Royal Patron of Restore Burn And Wound Research (formerly Stoke Mandeville Burns And Reconstructive Surgery Research Trust), January 1, 1994; and Patron of the Myalgic Encephalomyelitis Association (ME), December 11, 1996.

The Royal College of Surgeons elected Prince Edward an Honorary Fellow on October 30, 2002, and he was made an Honorary Fellow of The Royal Society of Medicine on July 20, 2010.

KING EDWARD VII's HOSPITAL SISTER AGNES

A hospital for sick and injured officers was the idea of His Royal Highness The Prince

27

of Wales, the eldest son of Queen Victoria and Prince Albert, later King Edward VII (1841-1910). Known today as King Edward VII's Hospital Sister Agnes it was set up in the main by Miss Agnes Keyser (1852 – 1941) and her sister Frances (Fanny), who were the daughters of a wealthy Jewish member of the stock exchange.

In February 1898, Miss Agnes Keyser had been introduced to the Prince of Wales at a dinner party at the home of his latest mistress, The Honourable Mrs George (Alice) Keppel. In December 1899, Agnes and Fanny Keyser turned their family home, No.17 Grosvenor Crescent, Belgravia, London, which they had inherited from their father, into a hospital for sick and wounded officers who were returning on hospital ships from the Second Anglo-Boer War in South Africa (1899-1902).

Queen Victoria died at 6.30 am on January 22, 1901, and the Prince, or Bertie as he liked to be addressed, became King Edward VII. When Agnes spoke of a name for the hospital the King offered his. He was now much in admiration of the sisters' nursing work and dedication, and he became the hospital's first patron.

Sister Agnes, as she became known, and her staff continued to care for officers in peacetime. In the modern age, care has been extended to all ranks of ex-service personnel. King Edward was a frequent visitor to the hospital, sometimes in the company of Queen Alexander and at others in the company of his favourite Alice Keppel, and they signed their names in the hospital visitors' register.

In 1948, the location of the hospital was moved to its present site in Beaumont Street, London. The world and the hospital have moved on since the humble beginnings of a twelve-bed ward in Sister Agnes' day to the larger and more modern dimensions of today.

Treating war wounds today

With the onset of wars in Afghanistan in October 2001, and Iraq in March 2003, the hospital has again been called upon to deal with major war wounds, including knee injuries and replacements, and also provides physiotherapy. The treatment that is carried out is on contract with the Ministry of Defence, working with Wellington Barracks in London. The Hospital also offers its services, where possible, to members of the armed forces preparing or returning from conflicts. Injured soldiers use the hospital's hydrotherapy pool providing their own physiotherapists. The hospital's facilities are also available to soldiers who have sustained an injury playing sports and who need to get fit for action in a hurry. A range of conditions are dealt with including postoperative rehabilitation, back and neck pain, and broken bones.

Treating general cases

The hospital now caters mainly for general cases. A badly needed Critical Care Unit has been installed, and a new Definition AS+ 128 slice CT Scanner acquired, both funded by The Michael Uren Foundation. The scanner has dramatically improved the hospital's CT service, due to the sub millimetre images and improved area coverage that it provides. The speed of scanning has been enhanced, making it a more pleasant experience for patients. The benefits provided by the new Unit are that patients receive state of the art treatment within the purpose-designed facilities. Dedicated care is now offered to the most seriously ill medical and surgical patients whereas, previously, they would have had to be transferred to other hospitals. Haemofiltration, which is a renal replacement therapy allowing a patient's blood to be cleaned, is available.

Operations are a vital part of the activity of the Hospital. To support this important hospital work carried out by a staff of over 80 surgeons, the Theatre Users Committee meets four times a year. It is made up of 12 surgeons representing major surgical specialties and sub-specialties, two anaesthetists, four senior nursing staff and the Chief Executive, who was for a number of years and until the spring of 2013, Mr John Lofthouse. Mrs Julie Watts, the Theatre Manager is the senior nurse who runs theatres and is supported by an experienced nursing team who are experts in infection control, blood transfusion, running specialist theatre sessions, planning efficient use of theatre equipment and time, through their knowledge of all the various operations and experience gained from working with surgeons in the operating theatres.

The most recent project for safety in theatres is the implementation of the World Health Organisation (WHO) Surgical Safety Checklist. This is designed to ensure that mistakes are not made regarding the wrong side and site of surgery, that allergies are noted, and that the nursing, anaesthetic, and surgical teams all have the correct equipment, medication, and blood for transfusion (if needed), for every procedure. This process encourages close teamwork because the staff working together in each theatre meet before their operating session begins.

Prince Edward opens the new
state-of-the-art Critical Care Unit

Prince Edward became President of the hospital in 1969, and on January 1, 1973, he became President of the Council. He has therefore been a long-term observer of progressive developments in surgical operations and after care.

In January 2009, Prince Edward was briefed on the versatility of the newly installed Agfa HealthCare IMPAX RIS and PACS solutions by Dr Julian Hague, Consultant Radiologist, during the Royal Opening of the hospital's new imaging department. In June of that year, to commemorate the 40th anniversary of his installation as President of the Freemasons' Grand Charity, Prince Edward, on behalf of the charity presented the hospital with a cheque for £50,000.

On November 24, 2010, Prince Edward opened the new state-of-the-art Critical Care Unit, named the Michael Uren Critical Care Unit that was fully funded by a generous £762,000 donation from the Michael Uren Foundation. The purpose-built Unit has four beds, catering for High Dependency and Intensive Care, and offering dedicated, continuous and specialist care. It has been designed to provide ventilation and haemofiltration, a renal replacement therapy, to patients concurrently as well as ensuring optimum hygiene at all times.

Building works had begun at the hospital in July 2010. Early that year, the Michael Uren Foundation, in an exceptionally generous gesture, offered to fund the Critical Care Unit. The Foundation has previously provided donations to the Hospital, including payment for a new CT Scanner in April 2009.

Mr John Lofthouse said:

"It's vital that any patient undergoing surgery at our Hospital knows that they are in the very best of hands. Our new Michael Uren Critical Care Unit means we can care for the most seriously ill patients and avoid the need to transfer to another hospital for specialist intensive care. … we can continue being at the forefront of private healthcare services. We're immensely grateful to the Michael Uren Foundation for its generous donation."

Fund raising

Fund raising for modern, expensive surgery and treatment is a crucial part of the life of the hospital. There are over 4,000 Friends who pledge their support to the hospital's charity. Each year, the hospital's staff sells raffle tickets to raise funds.

The Chairman, formerly Lord Glenarthur, currently Mr Robin Broadhurst, regularly briefs Prince Edward on what has been happening in the hospital, and he is very clearly and genuinely interested. Mr John Lofthouse said:

"During Prince Edward's visits to the hospital and his attendance at our annual Friends' Reception, he always asks questions, listens to answers, and shows real interest in what staff say and in what we are doing.

"I was very impressed when I attended his previous Private Secretary's, Mr Nicholas Adamson's, retirement event at Buckingham Palace, when he remembered my name, apparently unprompted, despite my having only having met him on a couple of previous occasions. He is clearly a genuine and caring man who is very easy to talk to."

Miss Caroline Cassels is Hospital Matron, having first come to the hospital 30 years ago as a Staff Nurse. Caroline was then promoted to Ward Sister before taking on the challenging role of Matron, which she has held for over 20 years. Driven by her commitment to maintaining high standards of quality care and professionalism, Matron remains involved in all aspects of the patient's stay. This hands-on, warm and caring approach, not only for the patients but also for those who work for her, ensures she remains personally involved in the life of the Hospital. Her devotion and hard work were recognised in 2004, when she received the MVO in the Queen's Birthday Honours List. More recently, she was awarded the LVO in the Queen's New Year Honours, January 2014.

Royal admissions 2012/13

The hospital experienced a busy 12 months during 2012/13, with a record number of four members of the royal family having been admitted during that time.

His Royal Highness Prince Philip The Duke of Edinburgh was taken ill with a bladder infection in the first week of June 2012, and spent five days in hospital. He was discharged the day before his 91st birthday, June 9. Leaving the hospital grounds by car and waving as he went, the Duke looked very fit and well, despite his advanced years.

The next royal to become a patient at the hospital was something of a surprise as it was announced by Buckingham Palace to the nation that Her Royal Highness

Catherine The Duchess of Cambridge, wife of Prince William, was expecting their first child and was suffering from chronic morning sickness, *Hyperemesis Gravidarumand,* and was not yet twelve weeks pregnant. To the joy and relief of the nation, Catherine, holding a bunch of delightful yellow roses, and accompanied by Prince William, walked out of the hospital three days later. Clearly, both were overjoyed at the prospect of becoming parents. They brought much happiness to the British people now that another heir to the throne was expecting to be born in July 2013.

The admission to the hospital of Her Majesty Queen Elizabeth II was even more unexpected. The Queen was driven from Windsor Castle on March 3, 2013, and remained in hospital where she was treated for symptoms of *gastroenteritis*. It was her first time in hospital in ten years and the 86-year-old monarch had to cancel an official trip to Italy. Leaving the hospital three days later, the Queen looked very well and, as usual, was smiling cheerfully, and was dressed in a beautiful, bright red coat.

Still the royal visits to the hospital were not at an end. On Sunday March 17, St. Patrick's Day, His Royal Highness Prince Edward The Duke of Kent was himself taken ill, and was admitted to University College Hospital, Euston, London, early that morning. Prince Edward was diagnosed with a mild stroke and remained in hospital for a few days and was then transferred to King Edward VII's Sister Agnes Hospital. He remained there for a short time, leaving on Sunday, March 24, in very good form and was able to resume his official engagements two weeks later.

In February 2014 the staff said farewell to Mr John Lofthouse. Matron became Acting Chief Executive until Mr Andrew Robertson joined the hospital on April 22 as the new Chief Executive.

LEUKAEMIA AND LYMPHOMA RESEARCH TRUST

Every 15 minutes someone in the UK is diagnosed with a blood cancer and it is unacceptable that nearly every hour someone dies from the same disorder.

Leukaemia and Lymphoma Research (LLR) is a British charitable organisation, established in 1960 by the Eastwood family from Middlesbrough, who started raising money, following the death of their six-year-old daughter, Susan.

Why do blood cancer patients need our help?
The LLR says: 'We tend to think of cancer as a disease we get when we are older, but this isn't necessarily true of blood cancer. Anyone of any age from a new-born baby to a grandparent can be diagnosed with one of over 100 different blood cancers. It's the diversity of the disease that makes it so hard to crack, but thankfully we're making more progress in blood cancers than many other cancers. We have grown a comprehensive research portfolio, making sure that the laboratory and clinical work as well as our clinical trials all have improvements for patients in their sight. Every 15 minutes someone in the UK is diagnosed with a blood cancer and it's unacceptable that nearly every hour someone dies.'

There are a number of different forms of cancer:

Lymphomas

Most lymphomas are non-Hodgkin, which can affect any lymph node or related tissue in the body. Hodgkin lymphoma is less common and tends to affect the lymph nodes in the head and neck.

Hodgkin lymphoma, previously known as Hodgkin's disease, is a type of lymphoma, which is a cancer originating from white blood cells called lymphocytes. It was named after Thomas Hodgkin who first described abnormalities in the lymph system in 1832.

Myeloma

Myeloma affects cells called plasma cells, which are also an important part of the immune system. The myeloma cells cluster in the bone marrow, preventing other blood cells from being made and causing serious damage to the bone. They also secrete large amounts of protein into the blood stream that can have detrimental effects on the body, including kidney damage.

Other blood disorders

The other, larger groups of blood disorders are myelodysplasias and myeloproliferative neoplasms but the LLR's work is also relevant to other less common blood cancers.

The blood cancers

There are more than 100 very different cancers. Generally, blood cancers affect the production and function of blood cells.

Most of these cancers start in the individual's bone marrow where blood is produced. Stem cells in one's bone marrow mature and develop into three types of blood cells: red blood cells, white blood cells, or platelets. In most blood cancers, the normal blood cell development process is interrupted by uncontrolled growth of an abnormal type of blood cell. These abnormal blood cells, or cancerous cells, prevent one's blood from performing many of its functions, like fighting off infections or preventing serious bleeding. That is why symptoms can include constant infections, tiredness, and bruising.

Leukaemia

Leukaemia patients produce abnormal white blood cells. These abnormal cells accumulate in the bone marrow and stop other important blood cells being produced. Most of the problems associated with leukaemia are caused by the lack of normal cells in the blood, rather than the leukaemia cells themselves. The various types of leukaemia are defined by the type of white blood cell that is involved. Leukaemias can progress rapidly (acute) or develop slowly (chronic), each requiring a different approach.

Lymphoma

Lymphoma appears as a solid tumour often in the lymph nodes of the neck, chest, armpit or groin. Swollen glands can be a common symptom for other diseases, so up to 5 per cent of lymphoma patients are misdiagnosed each year. People with lymphoma produce abnormal lymphocytes, a type of white blood cell. These are mainly found in the lymph nodes and lymphoid tissues, which make up the lymphatic system. The lymphatic system is the network of vessels that runs throughout the body carrying fluid containing important cells of the immune system.

The LLR is truly a voluntary organisation. Their income is derived entirely from voluntary donations. It really matters to them that they can show you how your money is beating blood cancer.

The vision of LLR is to beat blood cancer. Crucial to their success is research into cancers. In this respect, Leukaemia & Lymphoma Research is a unique organisation and they invest in basic laboratory research with clear potential for patient benefit, as they believe that really understanding blood cancers will enable them to stop them in their tracks. They also invest in translational research to translate the findings in basic research more efficiently into medical practice. Thanks to their considerable investment in both of these areas over the last 55 years, LLR now have sufficient understanding of the biology of blood cancers to invest more in clinical trials.

Young haematologists
All of these areas of research are supported with project, programme and trial grants as well as career development awards to ensure the continuity of career development for young haematologists, thereby ensuring that the talent will be available to continue this research in the future.

MRD test for children
The minimal residual disease (MRD) test for children with acute lymphoblastic leukaemia (ALL), pioneered by their researchers has now been adopted and funded as standard practice by the NHS. The MRD test detects leukaemia cells in the blood to an accuracy of 1 in 10,000 cells, enabling doctors to increase or decrease the intensity of treatment according to each child's needs. It has been so successful that the NHS is now paying for every child diagnosed with ALL in the UK to be given the MRD test as a standard part of their treatment.

Biobank
A biobank is a special store for human biological samples and related information. Biobanks allow researchers to analyse data representing larger numbers of patients than previously possible, and each sample can be used by many researchers in different ways. Biobanks represent a key investment in infrastructure that will significantly support drug discovery and development. Their biobanks catalogue specimens using genetics and other traits, such as age and gender, to enable their researchers to find very specific collections of specimens relevant to their research.

The national biobank for acute leukaemia in children and young adults is an internationally unique resource that places the United Kingdom at the forefront of research into childhood leukaemias. It has already been used to make important new discoveries about how leukaemia develops and can be managed. The Glasgow bio-bank for lymphomas has 8,500 samples from patients in the West of Scotland. Continued investment ensures that the collection is maintained and extended as well as ensuring the facility and associated research is shared.

Prevention
Understanding the causes of blood cancers and how they develop may enable LLR to treat patients before the disease really takes hold. The potential for screening to prevent blood cancer is a long-term goal but one that can clearly deliver the most patient benefit and remove the need for life threatening treatment. The work involves looking at all aspects of prevention, including the role of infections and treatment for a primary cancer, for all blood cancers.

Most common leukaemia
in adults: breakthroughs in research
Chronic lymphocytic leukaemia (CLL) is the most common leukaemia in adults and because of the age profile of the patients it is one of the most difficult to treat, as elderly patients cannot always withstand rigorous treatments. It would be much less risky for the patient if LLR could prevent the division of the CLL cells in the first place. It is known that in CLL the B cells, which are an important part of our immune system, multiply and fail to die. This is because of a protein called MYC that disrupts the cycle of cell birth and death. Professor Graham Packham in Southampton plans to target test drugs to MYC, which may then enable the prevention of CLL cell division. This could lead to clinical trials of new combinations of drugs in the future, which may prevent the development of CLL.

In 2009, 90 per cent of stem cell transplants in the UK were for treatment of blood cancer. Stem cell transplants can still be the only chance of a cure for many patients. When a patient has either a stem cell or an organ transplant, the treatment requires the suppression of the immune system, which leaves the patient at risk from viruses and infection.

Quality of aftercare
LLR's aim is to give each patient the best possible chance of survival, which in some cases will mean controlling the cancer with a good quality of life rather than a permanent cure. Controlling the symptoms of blood cancer and the side effects of anti-cancer drugs will mean better quality of life for patients both during and after treatment. For many patients, having control of their symptoms and a clear treatment plan to manage the disease should it progress is extremely reassuring and helps them to live life to the full.

Early detection
Early detection is critical to a successful outcome for patients, particularly for those with aggressive blood cancer. LLR are now able to diagnose specific types of blood cancer with more accuracy and they can even identify molecular and genetic differences between patients with what appears to be the same type of blood cancer.

**Early symptoms of blood cancers and
consistency and accuracy of early diagnosis**

The National Cancer Action Team have said that consistency and accuracy of diagnosis is probably 'the single most important aspect of improving outcomes in haematological cancers'. The challenges of diagnosing blood cancers include how quickly patients seek help when they experience symptoms, the knowledge and experience of the General Practitioner they visit and the time it takes for diagnosis. Other more specific challenges arise from the fact that many blood cancers are quite rare and initially present with common symptoms such as pain, tiredness, swollen lymph nodes, and breathlessness. They can often be misdiagnosed or there can be a delay in referral to haematology. There are many different types of blood cancer and accurate diagnosis is essential to ensure that the most effective treatment is given. A number of publications have raised concerns about the accuracy of diagnosis and the potentially damaging effect this can have on patient care. Recently this has been addressed in revised guidance from the Department of Health, which specified that the diagnosis of blood cancer should be carried out in specialised centres that are equipped with a full range of diagnostic technology and have access to appropriate expertise. Thanks to research and the availability of better technology, we know that to achieve the best patient outcome, treatment often needs to be targeted to specific molecular abnormalities. This means that it is important to combine results from a range of different tests to get the most accurate diagnosis.

Leeds and Yorkshire

Haematological Malignancy Research Network (HMRN) has unique access to data on patients' entire blood cancer journeys, from pre-diagnosis to prognostic predictions, treatments and outcome. This means HMRN is also uniquely positioned to analyse the effect of new treatments on groups of patients and bring doctors within the network up to date about the likely benefits of new drugs or protocols ahead of National Institute for Health and Clinical Excellence (NICE) guidelines, making patient benefit more immediate. This has exciting implications for Leukaemia & Lymphoma Research, informing health practice to benefit blood cancer patients across the UK.

LLR is already involved in discussions to replicate HMRN in other areas of the country. Based in Leeds and York and encompassing a population of 3.6 million, HMRN covers two cancer networks in Yorkshire which include 14 hospitals and has access to very detailed clinical information on all patients with blood cancer in these areas. This information, which is strictly anonymous, includes GP records, exact diagnosis, treatments received, response to treatments and the outcome for the patient. The demographic of Yorkshire has an overarching profile that closely matches that of the UK, so the data captured can be used to accurately represent that of the whole UK population, making it extremely valuable for informing the development of new treatment initiatives. Each time a patient is suspected of having a blood cancer in Yorkshire, their samples are sent to a central diagnostics facility, called the Haematological Malignancy Diagnostics Service (HMDS), in Leeds. This high-tech, centralised laboratory provides a range of diagnostic methods and is uncovering new sub-types of blood cancers. This blood cancer information is fed back into the HMRN database in York, funded by LLR, and provides a dynamic and highly accurate representation of how many patients are affected by blood cancer in Yorkshire, as well as any changes in incidence that may arise. These are the most up-to-date statistics of their kind in the world and are being used to understand more about how blood cancer affects people across the UK. Linking this clinical data to the genetic data contained in biobanks will provide LLR with an unparalleled understanding of blood cancer.

Targeting treatments to each patient's requirements

Overcoming drug resistance and understanding how to target treatments to each patient's specific disease is key to beating blood cancer. Although treatment has improved, much work is still needed to give each patient a truly individualised treatment that is more effective and less toxic. Removing the need for chemotherapy would change the world for cancer patients and their families, and LLR are doing all that they can to achieve this.

LLR have selected 13 centres around the UK, coordinated by a central hub in Birmingham, to set up more clinical trials in blood cancer, more quickly than ever before. This means that blood cancer patients will have access to trials, wherever they live in the UK. Running trials at all the centres also increases the catchment area, which results in more effective recruitment and quicker results. Clinical trials test new drugs or combinations of drugs in patients, a procedure that is really important because it is the only way to improve treatments for all patients in the future.

Importance of basic research

Basic research is the foundation of LLR's work, and is fundamental to beating blood cancer. Getting to grips with the biology of blood cancer cells and how they differ from healthy cells, as well as how they behave, grow, and interact with the immune system are vital questions that must be answered to progress effective new treatments to prevent and cure blood cancer

Information for patients and health professionals

Information plays a vital role for patients and health professionals. LLR aims to offer relevant, supportive information that empowers patients to ask questions and to take an active role in their treatment.

Community support, branches and fundraising

In the modern digitally connected world of advanced communications we enjoy a wider community that unites people across the country who share common experiences, have similar aspirations, and can offer friendship and support. Sufferers therefore know that they are not alone.

Branches and Fundraising Groups have sprung up around the country. LLR's community is reaching out even further uniting individuals, patient groups, sports enthusiasts, concert goers, Christmas shoppers, companies, in fact everyone with a passion to beat blood cancer. They like to meet in person as well as online, sharing experiences and ideas, and offering support and inspiration to each other.

LLR branches are at the heart of all that they do, providing support and sharing experiences with patients and their families and representing LLR in high streets across the UK.

Changing the world

LLR say: "You will by now have a sense of the extraordinary movement of people who make Leukaemia & Lymphoma Research (LLR) the successful charity that it is today. We believe that we can change the world; it is in our DNA. We started like that back in 1960, when a single family set up LLR, following the tragic death of their daughter from leukaemia. This was our first voluntary fundraising Branch."

Investing in cancer research

Financial uncertainty and a challenging world economy, means that LLR value every pound donated even more. They are in the position of being able to see more opportunities for improved patient benefit than ever before, but also need to make a bigger investment in research. LLR have experience and understanding of the biology of each cancer, the infrastructure through their Centres of Excellence, and Trials Acceleration Programme, and unparalleled talent in their community of researchers. All of these factors contribute to their ambitious plans to make one of their largest ever investments in research in the future. Programme renewals are required which is the research that develops the clinical potential of the laboratory work. They also need to expand the Trials Acceleration Programme to more centres, giving even more equality of access to patients throughout the United Kingdom. They have identified the value of the unique patient insight of their research nurses within the TAP centres and they plan to involve them in shaping key questions for the HMRN about the patient journey. This will also enable LLR to use the patient insight more purposefully at the heart of their decision-making. Using this insight and the evidence of their research, they will develop a policy and public affairs team to identify ways that they can enact policy change to provide more immediate benefit to patients.

President Sir Ian Botham

Sir Ian Botham has been President of LLR since 2003, and is known to millions around the world as one of the legends of English cricket. Sir Ian started participating in sponsored walks for Leukaemia Research in 1985. He was inspired to take action after a chance meeting with a group of children suffering from leukaemia in a Taunton hospital. Having been dismayed to learn they had very little chance of survival, he determined to do all he could to beat this terrible disease. "Beefy" as he is affectionately known, after children's best loved TV personality Guy the Gorilla, has raised vast sums of money for research into childhood leukaemia.

Prince Edward's involvement

Prince Edward has been Patron of Leukaemia & Lymphoma Research since June 1, 1972. Generous donations have been made over the years by the Freemasons' Grand Charity. In March 2007, 60 British vehicles lined up on Horse Guards Parade

Ground to commemorate the Diamond Wedding of Queen Elizabeth II and Prince Philip. All the vehicles were in production in 1947, the year of the royal wedding. They were then driven in a convoy to the Tower of London and displayed on the Wharf. At least a dozen of the vehicles were owned by Freemasons from all over the UK. It was particularly appropriate that Prince Edward, as Grand Master of the United Grand Lodge of England, was present on behalf of the Queen and Prince Philip. Prince Edward tasked the entrants with raising sponsorship for Leukaemia Research and the Stroke Association. Travelling with the vehicles and inspecting them, he talked with every owner. Sponsorship raised £10,000 for LLR.

Prince Edward has brought together his interest in the arts as well as his interest in LLR, by attending a gala event to celebrate the work of film composer and leukaemia survivor Patrick Doyle. At the event held at the Royal Albert Hall, he personally thanked the many people who had given generously of their time including the Director of the show Kenneth Branagh and performers including Jim Carter, Emma Thompson, Judy Dench and Derek Jacobi, as well as Patrick himself.

He has also been a great supporter of the "Calendar Girls", the Women's Institute members who have raised £4 million for LLR since the launch of their first "alternative" calendar in 1999. The charity felt very privileged to have him in attendance at the West End premiere of the "Calendar Girls" stage play, where he met the writer Tim Firth and leading actors.

Prince Edward has also demonstrated his personal interest in the charity by generously giving of his time to meet supporters and researchers involved. Most recently he visited laboratories in Birmingham, one of the LLR Centres of Excellence, to hear about research into Leukaemia & Lymphoma. He also thanked local fundraising Branches and supporters for the vital work that they do. Leukaemia & Lymphoma Research are very grateful for his continued support and great interest in their work.

STROKE ASSOCIATION

Every year, an estimated 150,000 people in the United Kingdom suffer a stroke. That is one person every five minutes. Most people affected are over the age of 65, but anyone can have a stroke, including children and even babies. There are over 1.2 million people living with the effects of stroke in the UK and more than half have disabilities that affect their daily life.

Brief history of the Stroke Association
The Stroke Association is a charity that was originally called The National Association for the Prevention of Consumption and for other forms of tuberculosis. The first meeting of the combined association (NAPT) took place on December 20, 1898, and their President was the Prince of Wales.

A handful of forward thinking physicians, eminent statesmen, churchmen, and academics were present. Over a 60-year period the NAPT provided health education, set up TB clinics, dispensaries, and open-air sanatoriums, and campaigned for better public health. With the early detection of TB, and the introduction of vaccination

17. HRH The Duke of Kent with stroke survivors.

and more modern treatments for the disease, the charity turned its attentions to other diseases: chronic bronchitis, asthma, lung cancer and heart disease. In 1959, it became The Chest and Heart Association and work continued throughout the 1960s with a programme of research, health education, and the publication of a newsletter, providing information and support to patients.

In the 1970s, strokes became more prevalent within the society, and the Chest and Heart Association's work became motivated in the direction of prevention. With help, it was found that people afflicted with disabilities like paralysis and/or loss of speech could be assisted to regain control of the affected area. Valerie Eaton Griffith MBE, pioneered a scheme using volunteers to help people regain their speech and language skills following a stroke.

In 1975, two pilot schemes in Oxford and the Chilterns were expanded under the title of the Volunteer Stroke Service. It is now known as Communication Support, running in partnership with local speech and language therapists and a newsletter Stroke News is published. In 1976, the charity changed its name to The Chest, Heart and Stroke Association (CHSA). On December 1, 1977, Prince Edward became President.

On June 3, 1986, Sir Eric Cheadle launched the National Stroke Campaign. Its objectives included providing information about the prevention and treatment of stroke, raising funds for research, the development of the Volunteer Stroke Service, and expansion of the stroke club network. A target of £2 million in funds was set, and a series of events and fundraising projects took place around the country.

In 1988, four junior doctors were awarded grants to work as CHSA Research Fellows on stroke patients in their hospitals. Clinical fellowships and bursaries are also financed for nurses and therapists, training in stroke research techniques, and careers in stroke services. In July 1988, the first Regional Advice Centre was opened in Southampton, and today there is a network of centres across the UK, which together with the central Stroke Information Service offers a range of support and information services. By the 1990s the charity was undertaking the provision of emotional support and advice to the families of individuals who had suffered a stroke and to victims living alone that is known as the Family and Carer Support Service.

Stroke Association

Chest disease, heart disease, and stroke, accounts for almost six out of 10 deaths in the UK. Stroke patients were therefore the most in need and the charity decided to concentrate on this area, and in January 1992 The Stroke Association was formed. In that year Professor Peter Fentem was appointed to the first Chair in Stroke Medicine in the UK at the University of Nottingham. The Stroke Research Unit there is a flourishing centre of excellence for stroke research, teaching and development of care. The first Life After Stroke Awards ceremony was held that year. Since then, the Awards have extended to the recognition of outstanding courage and achievements of people who have rebuilt their lives following stroke, as well as those who have cared for them with unstinting dedication.

Stroke Association today

Today the Stroke Association is working for a world where there are fewer strokes and all those touched by stroke get the help they need. The charity believes in life after stroke and supports stroke survivors to make the best recovery they can. It campaigns for better stroke prevention and care, and provides funds for research to develop new treatments and ways of preventing stroke.

The internet has proved a valuable means of communication for many, and the Stroke Association offers support and information via its website:

18. Watling Hospital Charitable Trust, Watling & District Nursing Home

www.stroke.org.uk. The charity relies on public donations to continue its vital work.

Scotland and Northern Ireland
The Stroke Association also has a long history of funding research into stroke in Scotland and Northern Ireland. In 2006, Speechmatters, a Northern Ireland charity working with people with aphasia, merged with the Stroke Association. In 2007, an office was opened in Edinburgh. There have been many thousands of stroke survivors in both countries.

The association was further broadened by involvement as a key member of the Stroke Alliance for Europe (SAFE). The Stroke Association provides the secretariat and the Research Project Officer for the 21 organisation strong body operating in 17 European countries.

Main aim of the Stroke Association
The main aim for the Stroke Association into the future is the implementation of national stroke strategies in England, Northern Ireland, Scotland, and Wales, that will improve activity along the whole stroke patient pathway, from prevention and awareness, and throughout long-term care. These measures should take place alongside the development of additional community support services. Currently, the charity runs over 350 local services and works with around 600 stroke clubs, supporting over 65,000 stroke survivors and their families every year.

Medical research is crucial
The Stroke Association has been, and continues to be the UK's key funder of research into stroke prevention, treatment, rehabilitation and long-term community care. Over the last 20 years, they have spent more than £40 million supporting vital stroke research. Medical research is essential to determine the best treatments and

19. Entrance to the Sun Lounge, Watling Hospital
Charitable Trust Watling & District Nursing Home.

20. Sun Lounge at Watling Hospital Charitable Trust Watling & District Nursing Home.

therapies for stroke patients. It also provides the evidence required to convince NHS commissioners to improve clinical stroke services in the UK. During those 20 years, medical research has led to dramatic improvements in the way we prevent, recognise, and treat strokes, meaning more people than ever before can walk out of hospital and return home following a stroke.

Action on Stroke Month

The Stroke Association introduced and runs the UK's first ever national awareness month, which takes place every year in May. Action on Stroke Month was launched in 2012, and has been making waves across communities and in the media ever since. The inaugural day saw Prince Edward open the charity's flagship Life After Stroke Centre in Bromsgrove, Worcestershire. Only a few years on, May is now firmly associated with stroke issues and they have seen the emergence of a stroke community. The charity has secured coverage in national and local newspapers and year-on-year has won extensive support from the BBC. Over the course of the month, hundreds of fundraising and community events happen around the country and as a result, the network of supporters has grown from 1,000 to a thriving community of over 7,000 ambassadors and campaigners. Following the endorsement by the Duke, the Month has won plaudits from stars and leaders such as Kirk Douglas, Julian Fellowes, Sir Alan Ayckbourn CBE, and Karren Brady, who was the first Life After Stroke Awards Patron. For the Stroke Association, Action on Stroke Month goes from strength to strength. It is an ambitious endeavour but the impact has been enormous.

Mr John Barrick, Chief Executive Officer of the Stroke Association had this to say of his experience of working with Prince Edward:

"It always feels like a true team effort, when 'the Duke' (as His Royal Highness is affectionately known within the charity) is involved. We're driven by a passion that isn't always easy to explain, or describe. But the Duke gets it, adds to it, gives it an energy and life force, which I will always remain in much gratitude for.

"I'm always taken aback by how much compassion the Duke creates around him. Mixed in with a gentle energy, sense of humour and calmness, everybody feels at ease and comfortable in his presence. He is thoughtful to help make them feel that way, especially those whose stroke is most apparent. He always takes the time to listen and involve himself with, and for them.

"There's always a glow in his wake, and true to his special commitment to us, he has been by our side at countless gatherings in the years I've been at the helm of the HMS Stroke. He makes it easy for me as CEO, as he is so much more than a figurehead. Like me, his very real passion for our cause is so clearly evident particularly in our private meetings where his knowledge of stroke is truly impressive. Our discussion is always vibrant and well informed, as much by his own keenness of mind and proactive interest in stroke.

"Can a CEO ask for any more from his President? I don't think so."

For more information please contact the Stroke Foundation website: http://www.stroke.org.uk/research/20-years-of-research

21. The Lounge at Watling Hospital Charitable Trust Watling & District Nursing Home

INSTITUTE OF OCCUPATIONAL
AND ENVIRONMENTAL MEDICINE
(UNIVERSITY OF BIRMINGHAM)

The Institute of Occupational Health, University of Birmingham, was founded in 1983, and was officially opened by Prince Edward on November 29. (It is referred to today as the Institute of Occupational and Environmental Medicine). Professor Malcolm Harrington CBE, Director of the institute, took Prince Edward on a tour of the medical services departments and he made further visits to the IOEM over the years, at which times he was updated on scientific progress. On June 1, 1984, Prince Edward was made Patron of the institute.

The institute runs an Occupational Health MSc/Postgraduate Diploma Course. The programme has been established for over 15 years, and more than 200 students from ten different countries have completed the course. It is based on a multidisciplinary approach to tackling a wide range of occupational health issues and is accredited by both the Institute of Occupational Safety and Health (IOSH) and the British Occupational Hygiene Society (BOHS) for graduate membership. It is also recognised by the Faculty of Occupational Medicine (FOM).

To understand progress it is worth going back to 1983, to the early days of the institute. Work was completed on their new building in February of that year. Professor Harrington writing of Prince Edward's visit emphasised that: "A particularly impressive part of that day was our ability to demonstrate the fully-equipped analytical and physical chemistry laboratories." [1] They had received a generous donation of £25,000 from the Birmingham Hospital Saturday Fund, which was matched by a similar amount from the university. They had received computers for use in epidemiological research and the handling of results direct from the analytical

22. HRH The Duke of Kent being admitted as an honorary fellow of the Royal College of Surgeons by the President of the college, Sir Peter Morris, 2002.

23. HRH The Duke of Kent with Sir Peter Morris, President of the
Royal College of Surgeons, and senior members of the college's Council.

chemistry equipment, and were linked to the terminal of the university's computer.

A generous donation from the Edward Cadbury Trust, supplemented by funds from the Arthur Thompson Bequest, and a bequest from the widow of one of the doyens of British occupational medicine, Dr AIG McLaughlin, had enabled them to set up their own library, which included one of the best collections of occupational health texts and journals in the Midlands.

Inauguration of a two-year medical course

The inauguration of a two-year course for doctors and nurses and other health and safety practitioners in preparation for the examination for the Faculty of Occupational Medicine was an important development in the teaching activities of the institute. The most prestigious project at that time involved a survey of offices, committee rooms, and plenary chambers of the European Parliament in the Palace of Europe in Strasburg as European Members of Parliament were unhappy with conditions there. There was a study of airborne micro-organisms conducted by staff at the Brompton Hospital, London, and of respiratory symptoms conducted by staff of Wythenshawe Hospital, Manchester. This was followed by what was considered the most valuable contract of the year which was to provide occupational hygiene and environmental advice to the Public Services Agency of the Civil Service, and to the salvage contractor engaged to demolish a large Ministry of Defence warehouse.

The institute had to make daily measurements to establish hazard levels of air-borne contaminants such as asbestos, lead, cadmium, and beryllium, in the breathing zone of workers, and to advise on the suitability of the protective clothing provided. The publication in 1984 of Occupational Health written by Mr Frank Gill and Professor Harrington provided pre-course reading for AFOM students. Prince Edward visited in 1988, and saw the progress that had been made.

Prince Edward made a further visit in October 1994, as did the Chief Medical Officer of the Department of Health. The success of the institute was by now to be measured in three broad areas: research, teaching, and consultancy, and research was their dominant activity.

Occupational epidemiology was strengthened by the appointment of Dr Tom Sorahan. Members of the institute were becoming key players in the area of work on exposure to non-ionising radiation. Mr Kerry Gardiner was appointed to the head of the hygiene section where research was being developed as an adjunct to epidemiology.

Worldwide, the institute had established itself as a major centre of expertise in occupational health. When Dr Kenneth Calman, the Chief Medical Officer for the Department of Health visited, Professor Harrington and the staff were able to show him their involvement in research issues of national importance, including work on auditing health services, the health care industry, studies of brain cancer, and exposure to electromagnetic fields, as well as research on the chronic low dose effects of organophosphate pesticides.

In occupational toxicology, Dr Len Levy worked on metal carcinogenesis and Dr Steve Faux was involved in the field of fibre carcinogenesis with active collaboration programmes in co-operation with researches in the UK and the US. In occupational psychology, Dr Anne Spurgeon extended the use of computerised neurobehavioural testing on the effects of organophosphate sheep dips, as she is a leading figure in developing strategies for the conducts of such tests within the European Union.

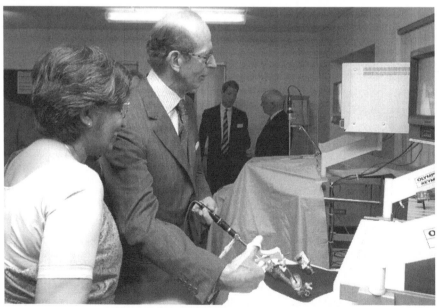

24. HRH The Duke of Kent visiting the Royal College of Surgeon's
Surgical Skills Centre, instructed in laparoscopic surgery by Miss Lelia Kapila.

Research and teaching programmes

The institute's research programme into the health of healthcare workers is on-going, with Mr Stuart Whitaker playing a national role in researching audit programmes for the effective delivery of health surveillance in the employee sector. The teaching programme at both undergraduate and postgraduate levels was developed through the work of Dr Ching Aw. The institute led in the development and delivery of new courses for the Faculty of Occupational Medicine Diploma courses. Dr Steve Sadhra has done an excellent job at furthering the future of hygiene consultancy.

Prince Edward's special interest

Professor Harrington was very impressed with Prince Edward's great interest in a range of work, and having also expressed a particular interest in being kept informed of the proposed collaboration between the institute and colleagues in Public Health and Environmental Health.

Financial and moral support has been vital to the development of the work of the institute as a world-class academic centre. Continued generous support from the National Grid Company and from the Colt Foundation were greatly welcomed and appreciated.

The University of Birmingham sees the institute as an important area of academic activity. The staff of the institute are committed and work hard to maintain standards and retain high quality outcomes. Professor Harrington considers the staff to be the basis of the institute's success.

Ten years of progress - into the 1990s

When Prince Edward visited in 1994, great strides forward had been made. Treating research as "the backbone of academic endeavour" and "the function of an academic department to expand the boundaries of knowledge," [2] Professor Harrington could expound in his 10th Anniversary Report that the institute had extended their work and become an important centre for the investigation of the neuro-behavioural effects of industrial solvents, of occupational-related skin disorders and of lung disorders caused by inhalation of particles. The research into lung disorders was being carried forward by multinational studies across Europe. Studies in epidemiology, notably of occupational cancer, had grown in scope and number. Experimental work in their laboratories had been extended to include tissue culture studies. The field of occupational hygiene had become a research area in its own right.

The National Health Service

The greater part of their medical consultancy is carried out within the National Health Service and therefore no fee is charged.

An Occupational Health Service of the Regional Health Authority was set up to provide a service for the benefit of the employees of the West Midlands Regional Authority which is also the source of occupational health advice and guidance for the 22 health districts within the region. To house the expanding activities a new three-storey building was added.

Tribute is to be paid to the dedicated staff of the institute and to the Birming

47

25. *HRH The Duke of Kent being introduced to Surgical Research Fellows of the Royal College of Surgeons during a visit in 2012.*

ham Hospital Saturday Fund and to the wise counsel and support of Sir Alex Jarratt, Chairman of the Advisory Board and Chancellor the University. Much appreciated direct support was received from Rolls Royce plc and the National Grid Company.

25th Anniversary of IOEM

Prince Edward visited the IOEM on March 18, 2009, as part of the celebrations for the 25th anniversary of the institute's work. The institute's scientists were warning then about a number of emerging environmental health risks, particularly in the developing world, that still remain with us today.

Asthma, cancer, and air pollutants

Occupational medicine at the institute had looked at the effects of work on health, most especially in occupations that can cause asthma or cancer. Work was also ongoing to highlight the importance of rehabilitation, in order to allow staff who had taken time off work for health reasons to return to work.

The institute is a leading centre for the study of human exposure to air pollutants, and measuring environmental health risks in large populations, and is leading the development of the University's overall approach to Environment and Human Health research. Ongoing projects include co-ordinating the first ever long-term study assessing the health risks to workers regularly exposed to radio-frequency radiation, particularly those in the telecommunication and broadcast industries, and work examining daily exposure to pollutant chemicals in the air.

Professor Jonathan (Jon) Ayres OBE, the institute's Director has said:

"Understanding the risks that both the occupational and non-occupational environment poses to human health is still a hugely important challenge. The sources of exposure and the chemicals involved have changed in the 25 years since the institute was founded with a substantial loss of heavy industry and the expansion of service-related jobs.

"Consequently, the methods we use to define these risks are constantly improving to meet the challenge. This means linking new technology that for instance greatly improve our ability to monitor chemicals with studies of large populations, to make clear links between exposure and health risks." [3]

The potential health risk from biomass smoke is one of the emerging environmental health threats. Across the developing world the burning of wood, animal dung, and crop residues is a major source of human exposure to pollutants with women and children being exposed to around 1,000 times higher levels of smoke during cooking than are in the outside air in the City of Birmingham.

Researchers in the institute are investigating these problems in Nepal and Malawi, particularly amongst children and how this translates into future health problems. Professor Ayres said:

"Biomass smoke is a huge health problem globally, causing nearly as much ill health as HIV/AIDS.

"Exposure, particularly in infants is very high across the developing world and this is of particular concern.

"Clearly in many developing countries biomass is the major source of fuel and heat. However, this does not mean that there aren't solutions that would allow us to reduce exposure. This could be as simple as encouraging people to cook outdoors or moving infants away from the source of smoke." [4]

In January 2015, Professor Ayes updated progress:

"Since then, the research activity in the department has continued in the field of occupational asthma, the effect of occupation on patients with chronic obstructive pulmonary disease (COPD, what used to be called chronic bronchitis), and occupational cancers. In conjunction with Imperial College, London, IOEM has developed a new approach to understanding how occupational exposures may cause COPD, and this will be used in the UK's Biobank cohort of 500,000 UK citizens. Their air pollution work has continued both in Nepal and in Hong Kong. They have been involved in the new field of nanotoxicology, assessing the potential for metallic nano-particles from car and lorry engines to have an impact on human health, a study which will have significant policy implications.

"Consequently there are many routes of research in which IOEM will be involved in the future." [5]

CHEST HEART & STROKE SCOTLAND (CHSS)

Mission statement:

"To improve the quality of life for people in Scotland affected by chest, heart and stroke illness through medical research, influencing public policy, advice and information, and support in the community."

The history of the present day charity, Chest Heart and Stroke Scotland, begins in 1899. The main killer diseases during that era were tuberculosis (TB), diphtheria, and scarlet fever. The victims were mainly children and young adults, and the biggest killer was tuberculosis which claimed 7,000 lives each year in Scotland. The situation was addressed initially in a primitive sort of way by a touring horse and cart going around with an exhibition warning people about tuberculosis.

The early charity was named the National Association for the Prevention of Tuberculosis (NAPT), and was formed under the patronage of The Prince of Wales. Distinguished doctors were brought together to work towards the eradication of tuberculosis through education in public health, and to relieve the suffering of those affected. There was then no cure for TB so the emphasis was on prevention of this and other diseases through cleanliness and public health precautions. Thousands were left debilitated and destitute, and with so many adult deaths, children became orphaned. A husband who lost his wife would be left with a family to bring up on his own. A wife who lost her husband fared much worse as the family had lost its breadwinner. Victorians had lots of children, for it was acknowledged that some of them would die either in infancy or in early childhood. There was safety in numbers in so far as at least some of the children were expected to survive into adulthood and become earners, thereby bringing money into the family home.

For the next 50 years, the NAPT addressed itself to raising public health campaigns and developing sanitoria and clinics that were based on the renowned Sir Robert Philip's pioneering dispensary in Edinburgh, supporting individual patients and their families. It was not, however, until after 1948 that the death rate from TB, known as the white plague, was reduced by nearly two-thirds. In the next decade, the introduction of new drugs like streptomycin, para-aminosalicylic acid (PAS) and izoniazid, began to eradicate a disease that had afflicted humanity for at least 6,000 years. The pioneering work was carried out in Edinburgh by a remarkable team under the auspices of Professor (later Sir) John Crofton, who for many years served as a member of the Chest Heart and Stroke Scotland Council.

Meanwhile, the NAPT broadened its scope, incorporating other chronic chest diseases such as bronchitis, and addressing the rising concern over the impact of heart and circulatory disease. In recognition of these developments, the charity changed its name in 1959 to the Chest and Heart Association, adding stroke in 1976. In 1991, they became known as Chest Heart and Stroke Scotland (CHSS).

Prince Edward became President of the Association on September 30, 1990. The Chief Executive today is Mr David Clark MA (Hons), and the Chair of Council is Dr Roger G. Smith MBChB FRCPEd FRCPGlas FRCPLon.

Changes in Scotland's health problems

The progression of change in the CHSS reflects the major changes in Scotland's health problems over the past century. Where once infectious diseases were the main killers, today Scots suffer from high rates of heart disease, stroke, and chronic respiratory illness, although these are now falling steadily due to improved medical treatment and public health.

Increase in the ageing population

The projection by the Department of Work and Pensions that one in six of the present UK population will live to age 100 could amount to as many as 10 million people. The numbers are expected to almost double between 2030-35, with nearly 97,300 centenarians. [6] The health problems associated with an ageing population are set to increase steadily. CHSS is committed to tackling these as they did during the Victorian and Edwardian, and post-First and Second World War eras. CHSS aims to improve the quality of life for people affected by chest, heart and stroke illness in Scotland, through medical research, influencing public policy, advice and information, and support in the community. It is the ongoing developments in public health and medical treatment that have produced a major impact on the improvements in the quality of the lives of ordinary people and it is crucial that the work continues.

Coronary heart disease is one of Scotland's biggest killers; stroke is the main cause of disability in the community; chest illnesses of various kinds are the biggest single reason people use the health service. These stark facts illustrate the challenges facing CHSS. The charity's strategy is to direct resources on a number of fronts.

Research

CHSS funds research into all aspects of prevention, diagnosis, treatment, rehabilitation, and the social impact of chest, heart and stroke illness.

Care and Support

CHSS provides care and support throughout Scotland for people affected by these conditions, as well as their families and other carers. More than 1,200 people affected by stroke, especially those with communication problems, benefit from the Volunteer Stroke Service (VSS), and more than 1,000 volunteers help operate it locally.

Advice Line

CHSS Scotland Advice Line offers a direct link to confidential, professional advice from trained nurses. This is backed up with booklets, facts sheets, DVDs and videos, available free of charge to patients and carers. Health professionals provide specialist advice and training to particular groups with specific needs. More than 100 local chest, heart and stroke clubs are affiliated to CHSS, and the Charity's Community Support Network brings practical help and advice to those whose need is greatest.

Education
CHSS works extensively in schools through the Active Expressions programme of dance-based activities, combined with healthy living messages. More than 50,000 children in 300 schools have taken part.

Welfare
The CHSS welfare grants programme provides direct financial aid to help patients and their families with some of the practicalities of living with a debilitating illness. Specialist Benefits Advice Services are reaching a growing number of those in need.

Funding
To maintain and expand this vital work in research and community services, CHSS relies almost entirely on the continuing generosity of the Scottish public, business, and community organisations. Every £1 sterling raised in Scotland is spent on research and services in Scotland. The main sources of funding include charity shops, of which there are a chain of 24 across Scotland, community fundraising ranging from local community initiatives to high-profile national events such as the famous Forth Rail Bridge Abseil, and the generous support of those who give directly.

RESTORE BURN AND WOUND RESEARCH
(formerly STOKE MANDEVILLE BURNS AND
RECONSTRUCTIVE SURGERY RESEARCH TRUST)

Restore's philosophy is to take the problem to the research laboratory and return the solution to the patient.

Restore Burn and Wound Research specialises in burn and wound research. Known formerly as Stoke Mandeville Burns and Reconstructive Surgery Research Trust, Restore was founded in 1991, as a trust to support research into burns and their treatment. Prince Edward became Patron of the Trust on January 1, 1994, and he takes an active interest in the scientific progress being made. The President today is Sir Desmond Fennell OBE.

Restore is advised by a Scientific Advisory Committee of some of the most highly regarded clinicians in the field in Britain. Research is based at Stoke Mandeville NHS Hospital Trust, an acute hospital, located at Mandeville Road, on the edge of the market town of Aylesbury in Buckinghamshire. The Trust is a registered charity and receives no grants from the government. Former President, Mr Anthony Roberts OBE MA BSc BM BCh FRCS FRCSG, who is a consultant burns surgeon, at that time led the foundation of Restore.

Brief history
The hospital started out in life in the 1830s. The village of Stoke Mandeville was very badly hit by the cholera epidemic that swept across England in the early part of the decade, and so a cholera hospital was established on the parish border between Stoke Mandeville and Aylesbury. It was financed out of monies provided by both

parishes.

By the start of the 20th century the hospital had developed into an Infectious Diseases Hospital, treating all infectious diseases. However, the town of Aylesbury was growing, and the distance between the town and the hospital was getting smaller, and people with infectious diseases could no longer be treated at the hospital because the risk of infecting the local community was too great.

With the start of the Second World War in 1939, the hospital was used to treat military casualties and was expanded to cater for extra patients. It was during this time that spinal injuries were first treated at the hospital.

Stoke Mandeville Games

In 1948, with the founding of the NHS, Stoke Mandeville became the main hospital in Aylesbury. On the opening day of the 1948 Summer Olympics in London, the hospital organised a sports competition for British Second World War veteran patients who had suffered spinal cord injuries. The games were held again at the same location in 1952, and Dutch veterans took part alongside the British, making it the first international competition of its kind. The Stoke Mandeville Games have been described as the precursors of the Paralympic Games. The Paralympics subsequently became a quadrennial event, tied to the Olympic Games.

Hospital developments 1950s to 1970s world centre for paraplegics

Throughout the 1950s, 60s and 70s the hospital was added to extensively, and a new Accident and Emergency Unit was opened. Also, during this period the Ludwig Guttmann Paraplegic Stadium was opened next door to the hospital, making Stoke Mandeville for the first time a world centre for paraplegics and spinal injuries. New wings have been built in recent years to cope with demand. Today, Stoke Mandeville Hospital is the largest acute care Trust in Buckinghamshire, and provides the largest dedicated spinal injuries facilities in the UK.

The Burns Unit

The Burns Unit was founded due to the dreadful injuries that were brought to the hospital during the Second World War. The objective of Restore is to support research into burns and their treatment, and to provide a foundation for innovative reconstructive surgery. The emphasis on research is rooted in the challenges faced by medical staff working with patients in the Burns and Plastic Surgery Unit. Restore's philosophy is 'to take the problem to the research laboratory and return the solution to the patient.' They are therefore one of the first teams to embrace and drive the modern paradigm of rapid translation. To achieve this aim, Restore employs clinicians in the role of Duke of Kent Research Fellows. These individuals can interact with patients and understand the issues facing them and their doctors. Subsequently, they take these problems to some of the major scientific laboratories in the country, including those associated with the universities of Oxford, Manchester, and London. Mr M.P.H. Tyler ChM FRCS(Plast), is Director of Clinical Studies, and more recently medical research is being carried out both by basic scientists and by trainee surgeons.

A two or three year Duke of Kent Fellowships scheme exists, and is offered to some of the country's most outstanding young doctors to continue developing the promising research of their equally talented predecessors. Four individuals, Catrin Griffiths BSc MSC, Fadi Issa MA BMBCh MRCS DPhil, Dan Markeson MBBS BSc (Hons) MRCS, and Hugh Wright BMBCh MRCS, have currently achieved this status through a national competitive interview. Through this scheme and the support of their Scientific Advisory Committee, the Trust's research has advanced significantly, and cost-effectively. Restore-funded research has received national and international recognition.

Recognising the burn and solving the problem

A burn, which only affects the upper layers of the skin, does not leave a scar. However a deeper burn can leave unsightly scarring. The pioneering research has already successfully identified some of the critical genetic and biochemical changes at this deeper level, and Restore scientists are now looking for ways to intervene to block the scarring process. The charity is an international leader in this respect and were the first to identify the critical depth of injury below which scarring is the inevitable and devastating consequence. Further, the ongoing work has established 179 chemical signals or markers within the skin which may provide the clues to how scarring may be ameliorated.

Restore believes that they are on the point of some exciting breakthroughs in this important area of medicine. Other related and vital work includes identifying the stem cells present in burn injuries and the DNA template that is switched on in abnormal wound healing. The next stage is to draw together all these significant strands to establish the network of interactions by which the identified signals trigger a harmful scar. Restore's researchers are thereby enabled to find treatments to eliminate or simply alleviate a painful and disfiguring process which can progress to limit an individual's movement or function.

Events to raise money for Restore

Restore is greatly honoured by having Prince Edward as their Patron. He has made several visits to Stoke Mandeville Hospital, and has been present at presentations of the work at events given by the Royal Society, and the Royal Society of Medicine. A series of events, some of which are annual, are held to raise funds to help finance the research. These have ranged from a cookery demonstration to a trek to Mount Everest Base Camp in Nepal.

In November 2006, at the annual Opera evening held at Milton Keynes Gallery and Theatre, supporters were able to enjoy viewing the work of Mexican artist Carlos Amorales at the gallery during a champagne reception which was followed by Glyndebourne Touring Opera's superb performance of Die Fledermaus by Johann Strauss II.

In May 2007, the Restore Trust was a beneficiary of part of the proceeds of a cookery demonstration presented by Stephen Bulmer of the Brook Hall Cookery School, and which was held in the grounds of Winslow Hall. In October, an event was held at the Royal Society of Medicine in the presence of Prince Edward to launch the charity's new identity, and to present its work. Some of Britain's best-known cartoonists donated original artwork for a cartoon auction to benefit Restore, and seventy lots went under the hammer raising a substantial sum of money.

In November 2008, Amanda Nicholson, a Trustee, and Sally Grant, embarked on a once-in-a-lifetime sponsored trek to Mount Everest's Base Camp, raising a substantial sum for Restore. This challenging undertaking saw them climbing to 18,000 feet above sea level, and braving rugged terrain, including rock-strewn precipices, rope bridges, and icy conditions, in what they rather gallantly described as "a truly unforgettable experience."

In 2009, a Clay Pigeon Shoot took place at Chilton, near Aylesbury, by kind permission of the Lord Lieutenant of Buckinghamshire. In glorious weather they raised £5,000. In that year also, Prince Edward brought the Trust £50,000 that was donated by the Freemasons' Grand Charity.

Restore held a ball in May 2010, at Stowe House, Buckinghamshire. Colourfully named The Scarlet Ball, it is so-called from the time in the 1880s when grand society parties were colour-coded. At Scarlet parties the ladies wore red gowns, and the gentlemen wore a red carnation in their buttonholes. The food, too, was coloured red! The 2010 ball raised the funds for the purchase of a technologically advanced microscope and camera, and the fitting out of a research laboratory. The new microscope would be used in the tissue culture laboratory to identify and record colonies of stem cells. This will aid the comparison of progenitor colonies grown from different sources and is a vital device for high quality investigation.

Ben Renshaw, a marine engineer, had very gallantly removed a bucket of burning petrol from the boat yard where he worked in September 2001, and in so doing, prevented a larger fire. Ben had to undergo major surgery, including skin grafts, after much of his body was badly burned. Ben was in the burns unit for three months but made a full recovery and returned to work. He showed Prince Edward the masks he wore to put pressure on the scars on his face. Prince Edward was "impressed with my progress", said Ben. "He did seem to know what he was talking about. I don't still wear the mask, but wore it as much as I could after the accident happened." By way of saying "thank you" to the hospital, which helped him make such a swift recovery, Ben ran the London Marathon to raise money for the burns unit.

Prince Edward also visited the hospital's Postgraduate Centre, where he listened to presentations on scarring and met five patients in the Occupational Therapy Burns Unit. Later in the evening, he was treated to a charity concert at the Church of St. Laurence in Winslow, which was raising money for the burns unit trust.

Prince Edward attends a seminar
Prince Edward visited Restore again on Monday March 1, 2010, where he spent much of the day. In the morning, he attended a reception and lunched at Hartwell House, where he met Trustees, Vice-Patrons, and a number of supporters and benefactors.

In the afternoon, he visited Stoke Mandeville Hospital where he was graciously received by Sir Henry Aubrey-Fletcher 8th Baronet, the Lord Lieutenant, who presented County and District leaders and Hospital principals.

A special seminar was put on by Restore for Prince Edward and attended by an invited audience in the Sir Henry Floyd Auditorium at Stoke Mandeville Hospital's Postgraduate Centre. Mr Anthony Roberts introduced Mr Mike Tyler, Mr Thanassi Athanassopoulos, Miss Jennifer Kean, and Mr Jon Pleat, who spoke about their research work. Professor Gus McGrouther spoke about the different possible directions for research in the future. The importance of the work done at Stoke Mandeville has been paramount and has received worldwide recognition. In conclusion, Ms Ann Eden, the Chief Executive of Buckinghamshire Healthcare NHS Trust spoke about the importance and value of research to the National Health Service.

Prince Edward graciously consented to appear in a short video introduction to Restore. He was filmed at St. James's Palace in June 2012, and he provided a powerful message of support for the charity and its objectives.

MYALGIC ENCEPHALOMYELITIS ASSOCIATION (ME)

Myalgic encephalomyelitis, commonly referred to as ME, and also known as chronic fatigue syndrome (CFS), and post-viral fatigue syndrome (PVFS), is a complex and debilitating disorder that nearly always follows a viral infection. The disease first came to prominence in 1955, following an outbreak of ME associated with a polio-like illness at the Royal Free Hospital in London. The outbreak was subsequently written up in the world's leading medical journal The Lancet.

Myalgic encephalomyelitis (ME) – sufferers and symptoms

ME affects around 250,000 people in the UK, some of whom are children and adolescents, where it is one of the commonest causes of long-term absence from school.

ME is characterised by profound exercise-induced fatigue and cognitive problems, particularly affecting short-term memory and concentration that do not improve with rest and are made worse by exercise. Other common symptoms include muscle weakness and pain, joint pain, on-going 'flu like symptoms, sore throats and tender glands, patches of numbness and pins and needles, headaches, problems with balance, and temperature control, un-refreshing sleep, and sensitivities to drugs and chemicals.

The symptoms tend to vary in intensity in each individual with around a quarter of all sufferers being in the severely affected housebound, even bed-bound group, at some stage. For many, the illness causes negative social and economic consequences and often results in long-term disability and loss of permanent employment.

Adding to the distress, sufferers sometimes feel polarised among the medical community as to the authenticity of ME, placing them in a very difficult and stressful situation and one that should not occur because it is a genuine illness that is classified as 'neurological' by the World Health Organisation, and fully recognised by the Department of Health as such.

ME-like symptoms can occur in a number of other physical conditions so the diagnosis is not always straightforward and many sufferers report long delays before a diagnosis is made or considered. Proper investigation to exclude other possible explanations is therefore essential.

The precise cause of ME remains uncertain but abnormalities in brain, muscle, the immune, and endocrine (hormone producing glands) systems, have all been identified.

The ME Association and the Ramsay Research Fund

The ME Association is a medical charity that provides information and support to people with ME, campaigns in relation to benefits and service provision, and funds biomedical research into the underlying cause of the illness through the Ramsay Research Fund (RRF). The RRF is currently co-funding a biobank at the Royal Free Hospital in London, where blood samples are being collected, stored, and made available for research purposes and, along with the Medical Research Council is funding a study at the University of Liverpool that is looking at muscle abnormalities.

Prince Edward opens a new clinic

Prince Edward became Patron of the Myalgic Encephalomyelitis Association on December 11, 1996. He officially opened a new National Health Service CFS/ME Service Centre, Wareham Clinic, at Wareham Hospital, Streche Road, Wareham, Dorset, on October 22, 1999.

Launch of new UK ME/CFS Research Collaborative

Prince Edward carried out the launch of the new UK ME/CFS Research Collaborative on April 22, 2013, at the Wellcome Collection in London. The ME Association was represented by the Trustees, Neil Riley, Dr Charles Shepherd, and Nikki Strong. The launch brought together a range of national agencies, ME/CFS charities, and over 70 working researchers in the UK. Their aim is to promote the highest quality of basic and applied evidenced-based and peer reviewed research into ME/CFS. The new research body will look into chronic fatigue syndrome in its different forms.

Five charities are involved in funding the research through a consortium that is supported by the Medical Research Council, the National Institute of Health Research, and the Wellcome Trust. The consortium will set up four work streams and quarterly meetings at which the researchers will liaise with charity funders.

As reported *by* Krishna Chinthapalli in the *British Medical Journal*, 24 April 24, 2013, the new UK-wide Chronic Fatigue Syndrome Myalgic Encephalitis Research Collaborative (CMRC) is being chaired by Professor Stephen Holgate who is professor of immunology at the University of Southampton.

WATLINGTON HOSPITAL CHARITABLE TRUST
WATLINGTON AND DISTRICT NURSING HOME

Watlington Cottage Hospital was opened in 1873, under the auspices of the 6th Countess of Macclesfield and local friends, and was supported financially by voluntary contributions. It became an NHS hospital in 1948. From 1948-56, it was administered by the Oxford and District Hospital Management Committee, and from 1956-1974 by the Nuffield Hospital Management Committee. At that time it was known as Watlington and District Hospital. Responsibility then passed to Oxfordshire Area Health Authority (Teaching) (1974), Oxfordshire Health Authority (1982), and Oxfordshire Community Health NHS Trust (April 1994). The hospital closed in 2000. Local residents, however, were not prepared to see valuable services disappear and it was decided to set up a Care Home in its place.

Watlington and District Nursing Home
Watlington Hospital Charitable Trust (WHCT) was formed in Oxfordshire. Founding Chairman Mr Charles Farrell MC, and the legal, medical, and financial expertise of his co-trustees, have won high praise for the work they put in to progress the new development.

On November 1, 2000, Prince Edward became Patron. Today's Chairman Mr Tom Holden, says: "After enormous efforts by the Trustees and the generosity of the local people, nearly £2 million was raised to purchase the site on which stood the shut-down hospital." WHCT appointed Sanctuary Care to take responsibility for building and running a new nursing home on the site and leased an area for the local General Practice to establish a new surgery. Watlington and District Nursing Home was then set up, and was opened officially by Prince Edward on July 23, 2004.

Range of care provided
Mrs Julie Cooper is Manager of Watlington and District Nursing Home. It is set in lovely gardens against a countryside backdrop that is within a designated Area of Outstanding Natural Beauty.

A wide range of care is provided for residents the majority of whom are publicly funded. There are 60 en suite rooms, and some 13 of the beds are NHS-funded and are used for recovery after hospital admission, thereby unblocking beds in the larger acute hospitals. About 30 beds are used for elderly or mentally infirm residents and the remaining beds are used for longer-stay nursing or respite care. The majority of these are funded by Social Services. Those with appropriate needs can usually be taken quite quickly. Social Services decide where to place mentally infirm residents and place them elsewhere if not at Watlington as do the NHS for intermediate care patients. The Trust purchased a minibus that transports patients, staff, and other users to and from Watlington and the surrounding area.

Quality of service
The charity's main task is to keep a watch on the quality of service given by the nursing home, which is taken very seriously by the Trustees. Priority is given to local people. WHCT is also responsible for raising and managing the patient fund that provides many of the vital facilities: the ambulance/people carrier, care of the gardens and estate, supply of conservatory and raised beds for the use of the residents, provision of in-room television sets, and payment of annual expenses such as insurance and professional services.

Annual Christmas Fair
Funds are always needed and the Annual Christmas Fair is the main fundraising

event for WHCT. The 2013 proceeds will go towards the furnishing of the Home's new Day Room.

Prince Edward's visits

Prince Edward visited the Care Home on April 23, 2013. On arrival, the Lord Lieutenant Mr Tim Stevenson presented Mr Tom Holden to His Royal Highness. In turn, Mr Holden presented Mr Steve Wood, Managing Director of Sanctuary Care, and then escorted His Royal Highness into the Nursing Home to meet the Manager, Mrs Julie Cooper, who accompanied him round the Care Home.

Prince Edward was shown the Dementia Ward, and then taken into the grounds to view the garden. He saw the latest developments, including a water feature in memory of Anna Thomas who had been a keen gardening volunteer, and he saw the raised seedbeds. Here, Prince Edward met the gardener, Mr Pete Hemmins. Returning via the Sun Lounge and Quiet Lounge, Prince Edward visited the Intermediate Ward, saw the Therapy and Activity Rooms, and watched an art lesson in progress. All the while he was meeting and chatting to a number of residents that included 100 year old Miss Leona Hughes. Inside the main lounge, Trustees Sir Christopher Payne and Mr Donald Chilvers were presented to His Royal Highness, together with the senior Medical Practitioner, Dr Steve Nicholson, Mr Ian Hill, Chair of the local Parish Council, the Reverend Canon Tony Williamson, and Mrs Janie Garforth-Bles, who chairs the main fundraising group. After tea and refreshments, Mr Holden said a few words and thanked His Royal Highness for his visit.

THE ROYAL COLLEGE OF SURGEONS OF ENGLAND

The Royal College of Surgeons of England (RCS), located at Lincoln's Inn Fields, London, is an independent professional body, and a registered charity, committed to promoting and advancing the highest standards of surgical care for patients, regulating surgery, including dentistry, in England and Wales.

The origins of the college date to the 14th century with the foundation of the Guild of Surgeons within the City of London. In 1800, the Company was granted a Royal Charter to become the Royal College of Surgeons in London. A further charter of 1843 granted them the present title of The Royal College of Surgeons of England.

A royal charter is a formal document issued by a monarch as letters patent, granting a right or power to an individual or a body corporate. They were, and are still, used to establish significant organisations such as cities (with municipal charters) or universities. A Royal Charter is produced as a high quality work of calligraphy on vellum. The British monarchy has issued over 980 and of these about 750 remain in existence. Charters still continue to be issued today by the British Crown.

The Royal College today

Consultant colorectal surgeon Professor Norman Williams became college President in July 2011. He is Professor of Surgery and Director of Innovation at the Academic Surgical Unit of Barts and The London, Queen Mary's School of Medicine and

Dentistry. His main clinical interests are sphincter preservation and reconstructive surgery, and his scientific interests are concentrated on Gastrointestinal (GI) motility and anorectal physiology. Gastrointestinal physiology is a branch of human physiology addressing the physical function of the gastrointestinal (GI) system.

Surgical research

Each year in excess of eight million people undergo surgery and as a result there are few people who have not benefited in some way, either directly or indirectly, from advances made in surgical research. Research is the foundation of good surgical practice and forms an essential source of knowledge for the surgeon, the surgical profession and medicine as a whole. In fact, research by surgeons over the past 50 years has probably done more than research in any other field to reduce mortality and disease and improve the quality of life for patients. The results of such work range from life-saving advances in heart and cancer surgery to life-enhancing procedures such as hip and knee replacement. Surgery remains the mainstay, indeed, only effective treatment for many diseases including solid cancers of the bowel, breast and lung, diseases causing organ failure (transplantation), victims of trauma, age-related disabilities, and disease or injury requiring reconstruction. [7]

The Freemason's Grand Lodge 250th
Anniversary Fund Surgical Research Fellowship Scheme

The college's formal relationship with English Freemasonry dates back to 1967, the year of their 250th Anniversary and when, it will be recalled, Prince Edward became Grand Master. To celebrate this occasion, every Freemason under the English constitution was asked to donate £1 to a research fund for The Royal College of Surgeons of England. When the fund closed three years later, a total of £594,850 had been raised, and the 250th Anniversary Fund was established in 1968. The fund is administered by officers of the United Grand Lodge of England and makes an annual gift to the college's Surgical Research Fellowship Scheme. Surgical Research Fellowships are offered to aspiring academic surgeons funding innovative projects based on clinically applicable need. Each Fellowship endows a full-time research programme lasting from one to three years and is supervised within a UK department of surgery, although a number have also taken place overseas. The college believes this is a powerful way of enhancing surgical research and a development that is of national importance.

Over the 45 years the fund has been in existence some £4 million has been donated to surgical research. However, the cost of modern, highly technological research has increased exponentially over the years, and as a result the fund has not kept pace with these increases. Each year the college aims to award in the region of fifteen to twenty fellowships, three of which are funded by the 250th Anniversary Fund. The number of excellent applications they receive, however, has doubled since the scheme was introduced. The college currently receives in the region of 120 research applications a year but is unable to support 80 per cent of those making application, due to lack of funds. The college receives no funding from the NHS and its ability to make awards to the most promising of cases is wholly dependent on raising voluntary income through, donations, gifts and legacies. [8]

Prince Edward becomes Patron

Prince Edward became Patron of the Grand Lodge 250th Anniversary Fund on November 10, 1997. To show their thanks for the support given by Freemasons over the years, the college elected Prince Edward an Honorary Fellow **on October 30, 2002.**

Royal Arch Bicentenary Appeal, Year 2013

To mark the bicentenary of the Royal Arch Lodge, an Appeal was launched early by the Supreme Grand Chapter in 2011 that ran until the end of 2013. The Appeal target was in excess of £1 million, and each Royal Arch Mason is being asked to support the appeal with a gifted aided donation of £10. The plan is to administer the fund in tandem with the 250th Anniversary Fund and to make an annual donation to the college's surgical research fellowships. Since the time of the launch the college has provided speakers at Royal Arch events throughout the country to support the Appeal and to date 95 presentations have been made.

With less than four per cent of national funding for medical research currently being applied to surgically-based projects there is a desperate need to redress this imbalance. Continued discrepancy in these funding arrangements will only diminish the ability of research findings to be translated into real benefits for patients. Supporting surgical research has always been a central tenet of the college because it is only through surgical research that there come advances in surgical technique and management of surgical conditions.

There is still much to do and surgical research continues to provide significant advances: in hip and knee replacements; the prevention of strokes; reconstructive surgery for trauma and war-wounded victims; less invasive surgery and quicker recovery; skilled operations to improve hearing and sight; and cancer survival rates. There is no doubt that future innovations in surgery will be driven by research, and further funding is urgently needed. Donations to The Royal Arch Masons 2013 Bicentenary Appeal will have helped to support advancements in surgical care for current and future generations. [9] Prince Edward has said of this important appeal fund:

> "I am delighted that we will mark our 200th anniversary in 2013, by working with The Royal College of Surgeons of England to establish The Royal Arch Masons 2013 Bicentenary Appeal.
> This campaign gives us an excellent opportunity to contribute further towards something that is helping to save lives and improve the quality of life for us, our children and grandchildren."

THE ROYAL SOCIETY OF MEDICINE

The Royal Society of Medicine (RSM) is a British charitable organisation, whose main purpose is as a provider of medical education, and they run over 350 meetings and conferences each year. Their headquarters are located at 1 Wimpole Street, London, wherein is housed one of the largest postgraduate medical libraries in Europe.

The society was originally founded on May 22, 1805 as the Medical and Chirurgical Society of London, following a split between leading members of the Medical Society of London to form a new society that would bring together branches of the medical profession "for the purpose of conversation on professional subjects, for the reception of communications and for the formation of a library."

They adopted the name The Royal Society of Medicine in 1907, when a number of independent societies, including the Epidemiological Society founded in 1850, merged with the Society under a new Royal Charter.

Prince Edward was made an Honorary Fellow of the RSM on July 20, 2010. The origins of the Honorary Fellowship may be traced to the first meeting in 1805, of the Medical and Chirurgical Society of London, when a resolution was passed: "That Gentlemen who have eminently distinguished themselves in Sciences connected with Medicine, but who are not of the Medical Profession, or do not practise therein, be admissible as Honorary Members."

Sources and Endnotes to Chapter 2

Sources

King Edward VII's Hospital Sister Agnes:

Richard Hough, Sister Agnes – The History of King Edward VII's hospital For Officers 1899-1999, pub. John Murray, London (1998); Chapter 1: The Keyser Origins; Chapter 2: The King Offers His Name.

Institute of Occupational Health:

J. M. Harrington, Director of the Institute of Occupational Health, The Report of the Director, 1983.

J. M. Harrington, Director of the Institute of Occupational Health The Report of the Director (10th Annual Report undated).

J. M. Harrington, Director of the Institute of Occupational Health, The Report of the Director; 1994; visit by HRH The Duke of Kent.

Endnotes

[1] J. M. Harrington, Director of the Institute of Occupational Health; Report of the

Director, 1983; p5. Introductory Remarks; (Internal publication).

[2] Malcolm Harrington, Director of the Institute of Occupational Health; The Report of the Director (10th Annual Report); p.8; (internal publication).

[3] Professor Jonathan Ayres, papers by, quoted on the website of the Institute of Occupational Health.

[4] Ibid.

[5] Statement provided by Professor Jonathan Ayres, January 16, 2015.

[6] Figures published by the Department of Work and Pensions, Autumn, 2011.

[7] Source: Mr Jonathan Fountain, Development Director, Development Office, The Royal College *of* Surgeons *of* England, 35-43 Lincoln's Inn Fields, London WC2A 3PE.

[8] Ibid.

[9] Ibid.

CHAPTER 3

BRITISH OVERSEAS TRADE BOARD
later
BRITISH TRADE INTERNATIONAL

In January 1976, aged 30 years, and having served his time in the British Army, Prince Edward became Vice-Chairman of the British Overseas Trade Board (BOTB) of which he was already a Member since February 1, 1975, and a Member of their Advisory Council from June 1 of that year.

The BOTB was an export promotion agency of the UK Department of Trade and Industry. It was made up of business leaders and representatives from the Confederation of British Industries, the Department of Trade and Industry, the Exports Credit Guarantee Department, the Foreign and Commonwealth Office and the Trade Union Congress. Its President was the Secretary of State for Trade.

There was some surprise and apprehension in the British newspapers [1] about Prince Edward's appointment to such an elevated position. But in his role previously as a member of the BOTB he had already travelled a good deal overseas promoting British business.

Overseas visits
The first overseas visit as the Queen's Special Representative undertaken by Prince Edward, aged 25 years, was in April 1961, when he spent a week at the Sierra Leone

Independence celebrations.

Between 1966 and 1975, Prince Edward carried out a number of engagements during some of which he represented the Queen and was accompanied by his wife Katharine, The Duchess of Kent. Katherine later, on June 9, 1977, for her work received the honour of Dame Grand Cross of the Royal Victorian Order (GCVO),

In February 1965, Prince Edward accompanied by the Duchess Katharine was the Queen's Special Representative at the Independence celebrations in The Gambia. The following year the Kents went to Guyana in May, Prince Edward again in the role of the Queen's Special Representative at the Independence celebrations. In October, Prince Edward opened the British Week at Lyons in France. That November, the Kents went to Barbados, Prince Edward representing the Queen at independence celebrations.

In July 1967, Prince Edward was again the Queen's Special Representative at the Coronation of Tāufa āhau Tupou IV, King of Tonga.

In 1967 the Kents also made a tour of Fiji, the Cook Islands, and Western Samoa. In 1968, they visited Canada, where Prince Edward opened the Stampede and Exhibition in Calgary.

In May 1969 Prince Edward, again accompanied by Katherine, made a tour to Australia and Papua and New Guinea. They visited Canberra and Darwin, whose peoples were celebrating their centenary. Prince Edward opened the Third South Pacific Games at Port Moresby in Papua and New Guinea. They also, that September, visited the British Solomon Islands and the New Hebrides.

27A. HRH The Duke of Kent, leading a mission to Indonesia and Thailand 1987. Left to right seated: Mr Don Holland, Chairman, Balfour Beatty; HRH The Duke of Kent; Sir Richard Buckley, Private Secretary to the Duke of Kent; standing: Mr Sebastian de Ferranti, Director of the General Electric Company plc; Mr Peter Lockton, Managing Director NEI Power Projects Ltd; Mr John Poston, Marketing Director, Overseas Division, British Telecommunications plc; Mr John Hall, Department. of Trade and Industry.

*27B. HRH The Duke of Kent, arriving in China
for the British Energy Exhibition in Peking, June 1979.*

In May, 1972, they attended the British Trade Drive in Copenhagen, Denmark. Later that year, they went to New York, where they attended the premiere of the film *Young Winston* that was held in aid of the Winston Churchill Foundation of the United States.

In September 1973, they visited Japan for the opening of the British Export Marketing Centre in Tokyo. That October, Prince Edward visited the Europalia '73 celebrations in Brussels – the major international arts festival held every two years.

The International Trade Fair in Teheran is popular worldwide. In 1975, Prince Edward and Katherine were in attendance on the opening day of the Third International Trade Fair as guests of the Imperial Court in Iran. Of that momentous occasion Prince Edward can still recall today:

"This was quite an important event, and it was strongly supported by the then Shah of Iran, who opened the Fair. There was a very strong British presence and this was one of the first events I attended as a member of the British Overseas Trade Board."

Prince Edward accompanied the Shah of Iran, Mohammad Reza Shah Pahlavi, on a visit to the British Pavilion on the opening day of the Fair, and the Shah performed the opening at the exhibition. On the British National Day they visited stands of companies in the British Pavilion that was organised by the BOTB. Their visit to the Pavilion concluded with a reception hosted by Her Majesty's Ambassador to Iran, Sir Anthony Parsons, KCMG, MVO, MC.

During his tour of the British Pavilion the Shah visited the stands of the 600 Group Ltd, Albright and Wilson Ltd, British Steel Corporation Ltd, General Electric Company Ltd, Lucas Industries Ltd, and Rolls Royce Ltd. It was noted that the Shah spent over 20 minutes on the stand of GEC Ltd, and that he expressed a particular

27C. HRH The Duke of Kent (centre) with Premier Chairman Hua Guofeng of the People's Republic of China, and leading members of the Communist Party; 2nd from left, Mr Timothy George, Counsellor at the British Embassy in Peking 1978-1980; third along from HRH on the right, Sir Percy Craddock, British Ambassador to China; 2nd from end on the right, Sir Richard Buckley, during the British Energy Exhibition in Peking, June 1979.

interest in GEC's involvement in the railway project between Tehran and Tabriz, and GEC's Marconi's Marine Position Fixing Systems. [2]

Prince Edward as Vice-Chairman
of the British Overseas Trade Board 1976

As Vice-Chairman of the British Overseas Trade Board from January 1976, Prince Edward continued to represent the Queen overseas. As is apparent he had considerable experience already of overseas trade and other appointments. Prince Edward and his Private Secretary, Sir Richard Buckley KCVO, worked closely together in corresponding rooms at St. James's Palace. Sir Richard emphasised that Prince Edward's new role involved "representing the United Kingdom at numerous trade fairs and conferences the world over, such as the World Economic Forum (WEF), at Davos." He was "an adviser to the government of the day on the promotion of overseas trade and export. He took a tremendous interest in, and was actively involved with, the work of BTI, promoting Britain and British companies throughout the world, by leading overseas trade missions and visiting companies across the UK." [3]

In December 1977, just under two years into Prince Edward's new job, his positive approach was discussed in a press report. [4] In order to more successfully promote British business during his overseas trips, Prince Edward toured businesses at home to discover how they operated and to assess their export capacity. He visited at least 50 British factories such as the giant British Leyland and the more modest 50-man company on Humberside who were selling oils to the Middle East. He also attended regional exporting conferences all over the country. Already he had made six overseas tours to Europe, the Middle East, the Far East and the Americas. Prince Edward's knowledge of British and overseas trading was apparent when he said:

"As a country we are pretty good at exporting. We sell £2,500 million-worth of goods a month in visibles alone, which is no small figure. We have recently managed to grab back an increasing share of total world trade from our rivals, and total volume has gone up 10 per cent."

He recognised that there was still a "problem of late deliveries" but acknowledged that the situation was improving. He said: "Certain firms give a terrific service. Call them on Friday night, and they'll have a chap out in Africa on Monday morning." Even at that early stage, Price Edward envisaged Britain's opportunities moving ever further into high-technology goods, and into newly-rich, non-traditional markets.

Sir Richard Buckley explained the voluntary nature of the work:

"There was no salary associated with the position, which remained unpaid throughout. The Duke was delighted with his new job and plunged himself into it whole-heartedly, and with an eagerness to learn about business and associated organisations.

28. Mr Damon de Laszlo then Chairman, Electronic Components Industry Federation (ECIF), welcomes HRH The Duke of Kent to the British Group exhibitors at Electronica, the Munich trade fair 1992.

29. HRH The Duke of Kent talks to Mr Dudley Ollis
and Mrs Monica Loeckman (interpreter) on the ECIF stand
at the Munich Trade Fair, 1992.

"The work involved him in travelling extensively abroad, representing the Queen and the British Government in fostering good trade relations with foreign countries and organisations. It was a position of the utmost importance and responsibility, and one to which the Duke was well suited, being of a calm and unassuming disposition, and having a good way with people whom he was often meeting for the first time." [5]

(As we shall see later in Chapter 20, these overseas trade trips enabled Prince Edward also to fit in visits to the many British Commonwealth War Graves).

The major part of the job for Prince Edward was in presenting the UK as an attractive, inward investment destination for foreign investors; creating more positive business conditions for British businesses investing overseas; and helping UK companies export their products to emerging and established markets. The work covered many areas that required strengthening bilateral relations with heads of state and heads of governments, visiting businesses large and small in their own environment, listening to their views and representing these back to the UK Governmen, receiving business leaders from the UK and around the world, and co-ordinating campaigns to win business in overseas markets, and hosting business events and receiving inward visiting leaders and business delegations at Buckingham Palace.

A 1982 British Overseas Trade Board Report speaks of Prince Edward's 'continuing programme to see as much of British industry as possible'. They printed photographs of him visiting business and industry. In one photograph taken in Wales, he is wearing a hard hat and protective clothing whilst visiting the Central Electricity Generating Board's new power station that was under construction at Dinorwic. In Manchester in February he opened an Export Europe Conference featuring four exporting case studies that was presented by radio and TV personality, the late Brian Redhead. In June he was visiting successful exporting companies in Leicester and was photographed at the premises of Camber Engineering Ltd. who specialised in the development, design, and manufacture of single jersey knitting machines. Another of his tours took him to the north east where he opened the new plant at Cleveland Bridge, Darlington. At these events Prince Edward was all the while learning from meeting with business experts and staff involved in the manufacture of British goods for export.

Sir Richard Buckley who was Prince Edward's Private Secretary for 28 years, today lives with his wife, Jane, Lady Buckley, at Coppins Cottages, Iver, Buckingham. Next door, across the lane, is the grounds of Coppins House, the former family home of Prince Edward's parents, where he lived as a child and into his adult years. A closed-off entrance almost directly opposite Sir Richard's living room window had provided a shortcut through the grounds to the house, so the relationship between employer and employee was very close indeed. For the sake of convenience, however, Prince Edward's family moved from Coppins House to London in 1972. Sir Richard has provided an important insight into Prince Edward's work:

"The Duke needed to be busy, and in 1976, through the offices of No.10 Downing Street [during the time Harold Wilson was Labour Prime Minister] he was invited to become Vice-Chairman of the British Overseas Trade Board, the first royal to be offered such a position. He began a programme of study to become familiar with science, industry, and commerce. This would lead on to his membership of the Royal Institution and all the other technical societies with which he is associated. Industry was delighted to get a Royal Patron who was so clearly interested in these topics. A truly huge programme of worldwide visits to promote British industry overseas was embarked upon.

"The Duke had learned to fly and a friendship developed" between him and "Sir George Edwards, then Chairman of the British Aircraft Corporation (BAC). It was at the time that Concorde [a turbojet-powered supersonic passenger airliner] was being developed, and the Duke was on an early flight out of Fulford, York, England." In January 1976, "he was the leading personality on the inaugural flight of Concorde to Bahrain.." This friendship with Sir George Edwards "also led to Prince Edward's association with the University of Surrey. Through him the University, which specialised in technology, got Prince Edward as the 'hands on' Chancellor with a knowledge of industry that they particularly wanted.

"But this was not enough, the Duke wanted a real job in industry. After checking with Buckingham Palace and with Mrs Thatcher [Prime Minister from May 1979 – November 1990] he became a non-executive director of ICC the electrical and engineering giant that included Balfour Beatty, [a world-class infrastructure services business, with leading positions in major markets]. He was a 'hands on' company director and acquired real experience.

30. HRH The Duke of Kent at the opening of Britannia House, the new headquarters of the Civil Service Motoring Association, 1980.

"Mrs Thatcher actively involved the Duke in trade matters, and he was invited to dinners at No.10 Downing Street to meet the heads of industry. He also hosted state dinners at St. James's Palace for industry.

"The job gave the Duke a new focus. Sir Percy Craddock GCMG was the British Ambassador to the People's Republic of China [1978-83], and was later Mrs Thatcher's foreign policy advisor. The Duke was the first royal to visit China, opening a British Engineering exhibition there in 1979 for the British Energy Exhibition. He met all the senior Chinese leaders. The Duke and the leading British businessmen were received by Chairman Hua, and dined with the leading members of the Communist Party in the Great Hall of the People.

"The formality of the 1960s was terrific! It was even a bit starchy. The Duke had lived through all the changes until by then 'anything goes'."

When Gambia became a Republic, February 18, 1965, Sir Richard had this to say:

"For the Gambia's Independence-day visit, a whole Britannia aircraft was made available for the Duke and Duchess representing the Queen. Prince Edward set an early good example by only taking one of each: one secretary, one servant, one policeman, etc. on the trip.

"As the first British settlement in Africa, there were some very symbolic sites to visit, involving a trip along the Gambia River. The Governor's launch sank at its moorings! I rang up the Royal Navy and asked if they

71

had a destroyer in the area. The answer was in the negative, but we could have the cruiser HMS Lion! It was sailed into, and managed to turn in, the river.' Sir Richard added wistfully: 'You couldn't do that now!' "

Sir Richard continued:
"Prince Edward has seen travel arrangements go from Royal conveyances, to First Class, to ordinary modes of transport." Once the two of them "were travelling together [with no other entourage] on a jumbo jet. As we were checking some papers an American lady asked if she might take a photograph of the Duke. He asked, charmingly, if she might not like a picture of them together. I obliged. That was typical of the Duke's kindness."

Sir Richard says they were not, however, always very high profile visitors:

"The Duke was then not so well known overseas as was the Queen's immediate family. During one visit to see the Rolls Royce operation in Mexico it was found that there wasn't a really good car at the Embassy [for their use]. On being told this, Rolls Royce sent one of their best, white limousines for official use."

Sir Richard laughed heartily:

"We were both very gratified to see so many people waving at us as we drove by them in the streets." Sir Richard went on, laughing and demonstrating the waves with both hands that they received everywhere they went. "We thought the Duke was a very popular visitor and were rather surprised that the population even knew who he was." When they mentioned this at a later gathering, someone pointed out that "the most famous courtesan in Mexico drove the only other white Rolls Royce in the country, and the people thought they were waving to her!" [6]

Prince Edward's Overseas trips, 1988-1997
The name British Overseas Trade Board changed in 1988 to British Trade International and Prince Edward remained Vice-Chairman. In total, he represented the UK for 25 years, during which time he made 60 overseas trips, a selection of which are discussed briefly here.

Visit to Hungary, 1988
Prince Edward visited Hungary during May 18-20, 1988, whilst it was still a Communist country. His elder son and heir, George the Earl of St Andrew's, then 25 years of age, was temporarily attached to the Foreign Office as a 3rd Secretary in the Hungarian Embassy. Mrs Veronika Bánki, wife of the well-known Hungarian artist and designer of postage stamps, the late Mr János Kass, (1927-2010), was Hungarian Secretary and translator for the Italian Ambassadors (1968-2006). Today

Mrs Bánki is a translator of famous books and still living in Budapest. Remembering Prince Edward's visit Mrs Bánki has provided the following account:

"His Royal Highness The Duke Of Kent was gracefully received by Károly Németh, President of the Presidential Council. He also met Miklós Németh, Secretary of the Central Council of the Hungarian Socialist Party of Labour, the Vice Premier and Minister of Foreign Trade, József Marjai, and Péter Várkonyi, Minister of Foreign Affairs.

"His Royal Highness had consultations with Tamás Beck, President of the Hungarian Chamber of Commerce on the future development of Hungarian-British economic and commercial relations. He also visited the International Fair of Budapest (MTI). His visit was recorded on the country's postage stamps and a special, first day cover was issued showing an aeroplane.

"During his visit, His Royal Highness carried out the official opening of the small concert room of the Academy of Music of Budapest. The Academy was founded at the end of the 19th century by Ferenc Liszt. Having been completely restored, the smaller concert room was dedicated to the famous orchestral and operatic conductor Sir Georg Solti KBE, the Soltis having helped with money and instruments. Solti was born in Budapest and studied music there and was known as a long-serving music director of the Chicago Symphony Orchestra. In the 1930s he was a répétiteur at the Hungarian State Opera until his career was interrupted by the rise of the Nazis as he was a Jew and he fled to Switzerland." [7] (See also Chapter 9).

Visit to World Expo 88 Brisbane
In June 1988, Prince Edward and his wife Katherine visited World Expo 88, a world's fair that was held in Brisbane, the state capital of Queensland, Australia, during a six-month period between Saturday, April 30, and Sunday, October 30, 1988. The theme of Expo 88 was Leisure in the Age of Technology, and the mascot for the Expo was an Australian platypus named Expo Oz. The A$625 million fair attracted more than 15,760,000 visitors who bought tickets worth A$175 million. The event therefore achieved its economic aims and secured excellent attendances. Queensland was also thereby successfully promoted as a tourist destination and there followed major re-development at the South Brisbane site. The core feature of the site was the international pavilions. Many of the exposition's sculptures and buildings were retained by various entities around the state and are still in use or on display decades later.

During the trip the royal couple also visited Kimberley, Canberra, and Melbourne. Katharine was a glamorous blonde and looking fabulously tanned and clad head to toe in stunning yellow so appropriate for outdoor wear in brilliant sunshine, she was photographed, cuddling a furry koala at Brisbane, and was featured in the Australian newspapers.

Changing into a soft pink suit, Katharine, along with Prince Edward, visited

31. HRH The Duke of Kent receiving a London Guildhall
University Honorary PhD certificate from Sir Brian Jenkins at the Barbican,
London, December 14, 1996.

Wesley Hospital in the Auchenflower suburb of Brisbane. The hospital is well known for its Kim Walters Choices Programme that supports women, men, and their families where a member has been diagnosed with breast or gynaecological cancer. The royal couple were excellent ambassadors on behalf of the royal family and the British Government.

That October, Prince Edward also carried out visits to Rabat, Casablanca, Marrakech, and Fez in Morocco. As part of the finale to his visit to Morocco he was received by King Hassan II.

1989 visits

In February 1989, Prince Edward visited Muscat and Salalah in Oman, where he opened Open with Britain week. The British Business Forum (BBF) in the Sultanate of Oman, that had been established over 20 years earlier, was composed of a group of business people with the objective of exchanging views and opinions about existing and potential business opportunities in the Sultanate. Its work to promote trade between the UK and Oman continues today. Each Month, BBF hosts an event in association with the UK Trade & Investment section of the British Embassy.

From February 8-10, Prince Edward undertook an intensive programme of visits in Norway interspersed with visits to Commonwealth War Graves, the Royal Regiment of Fusiliers and the Boy Scouts. He met leading Norwegian industrialists to study business activity in Norway and to assist the UK's export drive especially in the field of off-shore oil equipment. On February 9, he met the Confederation of Norwegian Business and Industry and had four further meetings and receptions with Norwegian businesses. That evening there was a black-tie dinner for Norwegian businessmen. There were two further meetings with businessmen on February 10, before he returned to the UK.

In June, Prince Edward visited the Supreme Headquarters, Allied Powers, Europe (SHAPE) in Brussels, Belgium, where he attended the Queen's Birthday Celebrations.

1990 visits

January 1990, saw Prince Edward at the Cologne International Furniture Fair in the Federal Republic of Germany that was first held in 1949. The exhibition focuses on contemporary furniture and interior design and showcases material and fabrics and lighting and technology.

That March, accompanied by Katherine, he went to the US, where he opened the Houston International Festival in Texas. Also known as iFest, it is a contemporary, multi-disciplinary, multi-cultural arts and music festival, held annually every April on 16 acres (65,000 metres) in downtown Houston's parks and plazas. The 10-day event is Houston's official city celebration of the visual and performing arts. The royal couple also visited New York.

In November, Prince Edward attended a British trade exhibition in Turin, Italy.

1991 visits

In November 1991, he attended a trade promotion in Germany, and in December as President of the Engineering Council, he attended an environmental conference in Hong Kong.

1992 visits

In May 1992, Prince Edward attended a trade promotion in Japan, and in June visited Italy for the Columbus '92 Expo in Genoa, followed that October by the Electronica trade fair at Munich.

The International Exhibition Genoa, Columbus '92 Expo was held from Friday, May 15 to Saturday, August 15. The theme was Christopher Columbus, The Ship and the Sea, and the Expo was timed to celebrate the 500 years since Christopher Columbus, a Genoese sailor, discovered America then thought of as the New World. Fifty-four countries were represented, and visitors numbered 694,800. The expo took place in Porto Antico, where the aquarium designed by the Italian architect

Renzo Piano, hosted the Seas Pavilion and the ship Italia hosted the Ships Pavilion. Other places of interest were Piazza delle Feste, a covered square, the Magazzini del Cotone, an old port structure, Porta Siberia, an historical port's fortress, and the Palazzina Millo.

In his address, Prince Edward said:

"Welcome to the British Pavilion at Columbus 92: Ships and the Sea, celebrating the 500th anniversary of Christopher Columbus' epic voyage.

"Italy and the United Kingdom, two sea-faring nations, have long-standing historical and contemporary links. The St. George's flag, a red cross on a white field, was adopted by England and the City of London in 1190, for their ships entering the Mediterranean to benefit from the protection of the Genoese fleet. The English Monarch paid an annual tribute to the Doge of Genoa for this privilege.

"Geoffrey Chaucer came to Genoa in 1376, to trade in wool at the Palazzo San Giorgio and many British artists and writers, including Gibbon, John Evelyn, Milton, Byron, Dickens, Addison, Smollett, and George Eliot, all spent some time in Genoa.

"British shipping traffic to Genoa intensified during the boom period of the Industrial revolution.

"In our display you will see the seals of the maritime trading companies, references to the Royal Observatory at Greenwich where the meridian line, probably the most important innovation in navigation techniques, was established; Captain Cook's navigation instruments, the working model of Harrison's chronometer, and Marconi's radio communications.

"The contemporary section, much the largest, includes satellite Communications, navigational aids, and conservation techniques for our natural resources, particularly those related to the sea.

"I very much hope that you have enjoyed visiting our display and that it has shown you that we in Britain continue to be your partners in the ever-closer links we are forging together within the European Community."

Mr Damon de Laszlo DL, Chairman of his own company Harwin plc since 1980, and then Chairman of Electronic Components Industry Federation (ECIF), welcomed Prince Edward on his arrival at the Electronica trade fair in Munich in the autumn of 1992. Speaking of trading relations between Germany and the rest of the world at that time, Prince Edward, who it will be recalled also speaks fluent German, said:

"British exporters must realise the importance of foreign languages and improve their skills – particularly in German. German is far more widely spoken as a native language than English, which is no more than on a par with French and Italian. The use of English in Europe is likely to be further reduced with the opening up of Eastern Europe where German is already a more obvious choice of language for those populations. There is a direct

32. HRH The Duke of Kent at the official opening
of the small concert room of the Academy of Music of Budapest,
1988; Valerie, Lady Solti, the widow of Sir Georg Solti;
and Mr Viktor Orbán, Prime Minister of Hungary.

link between export performance and proficiency in foreign languages. The removal of trade barriers in Europe, expanding world markets and ever increasing competition from overseas all make it imperative that British companies are able to compete on an equal footing. In the past there was no great need for British manufacturers to learn foreign languages in order to export goods as most of Britain's overseas trade was carried on with English-speaking countries. Companies are becoming more aware that language proficiency helps to build confidence in trading negotiations and in making and maintaining business contacts. However, language skills can also be vital for a company's first point of contact in its homebase – the telephonist, receptionist or telex operator, who need to be able to respond to sales inquiries from abroad." [8]

Twenty three years on, one would add computers, mobile/smart 'phones and

Blackberries to the list of much faster means of communication.

1993 visits
In October 1993, Prince Edward had an appointment to open a new S$100 million (US $62.5 million) manufacturing plant for Fisons at Jurong, Singapore. The plant was the largest capital investment for the company and its first outside of the UK. The facility manufactured nedocromil sodium, the active ingredient in the anti-asthmatic drug Tilade. The drug was launched progressively throughout Asia. The nedocromil sodium manufactured at the plant was for export to Fisons' European manufacturing unit at Le Trait in France and smaller plants in Italy and Spain, where it was formulated into Tilade for the worldwide market.

Prince Edward then travelled on to Kuala Lumpur, where he had a meeting with the Federation of Malaysian Manufacturers (FMM), established in 1968. The FMM is Malaysia's premiere economic organisation, having consistently led Malaysian manufacturers in spearheading the nation's growth and modernisation. Their vision is to make Malaysian industries Globally Competitive.

1994 visits
In June 1994, Prince Edward attended the Poznań International Fair (PIF), Międzynarodowe Targi Poznańskie, (MTP), the biggest industrial fair in Poland. (See Chapter 14, Part II).

At the end of a busy four days of trade visits and royal functions in Thailand in October 1994, Prince Edward took a memorable afternoon to visit two cemeteries associated with the notorious Death Railway, Kanchanaburi and Chungkai, where over 8,500 Commonwealth and Dutch prisoners are buried.

1997 visits
In mid-April 1997, Prince Edward was visiting Capetown, South Africa. On the morning of April 22, he opened a Britain Means Business Workshop at the BMW Pavilion, Victoria and Albert Waterfront. Located in the historic heart of Cape Town's working harbour the Waterfront provides the Nelson Mandela Gateway which offers boat trips to Robben Island, the Two Oceans Aquarium, and Chavonnes Battery museum. Situated between Robben Island and Table Mountain, it is set against a backdrop of panoramic sea and mountain views. It is South Africa's most-visited destination by foreign tourists and provides variety in shops and entertainment. Prince Edward also attended a meeting with the Western Cape Investment and Trade Promotion Agency. Today they offer a range of services to investors and exporters. In the afternoon, he presented the awards at an essay competition at a 2004 Olympic Bid reception, held at the Mount Nelson Hotel.

The Annual Meeting of the World Economic Forum (WEF), at Davos, Switzerland, took place on February 2, 1999, and Prince Edward was in attendance. The WEF is an international organisation committed to improving the state of the world by engaging business, political, academic, and other leaders of society to shape global, regional, and industry agendas. Their highest governance body is the Foundation Board, and they are 'committed to improving the State of the World.' Discussions focus around key issues of global concern, such as international conflicts, poverty, environmental problems, and possible solutions. Prince Edward's role also involved visiting companies inside the United Kingdom.

Prince Edward retired in 2001. The title of the job had changed and when that year, His Royal Highness Prince Andrew The Duke Of York took over the work the title was that of United Kingdom's Special Representative for International Trade and Investment.

Of the 25 years that Prince Edward promoted overseas trade with the UK, he said in 2012:

"For a number of years I was Vice-Chairman of what was formerly the British Overseas Trade Board, now UK Trade and Investment, and although I no longer hold that position, I have retained to this day a strong interest in our overseas commercial relations."

Endnotes to Chapter 3

[1] Reports in *The Times* and *Daily Mirror* 26th January 1976.

[2] Published in The Production Engineer, November 1975, Newsfeed.

[3] Interview with Lieutenant Commander (retired) Sir Richard Buckley, at his home, Coppins Cottages, 23rd February 2008.

[4] Reported in the *Sunday Telegraph* 4th December 1976.

[5] Op. cit. Sir Richard Buckley

[6] Ibid.

[7] Correspondence between Mrs Veronika Bánki and Celia Lee, November 2013. The Duke Of Kent's visit was also published in *Népszabadság* [The Liberty of the People] a daily newspaper, Saturday, 21st May 1988, article titled: *The Duke of Kent in visit to Károly Németh.*

[8] The address by HRH The Duke of Kent was also published in an article in *Language Matters* magazine, autumn 1992, and in the *Daily Telegraph,* 8th October 1992.

CHAPTER 4

EDUCATION AND TRAINING

Introduction

Prince Edward takes a keen interest in modern education. As we have seen in Chapter 1, he was educated at Ludgrove Preparatory School, Wokingham, Eton College, near Windsor, the prestigious baccalaureate school, Institut Le Rosey, Switzerland, that has educated royalties from around the world, and in 1953, he entered the Royal Military Academy, Sandhurst, to train as an army officer.

We shall encounter the term 'baccalaureate' in relation to education in this chapter, and the term refers to an educational qualification, for instance a degree or diploma, that is awarded at the end of an educational programme. In Europe and elsewhere it may refer to varying types of qualifications. The International Baccalaureate (IB), formerly the International Baccalaureate Organization (IBO), is an educational foundation headquartered in Geneva, Switzerland that was founded in 1968. IB offers a range of four educational programmes for children from age 3 to age 19 years.

In the mid-1960s, a group of teachers from the International School of Geneva (Ecolint) created the International Schools Examinations Syndicate (ISES), which would later become the International Baccalaureate Organization (IBO). The IB programme was established in 1968 for the development and maintenance of the Diploma Programme that would 'provide an internationally acceptable university admissions qualification suitable for the growing mobile population of young people whose parents were part of the world of diplomacy, and international and multi-national organizations', thereby offering internationally standardised courses and assessments for students aged 16 to 19 years.

Prince Edward also received an Honorary Doctorate of Civil Law (DCL) from the University of Durham in 1961. In 1981, he received an Honorary Degree from the University of York.

Prince Edward was President of the British Association for the Advancement of Science for the year 1980-81. Known today as the British Science Association (BSA), it is a learned society with the object of promoting science, directing general attention to scientific matters, and facilitating interaction between scientific workers. Speaking in his role as President of the association at its 150th anniversary Meeting at York Minister in 1981, Prince Edward delivered a stirring defence of science.

Prince Edward's mother, Princess Marina, The Duchess of Kent was the University of Kent's first Chancellor, March 30, 1966. At the Degree Congregations Ceremony, July 1989, Prince Edward received an Honorary DSc from the University. On January 1, 1990, he was awarded an Honorary Doctorate in Law by the University of Leeds.

Educational institutions and universities

The Honourable Society of Lincoln's Inn dates from the 14th century. Prince Edward was made Royal Patron in 2001. The Royal Society was founded in 1660. Prince Edward was elected as a Fellow in 1990. The Royal Institution was founded in 1799. Prince Edward became President in 1976. The Royal Geographical Society was founded in 1830. Prince Edward was made Honorary President in 1969. The University of Surrey dates back to 1891. Prince Edward was made Chancellor in 1976. Cranfield University was formed in 1946, and in 1989, Prince Edward became Royal Visitor. Cambridge University Scientific Society (SciSoc) was founded in 1995, and Prince Edward became a member in 2011. London Metropolitan University, from which Prince Edward holds an Honorary Doctor of Philosophy (PhD) (prior to its renaming), was established in 2002.

Educational institutions and universities of which Prince Edward is Patron or otherwise involved mentioned above are here presented in the date order of the year in which they came into existence.

THE HONOURABLE SOCIETY
OF LINCOLN'S INN

The Honourable Society of Lincoln's Inn, situated in Holborn, in east central London, is one of four Inns of Court to which barristers of England and Wales belong, and where they are called to the Bar. Originally, the term barrister was a purely internal or domestic rank, meaning a graduate of the Inn who had successfully negotiated the elaborate legal exercises. The other three are Middle Temple, Inner Temple, and Gray's Inn.

The exact date of the founding of Lincoln's Inn is unknown but the Inns of Court probably emerged around the 1340s, and may have been named after Thomas de Lincoln (died circa 1346), a sergeant-of-law who practised in the court of common pleas, and was known to own property in Holborn. During the 12th and 13th centuries in the City of London, Law as a subject was taught primarily by the clergy. In December 1234, a decree by King Henry III prohibited legal education in London and a Papal Bull prevented the clergy from teaching the common law. The common lawyers congregated in Holborn which was the place nearest the law courts at Westminster Hall in London.

The oldest known records documenting the Minutes of Lincoln's Inn's

33. The Honourable Society of Lincoln's Inn, London.

ing council, go back to 1422. The Old Hall dates from at least 1489.

Following a number of alterations over the centuries the Old Hall was refurbished in the 1920s and reopened by Queen Mary on November 22, 1928. What is held to be the Hall's most famous use as a law court appears in Charles Dickens' novel *Bleak House*, wherein the seemingly endless case of Jarndyce versus Jarndyce is played out. The Hall's present day use is for examinations, lectures, and social functions. Lincoln's Inn also possesses a Great Hall, a library, and a chapel. It is accessed via the Gatehouse that is the oldest part of the Inn, having been built between 1518 and 1521.

There are three levels of membership of the Inn: students, barristers, and Masters of the Bench who are commonly known as benchers. The term bencher as in the judicial bench, originates from when the Inns evolved in the Middle Ages or Medieval period that lasted from the 5th to the 15th century. Moots or mock trials conducted in the hall were a key feature of the legal education of students. The hall was set out like a court and the senior members of the Inn took the part of the judges and sat on a wooden bench. The first level, which is that of student, is open to those who possess a British university degree. Upon completion of the required number of qualifying sessions the student is thereby qualified to be called to the Bar. The process of formal education and examination for the Bar is regulated by the Bar Standards Board, (BSB) on behalf of the four Inns. Call to the Bar is made by the Treasurer of the Inn on one of the four call days in the year and the student then becomes a barrister.

After call to the Bar, Membership is for life and the barrister becomes a member of one of the four Halls. Barristers spend their professional lives as members of Hall. They are entitled to the rights and privileges of members which include, use of the Library, the ability to lunch and dine in the Inn, use of the Chapel for weddings and christenings, and access to Continuing Professional Development courses run by the Inn. Some members become circuit judges, tribunal adjudicators, arbitrators, and legal academics, and others become employed barristers with the Government Legal Service, Crown Prosecution Service, local authorities, and still others become non-practising barristers and make their way in fields other than the law. Several thousand members are from overseas and practise in their own home jurisdictions.

The highest level of membership is that of bencher, or more formally Master of the Bench. The benchers who form the governing body of the Inn meet once a month in term as a body in Council. The benchers also oversee the detailed affairs of the Inn through some 20 committees, which include representation from members of the Inn who are not benchers.

There are currently over 340 ordinary benchers, comprising mostly judges and senior barristers, the latter being in the majority. Many of the judges will have been first elected while still practising barristers, but it is customary to elect anyone appointed as a High Court Judge if they are not already a bencher. Barristers, typically, will have been Queen's Counsel (QCs) for seven or eight years at the time of their election as a bencher, but there are also usually at least 20 juniors, i.e. barristers who have not become QCs or 'taken silk' as it is known. In addition members of the Inn who, though not practising at the bar, have attained important positions in other walks of life, may be elected benchers. The election of benchers is by Council itself, but nowadays only after considerable input from Hall members. Election is for life but once retired from practice or from sitting as a judge a bencher is accorded emeritus status which carries all the privileges of being a bencher but without the right to vote in Council. There are also about 60 honorary benchers. Some may be members of the Inn who have for example achieved high judicial office overseas, but many are those who have achieved distinction in fields other than the law and have not necessarily been members previously. They cannot vote or hold office, but otherwise are full members of the Inn of the rank of bencher.

Royal connection

In addition to the honorary and ordinary benchers the Inn has a Royal Bencher who is in effect the Patron of the Society. The Inn has had long ties of allegiance to the Royal Family which it is able to recognise in this way. Previous Royal Benchers of the Inn have included His Royal Highness Prince Albert the husband of Queen Victoria; His Majesty King George V; His Royal Highness Prince George, the 1st Duke of Kent; Her Majesty Queen Mary who, in November 1943, became the first woman to be a bencher of any Inn; and Her Royal Highness Princess Margaret.

Prince Edward's role

Prince Edward has been Royal Bencher of The Honourable Society of Lincoln's Inn since June 6, 2001. He takes an informed and friendly interest in the affairs of the

Inn and particularly in its educational activities.

There are guest speakers before most dinners that students have to attend, and debates and moots in Hall after dinner. Residential weekends provide more in-depth forms of legal training such as advocacy. For those who have been called to the bar, particularly pupil barristers and new practitioners, there are further courses in the field of advocacy that are given by experienced barrister and judge members of the Inn.

Prince Edward's membership is also valuable as recognition of the Inn's place in the wider legal world and in the administration of justice. He occasionally dines at the Inn either privately with fellow benchers or on an Inn dining evening, when typically, he will take the opportunity to meet students and barristers.

Prince Edward was also very helpful when the Inn published a book edited by Angela Holdsworth, titled: *A Portrait of Lincoln's Inn*, having written the foreword, thereby promoting it to the membership and beyond. In the past the Royal Bencher has also from time to time graciously performed ceremonial duties when some significant event has taken place at the Inn.

In the three other Inns of Court there is a tradition that within their Inn the benchers are addressed and referred to as Master, for example Master Smith. That tradition does not prevail at Lincoln's Inn, where the benchers are simply referred to by their usual social or judicial forms of name. The Inn is led by the Treasurer and Officers who are elected annually, and the Treasurer is the head of the society. The year 2009 saw the election of the 500th, and first female, Treasurer of the Inn, Miss Elizabeth Appleby QC.

Lincoln's Inn as a location for films
Lincoln's Inn is frequently used as a location for film and television productions as well as still photography. Its varied architecture makes it especially attractive for period costume drama and for productions with a legal theme. It has been used for such productions as Arthur Conan Doyle's *Sherlock Holmes series*, Anthony Horowitz's *Foyles War*, Agatha Christie's *Miss Marple*, Charles Dickens' *Bleak House* and *Oliver Twist*, and Jane Austen's, *Sense and Sensibility*.

THE ROYAL SOCIETY

Mission statement:
"To expand the frontiers of knowledge by championing the development
and use of science, mathematics, engineering, and medicine for the benefit
of humanity and the good of the planet."

The Royal Society of London for Improving Natural Knowledge is known simply as The Royal Society (RS). Being of an intellectual persuasion, Prince Edward is drawn to societies of people with mutual interests. On March 15, 1990, he was elected as a Fellow of the Royal Society. On December 12, 1997, he also became a Royal Member of the Royal Society Club (RSC).

The Royal Society – A Brief History

The Royal Society (RS) possesses a rich scientific history, having been formed on November 28, 1660, and granted a Royal Charter by King Charles II. The RS came together initially to improve natural knowledge and was known as a learned society for science and is possibly the oldest such society in existence. It is believed to have been born out of a forerunner society that was known as the Invisible College, with its founders' intentions that it should be a place of research and discussion.

The Invisible College consisted of a number of natural philosophers, some of whose members later joined the RS. One of the most prominent was Robert Boyle FRS, who was a 17th-century natural philosopher, chemist, physicist, and inventor. Of Anglo-Irish extraction, Boyle is regarded today as the first modern chemist and also as one of the founders of modern chemistry, who pioneered experimental scientific methods. He is best known for *Boyle's Law*, which describes the proportional relationship between the absolute pressure and volume of a gas, if the temperature is kept constant within a closed system. His published work *The Sceptical Chymist* is still, today, viewed as a cornerstone book in the field of chemistry.

During the early 17th century, The Royal Society started out as a group of about 12 scientists. The founders and early members of the RS involved a number of gentlemen who were outstanding in several fields of science and related subjects: John Wilkins was a clergyman, natural philosopher, polymath, and author who had headed a college at both the University of Oxford and the University of Cambridge; Jonathan Goddard, an army surgeon to the forces of Oliver Cromwell was a physician; Robert Hooke was a natural philosopher, architect and polymath.

Sir Christopher Wren (RS President 1680-82) is one of the most highly acclaimed English architects in history. He was accorded responsibility for rebuilding 52 churches in the City of London after the Great Fire in 1666, including his masterpiece, St Paul's Cathedral. Educated in Latin and Aristotelian physics at the University of Oxford, Wren was a notable astronomer, geometer, and mathematician-physicist.

Sir William Petty first came to prominence serving Oliver Cromwell. Petty was an economist, scientist, inventor, philosopher, and entrepreneur. It is for his theories on economics and his methods of political arithmetic that he is best remembered.

The society splits into two groups

In 1638, due to travel distances the group split into two groups, the London society and the Oxford society. The Oxford society was more active because many members of the College lived there and it was established as The Philosophical Society of Oxford and was run under a set of rules still retained today by the Bodleian Library.

The London group met at Gresham College, London, primarily after lectures hosted by Sir Christopher Wren. Membership expanded and included William 2nd Viscount Brouncker, a mathematician whose work resulted in Brouncker's formula, and Timothy Clarke, a physician-in-ordinary to the royal household in 1663, and physician to the armed forces, and was a founding Fellow of the Royal Society.

From around 1645 onwards, the group discussed the new science, as promoted by Francis Bacon 1st Viscount St. Alban QC, in his novel *New Atlantis.* Bacon was a philosopher, statesman, scientist, jurist, and author. The primary goals were to organise and view experiments and communicate their discoveries to each other. It was forced to disband in 1658, during the English Protectorate, when soldiers invaded their rooms. Bacon served both as Attorney General and Lord Chancellor of England but sadly his political career ended in disgrace and he was committed to the Tower of London but was able to continue with his written work. He remained highly influential through his works, especially as philosophical advocate and practitioner of the scientific method during the scientific revolution.

The English Restoration of the Monarchy

During the English Restoration of the Monarchy, Francis Bacon was commonly invoked as a guiding spirit of the Royal Society. After the Restoration of King Charles II, meetings resumed at Gresham College. These groups are widely held to have inspired the foundation of The Royal Society. On November 28, 1660, a group of scientists from, and influenced by, the Invisible College, met at Gresham College, and announced "the formation of a College for the Promoting of Physico-Mathematical Experimental Learning", which would meet weekly to discuss science and run experiments. Sir Robert Moray was a Scottish soldier, diplomat, judge, and natural philosopher. His fields of study were chemistry, magnetism, metallurgy, mineralogy, natural history, pharmacology, and applied technology. Moray had attended the meeting of the committee of 12 men on November 28, 1660, that led to the formation of the Royal Society. Moray was able to announce that the King approved of the gatherings and a Charter was signed on July 15, 1662, which created the Royal Society of London, with Lord Brouncker nominated as the first President.

A second Royal Charter was signed on April 23, 1663, with the King noted as the Founder, and with the name of the Royal Society of London for the Improvement of Natural Knowledge. That November, Robert Hooke was appointed as Curator of Experiments. The initial royal favour has continued and since then, every monarch has been the patron of the society. The society's early meetings consisted almost entirely of demonstrations of experiments.

During the 18th century the number of scientific "greats" diminished compared to other periods and little of note was done. The number of Fellows, however, increased from 110 to approximately 300 by 1739 due to the reputation of the society having increased under the Presidency of Sir Isaac Newton from 1703 until his death in 1727. Editions of their journal *Philosophical Transactions of the Royal Society* were appearing regularly. In the second half of the century it became customary for the British Government to refer highly important scientific questions to the Council of the society for advice.

During 1777 there was a dispute over lightning conductors, one having been invented by the American, Benjamin Franklin, and another by the Briton, Benjamin Wilson, who was an English painter, printmaker, and natural philosopher in science and an electrical scientist. Wilson had been elected a Fellow of the Royal Society in 1751, and received its gold Copley medal in 1760 for his tourmaline experiments. Wilson opposed Franklin's theory of positive and negative electricity, and supported Isaac Newton's gravitational-optical ether. He was the first to presume that metal impurities affect the colour of the luminescence. His best experimental work was on the electrical properties of tourmaline, which gained him international recognition.

During the same time period it became customary to appoint society Fellows to serve on British Government committees where science was concerned, something that continues to this day. George Parker, 2nd Earl of Macclesfield was an English peer and astronomer. He had become a Fellow of the Royal Society in 1722, and had spent most of his time in astronomical observations at his Oxfordshire seat, Shirburn Castle. Here he built an observatory and a chemical laboratory. From 1752, until his death, Macclesfield was President of the Royal Society, and he made some observations on the great Lisbon earthquake of 1755.

The modern-day Royal Society

Presently, the Royal Society numbers approximately 1,500 Fellows and Foreign Members, including more than 80 Nobel Laureates. In the modern day Royal Society, Professor Sir John Beddington CMG, FRS, has (2008-2013), acted as the chief scientific advisor to the British Government and the society receives a parliamentary grant-in-aid. The society acts also as the United Kingdom's Academy of Sciences and funds research fellowships and scientific start-up companies. The President of the RS is Sir Paul Maxime Nurse PRS PhD, who is a British geneticist and cell biologist, and who works on what controls the division and shape of cells. He was (along with Leyland H. Hartwell and R. Timothy Hunt) awarded the 2001 Nobel Prize in Physiology or Medicine for their discoveries of protein molecules that control the division (duplication) of cells in the cell cycle. Members of Council and the President are elected from and by its Fellows, the basic members of the society, and it comprises a Fellowship of the world's most eminent scientists.

Through its Science Policy Centre, the RS acts as an advisor to the European Commission and the United Nations on matters of science. It publishes several reports a year. Fellows and Foreign Members are elected for life on the basis of scientific excellence, and have included such famous names as Sir Isaac Newton, Charles Darwin, Albert Einstein; the nuclear physicist Ernest 1st Baron Rutherford of Nelson; Mrs Dorothy Hodgkin the British chemist who confirmed the structure of penicillin and vitamin B_{12}, for which she was awarded the Nobel Prize in Chemistry; Francis Crick, an English molecular biologist, biophysicist, and neuroscientist, most noted for being a co-discoverer of the structure of the DNA molecule in 1953, together with James Watson an American molecular biologist, geneticist, and zoologist; Stephen Hawking the famous giant brain of modern science who is a British theoretical physicist, cosmologist and author. Among his significant scientific works has been collaboration with Roger Penrose on gravitational singularities theorems in the framework of general relativity, and the theoretical prediction that black holes emit radiation, often called Hawking radiation. Hawking was the first to set forth a cosmology explained by a union of the general theory of relativity and quantum mechanics. He is a vocal supporter of the many-worlds interpretation of quantum mechanics.

The Royal Society today is located at Carlton House Terrace, London. In the modern age, the RS views itself as a Fellowship of the world's most eminent scientists, emanating from the oldest scientific academy in continuous existence.

The RS has three roles: it is the UK academy of science, promoting the natural and applied sciences; a learned society; and a funding agency.

In 2008, they opened the Royal Society Enterprise Fund, intended to invest in new scientific companies and to be self-sustaining. It supports modern science, financing approximately 700 research fellowships for both early and late career scientists, along with innovation, mobility, and research capacity grants. Its Awards, prize lectures, and medals, are all accompanied by prize money intended to finance research, and it provides subsidised communications and media skills courses for research scientists.

The Royal Society's Aims

The aim of the RS is to expand the frontiers of knowledge by championing the development and use of science, mathematics, engineering, and medicine for the benefit of humanity and the good of the planet. Their priorities address the future of science in the UK and beyond. They aim to invest in future scientific leaders and in innovation; influence policymaking with the best scientific advice; invigorate science, mathematics and education; increase access to the best science internationally; and inspire an interest in the joy, wonder, and excitement of scientific discovery. As the UK's independent national academy, the society represents the British scientific community within Britain and in relations with individuals and groups of scientists throughout the world. The government recognises the Royal Society as a competent body for Tier 1 immigration.

350th Anniversary celebrations 2010, Hauksbee Awards

On March 10, 2010, Prince Edward attended the Royal Society Hauksbee Awards Ceremony. These are for excellence in the work carried out in science laboratories, research institutions, and schools, and in technology, engineering and mathematics. The Award is named after Sir Isaac Newton's assistant Francis Hauksbee and was created in recognition of those who work behind the scenes. They were made as part of the society's 350th anniversary celebrations and Prince Edward presented the Awards.

Convocation

Convocations of the RS take place only once every 50 years. The convocation held on Wednesday June 23, 2010, at the Royal Festival Hall, celebrated the 350th anniversary of the Royal Society. Along with Her Majesty the Queen, Their Royal Highnesses The Duke of Edinburgh, Prince William, and Princess Anne The Princess Royal, Prince Edward attended the Convocation. Guests included Fellows, their guests, and guests of the RS, the heads of foreign academies, and other significant representatives of the international science community. It was the first time that such an event had taken place since the 300th anniversary in 1960.

The Summer Science Exhibition

The RS annual Summer Science Exhibition is the main public event of the year. It is open to members of the general public as well as students and teachers, scientists, policymakers, and the media. Its purpose is to showcase the most exciting cutting-edge science and technology, and it provides an opportunity for members of the public to interact with scientists and ask them questions about their work. Prince Edward visited the RS Summer Science Exhibition in 2005, 2011, and 2013. These visits sometimes led to follow-up visits to particular exhibitors whose research has been of particular interest to him.

Chicheley Hall

In 2010, the Royal Society acquired a country establishment, Chicheley Hall, near Newport Pagnell, Buckinghamshire. Support was provided by The Kavli Foundation that supports the advancement of science and the increase of public understanding and support for scientists and their work and is based in Oxnard, California. The building is named The Kavli Royal Society International Centre.

The focus of the Centre is on strengthening UK and international science, and meetings that take place there include: Theo Murphy international scientific meetings, two-day scientific meetings which bring together top international scientists and engineers; Satellite meetings involving in-depth discussions which follow on from scientific discussion meetings held in London; International Scientific Seminars involving two-day meetings organised by Royal Society Research Fellows; National and International science policy activities, and science education activities. Training events also take place at the Centre. On Wednesday December 4, 2013, Prince Edward visited Chicheley Hall, where he was able to observe part of a scientific seminar on enhancing neuroscience.

THE ROYAL INSTITUTION
OF GREAT BRITAIN
and
ROYAL INSTITUTION OF AUSTRALIA (RiAus)

The Royal Institution of Great Britain (RI) is an independent charity dedicated to connecting people with the world of science. Based at Albemarle Street, Mayfair, London, the Institution was founded in 1799, by a group of leading figures: Sir Joseph Banks, 1st Baronet, was a naturalist, botanist, and a patron of the natural sciences. Sir Benjamin Thompson FRS, (later Count Rumford) was an American-born British physicist and inventor whose challenges to established physical theory were part of the 19th-century revolution in thermodynamics. Mr Henry Cavendish FRS was a natural philosopher, scientist, chemist, and physicist, who was noted for his discovery of hydrogen or what he called inflammable air. His experiment to weigh the Earth has come to be known as the Cavendish experiment.

In 1800, a Royal Charter was granted to the RI for "diffusing the knowledge, and facilitating the general introduction, of useful mechanical inventions and improvements; and for teaching, by courses of philosophical lectures and experiments, the application of science to the common purposes of life."

The first President of the RI was George Finch, the 8th Earl of Winchilsea, who had served in the British Army during the American War of Independence, and was a member of the Board of Agriculture. The initial proposal for its founding came from the Society for Bettering the Conditions and Improving the Comforts of the Poor. Those involved included Sir Thomas Bernard, 3rd Baronet, and Sir Benjamin Thompson, (Count Rumford). Bernard was an English social reformer, and having married a rich wife and acquired a considerable fortune, he devoted much of his time to social work for the benefit of the poor. He was active in promoting vaccination and improving the conditions of child labour.

Function of the Royal Institution

The RI's function throughout its history has been to support public engagement with science through programmes of lectures. The most famous of these are the annual Royal Institution Christmas Lectures, founded by Mr Michael Faraday FRS in 1825, and the Friday Evening Discourses for members also established by him in 1826. Faraday was an English scientist who contributed to the fields of electromagnetism and electrochemistry. His main discoveries include those of electromagnetic induction, diamagnetism and electrolysis.

Since its foundation, the RI has played a vital role in the advancement of science. Many notable scientists have worked in its illustrious laboratories, including Sir Humphry Davy, Mr Michael Faraday, Professor John Tyndall, Mr James Dewar, Mr William Thomas Brande, Mr William Lawrence Bragg, Mr William Henry Bragg, Miss Kathleen Lonsdale and Miss Dorothy Hodgkin. Fifteen Nobel Prize winners have been associated with the laboratories and the 10 chemical elements were discovered by those who worked there.

The inventions and discoveries that have happened at the RI have undoubtedly shaped the modern world. The invention of the Miners' Safety Lamp, by Humphrey Davy, electrification, the atomic structure of crystals, and the greenhouse gas effect, all had their origins at the Royal Institution.

John Tyndall FRS was a prominent 19th century physicist, known in the 1850s for his study of diamagnetism, and was professor of physics (1853-87) at the RI. Sir James Dewar FRS, was a Scottish chemist and physicist who invented the Dewar flask, which he used in conjunction with extensive research into the liquefaction of gases. He was also particularly interested in atomic and molecular spectroscopy and he worked in these fields for more than 25 years. William Thomas Brande, who studied medicine and later chemistry, was a contemporary of Humphrey Davy. He succeeded Davy at the RI, where he established a lecture course for medical students.

Sir William Henry Bragg OM, KBE, PRS, was a British physicist, chemist, and mathematician. His son, Sir William Lawrence Bragg CH OBE MC FRS, was an Australian-born British physicist and X-ray crystallographer and discoverer (1912) of the Bragg law of X-ray diffraction which is basic for the determination of crystal structure. In 1915, father and son jointly won the Nobel prize for their work on X-ray diffraction.

Dame Kathleen Lonsdale, DBE FRS, (née Yardley) was a crystallographer who, in 1929, proved that the benzene ring was flat by X-ray diffraction methods. Lonsdale was the first to use Fourier spectral methods while solving the structure of hexachlorobenzene in 1931. During her career she attained a number of firsts for a woman scientist. She was one of the first two women elected a Fellow of the Royal Society in 1945, (the other being Marjory Stephenson); she was the first woman tenured professor at University College London; the first woman president of the International Union of Crystallography; and the first woman president of the British Association for the Advancement of Science. Lonsdale won the Davy Medal in 1957.

The modern-day Royal Institution

The RI has always occupied its impressive Georgian building on Albemarle Street, London. It now also houses the Faraday Museum, substantial archives, modern research facilities, spaces for events, and a public restaurant.

Today, the RI is committed to "diffusing science for the common purposes of life". Science education and communication programmes reach millions of adults and children every year. The extensive public programme of lectures and events draw large audiences. The Christmas Lectures which are now broadcast on BBC Four are seen by over four million people in the UK and many more around the world, and the new and innovative RI Channel website, which was launched at the end of 2011, has nearing one million video views.

The RI's Maths Masterclasses that were started by Professor Sir Christopher Zeeman FRS in 1981, take place in 140 locations around the UK. Professor Zeeman is a Japanese-born British mathematician, known for his work in geometric topology and singularity theory. His main contributions to mathematics were in topology, particularly in knot theory, the piecewise linear category, and dynamical systems.

Prince Edward's visits

Prince Edward has been President of the RI since May 1, 1976, and is a regular attendee at RI events. He presides over the annual Fellows' Dinner which includes an after dinner speech from the current Christmas Lecturer. He has also attended many Friday Evening Discourses over the past 30 years, including those given by Nobel Laureates Sir Paul Nurse, Sir Harry Kroto, and Lord George Porter. Sir Paul Nurse believes that scientists should speak out about science in public affairs and challenge politicians who support policies based on pseudo-science. Sir Harold (Harry) Walter Kroto, FRS, is an English chemist, who shared the 1996 Nobel Prize in Chemistry with Robert Curl and Richard Smalley. George Hornidge Porter, Baron Porter of Luddenham, OM, FRS, (1920–2002), known for Flash Photolysis, was a British chemist, awarded the Nobel Prize in Chemistry in 1967.

Re-opening of the RI building 2008

Following its £24 million refurbishment, Prince Edward joined the RI's Patron Her Majesty Queen Elizabeth II and His Royal Highness the Duke of Edinburgh to re-open the Royal Institution on May 28, 2008. Welcoming the fresh start in the new premises on what he described as "this important landmark day in the history of the Royal Institution", Prince Edward gave the following address:

"When I became President in May 1976, roughly half way through the Directorship of Sir George Porter, the state of science, technology and the Royal Institution were very different from today as we celebrate the launch of the New Royal Institution. Computers occupied whole rooms and had the processing power of a modern pocket calculator; even in the 1980s 20Mb (or the size of a high quality image today) for a personal computer was considered extravagant. Mobile 'phones were unheard of; the internet and e-mail had yet to come into being; molecular biology was blue skies research and money came over bank counters rather than from holes in the wall.

"Year by year, as I have sat in the chair listening to Friday Evening Discourses, I have had a ringside view of how the application of scientific knowledge (much of it stemming from the basic research undertaken in this building by Faraday and Braggs), has transformed the way we live our lives. Who can imagine everyday life without all the electronic devices and tools that now surround us, or medicine without the genome or all the new scan technologies?

"Likewise, during the past 30 years the Royal Institution itself has evolved to meet the changing needs of the modern world. When I arrived the Royal Institution was still run very much as it had been since 1810, with a Committee of Managers and a Committee of Visitors which on occasion was an effective way to ensure that nothing happened. Perhaps one of Porter's most important legacies to the new Royal Institution was the decision in 1984, to merge these two committees into the Council. Other important legacies to the Porter era included the televising of the Christmas lectures, and the Mathematics Masterclasses which now flourish throughout the country.

"Yet Porter was quite clear that he regarded the Royal Institution primarily as a research institution with its public and educational functions as secondary. But it became increasingly clear towards the end of the last century that the pace of scientific and technological change, so bewildering to some, required that the Royal Institution should increase its public and educational programmes. Under the leadership of Baroness Greenfield, Director in 1998, the public programmes underwent a dramatic increase. The Science Media Centre has recently been established and last year also saw the opening of Adelaide the first overseas venture, Ri Australia, and the 'spirit of science' scheme, which bring underprivileged children from Australia to attend the Christmas Lectures.

"But alongside these innovations it is becoming more and more apparent that the infrastructure of the building would be unable to sustain this rate of growth – it was no longer fit for its purpose. Hence the decision to bring the building up to date with all the essential facilities required to enable the RI to 'provide a forum for everyone, irrespective of background, to discuss the challenges and excitements of science and technology in shaping our current and future society'. It is the successful completion of this project that we are celebrating today."

Prince Edward attended the President's Dinner on November 26, 2008. In his after dinner speech he said:

"I cannot tell you how much pleasure it gives me to be with you, the special friends of the RI, at this wonderful time in its history. Over the 32 years that I have been president, I have worked with 5 Directors and 16 Chairmen. The most recent Chairman, Winston Fletcher and his successor Sir David Arculus, both of whom I am so happy to see here this evening, stand at the end of a long line of exceptional individuals, all of whom I remember with great affection.

"During that time, I have been able to meet a significant number of Members during Friday Evening Discourses and other landmark events. However, I think I can safely say that the event that has stood out the most was when Her Majesty The Queen and His Royal Highness The Duke of Edinburgh attended the Grand Launch on 28th May. I am sure you will agree that, those who could come to such a unique occasion felt a real warmth and sense of teamwork that could never have been contrived. So many people remarked to me how wonderful it was to be back at the Royal Institution, which on the one hand, had not changed at all, but on the other, had changed so much. For me, it is this warmth and sense of fun combined with camaraderie that makes the science, which fascinates us all, such an enjoyable experience.

"I cannot thank you enough for joining me here this evening, since I feel that we are marking not just the decades of my Presidency, but the loyalty that so many of you have paid to the RI during the turbulent and difficult times of its two-and-a-half years closure. During this time, I realise that there was very little the RI could offer in return for the warmth, support and trust which you had in the RI Council, Director, and all the staff, so on a personal note, I would like to thank you as President. However, there are those that have been members of the RI for even longer than my 32 years, such as President Dr John Stevenson, a Member for 41 years.

"Let us hope that they and I continue to enjoy evenings such as this, and carry on, for decades to come, with the excitement of the science and technology that is a constant surprise and delight to us all.

"I treasure very much this wonderful photograph that reminds me of such a special day, and would just like to conclude by thanking you for all for the support and kindness you have shown me in making every visit I have made to the RI a special one."

Baroness Professor Susan Greenfield CBE, HonFRCP, is a British scientist, writer, broadcaster, and member of the House of Lords. She was Director of the RI for 12 years, and met Prince Edward there in September 2013. Of her introduction to him, Baroness Greenfield has said:

"I first met His Royal Highness The Duke of Kent in October 1998, in London. It was the first night that I, as the newly appointed Director of the Royal Institution, was hosting the opening of Friday Evening Discourse. These Discourses are formidable events: stretching back to the time of Davy and Faraday, a distinguished scientist is invited to lecture for an hour, and then to dine with a small group of distinguished guests in the apartment once occupied by Faraday and, where the resplendent gold Davy Cup graces the table – a gift from Czar Alexander I to Humphrey Davy for having saved so many miners' lives with the 'Davy lamp'. Perhaps not surprisingly the dress code is black tie, and the various stages of the evening are carefully orchestrated, highly formal, and timed to a split second. As if the prospect of ensuring the smooth-running of all this wasn't bad enough, a few days before the big night, I learnt to my consternation that the President of the RI himself wished to attend. Hosting occasions where royalty is present involves, as I was to learn, yet another layer of formality and rules. I was to await His Royal Highness on the grand staircase, with the staff sealing off all the possible entrances via which other attendees for the lecture might wander. Meanwhile, yet another staff member stood watch on the pavement to give the stand-by signal as the car approached carrying a detective, equerry, and the Duke himself. So far so good!

"However, after I had duly greeted His Highness, I had to escort him up the long flights of stairs – and it was here that my nerves got the better of me. We went on and on, me gabbling, the Duke smiling, until … we ended up at the very scruffy fire exit at the very top of the building. Not an auspicious start – but one that perhaps introduced me from the very outset to the Duke's kindness and sense of humour.

"Over the 12 years of my tenure at the RI, His Royal Highness was a regular visitor and supporter and I hope he remembers our various shared experiences with as much affection as I do. These are too numerous to record exhaustively, but several come immediately to mind.

"One occasion that will always stay as a truly fond memory was on the last day that Concord flew back from New York to London. Amazingly the RI had scored a huge coup in procuring Rod Eddington, the then Chief Executive Officer of British Airways, to give the Friday Evening Discourse. The Duke had been on one of the three returning Concord flights and came straight to the RI to preside over the evening.

"Yet another of the Friday night traditions is for the Director, and in this case also the President, to whisk the speaker away for a quiet and much needed drink, while the 300-strong audience filters out. At that time the RI was in sore need of refurbishment and Rod, the Duke, and I, ended up toasting Concord, and the RI, in a room only marginally larger than a broom cupboard, and about as well decorated.

"Then perhaps the most significant occasion of all was when, finally, we had raised sufficient funds for a complete facelift of the RI building and, after two years of grinding building work, were able to have a grand opening. So it was that in May 2008, the Duke arranged for Her Majesty The Queen and the Duke of Edinburgh to conduct the official opening ceremony. I was able to present my parents to the royal party and, as a friend remarked at the time, 'Now you can die and go to heaven'. I will always remember how the Duke made this all possible, and how he has supported me always, through challenging times as well as celebratory ones. Not just as President of the RI but as a truly generous spirited person, it has been an honour and pleasure to know him." [1]

ROYAL INSTITUTION OF AUSTRALIA (RiAus)

Australia is a country that is dear to Prince Edward's heart and he has this to say of it:

"There is so much to like about Australia. First, people are warm, welcoming and friendly, do not take themselves too seriously, and have a great sense of humour. Secondly, the country is endlessly fascinating with its immense size, its feeling of space, its extraordinary diversity of terrain and landscape, and not least the quality of its wine – and much more."

Prince Edward's reference (later) to the possibility that he might have spent some of his childhood in Australia relates to a time in his late parents' lives when they were to live there. King George VI invited his younger brother Prince George Duke of Kent to become Governor-General of Australia and succeed Lord Gowrie. He was to take up the appointment at the end of November 1939, and arrangements began several months in advance to ship some of the Kent's furniture out to Government House in Canberra. Choice of the colour schemes, furnishings, and fabrics were underway earlier that year. Prince George ordered household linen at a cost of £5,000, which he paid for himself, along with pink silk sheets, edged with satin, at a cost of £50 a pair.

The Kents invited visiting Australians to their country home Coppins House so that they could learn about the country. According to the *Sydney Sun* the Australian people were delighted with the choice of a royal duke. Winston Churchill described the appointment as a 'master-stroke of Imperial policy'. Prince Edward, who was approaching his seventh birthday on October 9, 1939, was excited about the adventure of his new home in this vast and beautiful country.

The sudden onset of the Second World War on September 3, brought the plan to an abrupt end. Princess Marina was listening to the radio in the music room at Coppins House when she heard the voice of the British Prime Minister Neville Chamberlain announce that war was declared.

Prince George would be needed to serve his country and was initially given an office job that he found boring but was soon promoted to Rear-Admiral. Lord Gowrie carried on in post. But for Prince George's untimely death in the 'plane crash in Scotland whilst on active service, he would have taken up his appointment at the end of the war.

Twenty-five years later, in 1964, Princess Marina visited Australia for the first time as ambassadress on behalf of Queen Elizabeth II. She saw Government House that would have been her home, still bearing signs of her late husband's taste: blue satin sofas, silk tweed rugs, and the pink satin sheets still in use after all those years.

Prince Edward becomes Patron of RiAus

As part of his role as President of the Royal Institution, in 2009, Prince Edward became Patron of the Royal Institution of Australia (RiAus). RiAus is a sister of the RI in London and is located in Adelaide, and is the first and only RI outside of the UK. It is housed at the Science Exchange that was Adelaide's former Stock Exchange building. The current Director is Dr Paul Willis, a renowned science communicator, palaeontologist, science journalist and broadcaster.

RiAus is a national scientific not-for-profit organisation, with a mission to "bring science to people and people to science". As a national hub for science communication, RiAus concentrates on promoting and supporting public engagement with science. It creates real-world and virtual spaces in which people listen, talk, and think about science in all its shapes and forms. Developing innovative and accessible ways of engaging people is designed to increase scientific awareness and debate on critical issues arising from science and technology.

RiAus was founded with government funds and some corporate support, mostly from Santos Ltd. Programs outside of The Science Exchange building are funded by government departments in different Australian states and territories to target specific audiences such as rural schoolchildren, teachers or those with little traditional engagement with science.

RiAus arose from recommendations made by Baroness Professor Susan Greenfield as Thinker in Residence for the South Australian Government during 2004 and 2005. Baroness Greenfield says of that time:

> "Then there was the trip together to Australia, to inaugurate the opening of our sister organisation, the RiAus: perhaps it was over the week or so that I accompanied the Duke through all the ceremony and procedure that I realised was the warp and weft of royal life, that I realised the kind of pressures he must face, and also saw how well he dealt with it all." [2]

Prince Edward performed the official opening of RiAus in October 2009. Having attended the RiAus Benefactors dinner held at the Science Exchange on January 31, 2013, he delivered a speech, excerpts from which are given here:

> "… it has since become a respected contemporary centre for science awareness in Australia. Since opening, the RiAus has formed strong links

97

with scientists, technologists, engineers, and mathematicians as well as the media, schoolteachers and importantly those business sectors dependent on scientific knowledge and innovation.

"Australia's future will increasingly be shaped by science and technology; this is particularly true in the case of South Australia, which quite clearly is in transition to become a major energy and resources state. You have seen a massive increase in mining exploration in recent years which has led to the discovery of vast mineral deposits including copper, gold, iron ore, and rare earths, as well as natural gas and, in addition, the world's biggest reserves of uranium.

"Alongside these natural resources, South Australia's industrial scene has been developing fast. The Woomera defence testing range, an area the size of England, has now been opened for exploration and I have been told that this will increasingly contribute to South Australia's export of resources. The development of scores of new mines, including the world's biggest, with the expansion of the trillion dollar Olympic Dam deposit, will require even more new skills and scientific expertise.

"The same is true with South Australia's resurgent defence industries, particularly with naval shipbuilding such as the Air Warfare Destroyers and the next generation of submarines to be built at Adelaide's Techport as well as your electronic warfare expertise at Technology Park. I am naturally pleased to learn that so many British defence companies are established here and that the University College, London, has opened its first overseas graduate department in Adelaide, appropriately in energy and resources.

"What is similarly impressive is South Australia's leadership in renewable energy and climate change policy and this, along with critically important water and environmental conservation in such a dry continent, will require the utmost scientific rigour.

"I understand that this state is also making a multi-billion dollar investment in health with the construction of Australia's biggest new hospital development, the new Royal Adelaide Hospital, as well as the adjacent Health and Medical Research Institute, a cutting edge research centre.

"One way of engaging minds is by ensuring that science stories and science heroes are made more visible in everyday life through mainstream media. This role in the UK, and I am pleased to say, also in Australia, has been championed with outstanding success by the Science Media Centres, established by the Royal Institution in the UK, and alongside the Royal Institution of Australia, co-located in this building. These Centres provide the media with information on request in times of international crisis and also by packaging data and commentary regarding newly released research publications. We increasingly see science moving from page 8 to a front page story associated with more informed and accurate comments.

"Increased awareness and interest in science is truly the focus of the Royal Institution of Australia. As Patron of RiAus, I would like to thank the many benefactors here this evening, from the private, corporate, and government sectors. In particular, the Government of South Australia and the federal Government, both of whom have been very generous. Santos has been a very long-standing supporter, and David Knox continues to give great service as a Council Member. Also the Myer Foundation and the Myer family. We are particularly grateful to Tim Cooper from Cooper's Beer and to Peter Gago of Penfolds for the most delicious beverages. And finally, I should acknowledge the support of Macquarie Capital."

ANZAC Day Commemorations, April 2015

Prince Edward returned to Australia for a week-long official visit from April 19-27, 2015 for ANZAC Day, during the hundredth anniversary commemorations of the Gallipoli campaign in 1915. Addressing a meeting of the Australian British Chamber of Commerce held at the Royal Automobile Club of Victoria on April 22, he said:

"Ladies and gentlemen, I cannot tell you what a pleasure it is to be back with you again in Melbourne and to be visiting this wonderful country once more, a country that I always remind myself I might have spent some of my childhood here had things turned out differently. It is an immense pleasure to be with you and to have the opportunity of speaking to you today."

Arriving in Adelaide on April 23, 2015, Prince Edward carried out the presentations at the Bragg inductions, attended by Australia's astronaut, Mr Andy Thomas, who was one of those inducted with Bragg membership of RiAus. On April 24, 2015, Prince Edward gave a lunch time speech to a Committee of the Economic Development of Australia (CEA) at the Conference Centre in Adelaide, having spoken of progress in business and in particular the importance of communication and technology, Prince Edward then addressed RiAus matters:

"Looking ahead to the future, if we are going to achieve the economic growth that we want and expect, we need highly qualified and imaginative leaders who in turn will be guiding the efforts of similarly well qualified and well trained workforces.

"This, in turn, presupposes that we shall have attracted enough students to take up STEM subjects [Science, Technology, Engineering, Mathematics]. Failure to do so could be very costly.

"This leads me to one of the main reasons for my visiting Australia, at the present time, which is to mark the recent 5th anniversary of The Royal Institution of Australia – or RiAus as many of you will know it. I am very pleased to hear that within such a short life, RiAus is playing a vital role in raising awareness of science and technology amongst the community as a whole and the next generation of future leaders with the upcoming launch of Australia's Science Channel, a single source for the Australian public on the best of Australian science, offering information on STEM careers and revealing the best of Australian innovation.

34. HRH The Duke of Kent with Australia's astronaut Mr Andy Thomas and Mr Peter Yates AM, during a visit to the Royal Institute Australia (RiAus), April 23, 2015.

be releasing its largest ever Ultimate Science Guide, the leading print guide in Australia on STEM careers, which is being distributed free to every secondary school in the country, that's no small undertaking.

"Recently, RiAus broadcast the views of the well-known physicist Professor Brian Cox to more than 16,000 students all over the country in more than 400 locations, allowing them to take part in teaching on the subject of the universe, which I imagine was especially vital to those in remote locations in this vast country who normally would not get this kind of opportunity.

"RiAus is working hard to have this kind of engagement with the community so as to inspire the next generation with these important subjects, in order that they may be properly prepared for the challenges ahead of them and to be able to play critical roles in driving the innovation and prosperity of the future in the way that Monash did 100 years ago.

"So I do congratulate RiAus for these recent develop-ments and for their impending launch which I am sure is going to be highly important and influential; and I do want especially to thank the BCCA for inviting me here today and I wish you well with all your future endeavours."

ROYAL GEOGRAPHICAL SOCIETY

The Royal Geographical Society, along with the Institute of British Geographers, was founded in 1830, under the name of the Geographical Society of London, for the advancement of geographical sciences. Today it is a professional body and world centre for geography. It supports research, education, expeditions, and fieldwork, and promotes public engagement and informed understanding of the world's peoples, places, and environments. The current President is Dame Judith Rees DBE, the first woman in the society's history to take on this role. She is a distinguished academic geographer and her main research interests include climate change and the governance of environmental resources and risk.

The society later absorbed the older African Association that was founded by Sir Joseph Banks 1st Baronet, in 1788, as well as the Raleigh Club and the Palestine Club. Banks had taken part in Captain James Cook's first great voyage (1768–1771). As was the tradition with other such like learned societies, it started out as a dining club in London where select members held informal dinner debates on current scientific issues and ideas.

Founding members of the society included: Sir John Barrow, 1st Baronet, FRS, FRGS, who was attaché on the first British embassy to China from 1792-94, and acquired a good knowledge of the Chinese language on which he subsequently contributed interesting articles to the *Quarterly Review.* Rear-Admiral Sir John Franklin KCH FRGS RN, who was a British Royal Navy officer and Arctic explorer. Rear Admiral Sir Francis Beaufort, KCB, FRS, FRGS, who was an Irish hydrographer and an officer in Britain's Royal Navy. Beaufort was the creator of the Beaufort
Scale for indicating wind force.

Under the patronage of King William IV, it later became known as the Royal Geographical Society, and was granted a Royal Charter under Queen Victoria in

35 HRH The Duke of Kent with
Australian astronaut Mr Andy Thomas during
a visit to the RiAUS, April 2015.

101

*36. HRH Duke of Kent at RiAus with
Prof Brian P. Schmidt AC, attending the presentation of
the Bragg Certificate, RiAus*

1859. Between 1830 and 1840, the society met in the rooms of the Horticultural Society in Regent Street, London, and from 1854-70, at 15 Whitehall Place. In 1870 the society moved permanently to 1 Savile Row. Lectures were held at a Civil Service lecture theatre in Burlington Gardens.

George Nathaniel Curzon, The Earl Curzon of Kedlestone, who was a former Viceroy of India, was elected as the society's President (1911-14). The society moved its premises to the present location of Lowther Lodge in Kensington Gore, Hyde Park, London, which was opened in April 1913. In that year also, history was made when the ban on female membership was lifted and they opened their doors to women.

Lowther Lodge was built in 1874, by Mr Richard Norman Shaw RA, one of the most outstanding domestic architects of his day. In 1929, new wings were added which included a new map room and a 750-seat lecture theatre. The extension was formally opened on the centenary celebration, October 21, 1930, by His Royal Highness the Duke of York, later King George VI.

The society was closely allied during its early years with colonial exploration in Africa, the Indian sub-continent, the polar regions and central Asia. It has been a key associate and supporter of many notable explorers and expeditions, including those of Charles Darwin, the originator of the theory of biological evolution by natural selection; Dr David Livingstone the Scottish pioneer missionary; Sir Henry Morton Stanley, journalist and explorer, famous for his exploration of central Africa and the Congo; Robert Falcon Scott, CVO, the explorer who led two expeditions to the Antarctic; Sir Ernest Shackleton the Anglo-Irish polar explorer; Brigadier Baron Henry Cecil Hunt, leader of the successful 1953 British Expedition to Mount

Everest; and New Zealander, Sir Edmund Hillary, one of the first to climb Mount Everest.

From the middle of the 19th century until the end of the First World War (1918), expeditions sponsored by the society were frequently front-page news. Shackleton was again press headline news in August 2010, when a case of his Whyte & Mackay whisky from the 1907 expedition that had been found frozen in the Antarctic was opened for the first time.

From the time of the society's foundation information, maps, charts, and knowledge that had been gathered on expeditions were sent to the Royal Geographical Society/Institute of British Geographers (RGS-IGB), and now form part of its unique geographical collections.

The first journal was published in 1831, and from 1855, accounts of meetings and other matters were published in the *Society Proceedings*. In 1893, it was replaced by *The Geographical Journal*, which continues to be published today.

The society was also pivotal in establishing Geography as a teaching and research discipline in British universities, and they funded the first Geography positions in the Universities of Oxford and Cambridge.

The Institute of British Geographers (IGB) was formed in 1933, as a sister body to the society. Its activities included, organising conferences, field trips, seminars, and specialist research groups. Its journal, *Transactions of the Institute of British*

37. Left to right: RiAus Chair, Mr Peter Yates AM;
HRH The Duke of Kent; and RiAus Director, Dr Paul Willis.

Geographers is now one of the foremost international journals of geographical research.

Royal Geographical Society today (RGS-IBG)

The Royal Geographical Society and the Institute of British Geographers co-existed for 60 years, until 1992, when a merger was discussed. By 1994, a merger was agreed, and in January 1995, the new Royal Geographical Society (with the Institute of British Geographers) was formed. Today RGS-IBG, as it is referred to, provides a voice and home for geography both nationally and internationally. It is the largest Geographical Society in Europe, and one of the largest in the world. It has 10 branches in the UK, plus branches in Hong Kong and Singapore.

The society supports and promotes many aspects of geography, including geographical research, education and teaching, field training and small expeditions, the public understanding and popularisation of geography, and the provision of geographical information. The society also works together with the other existing bodies serving the geographical community, in particular the Geographical Association and the Royal Scottish Geographical Society.

Facilities opened to the public

In 2004, the society took some futuristic steps. Its historical collections relating to scientific exploration and research, which are of national and international importance having been already available, were fully opened to the public for the first time. A new category of membership was also introduced to widen access for people with a general interest in geography. The new Foyle Reading Room and glass Pavilion exhibition space were also opened to the public, unlocking the society intellectually, visually, and physically for the 21st century.

The society is governed by its Board of Trustees called the Council, which is chaired by its President. Prince Edward has been Honorary President since 1969, and sits on the Council. The society has four specialist committees: Education, Research, Expedition and Field Work, and Finance.

Membership

There are four categories of individual membership: Ordinary membership, that takes in anyone with an interest in geography; Young Geographer, that is open to people between the ages of 14 and 24, currently studying or a recent graduate of geography or a related subject; Fellowship, is conferred on anyone over 21 years of age, who has a deep involvement with geography through research, publication or profession; Postgraduate Fellowship is open to anyone who is a postgraduate student in Geography or an allied subject at a United Kingdom university. In addition, since 2002, the society has been granted the power by the Privy Council to award the status of Chartered Geographer. This status can be obtained by those who have a degree in geography or related subject, and at least six years geographical experience or 15 years geographical work experience for those without a degree. Chartered Geographer, (Teacher), is a professional accreditation available to teachers who can demonstrate competence, experience, and professionalism in the use of geographical knowledge or skills, both in and out of the classroom, and who are committed to maintaining their professional standards through ongoing continuing professional development (CPD).

Research Groups, Awards, Medals and Grants

The society's Research and Study Groups bring together active researchers and professional geographers in particular areas of geography. Each group organises their own seminars, conference, workshops, and other activities.

The society also presents many awards to geographers that have contributed to the advancement of geography. The most prestigious of these awards are the Gold Medals, the Founder's Medal 1830, and the Patron's Medal 1838. These awards are given for "the encouragement and promotion of geographical science and discovery", and are approved by Her Majesty Queen Elizabeth II. Amongst those who have been awarded a medal is Harish Kapadia, who, in 2004 was awarded the Patron's Medal for contributions to geographical discovery and mountaineering in the Himalayas. In 2005, the Founder's Medal was awarded to Professor Sir Nicholas Shakleton for his research in the field of Quaternary Palaeoclimatology. The Patron's medal was awarded to Professor Jean Malaurie for a lifelong study of the Arctic and its people.

The society also offers over 90 research-student and touring grants, totalling over £180,000. They range from established researcher grants to expedition and fieldwork teams, photography, and media grants. The Ralph Brown and the Gilchrist Fieldwork grants are the largest awarded by the society and each is worth £15,000.

Translated into modern day practical issues the President of the society (2009-12) the well-known actor, writer, TV presenter, and comedian, and later documentarian, Mr Michael Palin CBE, FRGS, whose journeys took him to the North and South Poles, the Sahara Desert, the Himalayas, and elsewhere, has written of how "the more traditional activities of the society" continue to survive.

There is a rich and diverse Monday lecture programme where speakers cover subjects "from the Indus to Guyana, and from Tibet and Iran to Western Australia." They "learnt about conservation and flood risk" and there were scenes from The Frozen Planet the BBC1 "television success of the year". [3] Between 2007 and 2011, fifty world-leading speakers discussed the challenges facing the planet in 22 Council events, and 150 Monday lectures, at which a total audience of 100,000 people attended. In 2013, Michael Palin was made a BAFTA Fellow which is the highest honour the Royal Geographical Society can confer on a member.

Prince Edward often attends the Monday night lectures during which a wide variety of contemporary speakers provide informative and entertaining talks on their specialist subjects. Recently, Prince Edward attended a private view of Journey of a Lifetime, an exhibition of photographs taken by HRH The Princess Alice, Countess of Athlone, during the first British royal family visit to the Kingdom of Saudi Arabia in 1938.

105

UNIVERSITY OF SURREY
and
POSTGRADUATE MEDICAL SCHOOL

The educational institution that we know today as the University of Surrey dates back to its foundation in 1891, at which time it was known as Battersea Polytechnic Institute, changing later to Battersea College of Technology. Its humble beginnings at Battersea Park, southwest London, was part of the late-Victorian educational expansion and reform to provide specialist education for the poorer and artisan classes of London.

Today, the University of Surrey is a modern complex, having been established in 1966, at which time they received a Royal Charter. An early visitor in 1968 was the rock group Led Zeppelin, who performed the first show of their first British Tour under their new name at the University on October 25. In 1970, the University completed its relocation to Guildford.

Prince Edward became Chancellor of the University on June 1, 1976, and was formally installed in January 1977.

Achievement Awards

In 1991, the University was granted the Queen's Award for Export Achievement. In 1996, it was awarded the Queen's Anniversary Prize for Higher and Further Education in recognition of outstanding achievement in satellite engineering and communications, teaching, and research, by the Centre for Satellite Engineering Research and its associated companies. In 1998, the University's spin-out company, Surrey Satellite Technology Limited, won the Queen's Award for Technological Achievement. The Award was presented by Her Majesty Queen Elizabeth II, accompanied by HRH Prince Phillip The Duke of Edinburgh and Prince Edward.

The Duke of Kent Building –
The School of Health and Social Care

In March 2000, Prince Edward opened a new state-of-the-art healthcare education entre named in his honour. The Duke of Kent Building is today home to The School of Health and Social Care, part of the Faculty of Health and Medical Sciences. It is one of the most modern and well-equipped centres for healthcare, education, and research in the country. The School provides training for nurses, midwives, paramedics, and operating practitioners for nine NHS Trust hospitals in Surrey, and parts of West Sussex and Hampshire. Having cost £12 million to construct, the building has two floors of teaching rooms, a floor dedicated to computer rooms, laboratories which include dedicated clinical skills teaching areas, a community flat, an ergonomics research facility, a gait laboratory, shape, instrumentation, and a micro engineering laboratory.

The Faculty of Health and Medical Sciences

The Faculty of Health and Medical Sciences holds a major contract from

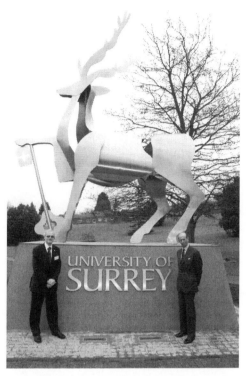

*38. HRH The Duke of Kent, Chancellor, and
Professor Sir Christopher Snowden, President and Vice-Chancellor of
the University of Surrey, pictured in front of the Surrey Stag
at its unveiling in February 2009.*

the National Health Service to train nurses, midwives, and other healthcare professionals to provide the workforce for the nine trust hospital health authorities, and the independent healthcare providers that are part of the Surrey and Chichester Education Consortium. These include the following NHS Trusts: The Royal Surrey; Frimley Park Hospital; Surrey & Sussex Healthcare; Surrey Oaklands; the Royal West Sussex; Sussex Weald & Downs; Surrey Hampshire Borders; Ashford & St. Peter's Hospital, Bournewood Community and Mental Health.

Portrait of Prince Edward

A new portrait of Prince Edward was painted by the respected Australian artist, Mr Paul Fitzgerald, having been specially commissioned by the university to mark the occasion of the new building, and was unveiled by Prince Edward. Many local dignitaries attended, and Vice-Chancellor, Professor Patrick Dowling, gave an introductory speech. During the ceremony, which took place on March 13, 2000, Prince Edward unveiled a plaque to commemorate the opening of the new building. In his address he said:

"I am very conscious of the challenges which face all those working in the field of healthcare and I hope the work undertaken in the European Institute will enable them to meet the changing needs of patients in the new millennium."

In May 2002, the university celebrated its 35th anniversary with a major event in the Cathedral Church of the Holy Spirit known as Guildford Cathedral. The unveiling of the Surrey Scholar sculpture by Mr Allan Sly FBS, marked the Golden Jubilee of Her Majesty Queen Elizabeth II, and was a gift to the people of Guildford. In that year also, the University was awarded the Queen's Anniversary Prize for Higher and Further Education in recognition of their internationally renowned research and development on optoelectronic devices and ion beam applications.

Postgraduate Medical School
On April 19, 2004, Prince Edward became Patron of the University's Postgraduate Medical School that has recently been renamed the Leggett Building, after the first Vice-Chancellor of the University, Dr Peter Leggett, who was Principal of Battersea College from 1960.

Professor Christopher Snowden became the University of Surrey's fourth Vice-Chancellor on July 1, 2005, having been appointed in recognition of his pioneering work in the fields of microwave engineering and compound semiconductors. He later received a knighthood in the 2012 New Year's Honours for services to Engineering and Higher Education. On October 26, 2005, Prince Edward was gracefully received by Professor Snowden and taken on a tour of the campus to inspect facilities in the I-Laboratory and the new Postgraduate Medical School building. Prince Edward viewed demonstrations of cutting edge research in the field of communications technology in a centre that weds advances in communications technology with the sociological and psychological needs of the end-user.

Prince Edward tries his hand at keyhole surgery
Prince Edward discussed research into pharmacoepidemiology that is the study of the use of and the effects of drugs in large numbers of people; traffic injuries; diabetes; and medical equipment evaluation. He then successfully tried his hand at an innovative laparoscopic technique used in keyhole surgery, where the user guides small surgical implements by viewing them on a TV monitor.

Future of sports
After lunch, Prince Edward discussed the future of sports at the university. Professor Snowden commented:

"In his role as Chancellor, His Royal Highness The Duke of Kent has always been a stalwart supporter of the University of Surrey. We are proud to be able to demonstrate to him some of the many advances that the University is making in the fields of science, medicine and sport."

Led Zeppelin's guitarist rewarded with a doctorate

The university's old friend from the rock-n-roll days of the 1960s, Led Zeppelin's guitarist Mr Jimmy Page was, in 2008, awarded an honorary doctorate for services to the music industry. Other honorary graduates of the University include: the England Rugby Union player Mr Jonny Wilkinson, famous for his drop goals; fertility pioneer Professor Lord Robert Winston; virtuoso violinist Yehudi Menuhin, Baron Menuhin, OM, KBE; the actress Dame Judi Dench CH DBE FRSA; broadcaster Sandi Toksvig (Sandra Brigitte) the Danish/British comedian, author, and presenter of News Quiz on Radio 4, and 1001 Things You Should Know on Channel 4; and 1996 Nobel Laureate, Professor Sir Harold (Harry) Kroto FRS, English chemist.

Prince Edward as Chancellor: 120th Anniversary

Prince Edward continues to be committed and enthusiastic about his role as Chancellor of the University of Surrey. He presides at the University's graduation ceremonies (typically two per annum) where he delights in meeting with and conferring degrees upon Surrey's new graduates. In 2011 he presided at a special graduation ceremony as part of the University's 120th anniversary celebrations. Paying tribute to its Battersea roots the University awarded honorary degrees to all former Battersea students. Veronica Hughes, aged 92 years, who completed her studies at Battersea Polytechnic Institute in 1941, was the first of nearly 400 graduates to receive a Bachelor of the University award from Prince Edward and Vice-Chancellor Professor Christopher Snowden, during the event at Guildford Cathedral. In his closing speech Prince Edward said:

> "As graduates of Battersea Polytechnic Institute and College of Technology, you have played an important role in making Surrey the forward-thinking, innovative University it is today. The University may have moved away from London, but the academic excellence and professional focus that defined the Battersea era continues to shape the lives of the University's students today.
>
> "Battersea Polytechnic Institute was founded with the aim of being a noble institution where the priceless treasures of Art, Science, and Literature shall be within reach of all. From the beginning the Polytechnic institute attempted to give students a rounded education, and to attend to their general welfare. This ethos lives on today here at Surrey. At a time when there is much public debate about access to higher education, Surrey is committed to ensuring that everyone who has the potential and talent, regardless of background, should be able to benefit from a university education."

The BBC's local radio station for Surrey and North-East Hampshire, (BBC Surrey), has its studios on the University's campus, and the University has its own student-run medium wave radio station, GU2 Radio.

Guildford School of Acting

From September 2009, the Guildford School of Acting (GSA), became a subsidiary of the University, and in January 2010, they moved to its new purpose-built headquarters on the University's campus. The building was formally opened by Prince Edward on April 26, and was attended by many of the GSA's high profile alumni, including the Oscar-nominated actress Brenda Blethyn, who has played many roles, having appeared in *A Midsummer's Night Dream,* Dalliance, The Beaux Stratagem, *Born Yesterday,* and such comedies as *Yes Minister* and Who Dares Wins, and the actress Penelope Keith of television fame in The Good Life and To The Manor Born, who attended the event in her role as Pro-Chancellor of the University.

Educational research and status

The University offers degree programmes across four Faculties: Engineering and Physical Sciences; Health and Medical Sciences; Economics, Business and Law; and Arts and Human Sciences. Some of the subjects taught at the University include, Sociology, studies allied to Medicine, Electrical and Electronic Engineering, Maths, English, Psychology, Physics, Chemistry, Tourism Management, Law with International Studies, Dance, Music and Politics.

Queen's Anniversary Prize

As a research-led institution, research at Surrey covers an extremely broad range of disciplines, from ion beams and nanotechnology to dance and the study of sleep. In 2011, the University was awarded its third Queen's Anniversary Prize for Higher and Further Education in the Diamond Jubilee round, recognising in particular the University's research expertise for improving access to safe water and sanitation. The award was presented by Her Majesty The Queen at a ceremony at Buckingham Palace in February 2012, at which Prince Edward was present, representing the University in his capacity as Chancellor.

Partnership with business and industry

Since its beginnings in Battersea, the University has nurtured strong partnerships with business and industry. Through these partnerships the University has been able to translate the results of its research into practical benefits for the individual, local communities, businesses, and world societies, through a range of knowledge transfer and enterprise activities.

The Surrey Research Park is a 28-hectare (69 acres) low density development which is owned and managed by the University, providing large landscaped areas with water features and facilities for over 140 companies and employing 2,500 staff engaged in a broad spectrum of research, development, and design activities, many of which relate closely to the work of the University's own faculties.

In 2012, Surrey was one of the first five UK Universities to secure funding from the Government's UK Research Partnership Investment Fund (UKRPIF) to create a world-leading research hub for 5G mobile communications based on the University's campus. The bid is underpinned by significant funding from a consortium of industry partners and will bring momentum to the success of new high tech business in the region and wider economy.

Outstanding academics

The University's outstanding academics include Alf Adams, pioneer of the strained quantum-well laser found in CD and DVD technology which was named as one of the Top Ten scientific breakthroughs of all time. In 2012 the University launched a new series of Annual Lectures named in honour of physicist Professor Adams. The inaugural Alf Adams Lecture was given by the distinguished professor in person at the Royal Society in London in the presence of Prince Edward. Jim Al-Khalili, the nuclear physicist, author and broadcaster; Aleks Krotoski, the technology journalist and broadcaster; Martin Sweeting, founder of Surrey Satellite Technology Ltd; and Nigel Gilbert, the sociologist pioneer in the use of agent-based models in the social sciences, are also some of the University's star academics.

In May 2009, Dr Andreas Mogessen, a researcher at the Surrey Space Centre, was announced as a new member of the European Astronaut Corps, part of the European Space Agency, to become the first Danish astronaut.

New Sports Park

The year 2010, saw the opening of the new multi-million pound sports facility, Surrey Sports Park, on the University's Manor Park campus. As one of Europe's premier sites for elite sport, physical activity, well-being, and leisure, it boasts a 50-metre swimming pool, three sports halls, a squash centre, 700 metres of fitness facilities, two artificial floodlit pitches, outdoor and indoor tennis courts, four real tennis courts, and a climbing centre. A 1,000-seat, indoor arena is home to Guildford Heath basketball team, former winners of the British Basketball League.

It is also the official training facility for Harlequins rugby club and was an official venue for the 2010 Women's Rugby World Cup, hosting 26 matches during the tournament. It provides the home ground for the Surrey Spartans Hockey Club that competes in both the Men's and Ladies South Hockey Leagues, and for the University's (UniS) Old Boys F.C. football team, which competes in the Surrey County Intermediate League (Western) at the 12th level of the English football league system.

2012 Olympic and Paralympic Games

In 2012, the Park was designated as an official pre-Games training base for the London 2012 Olympic and Paralympic Games, and played host to athletes from 16 nations in a variety of sports as they made their final preparations before competing. Tens of thousands of cheering supporters lined the Olympic Torch Relay Route on Friday, July 20, 2012, as Professor Lisa Roberts, the Dean of the Faculty of Health and Medical Sciences, ran with the Olympic torch flame past the entrance to the roundabout near Guildford Cathedral at approximately 6:15 p.m.

The university's highlights included a main stage performance by Guildford School of Acting (GSA), Rizzle Kicks, and the FA Cup display. Lisa commented: "I was absolutely thrilled to be representing the University of Surrey as an Olympic torchbearer. 2012 is our 'Celebrate Surrey' year at the University and I feel so proud to have been nominated to be part of this once in a lifetime Olympic experience."

CRANFIELD UNIVERSITY
"That's one small step for man, one giant leap for mankind."
(Astronaut Mr Neil Armstrong)

Cranfield University is a postgraduate and research-intensive university spread over two campuses (Cranfield, Bedfordshire and Shrivenham, Oxfordshire). The theme that runs through Cranfield's history is a commitment to, and a passion for, applied research and innovation which makes a positive difference to the world.

It was formed in 1946, as the College of Aeronautics on the former Royal Air Force base, RAF Cranfield, which had been opened in 1937. Some famous people have been associated with Cranfield University. Lord Kings Norton (born Harold Roxbee Cox, 1902 – 1997) was one of the leading British scientists, engineers and administrators of the 20th century. In 1943, as the vice-president of the Royal Aeronautical Society, Roxbee chaired two open meetings discussing the education and training of aeronautical engineers. Sir Richard Stafford Cripps (1889 – 1952) was a British Labour Party politician. During the Second World War, Cripps had served as Minister of Aircraft Production. He was one of a number of individuals who were instrumental in the foundation of the original College.

In 1967, the College presented the Privy Council with a petition for the grant of a Royal Charter for a new institution called Cranfield Institute of Technology and it was incorporated in 1969. The college was thereby given its own degree-awarding powers.

Several prominent figures have been awarded Honorary Degrees from Cranield University. One such was Sir Neil Armstrong (the first astronaut to walk on the moon). Born August 5, 1930, Armstrong will always be remembered for the words he spoke when he stepped onto the lunar surface on July 20, 1969: "That's one small step for man, one giant leap for mankind."

An academic partnership with the Royal Military College of Science (RMCS) at Shrivenham was formed in 1984. RMCS, whose roots can be traced back to 1772, is a part of the Defence Academy of the United Kingdom and forms the Defence College of Management and Technology, (DCMT), and from 2009, as Cranfield Defence and Security.

In 2008, the former National College of Agricultural Engineering, which had been established at Silsoe near Luton, Bedfordshire in the 1960s, was transferred to the Cranfield campus and became part of Cranfield University.

Cranfield has a worldwide reputation for excellence and expertise in aerospace, agrifood, defence and security, energy, environmental technology, management, manufacturing and transport systems. Known as the UK's most business-engaged university through its strong partnerships with industry and other organisations, Cranfield is renowned for some of the world's most practical, cutting-edge developments in science and technology. The international network of alumni now numbers over 58,000 and comprises leading figures who have contributed in making

39. HRH The Duke of Kent and Professor Sir John O'Reilly former Vice-Chancellor of the University, Cranfield University 2012, carrying out the unveiling at the naming of Kent House which houses the university's Executive Office.

a safer and more sustainable society.

Cranfield University has excellent facilities, some of which are unique to universities in the UK and many which are on an industrial scale. Specialist facilities include an oil and gas plant and an airport that serves both research aircraft and executive jets. Cranfield's commercial clients include aircraft and engine manufacturers, space organisations, Formula 1 teams, banks and financial institutions, commercial and not-for-profit organisations. They have strategic relationships with household names such as Rolls-Royce, BAE Systems, as well as Boeing, Shell and Nissan.

Cranfield also has a business incubation centre known as CUBIC to nurture new companies which was formed in 2005, and its own Technology Park with tenants such as the Nissan Technical Centre and Traffic Master plc. The Innovation Centre is also based on the Technology Park and accommodates a large number of and medium-sized enterprises.

Cranfield University consistently wins global accolades. Its School of Management rates highly in business school rankings both in the UK and internationally. Cranfield has been awarded the Queen's Anniversary Prize for Further and Higher Education three times – in 2005 for its Fellowship in Manufacturing Management programme, in 2007 for its role in humanitarian de-mining and again in 2011 for its work in aviation safety through research and training in air accident investigation.

Student Mr Padmraj Patil, who was studying for an MSc in Water and Waste Water Engineering, was on a 2011 Commonwealth Shared Scholar from India.

Padmraj participated in the London 2012 Olympic Games as a performer in the opening ceremony, and also as a marshal for the athletes. Padmraj's team was led by film director, producer, and Screenwriter, Danny Boyle, well known for his work on the film Slumdog Millionaire. Mr Boyle was the Artistic Director for the Isles of Wonder the opening ceremony of the 2012 London Summer Olympic Games. Mr Padmraj Patil says:

> "It was a once in a lifetime opportunity for me. I was completely lost in the moment when I saw a massive crowd cheer us. It's been an amazing experience, working with a talented team led by Danny Boyle, and making friends with the other volunteers."

Prince Edward visits Cranfield

Prince Edward who is the Visitor to Cranfield University, was appointed by Her Majesty the Queen, January, 1, 1989. It means that he has the right from time to time to direct an inspection of the university, including its teaching, research, examinations, and other work done by the University.

During Prince Edward's visit to Cranfield on Tuesday May 15, 2007, the then Vice-Chancellor, Professor Sir John O'Reilly showed him round the impressive facilities. Cranfield unveiled the University's involvement in several initiatives and projects that will improve the quality of all of our lives in the 21st century.

On May 14, 2010, Prince Edward visited Cranfield to unveil a painting of Field Marshal The Lord Vincent of Coleshill to honour his work and commitment as University Chancellor over twelve years. Lord Vincent was succeeded by Baroness Young of Old Scone, who had a 20-year career in health care and several years as Chief Executive of the Royal Society for the Protection of Birds. Created a Life Peer in 1997, Baroness Young is now active in the House of Lords, Chairman of English Nature and Chief Wildlife Advisor to the Government and Chief Executive of Diabetes UK. The painting was positioned in the Vincent Building (named after Lord Vincent) the newest building on the Cranfield campus. Prince Edward visited Cranfield's Bedfordshire campus on Friday November 4, 2011, and was greeted by by HM Vice-Lord Lieutenant of Bedfordshire, Colonel Colin Mason, The High Sheriff of Bedfordshire, Mr Andrew Slack, The Chancellor of Cranfield, Baroness Barbara Young of Old Scone, and the Vice-Chancellor of the University, Professor Sir John O'Reilly. The morning was spent touring the campus, viewing the extensive research facilities, including Cranfield's Accident Investigation Centre. Prince Edward was shown the extensive range of full-scale accident damaged vehicles including helicopters, fixed-wing aircraft and the carriages of a Pendolino tilting train involved in the Cumbria train crash in February 2007. Concluding his tour Prince Edward said:

> "The Accident Centre has contributed to the investigation of many high profile cases. It is very interesting to see the Centre first hand and to understand the complex nature of the work they undertake. I am reassured

40. A lecture in progress at Cranfield University.

to know that such investigations lead to technical improvements which make transport safer for us all."

On October 26, 2012, Prince Edward again visited Cranfield University. He was greeted at Bedfordshire Campus by Her Majesty's Lord Lieutenant, Mrs Helen Nellis, Mr Richard Carr, Chief Executive of Central Bedfordshire Council, and Professor Sir John O'Reilly. Prince Edward carried out the unveiling at the naming of Kent House which houses their Executive Office.

Professor Sir Peter Gregson succeeded Professor Sir John O'Reilly as Cranfield University's Chief Executive and Vice-Chancellor in 2013.

CAMBRIDGE UNIVERSITY SCIENTIFIC SOCIETY
(SciSoc)

The Cambridge University Scientific Society (SciSoc), is the largest student-run scientific society in the University, and welcomes undergraduates, postgraduates, academics, and members of the public. Although most members are students, people from across Cambridgeshire and as far as London often attend meetings. SciSoc was founded in 1995, in order to "promote all branches of science within the university and to make science accessible to all members of the university."

SciSoc has a membership of around 1,000, and a much wider interest base. There are another 3,000 people who are not members but have registered for the mailing list.

SciSoc hosts a number of events and every week during term time, they invite an eminent speaker from the scientific community and attendance is open to anyone. Often SciSoc is used as the first public exposure of new research and findings. Recent speakers have included such distinguished names as Professor Peter Atkins, Sir David Baulcombe, Sir John Beddington, Professor Daan Frenkel, Sir Richard Friend, Professor Michal Heller, Sir Colin Humphreys, Sir Tim Hunt, Sir David King, Professor David Nutt, Sir Roger Penrose, Conservative Member of Parliament, Mr David Willetts, and Sir John Walker.

To provide the widest range of events possible, other activities of the society include panel discussions and debates on scientific topics as well as social events such as the Annual Dinner and the Christmas Science Dinner. There was recently a society trip to the Diamond Light Source, the National Synchrotron facility, with a tour from the Chief Executive Officer, Professor Gerhard Materlik CBE. The society also had a successful trip to the Large Hadron Collider in Geneva.

Mr Filip Szczypiński who is studying for an MSc has been President of SciSoc during 2012-2013. The status and prestige of SciSoc is represented by its patrons, all of whom are distinguished scientists: Sir Michael Atiyah, Professor Antony Hewish, Sir Aaron Klug, Sir Salvador Moncada, Sir Paul Nurse, Professor Heinz Wolff, and Lord Martin Rees.

Prince Edwards' visits

Prince Edward was made an Honorary Member of SciSoc on April 19, 2011. He attended The Royal Institution's formal black tie dinner held at the University of Cambridge's Scientific Society on Saturday, November 26, 2011, where Sir Paul Nurse was in attendance. Prince Edward gave the following after dinner address:

> "I would like to thank you all for inviting me here tonight. It has been a pleasure to attend, and I had many interesting conversations with some of you about both your societies and your studies. The Royal Institution is a great establishment, which I have been fortunate to be involved with over the years. I have great passion for science and it is great to see that Britain not only has a great scientific past, seen here in this historic building, but a great scientific future too in today's students. I wish you well in your future endeavours and I hope you enjoy the rest of the evening."

LONDON METROPOLITAN UNIVERSITY

London Metropolitan University was established on August 1, 2002, by the amalgamation of the University of North London and London Guildhall University. In an earlier time, before the merger, Prince Edward was awarded an Honorary Doctor of Philosophy degree on December 14, 1996, which ceremony took place at the Barbican and the certificate was presented by Sir Brian Jenkins. The honorary degree was granted as a tribute to the contribution Prince Edward had made in the fields of British Industry, and commerce and trade, in relation to his work as Vice-Chairman of the British Overseas Trade Board.

The current university has campuses in the City of London and in Islington, and offers a vast range of courses in everything from business and banking to fine art, fashion, and science.

There is a museum, archives, and libraries. A university building is currently being fashioned into a new Archives and Special Collections unit that will include the Trades Union Congress (TUC) Collection; the East End Archive which is very largely digital in nature; the Irish in Britain; an Architectural Research Unit; the Cass Heritage Collection; the Atkins/Atcraft Archives; and the Frederick Parker Collection.

Engineering Award

On April 27, 2004, Prince Edward made the presentation to student Mr Glyn Bufton of the prestigious Cadzow Smith engineering award of £1,500 for his achievements and potential as an engineer. It took place at the Worshipful Company of Engineers' installation and awards livery dinner in Merchant Taylors' Hall, London, in the presence of the Master of the Worshipful Company of Engineers, Major General Ted Willmott.

The award was established in 1996 to recognise outstanding engineering undergraduates in universities within Greater London and to reward the most promising. The purpose is to identify young persons who have the potential to become tomorrow's captains of industry. The prize is given to the candidate who, in the opinion of the judging panel, displays the combination of academic ability and personality that will provide the most promise of leadership in engineering.

Mr Glyn Bufton said of the award: "It is a recognition that I've achieved something useful and produced work to a high level." Mr Keith Foster of the Worshipful Company of Engineers said:

> "Glyn's was a particularly interesting nomination, clearly intent from an early age on following a career in engineering. He appears to have chosen the course at London Metropolitan University's Polymer Centre with great care to suit his particular aspirations. A vacation placement with a company was so successful that he was offered a full-time contract, and has continued his studies part-time. He is now combining a successful job with excellent academic progress."

New Science Centre

In October 2006, the university opened a new Science Centre, part of a £30 million investment in its science department with a Super Lab claimed to be one of Europe's most advanced science teaching facilities, and 280 workstations equipped with digital audio visual interactive equipment.

Study of antique chairs: The Frederick Parker Foundation

The Frederick Parker Foundation is a registered charity whose aim is to maintain a collection of chairs for London Metropolitan University students to study at close hand their history, development, design, construction, and restoration. The Foundation seeks to promote and encourage the study of furniture history and in particular the design and development of British chairs.

Prince Edward opens fundraising event

Prince Edward opened a fundraising event on June 4, 2009, in The Frederick Parker Gallery at the Sir John Cass Department of Art, Media and Design at the London Metropolitan University in Commercial Road. The occasion was the 10th anniversary of acquiring the famous Chair Collection and placing it for study by furniture students interested in the history, design, restoration, and manufacture of chairs.

Prince Edward was introduced by Past Master, Mr Martin Jourdan, to senior members of the University, the Deputy Vice Chancellor Dr Robert Aylett, Head of the Department, Professor Brian Falconbridge, and Dr John Cross a senior lecturer and trustee of the Foundation.

Mr Jonathan Arnold, Chairman of the Foundation, then escorted Prince Edward around the gallery, and introduced him to supporters, including Masters and Clerks of the Furniture Makers and Upholders Companies. The monies raised contributed to a fund to extend the Parker Collection by purchasing further contemporary design chairs. On this special occasion the Frederick Parker Foundation started a membership scheme of Foundation Friends in order to purchase chairs to fill some gaps in their Study Collection and add some important modern items. The visit also marked a visit by Prince Edward's mother to the Parker Knoll factory some 50 years earlier.

Royal 'Red' chair

The development of chair design over the centuries reflects the changing social history and conditions of the time. The collection is an important and unique resource for members of the public to learn about the history of chair design in Britain. It includes the Prince of Wales Investiture Chair that was made specifically to seat the guests invited to Prince Charles' Investiture at Caernarfon Castle in July 1969. Known as The Red Chair, due to its scarlet upholstery, it was designed by Antony Armstrong-Jones, 1st Earl of Snowdon, (former husband of the late HRH The Princess Margaret), the stage designer Mr Carl Toms (1927-1999), and Mr John Pound, principle design officer with the Supplies Division of the Ministry of Public Buildings and Works. Afterwards, the chairs were sold to the public at £12 a chair and luckily, Lord Snowdon bought six.

Exhibition in Paris

That year also, a group of alumni, staff and students, from the department had exhibited their explorations of replacement seat solutions to the world famous No. 14 Bentwood chair at the Boutique Printemps Design au Centre Pompidou, Paris following a September showcase at Designersblock, London. The project and exhibition coincided with the 150th anniversary of the model No.14 Bentwood chair,

*41. London Metropolitan University, show-
ing the clock tower above the administrative
headquarters, Holloway, London (1896) and
the modern new Graduate Centre, designed by
Daniel Libeskind.*

also known as the café or consumer chair. Designed in 1859 by Michael Thonet, the No.14 is still in production today and is thought to be the best selling chair of all time.

Each member of the group created replacement seat proposals for the Bentwood chairs, driven by the knowledge that many of the chairs are out of service due to missing seats. But the iconic frames also presented the group with other, more expressive and experimental opportunities, resulting in six very different but equally stunning responses, including seats using mirrors, folded paper, Chinese checkers, and even a cup and saucer.

Coutts London Jewellery Week

As part of their Summer Show, the University also ran a Coutts London Jewellery Week, from June 8-14, 2009, organised by the London Development Agency and the City Fringe Partnership, with staff from The Sir John Cass Department involved in the planning. The jewellery industry united to showcase the UK's status as one of the leading centres of global excellence for jewellery. The week was designed to be an industry-wide celebration of all things jewellery, bringing together leading names and cutting edge designers, ultimately conveying the allure and diversity of

British jewellery.

Endnotes to Chapter 4

[1] Correspondence from Susan, Baroness Professor Greenfield CBE to Celia Lee, 7th May 2014.
[2] Ibid.

[3] Royal Geographical Society with IBG, Annual Review 2011, by Michael Palin, pp.1-2.

CHAPTER 5

YOUTH EDUCATION, WORK,
DISADVANTAGED AND DISABLED PEOPLE

Introduction
Prince Edward has for a number of years been Patron of several charities that cater for the development and future prospects of young people, and disadvantaged and disabled people. The name of each of the charities and the date he became Patron is as follows: Aidis Trust, (November 1, 1992), who help severely disabled adults and children. Endeavour Training, (November 28, 1979), a national youth and education charity. The Edge Foundation, (March 3, 1981), an independent education foundation, dedicated to raising the status of practical, technical, and vocational learning.

AIDIS TRUST

Mission statement:
"To improve independence for
disabled people through using assistive
computer technology."

The Aidis Trust was founded in 1975, and is a registered charity that helps severely disabled adults and children by providing support and information on communication aids, computers, and the special assistive technology that disabled people need to use them. It operates its services from an office located at the second floor of Richmond House, 15 Broom Street, Manchester, and also has a small office at Ironmonger Lane, London EC2.

Brief history
The organisation was founded in Poole, Dorset, when a boy was found to be suffering with Duchenne muscular dystrophy. As his condition deteriorated he could

121

42. An Aidis Trust assessment;
helping an individual to find technology suitable
to his or her needs.

no longer hold a pen but he wanted to continue his education and his writing. The Aidis Trust raised money and gave him a piece of what was at that time very modern technology, an electric typewriter. Since then, quite a lot has changed in the world of technology. By being able to just blink or move a finger, a severely disabled person can now use modern computers and software to communicate both in speech and in writing, enabling them to live more independently. They can learn on-line, work from home and can shop and make contact with services, friends, family, and support networks.

The Trust today
Aidis continues to support disabled people who wish to use computers or need help communicating. It offers free services to help its clients achieve independence in a number of ways discussed below.

Assessments
Software and hardware exists to help a disabled person use a computer. Aidis will talk with the individuals or their carers and determine what will be the most appropriate equipment to help them. When they visit, the individuals have the opportunity to use a computer with the adaptations. They are able to see how successfully they can

access a personal computer (PC) and how it will benefit them.

Training for individuals

The adapted software and hardware used by disabled people is unfamiliar and often complex. Without training, disabled people would struggle to use a computer with specialist software. Aidis provides free training to ensure that they understand how to use it. The trust maximises the benefit their clients can get from the equipment and ensure that they and their families know exactly how the software or hardware works, the different settings, and the opportunities on offer.

Training for disability groups

Aidis visit groups of disabled people and their carers to introduce them to technology they would not normally have the opportunity to see or try out. They demonstrate how a disabled person with no voice can communicate and how someone without arm movement can access a computer. These training events are designed to broaden expectations. If parents think their child can access a computer, they start to see what their child could achieve in the future. With the right help, teaching, and education, they see opportunities opening up.

Free Helpline

The free helpline telephone number 0808 800 0009; e-mail address: support@aidis. org offers support to disabled people with technical issues. Disabled people are using computers with technology most helplines will not understand, and if something goes wrong they are without their key to education or communication. The Aidis helpline exists so that any problem can be resolved quickly or extra training can be given. There is also a website which provides alternative help and support through live chat, Facebook, and Twitter: www.aidis.org

43. Some of the adapted computer equipment that the Aidis Trust uses to help disabled people.

*44. Aidis Trust training: Working with a group
of professionals to inform them how technology can
benefit disabled people.*

Why Aidis?

Aidis helps some of the most vulnerable members of society, those disadvantaged as a result of severe disability and poverty. They help them to lead more independent, less isolated lives through adaptive Information and Communication Technology. Aidis continues to help disabled people by expanding their own knowledge base of existing and new products. This enables the trust to assess and provide impartial and practical solutions to help overcome access issues.

Prince Edward's visits

Prince Edward has been Patron of the Aidis Trust since November 1, 1992. He visited Aidis on November 8, 2011, where he met Aidis' Trustees and members of staff. They showed how their services have developed over the past few years. Demonstrations were given on how Aidis can support and train computer users remotely, allowing them to be helped at a time that suits them and at a location that is most accessible to them in their own homes.

Prince Edward was also shown assistive technology, both computer hardware and software, some of which had been designed for disabled people and some not. Access to technology for those with disabilities enables them to communicate, work, and play.

Aidis are very pleased to have Prince Edward as a Royal Patron and have said of him: "The Duke of Kent has been our patron for many years now and we are extremely honoured and thankful for his continued support."

ENDEAVOUR TRAINING
National youth and education charity

Mission statement:
"To provide programmes of practical and challenging
experience to help young people to develop their potential as individuals, in teams and as active members of society."

Endeavour Training was founded in 1955, by Robert (Dick) Allcock OBE, and holds the Investors in People Award. Dick was a young man living on his parents' farm in Norfolk when, in 1940, during the Second World War, a group of evacuees from Bethnal Green, London, arrived in the area. They attended church on Sundays, and Dick realised that they needed a youth club and he set one up. He forged a new approach to personal growth and development that was made open to all young people.

Nearly 60 years later, in 1999, Dick attended the Town and Country Festival where he talked to everyone as they gathered on the abseil tower. Urging them to continue to provide leadership and role model status, he said that all that is good in society depends on leadership qualities and service to others. Today, Dick is still meeting and encouraging young people.

Endeavour

The modern day Endeavour is a national youth and education charity, working with the young, aged 8 to 16 years. Staff working for Endeavour are proud to be taking Dick Allcock's vision into the third millennium, applying the same principles, but in a multi-cultural and multi-racial society. Endeavour stands for shared human values of respect for others, personal growth, and relationships, as well as enjoying life to the full. They believe in understanding ourselves, and the roles we fulfil; taking personal responsibility for our actions; and making a positive contribution to society.

Over the years, Endeavour has adapted to change, and the young people it trains are creating their own small communities, and also getting on with the important job of doing fun things and growing into the leaders of tomorrow.

Purpose

The purpose of Endeavour is to provide developmental opportunities for children and the young. Their work emerged out of a tradition of using the great outdoors to challenge, inspire, and change the lives of young people, including young offenders.

Endeavour works with some of most disadvantaged and disaffected young people across the UK. In 2007 Endeavour worked with over 1,500 young people, putting in over 100,000 contact hours, helping them to change and therefore improve their life chances.

There exists a long-standing commitment to promote voluntary involvement through regional schemes designed to support those experiencing disadvantage, and to develop responsibility and leadership, which will continue into the next generation. The term NEET [Not in Education, Employment or Training] is an ugly tag to attach to a young person. The mission of Endeavour is to provide challenge and inspiration to young people who, for whatever reason, find themselves excluded from society.

The trainers employed are experts in building positive relationships with young people of all backgrounds, and they concentrate specially on motivating them to think about success in life. A range of targeted programmes is in place to assist young people in taking control of their futures, and in setting and achieving their goals. Regardless of his or her past a young person can be provided with support to conquer their fears and build up a future for his or her self. A critical element of the approach by the trainers is in providing character building and encouraging self-confidence and self-esteem.

Young people learn how to express themselves with confidence and how to trust and respect others. They experience the security of making friends, and working alongside colleagues as part of a team effort. It is in this way, that the individual can feel a sense of belonging and take a pride in his or her own work and objectives.

Endeavour specialises in providing a wide range of effective, personal, and social development programmes for young people who have been denied opportunities in life, that will enable them reach their full potential.

Skills, activity, and youth programmes

Indoor skills development focuses on kinaesthetic learning, which means that the student actually carries out a physical activity, rather than just listening to a lecture or watching a demonstration. Information Technology and skills helps the student with school and college exercises, and prepares him/her for a future job. Programmes include the use of presentational skills, ICT, use of digital camera, communication, and self-presentation, and literacy and numeracy.

There is a wide range of adventurous, outdoor activity, such as climbing, orienteering, kayaking, abseiling, raft building, canoeing, hill walking, and caving. Endeavour have found that for most of the young people they work with these activities and experiences are new, and are designed to develop confidence and skills which can be usefully transferred to the school or workplace environment. Youth programmes such as Up2Us, Team Endeavour, Wildside, and Gateway to Work, have sought to continue the work with young people.

The President of Endeavour is the Right Honourable, the Lord Phillips of Worth Matravers, The Lord Chief Justice, and the Chairman is Mr Richard de Lacy QC. Their Head Office is in Chesterfield, and they have centres in Scotland, Yorkshire, the Humber, the Midlands, the North East, and London.

Prince Edward's visits

Prince Edward became Patron of Endeavour on November 28, 1979, and takes a great interest in the development of young people. In July 2008, along with the Chief Executive, Mr Les Roberts, Prince Edward opened a new Leicester Centre. He spent the day there, meeting the youngsters, speaking with them, and sitting in on their activities, and watching them performing problem solving tasks.

On April 2, 2012, Prince Edward visited Endeavour's Challenge Teesside, where he was shown a range of projects that were on display at Coulby Newham Youth and Community

Centre, Middlesbrough. Endeavour has worked with young people in Middlesbrough and Teesside for over 30 years. Prince Edward was joined by Lord Crathorne, the Lord Lieutenant, Mr Peter Scrope, the High Sherriff and Mrs Scrope, Councillor Mr Ron Lowes, vice Chair of Middlesbrough Council, and Mr Kevin Parks the Council's Director of Regeneration, together with Endeavour trustees, Mr David White and Mr Kevin Ward.

Prince Edward saw young people from the Moving on Up, Inside Out and Youth Participation Project. He also discussed Endeavour's work with the Military to Mentors and Poppy Factory programmes that are training ex-servicemen to work with young people. Chief Executive Mr Les Roberts said:

"We were absolutely delighted that His Royal Highness came to meet the young people we work with, and showed his support for our work in the Teesside area. Many of our colleagues and partners attended the event, and gained real insight into our way of working with, and encouraging young people. We look forward to extending our work in the North East to bring new skills and new opportunities to the many young people we support."

Government figures in 2014 show that 1.04 million young people aged from 16 to 24 years in the UK were Not in Education, Employment or Training, a decrease of 38,000 from July to September 2013, and down 37,000 on the previous year. Endeavour, therefore, still has a great deal of work to carry out in assisting as many as possible of these young people towards a career.

The figures as at February 26, 2015, show that 963,000 young people are still not in education, employment or training and have the NEET tag attached to them. Of 16-24 year olds, 61 per are in NEET, and the remaining 39 per cent are in education or training. [1]

THE EDGE FOUNDATION

The Edge Foundation campaigns to raise the status of technical, practical and vocational education. At a time when parents and young people are worrying about job security, increases in tuition fees, and future employment, the practical skills acquired through hands-on training can offer a degree of comfort. Edge is located at No.4 Millbank, Westminster, London. Prince Edward became Patron in the time of Edge's predecessor Edexcel, on March 3, 1981. Sir Garry Hawkes CBE, was Chairman of Edge from its inception in 2004, until 2009, and its President 2009-12. Edge was established under Sir Gary's leadership with funds arising from the disposal of Edexcel to Pearson Group, to raise the status of technical, practical and vocational learning in the UK.

Development of technical, practical, and vocational learning
Mr John Cox CBE, one of the founding trustees of Edge, who is also Chairman of the UK Centre for Economic and Environmental Development, attributes the success of Edge in its early years to the inspiration of Sir Garry's vision of the importance of technical, practical and vocational learning as an aspirational choice, of equal standing with academic learning. Edge now sees itself as the champion of technical, practical, and vocational learning, at

*45. HRH The Duke of Kent meets students at the opening
of the Edge Hotel School at Wivenhoe House, September 2012.*

the leading edge of thinking and best practice, helping young people develop the skills and expertise vital to a successful career and to meet the needs of the future economy.

Edge campaigned for high quality and well regarded paths to success for young people particularly by raising the status of technical, practical, and vocational education. In 2009, Edge launched its Six Steps to Change Manifesto, designed to influence government and public opinion. This document was refreshed in 2012, and re-launched as Edge's Six Steps for Change, setting out what The Edge Foundation wanted the education and training system to do. This included such measures as providing technical, practical, and vocational learning as an integral and valued part of every young person's education and as a recognised route to success; from the age of 14 giving young people a choice of learning experiences and pathways based on their motivation, talents and career aspirations; ensuring that technical, practical and vocational education and qualifications are of high quality and valued by employers; and ensuring that all young people, whatever their different abilities and interests leave the system with confidence, ambition, and the skills to succeed and the skills the economy needs.

VQ Day

Since Edge's inception, it has supported a large number of projects. The charity established the annual VQ Day, meaning vocational qualifications for students, teachers and employers that is a celebration dedicated to the thousands of people who gain vocational qualifications each year. It sponsors WorldSkills and the Skills Show, to showcase vocational excellence and for the same reason also sponsors an Association of Colleges Beacon Award for excellence in practical learning in

46. HRH The Duke of Kent meets the Rt. Hon. Lord Baker of Dorking, CH, Chair of the Edge Foundation, at the opening of the Edge Hotel School at Wivenhoe. With them (centre) is Mr Harry Murray, MBE, Director of Wivenhoe House. September 2012.

colleges. Since 2009, it has sponsored two Academies in Bulwell, Nottingham, and Milton Keynes. Both Academies were officially opened by Prince Edward in 2010, and technical, practical, and vocational learning, forms an important part of their curriculum. A documentary film titled, We Are the People We've Been Waiting For, that was sponsored by Edge, was produced in the autumn of 2009, highlighting the importance and benefits of vocational education and training.

Young Enterprise and start-up programmes
In September 2006, Prince Edward announced that The Edge Foundation was to give a grant of £3 million to Young Enterprise. As part of a new initiative to promote vocational learning and skills-based training the funding went towards the delivery of a range of educational business and enterprise programmes for children and young people in UK. The scheme combined the experience and skills of both Young Enterprise and Edge to promote vocational learning for young people across the country. The benefits were reflected in IT capacity, expanding and creating shorter student business start-up programmes, and materials, and increasing recognition for teachers who incorporate Young Enterprise programmes in schools.

Edge continues to work to raise the status of technical, practical and vocational learning. Jan Hodges, Edge's current Chief Executive Officer, speaking about

Edge's strategic aims for the future stated:

"It's a very exciting time for The Edge Foundation. Having been through a period of reflection and review we have launched our Six Steps to Change, renewing Edge's commitment to practical learning. This offers future generations of young people the opportunities for 'learning by doing' at every stage of their education and training.

"One way in which we do this is by strengthening the evidence base that is finding and sharing research evidence to positively influence policy and practice. A prime example is the first-ever Edge Research Conference, which took place on 16th November 2012, as part of the Skills Show in Birmingham. We'll also promote debate. For example, we're working with the Cross Party Skills Group on the development of a Manifesto for Skills."

Baker Dearing Trust and University Technical Colleges
Edge is also involved in supporting the creation of innovative educational institutions. It is a key supporter of the Baker Dearing Trust, which is headed up by Edge's current Chair, Lord Baker of Dorking. The Baker Dearing Trust is the organisation behind the creation of University Technical Colleges (UTC), a new concept that offers 14-18 year-olds the opportunity to take a highly regarded, technically-oriented course of study. Each one is sponsored by a University or College and has the backing of key local employers. A total of 33 UTCs are currently either open or in development around the country with more to come. Lord Baker commented:

"Since Edge was first established it has taken great strides to champion technical, practical and vocational learning. Our vision is to be the leading edge in this thinking and best practice, helping young people develop the skills and expertise vital to a successful career and to meet the needs of the future economy. The development of a new network of University Technical Colleges is one way to address providing high-quality vocational pathways for 14-18 year olds.

"Each UTC is led by employers and a university, providing a gold standard education for young people who prefer a more practical and applied form of learning. I'm pleased to say that there are five already open and a further 28 have been approved so far to open in 2013 and 2014.

"Despite advances in the attitudes of many people, in the UK there is still a culture where high quality technical, practical and vocational learning is too often viewed as second best behind academic learning. Edge's mission is to change that.

The country needs people who can combine know-how with can-do, people who can invent and make, as well as remember and write. We have those people but we don't always give them the opportunity to discover and develop all their talents. We work hard to stay at the heart of the education agenda, influencing debate through research, working closely with opinion formers and educationalists, and supporting innovative projects."

*47. HRH The Duke of Kent performs the official opening of the Edge Hotel School at Wiven-
hoe House. With him is Mr Stephen Mannock, former General Manager of Wivenhoe House,
September 2012.*

By the spring of 2014, 17 UTCs had in fact been opened, with another 15
planned to open that September. A further 18 are due to open during 2015-16,
bringing the total number to 50, spread across the country.

Studio Schools Trust
Edge also supports the Studio Schools Trust, which supports the development of
Studio Schools. These are small schools for 14-18 year-olds of all abilities, which
seek to address the growing gap between the skills and knowledge that young people require to succeed and those that the current education system provides. Studio
Schools work in close partnership with employers and all students undertake work
experience.

University of Essex and Edge Hotel School
Edge is also a key partner along with the University of Essex in the Edge Hotel
School, a unique and innovative venture situated in Colchester, Essex. At the Edge
Hotel School students study for fast-track foundation and honours degrees in Hotel
Management and Culinary Management, whilst working alongside hospitality
industry professionals to operate a four-star commercial hotel. The Edge Hotel
School was opened by Prince Edward in September 2012.

Endnote to Chapter 5

[1] Source: Parliament website; Commons Library Standard Note, Published Notes

SN06705, February 26, 2015, author James Mirza Davie, Topic: Economic situation, Unemployment; fourth quarter of 2014.

CHAPTER 6

PROFESSIONS, BUSINESS, AND ENGINEERING
Part 1
Professions and Business

Introduction

Prince Edward's involvement with the professions and business and engineering has for many years been substantial and varied. He is Patron of: The Association of Men of Kent and Kentish Men, (May 1, 1968); Kent County Agricultural Society, (August 1, 1975); Institute of Export (IOE) International Trade, (November 1, 1976); and BCS, The Chartered Institute for IT (formerly the British Computer Society), (November 1, 1976).

Prince Edward was formerly a member of the Mountbatten Medal (Award) Advisory Panel. He is an Honorary Fellow of: the Chartered Management Institute (CMI), (January 1, 1981); The Institution of Engineering and Technology (IET), (April 1, 1977); and The Institution of Mechanical Engineers (IMechE), (February 8, 1994). He is a Royal Fellow of The Royal Academy of Engineering (RAE), (May 1, 1986), and President of The Engineering Council, (November 1, 1989).

Part 1

ASSOCIATION OF MEN OF KENT AND KENTISH MEN
and
KENT COUNTY AGRICULTURAL SOCIETY

The Association of Men of Kent and Kentish Men (known formerly as the association) was formed in 1897, at the Holborn Viaduct Hotel by ten businessmen. Their aim was to create an association that would further the good name of Kent and its people. They established the City of London branch, which met regularly until 1971. Other branches followed in Ashford, Canterbury, Central

48. HRH The Duke of Kent visiting the Institute of Export,
pictured with Rami Ranger and family.

Office Chislehurst, Deal & Walmer District, Dove, Faversham, Lynsted, Maidstone, Medway, Orpington Sittingbourne, Tonbridge, Weald, and Whistable. Ashford has recently celebrated its centenary.

Their aims and objectives are: 'to encourage good fellowship and citizenship and a sense of pride in the historic county of Kent; to protect the magnificent heritage of our towns and villages and the beauty of the countryside; to encourage and recognise educational activities in the youth of the County; to maintain a library of County literature and works by Kentish authors and to preserve records of historic and general interest in the County; to administer a Benevolent Fund; and, to promote interaction between members at Branch level through social and sporting activities.'

It is known that in the 1600s there was A Society for Kentish Gentlemen that was formed in London, and the aim of the County Society was to give charitable aid to the sons of poor Kentish men specifically for their training in the church. For reasons not recorded it vanished after the year 1700, and was then re-formed in December 1897.

Women's involvement

In an ironic twist of history, the association currently have more women than men members. It was not, however, until the early part of the 20th century that women were allowed to become affiliated members. Periodically debates take place about changing their title to include the ladies but tradition still prevails. All the branches are run like clubs and women play a good part in the running of them.

Prince Edward visits Kent County Show

The highlight of the year is the Kent County Show, which is primarily an agricultural show, presenting farm produce, livestock, and demonstrations of traditional skills like blacksmithery, and displays from the Royal Artillery. The three-day event brings together the very best of Kent, with animals, food, fun and excitement, and above all a sense of what the Garden of England has to offer. It is hosted, annually, by the Kent County Agricultural Society at Detling near Maidstone. The society was formed in 1923, and the first show was held in 1929. It attracts around 100,000 visitors each year.

On Friday July 11, 2014, at the Kent County Show, Prince Edward carried out the official opening of the new Kent Exhibition building as part of the celebrations of their 50 years at the Kent Showground. The 3,000 square metre building has capacity for up to nearly 5,000 people.

Prince Edward became Patron of the Association of Men of Kent and Kentish Men, on May 1, 1968, and Patron of the Kent County Agricultural Society on August 1, 1975. The society was delighted with Prince Edward's visit to the 2011 Kent County Show on Friday, July 15. Arriving at the Showground, he was greeted by Deputy Lord Lieutenant Viscount De L'Isle of Penshurst and his wife Isobel, Viscountess De L'Isle. Prince Edward met with civic dignitaries, society officials and staff, before beginning a tour of the Show. The Royal Party was escorted by Lady Astor of Hever, the society's President, who took on the role after her husband Lord Astor of Hever retired in 2010. Lady Astor and the society's Chairman Mr George Jessel, DL accompanied the party to Kent Young Farmer's area that is titled 'Why Farming Matters in Kent', located in the Show Gardens. The morning's tour was completed watching the Heritage Parade. The afternoon programme saw Prince Edward visit the 'Men of Kent and Kentish Men' display, before walking down to the new indoor Cattle Rings and Agricultural Area. Prince Edward was said to have enjoyed a marvellous day, and remarked that "the Show had highlighted the importance of food production and farming."

THE INSTITUTE OF EXPORT (IOE)
INTERNATIONAL TRADE

The Institute of Export (IoE) located at Export House, Minerva Business Park, Lynch Wood, Peterborough, Cambridge has been a Registered Charity since 1935, and was instrumental in establishing both the Institute of Export Australia, over 50 years ago, and the Institute of Export Canada, around 35 years ago. It is a founder member of the International Association of Trade Training Organisations, (IATTO). Prince Edward became Patron of the IoE on November 1, 1976.

Many of the IoE members hold qualifications based on those pioneered by the institute and their attempts to build competence and skill in trading internationally. In the United Kingdom the IoE and its qualifications has the Department of Education DoE OfQual awarding body status that is widely recognised internationally. The IoE is a non-profit making professional membership body, representing and supporting the interests of everyone involved in importing, exporting, and international trade. They offer a unique range of individual and business membership benefits as well as a world-renowned suite of qualifications and training. Dedicated to professionalism and recognising the challenging and often complex trading conditions in international trade markets, the IoE is committed to the belief that real competitive advantage lies in competence and that commercial power is underpinned by a sound basis of knowledge.

The IoE's mission therefore is to enhance the export performance of the United Kingdom by setting and raising professional standards in international trade management and export practice. This is achieved principally by the provision of education and training programmes. Offering all their courses through Distance or Online blended learning a mixture of tutor support and presentations, including webinars and chat rooms, IoE export qualifications will give the individual the knowledge to further his or her career in international trade. The range of qualifications on offer include: Young International Trader, aimed at 14-18 year olds; Certificate in International Trade, which is open to those aged 16 or over with no formal qualifications; Certificate International Trade Advisor; Advanced Certificate in International Trade; and a Diploma in International Trade. In 2012, a Professional Practice of International Trade Foundation Degree was launched to complement the study and take it into the University arena. It can take less than two years to start from the very beginning, and end up with a Diploma in International Trade, and in some instances formal qualifications are not required from the applicant.

Queen's Awards for excellence in international trade

The 2012 Queen's Awards for Enterprise in excellence in international trade was held at London's Radisson Blu Hotel. The institute's Director General, Ms Lesley Batchelor, having been part of the judging panel in the International Trade category of the awards hosted the first Gala Dinner for the winners. Some 151 companies were recognised out of a total of 209 recipients for their tremendous achievements internationally.

Prince Edward joined the celebrants for a drinks reception before dinner where he tirelessly enjoyed speaking to all the winners, and listening intently to their stories of growth and global trade. Congratulating the representatives of award winning companies, Prince Edward made his speech, expressing his pride in Britain's exporting talent. In his closing remarks he praised the success of UK companies making waves in international trade.

The Institute's Chair, Mr Doug Tweddle CBE, presented a special award to Mr Rami Ranger, Managing Director of Sun Mark for its achievement in being the only company to win a Queen's Award four years in succession. The Middlesex-based business, supplies and exports foodstuffs for major British and international companies as well as producing its own range of quality products.

The keynote speaker was Mr Richard Noble OBE, a holder of the land-speed record. A specialist in developing high-risk ventures, Mr Noble outlined his latest trail-blazing venture entitled 'Bloodhound Programme', to generate an all-British programme to break the 1,000 miles per hour land-speed record again, by engaging

49. HRH The Duke of Kent talking to members of the
Scout Association at the offices of BCS, the Chartered Institute for IT.

with the next generation of scientists, engineers, and mathematicians. The self-funding programme entails Mr Noble working with schools and sparking pupils' interests in harnessing key skills to progress long-term careers in key disciplines.

It was a great evening and a repeat dinner was planned with Prince Edward for September 2013. The institute prides itself on its relationship with the Prince and wishes him well in his superb work undertaken over many years, supporting international trade and the exporters of the United Kingdom.

BCS, THE CHARTERED INSTITUTE FOR IT
(formerly BRITISH COMPUTER SOCIETY)

BCS, The Chartered Institute for IT, formerly The British Computer Society (BCS), established in 1957, is a registered charity, having been incorporated by Royal Charter in 1984. They have offices off the Strand in Southampton Street, south of Covent Garden in central London. The main administrative offices are in Swindon, Wiltshire, and they also have an office in Sri Lanka.

BCS is the leading professional body and a learned society that represents those working in Information Technology (IT) in the United Kingdom and internationally. Membership is worldwide, with over 70,000 members in over 100 countries, including about 40 branches in the UK, 15 international sections, and around 50 specialist groups.

Its objectives are to promote the study and practice of Computing and to advance knowledge and education therein for the benefit of the public. BCS is licensed by the Engineering Council to award Chartered Engineer status (CEng) and Incorporated Engineer status (IEng). The institute also has a licence for the Science Council to award Chartered Scientist status CSci). BCS is also a member of the Council of European Professional Informatics Societies (CEPIS).

BCS – A Brief History

BCS emerged out of the London Computer Group (LCG), having been formed in 1957, from a merger of the LCG and an association of scientists, into an unincorporated club. That October, BCS was incorporated by Articles of Association as the British Computer Society Ltd. The first President was Dr Maurice Wilkes FRS. Charitable status was granted in 1966, and in 1970, BCS was given Armorial Bearings.

Prince Edward became Patron on November 1, 1976, and was BCS President during the Queen's Silver Jubilee Year 1982-3.

In 1985, BCS became a nominated body of the Engineering Council. It went through a transformation in September 2009, to ensure it remained relevant to the ever-changing world stage of IT, and the transformation included a re-brand as BCS, The Chartered Institute for IT. Changes include a modern new corporate identity, internal restructuring, and an overhaul of BCS Qualifications and Chartered IT Professional status to keep them relevant to the ever-evolving world of Computing.

Prince Edward opens BCS's new offices

On January 20, 2005, Prince Edward officially opened BCS's new offices that incorporate member facilities in central London. In the flexible meeting space which can cater for meetings of up to 120 people, facilities include working units with laptop docking stations that have internet access, and informal meeting areas with self-serving refreshment facilities, overlooking Covent Garden. Addressing nearly 100 members of BCS, Prince Edward said:

"I am pleased to note how the British Computer Society, in accordance with its Royal Charter, is playing a key role in raising professional standards and establishing the IT agenda for the nation. Also, how the society has dramatically transformed itself to become an all-embracing representative body for Britain's one million IT professionals as well as impacting on the education and work skills of the country.

"The BCS is now setting the pace for the nation's IT literacy programme so that our student and working populations are being taught to use computer technology in their schools, colleges, and places of work, while the BCS is also ensuring that society at large learns to use computing for enjoying its enormous benefits.

"The BCS still retains its key position at the forefront of supporting the nation's IT professional training and qualification programme. This ensures that thousands of young students who are looking to enter the IT

50. BCS's 50th anniversary celebration dinner in 2007 in a state room at St James's Palace.

profession every year are equipped with BCS accredited qualifications that are recognised as the best.

"And because the IT profession must also keep adapting to keep pace with the phenomenal speed with which technological advancements are unveiled almost every day, then so the society advises and delivers enhanced skills and career development services and products to its professional membership.

"I am greatly impressed by the new offices that the society has created to support its fast growing membership. Over one thousand IT professionals a month are now joining the BCS and these new offices gives the society the modern face with the facilities and location that its membership deserve."

Prince Edward also officially opened the new BCS headquarters in Swindon on June 6, 2006. He unveiled a plaque to commemorate the official opening of the premises, which BCS took over earlier that year in reaction to the society's rapid expansion, which at that point had reached more than 56,000 members. Prince Edward was taken on a tour of the building, accompanied by Mr David Clarke the Chief Executive Officer, BCS trustees, and members of BCS staff.

Scouts' IT Activity Badge

During the visit, the common interest of Prince Edward and BCS in scouting was highlighted. At that time BCS sponsored the Scouts' IT Activity Badge. A scout who had recently obtained his badge gave Prince Edward a demonstration of the website

139

he had developed. The launch of the Scout Association Staged IT Activity Badges to celebrate the sponsorship of the badges by BCS took place on a sunny September 17, 2005, at the House of Commons in the presence of Prince Edward.

The three-year deal included BCS creating resources to help members achieve each stage of the badge. At the launch, stages 1 and 2 were showcased and were met with much enthusiasm by the six Scouts from 2nd Swindon (Penhill), who attended the event. Scout Jamie Ballard said: "These resources look great. I am looking forward to being able to use them to help me get stages 2-5 of the badge as I have really enjoyed achieving Stage 1."

The launch was attended by around 30 Members of Parliament from all political parties, who mingled with the Chief Scout, Mr George Purdy, the then President of BCS, M. John Ivinson, and other BCS and TSA staff over tea and coffee and lovely cakes! This was followed by several speeches, including Mr Richard Allen the Member of Parliament who hosted the event, Prince Edward, Mr David Clarke and Mr George Purdy. To round off the event, and mark the beginning of a successful partnership with BCS, a large cake in the design of the IT badge was shared amongst all the attendees. Natalie Spencer, Head of Fundraising and Sponsorship at The Scout Association said:

"Both BCS and TSA are looking forward to a large percentage of the membership completing their IT badges and gaining the skills needed to keep apace with the technological advancements of the 21st century."

Mountbatten Medal Award

The Mountbatten Medal was established by the National Electronics Council in 1992, and named after Earl Mountbatten of Burma, who was the first Chairman of the Council. The award is made annually by the Institution of Engineering and Technology (IET) for outstanding individual contribution or contributions over a period of time to the promotion of electronics or information technology and their application that benefits the UK. It is supported by BCS and the Royal Academy of Engineering. The medal may be awarded only to UK residents, or international residents who have accomplished achievements of benefit to the UK. Contributions can be within the spheres of science, technology, industry or commerce, and in the dissemination of understanding of electronics and information technology is open to both adults and young people.

The Mountbatten Medal Advisory Panel, comprises the Presidents of the Institution of Engineering and Technology, the BCS, The Chartered Institute for IT, and the Royal Academy of Engineering. They meet in June, each year, to consider nominations for the award. In selecting a winner, criteria required involves the Panel giving particular emphasis to the stimulation of public awareness of the significance and value of electronics; spreading recognition of the economic significance of electronics and IT, and encouraging their effective use throughout industry in general; encouraging excellence in product innovation and the successful transition of scientific advances to wealth-creating products; recognising brilliance in academic and industrial research; encouraging young people of both sexes to make their careers in the electronics and IT industries; increasing the awareness of the importance of electronics and IT amongst teachers and others in the educational disciplines.

In the autumn of 2006, Mr John P. Leighfield CBE, Chairman of Research Machines Plc, and Deputy Master of the Information Technologists' Company was chosen by Prince Edward as the recipient of the prestigious Mountbatten Medal. Mr Leighfield experienced a long and very distinguished career in the UK IT industry. The award was made in recognition of his outstanding contributions to Information Technology and his achievements in the industry. Prince Edward presented the award to Mr Leighfield at the annual Mountbatten Memorial Lecture.

Patronage of His Excellency

Sheikh Nahayan Mabarak Al Nahayan

Under the patronage and presence of His Excellency Sheikh Nahayan Mabarak Al Nahayan, United Arab Emirates Minister of Higher Education and Scientific Research, BCS celebrated the official launching of its Middle East Section, which also marked the society's Golden Jubilee, on June 2, 2007. The event was held at the Emirates Palace Hotel in Abu Dhabi, and was attended by His Excellency Mr Edward Oakden, the British Ambassador to the United Arab Emirates (UAE). He was accompanied by a senior diplomatic team, in addition to the BCS Middle East Section members, including Information Technology Managers and Chief Executive Officers in the IT industry. Following the inauguration, His Excellency Sheikh Nahayan Mabarak Al Nahayan delivered his keynote speech, in which he said that he was pleased to see the inauguration of the Middle East Section of the British Computer Society; he expressed his admiration of the advanced level that the UAE Information Technology sector has achieved; and added that the mission of the Middle East Section which calls for developing and enhancing the IT Systems in the area will help in strengthening its position as a Technology Information centre within the region as well as internationally during the 21st century.

Professionalism in IT programme

BCS launched its Professionalism in IT programme with the goal to both increase professionalism in the field and change the way the entire IT profession is perceived. The initiative aims to ensure that companies understand the necessity of turning IT into an integral part of every business' infrastructure. Educating and training new generations of IT professionals and BCS members to carry out this and similar initiatives is yet another ongoing task in which the society is constantly involved.

There is a range of BCS membership grades available that cater for IT professionals as they progress through their careers. The top professional grade is Fellow of the British Computer Society (FBCS). It is open to individuals who meet certain criteria based on eminence, authority or seniority. Applicants typically have a minimum of five years' experience in a senior position in IT or, are outstanding individuals who have built a strong reputation as authorities in the IT field.

BCS also offers Chartered IT Professionals status (CITP). The standard has been developed in consultation with public and private sector employers and the academic community, to truly reflect today's IT profession. Aligned with The Skills Framework for the Information Age (SFIA), the UK Government backed competency framework, CITP as the benchmark of IT excellence. Holding CITP status reflects one's integrity, professionalism, and dedication to one's work.

Benefits of joining BCS

BCS members benefit from joining the society in more ways than one. Membership meetings give them fantastic networking opportunities, ensuring that they stay in touch with the latest trends in the IT and communications industry. The members of the UK branches meet regularly and discuss a series of topics related to IT, making their voice count with local committees and giving them a chance to grow professionally and build new professional networks.

Awards for years 2011-12

The annual BCS UK IT Industry Awards provide a platform for the entire profession to celebrate best practice, innovation and excellence. The Awards feature categories that cover: project, organisation, technology and individual excellence. These categories are open to organisations and individuals involved in IT across the public not for profit and commercial sectors. Previous winners include such organisations as Network Rail, RSC, BT, HMRC, and many more.

Probrand wins Queen's Award

With his interest in data and technology, Prince Edward decided to personally present the 2011 Queen's Award to Mr Peter Robins the Managing Director of Probrand, as the company enters its Platinum 20th year of business. The Award was for the continuous innovation behind its Information Technology procurement portal www.theITindex.co.uk which has been recognised for saving organisations millions of pounds sterling on product prices. The award is the first to recognise the growing global information economy and technology manufacturing community in the Midlands of England. It is recognition that Probrand has achieved the highest level of excellence in improving its performance and commercial success through continuous innovation over the last five years.

CHARTERED MANAGEMENT INSTITUTE (CMI)

Prince Edward is an Honorary Fellow of the Chartered Management Institute. It was over 60 years ago that the British Institute of Management as it was then, developed the UK's very first diploma in management studies. Today it is known as the Chartered Management Institute (CMI), and is located at 2 Savoy Court, London. CMI have constantly been at the forefront of all aspects of management training and thinking.

CMI are a chartered professional body in the UK dedicated to promoting the highest standards in management and leadership excellence. Over 100,000 managers use their unique services on a daily basis. CMI offers a range of qualifications for managers in business as for instance in leadership development, which is so crucial to the success of British business. The CMI's research has the purpose of making a difference to how you manage, and their policy is shaped by research into successful management techniques.

Part 2

Engineering

THE INSTITUTION OF ENGINEERING AND TECHNOLOGY (IET)

Prince Edward is an Honorary Fellow of The Institution of Engineering and Technology (IET) that is located at Savoy Place, London. It is the largest, multidisciplinary professional engineering institution in the world, having been formed in 2006, from two earlier institutions. Its worldwide membership is currently in excess of 153,000. The IET has the authority to establish professional registration for the titles of Chartered Engineer, Incorporated Engineer, Engineering Technician, and ICT Technician, as a Licensed Member institution of the Engineering Council.

THE INSTITUTION OF MECHANICAL ENGINEERS (IMechE)

Prince Edward is also an Honorary Fellow of The Institution of Mechanical Engineers (IMechE). Based in central London at Bridcage Walk, IMechE is an independent engineering society representing mechanical engineers. They have over 100,000 members in 139 countries in industries, including rail, automotive, aerospace, manufacturing, energy, medicine, and construction. They are licensed by the Engineering Council UK to assess candidates for inclusion on ECUK's Register of professional Engineers.

ROYAL ACADEMY OF ENGINEERING

The Royal Academy of Engineering (RAEng) is the United Kingdom's national academy for engineering, and brings together the country's most eminent engineers from all disciplines to promote excellence in the science, art and practice of engineering. Its strategic challenges are to drive faster and more balanced economic growth, to foster better education and skills, to lead the profession, to promote engineering at the heart of society and to build its organisational capability.

It all began at Buckingham Palace on June 11, 1976, when 126 of Britain's leading engineers gathered for the inaugural meeting of what was then The Fellowship of Engineering. For His Royal Highness Prince Philip The Duke of Edinburgh, who hosted the meeting as Senior Fellow of the new body, it was the culmination of years of effort, during which he was the most prominent advocate of what was to become known as The Fellowship. The result was the establishment of a body of the most distinguished British engineers drawn from all branches of the profession, to recognise the contribution of engineers to society, and to provide expertise and advice on engineering-related matters. Since then, The Royal Academy of Engineering (RAEng), as it became in 1992, has played an increasingly important role in policy advice to government and other bodies. Its promotion of best engineering practice through its support for engineering research, entrepreneurship, and innovation, its work to nurture engineering education and skills, its promotion of engineering and its leadership within the profession has also proved to be a catalyst of change within British engineering.

Prince Philip had previously become the founder President of the Council of Engineering Institutions (CEI), a body set up in 1965 by the major engineering institutions to promote the interests of the profession. This provided a focal point where the profession as a whole could debate matters of common concern, including the need for the formation of an elite body. Progress, however, was slowed by the lack of priority given to this initiative and uncertainty over the form the body should take. It was only in January 1976, thanks not least to steady pressure from Prince Philip and others, that this issue was resolved.

The Fellowship, once established, set up permanent membership arrangements. The founding Fellows had either been nominated by the chartered engineering institutions or had come from the engineers in the Royal Society. The Fellowship now established nomination procedures, with proposals to be scrutinised by four disciplinary groups representing mechanical, civil, electrical, and process engineering, whilst a ceiling of 1,000 Fellows was set, which was revised to 1,500 in 1994, and subsequently removed. A maximum of 60 Fellows was to be elected annually.

The Academy honours the UK's most distinguished engineers. It aims to take advantage of the enormous wealth of engineering knowledge they possess and, through the interdisciplinary character of its membership, it provides a unique breadth of engineering experience to further the art and practice of engineering in all its forms.

Election to The Academy is by invitation only, and Fellows are elected each year from nominations made by existing Fellows or by Presidents of engineering institutions. They are distinguished by the title 'Fellow of The Royal Academy of Engineering', and the designatory letters FREng. Honorary Fellows and Foreign Members who have made exceptional contributions to engineering are also elected.

The Academy's work programmes are driven by its strategic plan and the five strategic challenges articulated within it. Programmes and activities aim to provide a key contribution to a strong and vibrant engineering sector and to the health and wealth of society.

The Academy's vision is to put engineering at the heart of society, delivering a broadly based economy with many world-class engineering businesses. It sees the UK of the future as a nation of innovators and entrepreneurs, turning ideas into commercially useful products and services with more businesses based on the fruits of engineering innovation in the wider global market. Policymakers will understand the importance of fostering the right climate for success. The UK will be a world leader in engineering research and home to an education system that both inspires young engineers and equips them with the skills that the nation needs.

In this vision, society will recognise and value great engineering. The applications and implications of engineering will be integral to national development, engineers will be household names, and will inspire many more young people into a career in engineering. Engineering will become a desirable and natural career choice for people from all social, ethnic, and economic backgrounds. Young women in particular will become much better represented within the profession.

The Academy has a wide range of programmes and activities, each of which addresses one or more of its five strategic challenges and which, together, aim to progress towards achieving its vision. Its policy work focuses on complex and multidisciplinary areas that are rapidly developing and its support for research and innovation is targeted towards the most talented engineers in the UK. As a priority, it encourages, supports, and facilitates links between academia and industry.

The Academy celebrates engineering excellence and uses it to inspire, support, and challenge tomorrow's engineering leaders, increasingly through the media. It runs a comprehensive programme of awards and schemes to encourage engineering research and facilitate closer contacts between the industrial and academic worlds.

Prince Edward presents The MacRobert Award

The MacRobert Award, the UK's premier award for innovation in engineering, was established in 1969, and has been delivered by the Royal Academy of Engineering (RAE) since the early 1980s. In 2006, Optos plc, the company that has revolutionised eye care and the early detection of retinal defects with its ultra-wide retinal imagers, won the Award, securing a gold medal for the company and a £50,000 cash prize for the three team members. The announcement was made at the Academy's annual Awards Dinner in London, where Prince Edward, who has been a Royal Fellow of the RAE since May 1, 1986, was guest of honour and presented the award.

In 2012, the Academy established the Queen Elizabeth Prize for Engineering, a £1 million prize awarded biennially. It celebrates the engineers responsible for a ground-breaking innovation that has been of global benefit to humanity. The first prize was awarded to five people who had seminal roles in creating the internet and the World Wide Web.

One example of the work of the Academy is its annual Soiree and Exhibition that, in 2008, was held at the Science and Technology Facilities Centre (STFC), Rutherford Appleton Laboratory. During the day the exhibition was open to STFC staff and visitors, while in the evening it was attended by Prince Edward and the Royal Academy of Engineering Fellows and their guests.

Many STFC e-Science staff took turns to explain their subject on a stand in the exhibition. In the past RAL computing developments designed to meet the requirements of scientific research have produced technologies that have gone on to have a significant commercial impact. These include technologies for computer graphics and animation, and computer networking, for which research started in the 1960's has led to today's ubiquitous CGI and Internet. It is intended that such impact will be achieved by the success of grid technologies which STFC e-Science is developing to meet the requirements of today's scientific research.

The achievements of the UK National Grid Service is now supported by the European Grid Infrastructure. Presentations on the CERN (the European Organisation for Nuclear Research), LHC Computing Grid, and the EGEE Grid in particle physics, computational chemistry, and biosciences, were well received by the audience. The demonstration of the GridPP Real Time Monitor presented on the Magic Planet globe proved popular with many visitors attending the exhibition.

Mr Philip Greenish Chief Executive of The Royal Academy has said:

"The Academy values its Royal Fellows immensely. It recognises and greatly appreciates the long-standing support that Prince Edward has given to engineering and to the Academy in particular." [1]

ENGINEERING COUNCIL

The Engineering Council was created by Royal Charter in 1981. On November 1, 1989 Prince Edward became its President. As the regulatory body for the engineering profession it holds the national register of over 235,000 Engineering Technicians, Incorporated Engineers, Chartered Engineers, and ICT Technicians. It also sets and maintains the internationally recognised standards of professional competence and ethics that govern the award and retention of these titles. This ensures that employers, government, and wider society – both in the UK and overseas – can have confidence in the knowledge, experience and commitment of registrants.

Registrants must be a member of one of the 36 professional engineering institutions and societies licensed by the Engineering Council to assess candidates and accredit academic courses in universities and colleges. To gain the titles, applicants are assessed against the UK Standard for Professional Engineering Competence (UK-SPEC), published by the Engineering Council on behalf of the UK engineering profession.

The Engineering Council plays an active role internationally. It is a member of the International Engineering Alliance, which incorporates six international agreements governing mutual recognition of engineering qualifications and professional competence. The Engineering Council's International Advisory Panel is also the British National Committee of FEANI, which is the European Federation of National Engineering Associations – a federation that unites national professional engineering associations from 32 European countries. FEANI Index publishes an index listing over 14,000 university courses approved by FEANI as meeting the education component for EUR ING registration.

Prince Edward's role

In accepting the invitation to become the Engineering Council's first President, Prince Edward has helped to publicly raise the profile of the engineering profession. He has demonstrated his support for the work of the Engineering Council by attending many functions, meeting with committee members, and visiting the staff at their offices.

On October 19, 2007 Prince Edward opened new premises, designed to encourage joint working across the STEM (Science, Technology, Engineering and Mathematics) community. The open-plan building in Holborn, London, is the new collective home of the Engineering Council, the Engineering and Technology Board, SEMTA, STEMNET, Women into Science, Engineering and Construction, the Sector Skills Development Agency, and Engineers Against Poverty.

In his address, Prince Edward said:

"I am delighted to be here to open this essential STEM facility, which will help bring together crucial organisations from across the science and engineering communities."

Professor Kel Fidler, Chairman of the Engineering Council UK, said:

"I am delighted with the new offices and very pleased that the Engineering Council's President, His Royal Highness the Duke of Kent, has been able to mark the occasion of their opening."

Sir Anthony Cleaver, Chairman of the Engineering and Technology Board, said:

"By bringing together key representatives of the STEM community, this office will encourage collaboration and joined-up thinking. This initiative is already bringing the community together to help promote the crucial role of science and engineering in solving the challenges of the modern world."

Endnote to Chapter 6

[1] Correspondence between Mr Philip Greenish and Celia Lee, 11th May 2014.

CHAPTER 7

CIVIC DUTIES AND RELIGIOUS TRUSTS

Introduction

Prince Edward carries out a number of civic duties. He is High Steward (November 1, 1975) of the Borough Council of King's Lynn & West Norfolk; President (January 17, 1994) of The Henley Society; Royal Patron, (February 14, 1994) of the British-German Association; Royal Patron (January 20, 1998) of the Dresden Trust; and Patron (October 26, 2004) of the Canterbury Cathedral Appeal.

BOROUGH COUNCIL OF
KING'S LYNN AND WEST NORFOLK

Prince Edward became High Steward of the Borough Council of King's Lynn and West Norfolk on November 1, 1975. It is an honorary title bestowed by the council and dates back to the middle ages. The office of High Steward has its origins in the 16th century and the post-holder was originally the town's representative in the House of Lords. Initially, the office holder oversaw the administration of the borough courts on behalf of the lord of the manor. The role having been modified down through the centuries, today it involves Prince Edward's attendance at important functions.

Brief history of King's Lynn

King's Lynn is a picturesque and historic town and is mentioned in the *Domesday Book* of 1086 [1], where it is recorded that the property belonged to the Bishop of Elmham and the Archbishop of Canterbury. It was the Kingdom's fourth biggest port in the 13th century, known as Bishop's Lynn, becoming King's Lynn in 1537.

The town hall dates from the 15th century and there are a number of historic buildings, two theatres, museums, and other cultural and sporting venues. The Victorian Corn Exchange building is the main venue for concerts, stand-up comedy shows, and other live events. (The famous yearly King's Lynn Music Festival is included in Chaper 9 – Music). Literature Festivals are held during a single weekend in March (Literary Fiction) and September (Poetry), each year, usually in the town hall.

800th anniversary of the 1204 Charter
King's Lynn celebrated their 800th anniversary of the Charter of 1204, on September 10, 2004. The King's Lynn Charter granted by King John, provided the legal and economic framework for the already thriving town to continue to develop successfully as a commercial centre. The text was a grant by the King to the burgesses of Lynn, at the request of John de Gray, Bishop of Norwich, whereby the borough of Lynn should be a free borough for ever with rights of local jurisdiction, freedom from tolls, except in London, and a merchant guild. The original charter is a beautifully preserved document, written in Latin and housed in the borough archives of King's Lynn.

A banquet to mark the occasion was held in the Assembly Room and was attended by Prince Edward. Each course of the meal served signified one for each 100 years.

The Honourable Alderman Dr Paul Richards who was Mayor of King's Lynn (1998-2000) met Prince Edward. Dr Richards says:

"I had written a short History of Lynn (2004) for publication in our local newspaper *The Lynn News*. Its editor arranged for a copy to be nicely bound and I was asked to present it to Prince Edward at the Town Hall. This I did, when he was being introduced to people.

"It was pleasing to have the opportunity to present the book to His Royal Highness especially on the 800th anniversary of Lynn's 1204 Charter of borough freedom that had at least enabled a town council to be set up.

"Prince Edward seemed happy to receive the copy and looked most interested on what was a special and atmospheric evening for Lynn." [2]

Memorial service for All the King's Men 2011
A memorial service was held in the ancient church of St. Peter and St. Paul, West Newton on Queen Elizabeth II's Sandringham estate, Norfolk, on Sunday, September 12, 2011, in memory of All the King's Men, a reference to a company of the Norfolk Regiment raised at Sandringham that suffered very high losses at Gallipoli. Members of The Gallipoli Association and a large congregation filled the church to remember those who lost their lives during the Gallipoli Campaign, 1915, and especially those from Sandringham. Cadets from 42F Kings Lynn Air Training Corps along with cadets from Sandringham Army Cadet Detachment stood as an Honour Guard for the dignitaries attending.

Prince Edward was in attendance along with representatives from Turkey, New Zealand, and France, the Mayor of Kings Lynn and West Norfolk Councillor Zipha Christopher, and the Chairman of the Gallipoli Association, Captain Christopher Fagan. On leaving the church Prince Edward took the time to speak to each of the cadets on the Honour Guard. There was then an assembly in the Village Hall for a reception with displays of photographs, speechmaking, and tea with ANZAC biscuits.

THE HENLEY SOCIETY

The Henley Society was formed in 1961. At that time a major planning application submitted to Oxfordshire County Council which would have involved the demolition of the handsome Catherine Wheel Hotel in Hart Street, and its replacement with a row of 1960's style shops, was turned down. Local residents and visitors alike did not approve the plan of losing this historic building or its replacement with shops. The outcome was the formation of the Henley Society and the saving of the Hotel. Hart Street is considered one of the jewels in Britain's high street scenes and to imagine it without the Catherine Wheel façade would have been unthinkable.

Since then the society has flourished, ensuring that planning applications are examined by its own planning and conservation experts and it regularly brings its influence to bear on difficult and controversial applications. Particular attention is paid to Listed buildings and to buildings within the Conservation Area. The society has links with Henley-on-Thames Historical and Archaeological Group.

That is not to say they are opposed to modernising Henley, where it is favourable to so do. It is recognised that trade must prosper to enable the town to continue to flourish. The society also has links with The Henley Business Partnership and the River Thames Society. They arrange visits, lectures, and events for members to enjoy all manner of historic and interesting places, and to appreciate the need for continual vigilance on the environment. Their watchwords are to work to maintain the very best of the town for posterity and to ensure that the highest and most sensitive standards are applied to future developments.

Lord Camoys GCVO, PC, DL, who resides at Stoner Park, had been President of the society for some years. In 1993, following the death of the Vice-President Mr John Piper, Lord Carmoys accepted that position. Prince Edward was invited to become President and acceptance was duly made on his behalf by his then Private Secretary, Mr Nicholas Adamson. [3] His Royal Highness was introduced as President of the society on January 7, 1994, at their Annual General Meeting in the Leichlingen Pavilion, Mill Meadows. The society's Chairman, Major John Howard, also welcomed Prince Edward as "a Crocker End villager", saying: "He merely wants to feel closer to the town of Henley." Present also were the Secretary Mr Nic Rutherford, Vice-Chairman Mr Paul Clayden, and Treasurer Mrs Sandra Moon.

A talk was given on the Architecture of Royal Palaces by Mr Graham Keevil of the Oxford Archaeological Unit, who has considerable experience in restoration work and who, at that time was working at the Tower of London.

BRITISH-GERMAN ASSOCIATION

A renewed friendship between Britain and Germany began in 1946, when the Mayor of Reading, Mrs Phoebe Cusden, responded to an appeal for help from the Royal Berkshire Regiment that was then occupying the Rhineland. Mrs Cusden launched a Christmas appeal for food and clothing, and visited Düsseldorf in 1947 to see the situation for herself. In 1948 the first group of young people from Düsseldorf came to stay in Reading, Berkshire, and this started an exchange of youth that continued until 1992. The Reading-Düsseldorf Association is therefore one of the oldest Anglo-German links, the oldest of which is believed to be between Bristol and Hanover. The Southampton and other societies were also set up around the same time. The Reading-Düsseldorf Association continues today as an affiliate member of the British-German Association.

British-German Association (BGA)
An Association was founded in 1951, initially with the title of the Anglo-German Association (AGA). Prince Edward, who speaks fluent German, became its Royal Patron on February 14, 1994. In December 1995 the name was changed to the

51. The British-German Association marks the 300th anniversary of the Coronation of King George I. Left to right: BGA President Lord Watson of Richmond; Chairman Mr Stephen Watson; Patron HRH The Duke of Kent; Professor Monika Grütters Minister of State for Culture and Media in Germany; and the Rt. Hon. Ed Vaizey, MP.

British-German Association (BGA). Closer ties with both The Dresden Trust and The British-German Officers' Association for long-term association were under discussion. Of the BGA Prince Edward has said:

"The relationship between Britain and Germany is highly important to both our countries. As partners in Europe, in NATO, and with huge interests in business and commerce, it is vital that we continue to forge links and deepen mutual understanding. I have had a long relationship with Germany and it is a country I've visited many times. The British-German Association has played a pivotal role in furthering and shaping the relationship between Britain and Germany. Today, it is a thriving and vibrant Association, bringing together leaders in politics, business, and culture. It is also a place where many people, from all walks of life, can come together as friends and share their interest in our two countries. I am delighted to serve as the British-German Association's Patron and would like to encourage you to join and get involved."

Purpose of the BGA

The BGA exists to promote understanding and to forge links between Britain and Germany, and there are several branches in England and one in Scotland. The relationship has developed into a formal town twinning, supported by Reading Borough Council and the Landeshauptstadt Düsseldorf. There are regular exchanges between choirs, schools, sports clubs, churches, and many other groups.

The main aim of the BGA is the strengthening of understanding and friendship between the peoples of Britain and Germany. To this end, they provide an annual Programme of Interesting Events of various kinds, designed to promote understanding and foster friendship and which take place mainly in London. The programme includes a broad range of talks and discussions on cultural, historical, and political themes, musical performances, seminars in London and Berlin, and lectures and social events, all with a British-German theme.

They hold an Annual General Meeting, and there are various events each year, including a wine and cheese party with a talk on a topic that is related to Düsseldorf; an annual dinner; and a barbecue. The BGA is therefore an active membership-building organisation, attracting support from those involved in business, politics, and the arts, and they have an extensive network across business, with the diplomatic community, politics, and culture.

The strengthening of the relationship between Britain and Germany is being brought about by creating understanding and forging links. The BGA is therefore at the heart of the UK-German relationship, actively seeking to improve understanding and facilitate contacts and affiliations, and stimulating its relationship with affiliated societies.

Trading partners

Britain has also emerged as Germany's most important trading partner, and trade in

52. Anglo-German Remembrace Day Service at Penkridge on Sunday, November 9, 2014.

companies the UK is now their biggest investment destination.

BGA endeavour to take a public position when necessary on matters affecting British-German relations, and supporting the British and German business communities in the development of trade and commercial links.

A large number of British-German societies or town twinning associations around the country, all of which are independent of the BGA, are nevertheless affiliated to the BGA, in order to benefit from its contacts and its overview of the British-German scene. Periodically the BGA arranges a major conference for these societies, enabling them to discuss questions of mutual interest, learn from each other, get help from the BGA, and generally improve their contacts.

To assist in realising these aims they cooperate with the German Embassy in London and the UK Foreign & Commonwealth Office. They also seek to promote the strength of the UK-German relationship as partners in the EU and NATO.

Youthbridge or Jugendbruecke, supported by the BGA
BGA is a registered Charity and, in 1992, set up its own charity, the brainchild of Lord Watson of Richmond CBE and the then head of Lufthansa UK, Mr Tim Timmermann. Titled Youthbridge or Jugendbruecke, as the name suggests it is for the young. Their Chairman today is Mr Jon Corall. It raises funds that were originally obtained through the BGA's annual Nutcracker Ball, and now comes directly from companies, wherewith to encourage the learning of the German language in British state schools.

There is an annual award presented by the Ambassador for the best teacher of German, and they also promote school twinning and exchange visits as a catalyst for future friendship. There is an annual award and prizes for the best projects in the German language and on Germany, presented by pupils of Youthbridge schools. It also acts in many other ways to help these schools, for example by supporting exchange visits to partner schools in Germany as a catalyst for future friendship, by helping arrange master-classes for GCSE exams, and helping Youthbridge convince pupils in feeder schools to take up learning German.

Brief history of the AGA and BGA

After the Second World War (1939-45), the allied Military Government in Germany introduced a policy of non-fraternisation between the Allied troops and the local population as part of denazification. However, organised and controlled association did come about. County regiments were posted there and relationships developed between their home bases and the places where there were occupation troops, a classic case being Reading in England (home of the Royal Berkshire Regiment), and Düsseldorf (the location of the Headquarters of the British Zone of Allied Military Government). As a matter of policy, universities in the British Zone were paired with British universities in the hope that contact with the latter would influence the development of students in German universities. The relationship developed so well that, in 1949, the visiting student Chairman of Oxford-Bonn was asked if he would like to vote in the election that established Dr Konrad Adenauer (post-war Chancellor of West Germany) as Chancellor, and Bonn as the Federal Capital. The cities are now twinned and Oxford has a Bonn Square. Towns where there had been prisoner of war camps, for instance Manningtree, tended to produce Anglo-German Societies. All of these official organisations later became Affiliated Members of the Anglo-German Association.

Against this background, the 200th anniversary dinner for the birth of the German writer and statesman, Johann Wolfgang von Goethe was addressed in Heidelberg by Professor Sir George Catlin (father of Shirley, Baroness Williams née Catlin) who, on his return to England, attended another dinner at the Pen Club with the author Dr Thomas Mann and the Education Minister of Lower Saxony, Dr Adolf Grimme. They agreed that the time was now ripe and that an opportunity existed to take matters forward. They involved Professor Gilbert Murray OM, and the historian President of the Goethe Society, Dr G. P. Gooch. Discussion at the Catlin home and the House of Commons further involved Violet Bonham-Carter (daughter of a former Liberal Prime Minister H. H. Asquith), Harold Nicholson KCVO CMG, (diplomat and politician), and the publisher Victor Gollancz. With the blessing of the Foreign Office an Association was formed with Frank, Lord Packenham (later Earl of Longford) as its Chairman, and who had been Minister for Germany (1947-8), and was an Oxford don.

These events were followed by the famous letter to the *Times of* December 15, 1951 which was signed by many distinguished people, including Bishop Bell and Earl Russell. It invited applications for membership, and was accompanied by an immensely supportive leader that stated: "It cannot be too early to try to guide Anglo-German relations in the right Direction." These positive steps happened shortly after Dr Adenauer's visit to Britain, and one year after the founding of the

154

53. The Rt. Hon. Kenneth Clarke, Conservative MP, speaking at the British-German Association's Parliamentary Day at the House of Lords, 2014.

counterpart organisation, die Deutsch-Englische, now Deutsch-Britische Gesellschaft.

When, in 1995, the association changed its name to the British-German Association it was in order to prove that it was not excluding the Scots, Irish or Welsh. This fact was obvious in that the proposer of the change, George, later Lord Robertson of Port Ellen, (who had resigned from the Committee on becoming Minister of Defence) was very conspicuously Scottish.

The Association has had five Presidents: Field Marshal Earl Alexander of Tunis (the wartime commander), General Sir Brian Robertson (later Lord Robertson of Oakwood), former Commander-in-Chief of The British Zone of Germany, Sir Frank Roberts GCMG GCVO, Ambassador to the USSR, NATO, and Germany (1963-8); and Sir Nigel Broomfield KCMG, Ambassador to both Germanies. Today the President is Alan, The Right Honourable The Lord Watson of Richmond CBE, who was a former President of the Liberal Party, having been Chairman of the association for most of the 1990s. Mr John Faulder is Vice-President, having also become Chairman of the UK-EU Societies. Mr John Hobley is a Vice-Chairman, as is Dr Alan Russell.

Unlike its opposite number in Germany and most of the UK friendly societies with states in the European Union, the Association encouraged foreign (in this case German) members onto its board, and indeed elected a German, the Chief Financial Officer of Siemens UK, as its Chairman. The BGA's membership consists of individuals, Affiliate Members, and Corporates, some of whom elect to pay well over the minimum subscription and are gratefully known as Sustaining Members.

Early in the 21st century the British-German Officers' Association (BGOA) integrated with the BGA until it was dissolved in connection with the withdrawal of the British Army from the Rhine in 1994, at which time it was scaled down and its name changed to British Forces Germany who are due to leave by 2019.

Also, early in the 21st century the administration of the Dresden Trust was entrusted to the BGA, and a close relationship still exists between the two organisations.

In the past the BGA had premises at a number of sites in West London and, in 2002, arrived at 34 Belgrave Square SW1. The address was the location of the former Embassy of the East German Republic, and within a few minutes' walk of the Federal Embassy, whose moral support it has always enjoyed and the Ambassadors have always been among its patrons. These have always been men of very high calibre and three had already been head of the German Foreign Office, so highly was the London posting evidently regarded in Berlin. Two were also from very well-known German families, von Richthofen and von Moltke. However, the association never succeeded in its expressed ambition to create a club, where members and like-minded people could meet.

Not long after its foundation the association began publishing the *Anglo-German Review* which appeared fairly regularly for some 62 years, and which recorded its activities and kept in touch members who were scattered throughout the realm, a function that events could not achieve as they inevitably tended to be held mostly in or near London. The role of the former publication has now been taken over by the BGA's website.

The activities of the association were designed to foster the latent interests of members in each other's countries without, as far as possible, rationing participation by money. The most frequent events tended to be lectures, ranging from relevant current affairs to essays in historical information. Two major annual lectures emerged over the years: The Sir Frank Roberts Memorial Lecture – The expanding Europe: its relevance to both the British and the Germans, named after the former President; and The Prince Friedrich of Prussia Memorial Lecture – Britain at the heart of Europe, named after Kaiser William's grandson, who became an English country gentleman, exercising great influence for reconciliation. Among those giving the latter Lecture were a past President of the European Union, the Right Honourable Mr Roy Jenkins OM PC, a former British Prime Minister, the Right Honourable Sir Edward Heath KG MBE, and a former German Chancellor, Herr Helmut Schmidt, whilst the former was inaugurated at Lancaster House by the then Secretary General of NATO.

The first half-century was marked by an annual conference which tended to be combined with the Annual General Meeting usually held at Wiston House, West Sussex, and at which the evolution of British German relations was recorded. These years were also marked by The Young Koenigswinter Conference, an annual event that tends to make a deep impression on those young members who attend. The BGA regularly nominates delegates to participate in the conference that is organized by die Deutsch-Britische Gesellschaft.

Social occasions
There were of course a number of purely social occasions, several centring on the

German Embassy, but also including the Annual Dinner Dance, usually held at the Cafe Royal in Regent's Street, London. In the early 1990s, Karen, Lady Watson transformed it into the prestigious Nutcracker Ball. It became a splendid, pre-Christmas, fund-raising event, graced by a marching band from one of the Guards Regiments and was the highlight of the social calendar, where the Ambassador's wife usually became the Ball President. Nowadays the main social event is the New Year Reception and there are innumerable other opportunities to socialise around the many events the association arranges. In recent years the practice has grown up of arranging Members' visits to the premises of large German companies in the UK, most of which are Sustaining Members, such as the chemical and pharmaceutical company, Bayer, headquartered in Leverkusen, and the BMW motor vehicle company, that is headquartered at Munich.

Prince Edward as Royal Patron
of the British-German Association

To list just a few of Prince Edward's contacts with the BGA in his capacity as its Royal Patron, these started when, in 1995, his inaugural Annual General Meeting concluded with a splendid reception, complete with State Trumpeters at St. James's Palace, London, at which he presented the BGA's Medal of Honour to a number of recipients, one of whom, Dr Fred Hamblin, then a Vice-President, has since reached the age of 100.

In March 2003 Mr John Faulder was Vice-Chairman, and Prince Edward again very kindly made St. James's Palace available for a reception that was attended by delegations from each of the friendly societies within European Union states to celebrate the 50th anniversary of the Coronation of Her Majesty Queen Elizabeth II, which she attended with Prince Philip.

On September 26, 2005 the BGA celebrated 60 years of peace with Germany and a plaque was placed on the wall of Cannon Street Station, London, which Prince Edward graciously unveiled in the presence of the German Ambassador, The Lord Mayor of London, two former Foreign Secretaries, and several hundred members and their guests. The plaque read:

> "TO CELEBRATE sixty years of Peace between the peoples of Britain and Germany & TO COMMEMORATE six hundred years during which 400 Hanseatic merchants inhabited peacefully in the City of London from the X111th to the XIXth centuries a German self-governing enclave on this site known as the Steelyard, Stilliards or Stalhof."

On November 5, 2012, His Excellency the German Ambassador Georg Boomgaden hosted a gala dinner at his Residence for Prince Edward as the BGA's Royal Patron, to thank the association for its contribution to mutual understanding. The event was attended by members of the German Embassy and the BGA's Executive Board. Prince Edward took the opportunity to award the BGA's Medal of Honour to the ambassador for his own major contribution to relations between the two countries.

300th Anniversary of the Coronation of King George I

Following the death of Queen Anne (1665-1714), Georg Ludwig, Duke of Brunswick and Hanover and Prince-Elector of Brunswick-Lüneburg (1660-1727), became King of Great Britain and Ireland. Having adopted the English spelling of his first name, the new King George I travelled by coach to St. James's Palace where he stayed to be made ready for his coronation which was to take place on October 20, 1714, thus marking the beginning of the Hanoverian Accession. In those days Britain's kings also became rulers over part of what is today Germany.

Using an original manuscript found in the State Archives of Lower Saxony, the coronation service was reconstructed by Herr Arno Paduch, German musician and musicologist. Key parts of it together with a commentary were performed as a concert, created by Herr Paduch in Hanover, Göttingen, Halle (Saale), and several other cities in Germany, during the summer of 2014.

Special service at St Martin-in-the-Fields, London

Mr John Hobley found all the information relating to King George I's coronation in documents at the British Library, London, including the anthems that were sung. From these he put together a service with the help of Reverend Dr Sam Wells, and Dr Andrew Earis, both of St. Martin-in-the-Fields. The BGA held the Special Service at the church on Trafalgar Square, on October 20, 2014, to celebrate the 300th anniversary of the Coronation of King George I, and the Hanoverian Accession.

The church was packed to capacity with several hundred members and friends of the BGA, some of who had travelled from Germany and elsewhere in Europe and the US, especially for the occasion. Present were Prince Edward, Professor Monika Grütters, MdB, Minister of State for Culture and Media in Germany, His Excellency the German Ambassador and his wife, Mrs Marliese Heimann-Ammon, The Right Honourable The Lord Watson of Richmond CBE, President of the BGA, The Honourable Stephen Watson, Chairman of the BGA, Mr John Hobley, BGA Vice-Chairman, Alistair, Lord Lexden OBE, Official Historian to the Conservative Party and the Carlton Club, The Honourable Ed Vaizey, Conservative Member of Parliament and Minister of State for Culture, Sir Anthony Figgis KCVO CMG, Patron of Children and Families Across Borders, Mr George Mallinckrodt KBE, President of Schroders Private Banking plc, Mr Bruno Schroder, British Banker, Dr Katja Lembke, Director of the State Museum of Lower Saxony, Dr Ulrich Hoppe, Director General, German-British Chamber of Industry and Commerce, Professor Andreas Gestrich, Director, German Historical Institute, London, and Herr Arno Paduch and his son.

The Special Service

Herr Paduch had provided advice to Mr Hobley as to the likely composers of the music to the anthems sung. The lessons read and all but one of the anthems at the service on October 20, 2014, were the same as those performed at the coronation of King George I, at Westminster Abbey on that same day in the year 1714.

The Welcome was delivered by the Reverend Dr Sam Wells, Vicar of St Martin-in-the Fields. The First Address was given by Brendan Simms, Professor in the History of International Relations, The First Lesson, taken from Matthew 22 v.15-22, was read in German and English by Dr Ann Kennard, Chair of the Bristol-Hanover Council. The Second Address was given by His Excellency, Dr Peter Ammon, German Ambassador to the Court of St. James's. The Third Address was given by the Right Honourable The Lord Watson of Richmond CBE. The Second Lesson, taken from I Peter 2 v.13-17, was read by Prince Edward and was very much in keeping with the spirit of the occasion, containing the opening lines: "Submit yourselves to every ordinance of man for the Lord's sake: whether it be to the King, as supreme."

There was a selection of 17th and 18th-century music, sung by St. Martin's Voices and played by the St. Martin's Consortand Organist, Mr Richard Moore, all of which had been chosen by Mr John Hobley, Reverend Wells, and Dr Andrew Earis, Director of Music at St. Martin-in-the-Fields. These included extracts from Purcell, Bach, and Handel. The Organ Prelude was Purcell's Voluntary on the Old Hundredth, followed by the Processional Hymn, Hanover, by William Croft that contains the lines:

O worship the King, all-glorious above,
O gratefully sing his power and his love;
Our shield and defender, the Ancient of Days,
Pavilion'd in splendour and girded with praise.

In relation to the anthems that were sung at the King's coronation and that were again performed at the service, Herr Paduch has offered this further guidance on their origins:

"'I was glad' [from Psalm 122] by Henry Purcell [some musicologists say, that the composer is John Blow], 'The King shall rejoice' [from Psalm 21] by William Turner, and 'The Lord is a Sun and A Shield' [from Psalm 84] is by William Croft. The piece by Croft is the only one that was composed for the coronation. All the other pieces were composed for earlier coronations. The piece by Turner is also preserved in another manuscript with the title *The Queen shall rejoice*, so it was obviously composed for the coronation of Queen Anne in 1702, and remodelled for the Coronation of King George I."

The Blessing was followed by the British national anthem God Save The Queen, composed by Thomas Augustine Arne, the original title of which was God Save The King, having been first sung in 1745, during the reign of King George II.

At the conclusion of the service, Prince Edward was escorted from the church by the Reverend Dr Sam Wells, followed by members and guests, to attend a reception in St. Martin's Hall, in the 18th century church crypt.

Those present included the guests of honour, members of BGA's Executive Board, individual and Corporate members and societies, including Members from

Hanover, Oldenburg, Düsseldorf, Hertfordshire, Sussex, Bedfordshire, and Bristol.

The service was generously sponsored by Norddeutsche Landesbank Girozentriale, London, who were represented by Mr Christoph Trestler, Executive Vice-President, and Jon McLaughlin.

BGA's contribution to mutual understanding

Perhaps the words recently expressed by His Excellency the German Ambassador provide a flavour of the achievements of the association and, encompassing Prince Edward as Royal Patron:

> "I cannot praise highly enough your countless initiatives and tireless dedication, and would like to express my deep gratitude and appreciation to the members of the British-German Association. The service was not just the crowning glory of the many activities and events in the UK around the Hanoverian Accession, but a lasting expression of your devotion to British-German friendship and understanding".

DRESDEN TRUST

Today, such is the friendship between nations that towns as far distant as those in the UK and Africa are twinned. But on the nights of November 14, 1940, and February 13 and 14, 1945, the towns of Coventry and Dresden respectively, would be twinned in a very different and terrible sort of way. During the Second World War the Germans bombed Coventry in England, reducing it to a heap of rubble and killing hundreds of innocent civilians, and leaving many homeless. Coventry Cathedral, dedicated to St. Michael, was destroyed. In 1945 Anglo-American allied forces bombed the baroque city of Dresden in Germany to assist a Russian Army offensive into Saxony. Both cities had large, working-class populations, and escape in the face of sustained bombing from such a densely populated area was almost impossible. In the centre of the square in Dresden had stood the beautiful, Protestant Lutheran Church of our Lady the Frauenkirche. Three hundred residents had sought shelter in its crypt. It was not destroyed in the carpet bombing but collapsed due to the intense heat of the firestorm that followed.

Brief history of the church of our Lady the Frauenkirche

The church was built between 1726-43, and was designed by the city's architect George Bähr one of the great masters of the German Baroque style. It was different from other churches in that the altar, pulpit, and baptismal font were placed directly in the centre and therefore on view to the congregation. The altar was a relief depiction of Jesus' agony in the Garden of Gethsemane on the Mount of Olives by Johann Christian Feige. It was a fitting subject for the terrible night on which the temperature in that great building reached 1,000 degrees centigrade though, as if in an act of Christian defiance, it refused to melt and remained greatly intact.

In 1736, the church had been equipped with a Gottfried Dilbermann organ, which was dedicated on November 25, and the renowned composer Johann Sebastian Bach gave the first organ recital on December 1. So revered was its beauty and architecture that pictures of the church were painted by such distinguished artists as Canaletto and Bernado Bellotto. It was heart-rending for the citizens of Dresden to see that all that was left of the centrepiece of their town and their Protestant faith was a heap of rubble. To a religious community the desecration of a church is a terrible experience but the faith in God of the people of Dresden remained unshaken.

Towns of Coventry and Dresden twinned

Coventry and Dresden were officially twinned in 1956. Throughout the period of Communist rule in East Germany the Frauenkirche lay in ruins. It had been conserved as a war memorial and twinned with the ruins of Coventry Cathedral, which is designated an official war memorial in the county of Warwickshire in England. The inhabitants of Dresden, however, salvaged as many of the stones and pieces of religious ornaments as they could and numbered them in preparation for the day when the church might be reconstructed. A further reason that the church was so important was that it had been a meeting place for Christians opposed to Hitler.

During the 1980s the bombed site became a focal point for the East German peace movement and the removal of the Berlin Wall. In silence, they turned it into a shrine, adorning it with flowers and lighted candles.

The decision was taken in 1985 to rebuild the Frauenkirche. In 1989, a group of people headed by Ludwig Güttler, a noted Dresden musician, formed a Citizens' group, which blossomed the following year into The society to Promote the Reconstruction of the Frauenkirche. That year also the Communists left and East and West Germany were reunited in October 1990.

Fundraising got underway and work commenced in sorting the stones with a view to reconstruction. Other supporting organisations sprang up in Europe, America, and worldwide. The rebuild cost would be Euros 180 million (£70 million sterling). It would not be until after an appeal from Dresden in 1990 for help with its rebuilding which gained worldwide interest and support that work could begin.

Formation of the Dresden Trust

In response, the Dresden Trust was formed in Britain with Prince Edward as Royal Patron on January 20, 1998, and Colin James Bennetts, 8th Bishop of Coventry from 1998-2008, among its curators. Dr Paul Oestreicher, who is a canon emeritus of Coventry Cathedral and one of the founders of the Dresden Trust, underlined the importance of the Frauenkirche, comparing its status with that of St. Paul's Cathedral in London. Individuals and companies, including Rolls Royce plc helped to produce funds for the reconstruction of the church.

Tragically, the original orb and cross were destroyed, having melted in the extreme heat on the night of the bombing. Fortunately, however, the survival of the badly damaged cross, meant that it was available upon which to base a new one.

Bridge between Germany and the UK

In the 21st century, Dresden's Protestant Church has acted as a bridge between the two countries, and stretched a hand of friendship and co-operation across a peaceful Europe. On the 55th anniversary of the destruction of Dresden in the year 2000, as a symbol of millennium reconciliation, Prince Edward presented the city of Dresden with a new, 28-ton orb and cross for the church. It was paid for by British funds and was manufactured in London by the Gold and Silversmiths, Grant MacDonald, and was a gift from Great Britain's Dresden Trust. The British refer to it as the cross of peace. In a strange irony the maker was Mr Alan Smith, whose father Frank had been a member of one of the aircrew that had taken part in the bombing of Dresden. The cross and orb were forged of steel, with embossed work in copper and was matt fire-gilded. Care was taken to retain as far as possible the original 18th-century techniques.

Presentation of the cross and orb

Before delivery to the Frauenkirche the cross was exhibited for five years in churches across the United Kingdom, including Coventry Cathedral, Liverpool Cathedral, and St. Paul's Cathedral. It was shown to the President of Germany, Roman Herzog, during a state visit to the UK in December 1998, when he was staying at Windsor Castle as a guest of Her Majesty Queen Elizabeth II. The Queen accompanied by Prince Philip hosted a state banquet in St. George's Hall for President Herzog and his wife Christine. The banquet was attended by other members of the Royal Family and the Prime Minister, Mr Tony Blair and his wife Cherie. In her address the Queen told the President and his wife that they were the first visitors to Windsor Castle following the fire that had taken place there in 1992. During that year the Queen and Prince Philip had been on a state visit to Germany, having been taken on a tour of Dresden, amongst other places.

Symbol of reconciliation

The Queen emphasised the importance of the reconciliation between the United Kingdom and Germany as having been symbolised by the beautiful orb and cross, given earlier in the day as a gift from the British people to the people of Dresden. The Queen said: "It is a new symbol of the deep and ever increasing friendship between our two countries."

In 2000, the cross was handed over to the Frauenkirche by Prince Edward. A ceremony to remember D-Day June 6, 1944, was held in the presence of Chancellor Gerhard Schroeder and the Governor of Saxony Kurt Biedenkf. At the end of the ceremony the cross was raised 96 metres over the building and placed on the top of the dome to the sound of the people singing 'Give us Peace', that echoed throughout the square.

Consecration of the Frauenkirche

Work to the building was officially completed in 2005, a year ahead of schedule, and on time for the 800th anniversary of the City in 2006. During the Consecration the new Dresden Hymn was sung and the Bach Choir's rendering of the Messiah on December 9 and 10 resonated throughout the Frauenkirche. The Dresden Trust presented a beautiful new communion set to the church at Evensong. Once a month an Anglican Eucharist in English is held in the Frauenkirche with clergy from St. George's Anglican Chaplaincy in Berlin performing the service.

Prince Edward given highest order
On the eve of the inauguration and blessing of the Frauenkirche, October 29, 2005, Prince Edward was given the Federal Republic of Germany's highest order that can be awarded to a non-head of state, the Order of Merit of the Federal Republic of Germany at Grand Cross First Class Level. The honour was presented in Dresden by Georg Milbradt the President-Minister of Saxony who was representing the German President Horst Köhler.

In October 2006, Prince Edward was also awarded the Pro Humanitate prize of the European Foundation for Culture for his commitment to Anglo-German understanding. [4]

The cross will remain forever a symbol of reconciliation, peace, and friendship between nations. In his speech at the British Embassy, Berlin, on October 10, 2006, Prince Edward said:

> "I shall never be able to enter this wonderful Frauenkirche without recalling the glory of its reconstruction from a heap of rubble... To me it is not only a most beautiful building, but its recreation epitomises the reconciliation between nations, indeed the rebirth of the European home after the horrors of the 20th century."

Dresden Trust Medal 2015
On February 12, 2015, at the Kreuzkirche (Church of the Holy Cross) Prince Edward honoured Frau Helma Orosz, the Mayor of Dresden, with the Dresden Trust Medal in recognition of her work in furthering reconciliation and understanding of the city's history. At the same event, Eveline Eaton, Chairman of the Dresden Trust, presented the Mayor with a 'symbolic cheque' in acknowledgment of the trust's new project for the creation of a green area with trees and benches to take place in 2016.

On the occasion of the 70th anniversary of the bombing, Prince Edward was awarded the Dresden Prize by the friends of Dresden Deutschland at Semper Opera House on February 14, 2015. In his response to receiving this international peace prize, Prince Edward said:

> "It is a tribute to all supporters of the Dresden Trust who raised over £1 million to restore the city's famous baroque Frauenkirche. The award recognises their achievements and indeed the achievements of all people of good will in the United Kingdom and Germany, who have worked over the last 60 years to bring reconciliation between our two countries. Their success is an example to the rest of the world of what can be achieved through building trust and friendship."

In March, Prince Edward donated his £10,000 prize money that went with the peace award to the Dresden Trust to further their work.

On May 21, 2015, Prince Edward was again honoured with an award, the Saxonian Order of Merit which was presented aboard the German frigate FGS Sachsen, moored at London's West India docks. The award consists an eight-pointed, Maltase cross, covered with white enamel edged in green and with gold rim, and displays a small coat of arms of the Free State of Saxony. Prince Edward received the award from Saxony's Prime Minister, Stanislaw Tillich, who placed it round his neck on a green and white ribbon edged with gold. The award was in recognition of Prince Edward's services in fostering British-German relations and his work in assisting the rebuild the Frauenkirche. The Order of Merit was instituted in 1996 for outstanding services to the Free State of Saxony. It is their highest-ranking award and is presented to German and foreign persons for services which particularly benefit the general public in the political, social, cultural, and business fields or in connection with the envirionment.

Art exhibition London and Coventry 2015 – 16
Artist Monica Petzal, who is a Member of the Dresden Trust Board, opened her own art exhibition titled the Dresden Project which was on display in Dresden during January and February 2015. The exhibition will travel to Highgate Library and Scientific Institute, London, where it will be on display from 9-22 October 2015. From November 12 until Easter 2016, the exhibition will run concurrently at Coventry Cathedral and the Herbert Art Gallery & Museum, Coventry.

CANTERBURY CATHEDRAL
"Will no one rid me of this turbulent priest?"
(Attributed to King Henry II about St. Thomas Becket)

Canterbury Cathedral, which dates from the 6th century, is rich in interesting history. It was built under the auspices of a Benedictine monk who became known as St. Augustine of Canterbury. The Latin word for a seat is cathedra, from which the word cathedral is derived. Having been the prior of a monastery in Rome in the time of Pope Gregory the Great, Augustine was chosen by the Pope to lead a mission to Britain to convert the pagan King Æthelberht of the Saxon Kingdom of Kent to Christianity. He arrived on the coast of Kent as a missionary to England in 597 AD. The King's wife, Queen, Bertha, who was a Frankish Princess, was already a Christian. At his conversion the King allowed the missionaries to preach freely, giving them land to found a monastery outside the city walls. Augustine was consecrated Bishop of the English, and converted many of the King's subjects, including thousands during a mass baptism on Christmas Day 597.

Initially Augustine was given the church of St. Martin in Canterbury which is still in existence and is the oldest church in England still in use. Augustine became the first Archbishop of Canterbury in the year AD 598 and, since that time, there has been a community around the Cathedral which he founded offering daily prayer to God. Roman bishops were subsequently established at London and Rochester in 604, and a school was founded in Canterbury to train Anglo-Saxon priests and missionaries.

The cathedral may be the oldest organisation in the English speaking world, and the present Archbishop, The Most Reverend and Right Honourable Justin Welby, who was formerly Bishop of Durham, was enthroned as the 105th successor to St. Augustine, in March 2013.

Up until the 10th century the cathedral community lived as the household of the Archbishop. During that century it became a formal community of Benedictine monks that continued until King Henry VIII [5] dissolved the monastery in 1540.

Augustine's original building lies beneath the floor of the present church. It was extensively rebuilt and enlarged by the Saxons and, following a major fire in 1070, the cathedral was rebuilt by the Normans reaching completion in 1077. There have been many alterations to the building over the last 900 years, but the crypt, parts of the quire, and some of the windows and their stained glass, date to the 12th century.

Murder of St. Thomas Becket

The best-known event in the Cathedral's history is the murder of St. Thomas Becket. When, in 1162, Thomas was made Archbishop of Canterbury by King Henry II, he changed his allegiance from the King to the Pope and the Catholic Church. Henry, having previously appointed him Lord Chancellor, had expected his full support, and there were many conflicts between them, the final one being Thomas's excommunication of the Archbishop of York and the Bishops of London and Salisbury for their support of Henry's attacks on the rights of Thomas as archbishop.

Not only had the King's agents used Thomas's property while he was in exile in France but, in the summer of 1170, King Henry had his son crowned as his heir by these and other bishops, usurping a long standing right of the Archbishop of Canterbury to carry out coronations. The King was overheard in a rage to utter his infamous words about Thomas, "Will no one rid me of this turbulent priest?" although there are variations on what he actually said. In 1170 Thomas was murdered by four knights inside the cathedral. Three days after his death and burial in the Cathedral there began a series of miracles that were believed to stem from his martyrdom. Many of these are depicted in the miracle windows of the Trinity Chapel of the Cathedral.

Pilgrims began to flock to Thomas's tomb in the Cathedral. A year later King Henry, wearing sackcloth and walking barefoot, was among them. Thomas's murder had only increased the interest in him. Canterbury, always on the medieval pilgrim route to Rome, became an end in itself as thousands came to worship at his tomb especially after his canonization by Pope Alexander III in 1173. Geoffrey Chaucer's pilgrims in his famous poem, *The Canterbury Tales,* represented the hundreds of thousands who travelled to the Cathedral to pray, repent or be healed at Thomas's shrine. The shrine was later destroyed in 1538, on the orders of King Henry VIII. The work of the Cathedral as a monastery came to an end in 1540, when it was closed on King Henry's orders. The role of the Cathedral, however, as a place of prayer and the seat of the Archbishop continued.

Today, a simple candle marks the place where St. Thomas's shrine once stood, and the pink stone before it bears the imprint of thousands of pilgrims' knees. The tradition of pilgrimage is very much alive today, although the journey to Canterbury is faster and considerably more comfortable thanks to modern transportation.

Once the monastery had been suppressed, responsibility for the services and upkeep was given to a group of clergy known as the Dean and Chapter. Today, the Cathedral is still governed by the Chapter made up of the Dean, four Canons and five lay Members.

During the English Civil War of 1642-51, the Cathedral suffered damage at the hands of the Puritans. Much of the medieval stained glass was smashed and horses were stabled in the nave. After the Restoration in 1660, significant time and resources were spent in repairing the building.

The Second World War
Moving to modern events, during the Second World War (1939-45), the Precincts were heavily damaged by German Luftwaffe bombs, and the Cathedral's Library was destroyed. The Cathedral itself was not however seriously harmed, due to the bravery of the team of firewatchers who patrolled the roofs and dealt with the incendiary bombs.

Canterbury Cathedral in the modern age
Today, nearly 2,000 services are held each year at Canterbury Cathedral as well as countless private prayers from individuals, and the Cathedral offers a warm welcome to all visitors.

Save Canterbury Cathedral
Anglican Communion leaders witnessed the official opening of the International Study Centre at the Cathedral on April 16, 2002. Prince Edward unveiled the cornerstone plaque for the Phase 2 building. Great support came from the Episcopal Church USA, through the American Friends, chaired by the Reverend Dr John Harper of Washington DC.

The Cathedral Choristers sang, and Dean Robert Willis welcomed those who gathered. The Archbishop of Canterbury, Dr George Carey, gave the prayer of dedication. Also present were the former Dean and his wife, John and Ruth Simpson. Dean Simpson's vision for this centre began several years ago. He was present at the Lambeth Conference 1998, with the Bishops, when the corner stone for the building was being laid.

Prince Edward as Patron of the Canterbury Cathedral Fund
On October 26, 2004, Prince Edward became Patron of Canterbury Cathedral Appeal. Former US President George H. W. Bush is a President of the Appeal Fund. Like other English cathedrals, Canterbury receives no government help towards maintaining their fabric or buildings. The Canterbury Gift was for a time the major

fundraising effort for the Cathedral's conservation work. In 2007, the Freemason's Grand Charity donated £100,000 to the Save The Canterbury Cathedral Fund.

In 2008 Prince Edward joined a packed audience in the Cathedral for a concert by the famous English conductor, Harry Christophers, and 'The Sixteen' who are choral singers. Harry, himself a former chorister at Canterbury Cathedral when a boy, also spent three years in the BBC Singers. He founded the vocal ensemble 'The Sixteen' during 1979, and has directed them and their orchestra throughout Europe, America, and the Far East. Specialising in Renaissance, Baroque and 20th-century music, he has conducted recordings for 'The Sixteen' on a number of recording labels and has received several awards.

In December 2009, in their foreword to the English Heritage survey, the Archbishops of Canterbury and Westminster pointed out that cathedrals fulfil other roles as well as being places of worship:

"They are places of pilgrimage; many are also the focus of great national or civic events. They are cultural centres and, these days, tourist attractions. As public buildings, cathedrals are expected to meet certain standards and to provide modern facilities."

Prince Edward was guest of honour at a party in support of Canterbury Cathedral in 2012. Some 80 guests, many of whom were working in the City of London, met Prince Edward at Sarasin & Partners who kindly lent their offices overlooking St. Paul's Cathedral. Prince Edward urged the guests to visit Canterbury and see how necessary the conservation work is. Others attending included the Dean of Canterbury Robert Willis, Appeal Chairman Mr Richard Oldfield, and the Chairman of the Cathedral Trust Viscount De L'Isle. The Canterbury Gift raised more than £17 million but much more is needed.

Prince Edward visited the cathedral again, on February 11, 2013. He was warmly received by the Dean, the Receiver General, Mr Richard Oldfield, Chairman of the Cathedral's Development Committee, and Mr Andrew Edwards, Chief Executive of the Canterbury Cathedral Trust, formerly called the Canterbury Gift. Prince Edward has consistently supported the Cathedral in the past and they are always pleased to welcome him for a visit. He was given a tour of the Stained Glass Studio and the Stone Masons' Workshop, where he met the Director of Stained Glass, Leonie Seliger, and Head of Stonemasonry and Conservation, Heather Newton. Throughout the tour, staff and apprentices talked to Prince Edward and showed him their current projects.

The Canterbury Journey

For several years a project has been progressed named The Canterbury Journey, the purpose of which is to ensure that the visitors' experience of the cathedral is an unforgettable journey of discovery. Work is needed to be carried out to open up further aspects of the Cathedral and for which funds were required. An Application was made in 2012 to the National Lottery Fund for £10.6 million to fund work to the cathedral, including The Canterbury Journey project but it was not successful by 2013. Sixty-eight per cent of the money is needed for architectural work, particularly at Christ Church Gate and the West Tower. They tried again in 2014, and by May were delighted that a development grant had been ear-marked by the Heritage Lottery Fund for their now £19.4 million Canterbury Journey project.

The cathedral and its precincts were built for the use and enjoyment by everyone. Their established objectives are therefore: welcoming all people, increasing the involvement of local communities, and caring for the Cathedral, its community and its environment.

The Canterbury Journey project will provide a new Welcome Centre that will offer improved learning, hospitality, and public space. New trails will guide visitors through the cathedral and its newly landscaped Precincts, interpreting their journey and revealing unseen treasures from Canterbury's past. New visitors including children and families will be able to join the journey as a programme of outreach to schools and communities unfolds. A new Pilgrim Pass scheme will swell the company of contemporary pilgrims and deepen the cathedral's relationship with its neighbours. The fabric of the cathedral's western end, currently endangered, will be restored and enhanced, allowing Canterbury's journey to continue.

Endnotes to Chapter 7

[1] The *Domesday Book* housed at The National Archives, Kew, South West London, is the record of the great survey of much of England and parts of Wales completed in 1086, having been executed for William I of England (William the Conqueror).

[2] Correspondence between Honorary Alderman Dr Paul Richards, FSA, FRSA, Mayor of King's Lynn, (1998-2000) and Celia Lee, January 13, 2013.

[3] Letter from Mr Nicholas Adamson to Lord Camoys, January 19, 1994, Duke of Kent's files, St. James's Palace.

[4] Source for the Dresden Trust: *Dresden: a City Reborn*; edited Anthony Clayton and Alan Russell, foreword by HRH The Duke of Kent; pub. Berg, Oxford and New York, 2nd edition, 2005.

[5] King Henry VIII was the first King in England to adopt the grandiose title of His Majesty.

54. The installation of HRH The Duke of Kent as Grand Master
of the Freemasons at the Royal Albert Hall, London, on June 27, 1967.

CHAPTER 8

THE FREEMASONS' CHARITIES

Part 1

Who are the Freemasons?

Introduction

The Freemasons began as a group of men in a London coffee shop in 1717. It has remained a male organisation, although women have their own separate ladies charitable organisation, The Order of Women Freemasons, whose headquarters are located at Notting Hill, London.

The Freemasons address each other as 'brother' and Brother Nigel Brown, a former Grand Secretary of the Freemasons' United Grand Lodge of England, has described them in a Masonic pamphlet as having:

"... devised a non-sectarian, socially egalitarian forum in which men of integrity could fraternise, while avoiding the vexed issues of religion and politics. They took as their guiding metaphor the trade of stonemasonry, hence the symbols of Freemasonry – the square, compass and apron –

and its three degrees of evolution: Entered Apprentice, Fellow Craft , and Master Mason".

The Freemasons welcome people of all religions and as a leading Freemason Brother John Hamill, author of *The Craft A History Of English Freemasonry,* [1] has put it: "We insist that candidates have a belief in a Supreme Being because it is the one thing that unites us."

Today the headquarters of the United Grand Lodge of England and the principal meeting place for Masonic Lodges in London is located at Freemasons' Hall, 60 Great Queen Street, London. It is open to the public for guided tours and is conveniently situated near Holborn tube station. It is a Grade II listed building internally, and one of great beauty. The Grand Temple can seat 1,700 people, there are 21 Lodge Rooms, and an excellent library, and museum. The Grand Lodge has been in that location since 1775, and the present building is the third on that site. Built between 1927–32, as a memorial to the Freemasons who died in the First World War (1914-18), it is one of the finest Art Deco buildings in the UK. It has been used in the making of televised series of Agatha Christie's Hercule Poirot stories, and other television dramatisations, due to its Art Deco architecture and setting.

Freemasons' Hall Manchester
There is too, a Freemasons' Hall at 36 Bridge Street Manchester. Having been built in 1929, it is another building with an interior of great beauty. Boasting excellent banqueting, conference, and wedding suites it is suitable for all kinds of celebrations and is adorned with great marble pillars and Spanish galleries.

Prince Edward installed as Grand Master of the Freemasons
Prince Edward became a Freemason, joining the Royal Alpha Lodge No.16 on December 16, 1963. He was installed as Grand Master of the United Grand Lodge of Freemasons of England and Wales at a service in the Royal Albert Hall, on June 27, 1967. Within the precincts of the Freemasons his title is "the Most Worshipful Grand Master". Prince Edward is also Grandmaster of the Order of St. Michael and St. George, October 1, 1967; Patron of the Grand Lodge 250th Anniversary Fund, November 10, 1997; Grand Patron of the Royal Masonic Benevolent Institution (RMBI), January 1, 2002; Patron of The Royal Masonic Trust For Girls And Boys, January 1, 2003, and an Honorary Member of Old Wellington Lodge, November 5, 2005.

Sir Richard Buckley KCVO, who was Prince Edward's Private Secretary at St. James's Palace from 1961 until his retirement in 1989, said that he was not initially a Freemason but he was invited by the Freemasons to join them in a special lodge just before Prince Edward was installed as Grand Master. Sir Richard said "They thought it would be of great benefit if the Duke's Private Secretary were part of their system." Sir Richard was therefore present at the historic occasion of Prince Edward's installation as Grandmaster. The Freemasons, he said: "Love a lord, but the audience at the Royal Albert hall was a daunting one." It was huge, as at that time they numbered 750,000 members. "Those present were wise in the ways of the craft and would expect only the best from a new Grand Master. His Royal Highness carried off the ritual marvellously. More than that, he controlled the Hall. It was good fun!". [2]

In speaking of Prince Edward's attitude to his work, Sir Richard described him as "competent and confident", and that "he performs well at large set piece events. His investiture as Grand Master of the Freemasons was a good example." But in his early days, Prince Edward was "very shy until after his marriage to his wife Katharine nee Worsley the 2nd Duchess of Kent, who boosted his confidence and helped him get over it." Prince Edward was however "fine in the army, where he was taught to command men, but outside of that environment, formal occasions could be, and were, a real trial to him." [3]

The Freemasons – A Brief History
The Freemasons are mostly seen as a secret organisation, one mason identifying himself to another by a handshake, and by putting pressure on particular parts of the knuckles indicating which rank he holds.

When the Freemasons first set up a Lodge on June 24, 1717, it was limited to the Cities of London and Westminster. However, the stonemasons had organised about a century earlier and mention was made of them in the 1600s. They did not have certificates to prove that they had been properly qualified as stonemasons. Most could not read or write and the craft passed down through generations by word of mouth and by training, often father to son. The only method, therefore, by which a stonemason could indicate to a fellow mason that he was properly trained, was by that particular handshake. To avoid the untrained impersonating the trained and causing complications in the trade the signs were kept secret and known only to those who were qualified stonemasons.

These tradesmen were not rich and when work was scarce in one part of the country they had to walk to another, often to London, to find employment. Part also of the system of signs was that a mason who could provide accommodation for a fellow mason would put up a sign outside his lodging house or inn. A fellow mason arriving in London where he knew no one would look out for the sign and know when he saw it he was entering a place where he would be welcomed and given assistance by a brother mason. Some of these signs still exist today outside pubs with names like The Mason's Arms. The Freemasons as an organisation pre-date the trade union movement which existed from the 1860s.

Brother John Hamill, who is a highly recognised authority on Freemasonry, says:

"Most historians believe that Freemasonry as we understand it developed in the 17th century, which was a period of intense political and religious turmoil. Those who developed Freemasonry were seeking to provide a setting in which men of good will could come together in peace. By knowing what divided them, they could discover what they had in common and use that for the good of the community."

The Freemasons today

Events have moved on and today anyone can join the Freemasons through recommendation by a member, and who is prepared to subscribe to a code of moral conduct and to contribute to charity. Brother John Hamill says:

"The one thing we have in common is that we have a belief, however we practise it and whatever religion we may follow. Freemasonry in no way replaces that belief but its teachings of morality, tolerance, charity and kindness can support the individual's personal faith."

From their earliest days in history therefore the Freemasons held strong moral values, and were pledged to help one another and their fellow human beings, including those who were not stonemasons [4] and these values have been continued in the modern era.

The Freemasons' principles at their initiation in 1717 were: Brotherly Love, as a member of a tolerant and benevolent society; Relief, meaning the practice of charity in all its forms, not just giving money but showing caring towards other people; and Truth, i.e. obedience to moral precepts. These values are today taken collectively to mean charity and the obligation of giving to charitable causes. [5]

In relation to his role in the Freemasons Prince Edward has said:

"Freemasonry has taken a more prominent part in my life as Grand Master, visiting groups of Masons around the country. ... What I like to do is to go to Provinces and meet groups of Masons there, because one gets a better idea what they are thinking about. I try to meet as many as possible in an afternoon or evening.

"Another aspect is being involved in policymaking and talking to senior Masons about the future of Freemasonry and about problems as they occur; ... .

"I have been extremely fortunate in that I have been able to leave most of the day-to-day operations of the whole business of Freemasonry to my Pro Grand Masters. I've been extremely fortunate to be served by some wonderful people who have given a huge amount of time and energy to it, and by successive Grand Secretaries." [6]

Part 2

The Great Work of the Freemasons' Grand Charity

Current position of the Freemasons' Grand Charity

Prince Edward's role as Grand Master of the United Grand Lodge of England (which is not a charity) is different from his role as President of the Freemasons' Grand Charity but the two are intertwined due to the similarity of membership.

Prince Edward is not a trustee but is an Officer of the Grand Charity. His support for the Grand Charity and three other Masonic charities (that will be mentioned later), for each of which he is also Grand President, is extremely important to their members. General meetings of the Grand Charity are attended by several hundreds of members and sometimes Prince Edward is in the Chair. Proposals are currently being considered with a view in about a year's time to merging all the charities into one, single, over-arching charity. It is the Grand Charity and the other three charities, the Royal Masonic Trust for Girls and Boys, the Royal Masonic Benevolent Fund, and the Masonic Samaritan Fund, that are the focus of this study.

The Freemasons' Grand Charity, of which Prince Edward is Grand President, was set up in 1980, prior to which it was known as a Board of Benevolence. The Deputy Grand President is Brother Peter G. Lowndes, FRICS. The Vice Grand President is Brother Raymond J. Lye. Brother Richard M. Hone QC is President of the Grand Charity and Chairman of the trustees. Miss Laura Chapman is the Chief Executive. Brother Richard Cam-Jones is Secretary, having worked there for close on 50 years. Brother John Hamill is Director of Special Projects and Curator and Librarian of the United Grand Lodge of England. Their bookshop, Letchworths, is next door.

The hard work of maintaining and promoting the Grand Charity is therefore carried out inside Freemasons' Hall by the aforementioned officers and staff who have many years' experience.

Financial Assistance
The Grand Charity is the central grant-making body of all Freemasons in England and Wales, and is funded entirely by Freemasons and their families. They make a number of grants each year to Freemasons or their family members who are in financial distress, normally due to life-changing events beyond their control.

Relief Chest Scheme
The Grand Charity operates a Relief Chest Scheme, which means that the Charity holds the money on behalf of the Masonic lodges etc. who, in turn, maintain control over how the money is donated to any Masonic or non-Masonic charity or individual. There are approximately 4,500 Relief Chests with a total of over £26 million. In 2013, £5.6 million was donated to charitable causes via this scheme.

Beneficiaries Fund
Since 2002 the Grand Charity has managed the Beneficiaries Fund, which makes quarterly payments to the former beneficiaries of the RMBI Annuity Fund. Over 1,900 annuitants throughout the English Constitution and Districts overseas, receive quarterly payments and Christmas gifts to help make ends meet. In 1991 the total expenditure exceeded £1 million.[7] The Annuitants payments are made through the Beneficiaries Fund. At December 2007 there were 959 beneficiaries and for the financial year to November 2007, payments of £1,027,000 were made. [8] In 2013, there were 388 active beneficiaries, and during 2012/13 payments from the Fund totalled £433,115.

Grants
The Grand Charity also makes a number of grants to hundreds of nationwide non-Masonic charities as well as hospice and air ambulance services. At its General Meeting in Norfolk on November 15, 2014, they approved grants totalling £1,365,500 to non-Masonic UK causes. These charitable causes are supported because they aim to make a significant difference to people in need. Grants are provided for the purposes of: medical research; care for the most vulnerable people in society, including hospices for the elderly, and people with disabilities and those with health care needs; and providing opportunities for young people. Primarily, they make grants to: distressed Freemasons and their dependants; other Masonic charities; Non-Masonic national charities serving England and Wales; and emergency relief work on a worldwide scale, including disaster relief. Part of their policy expresses their devotion to duty and how they view themselves, quoted in their 275th Anniversary Souvenir Programme:

"We have always been at the fore in responding to appeals to relieve distress caused by floods, fires, earthquakes, hurricanes, cyclones, volcanic eruptions and similar calamities in all parts of the world." [9]

In the financial year ending November 30, 2014, 1,527 grants were made to individuals, amounting to £3,437,738. Some grants require the final approval of the Charity's members who, in general terms, are the members of Masonic Lodges.

Three Masonic charities
The Grand Charity does not make grants to the Masonic schools or care homes. Their needs are considered by three other Masonic Charities, which are separately constituted: Royal Masonic Trust for Girls and Boys, addressing the educational needs of Freemasons' children, the Chief Executive of which is Brother Les Hutchinson; The Royal Masonic Benevolent Fund, providing residential and nursing care for older Freemasons and their dependants, the Chief Executive of which is Brother David Innes; the Masonic Samaritan Fund, which helps to meet the costs of private medical treatment and of which the Chief Executive is Brother Lieutenant Colonel Richard Douglas, and the President is Brother Brigadier Willie Shackell CBE.

History of the Freemasons' health care
facilities and The Bagnall Report 1973
There had originally been five charities, the other two being the Royal Masonic Hospital for in and out patients, who were admitted on a means-tested basis, and the Fund of Benevolence, for donations to any charitable purpose.

Built in 1933, the Royal Masonic Hospital that was located at Ravenscourt Park, Hammersmith, south west London, was opened by His Majesty King George V in 1934. The hospital provided the highest standards of medical, surgical and nursing care for sick and needy brethren and their dependants. It had a fertility unit, a thriving outpatient department, an X-ray department, including a CT scanner, and a physiotherapy department. The Stamford Wing provided short-stay accommodation for acute cases as a department of psychological medicine, operating in partnership with Cygnet Health Care PLC. There was ECG facilities, chiropody, and dental clinics, and a department of nuclear medicine. The operating theatres were used by surgeons of the highest calibre, and the nurses were well-qualified professionals, retaining the tradition of providing warm and friendly care. It also had a pharmacy and pathology services.

In 1973, Prince Edward set up a Committee of Enquiry into the rationalisation of Masonic charities that reported under the Chairmanship of the Honourable Mr Justice Bagnell. The outcome was that the separate Girls and Boys Institutions became one, the RMTGB. Forty years on from its inception, and following the post-war period, the Royal Masonic Hospital was deemed to be no longer necessary and was sold. The care of the sick was vested in the Masonic Samaritan Fund. The Fund of Benevolence as it was then known, became the Grand Charity of today.

Part 3
Royal Masonic Trust for Girls and Boys

Brief history – girls

The name the Royal Masonic Institution for Girls was not adopted until 1868. The trust was the brainchild of a dentist, Chevalier Ruspini, who, in 1788, produced a scheme for establishing a school for the daughters of deceased and distressed Freemasons.

In order to secure a place at the school an application for support known as a petition would have to be submitted by a girl's parent, or if the girl was orphaned, a friend of the family – a petitioner – to be considered by the Petititons Committee, and therefore the girl was called a Petitions child.

The trust allowed for legitimate daughters of, and female children who were legally adopted by, Freemasons and who, from some unexpected calamity, were driven into poverty, to be educated at a Masonic school. In the beginning, there were only 15 girls between the ages of five and ten years who were admitted to the school which was set up in a rented house near Euston Railway Station, London. All the girls were boarders and were to be educated free of charge, unless it was considered that a parent's income was such that a contribution could be made. The girls came under the protection of Her Royal Highness, Anne, The Duchess of Cumberland, who was a member of the British Royal Family and the wife of Prince Henry, Duke of Cumberland and Strathearn. In 1795 a new, larger school was built at St. George's Fields, Southwark, London, to accommodate 65 girls. In 1853, they moved to St. John's Hill, Battersea Rise. By 1868, it was mostly secondary education that was provided, until a Junior School was opened in 1904.

An important aspect of girls' education was recognised in 1906 when it was accepted that a girl, who for reasons acceptable to the RMIG, was not admitted to the school might receive financial help to enable her to attend a school near her own home. During the 1914-18 War, the Junior School moved to Weybridge in Surrey, and by 1926, the numbers had increased dramatically. Freemasons numbering 3,500 had been killed in the war, and there was a post-war depression, which would account for the spiralling numbers of impoverished and fatherless children. In 1934, the Senior School moved to a 400-acre site in Rickmansworth Park, Hertfordshire, from where it still operates today.

The Royal Charter of 1952 made it quite clear that only daughters and female children legally adopted could benefit from RMIG, by being clothed, maintained, and educated. Fee-paying pupils were accepted from 1965, if they were daughters or legally adopted female children of a Freemason. Day-girls were admitted in 1972, when the doors were opened also to any fee-paying girl. The Junior School closed in 1973, due to falling numbers. The boys' school was eventually sold, but the Girls' School was set up as a separate foundation as a Girls' Independent School under the title of The Rickmansworth Masonic School (RMS). Today, it operates in the private sector in competition with all other schools in the area. Two injunctions were laid upon the school: any girl placed there by the newly formed RMTGB would be accepted, and if no Petitions child were at the school, the endowment would revert to the RMTGB to support Petition girls elsewhere. The term Petitions child here means that in the case of the dependent of a Freemason, they would petition the appropriate charity for example, as an entrant to the Masonic girls' school or to support the child in some way. This is what tends to happen for all the charities applicable to Freemasons as opposed to assistance given to other charities as donations. A girl would therefore be sent to RMS or supported at any other school, according to the needs of the girl.

The trust deed became active in 1986, whereby it assumed the duties and became responsible for the trusts of the former charities, the RMIG and the RMIB. The merger created one new body possessing wider terms of reference, and able to give greater assistance to the children of distressed Freemasons and when resources permitted, to give relief to children outside the Craft. In 1997, by the gracious permission of Her Majesty the Queen, the name of the school reverted to The Royal Masonic School for girls.

Brief history – boys
From 1798, there were two charities for clothing and educating sons of indigent Freemasons, following along on similar lines to that of the girls. The charities operated separately for nearly 60 years, each providing for the education of sons by sending them to the nearest school to which they resided. The privilege of the title 'Royal' was granted in 1832, and the name The Royal Masonic Institution for Boys was adopted. The first boys' school was at Wood Green in North London, where 25 boys started in 1857, following an amalgamation of the two charities in 1852.

A new school was built in Bushey in Hertfordshire in 1903. In 1926, the Institution was incorporated by Royal Charter, and an adjoining Junior School was added in 1929. By 1939, there were 800 boys aged eight to eighteen years at Bushey. A supplemental Charter was granted in 1958, which allowed fee-paying pupils, and a further Supplement Charter granted in 1966, allowed entry for day-boys. The RMIB did not exercise either of these options. In the late 1950s and 1960s, numbers declined sharply, and the two boys' schools merged in 1970, and also accepted boys from the age of eleven years. Due to a severe decline in numbers the school closed in 1977 and was sold. The money realised at the sale is used for supporting boys at whatever school is best suited to their needs.

In the early 1980s the RMIG and the RMIB were merged with the Royal Masonic Trust for Girls and Boys, which was given the overall aim of relieving poverty and advancing the education of children of all ages.

Part 4
Royal Masonic Benevolent Institution (RMBI)

Care homes – A Brief History

The Royal Masonic Benevolent Institution (RMBI) emanated from the time when the United Grand Lodge of England inaugurated the Royal Masonic Benevolent Annuity Fund for men (1842), and a Female Annuity Fund was set up in 1849. Its purpose for over 170 years has been to care for elderly Freemasons and their dependants. The first care home was opened in 1850 at Freemasons' Road, East Croydon, Surrey, at the time the RMBI was established. In 1955, the Home was transferred to Harewood Court, Hove, Sussex. The building was six-storeys high, providing 100 self-contained flats, where single or married Brethren, or their dependents, might continue to live an almost independent life, but with reassurance of having care and nursing facilities readily available should they be required.[10] Harewood Court still provides sheltered accommodation and, in the early 1960s, provision was extended to non-annuitants. There is now attached to it a 14-bed registered residential care home, as well as a 12-bed nursing home.

The demand in the 1960s and 70s was for residential care homes for the ambulant elderly, and that period saw a development in the range of care homes provided. Four more homes were opened between 1966-71, principally residential care homes, but with some sheltered accommodation. There then followed a period of diminishing demand for flats and bungalows, and the new phase saw the provision of residential care facilities only. Between 1960 and 1985, a further fourteen homes were set up or acquired in England and Wales. In the late 1980s the Institution was operating these Homes that were capable of accommodating well over 800 residents. Since that time, and with the increase in the numbers of elderly, four more homes have been opened.

A large number of people living in the community, including those whose names were on Homes' waiting lists, receive pastoral care visits from the Institution's Care Advice Team. Whereas in the earlier period, the elderly were seeking care in their 60s and 70s, with the ageing population increasing in number they are now living longer and mostly seeking residential care in their 80s and 90s and even at age 100. The present day increase in elderly who are pensioners is also very much due to the baby boom as it is called, and which refers to the large numbers of babies born after the end of the Second World War, and who are now approaching age 70. If they are not already, they soon will be requiring hospital care and places in retirement homes.

Masonic homes today
Newer and more modern projects have taken into account smaller groups of residents, enjoying a more comfortable existence. Rather than a very large Home for, say, 60 or more people living together, residents are accommodated in groups of eight in a setting more like their own home, whilst still having the company and companionship of others. Each group has their own sitting-room, dining-room, laundrette, and kitchen. Residents are encouraged to do a little in the way of light domestic work if they are able, like washing their own clothes and cooking some of their meals. The advantage of having their own kitchen is that they can put the kettle on for a cup of tea when they please. There are about 40 people on one site under the management of a Matron. They also have the use of a library, shop, licensed bar, and an area for parties or performances by visiting artists, and which also doubles as a communal meeting-place, a kind of common room, for the residents own day-to-day use. The RMBI is now the sixty-sixth largest registered charity in the country. They employ 1,500 full-time and part-time staff, and support more than 4,000 beneficiaries made up of 1,150 residents in their homes, and a further 3,000 people living in the community. [11]

The Masonic Housing Association
The Masonic Housing Association was formed in 1976, and specialises in providing sheltered housing accommodation for less active elderly people, who have a housing or social need. The accommodation comprises a small flat each, so that residents can lead a completely independent life and feel secure, as a Warden is employed to provide help when an emergency arises. The flats are rented and self-contained and each scheme has a residents' lounge with kitchen and laundry and the Warden's office and a guest room. Volunteers from the Province provide day-to-day management and welfare. The flats are furnished with the aid of public grants available to registered housing associations. Some flats are also made available to nominees of the local authority who may not have Masonic connections.

The RMBI currently operates seventeen care homes in England and Wales, all of which offer a high range of quality care. Prince Edward visits care homes and housing accommodation on special occasions, perhaps on the anniversary of when it was first opened or a reopening following upgrading and refurbishment. On Wednesday July 24, 2013 he visited the impressive James Terry Court Home in Croydon that had been rebuilt at a cost of £10 million. He carried out the reopening and gave an address, as did RMIB Chief Executive, Brigadier David Innes. The home offers places to people with dementia, dependent upon the individual needs of the person. Like others in the RMIB series of homes it is a safe and welcoming place where residents enjoy a range of trips, outings, and activities.

Part 5
Masonic Samaritan Fund (MSF)

The Masonic Samaritan Fund (MSF) which was set up by the Grand Charity, provides grants to eligible beneficiaries who have an identified health or care need and, faced with a long wait for treatment, care or support, are unable to provide their own private care. The Fund provides grants for applicants to receive treatment and care without undue delay or expense. Those eligible are Freemasons, their wives, partners, widows, and dependants. Once a grant is awarded, the interests of the applicant are paramount and the required treatment, care or support, is obtained through whichever hospital or care provider is the most appropriate, and near to where the applicant lives. The figures for 2014, show that the Fund has supported over 9,500 individuals at a total cost of over £60 million.

As well as providing grants to cover the associated costs of a diagnosed health or care need, the MSF funds medical research projects which aim to improve the treatment for many of the illnesses and disabilities that affect Masonic families and the wider community.

Medical and Dental Care

One may apply for a grant if they have a diagnosed health or care need and are faced with over twelve weeks wait for NHS treatment or support, or eight weeks or more wait for cardiac or cancer treatment, and are unable to afford private healthcare. Previous grants have included: orthopaedic surgery, cardiac surgery, gynaecological treatment or surgery, weight loss surgery, cancer treatment, IVF Treatment, prostate treatment, cataracts and other eye surgery. To restore dental function and promote good dental health, dental grants are available for functional treatment that is clinically necessary for good dental health and treatment that costs in excess of NHS charging rates. Previously these have included: NHS Band 3 dental treatment, root canal treatment, crowns, orthodontic, and bridgework.

Respite and Mobility Care

Respite care grants are available towards the cost of enabling a carer to continue providing vital support for a loved one during short-term, residential care breaks, domiciliary care in an individual's home, and day centre care. Grants have so far been offered to cover domiciliary in-home respite care, residential respite care, and day centre respite care.

In support of helping an applicant retain their independence, grants are available for mobility aids and equipment and home adaptations required for medical or mobility reasons. Grants offered have included: Scooters and Powered wheelchairs; Rise-recliner Chairs and Profiling beds; stair lifts; entry ramps and electric platform lifts; car hoists and adaptations and Motability contributions for specialist vehicles; bathroom adaptations and wet rooms; ground floor conversions; and specialist computer software, visual aids, and communication aids for adults and children.

Fund raising

The Freemasons Grand Charity and their families have been busy fund-raising in support of MSF. Following a six-year campaign in Derbyshire, they raised £2.4 million. The Brain Tumour charity that is based in Hampshire received £100,000.

In Cornwall in 2013, they celebrated raising £1,876,879 at their Festival Finale in Newquay. Cornwall Provincial Grand Master Brother Peter George proudly presented the cheque to Brother Brigadier Willie Shackell.

Every year, over 1,000 people in the UK and Ireland are paralysed, following an injury to their spinal cord. MSF and the Grand Charity have together donated £41,977 to Spinal Research, a charity dedicated to developing reliable treatments for paralysis caused by a broken back or neck.

The sum of £200,000 has been donated to Cancer Research UK's cutting edge research. This support is essential to improving the 3 per cent survival rate for people diagnosed with pancreatic cancer. They first provided £100,000 on behalf of the Masonic community during 2013, and have recently donated a further £100,000 towards the fight against one of the deadliest forms of cancers.

The University of Leicester received a donation of £33,000 for their Daily Remote Ischaemic Conditioning Post-Acute Myocardial Infarction. Known as DREAM, the project, which carries out research into the heart, is a randomised controlled trial currently being run in patients' homes across Leicestershire.

Part 6

Grants made by the Grand Charity
to other charities and worthy causes

Some idea of the extent of the work of the Freemasons' Grand Charity is apparent from examples of the generous funds they provide to help other charities and worthy causes. For example, grants for which extensive figures have been compiled and that were made during the year 2005 to deserving causes at home, totalled £4,702,897.

On the medical research side, grants were made as follows: the Alzheimer's Research Trust received £150,000 over three years; The British Heart Foundation received £64,000, over two years; The British Lung Foundation received £95,000, over two years. Cancer Research UK, received for research into improved treatments for bowel cancer that has spread to the liver, £64,000 over two years, and to fund research on chromosome translocation in leukaemia, a further £125,000 over five years. The Institute of Cancer Research received £1 million over 10 years to fund The Grand Charity's Chair of Molecular Biology for research into male cancers. Over a period of three years, the charity Funding Hope received £105,000 for research into a vaccine for meningitis B. The Motor Neurone Disease Association received £50,000 over two years to fund a PhD student to work with an established senior researcher on motor neurone disease. Tommy's, the Baby Charity, received £69,500 to fund research at John Radcliffe Hospital into whether vitamins C and E are effective in preventing pre-eclampsia during pregnancy.

In total, since 1984, nearly £10 million in medical research funding has contributed to successful treatments for a wide range of illnesses. Since 2007, £1.5 million has been donated to support air ambulance charities. All grants are made or recommended at the sole discretion of the Council of the Grand Charity, whose members are its trustees.

Other projects for vulnerable, older, and young people

With regard to such projects, £85,000 was paid to Abbeyfield UK to fund a new training programme for staff working with older people. Action Medical Research received £51,301 over eighteen months to develop standardised movement assessment tests for children over the age of eleven, suffering from dyspraxia. Centrepoint received £38,000, paid over 18 months to fund a project aimed at preventing homelessness. The Multiple Sclerosis Trust received £60,000 over two years. £125,666 was paid over three years to Emmaus UK to help homeless people by funding a central development officer and new Emmaus community in Sheffield. £10,000 was donated to Music in Hospitals to provide free musical performances by professionals to older people in hospitals, day care centres, and nursing and residential homes.

The St. John's Family Resource Unit received £40,000 to fund a nursery to help neglected or abused children to overcome profound developmental delay. £15,000 was donated to Touchstones 12 for drug rehabilitation. Vulnerable People – Disability and Health Care received £105,000 over three years to finance Breast Cancer Care. Down's Syndrome Educational Trust received £20,000. Elizabeth Foundation received £25,000 to fund an intervention programme for babies and toddlers who are deaf, to increase their ability to acquire speech and language skills. £60,000 was provided over two years to Home Farm Trust to fund a Carer Support Officer to support carers of people with learning disabilities. Youth Opportunities received £50,000, which went to the Depaul Trust over two years to support a Birmingham hostel for homeless young people. The Prince's Trust received over a period of two years £100,000 to fund new 'xl' clubs in schools for disaffected young people. Tall Ships Youth Trust received £50,000 over two years for disadvantaged young people to undertake a tall ship voyage. Throughout England and Wales, 217 hospices received a total of £502,600.

In 1981, over £120 million was donated by the Grand Charity to charitable causes. Since 1984, 290 hospices have received a total of £11.5 million.

Part 7

Disaster relief grants

Emergency grants for disaster relief

At an international level the Grand Charity provides for the victims of natural disasters. As Chairman of the trustees, only Brother Richard M. Hone QC has the authority to make emergency grants in times of national or international disasters.

Tsunami Disaster 2004

On December 26, 2004, twelve countries in Asia and Africa were struck by massive tidal waves, following an under sea volcanic eruption in the Pacific Ocean. One of the most dreadful calamities ever to hit mankind, it has become known as the Tsunami Disaster. The equivalent of five million tons of TNT in the form of water poured down on the inhabitants of villages and towns who were completely unprepared for such an event. The great work of the Grand Charity produced in twelve months, £850,000 in funding to the victims of the disaster. The Freemasons membership is today over 330,000, and through the 8,644 Lodges across England and Wales they donated the funds.

Within hours of the first reports of the disaster Prince Edward, in his role as President of the Grand Charity held a meeting. An emergency grant of £100,000 was authorised immediately to be paid to the British Red Cross. The grant helped to fund the first aeroplane the Red Cross sent out to the worst effected areas. It carried emergency relief items, including clothing, medical kits, cooking equipment, and emergency shelters.

At an early stage the Council of the Grand Charity decided to concentrate its support on projects that would provide relief to children orphaned or otherwise affected by the Tsunami. Funds were held in a relief chest and the money was provided for funding for projects that focused on the longer-term regeneration of the devastated areas. A leading international community development organisation named Plan was selected as its main delivery partner for projects in India, Indonesia, and Sri Lanka. It was also agreed to support an orphanage in Thailand as part of a project developed by the Light of Siam Masonic Lodge. £40,000 was sent to Schizophrenia Research Foundation of India (SCARF); £320,000 was sent to Villapuram; £200,000 was sent to Sri Lanka that included the rebuilding of a school; £100,000 was sent to Thailand; and £110,000 was sent to Indonesia. All together, £1 million was donated to help with the recovery process.

Later relief funds to distressed areas

Later relief funds to distressed areas included: £5,000 towards flooding in Carlisle, Cumbria, England; £15,000 to the Philippines Floods victims made via the Red Cross; £7,500 for victims of the Caribbean Hurricane, Bahamas/Turks; £10,000 to the Niger to the Severely Malnourished Children; £19,261 for the victims of Hurricane Katrina – Emergency Aid; £8,500 for Louisiana, Alabama and Mississippi. £100,000 was paid to Southern Asia Earthquake via the British Red Cross. The London bombings Relief Charitable Fund received £50,000, also in association with the Red Cross. £148,000 was donated to support relief efforts for victims of the Haiti earthquake.

Grand Charity grants made in 2012

The Freemasons' Grand Charity gave £450,000 to other organisations in 2012, as follows: British Autism Study of Infant Siblings (BASIS) received £25,000, for Autistica to fund the salary of the Family Liaison & Database Manager at BASIS. BASIS is a UK-wide network of research scientists studying young children who are at risk of developing autism, because they already have a sibling with autism. Autistica funds medical research to understand the causes of autism, improve diagnosis, and develop new treatments and interventions. Based in London, they are an autism medical research charity, and they are committed to funding translational research that will make a difference to people's lives. The International Spinal Research Trust received £25,000 to fund research based in Cambridge into the development of the enzyme chondroitinase for use in clinical trials with spinal cord injury patients. Keele University's Stafford-based project received £35,000, to fund the salary of a PhD student working on the characterisation of rodent and human fibrocyte cultures for cellular transplantation to prevent age-related hearing loss.

Youth opportunities

Depaul UK, based in London, received £25,000 to fund homelessness prevention. The charity has 42 projects across the UK, working with young homeless people. They operate a family mediation service and early intervention work in schools. £90,000 was given to Tomorrow's People to fund Working It Out, a work-related training programme for disadvantaged young people based in Sussex.

Vulnerable people

Action on Addiction whose headquarters are in Wiltshire, received £30,000 to fund the M-PACT service for children and families. The service focuses on the effect of adult addiction on children and uses specially trained counsellors to run programmes to help hard-to-reach families. A grant of £15,000 went to Addington Fund based in Cornwall to part-fund an affordable housing project with workshops for ex-tenant farmers. The charity aims to enable ex-farming families to remain in the countryside. Breast Cancer Care whose headquarters are in London received a £50,000 grant to fund Breast Cancer Care's services for people with secondary cancer. Services include a helpline and email advice, an online forum, publications, and Living with Secondary Cancer support group programmes. £25,000 went to Chailey Heritage Foundation in Sussex to part-fund the construction of a life skills centre for young people with complex disabilities. Changing Faces whose headquarters are in London, helps people whose lives are affected by conditions, marks or scars that alter their appearance. They received a grant of £30,000 to fund the salary of a practitioner in the children and young people's team who will provide one-to-one emotional support to parents as well as work with children, helping them to learn how to respond to curiosity, to handle bullying, and to make friends. £50,000 was granted to Clic Sargent to fund two part-time specialist Nurses in Cornwall over two years. There are eighteen principal treatment centres for children's cancer in England and the closest to Cornwall is in Bristol. Specialist Nurses enable some treatments to be undertaken at home and provide information, continuity of care and, if necessary, palliative care. Emmaus UK received a £30,000 grant to fund the salary of the Membership Services Director who oversees the development of new Emmaus Communities and supports existing groups. The charity, whose headquarters are in Cambridge, provides accommodation and employment opportunities for single homeless people. £30,000 was granted to Independent Age in order to fund the charity's advice service for older people. Independent Age is a well-established charity for older people whose headquarters are in London and has recently merged with Counsel and Care, and the Universal Beneficent Society. £25,000 was granted to Sense, to fund a Family and Support Worker in North West England. The project that is based in Lancashire supports deaf-blind people and the support worker will provide outreach assistance to forty deaf-blind children.

Reinforcing the dedication to charity work and to helping people in general from all walks of life, Prince Edward had this to say:

"Our charitable work is very extensive. The Masonic charities last year [2001] raised £20 million, but the effort is not devoted entirely towards Masons or Masonic objectives. The amount given to non-Masonic causes is also very large. The Grand Charity exists very largely to make donations and grants to causes which are nothing to do with Freemasonry. It gives money to a whole range of charities and charitable activities. It amounts to millions of pounds every year, and I would like that to be better publicised".

A powerful earthquake struck the Kathmandu Valley of Nepal on April 25, 2015. With their customary kindness and generosity the Freemasons' Grand Charity had two days later, donated £50,000 to the Red Cross to aid the stricken area.

Endnotes to Chapter 8

[1] John Hamill, *The Craft A History Of English Freemasonry*, pub. Aquarian Press, 1986.

[2] Authors' interview with Sir Richard Buckley, February 23, 2008.

[3] Ibid.

[4] In interviewing those who run the Freemasons' Grand Charity the authors found everyone fully co-operative, there appeared to be nothing to hide and they were sincere, hardworking, and dedicated to the Grand Charity.

[5] Source: Souvenir Programme 275th Anniversary of the Formation of the Grand Lodge of England, pub. 1992; *Freemasonry And the Future* by RW Bro. Cdr. M.B.S. Higham, RN, PJGW, Grand Secretary.

[6] Grand Secretaries are the senior officials who work full-time at Freemasons' Hall.

[7] Figures are taken from the 275th *Anniversary Souvenir* a booklet.

[8] Figures provided by Mrs Natasha Trewick, Freemasons' Grand Charity.

[9] Op. cit., *Souvenir Programme 275th Anniversary,* RW Bro. Cdr. M.B.S. Higham.

[10] Souvenir Programme; 275 Anniversary of the Formation of The Grand Lodge of England; and Internet 9th July 2006 print out.

[11] The Homes are as follows: Harewood Court, Hove, East Sussex; Devonshire Court, Oadby Leicestershire; Scarborough Court, Cramlington, Northumberland; Prince George, Duke of Kent Court, Chislehurst, Kent; Connaught Court, Fulford, York; Lord Harris Court, Sindlesham, Berkshire; Albert Edward, Prince of Wales Court, Porthcawl, Mid Glamorgan; Queen Elizabeth Court, Llandudno, Gwynedd; Eccleshome, Eccles, Manchester; James Terry Court, Croydon, Surrey; The Tithebarn, Great Crosby, Liverpool; Cornwallis Court, Bury St Edmunds, Suffolk; Zetland Court, Bournemouth; Cadogan Court, Exeter, South Devon; Prince Michael of Kent Court, Watford, Hertfordshire; Shannon Court, Hindhead, Surrey; Barnford Court, Hove, West Sussex; Prince Edward, Duke of Kent Court, Braintree, Essex.

CHAPTER 9

PRINCE EDWARD'S MUSIC
PATRONAGES AND HIS TASTE IN MUSIC

Introduction

Prince Edward is a great lover of opera and in particular of the works of Wagner. At age 18, he saw The Ring Cycle (Der Ring des Nibelungen) and it created a lasting impression upon the teenager, who has been interested in the composer's work ever since. Wagner took 26 years to write this series of four operas: Das Rheingold, Die Walküre, Siegfried, and Götterdämmerung. Briefly, it is the story of a magic ring that is stolen from a dwarf, Alberich, by Wotan, King of the Gods. He, in turn, has it stolen from him by two giants. The story is of Wotan trying to get the ring back.

There are a number of music organisations that are dear to Prince Edward's heart, and through his involvement with the London Philharmonic Orchestra, the late Sir George Solti KBE, (1912-1997), one of the leading conductors of the 20th century, became a personal friend. In 1961, Solti became musical director of the Covent Garden Opera Company. In 1972, he took out British citizenship. One of his most famous recordings is Decca's complete set of Wagner's *Der Ring des Nibelungen*, made between 1958 and 1965.

Prince Edward is President (January 1, 1969) of the Royal Choral Society; Patron (October 1, 1985) of Trinity Laban Conservatoire of Music and Dance; Patron (February 1, 1980) of the London Philharmonic Orchestra; President (October 1, 1989) of the King's Lynn Festival and Centre for Arts; Patron (February 15, 1996) of the South Bank Centre; Patron (January 18, 1999) of the International Musicians Seminar Prussia Cove; Patron (September 6, 2002) of Opera North; Patron (November 1, 1992) of the Hanover Band; Chairman of the Honorary Committee of Patrons (August 1, 1986) of the European Union Baroque Orchestra; and Patron (July 30, 2004) of the Mendelssohn Society.

Prince Edward's music patronages are discussed in this chapter in the date order of which he became their president or patron.

ROYAL CHORAL SOCIETY

The Royal Choral Society was formed in 1871, shortly after the opening of the Royal Albert Hall, London. Although it was an excellent location in terms of size, but having been built long before microphones were invented, natural acoustics produced an echo and it was a resonant disaster. The problem was not resolved until 1969, when an acoustic engineer installed a series of large, fibreglass, acoustic diffusing discs (commonly referred to as mushrooms or flying saucers) which were installed below the ceiling to reduce the notorious echo. These worked well and today they are still in place. The French composer, Charles Gounod, now famous for his Ave Maria, having fled to London from the Franco-Prussian War, conducted a choral concert at the Albert Hall that year to mark the opening of the International Exhibition which was taking place close by. Later that same year, Gounod was appointed as Conductor of the Royal Choral Society, which was now established as a resident choir. The aristocracy dressed in their finery and, led by Queen Victoria, packed the flower-adorned hall for concerts.

In 1872 the celebrated Joseph Barnaby, distinguished for his own Choir, became Conductor. Some highlights of the Royal Choral Society's performances included Barnaby's invitation to Giuseppe Verdi to conduct the British premiere of his Requiem in 1875, and Antonin Dvorák to conduct his Stabat Mater in 1884. Barnaby also established the annual Good Friday performance of Handel's Messiah in 1878, a tradition that has lasted to the present day. In May 1888, the choir gave a performance of Arthur Sullivan's The Golden Legend by royal command and Queen Victoria was present.

Frederick Bridge, the organist of Westminster Abbey, took over as Conductor in 1896. With his excellent administration and Queen Victoria's patronage, the choir continued to go from strength to strength. By 1899 the *Musical Times* could note that the choir comprised: 242 sopranos, 174 contraltos, 174 tenors, 236 basses and 16 superintendents, arranged as two separate choirs either side of the organ in the Albert Hall. The lady members all wore white dresses, with those on the right having red and those on the left having blue sashes.

On the death of Queen Victoria in 1901, her elder son the Prince of Wales became His Majesty King Edward VII, and the Royal Choral society continued its popularity throughout the Edwardian era. Ethel Smyth's Mass in D and Coleridge Taylor's Hiawatha were great favourites with the Edwardians. Scenes from the Song of Hiawatha were performed in 1900, conducted by Coleridge Taylor.

King Edward VII died in 1910, and was succeeded by King George V. In 1912, there was the inauguration of the choir's highly popular annual carol concert. The future of any musical society was inevitably subject to historical developments, and the First World War (1914-18) intervened. There was a decline in membership and the bombing of London decreased performances and the quality of music suffered. But Bridge adopted a mentality that was reflective of that of the British in general, 'the show must go on', and in 1915, introduced a Sunday afternoon concert series at the Royal Albert Hall.

In 1922, another organist, H.L. Balfour, who would become the longest serving chorus master, took over and served a series of guest conductors. Hiawatha was revived and, in 1924, there was the first of a series of staged versions of Hiawatha's Wedding Feast. The profits from these concerts supported the choir's ability to perform throughout the Great Depression of unemployment during the 1930s. The Death of Minnehaha and Hiawatha's Departure were performed by more than 1,000 braves and squaws, in extended seasons each June, until the Second World War in 1939. The stage set was enhanced with large painted waterfalls, wigwams, peace pipes, and various ethnic stage props. The audiences entered into the spirit by turning up at the theatre in their own variations of costumes.

In 1928, Sir Malcolm Sargent, (1895-1967), had been appointed permanent Conductor which post he would hold for 39 years. Sargent is today a household name as Conductor of London's internationally famous summer music festival, the Proms, from 1948 to his death in 1967. His flamboyant personality lent resonance to a man who was a leader of amateur singers and attracted a whole new generation of audiences to classical music. During the Second World War the society had to move to rather cramped quarters at the Queen's Hall in Langham Place, London. There were performances of the Messiah, Elijah, and Gerontius, until on the night of May 10, 1941 a German bomb wrecked the building. The society returned to the Royal Albert Hall and struggled on with their performances.

By the end of the war the Royal Choral Society was considered as the finest symphony chorus in the UK. Sargent and his musical team set about recruiting and training new members. At Sargent's death in 1967, by which time he had risen to fame world-wide as a conductor, the society had begun to tour overseas.

Prince Edward was greatly honoured to have been made President of the Royal Choral Society on January 1, 1969.

The society held its 125th anniversary Concert on May 8, 1997 at the Royal Albert Hall, which was attended by Prince Edward who was accompanied by the late HRH Princess Margaret. It was 125 years to the day since the society's first concert.

Wyn Morris held the post of Conductor for two seasons from 1968, until the appointment of Meredit Davies in 1972. Davis and his successor, Laszlo Heltay, prepared the choir for concert tours to the United States and Europe. There were performances of works by Raymond Premru, Anthony Milner, and Geoffrey Burgon, and performances at festivals as well as contributions to the Classic Rock and Hooked On series of recordings. Heltay's tenure as a conductor ended in December 1993. For the next two seasons the choir was led by guest conductors until Richard Cooke, who was formerly Chorus Master of the London Philharmonic Choir, was appointed in 1995.

In more recent years, the society has diversified its musical activities. They have joined with a number of charities for Gala Concerts, programmes of opera selections and popular choral music. They have performed at Westminster Abbey, St. Paul's Cathedral, and the cathedrals of Canterbury and Winchester, and at Symphony Hall, Birmingham, Bridgwater Hall, Manchester, St. David's Hall, Cardiff, and Palaise de Congés, Lille in France.

The Royal Choral Society performs all year round in England to huge audiences at Kenwood House, Marble Hill, Glastonbury, Milton Keynes Bowl, Crystal Palace,

55. Trinity Laban Conservatoire of Music and Dance symphony orchestra concert.

Hyde Park, Horse Guards Parade and Hampton Court. The choir was received with rugby euphoria when singing for England at international rugby matches in Paris and Twickenham.

A series of studio recordings were made in the 1990s, involving powerful versions of Handel's Messiah and Verdi's Requiem, conducted by Owain Arwel Hughes. There was a chart-topping Last Night of the Proms with Barry Wordsworth, and Carmina Burana, accompanied by the Royal Philharmonic Orchestra conducted by Dr Richard Cooke. The society has also appeared on television with singer Leslie Garrett CBE, and has made various films for television.

The society are, however, eager to stress that the broadening of their musical experience has not been at the expense of quality or standards. Dedication to maintaining traditional music has been upheld and in the last ten years, countless performances have been given of baroque, sacred music, oratorio, and 20th-century works.

The choir's musical knowledge is being expanded under Director, Richard Cooke. Rarely performed works by Berlioz such as Damnation of Faust and Grande Messe des Morts, the Mahler Symphonies and Schubert Masses have been performed to acclaim. Easter Messiahs have been sung successfully with the backing of a period instrument orchestra.

The Royal Choral Society now spans three centuries of making a major contribution to the musical life of the United Kingdom. Prince Edward regularly attends the choir's concerts.

TRINITY LABAN
CONSERVATOIRE OF MUSIC AND DANCE

Trinity Laban Conservatoire of Music and Dance is the United Kingdom's only conservatoire for both music and contemporary dance. It was formed from a merger of Trinity College of Music and Laban Dance, in 2005. Both Trinity College of Music and Trinity Laban have long and illustrious histories as centres of excellence for training in music and contemporary dance respectively, and they continue to flourish together as one unique institution.

Brief History of Trinity Laban

Faculty of Music

Trinity Laban Faculty of Music was founded as Trinity College of Music in 1872, by the Reverend Henry George Bonavia Hunt, to improve the teaching of church music. The College began as the Church Choral Society, whose diverse activities included choral singing classes and teaching instruction in church music. A year later, in 1873, the college became the College of Church Music, London, before being incorporated in 1976 into Trinity College. In the beginning, only male students could attend and they had to be members of the Church of England.

The college was established for practising and testing as well as for teaching, and Trinity developed the first examination board which thrives today as an international sister institution, Trinity College London. In 1881 the College moved to Mandeville Place, near Wigmore Street in Central London, close by Wigmore Hall. The College continued to expand until by 1922, it had extended into other buildings in Mandeville Place. In 2001 Trinity College moved to its present prestigious home, King Charles Court in the Old Royal Naval College at Greenwich, south east London. This complex comprises a series of classic buildings alongside the Thames, designed in 1694 by Sir Christopher Wren as a naval hospital for seamen. During the Victorian era the buildings became Greenwich Hospital, and when the hospital closed in 1873, it became the Royal Naval College for Officers. The Navy moved out in 1998, and Trinity College took up residence in 2001.

Greenwich is an illustrious centre of court and naval history and the location of countless momentous events down the centuries. It was a favourite palace of the Tudors and the birthplace of King Henry VIII, Queen Elizabeth I, and Queen Mary I. It was the scene of a change of royal dynasty when the nobility of England gathered in the Painted Hall to welcome the first Hanoverian King, George I, on his arrival in the country to succeed Queen Anne who was the last of the Stuarts. The body of Admiral Lord Nelson lay in state in the Painted Hall, following his death at the Battle of Trafalgar (1805).

Another famous resident of Greenwich Palace was Queen Caroline. As Princess of Wales, Caroline, having been abandoned by her husband, King George IV, dramatically followed him to Westminster Abbey and tried to enter the coronation

56. Trinity Laban Conservatoire of Music and Dnace annual CoLab event.

service on July 19, 1819. She hammered on the doors and demanded to be taken in but was turned away.

Rudolf Laban founds Trinity Laban Faculty of Dance

Trinity Laban Faculty of Dance began its life in 1948, at the Art of Movement Studio based in Manchester that was founded by Rudolf Laban, the Austro-Hungarian dancer, choreographer, and dance/movement theoretician. Laban is perhaps best known in the dance world as the inventor of Laban Movement Analysis, a system for interpreting, describing, visualizing, and notating all forms of human movement. It is used as a tool by dancers, athletes, physical and occupational therapists, and is one of the most widely used systems of human movement analysis.

In 1953 the school moved from Manchester to Addlestone in Surrey to enable further expansion. In 1975 it moved again to New Cross in south east London, whereupon it was renamed the Laban Centre for Movement and Dance, after its founder. In 1997 it was again renamed to the shorter Laban Centre London and, in 2002, its name was shortened still further, becoming simply Laban.

In 2002 the Laban Centre moved to its current location in Deptford in south east London, into award-winning premises, newly-built for the purpose. Designed by Herzog and de Meuron (of Tate Modern Art Gallery fame), the Laban Building was purpose-built for dance training, containing practice rooms with sprung floors, a state-of-the-art Health and Pilates studio, and one of London's largest dance theatres. In 2003 the Laban Building won the £20,000 Stirling prize for architecture and was named RIBA (Royal Institute of British Architects) Building of the Year.

The Laban Building also houses the Laban Library, the largest and most varied open access specialist research collection on dance and related subjects in the UK, which covers many aspects of dance in a variety of formats and languages.

Trinity Laban Conservatoire of Music and Dance

In 2005 the two colleges merged to form Trinity Laban Conservatoire of Music and Dance, becoming the United Kingdom's only Higher Education institution specialising in music and contemporary dance.

In its new location, Trinity Laban has the use of the Painted Chapel at the Old Royal Naval College, a chapel that rivals those of Oxford and Cambridge colleges, and which has become the focus of an increasingly strong reputation for choral music.

Nearby Blackheath Halls in Blackheath Village, south east London, is a wholly-owned subsidiary of Trinity Laban. These halls are reputedly London's oldest established purpose-built concert venue, providing a beautiful setting for music and the performing arts, and they provide the conservatoire with a regular base for large-scale rehearsals and performances.

Trinity Laban today

Today Trinity Laban is a thriving and prestigious institution with a growing international reputation for world-class teaching and artistic excellence. Under the leadership of the Principal Professor, Anthony Bowne, the two pre-eminent teaching faculties offer a wide range of programmes for undergraduate, postgraduate, and professional development, with input from many principal players, composers, conductors, dancers, and choreographers from the international stage. With links to such institutions as the Southbank, Kings Place, and Sadler's Wells, students have the opportunity to perform in professional venues, and the majority go on to pursue successful careers in the arts.

Community learning and participation programme

The conservatoire also has an extensive community learning and participation programme, which for over 10 years has brought opportunities to explore music and dance into the lives of many people in the more deprived areas of South East London. The Faculty of Dance offers a highly-regarded Centre for Advanced Training in dance, weekly dance classes for local school children, taster days, and summer schools. The Music Faculty opens its doors every Saturday for gifted and talented young musicians to join Junior Trinity. Other opportunities for community music-making include the World Choir for adults and Animate Orchestra for children and young people.

Prince Edward as Patron of Trinity Laban

Prince Edward has been Patron of Trinity Laban since October 1, 1985. He has been remarkably active and has presided over profound changes in the Institution. Extending his patronage from Trinity College of Music to the newly merged Trinity Laban in 2005, he marked the occasion with a visit to the Laban building to celebrate contemporary dance. One of Prince Edward's most significant engagements was in

2001, when he led Trinity College of Music in the procession down the Thames from Westminster Abbey to Greenwich, marking Trinity's move from its historic centre at Mandeville Place to its magnificent new home.

Over the past few years, Prince Edward's other engagements have included unveiling a bronze bust of Chopin, several events in conjunction with the 2012 London Olympics, with which the Conservatoire was closely connected due to its location, and Professor Derek Aviss' retirement concert. Always, he takes a particular interest in meeting students and encouraging the early development of their careers as performers.

Celebration of the bicentenary of Frédéric Chopin's birth

In September 2010 Professor Aviss, then Executive Director of Trinity Laban, welcomed representatives of the Polish Cultural Institute, the Polish Heritage Society, and distinguished guests to the Old Royal Naval College for a special event in celebration of the bicentenary of the birth of the Polish composer Frédéric Chopin. A bronze bust of Chopin was generously gifted to the Conservatoire by the Polish Ministry of Culture. While guests enjoyed a continental breakfast and music performed by Trinity Laban students, the bronze was being transported down the River Thames from Westminster Pier to Greenwich on the sailing ship named Frédéric Chopin. The highlight of the evening was the unveiling of the bust by Prince Edward, in the presence of Minister Counsellor Tomasz Kozlowski, who represented the Polish Ambassador Her Excellency Barbara Tuge-Erecinska. This special event brought together representatives from many Polish and British organisations, and was a fitting celebration for the famous Polish composer's life and work in the United Kingdom.

One of the most recent exciting events was the London 2012 Olympics, and, in its Greenwich location, Trinity Laban was privileged to be right at the heart of them. On Monday July 23, at 7.31 am, a huge group of people gathered to watch as the Olympic Torch Relay set off from the Laban Building at the start of its journey through the borough of Lewisham.

On September 26, 2012, Prince Edward was an honoured guest at the concert and reception given to celebrate the retirement of Professor Derek Aviss, former Joint Principal of Trinity Laban. The concert took place in the beautiful Old Royal Naval College Chapel, where Prince Edward addressed the audience, thanking Professor Aviss for all his work in furthering the cause of music and dance over many years. Other guests included many of Professor Aviss' students, past and present, the Mayor and Mayoress of Royal Greenwich, Lord Lipsey, and the Right Honourable Nick Raynsford, Labour MP for Greenwich and Woolwich.

Trinity Laban perform at the Polish Hearth Club London

On December 6, 2012, students from Trinity Laban performed at the Polish Hearth Club, South Kensington, London, in Prince Edward's presence. The event was part of an evening of cultural activities that included a Gala Dinner to pay homage to the writer Marcel Proust. (See Chapter 16) The music was provided by the dynamic young British Benyounes String Quartet, who were then the current holders of the

Richard Carne Junior Fellowship at Trinity Laban. Violinists, Miss Zara Benyounes and Miss Emily Holland, with Miss Sara Roberts, viola, and Miss Kim Vaughan, cello, played a programme of Mozart's String Quartet in C major K.157; Puccini's Crisantemi; Elgar's Salut d'amour and Chanson de Matin; and Tchaikovsky's Andante Cantabile from String Quartet no.1 in D major. Prince Edward later privately expressed his particular enjoyment of the music to the performers themselves.

Prince Edward attended the Principal's Dinner to celebrate Trinity Laban's recent Honorary Fellows in December 2012. This particular dinner signalled both the retirement of Trinity Laban's Chairman Sir Robert (Bob) Scott, and the election of the new Chairman, David, Lord Lipsey. Trinity Laban harpist Miss Alicia Griffiths performed during the reception, which was held in the Admiral's House at the Old Royal Naval College in Greenwich.

Over the years Prince Edward has attended Music Faculty graduation ceremonies to award degrees and prizes. He was present as Guest of Honour at the presentation, in January 2013, of the Isabelle Bond Gold Medal Award for Excellence in Performance to harpist Miss Claire Iselin, following her outstanding performance having competed against five other exceptional musicians in a showcase at King's Place, North London. It is the most prestigious award for a solo music performance offered by Trinity Laban.

LONDON PHILHARMONIC ORCHESTRA

The London Philharmonic Orchestra (LPO) is one of the world's finest orchestras and is based in London Southbank Centre's Royal Festival Hall. They have performed there since the hall opened in 1951, becoming Resident Orchestra in 1992. They have flourishing residences in Brighton and Eastbourne, performing at Brighton Dome and the Congress Theatre, and are the Resident Symphony Orchestra of Glyndebourne Opera Festival since 1964.

During the summer of 2012 the LPO performed as part of The Queen's Diamond Jubilee Pageant on the River Thames, and was also chosen to record all the world's national anthems for the London 2012 Olympics.

Touring abroad forms a major part of the orchestra's schedule and highlights of their 2014/15 schedule involved appearances across Europe, including Iceland, and tours of the USA's east and west coasts, Canada and China.

At the time of writing (May 2015) the Principal Conductor is Vladimir Jurowski, Principal Guest Conductor is Andrés Orozco-Estrada and the current Concertmaster is Pieter Schoeman, a violinist who studied under Sylvia Rosenberg and Eduard Schmeider. The Chief Executive and Artistic Director is Timothy Walker.

Brief history
The orchestra was formed in 1932, by Sir Thomas Beecham, and its founding associate conductor was Sir Malcolm Sargent. Its first concert was performed on October 7 that year at the Queen's Hall, London, and was conducted by Beecham. The Orchestra was led by Paul Beard and David McCallum, and included leading

58. The London Philharmonic Orchestra at the Royal Festival Hall

players such as Anthony Pini, Reginald Kell, Léon Goossens, Gwydion Brooke, Geoffrey Gilbert, Bernard Walton, and James Bradshaw. Compositions by Bach and Mozart were conducted by Beecham, and Elgar's Violin Concerto was conducted by the composer. The now famous Yehudi Menuhin, who was only 16 years old that November, played a programme of violin concertos. Throughout the 1930s the LPO was the orchestra for the opera season at the Royal Opera House, Covent Garden, with Beecham as artistic director. Beecham also conducted in a series of 78-rpm recordings for Columbia, including a critically-acclaimed, 1939 recording of Brahms' 2nd Symphony.

Women performing in orchestras were quite rare until after the Second World War. Most modern orchestras (and bands) employed men almost exclusively on all instruments until the middle of the 20th century. During the 1960s American orchestras began employing women as positions became available. Nadia Boulanger became the first woman to conduct the London Philharmonic Orchestra in 1936. Boulanger had for many years been a composer and music teacher and had taught some of the leading musicians. Today the idea of women leading an orchestra is, of course, perfectly accepted.

The Second World War and the post-war years
The Second World War took its toll on the orchestra as it did on all music and drama societies who were dependant upon packed theatre audiences for their survival. In 1939 the sponsors withdrew their financial support and the company went into liquidation. The players themselves then took control and had to make decisions about their affairs. Principal Horn, Charles Gregory, was elected first Chairman of the new company in September 1939. Despite the bombings and threats of

invasion, the orchestra continued to tour the country. In May 1941 the orchestra gave its last concert in the Queen's Hall before it was bombed in an air raid during which many of the orchestra's instruments were destroyed. The BBC broadcast an appeal for musical instruments and the response was enormous. The public donated instruments enabling the orchestra to continue.

The London Philharmonic Choir
In 1947 the London Philharmonic Choir was founded as the chorus for the LPO. Beecham had left, except for a brief spell of 18 months after the end of the war, but the orchestra still gave 248 concerts during 1949-50. The LPO's Managing Director, Thomas Russell, then invited Sir Adrian Boult, who had retired as Chief Conductor of the BBC Symphony Orchestra, to take up the principal conductorship. Sir Thomas Beecham famously commented that the problem with English singers was that their voices did not carry beyond the third row of the stalls. How wrong could he be?

Post-war period
The aftermath of the war in the late 1950s was a difficult financial period for the LPO. Conductors then included Constantin Silvestri and Josef Krips. Silvestri, who was reckoned to be the best orchestra trainer in Europe, left Roumania in 1956 and later conducted the Bournemouth Symphony Orchestra. Krips, who was Austrian, was also a fine conductor. He was the first to conduct the Vienna Philharmonic and the Salzburg Festival in the post-war period.

The LPO was obliged to abandon fixed contracts for its players in regard to holidays, sick pay, and pensions, and had to revert to payment by engagement. The Orchestra took part in the first concert at the newly-opened Royal Festival Hall on May 3, 1951. Having been invited to perform in the Soviet Union, they were the first ever British orchestra to appear there, on a two-week tour conducted by Principal Conductor Sir Adrian Boult. In 1958 William Steinberg was appointed as Chief Conductor and, as a noted orchestral trainer, did much to restore playing standards to their pre-war levels.

The LPO in the 1960s
By the 1960s the LPO was emerging from its difficult financial era and, in 1962, the orchestra undertook its first tours of India, Australia, and the Far East. Sir Malcolm Sargent and John Pritchard were the conductors. Pritchard was appointed the LPO's Chief Conductor in 1962, and Music Director of Glyndebourne Opera Festival. The Orchestra performed for the first time at Glyndebourne on May 21, 1964, under the name of the Glyndebourne Festival Orchestra, before reverting to its original name the following year.

In 1967 Bernard Haitink became the orchestra's Principal Conductor, remaining with them for twelve years. During this time the orchestra gave fund-raising concerts that included artists from outside the classical world. There were several popular and well-known Americans: actor, singer, dancer, and comedian, Danny Kaye; composer, pianist and bandleader of jazz orchestras, Duke Ellington; singer of popular music, show tunes, and jazz, Tony Bennett; comedian, vaudevillian, radio, television, and film actor, and violinist, Jack Benny; Danish comedian, conductor, pianist, and radio and television personality, Victor Borge; and English jazz composer, saxophonist and clarinettist, John Dankworth.

The LPO from the 1970s onwards

In the 1970s the orchestra broadened its sphere of musical influence, touring the USA in April 1970, and China in March 1973. Sir George Solti became the Chief Conductor in 1979. The LPO celebrated its golden jubilee in 1982. From 1983-87 Klaus Tennstedt was Principal Conductor, standing down through ill health. Franz Welser-Möst took over in 1990, although there were a number of critical reviews of his tenure. He left in 1996, and the orchestra was without a Principal Conductor for four years. Kurt Masur was then appointed, serving from 2004-7. Vladimir Jurowski had conducted the LPO in the past as a guest conductor, and in September 2007, the LPO's 75th anniversary season, he became their 11th Principal Conductor, and his services with the orchestra are ongoing until at least 2018.

LPO film soundtracks and recordings

The Orchestra launched its own record label in 2005. There are now over 80 releases available on CD and to download. Recent additions include Strauss's Don Juan and Ein Heldenleben with Bernard Haitink; Brahms's Symphonies Nos. 3 & 4 and Zemlinsky's A Florentine Tragedy with Vladimir Jurowski; Orff's Carmina Burana with Hans Graf; and Mahler's Das Lied von der Erde with Yannick Nézet-Séguin, Sarah Connolly and Toby Spence.

The orchestra has made several film soundtracks, including Lawrence of Arabia, Philadelphia, The Mission, The Lord of the Rings film trilogy, and some CD albums of music from the Square Enix video game series, Dragon Quest, composed by Kōici Sugiyama; and the Symphonic Poem: Hope for Final Fantasy XII and the soundtrack Xenosaga Episode I, composed by Yasunori Mitsuda. In the mid-1990s the LPO released tribute albums to rock bands like Pink Floyd, Led Zeppelin, and The Who. The orchestra also recorded most of the four CD set "Simply Rock Moods", covers of rock songs like Everybody Hurts, and Sailing by Rod Stewart, in classical form.

Prince Edward as President of LPO

Prince Edward has been President of the London Philharmonic Orchestra since February 1, 1980. He is a frequent attendee at their performances. One of the LPO's great highlights was the 80th anniversary celebration at which Prince Edward was present on June 27, 2012, at the Banqueting House, Whitehall, London.

The LPO's mission statement declares that its programmes 'will reflect the rich scope of contemporary London, inspiring its audiences, exciting its musicians and enriching people around the world through exceptional performance, recording, and education and community projects'.

80th Anniversary of Glyndebourne Opera Festival 2014
The annual Glyndebourne Opera Festival was founded in 1934, by the late John Christie and his wife, the opera singer Audrey Mildmay. Since that time it has become particularly known for its productions of Mozart's operas.

The festival is held at Glyndebourne House, near Lewes in the English county of Sussex. Gus Christie, son of the late Sir George Christie and grandson of John Christie became the Festival Chairman in 2000. As President of the LPO, Prince Edward is invited to the Glydebourne Festival in a private capacity.

Glyndebourne is "committed to presenting opera of the highest quality, commissioning new work, developing new talent, and reaching new audiences." Every year their work involves presenting six productions in a 1,200-seat opera house that was built in 1994; a Tour that takes three productions around the UK each autumn. The Festival and Tour together present about 120 performances to an audience of about 150,000. Their Music Education Programme hosts over 230 community and outreach events, and recordings of their work reaches worldwide audiences.

Sir Mark Elder, conducting the LPO, opened the Glyndebourne Festival in July 2014, with the famous and much loved La Traviata (The Fallen Woman) composed by Giuseppe Verdi, providing many column inches of high praise in the newspapers. The Festival's new Music Director, Mr Robin Ticciati, conjured up further great interest by the press and opera lovers when he produced the ever popular and rousing Don Giovanni by Jonathan Kent that was composed by Mozart at the height of his musical and dramatic prowess. It was followed by the challenge of a new production of the little-known La finta giardiniera (The False Garden-Girl), the earliest of Mozart's operas, directed by Frederic Wake-Walker. The story emanated from Samuel Richardson's historic novel *Pamela* (1740) and presents six characters in search of love.

Three further famous operas were performed at Glyndebourne. Richard Strauss's comic Der Rosenkavalier (The Knight of The Rose or the Rose-Bearer), staged by Richard Jones; Graham Vick's Eugene Onegin composed by Tchaikovsky, designer Richard Hudson, that is the story of a selfish hero who rejects the love of a bookish young woman, Tatyana, and lives to regret it and then foolishly indulges in a fatal duel with a friend; Rinaldo, composed by Handel, directed by Robert Carsen, is set in the time of the First Crusade and is a story of love, battle, and redemption.

KING'S LYNN FESTIVAL AND CENTRE FOR ARTS

The King's Lynn Festival, held in the market town of King's Lynn in the English county of Norfolk, began in 1950, and grew out of the celebration of the re-opening of the Guildhall of St George. It is reputed to be the oldest theatre in Europe and the famous English playwright, William Shakespeare, once appeared there.

The early 15th-century building in King Street, probably the largest and most complete surviving Medieval Guildhall in Britain, had become very dilapidated. It was saved from demolition and restored and adapted for the performance of concerts and plays by campaigners, including Ruth, Lady Fermoy (1908–1993). Having lived in King's Lynn from 1931, and being herself an accomplished concert pianist, Lady Fermoy demonstrated her affection for the town by organising lunchtime concerts to give local people the chance to hear professional music of the highest standard. Lady Fermoy and her husband had raised funds for the ambitious restoration project, and in 1951, to compliment the Festival of Britain, Lady Fermoy organised a triumphant festival, a week-long programme of music and the arts to mark the completion of the Guildhall's restoration. She was a close friend of the late Queen Elizabeth the Queen Mother who became the festival's Patron, carrying out the official opening of the newly-restored Guildhall in July 1951.

"Nothing but the best" was the maxim adopted by Lady Fermoy, and she was determined right from the start that its hallmark would be one of excellence. She single-handedly lined up a programme that read like a Who's Who of the world of music and the arts, including Benjamin Britten, Kathleen Ferrier, John Betjeman, Peter Pears, Osbert Sitwell, Shura Cherkassy, Peggy Ashcroft and Peter Ustinov. The BBC Home Service broadcast the official opening live, and the whole festival was a huge success. It rapidly went from strength to strength, quickly earning international renown.

The Guildhall remains a venue at the heart of the festival with other historic King's Lynn buildings also creating stunning backdrops, including St. Margaret's Church, the Town Hall, and St. Nicholas' Chapel. The Corn Exchange has always been used and has become a fine venue since its refurbishment in 1977. Concerts have also been held at Holkham Hall and in a number of West Norfolk churches.

Lady Fermoy was closely involved with the festival for 25 years, and, since she handed over the reins, those entrusted with staging the event have always sought to maintain the tradition of excellence. Classical music continues to provide the cornerstones of the programme and a succession of world-famous orchestras, ensembles of international renown, and big name soloists, have continued to draw audiences to King's Lynn from far and wide.

Prince Edward became President of the King's Lynn Festival on October 1, 1989. Pianist Freddy Kemfp, who is enjoying a meteoric career, is a vice-President of the festival and has become a favourite with audiences. Two successful competitors in the BBC Young Musician Competition, violinist Nicola Benedette and cellist Guy Johnston have delighted concert goers, as have established names such as pianist John Lill and violinist Tasmin Little. Historian David Starkey has informed and entertained audiences and is also a vice-President.

Festival organisers aim to cater for every taste and in recent years programmes reflect the huge range of entertainment on offer with top names who have attracted increasing numbers from all over Britain and abroad. They have included legendary names such as pianist Alfred Brendal and soprano Dame Kiri Te Kanawa; the Stars of the Bolshoi Ballet; singers Lesley Garrett CBE and Aled Jones MBE; actors Tom Conti and Corin Redgrave; percussionist Evelyn Glennie; cricket commentator Henry Blofeld; the Black Dyke Band, Jools Holland and his Rhythm and Blues Orchestra; and famed folk duo John Tams and Barry Coope.

Diamond Jubilee Year 2010

July 2010 was the Diamond Jubilee Year of the King's Lynn Festival and the 30th anniversary of Festival Too (a series of free concerts), and was celebrated with a two-week programme featuring major orchestras, world-famous musicians, and favourites from the world of comedy, folk and literature. It was opened by the renowned Black Dyke brass band, and appearing throughout the festival was the BBC Concert Orchestra with special guest, West End star Jodie Prenger. Also in appearance were Barry Cryer, the elder statesman of Britain's comedians with his "organically-grown" show; pianist Colin Sell, and the hugely popular Ukulele Orchestra of Great Britain. Folk stars Norma Waterson, Martin Carthy, and Chris Parkinson performed traditional folk songs and music.

Classical music provided the cornerstone of the festival programme and featured such famous names as the orchestra of the Age of Enlightenment, pianist Nikolai Demidenko, cellist Guy Johnston, who appeared with the Henschel Quartet. The Royal Philharmonic Orchestra, and a star cast of young singers performed operatic favourites at an opera gala, and the English Chamber Orchestra joined with the King's Lynn Festival Chorus in a programme that included works by Handel and Mozart.

William Shawcross CVO, author of the official biography of the Queen Mother, and cook and restaurateur, Prue Leith, spoke at the literary dinner. The festival's artistic director, Ambrose Miller said: "This milestone event will maintain the festival's tradition of excellence and offer something for everyone."

Mayor Michael Pitcher presented both organisations with his Award in recognition of their services to the community. The Festival Chairman was Alan Pask and the Chairman of Festival Too was Ron Ladley. Addressing 200 guests, Alan spoke of the "feel good" factor which Festival Too's free outdoor concerts created in the town for local people and which attracted visitors from far and wide.

SOUTHBANK CENTRE

The history of the Southbank Centre, located at Belvedere Road, London SE1, begins with the Festival of Britain, which ran from May to September 1951. In what was described as "a tonic for the nation" by the Right Honourable Herbert Morrison, the Labour Party Government Minister responsible for the event, the festival aimed to demonstrate Britain's recovery from the Second World War by showcasing the best in science, technology, arts, and industrial design.

Prince Edward became Patron of the Southbank Centre on February 15, 1996. Lord Hollick was appointed Chairman 2002. In 2009 Mr Alan Bishop took over the role of Chief Executive, and September 2005 saw the arrival of Mr Jude Kelly, as the Centre's Artistic Director.

Southbank Centre today

Today, the Southbank Centre is a complex of artistic venues in London, on the South Bank of the River Thames, between County Hall and Waterloo Bridge. It comprises three main buildings: the Royal Festival Hall, which is the only building from the time of the festival to have survived, the Queen Elizabeth Hall, and the Hayward art gallery. It is Europe's largest centre for the arts and, in all, the Southbank Centre manages a 21-acre (85,000 m²) site that includes the Purcell Room, Saison Poetry Library, Jubilee Gardens, and The Queen's Walk.

Visitors can relax with a glass of wine on Festival Terrace, wander through the Royal Festival Hall foyers, take part in one of hundreds of free events, enjoy a meal from an array of cafes and restaurants, browse through the shops and markets or visit one of the centre's iconic venues.

The centre is next to the popular Merlin Entertainments' London Eye, and is at the heart of an arts quarter stretching from the Royal National Theatre and National Film Theatre to Tate Modern and Shakespeare's Globe Theatre. More than three million people visit the Centre annually. Nearly a thousand paid performances of music, dance and literature are staged each year, as well as over 300 free foyer events, and an education programme in and around the performing arts venues. In addition, three to six major art exhibitions are presented at The Hayward Gallery yearly, and National Touring Exhibitions reach over 100 venues across the UK. It also manages the Arts Council Collection and organises the National Touring Exhibition programme in venues throughout the UK.

In 2000 a master plan for the entire Southbank Centre site was produced. This included the creation of three new public spaces around the Royal Festival Hall (Festival Riverside, Southbank Centre Square and Festival Terrace); modification of the Queen Elizabeth Hall undercroft and the lower two levels of the Hayward Gallery, providing a frontage onto Southbank Centre Square; and a new British Film Institute building.

A major development and refurbishment plan was implemented between 2004-7, providing a range of new shops and restaurants, inserted between the Royal Festival Hall and the approach viaduct to Hungerford Bridge. New shops were built to the low level Thames elevation of the Royal Festival Hall. The refurbishment of the Royal Festival Hall took place during 2005-7. In the auditorium the natural acoustic was enhanced to meet classical music requirements, while being flexible enough to suit the demands of amplified sound. Other features of the refurbishment included reconfigured seating and upgrades to production facilities and public areas, particularly a range of new bar areas.

There are further plans for modernisation but the massive stumbling block over the years has been funding, which was a key constraint, as has been agreement with Arts Council England and the Government about the arts-brief for the Queen Elizabeth Hall and the Hayward Gallery areas. Dione, Lady Digby, DBE, Darts(hc), DL was a member of the Arts Council of Great Britain when the Council took over the Southbank Centre from the Greater London Council (GLC) in the mid-1990s. Having been appointed to the new Board at the South Bank Lady Digby says:

"We made many plans to try to improve the site but the 'brutalist' architecture of the Hayward Gallery was a disaster and as an exhibition space it was a nightmare.

57. Steven Isserlis, cellist, in concert.

"There were no kitchen facilities in the Queen Elizabeth Hall and Purcell Room complex which required all food and drink for the audience to be carried over from the Festival Hall. At that time there was no money available for improvements."[1]

A solution appears to have finally materialised in May 2014, when the Arts Council made available a £16.7 million grant as part of the finances towards a £24 million backlog of repairs and maintenance work to restore some of the "crumbling" buildings. Work on refurbishing the interiors of the Queen Elizabeth Hall, the Purcell Room, and the Hayward Gallery, is scheduled to begin in late 2015. Mr Rick Haythornthwaite, Chairman of the Southbank Centre, expressed his gratitude to Arts Council England "for so generously supporting the urgent repair and maintenance of these iconic Sixties buildings." [2]

The resident orchestras at the Southbank Centre are the London Philharmonic, Philharmonia Orchestra, London Sinfonietta, and Orchestra of the Age of Enlightenment. Since 2008 artists in Residence have included Bellowhead, Cape Farewell, Shlomo, Lemn Sissay, and Rahayu Supanggah. A wide-ranging programme presents classical world music, rock pop, jazz, dance, literature, and the visual arts.

The year 2010 marked the 350th anniversary of the Royal Society, and Prince Edward along with other royal dignitaries joined 700 Fellows of the society and over 1,000 guests at the anniversary convocation at the Royal Festival Hall.

Prince Edward is also Patron of the South Bank Foundation and, in September 2002, unveiled a bust to Lord Goodman and afterwards attended a concert by the Vienna Philharmonic Orchestra at the Royal Festival Hall.

INTERNATIONAL MUSICIANS
SEMINAR PRUSSIA COVE

Brief history

The International Musicians Seminar Prussia Cove (IMS), was founded in 1972, by the virtuoso violinist, Sándor Végh, (1912-1997), who was best known as one of the great chamber music violinists of the 20th century, and Hilary Tunstall-Behrens, who had been a young instructor in the Outward Bound School at Aberdovey during the Second World War, and who is today Programme Director of IMS. Sándor Végh, who was first a Hungarian, and later a French violinist and conductor, believed that the remote location on the Atlantic Coast at St. Michael's Mount, Marazion, Cornwall, England, had an energy that could inspire and reinvigorate musicians. Here, as enshrined in Daphne Du Murier's dramatic novel *Rebecca*, in the setting of soaring cliffs and miles of crystal, blue sea and sandy beaches, musical genius is inspired. It is both a musician's and an artist's paradise. Renowned British cellist, Steven Isserlis, is Artistic Director, and American cellist, Ralph Kirshabaum, and Hungarian-born pianist András Schiff, are the Artistic Advisers. Sir Simon Rattle OM CBE is President of IMS, and Prince Edward became Patron on January 18, 1999.

It all began when, in 1971, Hilary Tunstall-Behrens invited Sándor Végh to Cornwall to attend a small music festival held at Prussia Cove that is a small inlet on the south coast of West Cornwall. The following year the first master class was held in Cornwall, with Végh as its Maestro. Sándor Végh, explains Hilary, "Kept alive through his teaching what he saw as the erosion of mid-European musical traditions." Quoting Végh Hilary had this to say: "Music was about speaking and sharing rather than shining and dazzling."

IMS Prussia Cove today

IMS Prussia Cove gives sixteen public concerts a year in different churches throughout west Cornwall. The concerts are run and supported by a strong and loyal network of Friends of IMS, who also arrange an annual autumn tour around the UK that culminates at the Wigmore Hall in London. They also put on various fundraising concerts and events throughout the year.

Each year, during the Autumn Open Chamber Music Seminar, promising young professionals are invited to participate and make ensembles with their professors, thereby combining youth and experience. Programmes for the concerts are decided by the players during the rehearsal week. The aim is to promote the work of the seminars and to build IMS's reputation as an integral part of the musical life of west Cornwall that is now the most sought after venue for young professional musicians.

The concerts that take place during both seminars are an integral and important part of the experience. Maestri concerts take place in the spring to enable students to hear their professors in concert, and the outstanding students are given an opportunity to perform in public. During the Open Chamber Music seminar the concerts are an opportunity for audiences to hear some of the chamber music that has been rehearsed and studied so intensively.

The Master Classes take place each year over a three-week period, and over 100 participants are involved. Over 120 young professionals attend classes for solo string players and pianists, string quartets, and chamber ensembles with piano. The classes have been running since 1972, when Sãndor Végh first invited his students to come to Cornwall and study with him. The seminars provide a totally professional atmosphere and aim to foster the highest level of advanced study, drawing inspiration from the central European tradition. String players predominate, with solo and string quartet classes, but also an important part of the course is the Piano in Chamber Music class, encouraging established ensembles ranging from duo to quintet.

The seminar takes place every September and has been running since 1975. International musicians of the highest level come together to sustain Sãndor Végh's original idea of a professor playing with his students. Participation in the Open Chamber Music Seminar is by invitation and many of the young performers taking part are the most promising players from the spring Master Classes. The seminar is divided into three separate weeks, with forty musicians taking part each week, rehearsing and performing 60 different chamber music works over the whole seminar. There are three public concerts each weekend in local venues and churches in the West Penwith area. Each ensemble is made up of experienced senior musicians and younger players, all contributing and working together to explore the chamber music repertoire.

A sample of the fine music produced and played by IMS Prussia Cove was to be found at London's Wigmore Hall on Monday, May 26, 2008 at 7.30 pm, held in the presence of Prince Edward. Bach Sonatas 1 and 2 were played on the cello by Steven Isserlis, with András Schiff on the piano, in a hall in which the acoustics are amongst the finest in London. There were works by Leos Janáček, George Enescu, and Zoltán Kodály. Steven Isserlis has this to say about IMS Prussia Cove:

"Some of my most satisfying musical experiences have been at IMS. The combination of the glorious setting, the close personal friendships that one forms there, while living in such close proximity, and the sense of pure musical idealism that has been the chief aim of the seminar since it began, produces a sort of magic that is unique. IMS is an important part of my life and, I believe, an important part of the lives of most people who attend the seminars." [3]

Every year, money raised by the Friends of IMS helps two students to attend the Master Classes. For instance, in 2010, they supported the German violinist Korbian Altenberger, and Canadian cellist Christian Elliot, both of who were chosen to perform in one of the public concerts during the seminar.

Jerwood Charitable Foundation

Jerwood Charitable Foundation has supported the International Musicians Seminar at Prussia Cove for many years. Their support is directed towards British musicians, giving them the opportunity to attend the master class series. In the idyllic setting of

*59. Dame Felicity Lott receives the Gold Medal
of the Royal Philharmonic Society from HRH The
Duke of Kent, Wigmore Hall, London, 2010.*

Prussia Cove, as intended by their deceased mentor Sãndor Végh, young musicians have an opportunity to succeed. Fifteen exceptionally talented young chamber musicians are selected to join other international musicians in the masterclasses each spring. András Schiff has said of IMS Prussia Cove:

"It means so much to musicians to come to IMS Prussia Cove. It's quite unique, and having been to some of the leading festivals of the world, I have enough experience to compare them. We can get together here, away from the hectic music business and concentrate on music itself. The seminars have been an invaluable contribution to British and International life." [4]

Prince Edward presents the gold medal
Prince Edward presented the Royal Philharmonic Society Gold Medal to András Schiff on December 21, 2013 at the Wigmore Hall, which was also the occasion of András's 60th birthday. The presentation followed a recital of Beethoven's Diabelli Variations and Bach's Goldberg Variations by András Schiff, the culmination of his all-Bach recital series at the hall during November and December. Mr John Gilhooly OBE, Director of the Wigmore Hall and Chairman of the Royal Philharmonic Society, read the citation in which he said:

"András Schiff is one of the most widely admired pianists of his generation and has made a pre-eminent contribution to the international musical life of Great Britain. He is one of the foremost ambassadors, throughout the world, of the music of Mozart, Schubert, Schumann and Beethoven. And his revelatory readings of J. S. Bach have helped to liberate his keyboard music from the increasingly narrow confines of period instrument performance."

WIGMORE HALL

In June 2015 Mr John Gilhooly spoke about Prince Edward's interest in the music performed at the Wigmore Hall:

"His Royal Highness the Duke of Kent has had a long association with Wigmore Hall, and has attended many concerts here over recent decades. We're always very pleased to welcome the Duke, who has an outstanding knowledge of piano, song and string quartet repertoire. Very often, he is accompanied by his sister Her Royal Highness Princess Alexandra, who also has a passion for the music we promote.

"The Duke of Kent has made a significant contribution to the public profile of the Hall. He joined us to present Dame Felicity Lott with the Wigmore Hall Medal in 2010, and also in 2013 to award Sir András Schiff the Gold Medal of the Royal Philharmonic Society – one of the highest honours in music. We were thrilled that the Duke could be part of these major events at the Hall.

"The artists who perform here and our loyal audience are always very happy to see the Duke, and we look forward to welcoming him for many years to come. His passion for music shines like a beacon, and it's wonderful to have such enthusiasm, encouragement, kindness and support from a member of our Royal Family."

OPERA NORTH

Brief history
Opera North was first established in 1977, as part of the English National Opera and is based in Leeds. The aim was to deliver high-quality opera to the northern area of England. The 7th Earl of Harewood, the late George Henry Hubert Lascelles KBE AM (1923-2011), was its founder. The founding Music Director of the company was David Lloyd-Jones who continued until 1981.

In 1978, under the title of the English National Opera North, they gave a performance of Camille Saint-Saëns's Samson and Delilah and Les mamelles de Tirésias by Francis Poulenc. In 1980 they performed The Mines of Sulphur by Richard Rodney Bennett, and A Village Romeo and Juliet by Frederick Delius. In 1981 the Company's name was changed to Opera North. They performed Prince Igor by Alexander Borodin in 1982, Beatrice and Benedict by Berlioz in 1983, Johnny Strikes Up by Ernst Krenek in 1984, and Intermezzo by Richard Strauss in 1986.

In 1990 Paul Daniel CBE took over as Music Director and the company continu-

61. Wigmore Hall presentation 2013. Left to right: HRH The Duke of Kent; Sir András Schiff; Mr John Gilhooly OBE, Director, Wigmore Hall and Chairman of the Royal Philharmonic Society.

tinued to bring operatic novelties and a wide selection of familiar works to audiences in the North of England and elsewhere. Performances have included Mozart's Il re pastore (The Shepherd King) in 1993, and The Secret Marriage by Domenico Cimarosa; in 1994, Oberto by Verdi, and The Reluctant King by Emmanuel Chabrier, both of which were British stage premieres; in 1995, Troilus and Cressida by William Walton, and Hamlet by Ambroise Thomas, and in 1996, Medea by Luigi Cherubini.

Following the departure of Paul Daniel, Elgar Howarth held the temporary post of Music Advisor until Steven Sloane was appointed Music Director in 1999, remaining until 2002. During those years, no fewer than 18 major performances took place including, Joan of Arc (1998), and Jerusalem (1990), both by Verdi, the latter being a British premiere performance. In 1991 there was The Jewel Box by Mozart, arranged by Paul Griffiths; Gloriana by Benjamin Britten (1993), and Paradise Moscow by Shostakovich (2001).

Prince Edward as Patron

Prince Edward became Patron of Opera North on September 6, 2002. The President **is** Sir Gordon Linacre, the General Director is Richard Mantle, the Music Director is Richard Farnes, and the Board of Trustees Chairman is Derek Netherton. Richard Farnes took over as Music Director in 2004, and Rachmaninov's Francesac da Rimini was performed, and later that year the British premiere of Love's Luggage Lost by Rossini. Performances have included The Fortunes of King Croesus by Reinhard Keiser (2007), which was a British premiere, and the Excursions of Mr

Broucek by Leos Janáček (2009).

World premieres

Opera North has given world premieres of Rebecca by Winifred Joseph (1983), Caritas by Robert Saxton (1991), Baa, Baa, Black Sheep by Michael Berkeley (1993), Playing Away by Benedict Mason (1994), The Nightingale's to Blame by Simon Holt (1998), Jonathan Dove's The Adventures of Pinocchio (2007), and Swanhunter Skin Deep by David Sawer and Armando Iannucci (2009). That year also, Opera North premiered Prima Donna, a new opera by Rufus Wainwright at the Manchester International Festival.

Musical theatre

Opera North has also given performances of musical theatre works like Jerome Kern's Show Boat in collaboration with the Royal Shakespeare Company (1989), and productions of Gershwin's Of Thee I Sing and Stephen Sondheim's Sweeney Todd.

The works of Kurt Weill have now become something of a speciality and there were productions of Love Life (1996), One Touch of Venus and The Seven Deadly Sins (2004), and Arms and the Cow (2006), and in 2009, Let 'Em Eat Cake, which was the sequel to Of Thee I Sing. The Company worked extensively with electronic composer Mira Calix, commissioning Dead Wedding for the 2007 Manchester International Festival, Onibus (2008), and the installation Chorus (2009) for the opening of the Howard Assembly Rooms, Leeds Grand Theatre.

In 2003, at Leeds, Prince Edward attended a performance of the company's translations of Francesca da Rimini, composed by Rachmaninov, and Pagliacci by Leon Cavallo. He was introduced to members of the cast on stage as part of the celebrations to mark 25 years since the company's inception. Mr Richard Mantle, said:

> "We were delighted that the Duke of Kent came to Leeds to celebrate Opera North's 25th birthday and our Eight Little Greats festival. As the Company's Patron he is a great supporter and takes a strong interest in our work. We are particularly proud that the two performances he sees this evening begin a series of twenty-two performances of opera at Leeds Grand Theatre over the next eleven days."

Awards

Opera North's success is growing yearly, and they are winning awards. In 2004 they won the Manchester Evening News Theatre Award for Opera, and again in 2008; the Audiences Yorkshire Award for Best Overall Marketing and Audience Development; the TMA Theatre Award for Outstanding Achievement in Opera, and again in 2007 for Peter Grimes directed by Phyllida Lloyd; the Royal Philharmonic Society Award for Opera and Music Theatre in 2007 for Peter Grimes; and the South Bank Show Award for Opera for its Eight Little Greats season of one-act operas in 2005, and in 2007 for Peter Grimes. They won the Manchester Theatre Award for

Opera 2011, 2012 and 2013. On Classic FM the public voted them winners of the Best Classical Music Education Initiative (In Harmony), Music Teacher Awards, 2014.

Future Fund for Opera North
On February 9, 2007, Prince Edward attended an afternoon Benefactors' Lunch at Harewood House, Leeds, and was received by Her Majesty's Lord Lieutenant of West Yorkshire, Dr Ingrid Roscoe. That evening, Prince Edward attended a performance of l'Elisir d'Amore by Opera North at the Grand Theatre, Leeds.

On May 8, 2009, in the Emerald Grand Hall, Leeds Grand Theatre and Opera House, Prince Edward officially launched a new financial initiative titled the Future Fund for Opera North, at a private reception in the presence of current and potential future supporters of the opera company. The target was to achieve a capital value of £10 million by 2012, and the Future Fund has secured several million pounds in gifts and pledges. The work that the Company will be able to deliver under the trust will be focused on aspects that are primarily more than opera, including valuable education work, outreach work, and the nurturing of young singers. The intention of the Future Fund is to provide top-up funding over and above those core funds received from the company's major stakeholders to enable Opera North to extend its work and accessibility beyond its regular programme of activity.

Opera North's creative projects
Opera North has embarked upon a range of creative projects. Their Orchestra's brass and percussion players perform concerts of the brightest, most stirring and majestic music written for their instruments. In 2010 they performed Monteverdi's *Toccata from l'Orfeo,* excerpts from Premru's *Divertimento for Brass*, Shostakovich's *Jazz Suite*, and further pieces by Gabrieli, Khachaturian and Beethoven. They provided an enchanting evening's entertainment with the orchestra performing in the Howard Assembly Room. Featured were the string and woodwind players of the orchestra in a programme that included Bach's Orchestral Suite in B minor, Dvořák's popular *Serenade* in E major for Strings, and the Slavonic-styled *Serenade* in D minor for Wind.

In 2011 the Company performed the Portrait by Mieczyslaw Weinberg, and have initiated an annual series of semi-staged concert performances of the four operas in Wagner's Der Ring des Nibelungen by performing Das Reingold in Leeds Town Hall. French Maestro Frédéric Chaslin and the Opera North Orchestra launched the season in a programme of Gallic romance: Saint-Saëns' Organ Symphony, pieces by Debussy and Ravel, and the World Première of Maestro Chaslin's Gypsy Dance from his haunting opera *Wuthering Heights*, influenced by the work of the great Yorkshire novelist Emily Bronte, about the fated lovers Heathcliff and Cathy.

Opera North's four-year journey through one of Prince Edward's favourite works, Richard Wagner's *Der Ring des Nibelungen (The Ring Cycle)*, has been internationally acclaimed. In June 2014 it was reaching its conclusion with Götterdämmerung. Their music director, Richard Farnes, has won high praise in the press for his "sensational" productions that were described as "a triumph of scarcely imaginable proportions." A big programme of opera that was begun in 2014 is continuing into 2015.

THE HANOVER BAND

The Hanover Band was founded in 1980 by Artistic Director, Caroline Brown, a flautist in the band. It has made many tours of the UK and is now an internationally renowned British period instrument orchestra. Hanover signifies the Hanovarian period 1714-1830 and Band is the 18th-century term for orchestra. The Band performs 17th-century, 18th-century and 19th-century music played on original period instruments or fine replicas. These instruments require specialist knowledge from the players, as they are constructed differently from their modern counterparts and they therefore make a different sound.

The Band has put in many appearances over the years, including at the Carnegie Hall, Amsterdam Concertgebouw, the Bridgewater Hall, Manchester, and in London at the South Bank Centre, the Royal Albert Hall, and the Wigmore Hall. They have made ten tours of the United States, and preformed in Canada, Mexico, Austria, Germany, Switzerland, France, Portugal, Spain Belgium, the Netherlands, Norway, Greece and Turkey. Over 160 recordings have been produced on Nimbus Records, Hyperion Records, Sony, EMI, Eminence, RCA, and other labels, including a complete cycle of the orchestral works of Johann Christian Bach for Cop.

Outstanding specialists in recreating the sounds of the past, the band has established an international reputation for the excellence of its performances and recordings. The band also has a history of big name guest-directors, Charles Mackerras, Roy Goodman, Nicholas McGegan, Anthony Halstead, and Richard Edgar.

At a private concert on November 1, 1992, at Claydon House, Buckinghamshire, Prince Edward became Patron of the Hanover Band.

Based at the Old Market, Hove, Sussex, the band has a long-term strategy to bring musical excellence to the South East of England, developing community links through an extensive education programme. The Old Market was built in 1828 as a market house but was derelict for some years. Funding by the National Lottery has helped pay for the redevelopment of the building, and has provided also a centre for local arts, community and education events. The restoration project began in 1995, and the Old Market Trust was set up to manage the project with work commencing in 1997. In May 1999 Prince Edward performed the official opening of the newly restored building, unveiling a commemorative plaque in the auditorium. A concert was held in celebration. A Grade II listed building, The Old Market stands in a part of Hove known as Brunswick Town which is an area of outstanding architectural heritage.

The Hanover Band's performances are too numerous to detail here but two recent concerts will provide the reader with a flavour of the quality of music. Their performance at St. Nicholas Church, Brighton, on a Sunday in January 2011 was described by one reviewer:

A fantastically well-played and varied programme proved the ideal way in which to enjoy a chilly winter's afternoon. The beautiful venue with its sublime architecture and warm, clean acoustic was the cherry on the cake. The highlights were Vivaldi's well known Trio Sonata La Follia, executed with a bravura passion, and the less well known solo pieces for harpsichord, in particular Rameau's Les Cyclopes and Couperin Les Baricades Misterieuses.

On Good Friday, April 2011, the band gave a concert at Chichester Cathedral (The Cathedral Church of the Holy Trinity), founded 1075, and which is the seat of the Anglican Bishop of Chichester. A magnificent building of Norman and Gothic styles from the late 12th through to the 15th century, the Cathedral with its superb acoustics was the ideal setting for the band's performance of Handel's best-known oratorio, Messiah, and Bach's St. John Passion. The Band was joined by the Hanover Band Chorus, directed by Andrew Arthur. Against a backdrop of towering gothic pillars, stained glass windows, rare medieval sculptures, modern art works and tapestries, many having been commissioned by Dean Hussey, the well-known churchman and lover of art, a contemporary audience enjoyed a wonderful opportunity to hear the same sound as audiences in the time of Handel in the 18th century.

The Worshipful Company of Stationers and Newspaper Makers, usually known as the Stationers' Company, is one of the Livery Companies of the City of London, dating back to 1403. It held a monopoly over the publishing industry and was officially responsible for setting and enforcing regulations until the enactment of the Statute of Anne in 1710. On September 9, 2013, the Hanover Band gave a concert at Stationers' Hall, which is near St Paul's Cathedral in the City of London. Prince Edward and the Right Honourable The Lord Mayor and Lady Mayoress of London were in attendance. The charity event was hosted by the Stationers' Company and all proceeds went to both the Lord Mayor's Appeal and the Stationers' Foundation. The Hanover Band performed a programme of music by Mozart, including the Horn Concerto No.4 K.495, Exsultate Jubilate for Soprano, and Orchestra Clarinet Concerto in A K.622. There followed a Candlelit Dinner in the Court Room and the event was deemed a huge success. Thanks were extended to Spicers, who are one of the Corporate Members, as well as to the Leather Bottle Trust, and Berforts Information Press, for their sponsorship.

EUROPEAN UNION BAROQUE ORCHESTRA

The European Union Baroque Orchestra (EUBO) was founded in 1985, and is an educational charity. It is supported financially by the European Union for which it acts as an official Cultural Ambassador, and also by private sponsorship. It has provided a major initiative to the European Music Year celebration of the 300th anniversaries of the great baroque musicians Johann Sebastian Bach, Domenico Scarlatti, and George Frideric Handel. Prince Edward became Chairman of the

Honorary Committee of Patrons on August 1, 1986.

EUBO is a training initiative of the European Union that allows young performers of baroque music from all over the EU to gain orchestral experience as part of their career development from conservatoire study into a professional career. The success of the project under the direction of the world's most eminent baroque musicians can be measured in the number of ex-EUBO members who now play in Europe's leading baroque orchestras.

Since its inception more than 500 full-time members of EUBO have given over 600 performances in 51 countries world-wide. The Ensemble performs at many of Europe's finest music festivals and concert halls, including the Amsterdam Concertgebouw, Opéra-Comique in Paris, the festivals of Ansbach and Musikalischer Herbst, in Germany, and the specialist early music festivals such as Utrecht, York, and Ambronay (a French opera and early musical festival). Outside of Europe, as well as tours of Japan, USA, and South Africa, EUBO has played in Ramallah and the Gaza Strip, Botswana, and Soweto.

The orchestra is completely renewed every year. Auditions take place in spring, with usually around 100 young baroque musicians applying for the 20-25 places in the ensemble. The successful applicants then come together for four tours which take place between July and December, and which take them across the EU and beyond. These tours are directed by such leading baroque professionals as Lars Ulrik Mortensen, Enrico Onofri, Roy Goodman, Petra Müllejans, Christophe Coin, Margaret Faultless, Edward Higginbottom, Rachel Podger, Andrew Manze, Ton Koopman, Favio Biondi and Christina Pluhar, who are amongst the artists that regularly work with EUBO.

Since 2008 EUBO has been Orchestra-in-Residence in Echternach, Luxembourg, working together with the City of Echternach, Festival International Echternach, and the new cultural centre Trifolion. The orchestra trains and plays together for only six months but during that time they perform at prestigious venues across the world and work with some of the finest international directors.

An instance of the international value of their work was when, in November 2002, they carried out a tour of Japan during which a 25-strong group of young musicians performed six concerts at five venues across the country. Associate Conductor of the English Chamber Orchestra Paul Goodwin was the conductor. Two concerts were performed in Tokyo, co-organised by NPO Triton Arts Network/Dai-ichi Seimei Hall and Allegro Music Tokyo Incorporated, and supported by the Japan Committee for UNICEF. The tour was financially supported by Matsushita Electric (Europe), JAS Forwarding (Japan), the British Council, the Royal Danish Embassy, Tokyo, and the Delegation of the European Commission in Japan.

The programme performed involved François Couperin's Huitième Concert dan le Goût Thétral; George Philipp Telemann's Concerto in E minor for Traverso Flute, Recorder, and Strings; Matthew Locke's Suite from The Tempest; and George Friedrich Händel's Water Music Suite, taken from Suites I, II, and III.

In his address, Ambassador Bernhard Zepter, Head of the Delegation of the European Commission in Japan emphasised that music can serve as an important bridge between the people of Europe and Japan:

"The Baroque period saw numerous exchanges between European musicians with many of the great composers of the age travelling to neighbouring countries to look for new ideas, new patrons and new audiences. Today, Baroque music represents the very essence of European culture and I am pleased to welcome the European Union Baroque Orchestra to Japan. I hope that these young musicians will encourage greater understanding of Europe through the medium of its rich musical tradition."

In his role as Chairman, Honorary Committee of Patrons, European Union Baroque Orchestra, Prince Edward has said:

"I was fortunate enough in 1985 to act as Chairman of the United Kingdom's celebrations for European Music Year. There were many exciting projects but the launch of the European Baroque Orchestra (as it was then, seven years before the Union came about) was one that has stood the test of time and proved of far-reaching value.

"In the quarter of a century since, I have been able to hear many of the orchestras that have been trained under the EUBO's auspices. I look at the continuing excellence of the music making and the constantly widening number of countries from which the participants are drawn as full justification of everything we instigated in 1985.

"Each time I hear the orchestra perform, I am amazed at the consistent brilliance each year's players manage to achieve in such a short time.

"It is a great source of pride that so many have made successful careers all over Europe."

MENDELSSOHN SOCIETY

The piano music of Felix Mendelssohn has long been a favourite with the British Royal Family. Queen Elizabeth II and Prince Philip walked down the isle of Westminster Abbey on their wedding day, November 20, 1947 to Mendelssohn's Wedding March. As noted in Chapter 1, Prince Edward's parents, Prince George and Princess Marina, were both musical. They were proficient pianists and Prince Edward grew up in a musical home. On July 30, 2004, he became Patron of the Mendelssohn Society.

The Mendelssohn Society was founded in 2002, with Kurt Masur, renowned conductor and Patron of the Mendelssohnhaus in Leipzig as its Honorary President. Its purpose was to promote appreciation of the life and work of Mendelssohn, and to support a Mendelssohn Scholarship Award and enable students of all background to attend Jewish music summer courses at the University of London.

The society was the idea of Geraldine Auerbach MBE, Director of the Jewish Music Institute (JMI), and Mrs Jackie Rosenfeld OBE, who became its Chairman. The inaugural event took place at the Royal Academy on Thursday, October 24. The outstanding young Jerusalem String Quartet performed Mendelssohn and Haydn quartets on Guarneri instruments, loaned by JMI Vice President, Dr David

Josefowitz, who introduced each instrument. It was followed by a tour of the Mendelssohn memorabilia in the York Gate Collection.

In December 2003, Malcolm Troup, Emeritus Professor of City University and JMI Trustee, paid tribute to the importance of this young society in *Piano Journal* of which he is Editor:

"The Mendelssohn Society's annual event at the Royal Academy of Music, last December, in the presence of HRH The Duke of Kent, featured the strings of the Fidelio Piano Quartet and the Belcea String Quartet in a programme of Dohnanyi and Beethoven, before joining forces in the Mendelssohn Octet. Lord Armstrong of Ilminster, whose father Sir Thomas had been a much-loved former Principal of the Academy, proved by his words to be himself a passionate advocate of the composer. The evening also served as a launch for Professor Larry Todd's new biography *Mendelssohn: A Life in Music* which has been described by Christopher Hogwood as 'A Bible for Mendelssohn's growing and hungry rank of supporters!'"

Funds have now been raised to send 22 young musicians of all backgrounds to study Jewish music at JMI's summer programme at the University of London.

Composer Felix Mendelssohn

Felix Mendelssohn was born in Hamburg on February 3, 1809, into a notable Jewish family. In 1811, the family moved to Berlin, where Felix was brought up as a Lutheran Christian. Mendelssohn is credited with being the most successful musician of the 19th century. His early success in Germany involved his revival of interest in the music of Johann Sebastian Bach.

Dr Richard E. Rodda, musical Programme Annotator, has described Mendelssohn's success as beginning with his being appointed, in 1835, as administrator, music director and conductor of the Leipzig Gewandhaus concerts. He raised the quality of musical life in Leipzig to equal that of any city in Europe and, in 1842, he founded the local Conservatory to maintain the standards of excellence he had set. The school would become the most highly regarded institution of its kind in the world for half a century. In 1841 he was Director of the Music Section of the Academy of Arts in Berlin that had been instituted by King Frederick of Prussia. This promotion demanded of Mendelssohn that he supervise and conduct a variety of programmes and to compose upon royal demand. Famous pieces followed: *A Midsummer Night's Dream, Italian Symphony,* the *Scottish Symphony*, the *Hebrides Overture,* his Violin Concerto, and his *String Octet.*

Arriving in England in May 1844, Mendelssohn rose to success and became highly respected and popular as a musician and composer. He conducted Beethoven's Violin Concert and presented *A Midsummer Night's Dream.* He served as soloist in his own G minor Piano Concerto, and took part in many social engagements and chamber music soirées.

In July he returned to Germany, where he completed his Violin Concerto for the Concertmaster of the Gewandhaus Orchestra, Ferdinand David. On the order of King Frederick he gave a performance of his oratorio *St. Paul.* By 1845 he was working on Elijah, premiered at the Birmingham Festival the following year, and he completed the String Quintet in B-flat major (Op.87) and the C minor Trio (op.66). Mendelssohn died on November 4, 1847, from exhaustion due to overwork, aged only 38 years. His C minor Trio was the last important chamber work of his career.

ROYAL OPERA HOUSE

Bob and Tamar Manoukian Production Workshop

Prince Edward carries out a number of engagements in relation to creativity for which he is not patron or president nor has any official role.

For every stage production there is required stage set and scenery that has to be expertly made and put together. For this purpose in December 2010, the Royal Opera House, London, opened the Bob and Tamar Manoukian Production Workshop at Thurrock, Essex, that is a set and scenery-making facility for their opera and ballet productions and which is part of a larger 14-acre site complex named High House Production Park, at Purfleet in Essex. The building was designed by Gibberd and constructed by Kier Eastern, who were appointed to build the facility in March 2011. The facility was designed by Nicholas Hare Architects and has won several design awards.

The state of the art workshop is designed to accommodate the sets and scenery of several productions being created at once. It features a fit up area as large as the Covent Garden stage, allowing the team to fully construct the set before it is transferred to the London stage, so that the designers can see their vision has been realised. All the productions for The Royal Opera, The Royal Ballet, and Birmingham Royal Ballet, are now made there.

The specially designed production workshop is home to a talented team of scenic artists, carpenters, draughtsmen, and metal workers. It has a paint spray room, and metal workshop, and welding bays, and large paint and carpentry workshops. On site, there are also beautifully preserved and refurbished Grade II listed barns which are used for community events and workshops and may be hired for meetings and weddings.

Prince Edward's visits

At the invitation of the Royal Opera House, Prince Edward was taken on a tour of High House Production Park on May 30, 2012. He was met by Royal Opera House Chief Executive, Tony Hall. Accompanied by the Lord Lieutenant of Essex, Lord Petre, Prince Edward was introduced to a number of important dignitaries. Tony Hall showed him the beautifully renovated farm buildings and formal gardens and then introduced him to members of the local community, people who have been involved in the creation of the Park, and members of the Royal Opera House Learning and Participation team which has been based on site since January 2011, although they started working in the community in 2006.

Prince Edward was then taken on a tour of the Bob and Tamar Manoukian Production Workshop, where he was introduced to members of the talented crafts team who are dedicated to creating the famous sets used in Royal Opera House productions. He was shown some of the dramatic scenery produced in the workshop, including the impressive set for director Paul Curran's production of *The Tsar's Bride*.

The Royal Opera House Learning and Participation team works closely with schools, colleges and the local community, making the Park a centre for community and cultural development. Prince Edward went to meet Year 6 pupils from Purfleet Primary School who were taking part in a creative workshop, helping to make costumes for the upcoming community opera Hot House. Two 11-year-olds spoke of their experience; Daniel Nistor said he was nervous about meeting a member of the Royal Family: "I was really tense. We had to tell him how the game on the smart board worked. It was good and fun." Lauren Steele didn't get to speak to Prince Edward but was excited to see and meet him. She had been printing patterns onto fabric for the opera costumes. Lauren said: "Making the costumes looks easy, but it's really hard."

At the end of a very special day, Prince Edward unveiled a plaque commemorating his visit to the workshop.

The Backstage Centre

Creative & Cultural Skills opened The Backstage Centre in October 2012, launching the building formally in March 2013, with a ribbon-cutting event with television personality Jools Holland OBE DL, who presents a weekly programme on BBC2, and has a touring band, the Rhythm and Blues Orchestra. In 2013 The Backstage Centre was highly commended in the British Construction Industry Awards.

The building was designed in consultation with theatre and music industry experts and provides a versatile training, rehearsal and technical space. Students come there to learn about backstage skills such as sound, lighting and pyrotechnics, and work alongside professionals from the industry to gain valuable work experience.

Acme Studios High House Artists' Studios

At the end of 2013, Acme Studios had also come on board in the Park. They are providing 39 artists' studios and four live/work spaces at low cost to artists ranging from installation artists to sculptors. They are also becoming integrated into the outreach work generated from the Park.

Community outreach and education projects

The Royal Opera House Learning and Participation team runs community outreach and education projects, focussing on the backstage and technical crafts. They provide teaching for students in practical skills to inspire them to think about working in theatre, stage, events, and music productions. The Royal Opera House Thurrock Community Chorus, numbering almost 150 members, was created and now gives performances in the local area and beyond, and RM19, a youth choir, has also been established for young people between the ages of 11 and 25 years.

Regular tours of the High House Production Park and Inspiration Days with creative workshops are offered by the Royal Opera House to schools, colleges, community groups, and to the public. For further information please visit www.roh.org. uk.

Endnotes to Chapter 9

[1] Correspondence between Lady Digby DBE, Darts(hc), DL, and Celia Lee, July 4, 2012.

[2] Report in the *London Evening Standard*, page 4 'News', May 29, 2014, article by Josh Pettitt.

[3] Celia Lee in correspondence with Steven Isserlis, 2008.

[4] Celia Lee in correspondence with András Schiff, 2008.

62. The Royal Box, Wimbledon tennis finals, 1977; front row, left to right: HRH Birgitte The Duchess of Gloucester; HRH The Duchess of Kent; HRH The Duke of Kent; Her Majesty Queen Elizabeth II; Air Chief Marshal Sir Brian Burnett, Chairman AELTC; HRH The Duke of Edinburgh; HRH Princess Margaret.

CHAPTER 10

WIMBLEDON TENNIS CHAMPIONSHIPS

PART 1
INTRODUCTION AND BRIEF HISTORY

Introduction
In a royal tradition that stretches back to Victorian times, Prince Edward is a tennis enthusiast and presents the prizes at Wimbledon Lawn Tennis matches each year. He is President of The All England Lawn Tennis and Croquet Club, (January 1, 1969). Prince Edward was made an Honorary Member (1962), and an Associate Member (June 1, 1984), of The International Lawn Tennis Club of Great Britain. He is also a Joint Associate Member of the Lawn Tennis Association (April 1, 1983). He was made Patron of the Wimbledon Lawn Tennis Museum (December 1, 1993).

Brief history – All England Lawn Tennis and Croquet Club
The All England Lawn Tennis and Croquet Club (AELTC), often referred to

as Wimbledon Lawn Tennis, was founded on July 23, 1868, at the height of the Victorian croquet craze and was first given the title of the All England Croquet Club. They held their first croquet competition in 1870.

Lawn Tennis Association

The Lawn Tennis Association (LTA) was founded in 1888, with seven-time Wimbledon champion Mr William Renshaw as its first elected president. The LTA is the national governing body of tennis in Great Britain, the Channel Islands, and the Isle of Man. Their overall purpose is to continue to grow and sustain the sport. As the LTA has a responsibility for all aspects of tennis within Britain, they have created a strong coaching structure to ensure that Britain has a very strong body of coaches that meet national standards.

International Lawn Tennis Club of Great Britain

In 1924, **Arthur Wallis Myers** CBE (1878–1939), always known as Wallis, founded The International Lawn Tennis Club of Great Britain (IC), with Arthur, Lord Balfour, (British Conservative Prime Minister 1902-1905). Wallis was a keen English tennis player and was active mainly in doubles. He was a tennis correspondent, editor, and author, and is considered to be one of the leading tennis journalists of the first half of the 20th century. He played in the mixed doubles at the 1914 World Hard Court Championships with Britain's **Mrs Phyllis Satterthwaite**, reaching the semi-finals. At the 1923 Monte Carlo tournament he teamed up with the Norwegian tennis player **Mrs Molla Bjurstedt Mallory,** who won a record eight singles titles at the US Championships. Wallis was the captain of British tennis teams on tour in Europe, South Africa, and India. With the First World War (1914-18) at an end, the post-war period at Wimbledon experienced a sudden surge in interest as a flood of new overseas tennis stars appeared. Wallis died in 1939, having been taken ill on his return from seeing Britain lose the Davis Cup tie against Germany in Berlin.

The strong revival of the IC movement took place in the postwar years from 1946 onwards. In the next five years, Belgium, (1947), Argentina (1948), Denmark (1949), and South Africa (1950) had formed clubs. By 1970 the total number of active clubs had increased to 16, and included Australia and India (1951), New Zealand (1956), Italy (1960), Canada (1965), Germany (1967), and Switzerland (1970) [1].

Open tennis

The arrival of open tennis in 1968 did nothing to diminish the numbers joining the IC but rather accelerated the interest, with Spain joining (1973), Mexico (1974), and Japan (1978). During the 1980s there was a flood of new clubs throughout the world led by Monaco (1980), followed by Uruguay and Luxembourg (1981), Brazil (1982), Pakistan (1983), Zimbabwe and Israel (1984), and the Bahamas (1988) [2]. At the 75th anniversary meeting at Wimbledon in 1999, 30 countries were represented. Today, the IC numbers 38 member nations.

63. The Duchess of Kent attends the trophy presentation at
the Wimbledon Lawn Tennis Championships, Wimbledon, 1986.

The ICs as they are known around the world, have as their core values: the enhancement of international understanding and goodwill through sport, specifically tennis; the playing of matches between nations among tennis players who have played representative tennis overseas; the maintenance, encouragement, and development of the highest standards of good sportsmanship among players of all nations; in particular the encouragement of the standards referred to above among young players; the enhancement of the lives of young people, many of whom may come from disadvantaged backgrounds, through teaching them the value of sport and tennis in particular; and the welcoming and entertainment of tennis players visiting their country from abroad.

The modern-day International Club (IC)
Mr Boyd Cuthbertson, Honorary Secretary, International Lawn Tennis Club of Great Britain, has provided an update on the modern- day International Club (IC) as follows:

"There are few major tennis playing nations who do not now have an International Club. In each country aspiring to have an IC, tennis needs to have reached a certain stage of maturity for a Club to be sustainable. To ensure that we can meet our objective of creating lasting international friendships, we will continue to encourage new nations to join.

"The fun side of what the IC does, is to play matches, nation to nation, in a series of bilateral, quadrilateral, and multilateral events. The events between two nations are numerous and often have their origins going

221

back many decades. For example, the French and the British have enjoyed biannual matches going back 81 years. The Americans and the Mexicans have an annual match, called the Coupa des Amigos, which goes back at least 30 years.

"The Council of ICs which administers the family of International Clubs worldwide, oversees a series of events that are hosted by clubs on a regular basis, usually to celebrate an important anniversary. These include the Windmill Trophy for players under the age of 45, and veterans aged 45 and over; the Mercelis Trophy for lady players under age 40, and ladies aged 40 and over; the Potter Cup for men veterans of age 45 and over; the Caretta Trophy for ladies between the ages of 50 and 60 and over; the Columbus Trophy for men aged 55 and 65 and over; and the Juego de Pelota for men aged over 70 and 75. Thus we achieve, through the promotion of these international competitions, our second objective of promoting good fellowship among international tennis players of the world.

"Our third and probably the most important objective is to maintain the standard of sportsmanship and understanding among players of all nations and young players in particular. The culture of good sportsmanship is seen throughout our events. It is rare to see a moment of uncontrolled anger or a serious line call dispute in IC matches. When this happens, a simple reminder that the perpetrator is taking part in an IC event usually results in good sense prevailing.

"To underscore this vital ingredient, the Council awards the Jean Borotra Sportsmanship Trophy to an international player who has shown outstanding sportsmanship on an individual occasion or throughout his or her career. The award has been won by **Stefan Edberg** (Sweden), **Chris Evert** and **Todd Martin** (US), **Maria Bueno** and **Gustavo Kuerten** (Brazil), **Pat Rafter** (Australia), **Kim Clijsters** (Belgium), **Mats Wilander** (Sweden), and **Roger Federer** (Switzerland).

"The objective of involving young tennis players carries a more important message. Young boys and girls who have set their sights on an international tennis career, often know little of the history of tennis and play very few team matches. We ensure that in some bi-lateral matches some of the more promising young players take part in these matches. In addition, in 2004, we introduced the IC Junior Challenge, where teams of boys and girls of 16 and under representing their countries take part in elimination competitions on their continent, followed by a final at a different venue. The boys and girls travel as a team and experience the pleasure of performing in a situation where interdependency is key. They are made aware of the requirements of fair play within the community of sport. In this way, we seek to achieve our fourth major objective, philanthropy.

"As a relatively senior institution in tennis, the notion of 'giving back' has taken hold. Recognising that with a network of 38 clubs around the world, we could do more, we have launched a philanthropic programme. We have benefited over many years from private donors and now run our

64. Marion Bartoli (France) receives the Rosewater Dish from HRH The Duke of Kent after the Ladies' Final, Centre Court Wimbledon Championships 2013.

own fund raising events. These funds are now spent in a structured manner by the IC Council's Philanthropic Committee on tennis programmes for disadvantaged children in South Africa, Mexico, Amsterdam, Barcelona, Ethiopia and Uruguay.

"By focusing our attention on less advantaged communities, the IC's Philanthropy Programme hopes to give those children an alternative focus to the streets and their inherent dangers of drugs, crime, and negative peer pressure. Through tennis, and the dedication and structure it provides, we hope the children in our projects will learn basics such as commitment, self-esteem, respect for fellow players, physical fitness, the benefit of nutrition, and how to play by the rules of fairness, all wrapped-up in an overall feeling of fun and enjoyment." [3]

Lawn Tennis Museum, Kenneth
Ritchie Library, guided tours and shop

Wimbledon Lawn Tennis Museum was inaugurated at the championship's centenary event in 1977. Having been refurbished in more recent years it was officially reopened to the public by Prince Edward on April 12, 2006. Today, located inside the grounds of the AELTC and accessed through Gate 4, it is the largest tennis museum in the world.

The museum has exhibits and touch screen computer consoles for visitors that are distributed throughout the museum hallways. Memorabilia from many famous players dating back to Victorian times and up to the present day are included in several different exhibits that change seasonally.

223

Many fabulous tennis trophies, including historic cups and dishes, are on display. These include the present Challenger Cup for the Men's Singles that was purchased in 1887, and the Venus Rosewater Dish that is presented to the Lady Champion each year, along with a variety of other gleaming silver trophies.

There is a viewing platform called CentreCourt360 that allows guests to sample the atmosphere of the Centre Court. Highlights of the museum feature a 200-degree screen that shows current films about the science of tennis. The famous US tennis player **Mr John McEnroe** has been created in a ghost-like-image. He reminisces about the dressing-room and his first meeting with fellow tennis player **Mr Jimmy Connors,** and how he emotionally prepared himself for matches.

There is a collection of past and present fashion, consisting Wimbledon outfits from those worn in the 1880s, to **Mr Rafael Nadal's** dri-fit 'pirate' trousers. Other features include Get a Grip, a rotating wheel of tennis rackets throughout the decades; The Reactor game, and an archive of great matches from past Wimbledon championships.

The museum is open throughout the year except during the championships week, where entry is possible for tournament ticket holders only. Guided tours are available, led by **London's Blue Badge Guides,** who take visitors around the grounds and behind the scenes of the All England Lawn Tennis Club and the Museum. Audio guides are available in eight languages, tours last 90 minutes and include access to Court No.1, Centre Court, the Press Interview Room, the players' restaurant and picnic areas, the terrace, the Millennium Building, and the water gardens.

The Kenneth Ritchie Wimbledon Library is the largest tennis library in the world and is home to a collection of books, periodicals, videos, and DVD's, relating to tennis, and is available to visitors by appointment. There is a shop at the entrance to the museum, selling tennis and casual clothing, towelling goods, sport bags, DVDs, books, jewellery, tennis rackets, souvenirs, and other tennis accessories.

PART 2

ALL ENGLAND LAWN TENNIS AND CROQUET CLUB

Part 2 (i)

The Early Years

The All England Lawn Tennis and Croquet Club (AELTC), situated at Church Road, Wimbledon, London, is a private members club. It is best known as the venue for the Annual Lawn Tennis Championships, the only Grand Slam tennis event still held on grass, and is commonly referred to as Wimbledon Tennis.

Association with British Royalty
British royalty has been associated with the championships since 1907, when Prince

*65. Andy Murray (Great Britain) receives the
Challenge Cup from HRH The Duke of Kent after the
Gentlemen's Final, Centre Court, Wimbledon 2013.*

George the Prince of Wales, second surviving son of King Edward VII, accompanied by his wife, Princess Mary, visited the previous club ground at Worple Road, Wimbledon, on Saturday, June 29. They were met by the Committee at the entrance and escorted to the Committee Box that had been fitted out temporarily as a Royal Box. True to the great British weather, a thunderstorm put an early end to the day's play. Before leaving, the Prince accepted an offer of the Presidency of the club and made his intention known of donating a challenge trophy. Prince George remained President until 1910, when he ascended the throne as His Majesty King George V. He then became Patron of the club a position that has been maintained by succeeding monarchs.

The King and Queen were regular spectators at the championships each year (excepting the First World War years) until 1934. In 1947 King George VI and Queen Elizabeth (later the Queen Mother) continued the tradition and were present to watch the Gentlemen's Singles final. The patron of the club today is Her Majesty Queen Elizabeth II, who visited the championships in July 1957, 1962, and 1977, during her Silver Jubilee year, which was also the occasion of the championships' Centenary, and again in 2010. In 2013 the Queen cheered on Britain's Andy Murray from the comfort of her sitting room at Buckingham Palace whilst watching him on television. His Royal Highness Prince Philip The Duke of Edinburgh attended in 1949, 1953, 1954, 1957, 1960, and 1977. His Royal Highness Charles The Prince of Wales, attended in 1970 and 2012, during the Queen's Golden Jubilee. Younger generations of royals also attend at Wimbledon; especially popular are the Duke and Duchess of Cambridge, William and Catherine.

Successive royal presidents

In 1929 Prince George, later the 1st Duke of Kent and third son of King George V and Queen Mary, became President of the AELTC. At Prince George's death in 1942, his widow Princess Marina The 1st Duchess of Kent, took over as President. Princess Marina died in 1968, and Prince Edward, being her elder son, became President on January 1, 1969. Prince Edward and his wife Katharine the 2nd Duchess of Kent have presented the prizes jointly at Wimbledon for many years. Previously, upon entering or leaving the Centre Court, players bowed or curtsied to members of the Royal Family seated in the Royal Box. In 2003, in order to simplify matters, Prince Edward decided to discontinue the tradition. Players now bow or curtsy only if Her Majesty The Queen or His Royal Highness Charles The Prince of Wales is present in the Royal Box.

AELTC Wimbledon Tennis Tournaments and Prize Giving

Brief history

AELTC is responsible for staging the world's leading tennis tournament at Wimbledon. Prince Edward became an Associate Member of AELTC, on April 1, 1983. Each summer, the tournament begins on the Monday falling between June 20 and 26, and lasts for thirteen days, ending on a Sunday.

The history of AELTC stretches back to 1868, to the time before lawn tennis was invented, when it was The All England Croquet Club. Major Walter Clopton Wingfield devised lawn tennis, which was added to the club's activities in 1875, and two years later the club changed its name to The All England Croquet and Lawn Tennis Club. The first Lawn Tennis Championship took place under the same set of rules by which it is played today, with one or two minor exceptions, like the height of the net and posts, and the distance of the service line from the net.

The Gentlemen's Singles was held in 1877, and was won by **Spencer Gore**, an Old Harrovian rackets player, and about 200 spectators paid one shilling (today 5p) to watch the final. The original ground was at Worple Road, Wimbledon, and in 1922, the club moved to the present site in Church Road, which was opened by King George V and Queen Mary.

The Ground

The lawns at the old Ground consisted of the principal or Centre Court in the middle and the others arranged around it. The title 'Centre Court' was retained when the club moved to the present site. Four new courts were brought into Commission on the north side of the ground in 1980, and two more were added in 1997, alongside the opening of the new No.1 Court. The 19 courts used are composed purely of perennial rye grass.

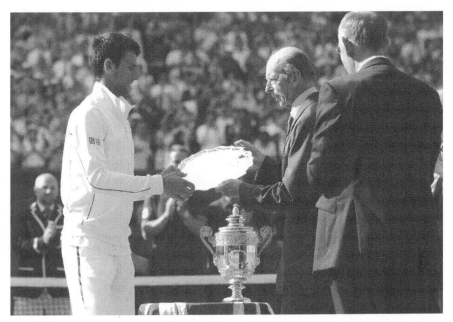

66. *Novak Djokovic (Republic of Serbia) receives the runners-up silver salver from HRH The Duke of Kent in the trophy ceremony after the Gentlemen's Final on Centre Court, Wimbledon 2013.*

General Election, women were admitted to the championships and the Ladies' Singles and Gentlemen's Doubles began in that year. Ladies Doubles and Mixed Doubles were added in 1913. Until 1922 the reigning champion had to play only in the Challenge Round against whoever had won through to challenge him in the All-Comers' Singles. As with the other three Grand Slam events, contestants were from the top-rank of amateur players, until the advent of the open era in tennis in 1968.

Until the victory of Scotland's **Andy Murray** in 2013, no British man had won the Men's Singles since **Fred Perry** in 1936, and no British woman has won the Women's Singles since **Virginia Wade** in 1977. However, **Annabel Croft** and **Laura Robson** won the Girls' championship in 1984 and 2008, respectively.

Children and the Disabled

Time has moved on from the days when the club recognised adults only as eligible to participate in tennis. There is now a greater recognition of the talents of children, young people, and the disabled. Today, Boys' and Girls' Singles and Doubles, and both Gentlemen's and Ladies' Wheelchair Doubles also take place.

Ball boys and girls

Ball boys and girls (BBGs), play a crucial role in the smooth running of the tournament and a good BBG should not be noticed. They are expected to do the job and melt away into the background rather than being a distraction from play. In the 1920s, ball boys were provided by The Shaftesbury Home for children, and from 1947, by Goldings, a Barnardos school. Since 1969 and 1977, boys and girls respectively have been provided by local schools as volunteers and may serve for one or two tournaments. To be selected, candidates must pass written, fitness, and mobility tests.

Wimbledon colours

The team spirit is emphasised with uniform colours in clothing. Dark green and purple (mauve) are the traditional Wimbledon colours. Green clothing was worn by the chair umpire, linesmen, and BBGs, until the 2005 championships. From 2006, for the championships, officials and BBGs were outfitted in navy blue and cream uniforms. The dress code for players is all white which means 95 per cent white in area.

Spectators, press, television, and radio

Wimbledon is the only grand slam where fans without tickets can queue up for seats. Many are so enthusiastic that in order to ensure entrance they camp out overnight so as to join the queue early in the morning. Fans arrive from all over the world with tents and sleeping bags to spend the night on the pavement.

The championships were first televised in 1937, and for over 60 years the BBC has broadcast the tournament with the added benefit of colour television since August 1967. Since 1992 Radio Wimbledon has broadcast from 8 am until 10 pm daily, throughout the championships. In America the US network NBC have made Breakfast at Wimbledon specials at weekends, and live coverage starts early in the morning.

Seeding

Seeding was introduced into tennis at Wimbledon in 1927. The definition of seeding is the system used to separate the top players in a draw so that they will not meet in the early rounds of a tournament. The top seed is the player the tournament committee deems the strongest player in the field. He or she and the second seed are placed at opposite ends of the draw so that if they both keep winning, they will meet in the final round.

The number of seeds is based on the size of the draw. Basically, the thinking behind seeding was to spread evenly through the draw those players whose past records on grass, taken with their current form, suggested they would proceed furthest. Seeding was viewed not as a reward for points scored but as a method of being fair to all the players and spectators [4].

These measures became easier to establish with the introduction of computer seeding in 1973. The 2001 event marked the first time in Wimbledon's 124-year history in which 32 players in the men's and women's draw were seeded, instead of the usual 16. This was accompanied by the introduction of a points system for the men, approved by their professional body the Association of Tennis Professionals (ATP), which acknowledged a player's past performance on grass.

67. Andy Murray receives the Challenge Cup from
HRH The Duke of Kent after the Gentlemen's Final, Centre Court, Wimbledon 2013.

Trophies

The Gentlemen's Grand Slam Singles champion receives an inscribed, silver gilt cup, which has been awarded since 1887. The Grand Slam Ladies' Singles champion receives a sterling silver salver, commonly known as the Venus Rosewater Dish, which is decorated with mythological figures. The winners of the Gentlemen's Doubles, Ladies' Doubles, and Mixed Doubles, each receive a silver cup. The runner-up in each event receives an inscribed silver plate.

The Davis Cup

The Davis Cup is the premier international team event in men's tennis. It is run by the International Tennis Federation (ITF) and is contested annually between teams from competing countries in a knockout format. The competition began in 1900, as a challenge between Britain and the United States. By 2013, 130 nations had entered teams into the competition. The most successful countries over the history of the tournament are the United States, winning 32 tournaments and finishing as runners-up 29 times; Australia, won 28 times, including four occasions with New Zealand as Australasia, and finishing as runners-up 19 times. Great Britain, and France have won the cup seven times; Spain has won five times, and Germany and the Czech Republic have won three times, and Russia has won twice. Italy, Serbia, Switzerland, South Africa, and Croatia have each won the cup once.

Prize money

In 1968 prize money was awarded for the first time at Wimbledon, when professional

229

players were allowed to compete in the championships. Before 2007, among grand slam tournaments, Wimbledon and the French Open awarded more prize money in men's events than in women's events. In 2007 the policy was changed, allocating the same amounts of money for both events. Prize money to the winners in 2008, reached an amazing £11,812,000 (US$23,500,000). The Gentlemen's Singles and Ladies' Singles Winners received £750,000, (US$1,470,000); the Gentlemen's Doubles and Ladies' Doubles, received £229,000 (US$448,000); and the Mixed Doubles Winners, received £90,000, (US$176,000), approximately. By 2009 the total had increased to £12,500,000 in prize money awarded, with the singles champions receiving £850,000 each, an increase of 13.3 per cent from the previous year. For the 2010 championships, the total prize money increased to £13,725,000, and the singles champions received £1,000,000 each. For the 2011 Wimbledon Championships it was announced that the total prize money would be £14,600,000, an increase of 6.4 per cent from 2010. Both male and female singles champions' prize money also increased to £1,100,000, a rise of 10 per cent since the previous year. For 2012, the total prize money was £16,060,000, a further increase of 10 per cent from 2011. The bulk of the increases were given to players losing in earlier rounds. In 2013 the prize money reached £22,560,000, the Gentlemen's and Ladies' Singles Champions each receiving £1,600,000. [Figures in US dollars are approximate due to fluctuations in currency].

Part 2 (ii)

Looking back

There was a new optimism amongst the British people at the end of the First World War in 1918. The situation of women was undergoing gradual improvement, with the introduction of the Franchise Act that allowed women over the age of 35, along with all adult males, the right to vote. There was a more prominent role for women in lawn tennis and less cumbersome clothing was acceptable. **Mrs Dorothea Lambert Chambers** was considered to be the first lady of British tennis, having won the Challenge Round seven times. At age 40, in 1919, Mrs Lambert Chambers played **Miss Suzanne Lenglen** who was younger by twenty years. Miss Lenglen won, though it was a close contest, and it was remarked that whilst she wore a loose dress coming to just below the knee, Mrs Lambert Chambers was trussed up in stays, and wearing the old style clothing of a tight-fitting, longer, and therefore more cumbersome, dress.

Move from Worpole Road to Church Road
Worple Road was now inadequate due to the increase in audiences and new ground was found at Church Road. The new Centre Court was designed by Captain Stanley Peach and was formally opened by King George V on June 26, 1922, in time for that year's championships.
Wimbledon Highlights of the 1920s and 30s
   In that year 1922, **James O. Anderson (Jo)**, won the Gentlemen's Doubles,

68. Andy Murray receives the Challenge Cup from HRH The Duke of Kent after the Gentlemen's Final, Centre Court, Wimbledon 2013.

partnered by **Randolph Lycett**. The UK's **Leslie Godfree** from Brighton won his first championship, the Gentlemen's Doubles in 1923, partnered also by Randolph Lycett. **Godfree** and his wife **Kitty** became the first married couple to win the Mixed Doubles in 1926.

Between 1919 and 1930, six men and three women shared the 12 singles titles. The first winner after the war was Australia's **Gerald Patterson**, who played **Norman Brooks**, the latter defending a five-year-old title. Patterson's 'heavy serving and powerful backcourt hitting' [5] was considered to have produced his success. Patterson won the Gentlemen's Singles in 1919, and again in 1922. The American **Bill Tilden** created the most impact of all the men at that time. Tilden was the first American to win the Gentlemen's Singles title in 1920. Known as 'Big Bill' and something of a character, Tilden was instantly recognisable sporting a 'grizzly bear' sweater.

The year 1924 saw victories for the French. They were champions at Wimbledon for six years in succession: **Jean Borotra** in 1924 and 1926; **René Lacoste** in 1925 and 1928; **Henri Cochet** in 1927 and 1929. They also won the Davis Cup for France, six years in a row, between 1927-32.

50th anniversary of Wimbledon

1926 marked the 50th anniversary of Wimbledon and was also the Royal Jubilee year. The Wimbledon Championships were celebrated as the Jubilee meeting. To mark the occasion, King George V and Queen Mary presented commemorative gold medals to 34 of the surviving champions on the Centre Court. Present were 71-year-old **Frank Hadow** the second champion in 1878, and **Maud Watson**, aged 63, who had been the first ladies' champion in 1884. To mark the occasion the

British champion **Kitty Godfree** and the Dutch champion **Kia Bouman** played an exhibition set against France's **Suzanne Lenglen** and the great American doubles player **Elizabeth Ryan** who, together, had won their sixth Wimbledon title in 1925.

The **Duke of York**, (later King George VI), broke with royal tradition and competed in the Gentlemen's doubles with his equerry, Wing Commander Major Sir **Louis Greig**, and was the only royal ever to compete at Wimbledon.

Athletic Englishwoman **Kitty McKane** and statuesque American beauty, the 18-year-old, **Helen Willis Moody**, had met in the final in 1924. Against all the odds, Kitty won, under the steady gaze of Queen Mary, seated in the royal box. Moody would go on to win again in 1927, 1928, and 1929.

The successes of **Suzanne Lenglen, Kitty Godree, Helen Willis, Bill Tilden,** and the three Frenchmen, meant that the Centre Court at Wimbledon was transformed into the world's most famous sporting arena. From 1927 BBC radio was broadcasting Wimbledon around the world.

In 1928 greater voting equality for women had been won. The first General Election to take place following that success was in May 1929. Women between the ages of 21 and 35 were now able to vote. The country was however, deep in an economic depression of unemployment, and hunger marches took place. 2.5 million people were unemployed, later rising to almost 3 million. That year also, 107 Nazis were elected to the Reichstag in Germany.

Prince George 1st Duke of Kent becomes President

In the midst of all these changes, in 1929, Prince George, later the 1st Duke of Kent, became President of AELTC, which involved giving out the prizes each year at Wimbledon. For Wimbledon spectators, transport had been increased by train and bus, making it much easier to attend the games. By 1932, it was reported that more than 219,000 spectators had attended.

In 1933, the King of Spain accompanied King George V and Queen Mary to the Wimbledon Championships.

UK's Fred Perry

In 1934 such was the popularity of the UK's **Fred Perry,** from Stockport in Cheshire that crowds queued all night to see him in the Gentlemen's Singles final. Perry was the World No.1 and had been the inspiration behind Britain's capture of the Davis Cup in 1933, and he won Wimbledon three times between 1934 and 1936. They were the first consecutive successes of the post Challenge Round era, and such wins would not be repeated for 42 years, until Sweden's **Bjorn Borg** came upon the scene.

UK's Dorothy Round

The UK's **Dorothy Round** (from 1937, **Mrs Little**), from Dudley in Worcestershire, was the Wimbledon Ladies' Champion in 1934. Dorothy was ranked in the world top ten from 1933-1937, reaching a career high of No.1 in 1934. [6]

The German, **Baron Gottfried von Cramm,** was considered the greatest pre-war player not to have won the championships. He was twice beaten by the UK's

Fred Perry in 1935 and 1936. But the courageous **Von Cramm** criticised Adolph Hitler and refused to join the Nazi party and was jailed for a year.

Britain's Fred Perry – and the birth of the Grand Slam

American **Donald "Don" Budge,** who was the champion in 1938, was the first of only four men to have won the singles without the loss of a set. Referring to Budge's competing in the forthcoming US Championships that year, *New York Times* columnist, **John Kieran,** wrote of the competition between **Budge** and **Fred Perry** in terms of its being 'something like a grand slam on the courts'. Kieran's throwaway remark gave rise to the concept of the 'Grand Slam', although he had first alluded to the term in relation to Australian **Jack Crawford's** 1933 US final against **Perry. Crawford** had won the Australian, French, and Wimbledon titles that year. **Perry** won the US Open Championship in five sets against **Budge**, meaning he obtained permanent possession of the Championship Cup. In 1938, however, **Budge**, did go on to achieve the first Grand Slam when he beat **Gene Mako** in the US final. [7]

Women's tennis was at that time dominated by **Helen Wills Moody**, who won the Grand Slam Singles in 1930, 1932, 1933, 1935, and 1938, bringing her tally to eight. Her success has been attributed to her game having been 'built on iron concentration, wonderful control of pace, and length on her ground strokes, and the fearless confidence that all great champions possess.' [8]

Dorothy Round who was a Sunday School teacher was a rival of **Moody** and won the Ladies' Singles title at Wimbledon in 1934 and 1937, by which time, long dresses worn by women tennis players on the court had been replaced by smart

69. *Serena Williams (USA) receives the Rosewater Dish from HRH The Duke of Kent after the Ladies' Final, Centre Court, Wimbledon 2013.*

tennis shorts.

Following on from **Fred Perry's** successes, Britain's morale in tennis was raised even higher.

Dark war clouds and the onset of yet another world war were, however, again on the horizon when American **Alice Marble** became the latest female tennis star to dominate Wimbledon. In 1939 she was the triple champion, changing the face of women's tennis 'by adopting the serve and volley technique.' [9] Serve and volley is a style of play in tennis where the player who is serving moves quickly towards the net after hitting a serve. The server then attempts to hit a volley (a shot where the ball is struck without allowing it to bounce), as opposed to the baseline style, where the server stays back following the serve and attempts to hit a groundstroke (a shot where the ball is allowed to bounce on the ground before contact is made).

Second World War 1939-45

Britain declared war on Germany on September 3, 1939. By May 1940 Winston Churchill had taken over as Prime Minister of a wartime coalition government. On October 11 that year, a German bomb fell on Wimbeldon's Centre Court, flattening one corner. At that time most of the staff was involved in the war effort. Nora Cleather became acting Secretary. One of the car parks was turned into a vegetable patch and another housed livestock. The main concourse was used as a parade ground for soldiers. Some of the buildings were occupied by various branches of the services like the Red Cross and St. John's Ambulance. However, the faithful Mr Edwin Fuller who was employed as grounds-man, and who had worked at Worple Road in 1916 during the First World War, when he was aged just 13 years, continued to take care of the ground during the war.

Wimbledon's President, Prince George, went into uniform as a Captain in the Royal Air Force. As has been mentioned earlier, whilst on active service, Prince George was killed in August 1942.

Princess Marina becomes President

Prince George's widow, Princess Marina, already serving as Commandant of the Women's Royal Naval Service (WRNS), took over her husband's role and, in 1943, became President of AELTC. Princess Marina would thereafter present the trophies to the winners at Wimbledon.

Post-Second World War period

From June 1945, matches between Inter-Dominions Services took place that included Britain, New Zealand, South Africa and Canada. Queen Mary attended the June match. Another took place in July, between the servicemen of Great Britain and Other Allies, attracting over 5,000 spectators. The Regent of Iraq, the Ambassadors of Belgium and France, and Winston Churchill's wife Clementine attended.

UK's Dan Maskell

The most popular tennis figure to emerge at this time was former **Squadron Leader Dan Maskell**, the All England Club's resident professional. **Dan** was British

70. Serena Williams receives the Rosewater Dish from HRH The Duke of Kent after the La-dies' Final, Centre Court, Wimbledon 2012.

professional tennis champion 16 times, and was coach of the winning British Davis Cup team of 1933. He had been engaged in war work helping to rehabilitate wounded airmen. Others who took part included: **Flight Lieutenant Donald McPhail**, who had been the Scottish No.1 before the war, **Flight Lieutenant CM "Jimmy" Jones**, and **Squadron Leader John Olliff**. **Staff Sergeant Charles Hare** the British pre-war Davis Cup player, now serving in the US Army, competed in the US team. **Dan Maskell** was awarded an OBE for his work. When the war ended he was barred from competing at Wimbledon because he was a professional player. He got a job at the BBC and from 1951 until 1991, as a tennis commentator, he became known as the 'voice of Wimbledon'.

At Wimbledon the bomb damage in the Centre Court caused a loss of 1,200 seats. With victory in war however, there was the traditional British stiff upper lip and 'carry on as usual' attitude, despite the tremendous bomb damage to London, and the British economy almost bankrupt. However, if Britain could win the war she could win the peace too! The attitude was the same where Wimbledon tennis was concerned.

US tennis tournaments
US tennis tournaments had continued throughout the war, whilst the British players had been unable to play or practise, many being on active war service. The new Wimbledon Committee organised a Championship with 23 nations represented. The Americans dominated the tennis scene in the post-war years for a decade, with seven US men winning once each, and five US women winning all 10 singles titles into

235

the mid-1950s.

New names and stars of Wimbledon tennis appeared. In 1946, Czech, **Jaroslav Drobny** defeated the US's **Jack Kramer** in the round of sixteen, but lost in the semi-finals. The tournament was won by France's **Yvon Petra**. **Petra's** powerful serves once broke a net and his 'thunderous serves' and 'audacious volleys' [10] guaranteed his success against the top seed **Dinny Pails**. Petra was the last French-man to win the Wimbledon Championships Gentlemen's singles title in 1946, beat-ing Australia's **Geoff Brown** in five sets in the final.

Death of King George VI

On February 6, 1952, King George VI died and the new Queen Elizabeth II and her husband, Philip Mountbatten, cut short their Commonwealth tour and returned immediately to England. The nation prepared for the monarch's state funeral. Soon, however, preparations were underway for the coronation. Nations around the world rejoiced when the serenely beautiful 27-year-old Elizabeth was crowned at Westminster Abbey on June 2, 1953. Many had rushed out to buy television sets as the ceremony was broadcast from the moment Queen Elizabeth left Buckingham Palace. Her mother, now known as the Queen Mother, and Prince Charles the heir apparent, aged only four-and-a-half years, watched from the gallery.

American successes continued

American successes continued at Wimbledon with **Ricardo Gonzales,** also known as **Richard** but usually called **"Pancho Gonzales,"** winning in 1950, 1951, 1952, and 1956. He was the world No.1 professional tennis player for eight years in the 1950s and early 1960s. He won two Major titles and 15 Pro Slam titles. What was unusual about this star of the tennis court was that he was largely self-taught. He had learnt by watching other tennis players on the public courts at nearby Exposition Park in Los Angeles. **Gonzales** was revered in the world of sport and a 1999 *Sports Illustrated* article about the magazine's twenty favorite athletes of the 20th century listed **Gonzales**, saying: 'If earth was on the line in a tennis match, the man you want serving to save humankind would be **Ricardo Alonso Gonzales**.' In 1969, aged 41 years, **Gonzales** had a disagreement with the umpire over the lighting at Wimbledon. Despite that upset the following day, he saved seven match points in taking the last three sets to win Wimledon's longest match after 112 games and five hours 12 minutes of play.

Australian successes

Australia's outstanding tennis player **Frank Sedgman** had won the Gentlemen's Singles in 1952, against **Jaroslav Drobny**. **Sedgman** had been trained by **Harry Hopman** who was Australia's world-acclaimed tennis player and coach. **Hopman** was the successful captain coach of 22 Australian Davis Cup teams from 1939 to 1967, winning the cup an unmatched 16 times. **John Barrett**, tennis player, commentator and author, wrote of **Sedgman's** style of playing which was influenced by **Hopman** who set a new standard and style in tennis, that it was: 'a breathtaking performance'. He said that **Sedgman's** 'ability to volley from any part of the court and his electrifying court coverage added a new dimension to the game which revealed the effect that **Harry Hopman** would have on tennis's development over the next 15 years.' [11] **Hopman's** techniques had been already in operation in the 1950s on other up-and-coming tennis stars: Argentina's **Guillermo Vilas**, Sweden's **Lennart Bergelin**, and one of the biggest names of all, Germany's **Boris Becker**.

The left-handed, **Jaroslav Drobny**, who had by now taken out Egyptian citizenship, would return, aged 33, as the only Egyptian to win the Wimbledon Championship in 1954, against Australia's **Ken Rosewall**, aged 19 years.

The US provided a successful end to the 1950s decade at Wimbledon with two American wins by the Davis Cup team-mates **Vic Seixas** in 1953, and **Tony Trabert** in 1955. **Seixas** was also a great doubles and mixed doubles player, in which his major victories include four consecutive mixed doubles crowns at Wimbledon 1953–56, the first three with the US's **Doris Hart**, and the fourth with **Shirley Fry**, also from the US.

During the post Second World War period, no fewer than eight American ladies dominated world tennis. **Maureen Connolly** and **Louise Brough** had the greatest of the successes at Wimbledon. Connolly was 'utterly ruthless as a match player, with powers of concentration and determination that intimidated her opponents.' [12] She won three consecutive victories 1952-54. **Brough** won four titles between 1948-55.

Australians keep winning
Australia's male tennis players dominated Wimbledon into the 1960s, five of them winning eight Wimbledon singles. The handsome **Lew Hoad** won the title twice in

71. Katie O'Brien (Great Britain), Kimiko Date-Krumm (Japan), AELTC Chairman Phillip Brook and HRH The Duke of Kent, at the opening of Court 3, Wimbledon Championships, 2011.

1956-57. **Ashley Cooper** won in 1958, the year he became one of only ten men to win three of the four Grand Slam events in the same year with his victory at the US Championships. **Roy Emerson** who could run 100 yards in 10.6 seconds when still only a boy aged 14, won the singles and doubles of all four Grand Slam titles. He won the Gentlemen's Singles at Wimbledon in 1964 and 1965, and the Doubles in 1959, 1961, and 1971.

The US's **Dennis Ralston** having failed to win Wimbledon in earlier years, bounced back in 1960, to win the Gentlemen's Doubles with 17-year-old **Rafael Osuna** of Mexico. Tragically, **Osuna's** career was cut short when he died in an air crash in 1969.

Australian **Rod Laver** was considered by some as 'possibly the greatest singles player of all time.' [13] He won four consecutive Wimbledons, having been twice Grand Slam winner in 1962 and 1969, and he won 28 consecutive matches at Church Road.

Australia's roller coaster of wins at Wimbledon was interrupted, temporarily, in 1963 when America's **Chuck McKinley** won the Gentlemen's singles. McKinley was one of only four men to have won the Championship without losing a set. The others were **Don Budge** (1938), **Tony Trabert** (1955), and **Bjorn Borg** (1976).

Australians **Fred Stolle** and **Bob Hewitt** won the Wimbledon Doubles together in 1962 and 1964. **John Newcombe** and **Tony Roche**, another of the great Australian pairs won the title five times between 1965 and 1974.

Women winners

America's **Althea Gibson** was the first black player to win a Wimbledon title in 1957, and she won again in 1958. She had also won the Doubles in 1956, 57, and 58. Turning professional, she toured with the Harlem Globetrotters. Another US woman victor was **Shirley Fry** who, having remained for some time in the shadow of the other great American players, in 1956 enjoyed a victory at Wimbledon.

Brazilian **Maria Bueno** won the Wimbledon Ladies' title in 1959, 1960, and 1964. Bueno was looked upon as 'the elegant queen of Brazilian tennis', whose 'every movement combined the grace of a ballet dancer with the controlled power of a top gymnast.' [14] At home in Sao Paulo, where she was something of a heroine, a statue was erected in her honour.

One of Britain's female hopefuls was Londoner, **Christine Truman**, who made her Wimbledon debut in 1957, aged 16, and reached the semifinals only to lose to **Althea Gibson**. **Truman** made a comeback in 1958, when she defeated **Gibson** in the Wimbledon champion for the Wightman Cup, returning this annual competition between the women of Britain and the United States to Britain, after some 21 consecutive defeats by the US. A few weeks later at Wimbledon, however, as the second seed, **Truman** was defeated in the fourth round by the American, **Mimi Arnold**. **Christine Truman** has remained a big name in British and world tennis, but she never won Wimbledon, although she was the French champion in 1959.

72. Petra Kvitova (Czech Republic) receives the Rosewater Dish from HRH The Duke of Kent after the Ladies' Final, Centre Court, Wimbledon, 2011.

Wimbledon in the 1960s

There was a new mood amongst the young in the 1960s of wanting liberation and to make their own decisions. Male youths grew their hair longer like the Beatles pop group. There were open-air pop concerts and the hippies wore psychedelic clothes and flowers in their hair. Fashion designer, Mary Quant, became the big name for girls' fashions, ushering in mini-skirts, more elaborate face make-up, and bouffant and straight hair styles. Mary Ramsay the wife of Major General Charles Ramsay remembers being caught out, when one day she was ironing her friend's curly hair on an ironing board to straighten it and suddenly the kitchen door opened and Prince Edward walked in on them. He was not in the least put out, and Mary and Charles always felt at ease in his company. [15]

First all-British women's final

The year 1961 saw the first all-British women's final at Wimbledon since **Mrs Dorothea Lambert Chambers** had won the last of seven titles in 1914 at Worple Road. Wimbledon was packed for a match in which only a British woman could take the title. The competition was between **Christine Truman** and **Angela Mortimer** from Plymouth. In true British style the rain came on causing a break at the end of the first set. In the second set, **Christine** suffered a fall and **Angela** would emerge victorious.

In 1962 the title was claimed by No.8 seed, **Mrs Karen Susman** from the US, who the previous year as **Miss Hantze**, had won the doubles with **Billie Jean King** nee **Moffitt**.

For the ladies, the 1960s decade under the old system of Wimbledon being for

73. *Kveta Peschke (Czech Republic), centre, and Katarina Srebotnik (Slovenia) are awarded their championship trophies by HRH The Duke of Kent in the Royal Box after winning their final round Ladies' doubles match against Sabine Lisicki (Germany) and Samantha Stosur (Australia), Wimbledon Championships, 2011.*

amateurs only, came to a close with wins by **Margaret Smith** (later 1967 **Mrs Court**), who was born in Albury, New South Wales, and who in retirement would become a Christian Minister in Perth. In 1963, **Smith** had beaten **Billie Jean King**, and in 1965, she beat Brazil's **Maria Bueno**. A strongly built, athletic woman, **Smith** was said to play the game 'like a man' and 'had a better serve than several of the lesser men.' [16] She kept herself very fit and could play for hours without tiring. **Smith** won 10 titles at Wimbledon and her total Grand Slam titles numbered 62.

Controversy over the surface at Wimbledon

The tennis court surface of grass at Wimbledon has been the focus of controversy over the years. Players who were used to a hard, concrete, surface, found it difficult to play the game whilst moving around at speed on what was often a slippery, wet surface due to the British weather.

Barkers Sports Ground, which sat alongside the All England Club, was purchased in 1966 for £150,000, no doubt with an eye to the future when the game would be expanded to include professional players and there were ever increasing audiences. That year, Spain's **Manuel Santana** beat the US No.1 **Dennis Ralston** in the Gentlemen's Singles. **Santana** who was ranked World No.1 didn't like playing on soft surfaces and he made the amusing comment: 'Grass is just for cows', and there were then, and still are, plenty that agree with him. **Santana's** words have practically become legend, having been quoted over the years, by players, commentators, and the public alike.

The big name from the US that came to the fore was that of **Billie Jean King**. King won her first singles title in 1966, when she beat **Maria Bueno**. The coveted trophy was presented to her on the court by Princess Marina.

The Wimbledon World Lawn Tennis Professional Championships were played in 1967, in co-operation with BBC Television, who broadcast them in colour. **Rod Laver** won the tournament against fellow Australian **Ken Rosewall**.

Tennis goes 'open' to amateurs and professionals, 1968

The decision to open tennis to professionals as well as amateurs was taken in March 1968, at a Special General Meeting of the International Lawn Tennis Federation (ILTF) that was held in Paris. Before that the only event for professionals held at Wimbledon had been the 1930 event that was open for teaching professionals. **Dan Maskell**, the resident professional, beat the Melbury Club professional, **Tom Jeffery**, in the final on No.2 Court. The Doubles, which had been played on the hard courts, was won by **Jeffery** and **Bill Dear,** who defeated Queen's Club teachers **Joe Pearce** and **Fred Pulson**.

Britain's **Ann Haydon-Jones** from Birmingham, at age 30, beat 27-year-old **Bille Jean King** in 1969, winning the Ladies' singles title.

Robinson's Barley Water has become a traditional beverage at Wimbledon, having been first made for Wimbledon tennis players in 1934. Today, 80 dozen

74. Laura Robson (Great Britain), the umpire, HRH The Duke of Kent and Daniela Hantuchova (Slovakia) before the opening match on the new Court 2 at Wimbledon, 2009.

bottles are delivered each year to the tennis courts and the squash is always on display.

When, in 1969, Britain's **Ann Jones** sported a bottle of Pepsi there were some raised eyebrows. Where the public are concerned, however, it is probably just a matter of taste!

During 1966 and 1975, a variety of gentlemen won at Wimbledon. One casualty however was reigning champion Australian **Roy Emerson** of whom great things were expected. In the 1966 quarter-final against fellow Australian **Owen Davidson**, **Emerson** came to grief when he crashed into the umpire's chair and was injured. However, **Emerson** would become the most successful player of that era. His two Wimbledon titles in 1964 and 1965 sit proudly alongside the ten other Grand Slam singles crowns he collected, two each in France and America, and six in his native Australia. At that stage he was only the third man behind **Perry** and **Budge** to have won all four Grand Slam singles titles.

Wimbledon – 1970s/80s

Partnering **Billie Jean King**, **Owen Davidson** went on to win the Wimbledon Grand Slam Mixed Doubles in 1967, 1971, 1973, and 1974. He won in total eight Grand Slam mixed doubles titles.

Mrs Margaret Smith Court won the Grand Slam in 1970, and was only the second woman after **Maureen Connolly** (1953) to achieve that feat. Her win against **Billie Jean King** in that year's Wimbledon final was considered to be the greatest Ladies' Singles final since the war. **Court** won her last Wimbledon title in 1975, whilst having become the mother of baby son.

Part 2 (iii)

Prince Edward becomes President of AELTC

Prince Edward became President of The All England Lawn Tennis and Croquet Club (AELTC) on January 1, 1969. His role would be to carry on in the tradition of his father and mother before him and present the tennis trophies to the winners and runners up at Wimbledon each year. In this he was joined by his beautiful wife, Katherine the Duchess of Kent. They became the golden couple of Wimbledon, seated in the royal box engrossed in the games of tennis, and then presenting the prizes jointly.

On some occasions since, Prince Edward has been accompanied in the prize giving by his sister, Princess Alexandra. At the time of Prince Edward's taking over as President, lawn tennis was making good progress, so the Duke and Duchess had a fine legacy to look back on and a promising future ahead. They would experience the development of the game which would unfold before their eyes for many years to come, not least opening the game up to professionals.

75. *Andre Agassi (who teamed with Steffi Graf) receives his trophy in the Royal Box from HRH The Duke of Kent and the Chairman Tim Philips after the mixed doubles match against Tim Henman and Kim Clijsters as part of the Centre Court Roof Opening Celebration at Wimbledon 2009.*

Wimbledon highlights of the 1960s and 1970s

Australia's **Rod Laver**, having won the Wimbledon Grand Slam Gentlemen's Singles in 1961, 62, and 68, won again in 1969. Australia's **John Newcombe**, partnered that year and on other years by fellow Australian **Tony Roch**, won the Grand Slam Gentlemen's Doubles.

In 1969 the UK's **Ann Haydon Jones** achieved victory over the US champion **Billie Jean King** in the Grand Slam Ladies' Singles final. A youthful, 18-year-old Princess Anne presented her with the winner's trophy. A photograph taken at the time shows a handsome Prince Edward standing nearby applauding. Australia's **Margaret Smith Court** who, having been partnered by **Judy Tegart Dalton**, won the 1969 Grand Slam Ladies' Doubles. Australian **Fred Stolle** and the UK's **Ann Haydon Jones** from Birmingham, won the 1969 Grand Slam Mixed Doubles.

Australia's tennis stars

Australia's **Margaret Smith** (known as **Margaret Smith Court** after she married Barry Court in 1967) was one of Wimbledon's finest tennis players, having won the Grand Slam Ladies' Singles in 1963, 1965, and 1970, and the Grand Slam doubles in 1964 and 1969, and the Grand Slam mixed doubles in 1963, 1965, 1966, 1968, and 1975. In 1970, **Court** became the first woman during the open era and only the second woman in history to win the singles Grand Slam in all four majors in the same calendar year. **Court** won a record 24 of those titles during her career. She also won 19 women's doubles and 19 mixed doubles titles, giving her a record of 62 Major titles overall. **Court** was the only woman to win the mixed doubles Grand Slam, and she won it twice.

John Newcombe was one of Australia's finest tennis players, having won the Gentlemen's Singles in 1967, 1970, and 1971. Partnered sometimes by **Ken Fletcher** and sometimes by **Tony Roche**, also two of Australia's finest, he won the Gentlemen's Doubles in 1965, 1966, 1968, 1969, 1970 and 1974. **Fletcher** won the Grand Slam Mixed Doubles in 1963, 1966, and 1968. Altogether he won 27 tennis titles. **Fletcher** had won the Grand Slam Mixed Doubles with **Margaret Smith** in 1963, and again in 1968. **Newcombe** and **Tony Roche** were considered by some to be 'the finest ever to appear at Wimbledon'. [17]

Australia's **Bob Hewitt** and South Africa's **Frew McMillan** were champions three times between 1967 and 1978, winning the Grand Slam Doubles.

In 1972, American Corporal **Stan Smith** competed with Roumanian Colonel **Illie Nastase**. **Smith** won and it was considered to be the best final since the end of the Second World War.

Coach **Vic Edwards** predicted in 1970 that his protégée, Australia's **Evonne Goolaong** would win Wimbledon within five years. **Goolagong** sprung a surprise on everyone by winning the Grand Slam Ladies' Singles the following year, beating **Margaret Court**. By 1972, America's **Billie Jean King** was back and beat **Goolagong**. In 1974 20-year-old American **Chris Evert** took the title in the Grand Slam Ladies' Singles over **Olga Morozova** the only Russian girl to appear in the singles finals thus far. **Evert** won the Singles again in 1976 and 1981, and the doubles in 1976. In 1979, **Evert** married the British tennis player **John Lloyd** and changed her name to **Chris Evert-Lloyd**.

The UK's **Roger Taylor** never won Wimbledon but in 1970, he played Australia's great **Rod Laver** a tough game in four sets on the Centre Court in the fourth round of the singles. **Taylor** then went on to beat America's 'Superman' **Clark Graebner**, but Taylor was himself beaten by Australia's **Ken Rosewall** in the semi-finals. **Taylor** was in the semi-finals of the Grand Slam singles in 1967, 1970, and 1973, and was a qualifier in the Doubles in 1968, 1969, and 1973.

In 1971, the tiebreak was introduced at eight games all in every set except the third for women and the fifth for men. The system prevailed until 1979, when it came into operation at six games all.

Swedish star Bjorn Borg

What has been described as 'Borgmania' came to Wimbledon in the 1970s. **Bjorn Borg** had won the junior title in 1972, aged only 16 years. He was cool, calm, and gentlemanly, and a powerful player. His youthful good looks meant he was besieged by 'teenybopper' girls wherever he went. **Borg** won five consecutive Wimbledon Grand Slam Singles in 1976, 1977, 1978, 1979, and 1980. Between 1974 and 1981, he won 11 Grand Slam singles titles. He is considered to be one of

76. Roger Federer (Switzerland) receives the runner-up trophy after being defeated by Novak Djokovic (Republic of Serbia) in the Gentlemen's Singles Final on Centre Court on Day 13 of the Wimbledon Championships 2014.

the greatest tennis players of all time. **Borg** was the first 'rock star' of professional tennis and the first player to earn more than US$1 million dollars in prize money in a single season in 1979.

Complimenting Borg's popularity and success was the Swedish pop group **ABBA** who won the Eurovision Song Contest in 1974. Up to 1982, **Abba** were the darlings of the British and European pop scene, topping the charts with such songs as Waterloo and *Dancing Queen*. There is a timelessness about their music, especially for the nightclub scene and, during these years **Borg** and **Abba** brought something new, bright, crisp, and fun from Sweden to the UK.

In 1973, Roumanian **Illie Nastase** lost in the singles to the US's champion **Alex 'Sandy' Mayer**. **Mayer** was however beaten by the USSR's **Alex Metreveli**. That year also, Czech **Jan Kodes** survived a gruelling semi-final against **Roger Taylor** to win the Grand Slam singles.

Two Americans dominated the meetings of 1974 and 1975. Left-hander, **Jimmy Connors**, aged 21, 'thrilled onlookers with the sheer exuberance and ferocity of his all-out attacking style.' [18] **Ken Rosewall**, now aged 39, just could not keep up with him and **Connors** won the Grand Slam singles in 1974, and again in 1982. American **Arthur Ashe** won the Grand Slam singles in 1975, beating Connors. Ashe was considered to be the first great male black player, and he was 32 years old when he won Wimbledon.

Billie Jean King totally dominated women's tennis at Wimbledon between 1966 and 1975. She won six of the ten championships during those years, despite having had to undergo several operations to her knees. Between 1961 and 1979, she also won ten ladies' doubles titles. She was described as 'the most dynamic and prolific winner ever to play' [19] at Wimbledon.

There was a dramatic increase in the development of tennis between 1976 and 1985. It took on a kind of show business dimension and tennis stars became multi-millionaires from their various earnings, both from tennis prize money, and income from advertising, and television appearances.

1977 marked the centenary of the Wimbledon Championships and it was celebrated with a lunch for the surviving champions. Prince Edward and the Duchess Katherine attended.

Land mark political changes took place in the UK and Europe during these years. Conservative Prime Minister Edward Heath had taken Britain into the Common Market on January 1, 1973. In 1979, Mrs Margaret Thatcher became Britain's first woman Prime Minister. Women had become more liberated. Ball boys were traditionally always used at Wimbledon to retrieve the balls, and 1977 saw for the first time ball girls doing the job.

Seating at Wimbledon was increased by an extra 1,088 seats to meet demand in 1981, and again in 1985, to provide a further 900 seats, plus the expansion of other facilities like restaurants. The First Aid Room was always staffed by St. John's Ambulance Brigade. Normally, about 2,000 people are treated for various ailments during the two-weeks of Wimbledon finals. In 1976 it was so hot that on one particular day over 500 people were treated for heatstroke.

Martina Navratilova

The name of Czech-American tennis player **Martina Navratilova** now enters the annals. **Navratilova** was one of the greatest tennis players ever to grace the Wimbledon courts, winning the Grand Slam Singles between 1978 and 1990, the Doubles between 1976 and 1986, and the Mixed Doubles between 1985 and 2003. **Navratilova** was a good friend of **Chris Evert** who partnered her in the Ladies' Doubles in 1976. American **Pam Shriver** then partnered **Navratilova** in the Doubles and she won four Wimbledon tournaments between 1981 and 1984.

Bjorn Borg and his regular practice partner **Vitas Gerulaitis** produced a spectacular final in 1977 to the last ball, with Borg winning 8-6 in the fifth set.

UK's Virginia Wade wins in 1977

That year the UK's **Virgina Wade** beat **Betty Stove** of the Netherlands in the Ladies' Singles. **Wade's** triumph was all the greater knowing that it was watched by Her Majesty Queen Elizabeth II and His Royal Highness Prince Philip. It was the Queen's Silver Jubilee year and it was also Wimbledon's Centenary. Accompanying the Duke and Duchess of Kent in the royal box also, was Her Royal Highness Princess Margaret. **Virginia Wade** was only the third British success since the Second World War. The crowd in the stands sang to her: "For She's a Jolly Good

77. *Novak Djokovic receives the Champion's Trophy after defeating Roger Federer in five sets in the Gentlemen's Singles Final on Centre Court on Day 13 of the Wimbledon Championships 2014.*

Fellow".

During these years Prince Edward and his serene and beautiful wife Katherine presented the prizes together, offering congratulations to the winners and hope to the runners up that their turn would come.

There was a proud moment in 1978 for Czech, **Ivan Lendl**, who won the Wimbledon junior title. Lendl would go on to capture eight Grand Slam Singles titles.

Bjorn Borg meets John McEnroe

America's **John McEnroe**, almost as popular for his tantrums on the court as his playing, was the latest attraction at Wimbledon in the 1980s. Audiences watched a final that lasted just a few minutes short of a gruelling four hours between **McEnroe** and **Bjorn Borg** in 1980, and which **Borg** won by 8-6 in the fifth set that 'produced some of the greatest shot-making ever seen on the Centre Court' [20] by both tennis players. **McEnroe's** day would come however, he was a great character who was an entertainment to watch and was held in high esteem the world over. He won the singles in 1981, 1983 and 1984 and today he is something of a legend.

Australia's **Peter McNamara** and **Paul McNamee** were the champions of the men's doubles in 1980 and 1982. America's brother and sister, **John** and **Tracy Austin** won the mixed doubles in 1980.

Britain's **John Lloyd** from Leigh-on-Sea, Essex, partnered **Wendy Turnbull** of

Australia in 1983, in the Grand Slam Mixed Doubles, and having won, he retained the title in 1984. It was the first such British male win at Wimbledon since Fred Perry in 1936.

Centenary of women's tennis

1984 was the centenary of women's tennis at Wimbledon. Those who attended included 17 of the 20 surviving lady champions who received a specially-commissioned Waterford Crystal vase presented by Katherine The Duchess of Kent. A great cheer went up for **Kitty Godfree** the champion of 1924 and 1926, who at age 88 years, still played tennis.

By 1985 America's **Kathy Rinaldi** had become the 11th ranked player in the world. In 1981, at aged 14 years, she had been the youngest player to win a round at the Wimbledon Championships. She was given the Wimbledon Tennis Award as the most Impressive Newcomer.

Germany's Boris Becker

German, **Boris Becker**, aged 17, became the star of Wimbledon in 1985, when he beat **Kevin Curren**, who was formerly from South Africa, in the Grand Slam Singles. No male so young had ever won the world's oldest title, and no German had ever achieved such a feat. This kind of fame and athletic celebrity status softened the edges in the aftermath of the 1939-45 Second World War wounds. The younger generations of Germans did not remember Hitler and the Nazis and had nothing in common with them. **Becker** was still only 20 years old when he won the men's singles in 1986, defeating **Ivan Lendl**. Such was **Becker's** popularity that the German President Richard von Weizsäcker attended the match. He was seated in the royal box with the Duke and Duchess of Kent, Princess Michael of Kent, King Constantine and Queen Anne-Marie of the Hellenes, Princess Alexandra, and her husband the Honourable Angus Ogilvy, the British Prime Minister Mrs Margaret Thatcher, and the Chairman of the All England Club, Mr Reginald (Buzzer) Hadingham. The Duchess of Kent presented **Boris** with a cheque for £140,000 less £3,080 which he, as the new Ambassador to the United Nations Children's Fund, had most generously donated to Unicef. **Becker** went on to win again in 1989.

In 1981, two Americans **Ken Flach** and **Kathy Jordan** would defeat **Martina Navratilova** and **Heinz Guenthardt** in the Mixed Doubles. However, **Navratilova**, teamed with **Pam Shriver**, claimed a fifth doubles title.

Australia's **Patrick "Pat" Cash** won the singles title in 1987, defeating **Ivan Lendl**. In his enthusiasm to see his family and share his joy with them, **Cash** clambered up the stands over the heads of the spectators, providing some entertainment for the film cameras and those at home watching the game on television.

Two Americans, **Ken Flach** and **Bob Seguso**, won the doubles in 1987 and 1988. **Jimmy Connors** of earlier fame made a comeback in 1987, against **Michael Pernfors** of Sweden, winning the Gentlemen's Singles. The following year the title was taken by Germany's **Patrick Kuhnen**.

78. Novak Djokovic (SRB) receives the Champion's trophy after defeating Roger Federer (SUI) in five sets in the Gentlemen's Singles Final on Centre Court on Day 13 of the Wimbledon Championships, 2014.

Germany's Steffi Graf

In 1988, the women's scene changed with Germany's **Steffi Graf** winning the Grand Slam Ladies' Singles, and also the Doubles. **Graf**, who had made her debut at Wimbledon in 1984, aged only 15, would go on to win the singles again in 1989, 1991, 1992, 1993, 1995 and 1996. During these years the women's singles at Wimbledon *was* **Steffi Graf**. Over a period of 13 years, between 1987 and 1999, **Graf** would achieve 22 Grand Slam successes, seven of which were at Wimbledon. **'Steffi'**, as she was affectionately known, was a charming girl, and her feminine, winning talents helped soften even further the memories of the war and post-war years.

Czech **Jana Novotná** was another big female name, winning the Ladies Doubles in 1989, 1990, 1995, and 1998, and the mixed doubles in 1989, and the singles again in 1998.

The US's **Sherwood Stewart** from Texas, aged 42, surprised everyone in 1988, by becoming Wimbledon's oldest Mixed Doubles winner, taking the title for the first time, teamed with fellow American **Zina Garrison**. **Garrison** went on to be a three times winner of the mixed doubles. That year also, Argentina's **Gabriela Sabatini** won the Ladies' Doubles.

One of the themes of the 1980s was the competition between Sweden's **Stefan Edberg** and Germany's **Boris Becker**. Edberg was a major proponent of the serve-

and-volley style of tennis. He won six Grand Slam Singles titles and three Grand Slam Gentlemen's Doubles titles between 1985 and 1996. In 1989, Becker took the title back but only for a brief period of time.

In 1995, Spain's **Aránzazu "Arantxa" Sánchez Vicario** won the Grand Slam Ladies' Doubles title partnered by with Czech **Jana Novotná**.

American **Andre Agassi**, who was known for his colourful clothes, won the Grand Slam singles in 1992, against Croatian **Goran Ivanišević** who put up a good performance. Such was the interest in **Agassi** and his fashion accessories that television audiences numbered a record 13.8 million. **Ivanišević** would go on to eventually win the Men's Singles in 2001.

Greg Rusedski of Canada and his Moroccan partner **Karim Aami** won the Boys doubles in 1991. In May 1995, **Rusedski,** having lived in England for some years, elected to play for Britain in the Davis Cup.

In 1991, Germany's **Michael Stitch** won the Gentlemen's Singles, and together with **John McEnroe** he also won the Gentlemen's Doubles.

The 1992 win of the Ladies Doubles by Puerto Ricon **Gigi Fernandez** and Belarusan **Natasha Zvereva** was the start of their success as an outstanding doubles pair. Together they won six Grand Slam titles during the years, 1992, 1993, 1994, and 1997.

Silver salver for Dan Maskell

In 1992, Katharine The Duchess of Kent presented **Dan Maskell** with a silver salver to commemorate his services to tennis, to the RAF and to broadcasting.

Like all sports, tennis has experienced tragedies. America's **Monica Seles'** chances of ever winning Wimbledon were destroyed when she was stabbed in 1992, at which time she was considered the greatest woman player in the world.

Wimbledon towards the 21st century

Wimbledon in the 21st century is acknowledged to be the premier tennis tournament in the world. A Long Term Plan was unveiled in 1993, to improve the quality of the event in the interests of spectators, players, officials, and neighbours. Stage one of the Plan was in place for the 1997 championships, involving building Aorangi Park the new No.1 Court that could accommodate a capacity of 11,000 spectators, plus a Broadcast Centre, two extra grass courts, and a tunnel under the hill for easy access, linking Church Road and Somerset Road.

In 1994 technology had progressed to the extent that it was possible to erect a huge TV screen at Aorangi Park that allowed those spectators who had not managed to get a ticket for the packed Wimbledon stands to enjoy watching the tennis matches on a huge BBC television screen. The park was named after London New Zealand Rugby Club's grounds, they having previously occupied the site.

Stage two of the Plan made way for the new Millennium building, providing facilities for the players, press, officials and members, with the extension of the West Stand of the Centre Court providing 728 extra seats. Stage three, which was begun in 2000, was completed in 2011, with the construction of a new Championship Entrance building, housing for club staff, museum, bank, and ticket office at Gate 3.

79. Chair Umpire Mr James Keothavong receives a medal after officiating the Gentlemen's Singles Final between Novak Djokovic and Roger Federer on Centre Court on Day 13 of the Wimbledon Championships, 2014.

Better facilities were provided for the public, involving an increase in seating capacity from 13,800 to 15,000.

Rod Laver's 25th anniversary
In 1994 there was a very proud moment for Australia who as a country has provided so many superb players for Wimbledon. Prince Edward presented **Rod Laver** with a Waterford Crystal vase to commemorate the 25th anniversary of his second Grand Slam. Laver had actually won 11 Grand Slams.

In 1995 the UK's **Martin Lee** and home-grown Wimbledon boy, **James Trotman** brightened up the UK's hopes when they won the Boys' Doubles being the first British pair to do so.

Switzerland's **Martina Hingis,** aged only 15, had won the Ladies' Doubles in 1996, with **Helena Sukova** to become the youngest player ever to hold a Grand Slam title. **Hingis** won the singles again in 1997, and the doubles 1996 and 1998.

The US's **Pete Sampras** won three consecutive Wimbledon titles between 1993 and 1996. **Sampras** looked pretty invincible winning the Gentlemen's Singles in 1994 and 1995. Between 1993 and 2000, he won the Grand Slam Gentlemen's Singles seven times, in 1993, 1994, 1995, 1997, 1998, 1999 and 2000.

Two great former champions **Boris Becker** and **Andre Agassi** competed in the 1995 Singles semi-final, which **Becker** won. But in the final it was **Sampras** who prevailed to take the title. **Sampras** reigned supreme during 1993-95 in the Gentlemen's Singles. **Becker** however took his defeats cheerfully, saying: 'The Centre Court used to be my back yard, now it belongs to Pete.' [21] The 6 feet 5 inches tall **Richard Krajicek** from Rotterdam eliminated **Sampras** and had victories over **Jacon Stoltenberg** and **MaliVai Washington** in 1996, also making him the first Dutchman to win a Grand Slam Singles crown at Wimbledon.

In the world-tennis scene the leading lights were **Boris Becker** and **Stefan Edberg**, along with their developing rivalry. Becker's 'serve was heavier' but 'Edberg's reflexes on the volley were quicker.' [22] They were contrasting personalities also on the court, '**Becker** was the extrovert, **Edberg** the introvert.' [23] The rivalry had begun some ten years earlier in January 1985, in Birmingham at the Young Masters, an under 21 event staged for the first time. **Edberg** was foot-faulted 21 times but still held his own with **Becker**. **Dan Maskell** commentating for the BBC in the commentary box said: 'I think today we have seen enough to know that within the next three years, **Boris Becker** will win Wimbledon.' [24] He would in fact win in six months' time. **Becker** won Wimbledon in 1989, **Edberg** in 1990. The Wimbledon patrons were assured of an entertaining time whilst the two giants of the tennis world inhabited that place. **Becker's** reign as The Grand Slam Gentlemen's Singles champion was ended abruptly in 1991, when fellow German **Michael Stitch** beat him in 'a dazzling display of power and finesse', whilst **Becker's** 'screams of self-disgust' [25] could be heard by the spectators, reverberating all around the stadium.

Andre Agassi too had his moment when, in 1992, he beat both **John McEnroe** and **Goran Ivanišević**, whose 'most penetrating approaches were fired down the lines' [26] to win the men's singles.

For three years two Australians **Todd Woodbridge** and **Mark Woodforde** won the doubles. **Woodbridge** won in 1993 and 1994, (which year he also won the mixed doubles), and again in 1995, 96, 97, 2000, 02, 03, and 04.

Canada's **Mary Pierce** was a newcomer to Wimbledon in 1995. She won the Grand Slam Ladies' Mixed Doubles in 2005.

PART 3

A NEW MILLENNIUM

During the years between 1996 and 2000, the world and Wimbledon was entering a New Millennium.

In 1996, **Kimiko Date** from Japan became the first player from her country to reach a Wimbledon singles semi-final, making her a national heroine.

In that year also, **Steffi Graf** passed the total of 19 Grand Slam successes she had shared with **Helen Willis Moody**, and in 1999, **Graf** retired from the competition.

As ever, there was a good deal of violence in the world in the 1990s. The incident that stands out as having shook the United Kingdom was when a crazed gunman went into Dunblane Primary School in an idyllic little town in Scotland on March 13, 1996, and shot dead 16 school children and their teacher. Some children survived by hiding in a cupboard and one of them was a little 8-year-old boy who would triumph to become today's British/Scottish hero and darling of the tennis courts, **Andy Murray**.

Ten past champions

Meanwhile, the courts at Wimbledon had experienced development, and in 1997, there was a new No.1 Court and a new Broadcasting Centre. The first day of play was marked with a ceremony and by the appearance of 10 past champions who had each won the singles title at least three times. Prince Edward presented each with a piece of Waterford Crystal.

Spectator attendance that year had reached record numbers at just under half a million people, averaging around 30,000 per day.

That year also, marked a watershed in the life of a great tennis player for in 1997, **Boris Becker** announced his retirement from Wimbledon.

1998 was the 50th anniversary of **Don Budge's** second Wimbledon title of 1938. To commemorate the occasion, Prince Edward presented the great American champion with a Waterford Crystal vase inside the Royal Box.

It was now the era of the internet and by 1999, internet visitors for the Championship's web site, designed and operated by IBM in association with the club, had reached more than 942 million.

That year, **Lindsay Davenport** from the US won both the Ladies' singles and Doubles.

New Millennium building

The new Millennium building was opened by Prince Edward during the week before the year's 2000 championships. It provided state-of-the-art facilities for the players, the tennis writers, the members, and the LTA Councillors. The popularity of **Pete Sampras** at Wimbledon, who played the US's **Pat Rafter** in the final, meant there were record television audiences of 12.5 million world-wide, and the club website received 2.3 billion hits.

The ballot applications for tickets for the championships between 1990 and 2001 had risen by almost 300 per cent. Television viewing, the quality of which has been somewhat enhanced by the split screen effect, had risen by 56.7 per cent.

Masters Tennis Cup

The Masters Tennis Cup was introduced in 2000 as a new event to replace the Grand Slam Cup, owned jointly by the Grand Slams Association of Tennis Professionals (ATP) and the International Tennis Federation (ITF).

Prince Edward's 40th anniversary
as President and a new roof for Wimbledon

January 1, 2009, was Prince Edward's 40th anniversary as President of the All England Lawn Tennis and Croquet Club, and he would reach his 74th birthday in October.

Retractable roof over Wimbledon

That year a great leap forward was made to prevent wet weather stopping play, when a new retractable roof was built in time for the 2009 championships. It marked the first time that rain did not stop play for a lengthy period of time on Centre Court. The club tested the new roof at an event titled A Centre Court Celebration, on Sunday, May 17, 2009, which featured exhibition matches involving **Andre Agassi, Steffi Graf, Kim Clijsters**, and **Tim Henman.**

The first championship match to take place under the new roof was the completion of the fourth round Ladies' Singles between Russia's **Dinara Safina** and France's **Amélie Mauresmo**. The first match to be played in its entirety under the new roof took place between the UK's **Andy Murray** and Switzerland's **Stanislas Wawrinka**, on June 29, 2009, and which the 22-year-old Andy Murray won. In the years that followed, fans would watch Murray's progress with interest, seeing a Wimbledon champion in the making.

Murray was also involved in the latest completed match at Wimbledon, which ended at 11:02 pm in a victory over Cypriot, **Marcos Baghdatis** at Centre Court in the third round of the 2012 championships. The 2012 Men's Singles Final on July 8, 2012, between **Roger Federer** and **Andy Murray** was the first final to be played under the new roof, which had to be activated during the third set.

A new 4000-seat No.2 Court was built on the site of the old No.13 Court in time for the 2009 championships and a new 2,000-seat No.3 Court was built on the site of the old Nos.2 and 3 Courts.

Grand Slam Gentlemen's Singles, 2001 – 2012

Between 2003 and 2012, **Roger Federer** dominated the Gentlemen's Singles, winning in 2003, 04, 05, 06, 07, 09, and 12. Carving a path through the big name success was Croatia's **Goran Ivaniševic**. He is the only person to have won the Gentlemen's Grand Slam Singles title at Wimbledon as a "wildcard" in 2001, having previously been runner-up at the championships in 1992, 1994 and 1998. The other winners in between **Roger Federer's** years of success were 2002, Australia's **Lleyton Hewitt**; 2008 and 2010, Spaniard **Rafael Nadal**; and 2011, Serbian, **Novak Djokovic**. **Andy Murray** had challenged **Federer** heavily but he had held him off until **Murray** beat him at the London Olympics in 2012, winning the gold medal.

Grand Slam Gentlemen's Doubles 2000 – 2012

There has been variety in players winning the Gentlemen's Doubles during the years 2000 to 2012, with faces changing yearly. Australia's **Todd Woodbridge** partnered by fellow Australian **Mark Woodforde**, won in 2000. **Donald "Don" Johnson** and **Jared Palmer** both from the US won in 2001. Sweden's **Jonas Björkman** partnered

Woodbridge and they won in 2002, 03, and 04. Australian **Stephen Huss** and South African **Wesley Moodie** won in 2005. The US's twin brothers **Bob** and **Mike Bryan** won in 2006 and 2011. Australian **Arnaud Clément** and France's **Michaël Llodra** won in 2007. **Daniel Nestor** from Toronto, Canada, and Serbian **Nenad Zimonjić**, won in 2008 and 2009. Australian, **Jürgen Melzer** and Germany's **Philipp Petzschner** won in 2010. The UK's **Jonathan Marray** from Liverpool, and Denmark's **Frederik Nielsen,** won in 2012.

Grand Slam Ladies' Singles – the US's Williams sisters

The arrival from the US of **Venus Williams** and her sister **Serena** from Los Angeles, sent delightful shock waves through Wimbledon and through the entire world of tennis. With just one year separating their ages, Venus having been born in 1980, and Serena in 1981, these two superb players dominated women's tennis year-on-year, competing against each other, making them the stars of the Grand Slam Ladies' Singles between 2001 and 2012. The sisters brought some colour to the tennis courts wearing beads in their hair. Unfortunately, some beads became detached during play and fell onto the court. A new rule had to be put in place whereby if this happened there would be penalties.

Venus Williams won the Singles in the years 2000, 01, 05, 07 and 08, and was ranked World No.1 in singles by the Women's Tennis Association (WTA) on three separate occasions. She became the World No.1 for the first time on February 25, 2002, and the first African/American woman to achieve this feat during the Open Era. She was ranked World No.21 in singles as of April 22, 2013. Venus is one of only four women in the open era to have won five or more Wimbledon singles titles. From the time of the Wimbledon Championships in 2000, until the 2001 US Open, Venus won four of the six Grand Slam Singles tournaments held. She is one of only five women in the open era to win 200 or more main draw Grand Slam singles matches.

Serena Williams won the Singles in 2002, 03, 09, 10, and 12, and the Doubles in 2000, 02, 08 and 09. The WTA has ranked Serena World No.1 in singles on six separate occasions. She became the World No. 1 for the first time on July 8, 2002, and regained this ranking for the sixth time on February 18, 2013, becoming the old-est world No.1 player in the history of the WTA. Having won 30 Grand Slam titles, Serena is the only player to have achieved a Career Golden Slam in both singles and doubles. She is regarded as one of the greatest tennis players of all time and is the only female player to have won over US$40 million in prize money.

Playing together, the Williams sisters won the Doubles five times. Their hold over the singles was broken three times during these years adding something in the way of challenge and variety to the game. In 2004, Russia's, **Maria Sharapova** won; France's **Amélie Mauresmo** won in 2006; and Czech, **Petra Kvitová** won in 2011.

Grand Slam Ladies' Doubles

The **Williams sisters** were not however so very dominant in the Grand Slam Ladies' Doubles but, considering their enormous success in the Singles, they achieved a great deal by winning the Doubles in 2002, 08, 09, and 2012.

The US's **Lisa Raymond** and Australia's **Rennae Stubbs** won in 2001. Belgian, **Kim Clijsters** and Japan's **Ai Sugiyama** won in 2003. Zimbabwe's **Cara Black** won in 2004, 05 and 07, partnered respectively by Australian **Rennae Stubbs** and South African, **Liezel Huber**. China's **Yan Zi** and **Zheng Jie** won in 2006. Taiwanese-American **Vania King** and Russian **Yaroslava Shvedova** won in 2010. Czech, **Květa Peschke** and Slovenia's **Katarina Srebotnik** won in 2011.

Grand Slam Mixed Doubles

In the mixed doubles for these years, one or two names from earlier games reappear. **Donald Johnson** partnered with **Kimberly Po** from the US won in 2000. Czech, **Leoš Friedl** and Slovak, **Daniela Hantuchová** won in 2001. India's **Mahesh Bhupathi** and **Elena Likhovtseva** of Russia won in 2002. **Leander Paes** of India won with **Martina Navratilova** in 2003, and **Paes** won again in 2010, partnered by **Cara Black**. Zimbabweans, brother and sister, **Wayne Black** and **Cara Black**, won in 2004. India's **Mahesh Bhupathi** and **Mary Pierce** won in 2005. Israel's **Andy Ram** and **Vera Zvonareva** from Russia won in 2006. Britain's **Jamie Murray** (the elder brother of Andy Murray), along with Serbian, **Jelena Janković**, won in 2007. **Bob Bryan** and Australia's **Samantha Stosur** won in 2008. **Mark Knowles**, from the Bahamas, and Czech **Anna-Lena Grönefeld** won in 2009. Austria's **Jürgen Melzer** and Czech, **Iveta Benešová**, won in 2011. **Mike Bryan** won again with **Lisa Raymond** in 2012.

PART 4

WIMBLEDON TENNIS FINALS WINNERS, YEAR 2013

The 2013 Wimbledon tennis finals were the 127th played of the Wimbledon Championships, and the third Grand Slam event of the year.

Stars **Roger Federer** and **Serena Williams** were the defending champions in singles events. But, for the first time since 1927, both defending champions were eliminated before the quarter-finals. New faces would people the Wimbledon finals and some well-known others from years gone by would return.

Men's Singles – Andy Murray

In the Men's Singles the world's eyes were on Britain's **Andy Murray** who was playing World No.1, Serbian, **Novak Djokovic**. It was a tense game played out in searing temperatures during a heat wave. Murray played hard and won, continuing his successes following the Olympic Games in London in 2012. In October at Buckingham Palace he was presented with an OBE by Prince William and, in December, he was voted BBC Sports Personality of the Year.

Ladies' Singles – Marion Bartoli
Marion Bartoli a former, French professional tennis player, won the Ladies' Singles title after previously being runner-up in 2007, and was a semi-finalist at the 2011 French Open. She also won seven WTA singles titles and three doubles titles.
Men's Doubles – the Bryan brothers
Identical twins, **Robert (Bob)** and **Michael (Mike) Bryan**, who are American professional doubles tennis players, won the Men's Doubles. They have won multiple Olympic medals, including the gold in 2012, and have won more professional games, matches, tournaments, and Grand Slams than any other pairing. As at March 2014, they had held the World No.1 doubles ranking jointly for 355 weeks which is longer than anyone else in doubles history.

Ladies' Doubles – Hsieh Su-wei and Peng Shuai
Hsieh Su-wei is a Taiwanese professional tennis player. By February 2013 she was ranked No.23 in the WTA Tour singles rankings, and is the highest ranked Taiwanese women's singles player ever. She was partnered by **Peng Shuai** of China, who reached a career high ranking of World No.1 in doubles by the WTA as at February 2014, making her the first Chinese professional tennis player to achieve such a ranking.

Mixed Doubles – Daniel Nestor and Kristina Mladenovic
Daniel Nestor originates from Belgrade, SFR Yugoslavia, being a Serbian-born Canadian professional tennis player from Toronto, Canada. He is one of the foremost doubles players in tennis history, having won 83 men's doubles titles, including a Gold medal at the 2000 Sydney Summer Olympics. He was partnered at Wimbledon by **Kristina Mladenovic** from Nord, Northern France, who is a professional tennis player of Serbian ancestry. As well as winning the 2013 Wimbledon Mixed Doubles, they also won the 2014 Australian

Girls' Singles – Belinda Bencic
Belinda Bencic, born in Flawil, is a Swiss tennis player of Slovak descent, holding dual citizenship. At age 16 she had won two singles and two doubles titles on the ITF tour and, in 2013, won the French Open and Wimbledon Girls' singles titles.

Boys' Doubles – Thanasi Kokkinakis and Nicholas (Nick) Kyrgios
Australian professional tennis players **Thanasi Kokkinakis and Nicholas (Nick) Kyrgios** are of Greek heritage. **Kokkinakis** represented Australia in the ITF World Junior Tennis Competition in 2010, and he was a member of Australia's Junior Davis Cup team that won the silver medal in 2012. **Kyrgios** won the boys singles event at the Australian Open. Together they won the Boys' Doubles at Wimbledon.

Girls' Doubles – Barbora Krejčíková and Kateřina Siniaková
Barbora Krejčíková and Kateřina Siniaková are Czech tennis players. On the ITF tour, **Krejčíková** won five singles and 11 doubles titles, and **Siniaková** won four singles and three doubles titles. Together in 2013, they won the French, the

Wimbledon Girls' Doubles, and the US Open Girls' Doubles titles.

Gentlemen's Invitation Doubles –
Thomas Enqvist and Mark Philippoussis

Thomas Enqvist is a former Swedish professional tennis player considered to be the only Swede who could follow in the famous footsteps of **Stefan Edberg** and **Björn Borg**, and he was ranked as high as World No.4. **Mark Philippoussis,** who is of Greek-Italian heritage, is an Australian former tennis player who turned professional in 1994. His career-high singles ranking was World No.8. **Enqvist** and **Philippoussis** won the Gentlemen's Invitation Doubles.

Ladies' Invitation Doubles – Lindsay Davenport and Martina Hingis

Lindsay Davenport, from Palos Verdes, California, is a former World No.1 American professional tennis player. She has won three Grand Slam singles tournaments and an Olympic gold medal in singles, and was ranked World No.1 on eight occasions. **Martina Hingis** from Košice in former Czechoslovakia, is a Swiss professional tennis player who spent a total of 209 weeks as world No.1. She won five Grand Slam singles titles (three Australian Opens, one Wimbledon, and one US Open), and nine Grand Slam women's doubles titles. **Davenport** and **Hingis** won the Ladies' Invitation Doubles.

Senior Gentlemen's Invitation Doubles – Pat Cash and Mark Woodforde

Pat Cash, now retired, is a professional tennis player who won six titles and reached a career-high singles ranking of World No.4 in May 1988. **Mark Woodforde, OAM,** is a former professional tennis player best known as one half of "The Woodies", the earlier mentioned doubles partnership with **Todd Woodbridge**. He is perhaps best known for his doubles success, having won 12 Grand Slam doubles titles in his career, one French Open, two Australian Opens, three US Opens, and a record six Wimbledons, making a total of 17 Grand Slam doubles titles. He reached World No.1 doubles ranking in November 1992. **Cash** and **Woodforde** also won the Senior Gentlemen's Invitation Doubles.

Wheelchair Men's Doubles -
Stéphane Houdet and Shingo Kunieda

Stéphane Houdet from France and **Shingo Kunieda** from Tokyo are wheelchair tennis players. Both have successful careers in tennis and are former World No.1s. **Houdet** has been a French US Open singles Grand Slam Champion and a Masters doubles champion. He won two titles in the 2013 season with victories achieved in Johannesburg and Sardinia, and also won two Grand Slam singles titles in Paris and New York. **Shingo Kunieda** was the ITF World Champion from 2007 until 2010. He was also the Year End Number One in doubles in 2007. In 2009 and 2010 **Kunieda** achieved the Grand Slam in singles. During 2007 and 2008 he won three of the four Masters series of events. **Kunieda** is the only player to retain the men's singles title at the Paralympic Games. He won the Gold medal in the doubles of the Paralympics in 2004, and has been part of two World Team Cup wins.

Wheelchair Ladies' Doubles – Jiske Griffoen and Aniek van Koot

Jiske Griffioen and **Aniek van Koot** are Dutch wheelchair tennis players. Both women have successful careers behind them having been World No.1. They have won a vast number of titles just a few of which are here mentioned. **Griffioen** is a nine-time Grand Slam champion in doubles, and a three-time Paralympic medallist. She is also a five-time Masters doubles champion and won her first singles title in Christchurch followed by successes at Bein, Cuneo, Prostejov, and Amsterdam. She was part of the winning team at the World team cup. **Aniek van Koot** has been an Australian Open and US Open champion. In doubles competitions with **Jiske Griffioen**, **van Koot** has been the Australian Open, French Open, Wimbledon, US Open, and Masters champion. In singles she was successful in Montreal and during the 2006 season she won doubles titles in Livorno. She won junior titles in Sydney and Nottingham during the 2007 season. **Griffioen** and **van Koot** also won the Ladies' Wheelchair Doubles.

Endnotes to Chapter 10

Note: Where US dollars are expressed as the equivalent of pounds sterling they relate to the time at which they were quoted. It is to be borne in mind that the value of the dollar to the pound sterling fluctuates over time.

[1] THE INTERNATIONAL LAWN TENNIS CLUB OF GREAT BRITAIN, a history, paper by Mr J. E. (John) Barrett MBE, titled: *An Idea is Born;* produced by the IC as a history of the club and primarily for internal use by the IC; pub 1991.

[2] Ibid.

[3] Quoted from material written by Mr B.N.A. (Barry) Weatherill CBE, former Chairman of the IC Council and current President of the IC of Great Britain.

[4] John Barrett, *Wimbledon The Official History Of The Championships,* pub. Collins Willow, 2001; rules on men's seeding; pp. 225-6.
[5] Ibid. Chapter 2, p.59.

[6] The Bud Collins History of Tennis: An authoritative Encyclopaedia and Record Book; pub. New Chapter Press, 2008.

[7] John Barrett, op. cit., Chapter 4, p.79.

[8] Ibid., p.81.

[9] Ibid., p.84.

[10] Ibid., Chapter 5, p.90.

[11] Ibid., pp. 94-5.

[12] Ibid., p.97.

[13] Ibid., p.117

[14] Ibid., p.112.

[15] Authors' interview with Mrs Mary Ramsay August 1, 2008.

[16] John Barrett, op. cit., Chapter 5, p.115.

[17] Ibid., Chapter 7, p.129.

[18] Ibid., p.141.

[19] Ibid., p.126.

[20] Ibid., p.126.

[21] Ibid., Chapter 8, p.149.

[22] Ibid., Chapter 9, p. 191

[23] Ibid., p.188.

[24] Ibid., p.188.

[25] Ibid., p.188.

[26] Ibid., p.190.

[27] Ibid., p.190.

[28] Ibid., p191 see also Biographies pp.193-4.

80. A leader skiing with a group of Ski Club of Great Britain members.

CHAPTER 11

SPORT

Introduction

Prince Edward has always taken a keen and active interest in sport, and skiing is one of his favourite activities. He is Patron of the Ski Club of Great Britain, (August 1, 1965); the Kandahar Ski Club, (January 1, 1969); and the Army Winter Sports Association (January 1, 1969).

Since his teenage years, Prince Edward has been a motoring enthusiast. He **is** Patron of the Civil Service Motoring Association, (February 1, 1972); the Institute of Advanced Motorists Motoring Trust, (November 1, 1986); and President-in-Chief of The British Racing Drivers' Club, (July 1, 1994).

Prince Edward became Patron of Kent County Cricket Club (June 1, 1967), and was made an Honorary Life Member of the Band of Brothers Cricket Club, (November 1, 1979).

SKI CLUB OF GREAT BRITAIN

The Ski Club of Great Britain is a not-for-profit members' club offering benefits and services to people who love skiing and snowboarding. Prince Edward became its Patron on August 1, 1965. It is the UK's biggest snow sports membership club with around 30,000 members.

Having been founded on May 6, 1903 at the Café Royal, London the club is regarded as a body of authority for recreational skiing in the UK. Its founders were a group of individuals who wanted to encourage other people to learn to ski, help club members improve, and take more enjoyment from their skiing, whilst bringing people together who were interested in the sport.

The club's current President since 2011 is journalist Mr Frank Gardner OBE, the BBC's security correspondent, who previously enjoyed a distinguished career in the army and in banking.

The Ski Club also offer tailored holidays (Freshtracks holidays) for their members and offer a leader service; a group of volunteer skiers who ski with members across several resorts in Europe and North America.

The Pery Medal – Gentlemen Winners

The Pery Medal was instituted in 1929, by the Honourable H.E. Pery, later the Earl of Limerick DSO, and President of the club from 1925-27. Having been first awarded in 1930, the medal is presented to a skier, individual, or organisation for an outstanding contribution to snowsports. Over the years it has been awarded to some famous and well-known names, including gentlemen skiers: Sir Arnold Lunn (1930), for valuable contributions to our knowledge of mountaincraft in relation to skiing. Vivian Caulfield (1932), for Development of ski technique. Stein Eriksen (1954), Olympic Gold Medal winner 1952, and World Championships 1954. Herman Geiger (1964), a pilot who rescued many mountaineers. Lord Hunt KG (1981), Leader of the ninth British expedition to Everest. Dr Michael Stroud and Sir Ranulph Fiennes (1993), Explorers. Franz Klammer (2003), Winner Combined in 1974, World Championships and Downhill at Winter Olympics 1976. Hermann Maier (2007), Contribution to ski racing and outstanding success at World Cup and Olympic level.

The Pery Medal – Lady Winners

Women skiers who were awarded the Pery Medal include: Miss A.D. Sale-Barker (1935), Downhill ski racer and one of the first ladies to compete. Mrs Gretchen Fraser (1948), Winner of Olympic Ladies Slalom and first English speaking skier to win an Olympic medal. Miss Evie A. Pinching (1949), Ski racer and Ladies World Champion 1936. Miss Lucille Wheeler (1958), Canadian ski racer and winner of downhill giant slalom World Championships 1958, Olympic bronze in slalom 1956. The Honourable Mrs Joan Raynsford OBE, (1975), Chairman/President of the Ski Club and Arlberg-Kandahar racer. Jenny Jones (2014), First Briton to win Olympic Bronze for Slopestyle, Sochi, 2014 Winter Olympics. Kelly Gallaher (2014), First

81. Members of the Kandahar Ski Club going skiing, left to right: Mr R. Cleeves Palmer (then chairman); HRH The Duke Of Kent; Mr Nick Morgan, (then club Vice Chairman); and Mr Beat Hodler (then club president).

ever Olympic Gold medal on snow for the UK Women's Super G, Sochi 2014 Paralympics.

KANDAHAR SKI CLUB

Skier, mountaineer, and writer, Arnold Lunn (1888-1974), sought to complement the speed, strength and bravery needed in a downhill skiing race by testing also the skier's balance, agility, close control and smooth turns, without needing any subjective marks by judges. Lunn turned the old, Norwegian style test called a slalom into a pure race, down a short course, tightly controlled by artificial marks. It meant that racers were obliged to ski between pairs of flags (rather than poles) doing particular types of sharp turns. In 1922 Lunn set the first slalom at Mürren, a traditional mountain village resort in the Bernese Oberland, in the Swiss Alps.

In January 1924, along with nine supporters who were Englishmen, Lunn established the Kandahar Ski Club at a dinner at his father's hotel in Mürren. The club was therefore founded as a racing ski club, and its declared objective was to promote downhill and slalom racing. It was named after the most famous skiing trophy of the time, the Roberts of Kandahar Challenge Cup that was in turn, named in honour of Field Marshal Sir Frederick Roberts (1832-1914), a former Commander-in-Chief of the British Army in India (1885), who donated the trophy.

82. Mr Nick Morgan, Kandahar
Ski Club, receiving the coveneted Roberts
of Kandahar Ski Cup from
HRH The Duke of Kent, 2009.

In 1931 Lunn succeeded in having the Alpine disciplines admitted to the International Ski Federation (FIS) Championship, and which were later recognised as the first World Championships. In 1932 the FIS Alpine Championships were held at Cortina d'Ampezzo, Italy. Switzerland's competitors won three Gold Medals, two Silver, and one Bronze. In the Men's Event, Otto Furrer won Gold in the Combined; Silver in the Slalom; and Bronze in the Downhill. In the Women's Event, Rösli Streiff won two Gold medals in the Slalom and Combined. David Zogg won a Silver Medal in the Men's Downhill Event. For the United Kingdom, in the Women's event, Durrell Sale-Barker won a Silver Medal and Doreen Elliott won a Bronze Medal, both in the Slalom.

In that year also, Lunn organised the first World Championships in Downhill and Slalom racing at Mürren. What has remained unique about the Kandahar Club is that members enjoy equal status and skiing is not viewed as the pursuit of only a few specialist elites.

Inferno Week

The focus of the members is on ski racing and Inferno Week, conjuring up Dante's famous 14th-century epic poem Inferno, is the biggest event at Mürren. This ski race was begun in 1928, by British skiing enthusiasts and featured both male and female competitors and has continued to take place annually in January. Over 100 members of the club and 1,800 competitors in total take part in this, the longest race in the world (15.8km), from The Schilthorn to Lauterbrunnen. The ski course is particularly arduous and those participating need to have all-round skiing experience and good mental stamina. The Roberts of Kandahar Challenge Cup, designed by Henry George Murphy, is presented to club members who have been awarded the Diamond Devil for consistently good results in the Inferno race.

Royal patronage
Prince Edward's father, Prince George, was Patron of the Kandahar Ski Club until his death in 1942, when his widow, Princess Marina The Duchess of Kent took over. Prince Edward became an Honorary Member in 1963, and after his mother died in August 1968, he agreed to become Patron on January 1, 1969. The Duke of Kent Cup had been given to the club during his parents' time, and the first event for the cup had taken place on January 9, 1937. Attracting over 100 entries, it was won by Arnold Kaech of Berne.

Duke and Duchess on four-day trip to Mürren
Along with his wife Katherine, Prince Edward visited Mürren in 1969, on a four-day trip for the Kandahar-Martini races, and it would be their first time to present the Duke of Kent Cup, and the Kandahar trophy. [1] Club Chairman Mr Nick Morgan described the arrival of the royal couple. They were greeted by local school children, who serenaded them with songs and presented them with flowers. A sleigh drawn by a white pony was waiting to convey them to their destination, and Prince Edward and the Duchess Katherine, "en-sleighed" with the club's President and Lady Silsoe, went "purring over the snow" to the Palace Hotel. During the skiing events, the Duchess "was at the finishing line on both days, where she spoke to many of the racers." Prince Edward, escorted by Ted Varley, "skied down the course, chatting to gate-keepers and expressing relief at not having to race himself."

The royal couple presented the Kandahar Cup at a glittering, celebratory dinner in the Palace Hotel that was attended by 100 guests. Club President Sir Arnold Lunn (having in 1952 been awarded a Knighthood for his services to skiing) spoke with his "usual brilliance" and was later photographed with Prince Edward.

When the prize giving was over some of the guests let their hair down and there was "carolling" in the cellar. One distinguished guest "sang Lily The Pink" a song that was a UK hit in 1968 for comedy group The Scaffold, whilst "Ted Varley performed an ethnic dance." Resonating throughout the cellar was the sound of "Count Rossi's rich tenor voice", singing "songs of the warm South." [2]

Prince Edward continues to award the Kandahar trophy each year, and club membership today numbers about 1,400.

Chairman Nick Morgan remembers
Mr Nick Morgan became Chairman of the club in November 2011, succeeding keen ski-racer, cricketer and golfer Mr Cleeves Palmer, who stepped up to become President. Nick says of his skiing career:

"I skied a lot as a child both in Mürren and elsewhere in Switzerland but did not join the club until 1993. Following joining the board in 1998, upon my return from many years living in New York, I became an active participant in club events. These included the Inferno and Amateur Inter-club Ski Championships which I helped establish in 2008, and which were hosted by the Down Hill Only Club (DHO) in Wengen in 2011."

The club has something of a family atmosphere about it. During Prince Edward's visit to Mürren in 2009, Nick was Vice-Chairman and the President was Mr Beat Hodler, a Swiss member, who is the son of Mr Marc Hodler, who was President of the International Ski Federation (1951–1998), and a prominent IOC member. Nick is the first Chairman to be the son of a former Chairman, his father Mr Andrew Morgan having been Chairman (1997-2001). Nick's wife, Carolyn, is no longer an active racer but was one of Prince Edward's regular ski and lunch companions during his visits.

Prince Edward does not mind the occasional joke at his own expense. During his visit to the club in 2009, Helen Carless asked His Royal Highness: "Did you ski in the Forces?" The freezing cold air in the Alps can play tricks on the ears and on the hearing, and it sounded to Prince Edward like: "Did you ski in your 40s?" Prince Edward replied: "How old do you think I am?" The then Chairman, Mr Cleeves Palmer intercepted: "Sir, I think Helen said Forces," meaning during his time in the Army. Cleeves then continued: "Anyway, Helen, if you get put in the Tower of London, I will visit you." Prince Edward roared with laughter.

In 2010 the Kandahar Ski Club got together with Barrogill, one of the great names in Whisky, and Prince Edward presented miniature bottles of whisky to the winners of the Inferno race. The North Highland's Mey Selections Barrogill had been sponsored by the Hulse-Palmer Cup, which is awarded to the three Kandahar teams with the best improved times in the race, and to the member of the club with the best overall performance.

Dr John Strak, Managing Director of Mey Selections, spoke of the "great tradition" of the race, which was the 66th event in Mürren, and praised the participants. "The traditions of the Kandahar Club, the Inferno and Barrogill Whisky", he said, "all fit perfectly together." Sam Hulse from the club said that the "race this year was as hard as ever", and that "the winners fully deserved their prizes."

The race coincided with Burns Night, the celebration of the famous Scottish poet Robert Burns, and many haggis were enjoyed and went down well with the whisky at a supper held in the Eiger Guesthouse Hotel. Mr Alan Ramsay, Proprietor of the Hotel who races in the Inferno each year, on this occasion wearing his kilt, personally organised the speedy delivery of a haggis to Prince Edward that was sent through the dazzling, picturesque, glistening snow and pines of the ski slopes.

ARMY WINTER SPORTS ASSOCIATION

The Army Winter Sports Association (AWSA) was formed at the behest of Field Marshal Montgomery, of battle of El Alamein fame, in 1947. "Monty", as he was affectionately known, wished to provide a break from routine training and operations in the immediate post-war years, whilst developing military and technical skills on snow and ice. These reasons are considered to be still as valid today as they were then.

Prince Edward was made Patron of the AWSA on January 1, 1969. The AWSA supports eight winter sports disciplines: Alpine, Bobsleigh, Cresta, Luge, Nordic, Snowboard, Skeleton, and Telemark. Ice Sports include the disciplines Bobsleigh, Luge and Skeleton, and Cresta, the latter only taking place in St. Moritz.

Annually, there are Army Championships in all of the eight disciplines and in addition there are four Inter Service (IS) Championships where the Army competes against the Royal Navy and the Royal Air Force. The Inter Service Snow Sports Championships comprises: Alpine, Snowboard and Telemark, the IS Ice Sports Championships (Bobsleigh, Luge and Skeleton), IS Nordic and IS Cresta.

The Army's annual Ice Camp gives novices the opportunity to try their hand at bobsleigh, luge (feet first on a sledge) and skeleton bobsleigh (head first on a tray). Reaching speeds in excess of 60 miles per hour (96.56 kilometres), competitors slip-slide their way down various tracks in Europe and Canada, only inches from the ice.

The Calgary track in Canada was built for the 1988 winter Olympics, famously remembered for the efforts of the Jamaican bobsleigh team that were immortalised in the film Cool Runnings. For the novice this event is an adrenaline-inducing test of bravery and commitment.

Prince Edward on skis

Prince Edward took part in the Army Ski Championships in 1961, aged 26 years, at St. Moritz. He competed in both the Downhill (DH) and Slalom (SL) races. He was in 101st place in the DH, when he fell in the gully. But he bravely put his skis back on and finished the race which practice is not permitted today. He was disqualified in the Slalom for presumably missing a gate. He fared much better in 1962, in St. Moritz, where he came 31st out of 111 in the DH, and 45th out of 80 in the SL, achieving a highly creditable 36th place out of 81 in the Combined event which was his best year. He came 55th in the new race the Giant Slalom (GS) in 1964. His last competition was in 1965, in St. Moritz, where he achieved 83rd in the GS, 73rd in the SL, and 95th in the DH, coming 71st overall. Prince Edward goes skiing for pleasure each year but he no longer takes part in competitions.

CIVIL SERVICE MOTORING ASSOCITION
(CSMA CLUB)

The Civil Service Motoring Association (CSMA Club) is a private home, motoring, and leisure organisation in the UK. It was established in 1923, and membership today is allowed to past and present members of the UK Civil Service and organisations that were formerly part of the British Civil Service, for instance Royal Mail and British Telecom, and membership is also extended to relatives of existing members.

CSMA Club is a mutual organisation and was founded by Mr Frank Vernon Edwards, an executive officer in the Ministry of Labour that was a British Government

*83. HRH The Duke of Kent attending the CSMA Diamond Jubilee
lunch, 23rd February 1973, with the late Barbary Sabey, CSMA
Chairman; the late Eric Haslam, CSMA Vice-Chairman, at the
RAC, Pall Mall, London.*

department in 1916, and who had an interest in motorcycle trials. Unfortunately,
he did not live to see the association blossom, having died the following year.

The club was expected to be a small motorsport organisation of around 300
members, but by 1930, the membership had increased to over 5,000. Membership
today stands at around 300,000.

Originally having concentrated on the sporting and leisure activities associated
with motoring, CSMA Club has since developed into primarily a provider of membership benefits in motoring and leisure areas. Today its member services include
insurance, banking, travel, leisure, and roadside rescue. These are provided through
relationships with Approved Partners, notably Frizzell Insurance, with which it has
worked since 1923. CSMA also owns and operates a number of Leisure Retreats
that includes: Wheel Farm Cottages, Manleigh Park, Treworgie Barton Cottages,
Cotswold Cottages, Ghyll Manor Hotel & Restaurant, Whitemead Forest Park, and
Parkergate.

Prince Edward became Patron of CSMA Club on February 1, 1972. On November 15, 1995, he carried out the official opening of the new office building that houses the CSMA Club, Britannia House, at Station Street, Brighton, East Sussex, where
he was joined by the Lord-Lieutenant of East Sussex, Admiral Sir Lindsay Bryson.

The National Motor Museum
Prince Edward enjoys looking at old cars and motoring memorabilia. In 1972, he
opened the National Motor Museum (NMM) at Beaulieu. The original museum
had been started in 1952, by Edward John Barrington Douglas-Scott-Montagu, 3rd

Baron Montagu of Beaulieu, as a tribute to his late father, John Walter 2nd Baron, who was one of the great pioneers of motoring in the UK. John Walter introduced the Prince of Wales (later King Edward VII) to motoring during the 1890s. John Walter was a British politician and the first person to drive a motorcar into the yard of the Houses of Parliament. The newly opened museum was a memorial to him; he was reputed to have kept six cars in the front hall of his home, Palace House, the home of the Montagu family since 1538.

Over the years, the museum has grown, and today the NMM houses a collection of over 250 automobiles and motorcycles, telling the story of motor vehicles on the roads of Britain from the dawn of motoring to the present day. The NMM appeals to all age groups. It includes World Land Speed Record Breakers like Sir Malcolm Campbell's famous Bluebird, and film and television favourites, including the 'Flying' Ford Anglia from J.K. Rowling's *Harry Potter and the Chamber of Secrets*, plus Superbikes. Visitors can take a trip in a space age pod where they experience Wheels, a dark ride through motoring history. The NMM welcomes over 350,000 visitors a year, having celebrated its 40th anniversary in 2012. To mark the occasion there was a May Day cavalcade of 40 cars, one for each year of the museum's life.

The Cotswold Motoring Museum

CSMA Club are also owners of the Cotswold Motoring Museum. Located in the picturesque village of Bourton-on-the-Water, Gloucestershire, the museum is overflowing with vintage car collections, classic cars, motorcycles, caravans, and an intriguing collection of motoring curiosities. A visit to the museum provides a great day out for all the family and is a place of fascination for children, or a weekend

84. Civil Service Motoring Association 90th Anniversary, June 2013. Left to right: Ann Whiffin; Hannah Ellams; Mr Bradley McCreary, CSMA Club Archivist; HRH The Duke Of Kent; and Mr Michael Tambini, General Manager, Cotswold Motoring Museum.

break in the Cotswolds. It is a truly magical journey for all ages through the 20th century.

90th Anniversary of CSMA

CSMA Club celebrated their 90th anniversary in June 2013. Prince Edward visited on June 12, to mark this historic occasion. He was welcomed by Chairman Mr Dave Farris. In his address Mr Farris said:

"In 1923, Frank Vernon Edwards wanted to share his passion for motoring and, as a result, our Association was formed. Ninety years later we are probably stronger as an Association than ever before, and we're really looking forward to our 10th decade."

Prince Edward opened the museum's exhibition titled Mud, Track and Tarmac, which celebrated the club's 90th anniversary. Escorted by museum keeper, Mr Michael Tambini, Prince Edward spent nearly an hour touring the museum's collections. Mr Tambini said of Prince Edward: "I could sense his enthusiasm and knowledge. He was taken with the Austin Seven Swallow and obviously knew a lot about Jaguar and their history."

Prince Edward spoke to all the volunteers, making their day all the more worthwhile. He unveiled a plaque to commemorate his visit and the club's 90th anniversary. He, in turn, was presented with a commemorative Winged Wheel by 82-year-old volunteer Mr Arthur Bartlett, who was born in the adjoining building.

INSTITUTE OF ADVANCED MOTORING TRUST
incorporating
THE AUTOMOBILE ASSOCIATION
MOTORING TRUST

The Institute of Advanced Motorists (IAM) is a charity based in the United Kingdom and serving nine countries. Their objective is to improve car driving and motorcycle riding standards, and so enhance road safety through the proper use of a system of car and motorcycle control, based on Roadcraft. The IAM merged its commercial arms into one organisation in April 2010, called IAM Drive & Survive, which offers on-line and on road driver training for companies of all sizes.

The IAM was formed in 1956, and has more than 100,000 members, all of who have taken and passed an advanced test in a car, commercial vehicle or on a motorcycle.

In 2006 two new assessments were introduced: DriveCheck and RideCheck. These checks provide the opportunity to have one's driving or riding ability assessed by an IAM observer. They are not, however, a test and there is no pass or fail.

At the end of 2006 the organisation formed the IAM Motoring Trust and took over the work of the AA Motoring Trust that had been formed by The Automobile Association (AA) in 2002.

In 2007 the IAM sought to address the needs of all road users by introducing

Bicycle Training, aimed primarily at the corporate market. IAM Cycling will provide professional training for people wanting to improve their cycling ability, skills and confidence and, in so doing, increase the numbers of people cycling to work. In 2010 IAM Cycling was strengthened with the publication of *How to be a better cyclist* (the third in the IAM Series), the others being *How to be a better driver* and *How to be a better rider*. The IAM now offers a special Cycling membership.

The IAM Motoring Trust has also taken on the former work of the AA Motoring Trust to form a new, independent road safety organisation that will be the research and advocacy arm of the Institute of Advanced Motorists (IAM).

Prince Edward became Patron of the Institute of Advanced Motorists Motoring Trust on November 1, 1986 and, to the delight of the management, is now also Patron of the two integrated organisations.

The Queen's Diamond Jubilee

The weekend of Queen Elizabeth II's Diamond Jubilee in 2012 was celebrated up and down the country. In honour of this historic event the IAM had been looking at how roads and highway safety has improved over the past 60 years. Back in 1952, when the Queen came to the throne, 13 people per day died in road accidents. Despite the numbers of vehicles increasing from 4 million to 34 million the figures have now been reduced to around five people per day losing their lives in road accidents. Mr Simon Best, Chief Executive of IAM in addressing these matters said:

> "Road Safety gets better by the year, and the technology of roads and cars improves all the time... I am delighted to say that road safety still receives royal support, in the form of from IAM's Patron, the Duke of Kent, and the Prince Michael International Road Safety Awards."

BRITISH RACING DRIVERS' CLUB

The British Racing Drivers' Club (BRDC) was founded in April 1928, by Dr J. Dudley Benjafield, one of an informal group of British racing drivers known as the Bentley Boys. There were originally only 25 members and it was primarily a socialising club. At the inauguration of the club they devised a set of objectives: to promote the interests of motor sport generally; to celebrate any specific achievement in motor sport; to extend hospitality to racing drivers from overseas; and to further the interests of British drivers competing abroad.

Prince Edward has been President-in-Chief of the BRDC since July 1, 1994, having followed in the footsteps of Prince Philip The Duke of Edinburgh KG KT, (1952-94), and his father, Prince George The Duke Of Kent (1932-42). He is an annual attendee at the British Grand Prix, and is particularly keen on the qualifying race that is held the day prior to the actual race. He takes an active interest in club affairs, and follows the career development of young British and Commonwealth drivers with a very thorough understanding. The clubhouse was officially opened by

Prince Edward in 1999, during the British Grand Prix weekend. It instantly became a landmark at Silverstone and a flagship of the British Racing Drivers' Club.

Sir Stirling Moss, OBE FIE, who is a megastar in motor racing world-wide, is Life Vice-President of BRDC. Moss raced from 1948 to 1962, and won 212 of the 529 races he entered, including 16 Formula One Grands Prix. He would compete in as many as 62 races in a single year, and drove 84 different makes of car over the course of his racing career, including Lotus, Vanwall, Maserati, Jaguar, Ferrari and Porsche. He competed in several formulae, very often on the same day.

Stuart Pringle

Mr Stuart Pringle has been Secretary of the British Racing Drivers' Club since 2006, and is only the tenth person to hold the position since the formation of the club. Prior to that he ran the Motorsport Department at Brands Hatch Circuit and was, for six years, Secretary of the Vintage Sports-Car Club. Before his career in motor sport, Stuart served for five years as an Officer in the 1st Royal Tank Regiment.

BRDC today

Today the BRDC is a membership body that represents the interests of professional racing drivers from the United Kingdom and the Commonwealth. It has over 800 people who hold a variety of membership status: Full Members, Associate Members, and Honorary Members. These include the young drivers who are part of the club's SuperStar and Rising Star schemes.

It is part of the BRDC's history that as early as 1929, they became involved in the promotion and organising of racing events. The first event was the 500-Mile Race at Brooklands that October. In the post-war era, they expanded their activities, taking over the lease of Silverstone race track from the RAC in 1952. In 1966 the club formed a subsidiary company, Silverstone Circuits Limited, responsible for the development of the British Grand Prix. In 1971, with financial assistance from the wider motor racing and motoring industries, they purchased the freehold of Silverstone Racing Circuit. Other notable BRDC-organised events at Silverstone included the BRDC International Trophy, which became a significant international race for single seater racing cars in its own right. Over the years the BRDC has also been an organiser of other International, National, and club races through its Race Department and has run a thriving Marshals' Club based at Silverstone.

The support and development of young British drivers has become an important part of the BRDC's existence, including its involvement in the annual McLaren AUTOSPORT BRDC Young Driver of the Year Award to honour and promote a young British driver who, in the eyes of the judges, shows the talent and potential to become a future Formula One World Champion. In 2008 the BRDC announced the creation of its SuperStars program, designed to advise and financially support Britain's most promising young drivers. The 1992 British Touring Car Championship champion, Tim Harvey, was appointed Director of the programme which provides both mental and physical fitness training, media training and all important simulator time.

85. HRH The Duke Of Kent with Sir Jackie Stewart OBE at the British Racing Driver's Club Clubhouse, British Grand Prix, 2008. The display behind them celebrates the 50th anniversary of Mike Hawthorn's Formula One World Championship – 1958 (the first F1 World Championship by a British Driver and BRDC Member.

The president of the BRDC has always been a notable figure in the world of motor sport. The current incumbent is Mr Derek Warwick, who was elected president in 2011. During his career, Derek contested 147 Grand Prix races and won the World Sportscar Championship and Le Mans 24-hour race in 1992 with Peugeot. His immediate predecessor was Damon Hill OBE, Formula One World Champion 1996, who held the position between 2006 and 2011, having taken over from three time Formula One World Champion, Sir Jackie Stewart OBE (2000 – 2006). The commercial business of the club is overseen by the Chairman of the Board of Directors. The previous chairman was Mr Stuart Rolt, who competed in international touring car racing in the late 1970s. The present chairman, Mr John Grant, was elected in October 2013. As a competitor, he has mainly enjoyed success racing historics, and a class win at the Nurburgring 24 hours. Mr Grant has enjoyed an outstanding professional career in the motor business having been with Ford, Jaguar, and Lucas.

Silverstone Circuit
As owners of the freehold of the Silverstone Circuit site, the BRDC are actively

273

nvolved in the management and promotion of Britain's Grand Prix circuit. Under the club's watchful eye, the 760-acre site (which straddles the Buckinghamshire and Northamptonshire border) has been developed to keep pace with modern motor racing safety standards and also commercial imperatives. Most recently, the circuit has been reconfigured to run infield for enhanced spectator viewing and a state of the art, multi-million pound new pit, paddock, and media centre building, named The Silvestone Wing, has been built. This dramatic structure now dominates the Silverstone skyline and, when not in use for motor racing activities, is the largest covered conferencing area between London and Birmingham. Stuart Rolt has said that the 'commercial potential of Silverstone and the Estate is significant' and they 'are seeking external investment' from third parties who share their vision. Mr Rolt said of his vision for the future: 'The BRDC has funded the new Grand Prix circuit, state-of-the-art Silverstone Wing complex, key developments around the venue, and the planning process for the Silverstone Masterplan.' A further investor is sought to help develop Silverstone even more into a world-class, multi-purpose centre for motor sport, high technology business, and training and education.

The BRDC Benevolent Fund

The BRDC Benevolent Fund was established in November 2000. The trustees are David Richards CBE, Chris Bliss and Michael MacDowel. The late Ken Tyrell and

86. HRH The Duke Of Kent meeting young British drivers (BRDC SuperStars) at the BRDC Clubhouse, British GP 2010, left to right: Mr Tom Onslow-Cole (British Touring Car Championship); Mr Oliver Webb (British Formula 3 Championship); Mr Adam Chrisodoulou (Mazda GT USA).

*87. HRH The Duke Of Kent with BRDC superstar Mr Alexander Sims
(F3 Euroseries), in the BRDC Clubhouse, British Grand Prix P 2010.*

the late John Britten gave generous donations of £25,000. The club matched this donation with the same, as did the President Sir Jackie Stewart, in 2002. The objective of the charitable trust fund is the relief of need by reason of youth, age, ill health, disability or financial hardship, for the public benefit, amongst persons involved in the participation, promotion, or administration of motor-sport, whether or not for remuneration, and their families and dependants. Mr Stuart Pringle has said:

> "It is not widely appreciated when the glamorous modern world of Formula One is viewed, that there was a time, not so very long ago, when motor sport was a poorly rewarded, insecure and dangerous place to earn a living. The BRDC Benevolent Fund provides invaluable, discreet support to many people who were involved in the sport in such times."[3]

BAND OF BROTHERS CRICKET CLUB

The Band of Brothers Cricket Club was founded in 1858, when Queen Victoria was still monarch. They are known throughout the cricketing world simply as "BB". Members are referred to as Brothers or Brethren. The original members were officers of the Royal East Kent Mounted Rifles. They formed themselves into a society, adopting as its name the title of a popular song of the Christy Minstrels called The Band of Brothers. Membership of BB is unique amongst wandering cricket clubs

88. Mr James Ryeland FICS, Managing Director, George Hammond Plc, member of the Band of Brothers Cricket Club, Kent, with HRH The Duke Of Kent in the Long Room of Lords Cricket Ground at the 150th anniversary dinner.

due to its strict territorial allegiance to Kent, with membership confined to those who were born, attended school or are domiciled in Kent.

In 1903 the club started a junior section, known as The BaBes, which continues to thrive and provide the lifeblood of future Brethren.

The earliest cricket match is recorded as having taken place on 12th August 1858 at Evington in Kent, on ground belonging to Sir Courtenay Honywood, against a side from Torry Hill. Competitive cricket fixtures have continued ever since, except for the interruptions during the two world wars. Torry Hill is still regarded as their primary ground. Their colours are black and Kentish grey.

The period from 1880 to 1914 is considered to span the golden age of cricket. Many matches were played during these years, and records show that out of 361 matches, 163 were won and only 84 lost.

George Robert Canning Harris, 4th Baron, GCSI GCIE, referred to as 4th Lord Harris, was a British politician, cricketer and cricket administrator and a leading light in promoting the club for many years, taking the lead from 1880 until his death in 1932. Harris played his first game for the Band of Brothers against St. Lawrence in 1867, when he was an Eton College schoolboy aged 16 years. He went on to play 224 First Class matches, represent Oxford University and Captain both Kent and England and later be appointed President of both clubs. He played his last game for BB against the Buffs in 1928, taking four wickets. Between these dates many centuries were scored and wickets taken against his name. Lord Harris became BB's first "Chief" in 1919 and was admired and respected for his inspiration, fairness, kindness, and generosity.

Post First and Second World War successes

During a match with the Royal Engineers (R.E.) on their own ground in 1935, the largest number of runs was made in a BB match. BB scored 403 for seven declared and 256 for five declared, and R.E. 343 and 289 for five: 1,291 runs in two days' cricket! After the end of the Second World War, play was resumed in 1947, and the members now in their 40's took up where they had left off.

Centenary 1958

By the time of their centenary in 1958 the cricket club had seen changes. During the years in between the two-day match, previously the staple fare of BB Cricket, had ceased to exist. The reduction in the armed forces swept away fixtures against the Kentish Garrisons, the Nore Command and the County Regiments, whilst the Town Clubs' interest in league cricket reduced their affinity with wandering clubs. Kentish schools matches however increased with a few London-based cricket clubs.

Matches were played to celebrate the centenary of the first matches against the Royal Engineers (1980), Royal Artillery (1981), Tonbridge School (1988) and Eton Ramblers (2000).

The club has enjoyed the support of the great names of Kent cricket over the past century and more. The "BB Books" contain some 20 leather bound volumes of a detailed record of the club's life and the scores of every match.

89. Mr James Ryeland with HRH The Duke Of Kent, the Long Room Lords Cricket ground, 150th anniversary dinner. On James's left Mr Peter Cattrall, the Club's Keeper of the Books that contain a complete record of every game played since 1858. On the HRH's right, Mr Nicholas Heroys, Band of Brothers' Ninth Chief

150th Anniversary 2008

Prince Edward became an Honorary Life Member of the club on November 1, 1979. In 2008 BB celebrated its 150th anniversary with, amongst other events, a dinner at

Lords Cricket Club at which Prince Edward was in attendance.

In 2010 BB held their first-ever Cricket Tour, a four-day trip to Paris, during which a strong group of BB cricketers played three cricket matches, winning them all convincingly.

BB cricket has withstood the test of time and triumphantly entered the 21st century with the same resilience and determination that gave it birth in the middle of the 19th century. [4]

KENT COUNTY CRICKET CLUB

Kent County Cricket Club (Kent CCC) is linked to the Band of Brothers through the 4th Baron Harris. Harris's father had become involved with Kent CCC as a committee member, rising to become club President in 1870. At his death in 1872, as his heir George Canning Harris 4th Baron became active in the club, becoming club Captain 1871-1889 and then President of Kent in 1875 and President of MCC in 1895.

The game of cricket being played in Kent has been traced as far back as the 17th century and Kent, jointly with Sussex, is considered to be the birthplace of cricket in England. Kent CCC is one of the 18 first class county cricket clubs which currently make up the English and Welsh national cricket structure.

Prince Edward was made an Honorary Life Member of Kent County Cricket Club, June 1, 1967.

The club currently plays most of its home matches at the Spitfire Ground, St. Lawrence in Canterbury, as well as playing home matches at The County Cricket Ground in Beckenham and the Nevill Ground at Royal Tunbridge Wells where they host the Tunbridge Wells Cricket Week.

KCCC ladies team

Kent CCC also have a ladies team. They play in Division One of the Women's County Championship which they have won six times. Home fixtures are played at The Spitfire Ground, St. Lawrence, County Ground, Beckham and Polo Farm, Canterbury.

Endnotes to Chapter 11

[1] A report and photographs of the events appeared in the 1969 *Kandahar Review* Vol.5 No.5.

[2] Ibid., detail from a report published by Peter Clarke.

[3] The detail relating to The British Racing Drivers' Club owes much to the efforts of Mr Stuart Pringle who acted as part-author and adviser throughout.

[4] Source: THE MYSTERY by the Band of Brothers, pub. 2014.

CHAPTER 12

ROYAL NATIONAL LIFEBOAT INSTITUTION (RNLI)
and
THE COMMUNICATIONS AND PUBLIC SERVICE LIFEBOAT FUND (CISPOTEL)

Part 1
The RNLI – who they are and what they do
"With courage, nothing is impossible."
(Sir William Hillary)

Introduction

The chapter on the RNLI is meant to introduce the reader to a basic understanding of the charity. Some snapshots of what they have achieved is provided but it is not intended to be a history or in-depth study of such a vast and extensive organisation.

The RNLI

Mr Paul Boissier is the Chief Executive of the RNLI. Mr Boissier graduated in Mechanical Engineering at The University of Cambridge, and then joined the Royal Navy, specialising in navigation. He served in, and then commanded, a variety of submarines, before moving to the surface fleet as Captain of an anti-submarine frigate. At Portsmouth Naval Base he was responsible for repairing and accommodating most of the Navy's ships. As Chief Executive of the Naval Support Organisation in Bristol, he worked closely with a variety of industrial partners and managed the three naval dockyards. Mr Boissier spent his last two-and-a-half years in the Royal Navy as Chief Operating Officer, integrating human resources, support, training, logistics, and procurement. Along with his wife Susie, Paul has sailed extensively in their boat *Snow Goose*. He has also written a book on the maritime rules of the road [1], and for three years was Commodore of the Royal Naval Sailing Association. He is a member of the Younger Brother of Trinity House, which is the official General Lighthouse Authority. [2]

Prince Edward became President of the RNLI on March 1, 1969. Her Majesty Queen Elizabeth II is their Patron, as was the late Queen Elizabeth The Queen Mother before her.

Prince Edward's former Private Secretary Sir Richard Buckley says: 'Curiously, though, he is not a good sailor!' [3] Prince Edward took over the presidency from his mother, Princess Marina. The RNLI honoured Prince Edward at their Annual Presentation Awards on the 40th anniversary of his Presidency in 2009, when they presented him with a diorama in recognition of his four decades of service and commitment.

RNLI Memorial Poole Headquarters 2009

In September 3, 2009, Prince Edward unveiled the first official RNLI memorial to lost lifesavers at their headquarters at Poole, Dorset, in a service that began at 12.00 noon. Throughout the UK and Ireland, RNLI lifeboat crews and supporters observed a minute's silence at 12.20 pm as a mark of respect. RNLI lifeboat stations, lifeguard units, and offices throughout the UK and Ireland lowered their RNLI flags. The memorial commemorates the lives of 778 people from the UK and the Republic of Ireland. Many relatives, friends, and crewmembers attended the ceremony. Mr Andrew Freemantle CBE, who was at that time Chief Executive of the RNLI, and who had undertaken a sponsored cycle ride to raise funds for the memorial said:

"The RNLI Memorial is a tribute to the many hundreds of people who have given their lives selflessly to save others over the last 200 years. Its location in front of The Lifeboat College here, in Poole, is truly fitting and will inspire generations of lifesavers from all over the British Isles who will train here in the years to come."

RNLI President Admiral The Lord Boyce, commented after the ceremony:

"Today has been a very special day for our charity. The new memorial, inscribed with the family motto of the RNLI's founder, Sir William Hillary: 'with courage, nothing is impossible', provides an enduring focus which will ensure that the sacrifices of our life savers will not be forgotten. It also reminds us of the seas that surround our islands and our volunteer lifeboat crews who will always be there when they are called upon. I hope that many people will come to Poole to see it."

The RNLI Memorial, designed by Mr Sam Holland ARBS, stands more than 4.5 metres in height, and depicts a person in a boat saving another from the water, symbolising both the history and future of the RNLI in its most basic and humanitarian form.

Admiral The Lord Boyce gave the Speech of Reflection. Six RNLI volunteers representing the six RNLI operational divisions recited the names of lifeboat stations where there has been loss of life. [4] The Bishop of Sherborne, Dr Graham Kings, conducted the Service of Dedication. St. Ives Coxswain/Mechanic, Mr Tommy Cocking, the descendant of three men named on the memorial (a great-grandfather and two great-uncles), gave a speech on behalf of all lifeboat crews.

Brief history of the RNLI

The RNLI was started by Sir William Hillary, 1st Baronet (1771–1847). An English soldier, author, and philanthropist, Hillary spent two years as Equerry to Prince Augustus Frederick, son of King George III. His duties included sailing with the prince in the Mediterranean, and it was there that he learned basic seamanship and navigation skills. Hillary was a religious man, a Quaker, and was married, but his father-in-law did not approve of his religious views. He and his wife separated and divorced, and Hillary settled at Fort Anne, Douglas, on the Isle of Man. It was there, on that rugged, treacherous coastline of the Irish Sea, that Hillary witnessed many ships being wrecked on the Manx coast, and he became involved in some dramatic rescues with the local independent lifeboat station crew at Douglas.

Hillary came to recognise the need for a unified rescue service. He drew up plans for a lifeboat rescue service staffed by trained crews intended for the Isle of Man and all of the British coastline. In February 1823 he published a pamphlet [5] on the subject, and in 1824 a charity was formed "a national institution for the preservation of lives and property from shipwreck", that is today the Royal National Lifeboat Institution.

The first lifeboats were rowing boats and therefore required a crew that was courageous enough to risk their own lives and go out in a storm to rescue sailors whose ships had got into difficulties, usually having run into rocks or run aground. The crews of the lifeboats were volunteers and were not paid for their services and the tradition continues today. Hillary was a fearless individual who bravely risked his own life to save others. Embedded somewhere deep in his psyche was the sensitive feeling that he could not sit by and suffer seafaring men to drown, and his heroism is now legendary.

In 1830 a massive storm was breaking near Douglas, off the coast of the Isle of Man. The paddle steamer St. George was impaled against the rocks and all hands on board would have perished. Hillary, then aged nearly 60 years, gathered together a crew and, though his usual lifeboat was damaged, he commandeered another and set out to the rescue. A massive wave smashed against the rudder and Hillary was severely injured and had six broken ribs and a crushed breastbone. But he continued, and he and his crew rescued the 22 men on the stricken paddle steamer. Truly, Hillary lived by his motto: 'With courage, nothing is impossible.'

HEROES AND HEROINES OF THE SEA
ENGLAND

Grace Darling

The women have not let themselves down either where daring is concerned. The Victorian heroine of the seas was one, Miss Grace Darling. Grace was born on November 24, 1815. Her father, William was Principal Lighthouse Keeper of the Longstone Lighthouse, on the Farne Islands, and her mother was named Thomasin.

90. *The RNLI Memorial, Poole, Dorset, designed by Mr Sam Holland ARBS, depicting a person in a boat saving another from drowning.*

Grace lived at the lighthouse with her parents, and at 4.15 am on the morning of September 7, 1838, during a howling gale, she saw from an upstairs window in the distance a ship in distress. At 4.00 am the paddle steamer Forfarshire carrying a cargo of clothes and hardware from Hull to Dundee had come to grief on the Big Harkar rocks. The engines had given up and the vessel was drifting southwards in the storm. At 7.00 am Grace, aged only 22 years, and her father, spotted survivors on the wreck trapped on the reef. William and Grace feared that the lifeboats from nearby Bamburgh and North Sunderland would not be able to put to sea in such bad weather. They set out together in the family cobble boat, and rowed for over a mile to the reef through mountainous seas and reached the stricken Forfarshire. Among the surviving crewmembers on board was a Mrs Dawson who was holding the bodies of her two dead children. The Darlings' small boat could only accommodate five people, and they rescued them and rowed back to the safety of the lighthouse where Mrs Darling and Grace attended to them. Then William and another man who was one of those who had been rescued went back to the wreck and rescued others, returning at 9.00 am. Later that day a lifeboat took off another nine survivors and landed them at Tynemouth.

An inquest on September 11, found that the ship had been wrecked due to the 'imperfections of the boilers' and that the ship's Captain Humble was considered negligent. He and his wife had perished in the disaster.

Grace Darling was besieged by scores of people after the story was published in the *Newcastle Journal*. She was said to have reacted with modesty to a national outbreak of hero-worship. She was hunted by the portrait painters, who were practically the equivalent of today's paparazzi. There are paintings in abundance of her, some considered to be a true image, others overly romanticised. Admirers wanted locks of her hair and poets wrote verses about her. The most famous pastoral poet of all, William Wordsworth, [6] wrote a poem about her. She received a number of awards, including a Silver Medal from the Royal National Institute for the Preservation of Life from Shipwreck (later the RNLI), and the Gold Medallion of the Royal Humane Society.

Grace died a month before her 27th birthday of consumption, now called tuberculosis, on October 20, 1842. The Duchess of Northumberland's physician attended to her in her illness, and she spent her last days at her sister Thomasin's house, having been cared for lovingly until the end.

Doris Tart

Mrs Doris Tart of Dungeness, Kent, is likewise revered in modern day RNLI circles. She was the daughter of Coxswain, Mr Douglas Oiller. The coxswain is the person in charge of a boat and his/her responsibility is the boat's navigation and steering. The term came from two words 'cox' meaning 'boat' and 'swain' meaning 'boy in authority', and originally meant 'boat servant'. The coxswain sits in the stern and steers the boat and motivates the rowers. Doris Tart served as a launcher of lifeboats for 44 years. Most of her life she lived in a fisherman's cottage close to the Dungeness lifeboat station. The constantly moving shingles there made launches difficult. Doris and her family and the Oiller family were at the foremost of a group of women who launched the lifeboats as most of the men formed part of the crew. The women had to haul the lifeboat out manually over greased planks of wood on top of the shingle on the beach. Only in 1979 was a tractor provided for the first time to carry out this task. On her retirement, Doris was awarded a Gold Badge. She died, aged 85, on April 30, 2007, at William Harvey Hospital, Ashford, Kent. Her mother-in-law, Ellen, and her aunt Madge were also both awarded the Gold Badge in 1954. They had helped launch the lifeboat for 50 years every time it put out to sea. Mr Douglas Oiller who had been Coxswain from 1916-1947, had received a Bronze Medal for Gallantry. Douglas' father and cousin and Doris' husband received gallantry awards as crewmembers. [7]

High status of the coxwain

During one of Prince Edward's visits to see a lifeboat station and its boats, he was invited to lunch at a local 'fine house'. On seeing the list of guests he remarked that the local coxswain had not been invited. The role of the coxswains in the past has been heroic and his/her presence is considered a mark of respect to all those who went before them, and the crews. Prince Edward refused to attend the lunch unless the coxswain was invited. [8]

Tragedies at sea

RNLI crews and lifeguards have saved over 140,000 lives since the RNLI was formed but there have been tragedies. In 1849, the South Shields lifeboat crew were on their way to rescue a vessel that had overturned in high seas but 20 of the 24 volunteers were themselves lost at sea.

Introduction of life jackets

In 1855 the first rather bulky life jackets were introduced made of cork and worn in a canvas vest. If the lifeboat got into difficulties the crew could stay afloat for a time but in a storm there was little chance of anyone picking them up. However, if their boat overturned, they stood some chance of staying afloat long enough to correct it and then clamber back inside and continue on their journey. They were, however, as much in danger of dying of cold in the sea as they were of drowning.

In 1868 the lifeboat Richard Lewis tried to rescue the crew of the North Britain, which was foundering off the coast of Penzance. The boat overturned, then righted itself but was forced to return to the shore with the coxswain and three crewmembers badly injured. An oarsman offered to try again, and a second crew set out. They managed to snatch the last of the sailors from the ship minutes before it broke up on the rocks.

During terrible storms which lasted two days during December 9-10, 1886, two lifeboats containing 27 volunteers of the Southport and St. Anne's lifeboat services were lost trying to save the crews on board the barque Mexico.

Locations of RNLI Memorials can be found on the RNLI's website.

Role of the lifeboat community

In shipping ports the townsfolk were naturally part of the lifeboat community. When a ship was stranded on the rocks a kind of hue and cry went up and the entire community close to the sea knew of the impending tragedy. Some of them would go to almost any lengths to save the crew of a stricken vessel. In January 1899 the Forest Hall had got into difficulties on the North Devon Coast. The gale was so fierce that the Lynmouth lifeboat could not put out to sea. The townsfolk took it upon themselves to haul the ten-ton lifeboat nine miles over Exmoor to Porlock to where it could be launched. It took them 10½ hours, and when they reached their destination it meant that the boat could be launched behind the wind and no lives were lost. In 1999 the local people re-enacted this feat of bravery.

Methods of launching the lifeboat

The launching of a lifeboat from dry land to the sea meant that for many years it was pulled along the road on wheels by a horse. From 1920 onwards, tractors began to be used to perform the task of hauling lifeboats into the surf. The first steam lifeboat was launched in 1890.

On February 22, 1908, the sailing ship SS Harold was 100 miles off the rocky fangs of Anglesey's Stacks in a fierce storm with winds gusting to 100 miles per hour. The steam-driven lifeboat the Duke of Northumberland came to the rescue.

By 1914 petrol driven lifeboats had been introduced. During a First World War blackout in 1914, a hospital ship the Rohilla struck a reef during a gale. The first attempt at rescue was by five oared lifeboats. Only one managed to save a few people and the others were driven back. A petrol-driven lifeboat the Henry Vernon arriving from Tynemouth proved its superiority on the high seas and saved 146 lives.

First World War 1914-18 – Henry Blogg

The courage of Mr Henry Blogg, a coxswain, is legendary in RNLI circles. In 1917 the Swedish vessel SS Fernebo was split in half by a German mine off the coast of Norfolk. Henry took out a crew on an oared lifeboat in high seas and rescued everyone on board. He served for 53 years and was awarded the RNLI's Gold Medal for Gallantry three times and the Silver Medal four times.

Throughout the First World War, 1,866 rescue launches were made, crewed by heroic veterans. In September 1918 the Lowestoft Lifeboat the Kentwell carried out a 5-hour rescue of the stricken Pomona. The lifesaving crew were not young as the younger men were away fighting the war. Of the volunteers, four were over 50 years of age, 12 were over 60, and two were in their 70s.

Second World War 1939-45 – Dunkirk rescue

During the Second World War (1939-45), during the battle of Dunkirk in France, thousands of British soldiers were trapped on the beaches and in danger of being killed or taken prisoner by the Germans. Hundreds of older men set out in small lifeboats across the English Channel and rescued approximately 300,000 men. Two lifeboats were manned by RNLI crews, the others were provided by naval personnel. On arrival in England the exhausted troops were fed by thousands of sandwiches and cups of tea prepared by women.

There are legendary stretches of treacherous coastline around the shores of England, Scotland, Wales, Northern Ireland, and the Republic of Ireland. During Victorian and Edwardian times and even into the 1940s, many sailing ships from European and foreign parts whose captains did not know of the dangers, met their end on the rocks, particularly in foggy weather when they could not see the warning light of the old, manually-operated lighthouse lanterns.

In January 1942 the Peterhead's lifeboat service were 52 hours at sea on the Julia Park Barry of Glasgow, saving 106 lives. It took Coxswain Mr John McLean to make 12 attempts at approach before he could rescue the 42 crew from the stricken ship. The average age of the lifeboat crew was 55 years.

WALES

The legendary Mumbles disaster took place in 1947. At 6.10 pm on Wednesday, April 23, the lifeboat from The Mumbles, Swansea, went out in a gale to assist the steamer Samtampa of Middlesbrough, Yorkshire. The steamer had been driven onto the rocks off Sker Point, 11 miles south-east of Swansea Bay. No one knows how the tragedy occurred, but next morning the upturned lifeboat was located on the shore, the entire crew having drowned. The coxswain Mr William Gammon had a very distinguished record. He had won the Institution's gold medal for conspicuous gallantry in October 1944, when he rescued 42 people from the Canadian frigate Cheboque. In his 17 years of service he took part in the rescue of 127 people.

The RNLI treated the 19 dependant relatives of the disaster, 11 of whom were children, as if their lost ones had been sailors of the Royal Navy, killed in action in the war, and they were awarded pensions. Princess Marina met the relatives on October 29, when they were presented to her at the Guildhall. The Princess was always good with people, her natural kindness showing through. Similarly, her son Prince Edward, when he met the descendants of the Mumbles disaster, at a memorial service for the 60th anniversary, held in All Saints Church on April 23, 2007 [9], showed the same understanding to the families who had lost loved ones.

SCOTLAND

The Fraserburgh Disaster

The story of the Fraserburgh disaster is particularly tragic. Princess Marina was invited to name a new lifeboat The Duchess of Kent after herself, on Wednesday, July 7, 1954, at the harbour at Fraserburgh in Scotland. The station has a proud history, having been in existence since 1858. It was an occasion of mixed feelings of joy over the new lifeboat and sadness in the wake of the loss of an earlier one The Charles Kennedy, that had capsized in February the previous year, whilst escorting fishing boats into the harbour. Hundreds of townspeople had witnessed the tragedy but were unable to provide assistance because of the heavy seas, and six of the seven crewmembers were lost. The only survivor, the Second Coxswain Mr Charles Tait, had very bravely volunteered his services again, when a new crew was formed twelve days after the tragedy. Miss Margaret Ritchie, daughter of the Coxwain Mr Andrew Ritchie who had lost his life, presented Princess Marina with a bouquet of flowers at the naming ceremony. The President, Lord Saltoun, Chairman of the Scottish Life-boat Council and President of the Fraserburgh branch, made a speech and pointed out that the new lifeboat was a 46-feet 9-inches Watson cabin type built out of RNLI funds. The BBC televised the event and extracts from the President's speech were broadcast. No one could know that 17 years later almost to the day, tragedy would also strike the new lifeboat.

On January 21, 1970, while on service to the Opal, a Danish fishing vessel located 38 miles off Fraserburgh, The Duchess of Kent capsized with the loss of five of the six lives on board. Prince Edward was now President of the RNLI, and stepped into the role of consoling the descendants of the deceased as his mother had done all those years earlier. Sir Richard Buckley can still recall that Prince Edward "was wonderful with the relatives of the Fraserburgh disaster." [10]

ORKNEY ISLANDS

Tragedy of the TGB, Orkney and self-righting lifeboats

During the 1950s diesel engines in lifeboats came into general use, making it somewhat easier and faster to ride the high seas to rescue stranded vessels. In 1956 VHF radio was introduced, followed by radar in 1963, but still tragedies occurred. In 1969 the lifeboat TGB left the Orkney village of Longhope in a severe storm to rescue a tanker that was out of control. The following morning the lifeboat was found capsized and the crew of seven had drowned.

In the disasters that have taken place over the years, many families were bereaved. At Orkney on that occasion there were seven women widowed and eight children left fatherless. This kind of tragedy prompted a return to self-righting lifeboats that, when capsized, did not sink but turned upright again in the water. In 1970 the new Atlantic 21 was introduced. Capable of a speed of 30 knots, this new type of lifeboat would save around 5,000 lives. Still the tragedies continued, though not on the scale of the earlier years.

Just before Christmas on December 19, 1981, the Penlee lifeboat Solomon Browne went out from Penlee Point to help a ship The Union Star which was in difficulties near Lamorna off the Cornish coast. The 8-strong lifeboat crew were from the tiny village of Mousehole. The lifeboat was lost in the fierce storm and all were drowned, as were the eight crew of the ship, including the captain, Mr Henry Moreton, and his wife and two daughters. Attempts had also been made to save them by a Sea King helicopter and a tug but neither could get close enough in the fierce sea, battling against winds gusting at 80-100 miles per hour. Such was the depth of feeling about this tragedy that local fundraising produced an amazing £3 million for the bereaved families. Every year on the anniversary of this tragedy the Christmas lights in Mousehole are switched off for an hour in honour of the memory of those who drowned.

SCOTLAND TODAY

The RNLI's 47 stations in Scotland launched a total of 417 times during the months of June, July, and August, 2012, an increase of 4 per cent compared with the corresponding period in 2011. Significant increases were experienced by stations on the west coast in Troon, Largs, Mallaig, Tobermory, and Campbeltown. The charity's newest lifeboat station at Leverburgh on the Isle of Harris, had seven shouts. The busiest inshore station was Queensferry, where the volunteers had 21 shouts.

Prince Edward visits Portpatrick
On May 25, 2012, Prince Edward visited Portpatrick lifeboat station, during part of his tour of RNLI lifeboat stations in the South west of Scotland. He met members of the volunteer crew of the new RNLI lifeboat, RNLB *John Buchanan Barr*, as well as members of the committee and fundraisers from the lifeboat shop. He was given a tour of the station, shop, and museum. Prince Edward also talked to pupils and teachers from Portpatrick School who, on a sunny morning, had walked to the lifeboat station to greet him.

Troon
The busiest station during the summer was Troon with 25 shouts. The increase in activity coincided with a period of good weather along the west coast of Scotland where the stations were busier than normal. Troon lifeboat station attended a wide variety of incidents, including a rescue that required the co-ordinated efforts of

the police, ambulance, Ayr coastguard, GANET SAR rescue helicopter 177 from Prestwick, and the Troon lifeboat in order to rescue a man in the water.

On July 23, 2012, the volunteer crew at Troon were diverted from a training exercise following reports of a flare sighting west of Troon. They found a man and his dog in a dinghy, the man having taken the decision to abandon his vessel after it capsized at approximately 2.00 pm the day before. They had been adrift and the man had been launching distress flares for approximately 30 hours, until fortunately a flare had been spotted by a vigilant member of the public, and the lifeboat crew arrived on the scene in the nick of time. Mr Colin 'Joe' Millar, Coxswain at RNLI Troon said:

> "It has been an unusually busy summer, we have been called out to a variety of yachts and small pleasure craft, including a windsurfer. We have been consistently called out to incidents to the north and south of the station."

The RNLI's volunteer crew at Tobermory had a huge increase in activity, with a rise from two shouts during the summer of 2011 to 15 during 2012, making them the eighth busiest station in Scotland. Mr Jock Anderson, Tobermory's full-time mechanic, said:

> "...the last three months have been a very busy time for the station. We have responded to a wide range of shouts, including medevacs, several yachts in difficulty, a fishing boat aground in the early hours, and two tragic incidents, which sadly saw two people lose their lives. ... When the pager goes off, the volunteer crew have no idea of what they are about to face but they never hesitate to respond."

Whales washed ashore
One of the more unusual challenges faced by RNLI volunteers occurred at the end of the summer 2012, when a large pod of pilot whales came ashore at Anstruther. The RNLI joined other emergency services in trying to save the whales. Although some of the whales died, Mr Gareth Norman, incident co-ordinator from British Divers Marine Life Rescue said: "The RNLI crew played an invaluable role, without them the rescue could have had a very different outcome." Mr Paul Jennings, the RNLI's Divisional Operations Manager for Southend Central and Shetland said:

> "Once again our volunteer lifeboat crews in Scotland have shown that they are committed and courageous individuals, on stand-by to save lives at sea come rain or shine. Behind the crews are a huge team of volunteers, the station management volunteers, shore helpers and fundraisers, to whom we owe our thanks for ensuring that the RNLI can keep on saving lives at sea."

WALES

Brief history of Porthdinllaen Lifeboat

Porthdinllaen Lifeboat Station is situated near Morfa Nefyn on the north coast of the Lleyn Penninsula in Gwynedd, North Wales.

The 19th century was the age of the sailing ship, both in deep sea and in coastal waters. An isolated region like the Lleyn Peninsula on the west coast of Wales was very dependant on shipping before road and rail transport became viable alternatives. Porthdinllaen, on the northern coast of the peninsula, with its sheltered east-facing bay, became important as a harbour of refuge and a busy seaport. Shipping returns for the period indicate the numbers of vessels that entered the bay: in 1804 there were 655; in 1840, there were 914; and in 1861, there was in excess of 700. Such high volume of traffic meant that many vessels came to grief with considerable loss of life.

In a severe northerly gale on December 2 and 3, 1863, about 18 ships that had been sheltering in Porthdinllaen Bay were driven ashore and wrecked. Mr Robert Rees of Morfa Nefyn, tied a rope around his waist and, with the help of four other men, succeeded in saving a total of 28 lives from the various vessels. For his gallantry Mr Rees was awarded the Bronze Medal from the Board of Trade and their Thanks on Vellum by the RNLI.

A few days later, the Reverend Owen Lloyd Williams of Boduan wrote to the RNLI headquarters in London, giving an account of recent gales and requested that a lifeboat station be established at Porthdinllaen. Formal approval took place at a meeting of the Institution's Committee of Management on March 3, 1864.

A 30 feet x 7 feet 6 inches, 10-oared self-righter lifeboat that had been built in 1858, was then altered and lengthened to a 36 feet x 8 feet, 12-oared self-righter at a cost of £198. The lifeboat arrived at Porthdinllaen on August 26, 1864, having been conveyed free-of-charge between London and Caernarfon by the London & North Western Railway Company, and was then sailed south to Porthdinllaen. The boat was provided out of a donation of £250 to the Institution from Lady Cotton Sheppard of Staffordshire, being the third lifeboat to be donated by that lady and, at a ceremony on September 9, 1864, the boat was formally christened Cotton Sheppard. The Reverend John Hughes was appointed Honorary Secretary of the new station, and Mr Hugh Hughes became the first Coxswain. The first boathouse was built in 1864 at a cost of £140. In 1888 a new lifeboat house and slipway were constructed at a cost of £1,200. In 1893 a special 15 feet long Boarding Boat was built for the station. During 1925-26 the boathouse was extended for the station's first motor lifeboat, and the slipway was extended to 351 feet.

Memorial to hero of the seas Mr Richard Evans

One of Wales' greatest heroes was Mr Richard (Dic) Evans of Moelfre, who rescued 441 people from treacherous seas in his 34 years of service with Moelfre Lifeboat. Mr Evans was awarded the MBE and two RNLI Gold Medals for his heroic sea rescues as Coxswain of the Moelfre Lifeboat. He won his first in 1959, when he led the rescue of the Hindlea of Cardiff that was in distress, having run aground in hurricane force winds gusting to 104 miles per hour. The second medal was presented in 1966, when in that year Dic led the rescue of the Greek motor vessel Nafsiporos. Mr Evan Jones who was a full-time mechanic with the lifeboat, knew Dic well and has this to say:

> "The sea had been his world since he was a small boy and he rescued many a life from the sea." Of the rescues from the Nafsiporos he said the Moelfre lifeboat managed to get alongside the stricken vessel "and took eight men to safety."

Mr Jones thought that a "memorial statue" to his friend "would put Moelfre on the map." He added:

> "Moelfre wasn't that popular before Dic was awarded the gold medal. He used to travel quite a bit after retiring to talk about his experiences."

A memorial statue to remember the life and work of Mr Dic Evans of Moelfre was planned by a group of organisations and individuals, and led by the island's county council. A statue was commissioned from sculptor Sam Holland. Located at the Moelfre Seawatch Centre the unveiling was carried out on November 23, 2004 by His Royal Highness, Charles, Prince of Wales, who also attended a small service in the local Carmel Chapel.

Porthdinllaen today

In 2012 a new boathouse was in the process of being built. Porthdinllaen's newest lifeboat is the Hetty Rampton a 47 feet x 15 feet steel hulled, Tyne Class, self-righting lifeboat, driven by two 425h.p, and General Motors 6V-92 TI Diesel engines that give a top speed of 18 knots. 'Hetty' has been on service at Porthdinllaen since April 27, 1987, having been built at a cost of nearly £560,000 by Fairey Allday Marine at Cowes on the Isle of Wight.The money was provided out of a gift from the trustees of Miss Hetty Mabel Rampton's Charitable Trust. It was a fitting tribute that, at the service of Dedication conducted by the Bishop of Bangor assisted by Reverend E. Wheldon the vicar of Nefyn, Hetty Rampton's neice, Miss Yolande Rampton, should christen the boat Hetty Rampton.

It was timely that a new boat the Tamar was launched in September 2012, re-placing the Tyne. Two kayakers issued a Mayday call. They had set off from Aber-daron Bay and were two miles offshore and were unable to make any headway due to deteriorating weather. The British Warship HMS Tyne was also responding to the Mayday call and making headway towards the kayakers when the RNLI lifeboat arrived first.

ISLE OF MAN

Brief history

The first lifeboat station was established at Douglas, Isle of Man in 1802, and closed in 1895. A second, established in 1874, is still at work. The first one would appear to have lapsed about 1851, and was reopened in 1868. Douglas was one of the earliest places in the British Isles to be provided with a lifeboat. One was sent there in 1802, having been ordered by the Duke of Atholl. It was one of 31 boats built by Mr Henry Greathead, builder of the first lifeboat station on the mouth of the Tyne in 1789.

On September 10, 1824, the Institution received a request from Sir William Hillary for a lifeboat for Douglas '... on account of the frequent gales and wrecks in Douglas Bay.' Built by Pellow Plenty of Newbury, Berkshire, the boat was sent in October 1825. Two years later, Cato of Liverpool built a larger boat, 29 feet long with 10 oars, and the two boats seem to have been in operation at the same time.

Heroic rescues and awards

During the years 1824 to 1851, it is reported that 91 lives were saved by the Douglas lifeboat. Sir William Hillary was awarded the Gold medal as founder of the RNLI, and won three other Gold medals for gallantry.

The other heroic rescues carried out by Douglas Lifeboat crews over the years are too many to list here. Since 1825, one other Gold medal and 15 Silver medals have been awarded to personnel from Douglas Station that includes Hillary's son Augustus, who was awarded a Silver medal in 1828.

On February 2, 1833, Coxswain, Mr Isaac Vondy, who went out with two lifeboats and rescued 52 people from the ship Parkfield, was exceptionally awarded two Silver medals for his services. Mr William Milburn rescued 8 people from the schooner Vernon on May 19, 1837, and was awarded a Silver medal. In 1881, the No.2 lifeboat with a crew of 13 capsized, having rescued 14 men and two women from the Barge Lebu of Liverpool in a heavy gale. Unfortunately, in the darkness, four members of the crew and seven of the rescued seamen were drowned. The Committee of Management voted £400 to the local fund for the relief of the dependants. In 1893 the Committee of Management voted £100 to the widow of the second Coxswain, Mr John David Hay, whose death was attributed to catching a cold on exercise in July, and Mrs Hay was left with three children to bring up on her own. She had been formerly married to one of the crew of the lifeboat who was also lost whilst on service in 1881, at which time she was left with four children.

In 1952 Douglas received the 150th Commemorative Vellum award. On January 5, 1997, a service was held to commemorate the 150th anniversary of the death of Sir William Hillary, and a Vellum was presented by the RNLI to record the occasion. In 1999 Coxswain Mr Robert Corran was awarded an MBE in the Queen's Birthday Honours List.

ISLE OF MAN TODAY

Today there are five lifeboat stations on the Isle of Man. The Tyne class lifeboat at

Douglas is named the Sir William Hillary, and Peel's all-weather lifeboat, the Ruby Clery is a Mersey class lifeboat. Lifeboat launches from the Isle of Man rose to 47 in 2012. Manx RNLI lifeboats rescued 68 people, the highest number since 2009. The most dramatic increase in 2012 was at Peel, where 26 people were brought to safety, nearly double the number recorded in 2011. Several of the callouts were to kayaks in trouble and it is thought that with more leisure time and more crafts on the water the callout rate may well increase. The crews have been presented with 21 awards for gallantry that include medals and vellums.

NORTHERN IRELAND

Due to the rugged, rocky coastline around Northern Ireland on the shores of the Irish Sea, there exists a long history of sailing shipwrecks and loss of life and rich cargoes. At the lifeboat station in Portaferry, County Down, on the shores of Strangford Lough, fishermen and women still put to sea today, along with other fishing villages in the area such as Cloughey, Portavogie, Ballywalter, and Ballyhalbert, situated on the Ards Peninsula, and Strangford, which is directly opposite Portaferry and is accessed by a car and foot passenger ferry across a mile-long stretch of Strangford Lough.

RNLI Portaferry – A Brief History

Two early lifeboat stations had been established in the area, one in 1865, at Ballywalter, and another in the small coastal village of Cloughey, in 1884, both on the Ards Peninsula. Their first lifeboat *The Faith* was commissioned in 1885. The Cloughey Lifeboat Station had been incorporated with Portavogie, a nearby fishing village, but it was closed in 1981, after the Portaferry Lifeboat Station was opened on May 1, 1980.

On the East Coast of Northern Ireland there are many hazards between Burr Island and Killard Point. They include some notorious danger points for boats and ships in days of old where they got into trouble on the rocks; the South and North Rocks, the Rig, the Butter Pladdy, and half-tide rocks off Ballyquinton Point. It was due to the large number of shipwrecks in the 19th century that lifeboat stations were established in the area. Between 1884 and 1978, Cloughey Lifeboat was called out on 152 rescue missions and saved 311 lives.

Some daring rescues

On December 19, 1982, a daring rescue was carried out at night in winds that increased from Gale 8 to Storm Force 10. The casualty was the yacht Frieda that had run aground at Jane's Rock in Strangford Lough. One of the crew was rescued and a search for the second crewmember was carried out amongst what is known in Northern Ireland as the pladdies (meaning an islet or bank in the middle of the water), in appalling weather conditions. For their bravery the Chief Helmsman, Mr Desmond Rogers of Portaferry was awarded the RNLI's Bronze Medal, and his crewmembers Mr Billy Ellison and Mr Francis Rogers were awarded the RNLI's Thanks on Vellum. Mr Roger's wife Bernadette has been Secretary of Portaferry

RNLI for over 30 years, and in 2005, received a Gold Badge, presented to her by Prince Edward for her 25 years of service.

Another memorable rescue

Another memorable rescue was that of the 12 persons on board the converted fishing vessel Tornamona that went aground and sank in the early hours of Sunday morning, May 26, 1985. The vessel had been on her way from Portaferry to the Isle of Man when she struck rocks near Killard Point at the entrance to Strangford Lough. Two of those on board were world famous motor cycling champion, Mr Joey Dunlop, and his brother Robert. Also on board was a cargo of eight racing motorbikes for use during the Isle of Man Tourist Trophy races. As the vessel began to sink, Portaferry Lifeboat arrived on the scene to find eight persons in a life raft and four others still on board. The lifeboat took several persons to safety, assisted by the Cuan Shore, which had been on its way to the scene.

Prince Edward visits Portaferry

In 1985 Prince Edward arrived in Portaferry as part of an official tour of Northern Ireland. He was met by the late Major William Brownlow the Lord Lieutenant of County Down, who was then Chairman of Portaferry Lifeboat, and by other local dignitaries. Prince Edward spent his time there talking to the crew and the staff, and then had dinner in the Portaferry Hotel on the quayside. [11] Captain Edward McGee and his wife Marie also met Prince Edward. [12] Captain McGee has given his recollection of Prince Edward on that important day in the life of this small seaside town, proudly receiving a member of the royal family:

> "His Royal Highness was a lovely, lovely, man, dressed in an immaculate grey suit. He was very knowledgeable about RNLI operations, and his questions were expert and to the point. This was not just a figurehead but someone who took a real interest in the work. He asked me about my work as Treasurer, (then raising about £15,000 a year).
>
> "He also made a special point of asking the mobile shop team about their work. This they very much appreciated, making them feel that their contribution really mattered and boosting their confidence. He was very 'hands on', sincere, and fitted in at every level with the people he spoke to. Everyone felt very comfortable with him, and the visit was a great boost to morale." [13]

Captain McGee was awarded the Bronze Badge in January 2003. Sylvia, The Lady Hermon, who is the Independent Member of Parliament for North Down to the Westminster Parliament, made the presentation. Captain McGee also received the well-deserved Silver Badge in 2008, for his tireless services to the RNLI over 20 years. His wife Marie has, since 1994, raised vast sums of money, and for the 25th anniversary ball provided beautiful flower arrangements. Along with Station Training Officer and Helmsman, Mr Jonathan Brownlee, Mrs McGee was awarded

91. Captain Edward McGee, RNLI,
Portaferry Branch, receiving a Certificate of Thanks
and a bronze badge from Sylvia, Lady Hermon.

the Certificate of Thanks, presented by the well-known Ulster television presenter, Pamela Ballentine.

Today, Major Brownlow's widow Eveleigh is President of Portaferry Lifeboats. Eveleigh related the following amusing and somewhat hair-raising tale to the authors about the day Prince Edward visited:

"My late husband went with His Royal Highness in his helicopter from Portaferry to Kilkeel and back to Newcastle. There we had lunch in my old home where I was born, The Turrett, now Enniskeen Hotel. In spite of His Royal Highness very kindly asking me to go in his helicopter too, [Eveleigh laughed heartily] the pilot said I would be too heavy! So I went with the security boys in their helicopter, skimming the Mourne Mountains with the doors open. It was one of the most beautiful, clear, sunny days, which I will never forget.

"The Duke is a wonderful President of the RNLI, we are very lucky to have him, his knowledge and enthusiasm is amazing." [14]

New lifeboat station for Portaferry

In 2008 the people of Portaferry and surrounding areas were busily collecting money to build the new RNLI lifeboat station in the town, directly opposite the quay on The Strand. [15] Captain Edward McGee, his wife Marie, and Mrs Eveleigh Brownlow worked very hard, selling gold bricks at £20 each, and in the region of £1 million

92. Mrs Marie McGee, RNLI, Portaferry Branch, receiving a Certificate of Thanks from ITV's Pamela Ballentine, January 2005.

was raised. Eveleigh, who in her role as President, was awarded an RNLI gold badge takes up the story again:

> "Our new *Atlantic 85* Lifeboat will make a huge difference to life saving – bigger, faster – it will take on extra crewmen and women, and also has radar which will take the research element out of the service as it should direct the crew straight to the casualty, and as a result rescue many more people from drowning. We have a wonderful crew, they won the Ardglass Award – an award that had never come to Ireland before."

In June 2014 Eveleigh got something of a surprise, when she received a letter from Buckingham Palace telling her she had been awarded an MBE in the Queen's Birthday Honours List to be presented to her that autumn.

TV's Blue Peter and the children
In December 1986 a new Atlantic 21 fast, inshore, lifeboat was presented to the Portaferry lifeboat station by Blue Peter, the British Broadcasting Corporation's (BBC's) children's television programme. Children from throughout the UK and the Republic of Ireland raised the monies to provide this and other Blue Peter lifeboats in former years. Named Blue Peter V, and with its close association with children,

the new boat was launched with a bottle of milk by 10-year-old Miss Paula Trainor. Paula was chosen to make the launch because she is a descendant of the family named Young of Cloughey, who provided so many coxswains and crewmembers for the former Cloughey lifeboat over many decades. Paula was photographed holding the RNLI's Bronze Medal that had been awarded in 1924 to her great great grand-uncle, Mr Andrew Young, and the Bronze Medal that was awarded in 1939 to her great grand-uncle, Mr George M. Young.

Portaferry has had an inshore lifeboat station since 1980. A new lifeboat house was built and opened in 2007. Captain Edward McGee, formerly of the Merchant Navy, has worked for the RNLI voluntarily as Honorary Treasurer since 1994. The work of the RNLI team based in Portaferry is testimony to the intensive fund-raising that takes place for the RNLI in general, and amounting to £20-£25,000 per annum. The funds helped the rebuild of the lifeboat station in Portaferry.

Miss Anna Classon, the RNLI Manager in Dublin, came up with the buy a brick scheme, whereby contributors could buy a brick for the new building, one brick £5 (bronze), two bricks £10 (silver); four bricks £20 (gold). Everyone making a contribution received a certificate, sent out by the Belfast Office.

The Portaferry RNLI Station costs about £12,000 a year to run and their Guild raises nearly twice that sum per annum. They are therefore able to assist the other local RNLI stations with their surplus. As Captain McGee explained to the authors:

"Fundraising for the RNLI reaches across the so-called political divide and all the churches and schools contribute generous sums." Dr David Peacock, Captain of the Kircubbin Golf Club and a well-known general practitioner at the Portaferry Health Clinic, organises donations of £5-6,000 a year. Tesco's and The Wildfowlers, Newtownards, collect respectively, £1,500 and £500-£1,000. Every Easter Monday there is a collection at the Ferry Slip in Strangford that raises £2,000."

Round the corner from the lifeboat station in Castle Street is Portaferry Visitor Information Centre, located in the precinct of the former stables of the historic, stone-built, 16th century castle of the Savages of the Ards. Mrs Linda Ritchie who is well-known in the community is the Visitor Information Adviser.

Another new Blue Peter lifeboat

Portaferry is, today, one of seven RNLI lifeboat stations operating a lifeboat that is funded by viewers of the BBC's television programme Blue Peter. There has been in recent years an increase in pleasure boating and yachting activity in Strangford Lough, with many yachts moored at Portaferry slip. Apart from the expanse of sea for boating, fishing, and sailing activities, the added attraction is that Portaferry and Strangford Lough are areas of outstanding natural beauty and wildlife preservation. On June 6, 2010, a new Atlantic 85 lifeboat was presented to the Station by the BBC's Blue Peter, also named Blue Peter V. The new lifeboat carries a crew of four and has updated electronics such as radar and direction finding equipment.

During 2011 the latest Blue Peter V was launched on service 30 times and rescued 23 people, during which the lifeboat crew spent 179 hours at sea. In addition to shore-based training the station's volunteer crew also spent 365 hours at sea whilst on exercise. During 2012 the lifeboat was launched to incidents on 23 occasions, 11 of which were in darkness. They rescued 16 people which meant they spent 252 hours at sea.

2014 World Championships

During the 2014 GP14 sailing World Championships on Strangford Lough, an incident took place outside Killyleagh Harbour on August 12. High winds and freak waves created a ferocious squall, causing many vessels to overturn, and 20 sailors were tipped into the sea. A major rescue operation took place from Portaferry Lifeboats, backed up by helicopters sent in from Dublin. Modern life-saving, training, and equipment ensured that all the sailors were rescued and the race went ahead.

Lifeguards

RNLI Lifeguards were first introduced into Northern Ireland in 2011, operating on seven beaches along the Causeway coast. They now cover an additional three beaches in County Down, Newry, and Mourne. There were 413 calls for help to the RNLI lifeboats and lifeguards in Northern Ireland in 2012, and the lifeboats were launched 255 times. Over the course of a year, across the region, 201 people were rescued by volunteer lifeboat crews operating from the 10 RNLI Lifeboat Stations. Crews spent over 1,726 hours at sea, while the newly introduced RNLI lifeguards operating on seven beaches along the Causeway coast recorded 114 incidents and helped 123 people. Of the services provided, 111 took place in darkness. Including training exercises, crews collectively spent 2,193 service hours at sea.

Lifejackets for Lifesavers campaign

The RNLI's Lifejackets for Lifesavers campaign saw every lifeboat station in Northern Ireland take delivery in 2012 of new, specially-designed lifejackets. The lifejackets were commissioned by the RNLI for search and rescue work and have been given the seal of approval by lifeboat volunteers. The cost was estimated at £26,500.

Bangor Lifeboat Station, County Down

Bangor Lifeboat Station situated on the north east coast on the shores of Belfast Lough, was the busiest, launching to 53 requests for help with the crew rescuing 53 people off the County Down coast. The station operates a B class *Atlantic 85* lifeboat, and has provided search and rescue cover for the area for over 40 years.

The Queen's Diamond Jubilee Medals awarded

A combined total of 360 years' service to the RNLI by 20 members of the Bangor Lifeboat Station was recognised with a presentation of the Queen's Diamond Jubilee medals at the Royal Ulster Yacht Club in 2012. Mr Ewan Scott and Mr

Tommy Burns were awarded Long Service medals at recent RNLI ceremonies. Both Helmsmen, who are also Quay Marinas Berthing Masters, were awarded the medals in recognition of their many years of devoted service to the RNLI. Both Ewan and Tommy agree that over the years, there have been many improvements to the lifeboats and the equipment and training, all of which has greatly enhanced the RNLI's ability to save lives at sea. Even after 20 years of service, Ewan and Tommy continue to freely give of their time and effort. They are considered by all to be the most experienced helmsmen at Bangor station, and are actively involved in the training of crew and other volunteers. During their 20 years of dedicated service, RNLI Bangor Lifeboat has undertaken a total of 845 rescues, resulting in the saving of 98 lives.

Donaghadee Lifeboat station, County Down

Situated on the north east coast of County Down, Donaghadee's first lifeboat station was set up in 1910, by a team of local businessmen, along with many from the fishing industry and boatmen. On July 10, they received their first Lifeboat, the *William & Laura,* a Watson Class with sails, 10 oars, and a 40-horse power petrol engine. It cost £3,599 and was launched 61 times, saving 65 lives.

Prince Edward visited Donaghadee Lifeboat station in 1985, and much enjoyed the warm reception, hospitality, and the lovely views from the harbour across the sea. [15]

The Princess Victoria sinks, 1953

Donaghadee Lifeboat was involved in one of the most dramatic rescues ever, when MV Princess Victoria sank on January 31, 1953. Built in 1947, the vessel was one of the earliest roll-on/roll-off (ro-ro) ferry services, operating between Stranraer, Scotland, and Larne, County Antrim. Captained by Mr James Ferguson, the Princess Victoria left Stranraer at 07:45 am carrying 44 tons of cargo and 128 passengers and 51 crew. There was a severe storm and in the North Channel, the vessel started taking in water on the car deck and began to sink. Two ships went to the aid of the stricken vessel but the storm was so severe and visibility so poor they had difficulty seeing it. Small lifeboats that could have been launched were in danger of being dashed to pieces against the sides of the ships. All they could do was provide shelter from the worst of the storm until the Donaghadee lifeboat, the Sir Samuel Kelly, arrived and was able to bring survivors on board.

Of the 180 people on board the stricken vessel, 133 drowned, including the Deputy Prime Minister of Northern Ireland, Major Maynard Sinclair, and the Member of Parliament for North Down, Lieutenant-Colonel Sir Walter Smiles. It was the worst maritime disaster in United Kingdom waters since the Second World War. The lifeboat crew on the *Sir Samuel Kelly* rescued 34 passengers, but sadly, there were no women or children among the 40 survivors. The Coxswain, Mr Hugh Nelson, was awarded a Bronze Medal and the British Empire Medal for the skill, courage, and initiative, shown during the rescue. 2013 was the 60th anniversary of the tragedy. The lifeboat *Sir Samuel Kelly* has been preserved in the Ulster Folk and Transport Museum, Hollywood, County Down.

Donaghadee RNLI today

The crews of the Donaghadee Lifeboat have been presented with three awards for gallantry that includes a Bronze Medal. Today, Donaghadee is home to one of the most modern lifeboats in the world. An all-weather Trent Class lifeboat named *Saxon* that cost about £1.3 million has a top speed of around 25 knots, and an operating distance of over 100 miles. It is equipped to carry out sea rescues in even the very worst of conditions in the Irish Sea and beyond.

Nine Lies rock band raises funds

A Northern Ireland rock band, Nine Lies, released a single titled *Tragedy* to raise money for the RNLI. The track is available along with a video from all major online retailers. Speaking about the song, Donaghadee RNLI Coxswain Mr Philip McNamara said: "We are delighted that a group from Northern Ireland have chosen the RNLI to benefit from the sale of their single Tragedy."

Enniskillen, County Fermanagh

Enniskillen has the newest lifeboat station in Northern Ireland. It operates from two bases on Upper and Lower Lough Erne. It is Northern Ireland's only inland RNLI station and is classed as a Discover station meaning the boathouses are open to visitors during the summer months. In 2012 lifeboats were launched 46 times bringing 50 people to safety. Twenty of these services were carried out in dark of night, and crews spent a total of 169 service hours on the water.

A new lifeboat station is in place at Carrybridge, Upper Lough Erne. It cost £60,000 and the money was provided by subscriptions and fund-raising events, and it was built by Woodvale Construction, Omagh, County Tyrone. At the hand-over on March 25, 2015, Mr Derek Potter, RNLI Divisional Technical Manager who is well pleased with the new station said:

> "From the outset, we wanted to build a modern station with full crew facilities, with areas for the crew to change and train, and space to keep the lifeboat and rescue watercraft and lifesaving kit safe. We now have those facilities ... and are delighted with both the design and quality of the building."

Portrush, County Antrim

Portrush Lifeboat Station, situated on the Causeway coast, has been in operation for over 145 years. In 2012 lifeboats were launched 33 times and rescued 33 people in 2012. They were extraordinarily busy in 2014, when the temperature reached 27 degrees Celsius. The lifeboat crews have been presented with 28 awards of gallantry.

Portrush is also classed an Explore station, meaning it offers the best visitor experience for those wishing to go in and look around or book a tour. A Raft Race has been held each year for over 30 years, and involves events for all the family. Today it is watched by hundreds of spectators and the emphasis is on raft design and crew costumes rather than speed. The 2014 race raised £3,000.

REPUBLIC OF IRELAND

Dun Laoghaire (Dun Leary) Lifeboat Station – Brief History
Lifeboats have been based on Dublin Bay for more than 200 years, and this service is one of the oldest in the world. The first lifeboat for the area was placed at Sandycove in 1803, by the Dublin Ballast Board. In 1817 they placed another at Old Dunleary. Before the RNLI took over the lifeboat stations, many rescues took place off the coast of the Irish Sea which sweeps out to the Atlantic Ocean. A number of medals have been awarded, one Gold in 1829, and seven Silver between 1844 and 1861. In 1861 the RNLI took over the lifeboat station. [16]

Medal awards and heroism
In 1868 Silver Medals were awarded to Mr Edmund Gray and to Mr John Freeney for saving five men from the schooner Blue Vein. A Silver Medal was awarded to Coxswain Mr Henry Williams in 1881, for carrying out a rescue to the wreck of the ship the George H. Oulton. On December 24, 1895, No.2 lifeboat capsized on service to the steamship Palme, and 15 lifeboat crewmen lost their lives. The No.1 lifeboat also capsized but fortunately all the crew were able to get safely back to shore. The next day, Mr Thomas McCombie, Captain of the steamship Tearaght, rescued the 20 crewmembers off the Palme, for which he was awarded a Gold Medal. There is a memorial to the 15 life-boatmen overlooking the harbour, close to the lifeboat moorings.

In 1947 The Thanks of the Institution Inscribed on Vellum was awarded by the RNLI to Acting Second Coxswain Mr W. Kelly for saving 45 people from the Bolivar. A Bronze Medal was awarded to Coxswain/Mechanic Mr Eric Offer in 1969 for rescuing two men from their capsized dinghies. He was also presented with the Maud Smith Award. The station was presented with a 150th anniversary Vellum in 1975. Mr Eamon O'Leary, who rescued, single-handedly, five men, one of who had suffered a heart attack, and a young boy from a capsized dinghy was, in 1990, awarded The Thanks on Vellum. To date two Gold Medals, 10 Silver Medals, one Bronze Medal, and four Thanks on Vellum have been awarded. In 2001 a new D class lifeboat, Tony Heard, was placed on service, having been funded by a legacy from Mr Tony Heard.

REPUBLIC OF IRELAND LIFEBOATS TODAY

That the work of the RNLI covers the whole of the United Kingdom and the Republic of Ireland is a fine demonstration of the ability of sea-farers to rise above any and all difficulties in the interests of those at peril on the sea.

There are 34 lifeboat stations in the Republic of Ireland, and in 2013, they rescued over 832 people. The majority of callouts were to pleasure craft, making for 430 launches, and to fishing vessels, 121 launches.

Dun Laoghaire RNLI brought the highest number of people to safety, with 67 individuals rescued by their volunteer lifeboat crews during 58 callouts.

RNLI Lifeboat Operations Manager for Dun Laoghaire, Mr Stephen Wynne commented:

"The two RNLI lifeboats at Dun Laoghaire recorded a sharp increase in the number of people rescued in 2012 and 2013, which we attribute to the nature of a number of incidents that occurred. Like our colleagues around the coast, station volunteers train weekly in preparation for a variety of situations."

Dun Laoghaire RNLI's all-weather lifeboat and Howth RNLI's inshore lifeboat rescued six people on Dublin Bay in August 2013, after their boat capsized and they were left clinging to the upturned hull.

In July 2013 30 people were rescued by Kinsale and Courtmacsherry lifeboat crews, when the tall ship Astrid was blown onto rocks and started to take on water and later sank.

In 2014 a Trent class all-weather lifeboat (ALB), RNLB Anna Livia, and a D-class (ILB) inshore lifeboat Realt Na Mara, were stationed at Dun Laoghaire, where there are 35 volunteers involved in lifeboat operations. They have fund-raising volunteers and there is also a gift-shop.

Lough Ree Coosan Point Lifeboat, located on the River Shannon on the south lake of the shores of Athlone in County Westmeath was newly opened in 2012. Operating a 75 Atlantic Class lifeboat, the station has 18 volunteer crewmembers. During the summer of 2014 they received 43 callouts, four of which were within a 24-hour period.

Following a 16-year campaign, a new lifeboat station was opened in 2014, at Keelbag Pier, Union Hall, County Cork, bringing the number of stations in Ireland to 45. Their B Class Atlantic 75 lifeboat is in operation as a declared search and rescue asset, and there is 16 volunteer crewmembers including six helms. Village children lined the pier, cheerfully waving flags in welcome of the vessel.

Prince Edward's 2013 tour

During May 1 to 3, 2013, Prince Edward, accompanied by the British Ambassador Mr Domnick Chilcott, carried out a tour of visits to RNLI stations in the Republic of Ireland.

Prince Edward visited the Youghal RNLI station. Considered one of Ireland's premier seaside costal resorts, the town of Youghal sits on the estuary of the River Blackwater in County Cork. Mr Fergus Hopkins, Youghal RNLI Lifeboat Operations Manager, and Mr Tadgh Kellegher, Chairman of Youghal RNLI, welcomed Prince Edward. He was then taken on a tour of the station, where he chatted with members of the crew, station personnel, and the fundraising committee.

Prince Edward then went on to visit lifeboat stations in Helvick, Tramore, and Dunmore East, Co Waterford. Again, he met local dignitaries, including the Mayor of Dungarvan Councillor Mr Micheál Cosgrove, and Waterford County Deputy Mayor Mr John Pratt. In his words of welcome, Mr Eamon Mansfield from Helvick Head RNLI said:

"A Shoilse Riogach, Ambasadoir na Breataine, agus a uaisle go leir. [17] Your Royal Highness, Your Excellency, in welcoming you Sir to Helvick Lifeboat Station, I am conscious of the honour you do us as President of the RNLI in recognising the long association which we have with the Institution, an association which goes back for over a century."

Mr Mansfield went on to say that he had been present at Poole in Dorset, when Prince Edward dedicated the memorial to the lifeboat men who had given their lives in the course of their duty and that:

"… on the memorial were inscribed the names of six men from this area who made that ultimate sacrifice. The crew you honour by your presence here today are worthy successors of these men and continue a tradition of courage and of service which in these islands binds us together in our common purpose of saving lives at sea."

In thanking Mr Mansfield and the crew, Prince Edward said:

"You are all very special ordinary people doing the extraordinary, and you deserve great credit for this. It takes an enormous commitment to keep a station afloat and to provide the latest safety equipment and training for our brave crewmembers, and the fundraising committee are the backbone of this."

Prince Edward was presented with a piece of exquisite Irish Criostal na Rinne (Ring Crystal), designed and cut by former RNLI crewmember, and now Deputy Launching Authority, Mr Eamonn Ó Turraoin.

THE CHANNEL ISLANDS

The Channel Islands are an archipelago of British Crown Dependencies in the English Channel, off the French coast of Normandy. They include two separate bailiwicks: the Bailiwick of Guernsey and the Bailiwick of Jersey. They are considered the remnants of the Duchy of Normandy, and are therefore not part of the United Kingdom.

The Channel Islands Air Search Service works closely with the RNLI Channel Island lifeboats based in Alderney, Guernsey, and Jersey, and search operations are co-ordinated by the harbourmaster of the island closest to the search area.

JERSEY

St. Helier Lifeboat Station

For over 120 years a lifeboat has operated from St. Helier, excepting the years of the

Second World War, when Jersey was occupied by the Germans.

RNLI Jersey is a highly trained team of volunteers operating from two lifeboat stations, St. Helier and St. Catherine's. During the summer months, they are supported by paid lifeguards, who patrol Jersey's western beaches. The St. Helier lifeboat launched 26 times in 2012. Crewmembers from St. Helier Lifeboat Station have been awarded four Gold Medals for gallantry, nine Bronze Medals, and seven Silver Medals. Mr Andy Hurley, the RNLI regional operations manager, said:

> "I'm delighted to say the numbers [of lives lost] are down which I hope means our prevention messages are getting through to people before they go onto the water.
>
> "However we have seen a rise in the number of fishing boats needing our assistance and in rescues of people ashore – that's folk who are perhaps injured, trapped or cut off by the tide around the sea shore and cliffs."

GUERNSEY

St. Peter Port Lifeboat Station

The first Lifeboat Station on Guernsey was established at St. Sampsons in 1803, following representation to the then States of Guernsey by the Douzaine (local parish council) of St. Peter Port. The Station was taken over by the RNLI in 1861, and subsequently moved to the capital St. Peter Port, in 1881, where it is still based today. It is one of only four stations in the Channel Islands. The island has always been proud to support the lifeboat station and crews. They operate an all-weather lifeboat and they have been honoured with several awards for gallantry.

The station has seen a variety of lifeboats over the years. In 1973 a special appeal raised a considerable sum towards the cost of the Arun class Sir William Arnold. In the 1990s an appeal was launched to raise £1 million to support the building of the Spirit of Guernsey. Thanks to the generosity of friends in Guernsey, Sark, Herm, and further a-field, the target was achieved within one year. The Severn class Spirit of Guernsey is the lifeboat currently in use.

The Severn

The Severn class lifeboat is the largest lifeboat used by the RNLI. The class has been named after the River Severn, the longest river in Great Britain. There are 46 Severn class lifeboats serving the RNLI around the coast of the UK and Ireland, since the introduction of the class in 1996. It carries a Y Class inflatable boat, which can be deployed by an on-board crane for use in shallow water.

Severns have a comprehensive electronics fit, including full MF and VHF DSC radio equipment, DGPS Navigator, an electronic chart system, VHF/DF, radar and weather sensors. For added manoeuvrability, in addition to twin engines, the Severn also has a bow thruster fitted. The propellers are enclosed so the Severn can take ground without damaging them. The Severn is constructed of fibre reinforced composite material, and the hard chine semi-displacement hull built to a two-compartment standard, means it can stay afloat with two of its five compartments flooded. Provision for survivors includes comprehensive first aid equipment, stretchers, oxygen, and Entonox. Severns carry a portable salvage pump in a watertight container, and can also carry out pumping and fire-fighting tasks using the engine driven general service pump.

Part 2

The modern-day RNLI

There are four main aspects of the RNLI today: **lifeboats, lifeguards, safety advice, and flood rescue.** In addition, there is their International work which is treated separately in the section following.

RNLI – Their purpose, values, vision, and achievements

There are now, in 2015, over 230 lifeboat stations located in England, Scotland, Wales, Northern Ireland, the Republic of Ireland, the Isle of Man, and the Channel Islands.

The combined figures for 2013, show that RNLI lifeboats and hovercraft were launched on service on 8,304 occasions, rescuing 8,384 people and saving 325 lives. There is the usual peak during the summer months when more boats and people take to the sea. Launches to vessels suffering machinery failure still account for the largest number of callouts. The busiest beaches were Perranporth with 872 incidents, Gwithian with 466 incidents, Porthtowan with 429 incidents in Cornwall, and Bantham in south Devon, with 429 incidents.

The RNLI views itself as the charity whose purpose is to save lives at sea. They provide an on-call-24-hour-a-day lifeboat search and rescue service, and a seasonal lifeguard service. Their values reflect the way they perform as an organisation. Their vision is to end preventable loss of life at sea and their lifesaving service is provided, wherever possible by unpaid volunteers. They possess exceptional expertise in the preservation of life at sea and on the water, through prevention and rescue. They are dependable, always available, committed to doing their part in saving lives with professionalism and expertise, continuously developing and improving, and working in and for the community. Aware of a changing and challenging environment, they are determined in their mission to save more lives at sea.

Volunteers

The people of the United Kingdom, the Republic of Ireland, the Isle of Man, and the Channel Islands, depend on the RNLI, and the RNLI depends on its network of volunteers. They are at work on lifeboats, at lifeboat stations, on beaches, as community fundraisers, in RNLI shops, as education presenters in schools, at events, as sea safety officers in coastal communities, at museums, and in their offices. The services required of volunteers involves crewing the lifeboats, raising vital funds for the RNLI, using professional skills in their offices, and a wide variety of other volunteer roles, including occasional volunteering where regular volunteering is too much of a commitment for the individual.

Lifeboat and shore crews

It is the RNLI's volunteer crewmembers that are the backbone of the lifeboat service, physically saving lives at sea. There are more than 4,600 volunteer lifeboat crewmembers at stations, and another 3,000 volunteer shore crewmembers supporting them. They are available 24 hours a day, 7 days a week, and throughout the year, whatever the weather, to rescue those who need help.

In addition to the crew, it takes many more volunteers to run a lifeboat station effectively. The Lifeboat Operations Manager is in charge of authorising launches and the day-to-day station management. The Lifeboat Management Group, also made up of volunteers, represents the station in the local community. Each station has a volunteer Lifeboat Press Officer who produces press releases and promotes the station's activity in local and regional media. There is also a Lifeboat Medical Adviser at every station, performing the crews' medicals, and giving casualty care and scenario training.

Lifeboat fleet

The RNLI has an active fleet of over 340 lifeboats, ranging from 3.8m to 17m in length, as well as a relief fleet. There are also four active and three relief hovercraft. Different classes of lifeboat are needed for various locations, depending on geographical features, the kind of rescue work that the station is asked to do, and the cover provided by neighbouring stations.

RNLI lifeboats are divided into two categories: all-weather and inshore. All-weather lifeboats (ALBs) are capable of high speed and can be operated safely in all weather. They are inherently self-righting after capsize and are fitted with navigation, location and communication equipment. Inshore lifeboats (ILBs) usually operate closer to shore than ALBs, and in shallower water, close to cliffs, among rocks or even in caves. Hovercraft can operate in areas such as mud flats or river estuaries that are inaccessible to conventional lifeboats.

Prince Edward visits RNLI Headquarters Poole, 2010

Prince Edward made a special visit to the RNLI's headquarters at Pool, Dorset, on Thursday April 22, 2010. Having put on a life jacket he was taken on a trip out to sea by staff and crew, aboard the charity's newest lifeboat the Fast Carriage Boat 2 (FCB2) that was then undergoing sea trials.

Back on dry land, he toured the boatyard, where staff explained the work carried out there, including the important service, repair and maintenance procedures that ensure the lifeboats remain fit for service.

Prince Edward was then taken to The Lifeboat College, where RNLI crew training takes place and he talked to staff involved in the development of FCB2, to find out more about the design and technology behind the vessel, most especially, how it would benefit the RNLI's volunteers when it became fully operational. Mr Chris Eves, RNLI FCB2, Project Manager, said:

"It was a great honour to welcome The Duke of Kent to RNLI headquarters today. As our President, he shows a great deal of interest in the charity and its lifesaving work. It was very exciting to be able to show him the FCB2 experimental lifeboat and take him afloat on it, and thereafter show him the design and development of the prototype. He seemed to enjoy his visit and found out more about the work that goes on behind the scenes to ensure the RNLI's volunteer crews have the very best lifeboats and equipment to continue saving lives at sea."

The Shannon-class lifeboat has since succeeded the FCB2 and is the latest class of lifeboat currently being deployed to the RNLI fleet. [18]

RNLI Inshore Lifeboat Centre

The RNLI constructs up to 60 per cent of the lifeboats it needs in its own purpose-built manufacturing facility the Inshore Lifeboat Centre (ILC) in East Cowes on the Isle of Wight, which is easily reached from the mainland by regular ferry service. Fifty lifeboats are now constructed at the centre each year, with up to 200 being serviced and refurbished. They produce Atlantic 85 rigid, inflatable boats (RIBs). The facility on the Isle of Wight is highly respected across the globe as a centre of excellence for the building and maintenance of inflatable and rigid inflatable lifeboats, including the B class and D class lifeboats, and the lifeguards' inshore rescue boat, the Arancia, which are constructed under licence from Arancia of New Zealand. The centre also constructs lifeboats for other countries, and recently, craft have been supplied to the Dutch and Icelandic lifeboat services, and the Police and Irish Coast Guard.

The work is very skilled and a team of over 70 boat-builders, fitters, electricians, and solutionists, are employed, including apprentices and supporting office and stores staff. They give support to lifeboat stations and lifeguard units on all aspects of inflatable and rigid inflatable boat supply and maintenance. Just like RNLI crews, their work and attention to detail is vital for saving lives at sea. The ILC are pleased to host visits by schools and other organisations.

The RNLI now has an All-Weather Lifeboat Centre under construction at Poole, with plans to ultimately build all of their lifeboats in-house. Estimated at a cost of £11.2 million and built on RNLI land, it will, when completed, save the charity in the region of £3.7 million a year. (See also section headed Financing the RNLI).

Southend-on-Sea, Essex – Hovercraft and D-class

As part of his Lord Lieutenant's visit to Essex on Thursday July 16, 2013, Prince Edward took part in a ceremony to officially open the Southend-on-Sea RNLI lifeboat station's new inshore boathouse. It houses the station's hovercraft and D-class inshore lifeboat that is crucial to saving lives at sea. The boathouse will also provide space for the all-important crew training. The RNLI charity appeal had been in operation from 2006 to raise funds for the new boathouse. Present were Southend Lifeboat Operations Manager, Mr John Foster and Mr Ray Austin, who was representing various donors who made the new building possible. Credit was given to the people of Southend and the RNLI, thousands of who were involved in the fund raising. Mr Paul Boissier, Chief Executive of the RNLI, said: "This new building is a symbol of the spirit, generosity, and selflessness in the community that has made it all possible."

Prince Edward unveiled a commemorative plaque and said:

"Southend-on-Sea lifeboat station has a tremendous record of saving lives at sea, going back to the early 19th century, approaching the foundation of the RNLI itself. It also has a reputation of being one of the busiest stations in the whole of the RNLI, with three lifeboats and a rescue hovercraft, so it's entirely right they should have this wonderful boathouse. It is therefore a great pleasure for me to declare this station officially open, and may it serve you all extremely well for many years to come."

Lifeguarding service
RNLI lifeguards now patrol over 200 beaches around the UK that include the UK and the Channel Islands. In 2013 they attended 19,594 incidents and assisted 21,938 people, which involved rescuing 1,561 people and saving 100 lives. The RNLI's aim is to expand their lifeguarding service so that every region that needs lifeguard cover on its beaches has seasonal patrols. Two out of three people in the UK will head to the seaside at least once each year. Most beach goers will have an enjoyable and relaxing time. But every year, around 7,000 of them get into serious difficulties. When something goes wrong, RNLI lifeguards come to the rescue. For the best chance of survival, you need someone on the beach who can see the dangers develop or someone who can prevent accidents before they happen and respond instantly if they occur. That person needs to be a trained lifeguard; 95 per cent of a good lifeguard's work is preventative.

Saving lives from the beach to the open sea
In addition, RNLI lifeboat volunteers, or search and rescue helicopter crews, can respond within minutes and often save lives close to the shore. Time is of the essence if someone is drowning or a boat or sea-going vessel has got into difficulties and has either capsized or is sinking. In these circumstances, each second counts.

Safety Advice: wear a lifejacket
For many, the seaside provides a pleasant day out bathing and picnicking on the beach. However, the sea needs to be treated with caution, as it can be extremely unpredictable. At certain times of the day the tide may come in very quickly and in strong waves. It is vital to wear a lifejacket or buoyancy aid when going out in a boat even on the calmest day as true to the great British weather a storm can blow up suddenly and without warning. The RNLI believes that lifejackets save lives and are useless unless worn. If, for any reason, you find yourself in the water, a lifejacket or buoyancy aid could save your life. It is, however, very important that it is the correct size and type for you, properly fastened and maintained, and that you understand how to operate it. Of all the bodies that the RNLI have pulled from the water, precious few were wearing lifejackets. If they had been, they might have been

spotted earlier or survived longer, perhaps long enough to have been found alive.

Flood Rescue Team

The flooding of people's homes has been much featured on the news in recent years, with rivers bursting their banks due to unusual climatic changes around the world. The RNLI Flood Rescue Team is available 24 hours a day, seven days a week, to deploy to flooding events in the UK and the Republic of Ireland, and if requested, overseas too, to perform search and rescue operations. The team was formed in the year 2000, and comprises lifeboat crews and staff from the RNLI, who have been specially trained for the risks involved when working in or around fast moving flood water. There are now six divisional teams strategically positioned to respond to a flood anywhere in the UK or the Republic of Ireland within six hours, with a total of 250 team members. Fifty of these team members form the international Flood Rescue Team who can deploy anywhere in the world within 24 hours.

The Flood Rescue Team relies upon voluntary donations, and is currently supported by Toolstation. The team does not receive government funding for responding to UK floods and the cost of international deployment is borne by the UK Department for International Development.

Each team has two boats, a rescue van, and a Land Rover, as well as all ancillary equipment to allow the team to operate self-sufficiently for 48 hours. These include an operational base gazebo, electric generators, food, refreshments, scene lighting, and maintenance equipment. When deployed, the team integrates with the Fire and Rescue Service Command and Control system. They operate within the guidelines set out in the Department for Environment, Food and Rural Affairs (DEFRA) Food Rescue National Enhancement Project Concept of Operations.

The RNLI's international Flood Rescue Team (iFRT) is a group of specially trained volunteers, both male and female, who are ready to travel anywhere in the world to assist in flood relief work. They have additional skills for working overseas, including previous experience in developing countries and disaster zones, as well as specific skills such as being a doctor, paramedic, linguist or mechanic. They also have all necessary vaccinations to enable them to deploy at a moment's notice.

They are all experienced crew, but the situations and environments they may find themselves in during inland flooding are very different to those they encounter during sea rescues. Regular training exercises are vital to ensure team members can work safely and effectively in the unfamiliar terrain and diverse, high-risk environment of flood-affected areas. They are given additional training to become Floodwater Rescue Technicians and Flood Water Rescue Boat Operators. This training covers such skills as: operating boats in fast flowing water in narrow spaces similar to the streets of a town; performing rescues from weirs safely, using two boats; navigation; technical rope work; reconnaissance techniques; and how to deal with submerged hazards.

RNLI College

Lifesavers are trained at RNLI College, Poole, Dorset, which is a unique harbour-side location for conferences, training, and team building. Overlooking Poole Harbour on England's south coast, the college welcomes RNLI lifeboat crewmembers and lifeguards from all of the charity's locations, who visit for training courses and to make use of the training facilities. These include a huge lifeboat bridge simulator, sea survival pool where training provides a situation similar to that encountered in a real- life rescue out at sea. They run a successful Internship programme which is open to both graduates and those with work experience. The College is also used to raise funds, through hosting conferences, wedding receptions, social, and other functions, as well as welcoming film crews, and holidaying RNLI supporters.

Part 3
International Development

With nearly 200 years of accumulated knowledge, and world-class resources and capabilities, the RNLI is in a unique position to help new or developing lifesaving organisations.

Tackling the international drowning epidemic

Drowning kills more people each year than malaria, claiming an estimated 1.2 million lives around the world. In some countries, particularly in areas of Asia, Africa, and South America, drowning is the leading cause of child death. Most drownings occur in the world's poorest countries, which have either very limited lifesaving services, or none at all. Despite the scale of the problem this hidden epidemic is barely recognised.

The RNLI's international work aims to help emerging and developing search and rescue-related organisations worldwide by providing them with knowledge, equipment, and skills to save more lives and try to reduce this staggering loss of life. The RNLI is helping them to improve their own capabilities and is making a clear and measurable difference by delivering training, equipment, and advice to reduce global drownings.

Drowning is preventable

A large proportion of the 1.2 million global drownings each year occur in coastal locations, in floods, or in other large bodies of water, and areas in which the RNLI has expertise in saving lives and can offer help. The RNLI is not setting up services overseas, but they are providing others with the means to help themselves through a range of initiatives to other search and rescue-related organisations. In each case, they assess their current capabilities and needs, to decide how best they can help. This help might take the form of bespoke training, supply of equipment, safety education, or guidance on search and rescue operations, and flood resilience. Small interventions can make a huge difference. For example, in March 2012, two RNLI lifeguard trainers spent a week in Bangladesh, teaching lifesaving skills, which now means Bangladesh has its first lifesaving club, with trained volunteers who have already begun saving lives.

RNLI GLOBAL PROGRAMMES

Future Leaders in Lifesaving training course

In August 2012 the RNLI welcomed key representatives from eight overseas lifesaving organisations, who received two intensive weeks of tuition on how to run effective coastal lifesaving services. They invited representatives from Senegal, Cameroon, Bangladesh, India, Uganda, Mauritius, Thailand, and the Philippines. The Future Leaders course was run again in the summer of 2013.

Delegates were taken through a bespoke RNLI course, designed to equip them with essential skills to run lifesaving organisations in their home countries. A vast range of subjects were covered, including causes of drowning, the role of a lifeguard, equipment needed to run a lifesaving service, managing incidents, practical lifesaving skills, conducting beach risk assessments, writing training programmes, and how to run safety education initiatives.

All parts of the course were tailored to help participants apply what they have learned to their specific environments. The course was based at RNLI College, Poole, Dorset. Mr Austin Andemani from Uganda commented afterwards:

"This has been a very wonderful and fantastic opportunity. The skills the RNLI are providing are so great for our kind of work ... I will be able to push lifesaving activity further from where it has been in Uganda. The content, the people ... everything has been fantastic. It is so important for us to remember that although water gives life, it can also take life away."

Lifesaving training resources
for new and developing organisations

New and developing lifesaving organisations can struggle to implement effective coastal drowning prevention strategies due to limited training and resources. Together with the International Drowning Research Centre Bangladesh (IDRC-B), the RNLI has developed a beach lifeguard course, specifically designed for use in areas where specialist equipment and facilities are unavailable.

The instructor's manual is a simple toolkit for lifeguard trainers to refer to, and accompanies a basic student manual and optional teaching aids. Organisations and individuals are free to copy parts of the manual for teaching and learning purposes. It is hoped that by sharing knowledge and understanding of the beach environment and lifesaving skills the RNLI can help save more people from drowning worldwide.

Bangladesh – Saving and
changing lives through lifeguard training

Bangladesh has one of the highest drowning rates in the world, with drowning being the lead killer of children, claiming around 18,000 lives a year. Hundreds of lives could be saved there every year now the country's first ever lifesaving club has been set up with the RNLI's help.

Working with the International Drowning Research Centre Bangladesh, RNLI Lifeguard Trainers Mr Darren Williams and Mr Scott Davidson spent two weeks in March 2012, delivering much-needed lifesaving training to 15 Bangladeshi volunteers. The volunteers are using their newly acquired skills to run Bangladesh's first beach lifesaving club and have already started saving lives. The course covered crucial first steps including: personal fitness, beach surveillance, risk assessments, recognising when a person is in distress, understanding rescue equipment, and reaching, retrieving, assessing, and treating a casualty. They also delivered a Train the Trainer course manual, enabling the volunteers to teach the skills to others that they had been taught.

In October 2012 Mr Williams and Mr Davidson returned to Bangladesh to oversee the delivery of training to 45 more lifeguards. They supported the local lifeguards, who had been trained back in March, and who led the sessions using a training manual developed by the RNLI specifically for use in countries where specialist equipment and facilities are not available. They also taught the lifeguards how to deliver water safety education talks in schools. If the newly trained lifeguards can give vital advice to thousands of school children it would mean that many more lives could be saved each year. Representatives from Bangladesh attended the Future Leaders in the Lifesaving course that the RNLI ran to further develop their lifesaving skills.

Coast Guard development

The RNLI is working with the Bangladesh Coast Guard, providing guidance to help them develop an effective search and rescue training programme. Two coast guard officers visited RNLI College in 2012 for an introduction to search and rescue training and management. In October a team of RNLI lifeboat trainers visited the Bangladesh Coast Guard to fully assess their training needs and provide further search and rescue training to key officials. During the three weeks, RNLI Lifeboat Trainers Mr David Riley, Mr Alex Evans, and Mr Bernie Mannings, gave 40 Bangladesh Coast Guard officers an introduction to the essential aspects of search and rescue coordination, before moving on to deliver in-depth training on operating all-weather lifeboats for search and rescue. The RNLI training, comprising a mixture of classroom-based theory and at-sea practical work, aimed to improve their knowledge and skills to enable them to carry out rescues more efficiently and effectively, to help save more lives. They covered search and rescue theory and co-ordination, practical search exercises, and Train the Trainer skills.

Flood prevention and flood rescue in Bangladesh

Flooding in Bangladesh has been for many years a serious problem. Each year, around 18 per cent of the country is flooded, killing over 5,000 people and destroying seven million homes. The RNLI is running two new programmes in the country to help Bangladesh prepare for floods and save more lives from drowning. Three members of the charity's Flood Rescue Team are delivering the programmes. The first is for 40 members of Bangladesh's Fire Service and Civil Defence. Over a four-day period they will learn about swift-water swimming techniques; crossing moving water; using a rescue boat; assessing risks and keeping themselves safe; rescuing others; and taking command of an incident.

The team will train 25 personnel from other charities operating in Bangladesh, including Save the Children, Voluntary Services Overseas, and Plan International. These organisations which provide important support to local communities, will learn about the dangers of flood water; protecting themselves should they end up in the water; types of rescue boats and how to load them safely; using suitable safety equipment; paddling a boat in flood waters; and what to do in the event of a capsize. One of the RNLI team delivering the training is Mr Martin Blaker-Rowe, who was among three RNLI Flood Rescue Team members awarded a Pride of Britain Award in 2013.

Brazil – Operational development

The RNLI and the Swedish Sea Rescue Society jointly assessed Brazil's search and rescue service the Anjos do Mar (Sea Angels), and created plans to help build it into a stronger, more effective rescue service. After an initial assessment to determine its operational capacity and organisational structure, the RNLI gave advice to help it develop a sustainable operational platform. They are continuing to advise Sea Angels and hope to also help with rescue craft and training.

Cameroon – Swim and Survive training

Volunteers in Cameroon learned essential lifesaving and swimming skills, delivered through a joint initiative between the Swimming Teachers' Association (STA) and the RNLI. The RNLI joined forces to deliver a Swim and Survive Train the Trainer project in the country, following a request from Royal Lifesaving Society Cameroon. Mr Ross MacLeod, RNLI Coastal Safety Manager, and Mr Tim Doran, RNLI Lifeguard Supervisor, travelled with Mr Gary Seghers, STA Qualifications Development Manager, to deliver a five-day course covering basic first aid, resuscitation, safety in open-water environments and the technical knowledge and practical skills required to teach basic swimming and survival skills. The aim of the course was to train local instructors who would then deliver high-quality swimming lessons in their own communities. Twenty-three candidates attended the course in Kribi, a popular southern coastal town. Of those who completed the course, 14 achieved the International Swimming Standards teaching qualification, while six were awarded a Certificate of Attendance that entitles them to be assistant teachers who work alongside a qualified instructor. They each had to complete practical and theory tests in swimming and survival skills. Representatives from Cameroon will attend the Future Leaders in Lifesaving courses. A representative from Cameroon attended the Future Leaders in Lifesaving course in July 2013.

China – Training and technical development

The RNLI have been working with the Chinese Ministry of Transport's Rescue and Salvage Bureau since 2003, to help them develop their rescue service. Their fleet mainly comprises deep-sea salvage tugs but to expand their search and rescue services, they needed smaller, shallow-draught boats. The RNLI have sold 20 former RNLI lifeboats to China to help them meet this need. Ongoing training is also being provided by the RNLI for the crew, who are now operating the lifeboats, plus technical support, maintenance, feedback, and recommendations.

Kenya – Lifeguard training

Two members of the RNLI's Lifeguards team visited Kenya in 2008, to help equip 16 local people with essential lifesaving skills as part of the Crisis Response Development Foundation's (CRDF) maritime community project. They spent two weeks at a public beach in Mombassa, where they taught a group of Kenyan people to become lifesavers. Lifeguard training in Kenya was non-existent before the RNLI's visit, and their equipment was improvised: old windsurfing boards became rescue boards and palm trees were used as flagpoles.

A year later the lifeguard trainers returned to deliver Train the Trainer sessions, enabling the Kenyan lifeguards to share their skills with others and help secure the long-term future of lifeguarding in the country. Since they received their RNLI training, the number of drownings on that beach has reduced from an average of three per month to zero. Representatives from Kenya attended the Future Leaders in Lifesaving courses being run by the RNLI in August 2012 to further develop their lifesaving skills and candidates from Kenya attended the course also in July 2013.

Saint Lucia – Beach safety management consultancy

Beach safety and bathing water quality are crucial for tourism on small island states like Saint Lucia. The variety of Saint Lucia's beaches in terms of appearance, size, composition, and use, make them challenging to manage. Working with other key groups and agencies, the RNLI provided guidance on beach risk management, which will lead to the development of national beach safety standards for the island. The RNLI assessed the importance of beach safety for local communities and tourism, helped set up systems to monitor water quality, and devised a way of classifying the island's beaches according to safety features. Saint Lucia's government is now using the RNLI's guidance in its coastal safety plans.

South Korea – Coastal risk assessment consultancy

The RNLI has been working with Lifesaving Society Korea in South Korea to provide advice and training on coastal risk assessment. This has included setting up systems to enable them to carry out coastal risk assessments and manage any risks identified.

Uruguay – Training and technical support

The RNLI has been supporting Uruguay's volunteer lifeboat service, Asociación honoraria De Salvamentos maritimous y fliuviales (ADES), through the sale of former lifeboats and training. ADES is made up of volunteers, operating five stations along the mouth of the River Plate. It operates all-weather lifeboats and inshore lifeboats, and is run with very little funding from government or local institutions.

During 2011-12, ADES took delivery of two former Tyne class lifeboats, purchased from the RNLI to modernise their existing fleet and which included former RNLI Waveney class and Solent class lifeboats. In that year also, two RNLI instructors trained the ADES crews who will be operating the lifeboats. The RNLI hope to deliver further training in Uruguay, to continue the work of strengthening their search and rescue service.

Senegal – Lifeguard Training

In December 2012 RNLI lifeguards Mr Tim Doran and Mr Vaughan Lawson travelled to Senegal to help develop the first dedicated lifeguard service in the capital of Dakar. They delivered two weeks of rigorous training to both volunteer and full-time lifesavers, equipping them with vital knowledge and skills to help save more lives from drowning. During the two weeks, Tim and Vaughan trained 25 volunteer and full-time lifeguards and members of the fire service, who undertook regular beach patrols, and six instructors as specialists, and that will, in turn, teach lifesaving skills to others to help establish a long-term, sustainable lifesaving service. The course covered the important first steps of lifeguarding, including: recognising when a person is in distress; how to use rescue equipment; beach surveillance; risk assessments, and rescuing and treating a casualty. Two of the Senegalese lifeguards, Mr Idrissa Ndiaye and Mr Moustapha Diene, had attended the Future Leaders in Lifesaving course which took place at the RNLI's headquarters in August 2012. The visit by Tim and Vaughan was the RNLI's first to Senegal, following the training delivered to Idrissa and Moustapha in August. Tim and Vaughan assessed how the two have implemented what they learnt and helped them further develop their skills, while also training other Senegalese lifeguards for the first time.

Mr Steve Wills, the RNLI's International Development Manager said in 2012:

"Drowning is, very sadly, a common occurrence in Senegal – earlier this year, nine boys drowned off the coast of Dakar. They had been playing in the water when a current took them. There were no lifeguards around to save them. During this visit to Senegal, we have taught the lifeguards vital skills to help them set up, run, and expand an effective lifesaving service and, ultimately, save more lives from drowning."

Mr Tim Doran, RNLI Lifeguard Supervisor, who was involved in delivering the training, said:

"Last year there were 55 recorded drownings on the beaches just around Dakar. Over the course of their season, that's around two drownings per week. It really highlights the work that we're doing here, and hopefully what we're doing will have an impact for future seasons."

British Virgin Islands

Two lifeboat trainers from RNLI College spent a week in the British Virgin Islands in November 2012, delivering training to Virgin Islands Search and Rescue (VISAR) crewmembers. VISAR is a voluntary organisation dedicated to saving life at sea. It is the officially recognised search and rescue service in the British Virgin Islands, where it provides 24-hour cover every day of the year in close co-operation with the Royal British Virgin Islands police, fire, and ambulance services. The trainers taught search techniques, advanced navigation, rough-weather handling, slow-speed transfers, high-speed helming, distress situations, and practical and theoretical search pattern sessions. They worked with a large number of crewmembers of different levels of experience.

Africa – New Aquatic Survival Programme

A first-of-its-kind lifesaving programme is being run by the RNLI in Tanzania and is expected to save the lives of hundreds of African children. The new Aquatic Survival Programme has two key aims – first, to deliver water safety messages to school children and, second, to teach children basic survival swimming. The RNLI is training local teachers, community leaders and scout leaders to deliver the vital water safety lessons to such a vulnerable group.

They are working closely with a local Zanzibari community- based organisation called The Panje Project which is providing important on-the-ground support, involving local people and schools in the programme. In the village of Nungwi in Zanzibar, 10 local people are being trained by the RNLI to deliver key water safety messages. Five of them are receiving additional training in how to teach self-survival and rescue or basic survival swimming. Once the local people have had this training, they will then deliver the sessions to local children thereby putting their learning into practice immediately. Over the course of two weeks, at least 300 children aged 7-14 are being taught important water safety messages, and 30-40 children are being taught self-survival and rescue.

The World Health Organisation estimates that Africa has the highest continental drowning-rate in the world. There is currently no global swim-survival programme for low resource countries so the RNLI has worked closely with other key organisations including UK Sport, Plan International, the Swimming Teachers' Association, Nile Swimmers, and Royal Lifesaving Society Commonwealth, to create this unique programme. Using their combined experience and expertise the organisations created an Aquatic Survival Programme manual designed specifically for Africa. The manual is being used to deliver the training to local people, and will thereafter be available as an open-source resource for the local people to use. The manual covers every step in how to set up and run the Aquatic Survival Programme, from finding a suitable location to sourcing funding and delivering the training. Mr Steve Willis who is the RNLI's International Development Manager, explains:

"Before the start of the Aquatic Survival Programme in Zanzibar, three RNLI lifeguard trainers ran a lifeguard training programme in Dar es Salaam. They taught essential lifeguarding skills to 30 participants from Tanzania, Zanzibar, and Uganda. They covered crucial first steps of lifeguarding and also delivered a Train the Trainer course, enabling the trainee lifeguards to teach the skills they learn to others, again ensuring they are able to set up and sustain their own lifeguarding service."

What is the RNLI offering to other countries?

The RNLI is offering other countries a range of options to other lifesaving organisations, dependent on their capabilities and needs. Areas in which the RNLI can help are: training – operational, first aid, search and rescue, and management; equipment – lifesaving and personal protective equipment; safety and education – programme design and development; lifeboat and lifeguard services – search and rescue framework, governance and strategy, flood preparedness and resilience.

The RNLI will be delivering and monitoring programmes by working with key local, national and international groups. With nearly 200 years of accumulated knowledge, and world-class resources and capabilities, the RNLI is in a unique position to help new or developing lifesaving organisations.

RNLI's attitude to the environment

The RNLI takes a highly responsible attitude towards preserving the environment free from pollution and contamination. They aim to reduce energy consumption, which will improve their carbon footprint and also reduce costs which means donations go further. Projects that reduce their impact on the environment include ground source heat pumps at new lifeboat stations, a wind turbine that powers Aith Lifeboat Station, and a variety of energy saving measures in their offices. Their long-term plan is to slow their carbon footprint expansion, reach a steady state, and then achieve year-on-year reductions, while still meeting their need for increased operational activities.

Financing the RNLI

The RNLI has always been funded by voluntary contributions from the general public. Even during its early days in 1849, people gave generously to the lifeboat service. The Institution's total income for that year was £354-17s-6d. The first RNLI Lifeboat Day took place in October 1891, in Manchester, and raised over £5,000, today's equivalent of more than £2 million.

Today the RNLI is dependant upon voluntary donations from the public and upon legacies, together with tax reclaims. In 2013 the RNLI's income was £182.7 million, while its running costs were £144.4 million, and capital costs were £48 million. What has to be taken into consideration in the modern world is the use of larger more efficient, and therefore more expensive, vessels. Every year newer and more modern all-weather and inshore lifeboats are required for the fleet, which are expensive to build and maintain. Lifeboats eventually wear out and have to be replaced at considerable expense.

RNLI bring lifeboat building in-house

With the technology of their lifeboats becoming ever more advanced, there are fewer boat builders that can meet their specific requirements. And with fewer suppliers it is harder to negotiate costs. The RNLI have therefore brought lifeboat building in-house, putting them in control. It will enable them to better monitor quality and costs and will save them in excess of £3 million a year once the facility is fully operative. The building and fitting out of their own All-weather Lifeboat Centre has been costed at £14.5 million. They are appealing for £5 million from the public to help fund this project. The RNLI can cover the rest of the cost thanks to a three-year programme of driving efficiencies right across the RNLI that has led to £20 million savings annually, some of which has been allocated to the project. The RNLI has a guaranteed order book: £20 million worth of work will flow through the facility each year, building 6 new £2 million all-weather lifeboats every year (one every two months), and maintaining a fleet of 160 all-weather lifeboats, plus refitting seven all-weather lifeboats annually to double each vessel's operational life.

Running costs

The RNLI does not seek central government funding. They operate through local teams, centrally directed and resourced. Keeping a modern fleet of lifeboats ever-ready to go to the rescue from 235 stations and two trial stations is an expensive business. Added to the cost is crew-training, running a lifeguard service on more than 210 popular beaches, and campaigning for water safety, and the expense soon mounts up.

It costs around £385,000 a day to run the RNLI. This might sound like a lot, but the RNLI think that the 23 people rescued per day (on average) are worth it. Here is a breakdown of some of the costs: Lifeboat fleet: Tamar class £2.7 million; Shannon class £2 million; B class £214,000; D class £41,000, E class, £350,000. Hovercraft £300,000. Lifeguards equipment: Inshore rescue boat £12,000; Patrol vehicle £24,207; All-terrain vehicle £6,000.

To kit out one person for lifeboat service, costs more than £1,345. A small sample of the more expensive specialist clothing and accessories required includes: all-weather lifejacket £368; waterproof trousers £210; waterproof jacket £305; inshore drysuit and boots £700; thermal suit £210; and a lifeguard's full wetsuit £85.

Out on a shout!

Lifeboat crews launch on average 24 times a day. Crewmembers of RNLI lifeboat stations have a well-known saying. When they are called upon to carry out a rescue they refer to it as "Out on a shout!"

Part 4

THE COMMUNICATIONS AND PUBLIC
SERVICE LIFEBOAT FUND (CISPOTEL)

The Communications And Public Service Lifeboat Fund or The Lifeboat Fund as it has become known, was founded in 1866, when a group of civil servants met with the intention to raise sufficient funds to present a lifeboat to the Royal National Lifeboat Institution (RNLI). They formed a committee and put out an appeal to government offices, asking for £300. This amount was raised before the year was

93. A modern RNLI lifeboat provided by
The Communications And Public Service Lifeboat Fund.

out, and paid for a lifeboat that was given the name *Civil Service*.

The title of the fund has changed over the years, and initially, the committee was known as the Civil Service Lifeboat Fund. Later it was changed to The Civil Service, Post Office and British Telecommunications Lifeboat Fund (CISPOTEL). It was altered again, in 1969, when the Post Office left the Civil Service, and again in 1983, when British Telecom did likewise. In 2002, when the Post Office changed its name to Consignia, the fund changed its title to The Communications and Public Service Lifeboat Fund, with a working title of The Lifeboat Fund. When Consignia was renamed Royal Mail, no further change was made to the name.

Prince Edward became Patron of the Lifeboat Fund on July 1, 1997, as successor to Her Majesty Queen Elizabeth II. A new lifeboat, The Duke of Kent, was named in his honour.

The sole object of the fund has always been to raise money to further the work of the RNLI, by providing lifeboats or other items that they require. Every year the fund launches an appeal for donations. Supporters are encouraged to fundraise, and collections and events are organised across the UK Civil Service. Retired civil servants and Royal Mail pensioners subscribe mainly through pension payroll, and British Telecom employees use payroll giving.

The Lifeboat Fund's work is highly valued by the RNLI, and the charity is by far its largest single regular contributor. Since 1866 the fund has provided the RNLI with 52 new lifeboats, which have saved over 4,700 lives. In 2011 the fund's appeal raised £122,000 for the purpose of helping train and equip the RNLI's brave volunteer crews. In 2014 their goal was to donate £280,000, which is a sufficient sum to train one crew member at every lifeboat station in England, Scotland, Wales, and Northern Ireland.

The Charles Dibdin, which was the fund's 51st lifeboat, went into service in November 2009, at the New Brighton Lifeboat Station, Merseyside.

The Lifeboat Fund's first lifeboat in Northern Ireland since the year 2000, the 52nd lifeboat, was named David Roulston. The volunteer RNLI lifeboat crew took delivery of their brand new state of the art Inshore Lifeboat in September 2010, and wasted no time in putting it through its paces, operating out of Portrush. It was officially named and handed over in April 2011, at Portrush, by the fund's Chair, Sir Peter Housden KCB, Permanent Secretary of the Scottish Government.

Civil Service No.52 lifeboat, cost £35,000, and was so named in memory of Mr David Roulston, a member of the Northern Ireland Tourist Board who had drowned tragically, while taking recreation with his family. The staff of the Tourist Board fundraised to pay for the lifeboat's upkeep and maintenance. The new D-Class lifeboat measures five metres in length, can operate close to shore and is much faster than its predecessor. It will thus be ideal for saving lives around the North Coast of Northern Ireland.

Lifeboat Operations Manager Mr Robin Cardwell said:
"The crew are very impressed with the performance of their new lifeboat. They have already had intensive training sessions on the boat and are delighted to have it on station in Portrush. The new boat has arrived just as the Station is celebrating its 150th anniversary."

The Lifeboat Fund has recently been pleased to attract new supporters from within the UK Civil Service. Scottish Government colleagues also responded well, following registration of the charity by the Office of the Scottish Charity Regulator late in 2010. This is very heartening as is the strength of donations to recent annual appeals, given the prevailing economic conditions.

The Lifeboat Fund updated its branding and communications in 2011, and now has a new logo and website the latter providing a range of new ways to donate at http://thelifeboatfund.org.uk.

The fund's 2012 appeal continued the recent theme of supporting crew safety and local life-savers. This serves to extend the impact of its fundraising to assist RNLI volunteers around the UK.

The RNLI asked the fund to pay for lifeguard training of one person at every RNLI life-guarded beach; the kitting out of their crew in the latest safety lifejackets, to help with the current 'roll out'; and maintenance at those lifeboat stations where their boats are in service in order to keep them in top condition.

Prince Edward in his message, which is stated at the introduction to the charity's 125th anniversary booklet said:
"The staff of the Civil Service, Post Office and British Telecom hold a unique record of support for the Royal National Lifeboat Institution. ... I should like to offer my most sincere thanks to ... the Fund for their constant help, which I know is deeply appreciated by our lifeboat crews. Whatever

happens in the future, there will always be lives to save at sea."

Endnotes to Chapter 12

[1] Paul Boissier, *Understanding The Rule of the Road,* pub. John Wiley & Sons, 2006; ISBN No. 1898660999.

[2] The Corporation of Trinity House of Deptford Strond, known as Trinity House, is the official General Lighthouse Authority for England, Wales, and other British territorial waters, with the exception of Scotland, Northern Ireland, and the Isle of Man.

[3] Authors interview of February 23, 2008, with Sir Richard Buckley, former Private Secretary to HRH The Duke of Kent.

[4] Scotland, Dunbar Mechanic Kenneth Peters; Ireland, Dun Laoghaire ex-crew member William Scully; West, The Mumbles Deputy Launching Authority Roy Griffiths; North, Humber Superintendent Coxswain David Steenvoorden; South, Lyme Regis Deputy Launching Authority/ex-crew member Garry Gibbs; East, Shoreham Coxswain Peter Huxtable MBE.

[5] Sir William Hillary, *An Appeal To The British Nation On The Humanity And Policy Of Forming A National Institution For The Preservation Of Lives And Property From Shipwreck*; pub. 1823.

[6] The Grace Darling Museum in Bamburgh, Northumberland, UK, commemorates the life of Victorian Britain's greatest heroine on the high seas, and the story of the wreck of the SS *Forfarshire* in 1838. The museum features the famous rescue coble, Grace's dresses, letters, and family belongings, and a cornucopia of commemorative ware.

[7] Source: material and newspaper reports provided by the library of the RNLI.

[8] Op. cit., Sir Richard Buckley.

[9] Ibid.

[10] Ibid.

[11] Authors interview of August 18, 2008, with Captain Edward McGee.

[12] Celia Lee in conversation with Prince Edward, May 1, 2001, regarding his tour of Northern Ireland.

[13] Op. cit., Captain Edward McGee.
Endnotes Chapter 12 contd.

[14] Authors Interview with Mrs Eveleigh Brownlow MBE, 2008; letter from Mrs Brownlow to the authors, August 28, 2008.

[15] Authors in conversation with HRH The Duke of Kent, 2001.

[16] It is worth recalling that at this stage in Ireland's history, all 32 counties were still part of the United Kingdom. When 26 counties became independent the RNLI continued to operate there despite being British in origin.

[17] Translation from the Irish: 'Your Royal Highness, British Ambassador, and all the gentlefolk/gentlemen.'

CHAPTER 13

ART, DRAMA, LITERATURE, AND PHOTOGRAPHY

Introduction

As we have seen in Chapter 1, Prince Edward's well-rounded education provided him with a good understanding of most aspects of the Arts. Thus Chapter 13 encompasses four somewhat diverse organisations. *The Catalogue Raisonné of Works*, of which Prince Edward is Patron, October 4, 2007, is a collection of the paintings by the artist Philip de László. The P G Wodehouse Society (UK) of which Prince Edward became Patron, March 12, 2007, was set up to celebrate that author's life and works. The Noël Coward Society of which Prince Edward became President, September 16, 2005, celebrates the life of this prolific writer. Prince Edward became an Honorary Member of The Royal Photographic Society of Great Britain, April 4, 1978, as he is a keen photographer.

THE CATALOGUE RAISONNE OF WORKS
By Philip de László m.v.o., prba, (1869-1937)

In his lifetime, Hungarian-born Philip de László (1869-1937) was recognised as one of the most important portrait painters of his generation. His sitters included influential politicians, artists, musicians, industrialists, scientists, businessmen, and the royal families of Europe. With a career spanning almost fifty years, and an estimated body of 5,000 works, his oeuvre constitutes a remarkable overview and testimony of the period 1889-1937. His portraits of leading world figures like Pope Leo XIII (1900), Theodore Roosevelt (1908), Field Marshal Earl Roberts of Kandahar (1911), Sir Ernest Rutherford (1924), Her Late Majesty Queen Elizabeth The Queen Mother when Duchess of York (1925), and Princess Elizabeth of York (1933) later Her Majesty Queen Elizabeth II, count amongst his most famous works.

The aim of the catalogue raisonné is to provide the definitive record of the complete works of de László by tracing, photographing, and cataloguing every known painting and drawing made by him. A scholarly enterprise, it aspires to be an authoritative source of information to researchers, academics, and students alike, and to allow authentication of works by scholars, dealers, and auction houses worldwide.

The Honourable Mrs Sandra de Laszlo, an art historian and the wife of Da-mon, one of Philip de László's 17 grandchildren, started *The Catalogue Raisonné of Works by Philip de László* in 1989, originally working on her own. As the project has developed she has gathered a team of editors and a number of volunteer re-searchers and genealogists across the world, thus building a reliable network of ex-perts. To date some 3,750 works by de László have been recorded by the catalogue raisonné team and 700 entries with biographical notes and professional photographs have been uploaded to the online catalogue raisonné. [1]

Prince Edward became Patron to the catalogue raisonné in October 4, 2007. He is particularly familiar with Philip de László's work as the artist painted three portraits of his mother Princess Marina in 1934, at the time of her wedding to Prince George, whom de László also portrayed. The artist painted Prince Edward's grand-mother, Princess Nicholas of Greece and many other relatives. Prince Edward has been supportive of the aims of the catalogue raisonné from the outset and is com-mitted to its ambition to reassess de László's oeuvre. In March 2010 in an informal capacity, Prince Edward attended the opening of a display dedicated to the artist Philip de László, Portrait, at the National Portrait Gallery, London.

P G WODEHOUSE SOCIETY (UK)

Sir Pelham Grenville Wodehouse KBE (15 October 1881–14 February 1975), writing under the name P G Wodehouse, is widely regarded as the greatest comic author of the 20th century. An English humourist, who wrote more than 70 novels and 200 short stories, his work also includes plays, poems, song lyrics, and numerous pieces of journalism. Wodehouse enjoyed enormous popular success during a career that lasted more than 70 years, and his many writings continue to be widely read.

Much of Woodehouse's life was spent in France and the US, but he remained a part of pre- and post-First World War English upper-class society. An acknowledged master of English prose, Wodehouse has been admired both by contemporaries such as Hilaire Belloc, Evelyn Waugh, and Rudyard Kipling, and by more recent writers such as Stephen Fry, Christopher Hitchens, Douglas Adams, John Le Carré, and J. K. Rowling.

Jeeves and Blandings Castle stories
Best known for his *Jeeves* and *Blandings Castle* novels and his short stories, Wodehouse was part author and writer of 15 plays and of 250 lyrics for some 30 musical comedies. He is featured in the Songwriters Hall of Fame, and many of the works in which he participated were produced in collaboration with Jerome Kern and Guy Bolton. He also worked with Cole Porter on the musical Anything Goes (1934), wrote the lyrics for the hit song Bill in Jerome Kern's Show Boat (1927), wrote lyrics to Sigmund Romberg's music for the Gershwin, Romberg musical Rosalie, and collaborated with Rudolf Friml on a musical version of The Three Musketeers, (both in 1928).

Wodehouse is most famous for The Jeeves and Wooster Series of multiple short-stories and novels, including *Thank You Jeeves*, *Right Ho Jeeves*, *Very Good*

*94. HRH The Duke Of Kent enjoying
a cup of tea with P G Wodehouse members
Camilla Cazalet and Sir Edward Cazalet
in Camilla's kitchen.*

Jeeves, Carry On Jeeves, The Code of Woosters, Joy in the Morning, The Mating Season, The Inimitable Jeeves, and so on. The plots follow the character of Bertie Wooster, an upper-class gentleman and Jeeves, his faithful butler, through everyday life with its ups and downs. [2]

Blandings Castle Saga [3] is a collection of books which include: *Something Fresh, Leave it to Psmith, Summer Lightning, Blandings Castle and Elsewhere, Uncle Fred in the Springtime, Pigs Have Wings,* and so forth.

The reader is introduced to the absent-minded 9th Earl of Emsworth, owner of Blandings Castle, and the head of the Threepwood family, who has a love of pigs and gardening, and a plethora of sisters, nephews and nieces.

The Drones Club stories is a collection of short-stories set around the fictional Drones Club and consisting of Egg, Beans and Crumpet stories, and involving the young rich and not-so-rich social aristocrats who were then part of the London scene. Very few members of the Drones Club were wealthy, all the stories are about members trying to rustle up some ready cash.

Wodehouse's characters play a robust and leading role in all his novels, and are often so colourful and forceful as to be as well known as the titles of his books in which they are featured. They are always eccentric and are often based on the impecunious members of the English gentry, Earls and Lords, Eton and Oxford educated men, juxtaposed alongside domestic staff such as butlers and secretaries.

P G Wodehouse Society (UK)

The P G Wodehouse Society (UK) celebrates the life and works of the author and they organise many enjoyable social events for members to meet fellow enthusiasts. They also produce an excellent quarterly magazine titled *Wooster Sauce*, as well as additional papers and supplements.

Prince Edward's role

Prince Edward became a Patron of The P G Wodehouse Society (UK) on March 12, 2007. An enthusiastic Wodehousean, Prince Edward has demonstrated an obvious theatrical flair by taking part in the evening's entertainment at each Biennial Society Dinner since 2004.

Prince Edward's interest in P G Wodehouse is not surprising as his mother was Patron of the Central School of Speech and Drama. Prince Edward hated school and from boyhood found escape in Wodehouse's stories and has this to say of his experience:

"I was first introduced to P G Wodehouse at school, and I remember that the first Wodehouse I read was *Joy in the Morning*. The Jeeves and Wooster stories have always been favourites, as have those concerning Blandings Castle. Wodehouse has a unique way of expressing himself which to me is inherently humorous; both from the situations which he creates, some of them ludicrously complex, and the actual language which contains so many memorable phrases and so much vivid imagery. Having been an avid Wodehouse reader now for over 60 years, I still get as much pleasure from reading and re-reading his novels as I did when I read the first one, and I feel proud to be a Patron of the society which is named after this great writer."

In 2010 Prince Edward played The Voice of the Author – not a huge part but obviously a crucial one – and it was written about by Miss Ellie King in *Wooster Sauce*:

"HRH The Duke of Kent set the scene with theatrical flair – in an English republic one could see him make a new career as a TV announcer. We were at times reduced to helpless laughter as the drama developed in its rather complicated way.

"After dinner there was an entertainment consisting of a short musical adaptation of the classic Wodehouse short story Uncle Fred Flits By, masterfully performed by a stellar cast including Tim Brooke-Taylor, HRH the Duke of Kent, and a couple of Wodehouse's descendants – the Cazalets. All in all it was a wonderful evening and I'm pretty certain that a merry time was had by all who attended."

P G Wodehouse Biennial Dinner 2012

The P G Wodehouse Biennial Society Dinner for 2012 was held at Gray's Inn,

326

95. HRH The Duke of Kent
attending a P G Wodehouse Society dinner.
in October 2012.

London, on October 25. Following Grace before the meal, which was recited in Latin, the Chairman of The P G Wodehouse Society (UK), Mrs Hilary Bruce, hosted the evening. Mr Tony Ring, who is a member of the Committee of the P G Wodehouse Society (UK), Editor of *The Wit and Wisdom of P G Wodehouse*, and author of several books about Wodehouse and his work, including the eight-volume *Concordance*, introduced the speaker Mr Simon Brett, who had a career with the BBC, having produced the first episode of *The Hitchhiker's Guide to the Galaxy*, as well as many episodes of cult comedy series. [4] Turning his hand to writing, Mr Brett has penned such successes as *A Shock to the System* (1984) that was made into a film starring Michael Caine, and he has also written some highly successful radio and television series. *No Commitments* is one of his comedy dramas that was broadcast on BBC Radio 4. It portrays the day-to-day lives of three very different sisters played by well-known names like Rosemary Leach, Celia Imrie, and Stephen Moore. *After Henry is a* sitcom from the heart of Middle England that follows the fortunes of Sarah France, with Prunella Scales playing the part of the well-to-do general practitioner's wife who is getting on with life after the death of her husband Henry, who was killed in a car crash. The female members of the family are all sandwiched together on different floors of their large Edwardian house.

In his talk Mr Brett reflected on the occasional humiliations of being a writer when called upon to give a talk. During a book tour in Finland the only person who turned up had been hired to play the piano in the interval. Despite his good Oxford degree in the late 1960s, the only job he could find was as a temporary Father Christmas in a department store in Sutton.

Prince Edward plays a role

There followed colourful cabaret in which Prince Edward played a role described by Mr Paddy Briggs, journalist and writer:

> "There was also to treasure a measured and entirely convincing portrayal of Jeeves from the Duke of Kent, who, one felt, if the dice had rolled slightly differently, could have been an outstanding Gentleman's Gentleman. Which prompts the thought that you can 'Say what you will, there is something fine about our old aristocracy.' "

Reginald Jeeves, the fictional character in the short stories and novels of P G Wodehouse, is the valet of Bertie Wooster (Bertram Wilberforce Wooster). Created in 1915, Jeeves was Wodehouse's most famous character, continuing to appear in his work until his final completed novel *Aunts Aren't Gentlemen* (1974). In a conversation with a policeman in *Jeeves and the Kid Clementina*, Jeeves refers to himself as both a "gentleman's personal gentleman" and a "personal gentleman's gentleman." This means that Jeeves is a valet, not a butler—that is, he serves a man and not a household.

Sir Terry Wogan becomes President

There was a farewell from Mrs Hilary Bruce, who welcomed the new President, Sir Terry Wogan KBE, DL, the much loved star presenter of TV and radio, and stalwart of the Eurovision Song Contest for which he was for many years the BBC's off-screen commentator. Sir Terry said:

> "I've just taken the reins of office as President of the society that rightly honours the great Plum, but I'm fully conscious of His Royal Highness, the Duke of Kent's support. Not only that, I have applauded his scintillating cameo performance at the society's dinner last year, when he stole the show as Jeeves. The Theatre's loss is our gain." [5]

Sir Terry expressed his admiration for Wodehouse in a BBC documentary Wodehouse: Life & Works, on January 13, 2012, reflecting back to Desert Island Discs of May 21, 1983. Then Stephen Fry and the late Richard Briers CBE, who was at that time President of the P G Wodehouse Society, gave readings, and Joanna Lumley star of the BBC TV series Absolutely Fabulous was interviewed along with many others.

There was an old recording of Wodehouse being asked in interview about a broadcast he made for the Germans when he was held prisoner in Germany during the Second World War in which he replied: "I made an ass of myself." For that blunder he was obliged to live in exile in the US until practically the end of his life. Finally forgiven, he was awarded a Knighthood in 1975.

The BBC's adaptation of Blandings, 2013 and 2014

The BBC's new adaptation of Wodehouse's *Blandings*, starring Jennifer Saunders and Timothy Spall, and serialised in January 2013 and February 2014, has been a real entertainment. Wodehouse's work adapted well to the screen. The lovable pink pig The Empress (though as one reviewer pointed out, in the original work she was actually black), performed well in the first series. She was so over-indulged by her owner that she could tuck into sumptuous, pink blancmanges for dessert, eat apples and grow fat, basking in a bed of straw. Sadly, by the time the second series was screened in 2014, this delightful creature had passed away (no doubt happily and peacefully) and was replaced with yet another, somewhat paler pink Empress.

THE NOËL COWARD SOCIETY

The Noël Coward Society is an international society that was founded in 1999, to celebrate the life and work of Sir Noël Peirce Coward (December 16, 1899 – March 26, 1973), on the 100th anniversary of his birth. Noël Coward is considered to have been one of the finest writers of high comedy in the English language, following on from the tradition of William Congreve, Richard Brinsley Sheridan, and Oscar Wilde. In more recent years, Harold Pinter, who directed Blithe Spirit at the National Theatre, and Edward Albee, author of *Who's Afraid of Virginia Woolf?* were greatly influenced by Coward's plays.

The aims of the society are to study and promote, enjoy and celebrate the myriad aspects of Coward's achievements as a playwright, composer, librettist, theatre and film director, actor, novelist, short story writer, poet, cabaret artist and wit. It owns an extensive archive of recordings and written works and is attempting to become the official on-line archive of all things 'Coward'.

Centenary Year – 1999

Noël Coward was born at Teddington, south west London. During 1999, a year that marked the centenary of his birth, a Committee chaired by Michael Imison, retired television director and one of the original directors of the Doctor Who series, organised a series of performances of plays, films, concerts, meetings, and a conference at the University of Birmingham which houses the Noël Coward Special Collection. The ornamental sword used by actor Edmund Kean (1789-1833) in his performances of Shakespeare's Richard III was presented to the University at a special session of the Centenary Conference to mark their agreement to house the archive of papers, books, and memorabilia.

New York celebrations

Prince Edward unveiled a statue of Sir Noël Coward at a gathering of the Broadway theatre community on Monday, March 1, 1999, in the Broadway Hall of Fame at the Gershwin Theatre. Present was the sculptor of the life-size statue, Angela Conner. The ceremony was the first in a year-long series of events in New York, celebrating the Centenary of Coward's birth. The Master of Ceremonies was Coward historian, Mr Barry Day OBE, current Vice President, and a prolific writer on the theatre, and Editor of *The Complete Lyrics of P G Wodehouse* and *P G Wodehouse in His Own Words*. There were remarks from the Broadway producer Mr Alexander Cohen, Prince Edward, and long-time friend, Graham Payn. Cabaret artist Steve Ross sang Noël Coward's most famous song, Mad Dogs And Englishmen. Jeannie Lehman, then in the Broadway company's The Sound Of Music, sang I'll See You Again.

Pizza-on-the-Park musical evening

In May 2000, an unusual event entitled Pizza-on-the-Park, featuring an evening of George Gershwin and Noël Coward, was staged in Hyde Park, London. It began with I Got Music that was a celebration of the life and music of George Gershwin. Michael Law, at the piano, sang a selection of Gershwin numbers with style and panache. Between the songs, Ruth Leon who is Gershwin's biographer, spoke about him with great warmth and vivacity. The event was packed with an elegant audience and to everyone's surprise Prince Edward and his sister Her Royal Highness Princess Alexandra LG GCVO, were seated together at a table. Their father Prince George is well known to have been a friend of Noël Coward. There was no pomp and circumstance but the royal presence certainly spiced the evening with a very Cowardesque touch.

Sheridan Morley took to the stage in cabaret for Noël Coward Lost and Found. He told amusing 'Noël' stories, made all the more immediate because of his own friendship with The Master. Sheridan's narration was interspersed by Michael Law performing a medley of songs: Uncle Harry, We Must All Be Very Kind To Aunty Jessie, This Is A Changing World, and Something Very Strange.

Noël Coward was well known to the Kent family and had been a guest at the wedding of Prince Edward and Miss Katharine Worsley on June 8, 1961. Soon after the night of songs and pizza in Hyde Park, Prince Edward became President of the Noël Coward Society on September 16, 2005.

Tenth Anniversary

The society's 10th anniversary celebration was a cabaret event titled *Don't Put Your Daughter on the Stage,* arranged and produced by Mrs Barbara Longford at her London club Hurlingham, on September 10, 2009. The cabaret was led and directed by the society's distinguished music expert Mr Dominic Vlasto.

Prince Edward was unable to attend as he was in Australia on official business but his Equerry, Mr Andrew Palmer GMC CVO, accompanied by his wife attended. On behalf of the society, Barbara presented Mr Palmer with the official scroll, which he kindly accepted on Prince Edward's behalf as it is the Duke's official scroll, marking his presidency of the society. Of that evening Barbara said: "Andrew and his wife were the most delightful company."

The celebrations continued at the Musgrave Theatre, adjacent to the Palm Court, in an evening's entertainment which began with a compilation film about Noël Coward provided by Ken Starrett and edited by John Knowles, containing previously unseen footage. Barry Day's book *The Essential Noël Coward* was on sale with Barry present, signing copies.

Barbara Longford speaks about
Prince Edward and the NCS connection

Mrs Barbara Longford, Chairman of The Noël Coward Society, (2004–2010), and currently Chairman and Founder of the Terence Rattigan Society, has kindly provided a most valuable background portrait to Prince Edward's connection with the Noël Coward Society:

"At a Committee meeting of the Noël Coward Society (NCS) on July 26, 2005, members discussed who might be invited to become the next President. British film and stage actor, Sir John Mills, CBE, had died on St. George's Day that year and as a close friend of the late playwright, he had been President since the inception of the society in the centenary year.

"Committee member, Robert Gardiner, also trustee of the Noël Coward Foundation, had experienced the honour of meeting The Duke of Kent at a dinner in St. Petersburg and recalled hearing him speak most warmly of Noël and his friendship with the family. His Royal Highness was known to have a genuine knowledge and admiration for Coward's work, and society members had been delighted to see him at a very informal cabaret venue 'Pizza-on-the-Park' in May of that year, accompanied by his sister, Princess Alexandra. They were enjoying a performance of Gershwin and Coward music, narrated by the then Vice President of the NCS, Sheridan Morley. The decision was taken that Robert Gardiner would ask his friend John Julius Norwich (Viscount Norwich) to approach the Duke of Kent on the society's behalf and outline the society's modest expectations of the role. I was encouraged to write to His Royal Highness and a letter was despatched on August 10, 2005. The following paragraphs are an extract from that letter:

'In the past two years we have arranged some exciting events. The latest was on 22nd May, when we officially welcomed Mr Stephen Fry as one of our Vice Presidents at a private showing of the 1935 Hecht and MacArthur film 'The Scoundrel' in which Noël starred. The event was a resounding success, made all the more pleasurable as we were able to announce the fact that the Albery Theatre was going to be re-named The Noël Coward Theatre.

'Each December, on the Saturday closest to Noël's birthday, we have a flower-laying ceremony, at the statues of our hero at the Theatre Royal, Drury Lane and the Gershwin Theatre in New York. In 2004 Lord

Attenborough was our Guest of Honour and previous performers of the ceremony have included Elaine Stritch and Alan Rickman and Lindsay Duncan. This December, a group of UK members is going over to New York for several events, including the official naming of a Noël Coward Suite at the Algonquin Hotel. Sir Phillip Thomas, the British Consul-General, will be performing the ceremony, which will be followed by a Coward cabaret in the Oak Room.

'I hope that you will think that our efforts are worthwhile especially as they are all organised and managed totally by unpaid members, who pay an annual subscription of £20.

"We realise, of course, that your Royal commitments are very exacting and demanding and may I assure you that, if you felt able to accept our invitation, we would not wish to encroach on your valuable time in any way. Of course you would learn of all our activities well in advance and be fully aware of everything we were doing, but the honour of having you associated with us is really all we are asking. We feel that Noël Coward's immense and multifaceted contribution to British culture should be recognised and promoted by a professional society, with a man of substance at its helm. I do hope that you will feel able to become President of The Noël Coward Society'."

Barbara Longford goes on to say:

"On September 16, I received a reply from Mr Nicolas Adamson, Private Secretary to His Royal Highness, saying:

'The Duke of Kent has asked me to thank you for your letter of 10th August, and to say that he would be delighted and honoured to accept your invitation to become President of The Noël Coward Society.'

"Needless to say, the Committee and members of the society were delighted and honoured also. We felt that it was a fitting tribute to the long friendship of His Royal Highness's parents, the late Prince George, Duke of Kent and Princess Marina, with Noël. The couple married in 1934, and were regarded as the most attractive, popular and, above all, stylish royal couple of their generation. Prince George met Noël in 1923, just as his career was taking off. Both men had immense charm and astonishing good looks and represented the crème de la crème of glittering 1920's London Society. On reading the terrible news of Prince George's death in an air crash, in August 1942, aged only 39, Noël wrote in his diary:

"A dreadful morning. Headlines in the papers saying that the Duke of Kent was killed in an air crash. I can hardly believe it, but of course that is nonsense because I believe it only too well. It is never difficult to believe that someone young and charming and kind is dead. They are always dying... Well, there goes a friendship of nineteen years. I shall miss him most horribly..."

Barbara says:

"Noël's friendship with the elegant Princess Marina continued throughout her life. His diaries written from the 1940's onwards, and his journals for the 1950's and 60s were liberally sprinkled with references to Princess Marina. On June 25, 1951, he wrote:

'Went with the Duchess of Kent to Covent Garden to hear Boheme – Victoria de los Angeles sang well but looked like a musical bun.... . Took the Duchess to dine at the Ivy, and then on to the Palladium for the Sid Field Benefit ... Highest spot – Judy Garland.'

Barbara asserts:

"As the years passed there were other references, some more fleeting than others:

'Lunched with the Duchess and Princess Alexandra...'
'Had tea with Princess Marina'

and so on.

"Noël was a genuine friend who adored being with the Duchess, whether entertaining her in lavish style, or merely dropping in for a quiet chat over a drink or two. Princess Marina died in 1968, aged only 61, from an inoperable brain tumour. Noël visited her for tea on the day she returned from hospital and wrote afterwards:

'... she was in bed and looked very papery. I am worried about her. She was very cheerful, however, and we gossiped and giggled.'

Barbara goes on to provide us with her own, unique experience of Prince Edward and knowledge of Noël Coward:

"I had the honour of meeting His Royal Highness at his pre-Christmas drinks party in the State Apartments of St. James's Palace in December 2009. The Duke spoke animatedly and warmly of his friendship with Noël Coward and recalled a private dinner party they had in New York when Noël had entertained the Duke and Duchess with very amusing anecdotes and songs.

"Noël Coward was born into genteel poverty at the end of the 19th century. No silver spoon for him, no private education, no university, no connections. However, through his own achievements and sheer magical genius, he rose to become one of the most celebrated artists and personalities of the 20th century. He was accepted and indeed loved in the highest circles and His Royal Highness The Duke of Kent, has honoured his memory in the most appropriate and moving way, by becoming the society's President. Sir Noël Coward, CBE, would be immensely proud."

THE ROYAL PHOTOGRAPHIC
SOCIETY OF GREAT BRITAIN

The beginnings of attempts to reproduce images (other than through art) in primitive photographic form dates back to the 6th century CE. Byzantine mathematician Anthemius of Tralles used a type of camera obscura in his experiments. Chinese philosopher Mo Ti, and Greek mathematicians Aristotle and Euclid, described a pinhole camera in the 5th and 4th centuries BC. Wilhelm Homberg described how light darkened some chemicals, known as the photochemical effect, in 1694.

Other developments more relevant to the present age were carried out by Thomas Wedgwood (1771-1805) the son of Josiah, the famous potter, and Humphry Davy, inventor of the miners' lamp [7], who were early experimenters in photography.

Wedgwood is credited with a major contribution to photography as the first man to think of and develop a method to copy visible images chemically to permanent media. In his many experiments with heat and light, Wedgwood first used ceramic pots coated with silver nitrate as well as treated paper and white leather as media of print, and had the most success with white leather. His major achievements were the printing of an object's profile through direct contact with the treated paper, thus creating an image's shape on paper, and, by a similar method, copying transparent paintings-on-glass through direct contact and exposure to sunlight. He advised James Watt (1736–1819) on the process of photography, circa 1790 or 1791.

Wedgwood met the young chemist, Humphry Davy (1778–1829). Davy wrote up Wedgwood's work and titled it: *An Account of a Method of Copying Paintings upon Glass, and of Making Profiles, by the Agency of Light upon Nitrate of Silver*, which he published in the *Journal of the Royal Institution* (1802). The paper detailed Wedgwood's procedures and accomplishments. The *Journal* was little known in those days, but the paper and Wedgwood's work directly influenced other chemists and scientists delving into the craft of photography, as subsequent research has shown that it was quite widely known.

Johann Schultz (1687–1744) was a German professor and polymath [8] and is best known for the discovery that certain silver salts, most notably silver chloride and silver nitrate, darken in the presence of light, and for using those effects to capture temporary photographic images. In an experiment, conducted in 1724, he determined that a mixture of silver and chalk reflects less light than untarnished silver. Though his discovery did not provide the means of preserving an image as the silver salts continued to darken unless protected from light, it provided the foundation for further work in fixing images.

334

The French inventor Joseph Nicéphore Niépce had succeeded in photographing camera images on paper coated with silver chloride in 1816, but could not make the results light-fast. Niépce produced the first photograph in 1826, in which he used a polished pewter plate that he covered with bitumen of Judea. The bitumen hardened when exposed to light and the unhardened material could then be washed off. An image in dark and light was then produced on the plate. The process was the precursor to the work of Louis Daguerre who, in the mid-1830s, discovered that if a silver plate was exposed to iodine vapour, a latent image was formed which could be developed using mercury fumes. The image could then be made permanent, or fixed, by washing it in a salt bath.

The earliest known photograph that includes images of people, titled Boulevard du Temple, was taken in a busy thoroughfare in Paris by Louis Daguerre, circa 1838-39. Because it took over ten minutes to develop the photograph the traffic had moved past and does not appear. There are however two people visible in the bottom left corner of the picture who remained throughout the time it was being developed as one was polishing the others boots!

Photography

The term *photography* came into use in 1839, first coined by Sir John Frederick William Herschel, and is derived from the Greek words phōs (genitive: phōtós) light, and gráphein, meaning 'to write'. The first permanent camera photograph of this type was however made in 1835, by William Henry Fox Talbot, (1800 –1877). Talbot was a British inventor and photography pioneer who invented the calotype process, a precursor to photographic processes of the 19th and 20th centuries. His work in the 1840s on photo-mechanical reproduction led to the creation of the photoglyphic engraving process, the precursor to photogravure. He made some important early photographs of Oxford, Reading, and York, England, and of Paris, France.

At an early period, Talbot had begun his optical researches, which were to have such important results in connection with photography. He said he began his photographic experiments in early 1834. He showed his five-year-old pictures at the Royal Institution of Great Britain in London, on January 25, 1839. Talbot's original contributions included the concept of a negative, from which many positive prints can be made, and the use of gallic acid for developing the latent image. Talbot's negative/positive process eventually succeeded as the basis for almost all 19th- and 20th-century photography. In 1842, for his photographic discoveries later detailed in his paper *The Pencil of Nature* (1844), Talbot received the Rumford Medal of the Royal Society.

The formation of the Photographic Society

In the winter months of 1851-52 informal discussions took place concerning the possibility of mounting a photographic exhibition. A provisional committee was formed under the leadership of Mr Roger Fenton (1819-1869) a pioneering British photographer and one of the first war photographers. On December 22, 1852, an exhibition of 784 photographs provided by 76 photographers was held in the gallery of the Society of Arts. The exhibition acted as a catalyst to the formation of a photographic society and a public meeting was held on Thursday January 20, 1853. The Photographic Society of London was formed with the objective of promoting the Art and Science of Photography. It became known as the Photographic Society and was granted the use of the Royal prefix in 1894.

The Royal Photographic Society
Today, The Royal Photographic Society whose headquarters are at Fenton House, Bath, Somerset, is an educational charity. A Royal Charter was granted on July 27, 2004. Prince Edward who is a keen amateur photographer was made an Honorary Member of the Society on April 4, 1978. The President is Mr Dirk C. Birch, ASIS HonFRPS, and the Director General is Dr Michael Pritchard, FRPS. Membership is international and is open to anyone with an interest in photography.

Each year the society presents a series of medals and awards to photographers and other individuals in photography. The most important of these is the Progress Medal, which was instituted in 1878, in recognition of any invention, research, publication or other contribution that has resulted in an important advance in the scientific or technological development of photography or imaging. It also carries with it an Honorary Fellowship of the society.

Prince Edward's love of photography has continued throughout his life. In February, 2015, he told the author: "I have enjoyed photography ever since I was given my first camera. It is a hobby of mine." [9]

Endnotes to Chapter 13

[1] The catalogue raisonné online is a free resource:
www.delaszlocatalogueraisonne.com

[2] P G Wodehouse *Joy in the Morning*, pub. Arrow Books, 2008.

[3] P G Wodehouse *Blandings Castle*, pub. Arrow Books, 2008.

[4] Other of Simon Brett's works that have been broadcast have included: *The Burkiss Way*, comedy series; *I'm Sorry I Haven't a Clue,* and a comedy panel game *Just a Minute*, plus three series of detective novels and several mystery plays.

[5] Correspondence between Miss Victoria Packenham, Sir Terry Wogan's Manager, and Celia Lee, March 17, 2014 on behalf of Sir Terry Wogan.

[6] Later Sir Humphry Davy, 1st Baronet FRS MRIA FGS (17 December 1778 – 29 May 1829), an English chemist and inventor. In 1815 he invented the Davy lamp, which allowed miners to work safely in the presence of flammable gases.

[7] Johann Heinrich Schulze or Schultz was from Colbitz in the Duchy of Magdeburg.

[8] Correspondence between HRH The Duke of Kent and Celia Lee, February 27, 2015.

CHAPTER 14

COMMONWEALTH AND INTERNATIONAL
ORGANISATIONS AND OVERSEAS VISITS
Part I

THE DUKE OF EDINBURGH'S
COMMONWEALTH STUDY CONFERENCES
AND CSCLEADERS

The Commonwealth of Nations, normally referred to as 'the Commonwealth', is an intergovernmental organisation of 54 independent member states. All members, except Mozambique and Rwanda, were part of the British Empire, out of which the Commonwealth developed. Her Majesty Queen Elizabeth II is Head of the Commonwealth and is also monarch, separately and independently, of 16 Commonwealth members, which are known as the Commonwealth realms. It is therefore rather fitting that the Queen's husband His Royal Highness Prince Philip, The Duke of Edinburgh KG KT, should be founder of the Duke of Edinburgh's Commonwealth Study Conferences.

The first Duke of Edinburgh's Commonwealth Study Conference (CSC) was held in Oxford, England, in 1956, to study the human aspects of industrial issues across Commonwealth countries. The conference provided an opportunity for people from all over the Commonwealth and all walks of life to leave their usual roles and, with a diverse group of people, examine the relationship between industry and the community around it. In 1956 Prince Philip described the objective as being "for members to look, listen, and learn in the hope that the process will help them to improve the quality of their decision-making when they reach the peaks of their occupations."

Participants at the conferences are drawn from all sectors of society and particularly include people from government bodies, non-governmental organisations (NGOs), businesses, and trades unions. On average, 300 people attend such conferences and are afforded a unique opportunity to examine a broad range of society, how each component functions, and its interactions with others.

The success of the first event, and the enthusiasm that others should benefit from the experience, led to the establishment of a secretariat to enable the continuation of CSCs. Since then, 10 conferences have been held in the UK, India, Australia, Malaysia, Canada, and New Zealand. A number of related Regional conferences have also been held in the Pacific and the Caribbean.

Influence of Canada

In 2006 a comprehensive book, *Leadership In The Making,* was published in Canada, celebrating the 50 years since the first conference. Prince Philip described how the idea came about:

> "The idea for the conference arose as a result of my visit to Canada in 1954. I had asked to visit some of the new and developing industries in Canada's far north on the way home from the Commonwealth Games in Vancouver.
>
> "Two things struck me. The great majority of these developments were 'single-industry' enterprises and, in most cases, the towns associated with the industries were 'company towns'. This is not typical for an industrialised country, but it had the effect of drawing my attention to one of the basic problems faced by industrial communities. While a company in control of an industrial enterprise has to be based on a system of managerial and technical qualifications, the town in which all the workers and the management have to live needs to be managed by some democratic system involving all the inhabitants as citizens.
>
> "The purpose of the conference was to look into the tensions, problems and opportunities created by this dichotomy between industrial enterprise and community development."

Each conference has addressed similar themes and each has provided members assessed as having the potential to rise to positions of significant influence in their communities with a unique leadership development opportunity. This opportunity has consistently been built around learning from the experience of others – both good and bad - through the application of the look, listen, and learn features as described by Prince Philip.

Prince Edward becomes Chairman of the Trustees

On January 1, 1982, Prince Edward became Chairman of the trustees of the Duke of Edinburgh's Commonwealth Study Conferences United Kingdom Fund. He is an active supporter of the CSC conference over and above his formal governance role. Over a number of years he has met with conference groups during their study tours and has hosted formal and informal receptions and dinners to meet and discuss issues with conference participants. His work in relation to the conferences complemented his work (discussed in Chapter 3).

In 2007 Prince Edward travelled to New Delhi to the Commonwealth-wide conference that was the last that conformed to the traditional format, where he made the opening address and welcomed participants to the conference in India and Malaysia.

In June 2011, when Prince Philip stepped down as President of the trustees and became Patron of the CSC (UK Fund), Prince Edward accepted the invitation of the trustees to become their new President. Mr David Ward and Mrs Libby Gawith are trustees of the UK Fund and were instrumental in establishing the partnership with Common Purpose and the first CSCLeaders program held in March and June 2013.

CSCLeaders for the 21st century

Commonwealth Study Conferences have successfully followed the format established in 1956 for over 50 years, and have rotated to a different part of the Commonwealth approximately every six years. Since 1977 there have also been several national conferences, including the Canadian Governor Generals conferences and the interim conferences in the United Kingdom.

In 2006 wide-ranging discussions were held with alumni and interested parties to review and refresh the basic concept. In 2011 building on that review, the UK Fund contracted with Common Purpose, the international leadership development organisation, to develop CSCLeaders making for a renewal of these ground-breaking Study Conferences for the Commonwealth of the 21st century.

The design for CSCLeaders represents a departure from the past, whilst maintaining its historical roots of assembling a diverse community of equals. It includes precursor conferences held in Oxford, England, and Johannesburg, South Africa, for students, followed by a linked, follow-up conference for exceptional leaders drawn from around the Commonwealth and held in the UK.

CSCLeaders is delivered by a partnership between The Duke of Edinburgh's Commonwealth Study Conferences (UK Fund) and Common Purpose, the international leadership organisation, operating in 18 countries, and which has been giving people the inspiration, skills, and connections to become better leaders both at work and in society for over 21 years.

The International Liaison Group

A number of CSC organisations around the Commonwealth were formed in the years following the original CSC conference. Their activities are co-ordinated by the CSC International Liaison Group (ILG), which was renamed in 2007 to Commonwealth Leadership Development Conferences (CLED).

At around the same time that the UK trustees were undertaking their 50-year review for the Commonwealth-wide event, a regional format under the title of Emerging Leader's Dialogue was developed by CSC Australia and CSC Canada. These conferences follow the principles of the 1956 conference and have been held in the Pacific (EPLD), sponsored by CSC Australia, and the Caribbean (CCELD) sponsored by CSC Canada, with an Emerging Leaders Dialogue in Africa (ACELD) in 2013, also sponsored by Canada. A South Asia Emerging Leader Dialogue was also taking place in 2014, sponsored by Australia.

There is now a growing network of regional and Commonwealth-wide conferences held on a regular basis around the Commonwealth. They provide an opportunity for up-and-coming leaders to examine the relationships between industry and community in real life settings, and to be challenged on their assumptions and preconceived notions of what it takes to be a leader at three key stages of leadership; student, emerging leader, and exceptional leaders on the verge of global influence.

Her Royal Highness The Princess Anne, the Princess Royal is President of the international CSC (CLED) and works with Prince Edward, who leads the UK CSC, to ensure the effectiveness of these interlocking arrangements for the Common-wealth-wide, UK-organised CSCLeaderas and the CLED regional conferences.

Emerging Pacific Leaders' Dialogue (EPLD 2006)
The CSC Australia and New Zealand, supported by Alumni and sponsors across the region, organised the Emerging Pacific Leaders' Dialogue from June 28 to July 12, 2006. Men and women from 19 Pacific nations were offered 120 places of high calibre. The chosen ten study tour destinations included Papua New Guinea, Fiji, Solomon Islands/Vanuatu, Samoa, Tonga, Kiribati, Auckland/Cook Islands, and New Caledonia. The theme of the two-week event was Navigating our Future Together. It opened in Brisbane and closed in Auckland. During the study tours, participants had the opportunity to observe communities in action and the leadership challenges that arose within them.

Commonwealth Leadership Development Conferences
The Commonwealth Leadership Development Conference which replaced The Duke of Edinburgh's Commonwealth Study Conference, continued with the conferences in 2007.

Malaysia 2007: 10th Commonwealth Study Conference
Thirty-eight delegates from various Commonwealth Countries were in Malaysia from March 18 – 25, 2007, to attend the study tours hosted by the Commonwealth Study Conference Association of Malaysia (COSCAM).

COSCAM was honoured to co-host the Tenth Commonwealth Study Confer-ence under the patronage of the Duke of Edinburgh, together with India as main host. The host organisers in India were the Confederation of Indian Industries and the conference was held from March 16-29, 2007.

Emerging Pacific Leaders' Dialogue (EPLD), 2010
The Emerging Pacific Leaders' Dialogue (EPLD) 2010, opened in Samoa on March 11, and closed in the Kingdom of Tonga on March 23. The Dialogue brought together 120 individuals to examine, discuss, and report on current strategic issues across the Pacific. The theme, Navigating Our Future Together, conveyed the idea of charting a course, working together, and negotiating the shifting tides and currents. The study tour destinations included Papua New Guinea, The Solomon Islands, Vanuatu, New Caledonia, Fiji, Kiribati, Samoa, Tonga, Australia, and New Zealand.

Caribbean-Canada Emerging Leaders' Dialogue (CCELD), 2011
On May 28, 2011, participants assembled in Gatineau, Quebec, Ottawa, Canada, for three days of Opening Session discussions on important economic, social, environmental, and regional development issues. Participants were then divided

into 10 study tour groups and travelled for a further four days to a diverse number of locations in six Provinces to build their understanding of how these issues impact on decision-making and leadership. Thereafter each group travelled to one of 10 Caribbean countries for similar visits for a further four days. The groups reconvened in Bridgetown, Barbados, from June 8-12 to report on their leadership learning experiences.

HRH The Princess Anne served as President of the Dialogue. The Princess gave freely of her time and met with each study group. Her thought-provoking and insightful observations were truly appreciated by all participants. She also visited some groups during their study tours. The success of this method of study group was that 120 Leaders, (40 Canadian and 80 Caribbean), emerged from this first-ever Caribbean-Canada Dialogue.

Conferences and themes

The underlying theme of the conferences since 1956, has been the impact of industry and commerce on people and their environment, but each conference has interpreted it to reflect prevailing concerns of the time.

New Delhi Conference, 2007

The 2007 Conference at New Delhi on India and Malaysia has been selected for readers as an example of the kind of progress that is being made in promoting good business relations between countries.

Prince Edward attended the Duke of Edinburgh's 10th Commonwealth Study Conference (CSC) that was held in New Delhi during March 2007. It was also the 60th anniversary of India's independence and the theme of the conference was centred on India and Malaysia who were twinned, and the title was Working Together for Inclusive Growth & Development. Mr Dhruv M. Sawhney was Conference Chairman. Also present were Mr Kamal Nath, Minister for Commerce and Industry, India; Mr Dick Warburton, Chairman, CSC Liaison Group; and Mr R. Seshasayee, National President, Confederation of Indian Industry (2006-7). Taking part were 188 delegates and CSC alumni from around the world. They represented 30 countries and were from varied backgrounds, and one-third of delegates were women.

Mr Sawhney in his reports of the conference says that India and Malaysia typify the opportunities and challenges of the 2007 conference theme in a number of ways, and the most obvious is that they are both multi-lingual, multi-ethnic, and multi-religion societies.

The growth of the modern-day domestic services sector has created the necessary environment for enterprise to prosper. The 2015 figures for trade volume between Britain and India are expected to show that it has doubled. Currently it is worth in the region of £23 billion. Between 2010 and 2011, trade between the two countries grew by 23 per cent, the total trade volume at 2011, standing at £16.8 billion. [1] From an economic perspective, Goldman Sachs has said that India will sustain over 8 per cent growth until 2020.

Mr Sawhney, in opening the conference, emphasised that it was a "unique time in India's history" as it was "the first such comprehensive study ever to be organised

96. Duke of Edinburgh's Commonwealth Study Group, Tenth Commonwealth Study Conference, India; left to right: Mr R.S. Pawar, Chairman NIIT Ltd; Mr T. Das, Chief Mentor CII; Mr Dhruv M. Sawhney, Chairman, Tenth Commonwealth Study Conference; HRH The Duke of Kent; Ms S. Rajan, CEO, OIFC; Ms S. Pandhi, Director CII, and Mr P. Balaji; Vice President, Ericsson.

in India." Pointing to the success of India's economy, Mr Sawhney said: "The last few years have witnessed unparalleled growth in the economy. ... Trade in and of India is also growing at an increasing pace." There were, he said, "young entrepreneurs brimming with confidence." Delegates would see almost "all of India, 18 States and Union territories" during their period of study.

Prince Edward, who is rather fond of India, said in his address what a "great pleasure" it was to be there:

> "The Commonwealth, which houses a third of the world's population is diverse in culture, but the core values of the countries have remained the same. It meant that the socio-economic challenges were similar for all countries and therefore every tour finding would be relevant to all countries at different stages of development.
>
> "If I am asked to define the conference idea, it could be summed up as 'learning by inter-action'."

Prince Edward went on to affirm the importance of the aims of the conference:

> "It is aimed to bring out contrasting experiences of two developing countries – India and Malaysia. The key questions to be looked at were:

97. *Duke of Edinburgh's Commonwealth Study Group, Tenth Commonwealth Study Conference, India, left to right: Ms Naina Lal Kidwai, CEO & Country Head, HSBC Ltd; HRH The
Duke Of Kent; Mr Dhruv M. Sawhney, Chairman Tenth Commonwealth Study Conference;
Mr Kamal Nath, Minister of Commerce & Industry, Government of India; Mr Richard Warburton, Chairman , CSC Liaison Group.*

"How can government help or hinder enterprise? Is education and
training of the highest quality and is it available to all? Are resources being
put to their best uses? And, are public and private institutions maintaining
high standards of transparency and accountability."

Prince Edward then went on to provide guidance to participants: "I urge you to
use your power of observation, prepare to talk and argue, but don't forget to listen."
He pointed out that the plan was for the "Study Groups, 12 in all, nine in India
and three in Malaysia" was "to disperse to different regions in India and Malaysia to
carry out programmes of local visits." The "tours", he said, were to be "the core of
the Study Conference" that would enable participants "to see the industrial and commercial enterprises of many kinds, and to appreciate their contribution to economic
and social progress, while at the same time considering their effects on communities
and on the environment."
Prince Edward emphasised: "Two issues that will undoubtedly feature promi-
nently in your study tours are those of poverty and development, topics of crucial
concern to many... ." He advised:

"Whilst sustained growth may well be the main driver of economic

344

development, you will also want to consider the need for a fair and balanced trading system that does not put poorer and weaker nations at a disadvantage. Here is important area where the Commonwealth could have real influence."

Ever mindful of the gradually changing role of woman, Prince Edward said:

"The economic role, especially of women, has until only recently barely been recognised or acknowledged, yet their contribution to overall development is clearly of enormous significance."

Mr Kamal Nath spoke of "Agriculture" being "at the heart of India's challenges today." He said: "Its sustainability would determine India's approach to double-digit growth in the coming years."

Indian companies in global competition

The two-day conference encouraged Indian companies to compete in global competition. It had provided a significant opportunity for people from Commonwealth countries to work together and consolidate lifetime associations. India had demonstrated that technology can change the lives of people without making huge capital investments. Millions of cellular 'phones are entering into the market in India each month, increasing connectivity and market information and thereby productivity and income levels. The conference experience had provided most crucially for its participants a course in leadership. Three key facets in India's remarkable turnaround were considered to be technology, entrepreneurship, and its democratic institutions. There were still, however, large challenges ahead, bearing in mind that there are over 400 million people under the age of 22, and employment for them is crucial.

Malaysia

The presentation on Malaysia talked about the promotion of environmental tourism. Mr Sawhney concluded that: "The study conference was a major opportunity for young minds from around the world to hold the mirror to decision makers in India and Malaysia." The twelve study groups, he said: "displayed deep understanding of the key challenges that India and Malaysia face today." These "learnings" came through following "a very short period of ten days to a fortnight's travel across the regions."

Following the 2007 conference, Mr Dhruv M. Sawhney and Mr Robert F. (Bob) Taylor, Canada, Chair, International Liaison Group, have been meeting with Prince Edward each year ever since. [2]

A history of The Duke of Edinburgh's Commonwealth
Study Conferences by Mr Edward Guinness CVO
Mr Edward Guinness, CVO, is a member of the famous Guinness brewing family. He

will be 91 years of age in 2015, and was one of the first intake of the Commonwealth Study Conference groups and is a former Chairman of the UK trustees. We are indebted to Mr Guinness for an impeccably kept record of his own experience of the first conference in 1956, just eleven years after the end of the Second World War, and which is in itself an historical document. [3] Mr Guinness has provided us with an insight into the responsibilities Prince Edward would eventually take over some 26 years later in his role as Chairman of trustees.

Mr Guinness says:

"I first became aware of the intention to hold a conference, presided over by Prince Philip in March/April 1956. The preliminary preparatory work had been started in the winter of 1953-54, and by March 1956, all was in place to start the recruitment of members both in the United Kingdom and through the Commonwealth and Empire (as it was at that time).

"Throughout the conference, great stress was laid on the fact that we were there as individuals, learning what was on offer for ourselves, and not as representatives of any industry, firm, or trades union. Nevertheless a start had to be made somewhere and so industrial organisations and trades unions were invited to put forward nominees who were in their late 20s and early 40s that were active in pursuits outside their immediate jobs, and who were regarded as being 'up and coming' and thereby likely to be influential within their communities in the future. The theme was very much The Influence of Industrialisation on Society and vice versa, and the 300 members of the first conference aged 30-42, were drawn exclusively from industrial organisations or trades unions throughout the Commonwealth.

"One of the organisations approached was the Brewing Industry in the UK and to my surprise I was their nominee. I was 32 years of age, and was Labour Manager of the Guinness Brewery at Park Royal, London. I was already much involved with bodies such as the Industrial Welfare Society, the Institute of Personnel Management, and several Charities, and had the qualification, but I was grateful to others for placing me in the up and coming category.

"I was interviewed twice in my office and attended a small selection lunch in London with other nominees, with the result that on the afternoon of Sunday, July 8, 1956, I stood on the platform of London's Paddington Station to catch the Special Conference Train to Oxford. We were especially asked to travel by this train and not to drive to Oxford by car so that bonding could start at the earliest moment. So began a three-week experience which was to have a profound effect on my future thinking and indeed upon my life.

"I was very excited and as the train was about to leave, a large Chief in flowing white robes said farewell to three ladies all said to be his wives, and I realised I was embarking on something completely different to what I was accustomed. Surprisingly, this gentleman turned out to be the General Secretary of the Construction Workers Union from the then Gold Coast.

He subsequently appointed himself to be Prince Philip's bodyguard and in photographs was seen to be standing behind the Prince.

"From Oxford Station we were bussed to our various colleges, Christ Church, Pembroke, Oriel, and University College, and one could see on a beautiful evening, that 'the dreaming spires' and the colleges we passed were having a remarkable effect on my new-found colleagues from the Commonwealth and this was important in orientating us to the conference proper.

"The following morning, L.C. Katilungu, General President of the Mineworkers Union in the Northern Rhodesia Copperbelt received a cable from his senior colleagues in Kitwe, asking him to authorise a strike. His immediate reply was that for three weeks he was a member of Prince Philip's conference and the decision must be taken by them, not him. This brave response spread very quickly among us and had a marked effect on attitudes to the conference."

The 300 conference members were divided into a number of study groups each with 15 people. Mr Guinness continues:

"In three weeks, people were adjusting very quickly in terms of personal relationships and this to the members proved to be one of the key benefits as it would have a lasting effect, long after the conference period had ended. The calming influence of Oxford and its colleges, especially Christ Church wherein for the first five days we all ate and some slept, was very marked. After Prince Philip had made his remarkable Opening Address in the Sheldonian Theatre, we divided our time between getting to know each other in our Study Groups and listening to some very illuminating talks by leaders from the UK and the Commonwealth which were delivered in Rhodes House, the Rhodes Scholars being an important part of Oxford life, and Rhodes House itself had very historic connections to the Commonwealth.

"One of the later speakers was Mr Harry Oppenheimer [one of the richest men in the world] a South African Member of Parliament and very influential in finance and mining circles in South Africa and the Copperbelt. His subject was Industrial Relations in a Multi-Racial Society. In 1956, South Africa and the Rhodesias were both fully members of the conference. Many of the black African members had met and agreed that the moment Harry Oppenheimer rose to speak, they would stage a walkout. The walkout did not happen. The prevailing atmosphere that had been generated by then showed that as far as the conference itself was concerned such an act of protest would achieve nothing. Speaking to people afterwards it was clear that the majority felt that a very controversial subject had been handled in the Oppenheimer speech in a humane and rational way, and that we had been listening to something which could not have been delivered in his own country. The conference was already history-breaking in terms of tolerance.

Working together

"With regard to the early settling in of the Groups, … Study Group Chairmen had been selected … and they had attended seminars [in advance] preparing them for their crucial roles. Clearly a priority in their coaching had been addressed to the problems of bringing people from such varying backgrounds to work cohesively in groups of 15 people… I felt that the people who had the greatest difficulty in this respect were the trade unionists. In 1956, the unions were contrasting in that at the head of many of them were some very statesman-like men and women, whose actions were always both constructive and patriotic. Many of them had played significant roles in the organising of the conference. Underneath this tier was a substantial body of trade union members who were apathetic to union politics and were mainly concerned about the retention of their jobs and the welfare of their families (and football team!). But there was a third group – Communist-inspired – who saw industrial unrest as a means of bringing about a new order and those were operating on a global basis. They were infiltrating the trades unions and at plant level were exploiting procedural rules to obtain influential roles as shop stewards. Post-War industrial and social conditions presented problems, which were undoubtedly an additional factor, but the militancy in the trade union ranks meant that strikers and the threat of strikes and go-slows were very rife at this time. Management as a whole was unprepared for the new situation and concessions granted in negotiations must have convinced many of the silent majority that the lead of the militants was worth following. … Foremen/supervisors felt that their traditional roles had been completely undermined and they were receiving no training in how to cope with the new challenges facing their authority.

"In 1947, my Company, Guinness, had suffered its first strike in its 190-year-history. It was unofficial as Guinness had already signed an Agreement with the Unions, which included dispute procedure. Although they [those attending the conference] had been carefully selected, some trades union members were not conditioned to be co-operative with Management, indeed at the start, one or two saw the conference as an Establishment ruse to blunt trade union power. The background papers however and the early addresses had emphasised that the issues with which the conference was concerned could be summarised as a study of the effect Industrialisation was having throughout the Commonwealth on Communities and the effect society with its Post War aspirations was having on Industry. The conference was not concerned with wages and working conditions but those wider issues which impinge on the lives of so many of us and cannot be settled round a negotiating table.

Investment of American capital in Scotland

"Taking one example, after our time in Oxford and a short period in London where we attended a Buckingham Palace Garden Party, my Group 'I' travelled to the Scottish Border Towns and thence to Edinburgh University where, inter alia, we were told by a professor from Glasgow that at that stage 80 per cent of all American capital that was invested in the UK had come to Scotland. This manifested itself when we came to Dundee."

Here, Mr Guinness broke off to relate an amusing story about the Prince of Wales, later King Edward VIII, who abdicated in 1936 to marry Mrs Wallace Simpson, and who was very much a man of the people and visited the ordinary workingmen and trades unionists at their places of work:

"In the 1930s the Prince of Wales went to lunch with some trades unionists in a hotel. The trade union chap who arranged the lunch especially for the Prince hadn't a clue about etiquette. The trades union leader sat at the top of the table with the Prince next him instead of the other way round. When the soup was served the man at the top of the table was naturally served first. The Prince didn't bat an eyelid! The ice bucket was placed on the table and the trade union chap helped himself to an ice cube but instead of putting it in his glass of water, he dropped it into his soup! Rather than embarrass the man, when Prince Edward picked up an ice cube he, too, dropped it into his soup."

Mr Guinness continued in relation to the conference:

Employment of women

"This influx of capital had resulted in the building of new factories (for example the National Cash Register Company), and a high proportion of the employees were male. Traditionally, Dundee had been the centre of the Jute Industry that had fallen away but was then enjoying a revival. The labour force however, had been absorbed by the factories, and in desperation the jute employers had established crèches at the factories to attract women with young families back into employment. Visiting them we found it meant that mothers were leaving their homes very early with their babies or toddlers and travelling in often bitterly cold weather conditions to hand them over to the nurses at the crèche while the older children left later in the morning for school with the house key tied round their neck so that when school finished they were able to let themselves into an empty, often cold house, with no meal prepared for them until their mother returned home from work.

"For the ensuing discussion on this subject we were joined by an employer, a union official, and the lady who had overall responsibility for the crèches. The two in our group who were from India and Ceylon (later Sri Lanka) were appalled and vehemently argued that no economic condition could justify such a practice. The discussion was indeed lively and all participants realised that they were expressing their own views and not representatives' views of their organisations. Out of this [method of discussion] developed what we called an ésprit de Group, so that by the time we arrived back in Oxford to prepare our final reports to be delivered in plenary session before Prince Philip, we had achieved a harmonious coherence with each member willingly playing his or her agreed part in that preparation. To have achieved this was a great relief to us all, especially to the trades union members who became far more relaxed in enjoying the experience. I, myself, was fortunate in that as Labour Manager of Guinness at Park Royal, I had five years' experience in forging relationships with the trades unions, both at the plant and at national level, and it had enabled me to help our Study Group Chairman a good deal.

"I belonged to study Group 'I' which was housed in Christ Church College, Oxford. It was a memorable experience in itself for those of us who had not been to a university as part of our education. After the four-day shake down period, we travelled to London for an afternoon where we attended a Buckingham Palace Garden Party; then to Shell Mex House for a briefing on our Study Tour Itinerary; and then by sleeper train to Scotland, where we started in the Border Towns of Hawick, Selkirk, and Galashields, with discussion points with local people at each, followed by a day in Edinburgh, and luncheon at Edinburgh Castle, followed by a talk in the afternoon at Edinburgh University about Scottish Industry.

"We then travelled on to Dundee and St. Andrews, where we spent an evening with the Scottish Trades Union Congress, who were in conference. The following morning, we discussed relations between University and Industry with the dons and then to the envy of local residents we lunched at the Royal and Ancient Golf Club of St. Andrews." [4] (See also Chapter 17).

The merry party then went on their way to their next place of interest, which was "to go down a local coalmine at Glenrothes." [5] Planned in the late 1940s as one of Scotland's first post-Second World War new towns, the purpose of Glenrothes was to house miners who were working at a newly established coalmine, The Rothes Colliery. Mr Guinness continues: "The group encountered the problems associated with starting a New Town – in this case by a coalmine – which was experiencing its own problems."

The group then went south to look at how "'the New Towns, especially Stevenage, were coping with a variety of issues, including the problem of alienation caused by being moved there from the East End of London." Finally, they arrived "at Heathrow Airport to look at the problems that had arisen in establishing it as London's No.1 Airport, and where finding housing accommodation for those employed there was a major concern."

Final six days of the Conference

Mr Guinness continued:

"On July 1, the study groups returned to their base at Oxford for the final, all important six days of the conference. In the evening at Rhodes House, Sir Harold Hartley the Conference Chairman, gave a very far-seeing address on his views as a technologist of the causes for the rapid changes which were then taking place and the material and spiritual problems arising from these changes which mankind now had to face. He foresaw global water supplies as a matter for particular concern for the future.

"Overseas commentaries by speakers from the Gold Coast, India, South Africa, and Canada (W. J. Bennett) were given at intervals at Rhodes House during the next few days.

The programme

"The programme was organised so that Monday would see the start of the work on the final Study Group Reports to be delivered on Thursday of that week. The groups (each still numbering 15 members) were divided up into five teams, and were allocated a particular subject within the category of Industry and Community on which they were to report on an Inter-Group basis. One aspect was that the Group Report was to be prepared for presentation at the final plenary session on Thursday.

"From our Group 'I', Mr Evan Wong, Mines Superintendant at the Demerara Bauxite Company in British Guiana, Mr Andrew Torrance, the Assistant Personnel Manager at the Mufulira Copper Mines in Northern Rhodesia, and myself, were chosen. Our Report for the plenary session was entitled *Industry and Community* and the opening paragraphs covered our many findings on this relationship in the course of the Tours. Thereafter in individual sections we covered Housing, Family Life, Education, the Position of Old People, and the Size of the Community.

"It was held afterwards that our Report and that by Group 'F' on *Organisations and Relationships at Work* were two of the best. The 1956 conference was fully documented and, fifty years on, the Report makes interesting reading with so many of the questions posed in our findings still unanswered.

Final day of Conference

"On the final day, Friday, July 27, the Vice Chancellor of Bristol University made the important observation in his summing up that from the point of view of the members the success of the conference lay in the fact that we had come to learn and not to teach. All of us had learned so much that was new to us and outside our experience. I think we all felt great pride in knowing ever afterward we would be able to say those wonderful words 'I was there'."

Prince Philip closes the 1956 Conference

Prince Philip then aged 35, closed the conference, with an inspiring address in Rhodes House that was followed by a final dinner at Christ Church Hall. Mr Guinness comments:

"Although only in his early 30s and with the Queen in the second year of her reign, Prince Philip had established himself as a leader and a speaker which had earned him widespread respect. From the start, he very closely and actively identified himself with the project and throughout I was amazed by how much time he was able to devote to us, encouraging us so much by his example. This was fundamental. A personal invitation from Prince Philip would bring the Great and the Good to Buckingham Palace, St. James's Palace, or Congress House [headquarters of the Trades Union Congress]. It was a joy, post-conference, to hear those involved offering their personal services. The inspiration of the spirit of enthusiasm and co-operation coming from Prince Philip has been the vital ingredient for later conferences.

Keeping in touch

"Afterwards, all the groups met individually for a final time. We were exhausted but quite emotional. Three weeks before, we had come together as complete strangers. In Group 'I', we were leaving as firm friends with a silent prayer that the ésprit de Group we had generated would live on in each of us.

"Next morning, Prince Philip was on the platform at Oxford railway station to wave us goodbye as we departed on another Special Train."

Plans for the future

Mr Guinness says that in the beginning, "It had been believed that the conference was a one-off with no plans to continue it into the future." A group including Mr Guinness were very eager that it should continue, and he says: "so already in the early post-conference months we were meeting at different locations and formulating proposals."

Influence of Canada 1962 Conference

As it transpired they were not alone. Mr Guinness continues: "Fortunately, Conference members in Canada and Australia were thinking along the same lines. The 1962 conference in Canada was to prove the turning point for the definite continuance of future activity." The Conference Treasurer Mr E. P. Taylor, played an important role, having raised a surplus which made it possible to form "a Central trusteeship and secretariat." It "was agreed to set up a secretariat in London, chaired by Sir Harold Hartley who, it will be recalled, had chaired the 1956 conference. Sir Harold arranged a weekend gathering of the 1956 conference members at the Central Electricity Generating Board's Training Centre in Surrey." Those present as members were: "Mr Reginald Verdon-Smith (Vice-Chair); Mr Alexander Fleck (Chairman of ICI and Membership Committee, 1956); Sir John Hanbury-Williams (Chairman of Courtaulds and Treasurer, 1956); Mr Tom Williamson (General Secretary, General and Municipal Workers Union GMWU), and Mr Tom King, (General Manager, Administration, Shell Mex and BP, and Study Group Chairman 1956). Miss Suzanne Walker who was Harold Hartley's secretary became Secretary to the new Committee. Shortly afterwards they were joined by Mr Jack Cooper who had been a Study Group Chairman in 1956, and who succeeded Mr Tom Williamson of the GMWU."

At the weekend gathering in Surrey, "unanimous agreement" was reached that they "should continue, and set up planning for the future. It was further agreed that there should be set up a Central Committee of Study Groups whose membership should not be confined to conference members. Prince Philip was informed and once again, he gave his whole-hearted personal support. The setting up of the Central Committee of Study Group 'I'" of which Mr Guinness "became Founder Chairman was also agreed."

Mr Guinness continues: "Over the next months we formed about 15 Groups round the country." The subjects they considered were: "The Introduction of Shift work into an Area; Training of Young People; The Optimum Use of Leisure; (in the 1960s there was a widespread belief that technology would bring about shorter working hours and thereby greater leisure); Redundancy and Retirement, the recommendations of which formed the basis of the Government's Redundancy Act."

The weekend locations where their meetings took place: "varied from Butlins Holiday Camp at Bognor Regis; Company Training Centres, and Keele and Manchester Universities. Prince Philip invariably attended them on the Saturday evenings and was a great inspiration and discerning in his comments."

By the early 1970s "Harold Hartley had died and Miss Suzanne Walker became conference Organiser at St. George's House, Windsor." In 1972 Mr Guinness "took over the Chairmanship of the UK trustees from Sir Michael Clapham who had become President of the Confederation of British Industries (CBI) and Chairman of ICI." Mr Guinness "then became a member of Prince Philip's Council, preparing for the 1974 UK conference", in which he and Miss Betty Sharp his Personal Assistant "became actively involved."

Change to interim mini-conferences

Mr Guinness says that: "After the 1974 Conference it was agreed that rather than resurrect the Central Committee of Study Groups, it would be better to organise Interim mini-conferences confined to UK members. The first was held in Holland in 1977."

Mr Guinness hands over the Chairmanship to Prince Edward

Mr Guinness remained Chairman of UK trustees, until he "handed over to The Duke of Kent," having "consulted with Prince Philip on the matter" and that "Prince Edward was Prince Philip's choice."

Prince Edward was made Chairman of UK trustees on January 1, 1982. Mr

Guinness says that the interim period "resulted in a good friendship with His Royal Highness" and that "from the start he was enthusiastic and anxious to learn his role as quickly as possible. He attended trust committee meetings" and at

"a regional mini-conference in 1983 at Aston University, Birmingham, he presided over the final session and commented on the group presentations in the manner Prince Philip had adopted."

Mr Guinness also recalls

"Prince Edward attending the 1986 conference in Australia, and the 1992 conference in the UK."

On that occasion

"the final dinner was held at Blenheim Palace and was graced by the presence of three Dukes: Edinburgh, Kent, and Marlborough."

Mr Guinness observed in particular, Prince Edward's "ability to relax people" [6] who were perhaps meeting him for the first time.

Historic get together in 2013

Mr Guinness took a trip down memory lane when he was a guest at the St. James's Palace reception for members of the Duke of Edinburgh's Commonwealth Study Conference in the spring of 2013. Says Mr Guinness: "Prince Philip stepped back from the group with whom he was chatting and said to me: 'You ought to be in a glass case.' " Never short of an answer, Mr Guinness replied: "If that is so, Sir, I hope you will join me as by now you and I could be the only survivors of the 1956 conference." [7]

Sir Alan Parker, Chairman and founder of the Brunswick Group LLP, is the current Chairman of the Duke of Edinburgh's Commonwealth Study Conferences UK Trust. His father, Sir Peter Parker, was the Conference Director of the founding Conference in 1956.

Endnotes to Chapter 14 Part 1

[1] Figures from the *Economic Times*, 23rd February 2013.

[2] Sources: the papers of His Royal Highness The Duke of Kent, St. James's Palace. Report of Mr Dhruv M. Sawhney, Chairman, The Duke of Edinburgh's 10th Commonwealth Study Conference, India, 2007. The written accounts of Mr David Ward, trustee of the UK Fund and Mrs Libby Gawith, trustee of the UK Fund, provided to Celia Lee, February 12, 2014.

[3] Source: manuscripts written by Mr Edward Guinness CVO; August 6, 2010, from his original report; and, from the report of 1956 Aftermath and Formation of Central Committee of Study Groups, 16th October 2005.

[4] Ibid.

[5] Telephone conversation of 20th January and written correspondence from Mr Edward Guinness CVO, of 6th and 21st February 2013.

[6] Source, Letter from Mr Edward Guinness CVO to Celia Lee, 6th February 2013.

[7] Letter from Mr C.E. Guinness, CVO, December 4, 2013 to Celia Lee.

CHAPTER 14
(continued)

COMMONWEALTH AND INTERNATIONAL ORGANISATIONS AND OVERSEAS VISITS

PART II

Introduction

As is apparent from earlier chapters, Prince Edward has fostered good relations with many organisations and other countries, and made a vast number of overseas visits, creating friendship between the UK and other countries. This chapter covers The Special Relationship With Poland; The Anglo Jordanian Society of which he is a co-Patron; and the visits he made in 2012 to Uganda, Ascension Island, and the Falkland Islands.

THE SPECIAL RELATIONSHIP WITH POLAND

Prince Edward's special relationship with Poland was, like so many other friendships in the UK, in the main born out of a wartime situation and originally involved his parents.

Brief history

In August 1937, during a peasants' strike and prior to the outbreak of the Second World War in 1939, British backing was sought for Poland, and King George VI and Queen Elizabeth were invited on a visit. Prince Edward's glamorous parents, Prince George and Princess Marina, were sent in place of the monarch. During their time there they stayed in Count Potocki's Castle Łańcut that was some 300 kilometres from Warsaw. Their visit was announced on Pathe News in British cinemas as being a traditional European holiday, rather than an official visit, and newsreel was shown of the royal couple being driven about in a horse-drawn carriage, and posing for photographs on the castle steps with the Potocki family.

98. HRH Prince George Duke Of Kent and
HRH Princess Marina Duchess Of Kent, who
visited Poland, August 1937.

The decision to send the Kents to Poland was due to Princess Marina having known Zoia de Stoeckl since they were young girls living in Paris, at which time they became life-long friends. Whilst living in London, Zoia had married Mr Alfons Poklewski Koziell a member of the Polish nobility.

Alfons then got a job working for a company in Poland, running a smelting and mining business and they returned there. Their son, Vincent Poklewski Koziell, remembers the Duke and Duchess of Kent staying at his family home at Łańcut, and his mother Zoia riding in the carriage with them. At the outbreak of the Second World War, Alfons was Managing Director of the company. But due to the war situation they were obliged to leave and return to live in London.

During the London blitz of 1940, children were evacuated to the countryside. Vincent, having been born at St. John's Wood in 1929, can recall that, aged eleven he, and his parents, were taken in by the Kents to live in their country home, Coppins House at Iver in Buckinghamshire. Later, when two cottages known as Coppins Cottages that normally housed estate staff became vacant, Vincent's family occupied one and his grandmother, the Baroness Agnes de Stoeckl who was Zoia's mother, lived in the other. The friendship between the two families blossomed even further and there were frequent visits to the Kent's home where other guests included the Princesses Elizabeth and Margaret, and even on occasion, King George VI

99. HRH The Duke of Kent attending the unveiling of the statue of General Sikorski, Portland Place, London W1. September 24, 2000.

and Queen Elizabeth.

Vincent saw a good deal of Prince George and Princess Marina and their son Prince Edward, and the two boys became friends from when they were school-boys. Zoia was invited weekly by Princess Marina to lunch at the Kent's home, and there were get togethers and Christmas parties at the cottages, and Zoia later visited Princess Marina at other of the Kent's royal homes, including Kensington Palace, London.

Just before the fall of France to Nazi Germany, General Sikorski, who was also Commander-in-Chief of Polish Forces, moved from Paris to London in September 1939. The British Embassy in Poland and the British Council (Warsaw Office) were also operating in exile, and all were reporting to the British Foreign and Common-wealth Office. Poland having been occupied first by the Germans and then by the Russians, saw the entire Polish Armed Forces and Government-in-exile run from London.

After the Nazi and Soviet attacks on Poland in September 1939, some of the first to arrive in the UK to offer their services in the continued fight were Polish pi-lots. Being himself a pilot on active war service and due to his involvement with the Welfare Section of the Royal Air Force, Prince George was fully aware of the plight of his fellow pilots and was very supportive. Being mindful of the cultural needs of the First Ally, he became very involved in the initiative.

Mr Alfons Poklewski Koziell was now President of the Polish Red Cross, which organisation had been relocated to The Polish House, as it was originally referred to, that is today the Polish Hearth Club, South Kensington, London. General Władyslaw Sikorski, Prime Minister-in-exile of the Republic of Poland, used to visit Mr Poklewski Koziell at the cottage in Iver. General Sikorski and Prince George knew each other rather well, due to the Prince being an officer in the British Royal Air Force (RAF). Having reached the rank of Air Vice-Marshal, during the war, Prince George waived rank and reverted to being a Group Captain. In 1941 he became an Air Commodore in the Welfare Section of the RAF Inspector General's staff, which meant he went on official visits to RAF bases to help boost morale, and these included Polish pilots who were fighting with the British RAF.

The Polish House that is today
Ognisko Polskie, the Polish Hearth Club

Due to the increasing numbers of Poles arriving in London it was at the Polish Embassy, in November 1939, that His Excellency the Polish Ambassador Mr Edward Raczynski first discussed with Lord Lloyd, the British Colonial Secretary who was also Chairman of the British Council, the idea of setting up a Polish House in London (known in Polish as: Kasyno Polskie w Londynie), Kasyno meaning Little House. A house was leased from the British Government in South Kensington, in order to have a centre where the Free Poles would feel at home.

The Polish house then referred to as the Polish Hearth and known today as the Polish Hearth Club (Ognisko Polskie) was set up on July 1, 1940, under the patronage of the British Council which had just received its Royal Charter in April 1940. The inclusion of the word Ognisko meaning hearth, in the club's title is two-fold. It gave the impression of the welcoming hearth of home in relation to the return of soldiers from the First World War. The notion had been popularised in a song by Ivor Novello (1914), titled Keep the Home-Fires Burning ('till the boys come home). It was also due to the National Hearths that was a British Foreign and Commonwealth Office initiative, run through the British Committee for Relations with Other Countries that had been set up in 1934. Mr Stanisław Stronski, who was a former Polish Minister of Information and a close associate of the BBC Polish News Service, is recorded as having used the name Ognisko Polskie in relation to the Polish House, and it was also printed as such in *The Times* on July 15, 1940. The Anglo/Polish Society met at No.45 Princes Gate, Exhibition Road in 1940, and Cultural Propaganda operated out of No.55, from 1940-45. After the war, No.55 was named the Polish Hearth and became a modern club and the name was later lengthened to the Polish Hearth Club.

Setting up the Polish House

Meetings to set up the Polish House as it was then known took place in preparation for the arrival of the Polish Government-in-exile. Its establishment was done relatively swiftly through the efforts of the Polish Ambassador in London with help from Lord Lloyd and Prince George in his capacity as a member of the RAF Welfare Section. The Foreign Office of both Britain and Poland were involved in the behind the scenes operation with Sir Frank Savery CBE, who was Consul General at the British Embassy in Warsaw from July 1919 until September 1939.

Sir Frank Savery became the First Chairman of the Polish Hearth, serving until

1949. Count Jan Balinski Jundzill was Vice Chairman from 1940-49, and again from 1949-73. The First Director was Professor Bernard Massey for a few months from November 1939, and Mr Ronald Braden took over in 1940.

The rapid fall of France to the Germans had just taken place when Mr Braden oversaw the inauguration of the Polish Hearth by Prince George in his role as President, accompanied by his wife Princess Marina, on July 16, 1940. Amongst those in attendance on this special day were the President of Poland His Excellency Mr Raczkiewicz, General Sikorski, and members of the Polish Cabinet. The event was also well attended by prominent Allied representatives fresh from France, and among the British dignitaries were Lord Halifax, the Foreign Secretary, Lord Lloyd, and His Eminence Cardinal Hinsley. The Polish Hearth was blessed by the Right Reverend Bishop Gawlina. The Polish Naval Choir sang to the accompaniment of the Empire Trio, before and after the ceremony. It was reported in the British press that His Royal Highness Prince George The 1st Duke of Kent had said:

"It is a great sign of strength that we are able, while devoting our whole energy to the war, to keep the machinery of civilization running smoothly. The losses Poland have suffered are not only material, but threaten to strike at the national spirit of the country. By giving them that house we should be able to express our admiration and thanks for their support in our joint cause."

There was then, and still is, at the Polish Hearth Club a lovely Victorian marble fireplace that is the centre piece of the ground floor restaurant and, like the wall chandeliers, it is adorned with an original, Josiah Wedgwood, blue macaque panel. Lighted, scented candles, glisten on the mantle-piece next to floral arrangements to the memory of those who gave their lives for Poland in two world wars.

One can still today visualise gatherings taking place there long ago, around a crackling, log-fire on cold, foggy winter's nights, during the time it was used as a Polish Officers' mess. When the officers arrived they were obliged to remove their firearms and leave them in the hall before entering the club. General Władysław Anders, a general in the Polish army and later a politician in the government-in-exile in London, had a favourite table that is tucked behind a gothic pillar in the right-hand corner, just inside the entrance door to what is today a flourishing and popular restaurant and bar. The club is steeped in history and portraits of the late generals Anders and Sikorski adorn the wall above the bar. There lingers about the place in the gloaming of the evening, when the sun is setting through the window, an atmosphere of Polish officers in the 1940s wearing smart uniforms decorated with bright medals, the crunch of big leather boots on a wood floor, the chink of vodka glasses sparkling in the light of a log fire, laughter, and talk of war and how to win it, and then, after all their efforts, having to face eventual exile from their beloved Poland.

More than 200,000 Polish armed forces personnel fought under British command during the war. They were barred from marching in the Victory Day Parade through London on June 8, 1946, for fear of angering Joseph Stalin, who had ordered his troops to take over the whole of Poland that was now under complete Russian occupation.

In 1942 the Polish Hearth had to move temporarily from South Kensington to the larger premises of 45 Belgrave Square, London, SW1, having received a donation towards the expense from the British Consul. The club was the centre for Polish social and cultural life and was used by Ministers of the Polish Government-in-exile who met there, and was visited by leaders of other nations-in-exile including the Hungarians to whom there is a plaque on the exterior wall.

Various other buildings were leased to house the different Polish ministries and departments and associated organisations, at another address at Kensington Palace Gardens, London W1. The Rubens At The Palace Hotel, Buckingham Palace Road, London SW1, housed the Polish General Headquarters and the office of General Sikorski and his Free State Polish Army, and there remains a commemorative plaque at the entrance to the hotel.

The Belgrave Square premises however, proved too expensive to keep up and, in 1945, the club returned and took up permanent occupation again at No. 55 Princes Gate, Exhibition Road, South Kensington.

Prince Edward's special relationship with Poland

Prince Edward's special relationship with Poland therefore originates from the time of his father Prince George. General Sikorski wanted a Central European Federation and it was the Polish peoples' wish that Prince George should be King of Poland after the war when it was hoped that Poles would be in control of their homeland. Sadly, that was not to be for as we have seen in Chapter 1, Prince George was killed in a 'plane crash whilst on active service on August 25, 1942, just six weeks before Prince Edward's 7th birthday. With the Soviet Union in control of Poland a monarchy was out of the question and in any event as we have seen in Chapter 4, the King wished Prince George to become Governor-General of Australia at the end of 1939, which post could not be taken up by him either due to the outbreak of the Second World War that year.

Ten months later, on June 23, 1943, Princess Mariana, now a war widow, paid a visit to the Polish Hearth that was then at Belgrave Square, where a small reception was organised in her honour. The interest shown by the Kent family in the Polish community continued after the end of the war. Princess Marina took on the duties of her late husband, becoming a frequent visitor to and supporter of the club relocated to 55 Princes Gate. On the 20th anniversary of the club's opening, June 20, 1960, the Princess was present and was photographed shaking hands with and welcoming those attending. (For further reading on the Polish Hearth Club see Chapter 16).

International Trade Fair Poznań, Poland

The Polish people would suffer the tactics of the Soviet Union's leader, Joseph Stalin, and his successors, during the occupation of Poland, until the last of their troops left their beloved homeland in 1993. Their heels were scarcely out of the country when, in June 1994, Prince Edward left with his entourage to attend the Poznań International Trade Fair. This event is the biggest industrial fair in Poland

and is held on the Poznań fairground in the centre of the city of Europehttp. There are in the region of 13,200 exhibitors, including about 3,000 foreign companies from 70 countries, participating in 80 trade fair events. The itinerary is an example of the amount of work Prince Edward undertakes during an official overseas visit.

On arrival, June 12, at 15.00 hours, Prince Edward was met by His Excellency Mr Michael Llewellyn Smith CMG, British Ambassador to Poland, Mr Wokciech Kaczmarek the Mayor of Poznań, and several other important dignitaries. He attended a reception laid on to mark the opening of the fair, hosted by Mr Leslaw Podkanski the Minister for Foreign Economic Co-operation. There was then a meeting with the Prime Minister Mr Waldemar Pawlak, and an exchange of gifts.

Moving on to Zakrzewo and arriving at 16.45 hours, Prince Edward was met by the President of the Bank Wielkopolski. There was a short welcoming ceremony, followed by an opportunity to rest.

By 19.30 hours, Prince Edward had arrived at Kórnik, where he was taken on a short tour of historic Kórnik Castle. Once the home of Count Władysław Zamoyski, who had willed it and its extensive art collection and the Kórnik Arboretum to the Polish state, and it houses also a museum and library.

There was a dinner at 20.00 hours, hosted by Mr Wlodimierz Lecki in the name of the President of Poland with around 30 guests in attendance and a further exchange of gifts.

On June 13 Prince Edward arrived at Poznań International Trade Fair, where he was met by Mr Laskowski, Director of the Fair. He was taken on a tour of the stands of the British participants and the press were present.

On June 14 Prince Edward arrived in Warsaw. At 11.57 hours, he visited Belweder Palace that is the residence of the President of Poland and used for ceremonial purposes. He was met by His Excellency Mr Lech Walesa, President of the Republic of Poland, and there was another exchange of gifts. Somewhat nostalgically, the palace had belonged to the last King of Poland, Stanisław August Poniatowski, who had used it as a porcelain-manufacturing plant.

Lunch took place at the British Embassy's Commercial Section with Polish and British businessmen. In the evening at 19.00 hours, Prince Edward visited the Warsaw Chamber Opera, where there was an invited audience for a performance of Venus and Adonis by John Blow, followed by a short reception.

During his stay in Poland, Prince Edward was also taken to visit several places of historic interest including Farny Church, the Museum of Musical Instruments, Lednica Open Air Ethnographic Museum, Wawel Castle the seat of Poland's former Kings, an exhibition of Eastern Arts, Wawel Cathedral, and Jagiellonian University.

Prince Edward is awarded the Grand Cross of the Order of Merit
Mr Andrzej Morawicz who was Chairman of the Polish Hearth Club, for 20 years until 2012, said of Prince Edward in interview:

"His Royal Highness was awarded the Grand Cross of the Order of Merit of the Republic of Poland (Order Zasługi Rzeczypospolitej Polskiej) on April 2, 1997. His Excellency the Polish Ambassador Mr Ryszard Stemplowski

100. George, The Earl of St. Andrews addressing the audience at the Last Night of the Proms, Cracow, Poland, 2005; next him, Mr Patrick Davies OBE, British Vice Ambassador. The concert was sponsored by Price Waterhouse Coopers.

held a dinner at the Polish Embassy in London to mark the occasion. The Award is accorded to those who have rendered great service to the Polish nation and it is a great honour for his Royal Highness to have it bestowed upon him. Having been created in 1974, it is granted to foreigners or Poles resident abroad and as such is a traditional diplomatic order."

Last night of the Proms, Cracow
In 1995 Cracow Industrial Society decided to organise a replica of London's Last Night of the Proms in Krakow. It was the idea of two CIS members, Grzegorz Łuczkiewicz and Richard Lucas. The instant success of the concert prompted the society to turn it into an annual event. Today many soloists from Poland and abroad perform in front of audiences at this prestigious and fun event. The concert is dedicated to the British people who work in Poland and is a meeting place for the international business community as well as music lovers. Prince Edward was made Royal Patron on January 1, 1999.

The Earl of St. Andrews and Lord Nicholas Windsor visit Poland
Stepping into their father's role, Prince Edward's two sons, George, The Earl of St. Andrews, and Lord Nicholas Windsor, attended the Last Night Of The Proms that was the 10th Jubilee concert, held at The Cracow Philharmonic Hall, on Sunday, September 10, 2005, which event was sponsored by PriceWaterhouseCoopers. Also

101. George The Earl of St. Andrews with his brother Lord Nicholas Windsor, representing their father HRH The Duke Of Kent at the Last Night of the Proms, Cracow 2005.

attending from England were Committee members the Right Hononourable Lord and Lady Belhaven and Stenton, (Robin and Malgosia Hamilton), and the Right Honourable Baroness (Betty) Boothroyd OM PC, former Speaker of the British House of Commons. The concert was held in the presence of His Excellency Mr Ryszard Kaczorowski GCMG, President of Poland, and His Excellency the British Ambassador Mr Charles Crawford CMG.

Prior to the commencement of the concert, Mr Tadeusz Syryjczyk, Chairman of Cracow Industrial Society, and George, The Earl of St Andrew's, made formal addresses to the audience.

There was a packed programme of classical music with Łukasz Kuropaczewski, guitar; Tomasz Kuk, tenor, Przemysław Firek, baritone, Rafał Songan, baritone; the Polish Radio National Symphony Orchestra, and the Cracow Philharmonic Choir, under the baton of special guest Mark Fitz-Gerald. The compositions performed included Portsmouth Point overture, The Sea Hawk Suite, and concluding with the three pieces of traditional music that are so popular at the London Proms the Pomp and Circumstance March, Rule Britannia, and Jerusalem.

Prince Edward honours
code breakers at Bletchley Park, 2000

At Bletchley Park, the former and now famous headquarters of the British Government code-breaking centre in Milton Keynes, Buckinghamshire, on July

11, 2000, Prince Edward, accompanied by the last Polish President-in-exile, His Excellency Mr Ryzard Kaczorowski, unveiled a memorial in the shape of a book, engraved with a tribute to three Polish mathematicians. Marian Rejewski, Jerzy Rozycki, and Henryk Zygalski who, having first cracked the Germans' Enigma code messages in 1932, were involved in crucial code-breaking on the Enigma machine at Bletchley Park during the Second World War, where they worked every day with British code breakers on codes that changed daily. Descendants of the code breakers were present at the unveiling, along with the late Sir Christopher Chataway, the well-known middle-and-long-distance-runner and television newscaster who, as Chairman of the trustees had helped save Bletchley Park as an historical site. (See also Chapter 19).

70th Anniversary of the Second World War, 2009
In 2009 Prince Edward commemorated the 70th anniversary of the outbreak of the Second World War (September 1, 1939) at a reception held at the Polish Embassy in London, where he was received by the Ambassador of the Republic of Poland, Her Excellency Mrs Barbara Tuge-Erecińska, and Madame Maria Kaczyńska, wife of Mr Lech Kaczyński, President of Poland (2005-10). On that date, Nazi Germany attacked Poland by land, sea, and air, and Britain declared war on Germany two days later.

70th Anniversary of the victory of the Polish Air Force, 2010
For the 70th anniversary of the Polish Air Force's commemoration of their contribution to the victory of the Royal Air Force during the Battle of Britain (July – October 1940), on September 11, 2010, Prince Edward unveiled a plaque at the National Arboretum in Staffordshire to the Polish pilots who lost their lives.

Continuing the commemorations, a gala dinner was hosted by Her Excellency Mrs Barbara Tuge-Erecińska and the head of the office for war veterans, Minister Jan Stanisław Ciechanowski, at the Rubens At the Palace Hotel, on Monday, September 20, in the presence of Prince Edward. Air Chief Marshal Sir David Parry-Evans gave the Polish Air Force Tribute.

The National Memorial Arboretum in Staffordshire, 2013
Poland's contribution to winning the Second World War was enormous and involved great sacrifice. On September 19, 2013, Prince Edward together with Her Excellency Mrs Barbara Tuge-Erecińska, visited The National Memorial Arboretum in Staffordshire, where he unveiled a war memorial that comprises four sculptures of branches of the services that fought in the war: the Air Force, the Army, the Navy, and the Polish Underground Home Army. [1]

Princess Alexandra, 2014
Prince Edward's sister, Princess Alexandra, (who we shall hear more of in the section on the Polish Hearth Club, Chapter 16), is also associated with Poland. Her Royal Highness attended a Chopin Society London Guildhall Gala concert held in honour of the Polish composer, on December 15, 2014, where she was Guest of Honour

along with the Polish Ambassador His Excellency Mr Witold Sobkó. The Princess could reminisce in her written greeting in the event programme note: "Guildhall has a long association with Poland. In the 1830s and 40s, annual Polish Balls and Concerts were held here, organised by the Literary Society of the Friends of Poland. ... I am delighted to be here to celebrate with Polish people in this country." [2]

102. HRH The Princess Sarvath El Hassan
of Jordan and HRH The Duke of Kent, attending the
Anglo Jordanian Society's biennial dinner, 2012.

THE ANGLO JORDANIAN SOCIETY

The Anglo Jordanian Society (the AJS) was set up in 1981, on the initiative of His Royal Highness Prince El Hassan bin Talal, who is a member of the Jordanian Royal Family. Today the AJS has well over 400 members, made up of British people who have come to know and love Jordan, and Jordanians living and working in the UK. They accept into their membership both adults and young people.

The purpose of the AJS is to advance understanding and friendship between the United Kingdom and Northern Ireland, and Jordan. They provide for the relief of need, hardship, and distress in Jordan, and in exceptional circumstances in association with Jordanian charitable societies also in the countries of the wider Levant. To further these objectives the AJS organises lectures, conferences, film shows, art exhibitions, concerts and similar functons.

366

103. Left to right: His Excellency Mr Mazen Homoud, Ambassador to Jordan; Sylvana, Countess of St. Andrews; HRH Prince Hassan El bin Talal of Jordan; and Lady Olga Maitland, former Chairman, at the Anglo Jordanian Society's biennial dinner, 2012.

Their Royal Highnesses Prince Hassan and Princess Sarvath of Jordan, and Prince Edward are the Patrons of the AJS, Prince Edward having become co-Patron in June 1981. The Ambassador for Jordan in the UK, His Excellency Mazen Kemal Homoud, is joint Honorary President of the AJS, with the British Ambassador to Jordan, His Excellency Peter Millet.

Every two years, their main fundraising event is a biennial dinner, held under the patronage of the three co-patrons. In 2012 it was held on June 21, at the Millennium Hotel, Grosvenor Square, London, in the presence of His Royal Highness Prince El Hassan bin Talal, Her Royal Highness Princess Sarvath, and Prince Edward.

The AJS has contributed over £120,000 to charities in recent years, and in 2010 alone, they raised an additional £60,000. They will give a warm welcome to anyone interested in Jordan and in furthering understanding between Jordan and the UK, and wanting to help Jordanian charities. Fundraising events have included a musical tour of Westminster Abbey, a tour of thfe Royal Military Academy at Sandhurst, an event in the Locarno Room of the British Foreign and Commonwealth Office (FCO), London, and lectures on Jordanian archaeology, history and culture.

Young Anglo Jordanian Society (YAJS)

There is also a Young Anglo Jordanian Society (YAJS) that was set up in 2004, by a group of people who had worked in, and knew and loved Jordan and its people. Today they number around 300 members. YAJS encourages like-minded young people age 16 and over from all backgrounds, social, academic, business, diplomatic, and different nationalities, to meet and to network, share, and connect with each other. The group is diverse, but fundamentally what unites them is their communal interest and love of Jordan. YAJS also fundraises for very worthwhile charities in Jordan which primarily benefits disadvantaged children. They host events throughout the year to celebrate and promote British ties with Jordan among the younger generation. The development of Facebook and Twitter pages act as a focal point where anyone interested can learn more about other fun Arab-orientated events taking place in London.

PRINCE EDWARD'S OVERSEAS VISITS 2012

Introduction
A programme of visits took place by members of the Royal Family to Realms and Overseas Territories in 2012, to mark Queen Elizabeth II's Diamond Jubilee. Prince Edward represented the Queen in visits to Uganda, Ascension Island, and the Falkland Islands.

VISIT TO UGANDA 2012

As part of the programme of visits, Prince Edward and his entourage arrived, on a British Airways flight from London, at Entebbe International Airport, Uganda, in the early hours of the morning of Friday, October 5, 2012, to conduct a commemorative tour of Uganda. Prince Edward was representing Her Majesty Queen Elizabeth II on an official visit for the occasion of two jubilees: the celebrations for Uganda's Golden Jubilee after 50 years of their independence [3], due to take place on Tuesday, October 9, and the Queen's Golden Jubilee in the 60th year of her reign. The jubilee celebrations were being held under the theme title: 50-year Journey since Independence (1962-2012): A Good Foundation for Social and Economic Transformation. Prince Edward was met at the airport by the Minister of Water and Environment, Professor Ephraim Kamuntu.

It was a great honour for all of those countries involved in the Uganda celebrations that Prince Edward was the Queen's representative. As a senior member of the royal family, he is very experienced in carrying out royal duties both at home and abroad. Prince Edward is a first cousin to the Queen, his father Prince George, having been a brother to Prince Albert, who became King George VI.

Visit to Uganda 1962
It was an historic moment as, on his 27th birthday, October 9, 1962, Prince Edward had represented the Queen in Uganda, when that country gained its independence, moving forward from being a protectorate of Great Britain. The instruments of power were then handed over to the newly-elected Prime Minister, Mr Apollo Milton Obote. The country and its people therefore hold fond memories for Prince Edward. On that occasion he had reminded them that Uganda was now a full Member of the Commonwealth, the Head of which is Queen Elizabeth II. On the day that Uganda became self-governing, the Governor became the Governor General; Kampala replaced Entebbe as the capital of the country; and the 4th Battalion of the King's

African Rifles became the 1st Battalion Uganda Rifles. The following day, Prince Edward took part in the State Opening of Parliament in Kampala.

Visit to Uganda 2012

Shortly after arrival on October 5 2012, Prince Edward travelled to Masindi district to undertake a tour of projects by Soft Power Education (SPE), a British-funded charity. He was met by Mr Godfrey Opira, the representative for SPE at the Masindi Hotel where the event was being held and which is Uganda's oldest hotel, having opened in 1923.

Prince Edward accompanied Mr Opira on a tour of an exhibition of photographs, literature, and artefacts, showcasing Murchison Falls National Park. Topics ranged from early explorers to the current poaching crisis. Mr Opira explained to Prince Edward the history of Uganda's tourism, and their Conservation programme. SPE runs three programmes in Buliisa district, which include the Conservation Education Community Outreach Programme (CECOP) and the Murchison Memories Museum Exhibition. Through the project, communities are taught practical skills to earn income through conservation including ICT, tailoring, knitting, and agriculture. Prince Edward displayed his customary warmth and cordiality as Mr Opira walked him from one poster board to the next. He said that when he arrived in Uganda in 1962, with his wife Her Royal Highness Katharine The Duchess of Kent, they flew over the Murchison Falls. They had enjoyed an enviable panoramic view of the area.

Bending over, looking at a disturbing picture of poachers with their hippopotamus prey, Prince Edward asked: "What approaches are you using to conserve the park?" Mr Opira explained that through CECOP, SPE promotes community conservation by educating communities on why it is important to protect the national park. The charity offers alternative livelihood projects to communities to prevent them from poaching and encroaching on the natural resources of the park. Prince Edward listened attentively to Mr Opira and to Mr Rob Johnson, who took him through the wildlife conservation in Murchison Falls National Park. It is a programme that Prince Edward is passionate about, for in the tradition of the British royal family he is a lover of animals. Mr Opira advised: "This way we raise awareness of the benefits of conserving while also providing businesses for the people to continue living a normal life alongside the plants and animals in the parks."

On Sunday October 7, Prince Edward was hosted to luncheon at the Masindi Hotel by the British High Commissioner to Uganda, Miss Alison Blackburne, and other district leaders. He mingled freely with excited guests, shaking hands with them. In his address, Prince Edward said that it was his recollection of Uganda during his first visit in 1962 "of meeting kind and warm people." Miss Hannah Small, a founder and trustee of the SPE project said it aimed at helping local communities appreciate and preserve their environment. Prince Edward had, she said, noted that despite some struggles, the population of wild animals in the park had increased. Murchison Falls is Uganda's largest national park and is home to lions, giraffes, chimpanzees, hippopotamidae, and more than 450 species of birds.

Prince Edward visits Uganda Breweries Limited

On the morning of October 8, accompanied by Miss Blackburne and the Honourable Amelia Kyambadde, the Minister for Trade Industry and Cooperatives, Prince Edward visited Uganda Breweries Limited (UBL) in Luzira, Kampala. UBL is a subsidiary of East African Breweries Limited (EABL) that is associated with Diageo Plc, a British multinational company headquartered in London. Diageo is the world's leading premium drinks business, trading in over 180 markets around the world. Prince Edward commissioned a mash filter which would ensure production capacity at the plant increased by 50 per cent. The benefit to the brewing company of the new mash filter is that it takes up less floor space. This facility worth USh56 billion (£14 million) is a direct investment from Diageo who have a majority stake in EABL. It is part of the UK's commitment to boost trade and investment in Uganda that will aid its economic growth. Mr Alasdair Musselwhite, Managing Director of UBL said:

> "This new investment represents a key milestone in the journey towards achieving our local raw material sourcing program and which strongly leverages on the three-prong partnership between government, farmers and UBL. Besides creating a step-change in our capacity to brew, using local raw materials, it goes a long way in support of the government's focus for value addition to local raw materials and growth of local manufacturing industry."

More than 17,000 farmers have benefited under the UBL Sorghum and Barley farmer programmes across the country, through which they have access to quality seed and fertilisers, equipment, and extension services. The Honourable Amelia Kyambadde said:

> "As the government of Uganda we are strongly advocating for greater use of local raw materials so it gives me great comfort to hear that with UBL's mash filter, small scale farmers and rural communities are set to benefit through the guaranteed market. With the additional investment in research and capacity building, I am confident this will go a long way in supporting the farmers acquire the skills and expertise required for modernisation and higher productivity."

Ugandan Rapid Deployment Corps

The next stop was a visit to the Ugandan Rapid Deployment Corps, and the Ugandan Army Senior Command and Staff College at Kimaka in Jinja, where Prince Edward was welcomed by Major General Francis Okello, the Commandant, former Force Commander of the African Union Mission in Somalia (AMISON). The centre was built using UK funding as part of the UK's commitment to the East African Standby Force (EASF). Its aim is to provide a centre from which Uganda can rapidly deploy a force HQ for peace support operations on behalf of EASF.

The building is also used for seminars and workshops for the Uganda People's Defence Force (UPDF), some of which are undertaken by UK training teams. Prince Edward's visit was meant to highlight the support the British government renders to the UPDF and its operations in Somalia, and he commended Major General Okello and the UPDF for their professionalism and commitment in Somalia.

Moving on to the Staff College, Prince Edward was welcomed by Brigadier Apollo Kasiita. The college provides training in the latest military ideas and systems, producing professional officers who will lead the UPDF and other regional armies in the coming years. The UK is very proud of its long-term support for UPDF staff course training, which took place at the Junior Staff College until 1995. Since then the UK has continued to provide material support as well as lecturers in specialist areas. In his address Prince Edward said: "It is a great pleasure to be back, having come in 1962 to represent the Queen and hand over independence. In 1962, it was the time that the King's African Rifles were wound up." As President of the Commonwealth War Graves Commission, Prince Edward went on to tell UPDF soldiers of his visit earlier that day to the Jinja War Cemetery, where he paid his respects at the graves of over 300 Ugandan and British servicemen:

> "I have been to the cemetery and found some of the soldiers that fought in the two world wars. The courage of Ugandan forces in Somalia is recognised all over the world. I congratulate and express thanks to Ugandan troops and offer condolence for the soldiers who were lost. In all you are doing, take into consideration that it's the people who you are commanding that are crucial. The days of using force are becoming rare, it is non-combatant methods that are often used." (See also Chapter 21).

When luncheon was served, Prince Edward reverted to the practice of his youthful days as a cadet at the Royal Military Academy, Sandhurst, standing in line with everyone else in the queue to be handed his lunch on a tray.

That evening Prince Edward attended a State Banquet given by the Government of Uganda in Kampala that was held for all the special dignitaries at Entebbe State house.

A day of celebration of two Golden Jubilees
The day of joint celebrations for Uganda's Golden Jubilee and the Queen's Golden Jubilee, October 9, dawned, a typically hot day in Uganda. It was also Prince Edward's 77th birthday. Countries whose heads of state arrived to take part included Rwanda, Tanzania, Burundi, Kenya, Ethopia, Somalia, Democratic Republic of Congo, South Sudan, Egypt, Somalia, Congo Brazzaville, Central African Republic, Malawi, and Benin. Among the presidents who attended the ceremony were Dr Thomas Yayi Boni, the President of Benin; Mr Paul Kagame of Rwanda, Chairman of the African Union; Mr Jakaya Kikwete of Tanzania; Mr Pierre Nkurunziza of Burundi; South Sudan's Mr Salva Kiir Mayardit; Mr Mwai Kibaki of Kenya; Mr Joseph Kabila of the Democratic Republic of Congo; Zimbabwe's Dr Robert Mugabe, and the newly-elected presidents: Mr Mohammed Morsi of Egypt and Somalia's Mr Hassan

Mohamud. Countries whose leaders sent delegations included China, the United Kingdom, South Africa, USA, Nigeria, and the Sudan.

The main ceremony was held at Kololo Airstrip on the outskirts of Kampala, which could hold 5,000 people. It was there on October 9, 1962, that the ceremony to mark Uganda's independence had taken place. The 2012 Jubilee Celebrations would prove one of the most historic days in the journey of Uganda, which is looked upon as the Pearl of Africa. The programme was organised with military precision. By 11.15 am the heads-of-state and foreign dignitaries had arrived. Thousands of Ugandans thronged the airstrip. The President of Uganda, Mr Yoweri Museveni, arrived with his wife, the First Lady, Mrs Janet Museveni, to a joyous reception from the crowd. Prince Edward took his seat in the front row, third in line to the President and the First Lady, and next to Mr Paul Kagame.

At 11.20 am the Uganda national anthem was sung. A colourful scene of entertainment from various groups then unfolded on the stage. Pablo, the popular comedian, made people laugh. The talented Ndere Troupe kept the guests and the massive crowd entertained with lively dances and songs.

At 11.40 am President Museveni started out in a military jeep on an inspection of the guard of honour. Tunes from the military band played in the background. By 11.59 am the President was being driven back to the presidential tent. There, he witnessed the raising of the national flag of Uganda that had been designed by the Justice Minister, the late Mr Grace Ibingira. The flag was hoisted into place at 12.05 pm, whilst the band played the national anthem that had been composed by the late Mr George Wilberforce Kakoma, who had been a graduate of Trinity College of Music, London, and who sadly did not live to see the day, having died in April 2012.

It was a moment when, undoubtedly, all present remembered with nostalgia the late Milton Obote, the first Prime Minister of Uganda, into whose hands passed the instruments of power from Her Majesty the Queen's representative, HRH Prince Edward The Duke of Kent, that historic day 50 years ago, when Uganda came into its own. As the Uganda flag slipped into place there was thunderous applause and cheering from the crowds. To add to the nostalgia the young man who had raised the Uganda flag at midnight, Major Kenneth Akirimo, then aged 31 years, now, aged 81 years, emerged from the crowd to more thunderous applause, and stepped up to the podium. Speaking over the microphone he said: "Congratulations Your Excellency for all that you have done for this country."

At 12.11 pm it was time for prayers. The outgoing Archbishop of the Anglican Church of Uganda, The Most Reverend Henry Luke Orombi, addressed the people: "We pray for a future where our politics can give hope to the people of Uganda where Uganda is the head, and not the tail." He was followed by the Mufti of Uganda, Sheikh Shaban Mubajje, who offered his prayers: "God blesses, guides and protects the leader of Uganda, Yoweri Kaguta Museveni." American gospel singer, Judy Jacobs, charmed the vast audience with some wonderful spiritual singing.

At 12.28 pm there was a military march past in slow and quick time, and civilian groups joined in the music that was played by police bands. A 15-minute air display started at 1.35 pm, put on by the UPDF Air Force. Performing breath-taking manoeuvres, the boom of low-flying, newly acquired, military jet fighters that zoomed over the heads of the crowd was the major highlight of the day.

The youthful Golden Jubilee Choir then took to the stage at 2.10 pm. They were a colourful sight wearing black, adorned at the waist with sari-like sashes in Uganda's national colours, black, yellow, and red. Their singing was joyous, peaceful, and harmonious.

At 2.20 pm, to loud cheers, President Museveni, wearing his customary cream hat and yellow tie began his Jubilee Speech to the nation. He reminded Ugandans that the discovery of oil and the completion of Bujagali Hydro Power station meant that Uganda is on its way to economic prosperity. He spoke passionately of adding value to their raw materials, particularly bananas, that are the nation's staple food, and drew attention to the value of sectors of the economy like oil, agriculture, and industry. Reflecting on the progress made over the years, President Museveni pointed out that the number of primary school children has risen tremendously today from what is was 50 years ago. He spoke of the beliefs that shape the country's prosperity, nationalism and anti-sectarianism.

The Egyptian President, Mr Mohammed Mursi, had travelled from Egypt, accompanied by a choir. At 2.45 pm, wearing magnificent, pure white drapes, they began singing in peaceful, soothing tones.

Next there were dancers and other Ugandan groups who remained undeterred by the sudden shower of rain. Local entertainer Alex Mukulu's group, even on a wet stage, put on a determined and lively performance with their dancing and singing that reminded all Ugandans what a great day this was and one to be remembered. Further performances took place and the day felt as though it might never end and that no one wanted it to end.

When it did come to an end, everyone stood for the Ugandan national anthem and the East Africa anthem, followed by synchronized marches past that went on from 3.35 until 4.25 pm.

Prince Edward enjoyed his visit enormously and summed it up in his own words of tribute: "A journey that has brought back pleasant memories of a nation in jubilation, a beautiful country of potential and wonderful people."

VISIT TO ASCENSION ISLAND 2012

Prince Edward departed on the evening of November 7, 2012, from Royal Air Force Brize Norton for RAF Ascension Island. The Island is named after the Feast day on which it was recorded to have been discovered, Ascension Day, May 9, Holy Thursday, which in accordance with the Bible commemorates the ascension of Jesus into heaven, having risen from the dead following his crucifixion.

The island is located in the equatorial waters of the South Atlantic Ocean about 1,600 kilometres (1,000 miles) from the coast of Africa, and 2,250 kilometres (1,400 miles) from the coast of South America. The climate is tropical, with temperatures at the coast ranging from about 68 to 88 degrees Fahrenheit (20–31 °C), and about 10 degrees Fahrenheit (5 to 6 degrees Celsius) cooler at the highest point.

The island's first inhabitants

Organised settlement of the Island began in 1815, when the British garrisoned it as a precaution, having imprisoned Napoleon I, Emperor of the French, on the island of Saint Helena to the south east. On October 22, the Royal Navy claimed the island for King George III and it was garrisoned by the British Admiralty until 1922. The location of the island made it a useful stopping-point for ships and communications. The Royal Navy used it as a victualing station for ships, particularly those of the West Africa Squadron working against the slave trade. A garrison of Royal Marines was also based there from 1823. In 1922 the island became a dependency of Saint Helena and was managed by the head of the Eastern Telegraph Company until 1964, when the British Government appointed an Administrator on the island to represent the Governor who lived on the island of Saint Helena.

Charles Darwin and Joseph Hooker visited

In 1836, during his trip around the world on the HMS Beagle, studying exotic plants and animals, the naturalist Charles Darwin visited the island. In 1859, he published his famous book *On the Origin of Species* in which his description was of an arid, treeless island with nothing growing near the coast. Sparse vegetation supported "about 600 sheep, many goats, a few cows and horses." There were large numbers of guinea fowl as well as rats and mice and land crabs. The springs were carefully managed by the inhabitants, "so that a single drop of water may not be lost." There was a saying of the people of Saint Helena that Darwin quoted: "We know we live on a rock, but the poor people at Ascension live on a cinder."

In 1843 Darwin's closest friend, botanist and explorer, Joseph Hooker, Director of the Royal Botanical Gardens, Kew, London, visited the island. Hooker later advised the Royal Navy that with the help of Kew Gardens, they should ship trees to the Island because planted trees would capture more rain and improve the soil. From 1850 onwards, visiting ships carried plants and trees to the Island, and by the late 1870s Norfolk pines, eucalyptus, bamboo, and banana trees grew at the highest point of the island, Green Mountain, creating something of a tropical forest.

In 1899, the Eastern Telegraph Company, today part of Cable & Wireless Worldwide, installed the first underwater cable from the island.

Strategic advantage

Historically, the Island played a role as an important safe haven and coaling station to mariners and for commercial airliners, during the days of international air travel by flying boats.

During the Second World War (1939-45) it was an important naval and air station, providing antisubmarine warfare bases during the Battle of the Atlantic and throughout the war. In order to support amphibious aircraft antisubmarine patrol operations, the United States built an airbase on the Island, known as Wideawake. The airfield was used by the US military as a stopping point for American aircraft crossing the Atlantic Ocean on their way to theatres of operation in Europe and Africa.

The Cold War and the US

After the war the Americans left the island and the airbase fell into disuse. But with the onset of the Cold War with the Soviet Union and the ensuing Space Race, the Americans returned to the island in 1956. Wideawake Airfield was expanded in the mid-1960s, with its runway having been adapted to allow it to be used by large aircraft. It later acted as an emergency runway for the Space Shuttle although it was never used. In 1967 the National Aeronautics and Space Administration (NASA), the agency of the United States government that is responsible for the nation's civilian space program and for aeronautics and aerospace research, established a tracking station on the island which remained in operation for more than 20 years until 1990. The BBC Atlantic Relay Station was installed in 1966 for short-wave broadcasts to Africa and South America.

Falkland Islands War 1982

Ascension Island was used extensively by the British during the Falkland Islands War of April 2 to June 14, 1982. An RAF British task force used the Island as a staging post and as a base to supply the task force. The Royal Air Force deployed a fleet of Vulcan bombers and Victor tankers at the airfield. The beginnings of the British offensive, called *Operation Black Buck,* was launched in Vulcans from the Island. The Royal Navy's fleet also stopped at the Island for refuelling.

Following the war the British retained an increased presence on the island, establishing a station, RAF Ascension Island, and also providing a refuelling stop for the regular airlink between RAF Brize Norton in Oxfordshire, England, and RAF Mount Pleasant in the Falkland Islands.

The space age

Located on the island today is *RAF Ascension Island*, a Royal Air Force station with a United States Air Force presence, a European Space Agency rocket tracking station, and the BBC World Service Atlantic Relay Station. The Island hosts one of five ground antennae that assist in the operation of the Global Positioning System (GPS) navigational system. The United States Air Force uses the Island as part of its Eastern Range. The European Space Agency operates an *Ariane* monitoring facility.

Political status

Today Ascension Island is governed as part of the British Overseas Territory of Saint Helena and Tristan da Cunha. The Governor resides in Jamestown, Saint Helena, and an Administrator represents him on Ascension Island. In 2008 elections were held on the Island and seven candidates were elected to form a new Island Council, which was sworn in on October 28. Executive authority is vested in Queen Elizabeth II, who is represented by the Governor, His Excellency Mr Mark Capes, who is based at Saint Helena. Mr Colin Wells, who has been a career member of Her Majesty's Diplomatic Service since 1987, was sworn in as the Administrator of Ascension Island on October 27, 2011 in the presence of members of the Island Council.

The island has its own local system of law and the Island Council advises on new or revised laws. Employment legislation consists a mixture of contract law and the Workmen's Protection Ordinance, which guarantees a contract as well as obliging employers to provide free accommodation, medical cover, food (or a food allowance), and travel etc. The Order of 2009 was made by Her Majesty the Queen and the Privy Council on July 8, and came into operation in September. The new Constitution limits the Governor's powers, includes a Bill of Rights, and establishes independence of the judiciary and the public service.

Plants on the island

Being a tropical island the climate is particularly conducive to plants and vegetation. But, in 1843, it was nearly barren due to the plants having been eaten over the years by goats. The introduction of new species of plants by the British transformed the Island's Green Mountain into one of the few, large-scale, planned forests, and it is growing richer yearly. The Green Mountain National Park was opened in June 2005. Its highest point is at 2,817 feet (859 metres). Non-indigenous plants flourish there, the most outstanding being bamboo, along with tall Norfolk Pine trees *Araucaria heterophylla*.

Animals, fish, and birds

The largest native land animal is the land crab Johngarthia lagostoma. In the sea there is a variety of open-ocean fish, including sharks, wahoo, tuna, bonito, barracuda, marlin, blackfish and sailfish. From November to May the protected green turtles come ashore to lay their eggs on the beaches.

Sooty Terns or Wideawake Birds nest in great seashore lava fairs. Other sea-birds include some types of boobies, petrels and tropicbirds, White Tern, Brown Noddy, Black Noddy, and Ascension Frigatebird. Off the east coast of the Island is the islet of Boatswain Bird Island, that is a safe haven for sea birds. On land are colourful canaries, francolins, mynas, sparrows, and waxbills. The Island has been identified as an Important Bird Area by BirdLife International as it is a breeding site for seabirds. These include Red-billed Tropicbirds, Ascension Frigatebirds, Sooty Terns and Black Noddies.

Prince Edward visits Ascension Island

Arriving on the morning of November 8, 2012, Prince Edward spent the early part of the day on Ascension Island. He carried out the official opening of the Jubilee View Picnic Site on Cross Hill, and met with members of the Island's community.

Earlier in the year the area had been prepared and made suitable for islanders who wanted to picnic, hold barbecues, or socialise. The site was dedicated to the community of Ascension Island in honour of Queen Elizabeth II's Diamond Jubilee. Now fully functional it offers spectacular panoramic views of Georgetown, Long Beach, and Clarence Bay, as well as further north towards English Bay, with a back-drop of Green Mountain.

Prince Edward met with the Island Council, Heads of Organisations, Scouts, Guides, and the teachers and pupils of Two Boats School. He also met all those involved with the organisation and preparation of the Diamond Jubilee celebrations and the creation and construction of the Jubilee View site.

After greeting everyone, Prince Edward, escorted by The Administrator Mr Colin Wells, was given a tour of the HMS Hood Guns at Cross Hill. The history of the two guns is that they were originally on *HMS Hood,* which was the largest battlecruiser ever built. The ship was the first of its kind to be completed, and was launched in 1918. HMS Hood also remained in service during the Second World War. When the German battleship *Bismarck* was sent out as a raider it was intercepted by *HMS Hood,* along with the battleship *HMS Prince of Wales* in May 1941, and a stand-up fight ensued. The *Bismarck*'s 15-inch shells caused a magazine explosion in *HMS Hood*, sinking her. However, two of the ship's 5.5-inch guns have survived, having been taken off the ship in 1935, and placed on Cross Hill overlooking Georgetown. Over the years the guns fell into a state of severe disrepair, until they were rediscovered by the Royal Air Force in 1982, during the Falklands war. The Global Environmental Facility restored them and the guns were handed over to the Ascension Island Historical Society. The story of their preservation appeared in *Royal Air Force News* issue 14th December, 1984.

At this point, Prince Edward was informed that due to adverse weather conditions on the Falkland Islands his stopover on Ascension Island was going to be extended for six hours. He was taken to the residence of the Administrator for lunch. The Residency is a former Royal Navy hospital, built in 1867, and located half way up Green Mountain at what was deemed to be a healthy altitude. There, Prince Edward had an opportunity to relax and take a little time out of his busy schedule.

On the way back to the airbase Prince Edward made good use of his extra hours on the island, making an unscheduled detour to visit the few Commonwealth war graves on the coast. The Island's New Cemetery contains six Commonwealth burials of the First World War, two of which cannot now be traced and are represented by special memorials, and one Commonwealth burial of the Second World War.

VISIT TO THE FALKLAND ISLANDS 2012

Falkland Islands motto:
"Desire the right"

Continuing the programme as representative of Her Majesty The Queen, Prince Edward arrived on the Falkland Islands a little late on November 8, due to bad weather conditions having caused his flight to be delayed.

It had been decided that it would be fitting for his visit to coincide with Remembrance Day, as 2012 was also the 30th anniversary of the Falklands War, Britain's conflict with the Republic of Argentina over ownership of the islands. During the 74-day conflict in 1982, over 900 people lost their lives, 649 Argentineans, 255 British soldiers, and three Falkland Islanders.

Prince Edward's 'plane touched down at Mount Pleasant Airport at 21.15 hours, and he was met by the Governor, Mr Nigel Haywood CVO, Brigadier William (Bill) Aldridge CBE (CBF), Commander British Forces, and Mr Dick Sawle a Member of the Legislative Assembly (MLA).

377

The Falkland Islands – a brief history

The Falkland Islands were uninhabited when discovered by Europeans. The first reliable sighting is usually attributed to the Dutch explorer Sebald de Weert in 1600, who named the archipelago the Sebald Islands, a name that appeared on Dutch maps into the 19th century. The islands are also known in Argentina as Islas Malvinas (the Malvinas) and are about the same size as London, England, (including Greater London), or the State of Connecticut in the US, or the six counties of Northern Ireland. The archipelago is located in the South Atlantic Ocean on the Patagonian Shelf. The English name was taken from Falkland Channel (today named Falkland Sound), which was bestowed upon the channel that runs between the two main islands by Captain John Strong, who landed there in 1690. Strong chose the name in honour of Anthony Cary, 5th Viscount of Falkland, who was Commissioner of the Admiralty and who had financed the expedition. Claims to ownership of the islands have alternated over a number of years, and has involved France, Britain, Spain, and the Republic of Argentina. Britain had established its rule over the Islands in 1833, at which time there were no other settlers. The Spanish name, las Islas Malvinas, is derived from the French name, Îles Malouines, named by Louis Antoine de Bougainville in 1764 after the first known arrivals who were mariners, and fishermen from the Breton port of Saint-Malo in France. The Republic of Argentina only came into existence in 1853, so their claims to the islands are not legitimate.

The principal islands of the Falkland Islands are about 310 miles (500 kilometres) east of the Patagonian coast at a latitude of about 52°S. They span an area of 4,700 square miles (12,173 square kilometres), and comprise East Falkland, West Falkland, and 776 smaller islands. The archipelago of the Falkland Islands is classified as part of the Antarctic Ecozone and Antarctic Floristic Kingdom.

Falkland Islands strategic importance during two World Wars

The Falkland Islands became of strategic naval importance to Britain during the First World War (1914-18). A new harbour had been built in the capital of Stanley, which is also known as Port Stanley. The Battle of the Falkland Islands, a British naval victory over a German fleet, took place in December 1914.

During the Second World War (1939-45), Port Stanley again served as a Royal Navy station, servicing ships that took part in the 1939 Battle of the River Plate. The powerful German pocket battleship Graf Spee had sunk nine British merchant vessels in the South American shipping lanes. The predator was found by three small cruisers, Exeter, Ajax, and Achilles, operating out of the Falkland Islands. On December 17, rather than be taken the Commander of the Graf Spee, Hans Langsdorff, scuttled the ship. Moving out of Montevideo the chief port of Uruguay, and watched by thousands, the ship spectacularly exploded in a ball of fire. Langsdorff and some of his crew were taken to Buenos Aires, where he shot himself wrapped in the German ensign.

Argentina's intentions raised
at British Overseas Trade Board Meeting

Concern over Argentina was raised at a meeting of the British Overseas Trade Board

105. Major General Julian Thompson's Brigade Tactical Head Quarters on the Falkland Islands on the shoulders of Mount Kent on the morning of the Argentine surrender, June 14, 1982.

of which it will be recalled from Chapter 3, Prince Edward was Vice-Chairman. Lieutenant (Royal Navy Volunteer Reserve) Guy Huntrods CBE, (retired), now aged 92 years, and a seasoned veteran of the Second World War who commanded an assault landing craft carrying Randolph Churchill's detachment of the Special Air Service (SAS) on a wartime raid on the coast of Sicily in 1943, remembers the difficult trading situation in relation to Argentina in early1980. Lieutenant Huntrods says:

"I was a member of the British Overseas Trade Board (BOTB) in the 1980s, during the time I was also Director of the Latin American Division of Lloyds Bank International. Largely through its subsidiary the long-established Bank of London and South America it had many branches and interests throughout the area and especially in Argentina. I was thus a regular and frequent visitor to Latin America with a wide range of contacts at all levels. For two years from 1977, I also chaired the Latin America Trade Advisory Group, which reported to the BOTB.

"For years the long standing UK dispute with Argentina over the sovereignty of the Falkland Islands had ebbed and flowed with intermittent crises but, in early 1982, matters became acute after the relative breakdown of inter-governmental talks in New York. Argentina had a new President

106. Major General Julian Thompson's Head Quarters being packed up in a blizzard during the Falklands War, 1982.

General Galtieri, and a seriously worsening economic and political situation. I was worried that overt steps would be taken against British interests in Argentina. I did not, however, think that they would invade the Falklands Islands.

"My return from a visit to the area in February/March 1982 coincided with a scheduled routine meeting of the BOTB on March 18. I raised my concerns under Any Other Business saying: 'I would like to raise the question of the Falkland Islands. I believe that the situation is deteriorating and will have a serious effect on our trade with the Argentine. The Argentines are experiencing problems with their economy.'

"After some discussion, including comments by the Foreign Office, the Chairman stressed that 'the record should show that the Board were very concerned that our export trade should be compromised by an escalation in the dispute.'

"Just two weeks later the Falkland Islands were invaded by Argentina. The BOTB's next Board Meeting was held on May 18, and the Minutes read: 'Argentina: Recalling Mr Huntrod's prediction at the last meeting the Chairman invited Mr Huntrods, who had just returned from Montevideo, to report. Mr Huntrods said he felt no satisfaction about being right. ...'

"What the Minutes of the Meetings of March 18 and May 18, 1982, (now located at the National Archives, Kew, London), have discreetly not recorded is the Duke of Kent's comment: 'Before we start we must ask Guy where he got his crystal Ball.' This was typical of the relaxed charm and humour of His Royal Highness which, combined with his dedicated and professional approach, did so much for the successful promotion of British interests worldwide." [4]

Falklands War between Britain and Argentina 1982

On April 2, 1982, Argentina invaded the Falkland Islands and other British territories in the South Atlantic, in an attempt to claim Argentine sovereignty over them. The United Kingdom sent an expeditionary force 8,000 miles to retake the islands. After a war that lasted two-and-a-half months, the Argentine forces surrendered on June 14.

Under the British Nationality Act of 1983, Falkland Islanders are legally British citizens. The United Kingdom's claim to the Falkland Islands is based on its position of continuous administration of the islands since 1833, and that the islanders themselves have a 'right to self-determination, including their right to remain British if that is their wish'. Following the war the British increased their military presence on the islands, constructing RAF Mount Pleasant and increasing the military garrison. Diplomatic relations between the United Kingdom and Argentina were, however, re-established in 1990.

Falkland Islands economy

The Falkland Islands are mountainous and have arid lands fit for grazing thousands of sheep. The major economic activities are fishing, sheep farming, and tourism, of

107. 45 Commando during the 1982 Falklands War being taken across San Carlos Water in a landing craft before starting their epic 'yomp' to Stanley 70 foot miles away. The gentleman wearing glasses and smoking a cigarette is the 45 Commando's chaplain Rev. Wynn Jones.

which fishing is the largest and tourism is enjoying a substantial increase. There is a regeneration project underway on the islands, part of which involves road links to all occupied mainland settlements. The islands have become a regular port of call for the growing market of cruise ships. During the 2008-2009 season, almost 69,000 tourists visited the islands, with 62,600 of these arriving onboard cruise or expedition vessels. Overall tourist arrivals increased by 7 per cent during the period 2000-2012. The Falklands Tourist Board recorded that in 2012, 67.8 per cent of all business tourists visited the islands.

During his visit to the islands, Prince Edward said in an after dinner address to the Members of the Legislative Assembly (MLAs), at the Café Carancho on Re-membrance Sunday, November 11, 2012:

"If the size of the new restaurant extension at a certain waterfront hotel is anything to go by the Islands are on the cusp of some very exciting times, with increased revenue providing new opportunities and new economic security."

The tourism figures also show that apart from defence, the islands are self-sufficient, with annual exports worth in excess of £100 million and imports of just under £90 million and the Falklands pound is backed by the British pound sterling.

Offshore oil discovery
Since the time of the Falklands conflict events have moved on. Whereas at that time ownership of the islands and their economic produce was the main point of disagreement with Argentina, in 2010, valuable oil deposits were discovered in the Atlantic Ocean. The oil is claimed by Britain and exploration is licensed by the Falkland Islands Government. However, Britain very generously offered to share the proceeds of the profits of the oil revenue with Argentina but the Argentine Government has refused to co-operate. A 1995 Agreement between the UK and Argentina had set the terms for exploitation of offshore resources, including oil reserves, but in 2007 Argentina unilaterally withdrew from the agreement. Rockhopper, the exploration company, have been drilling in the Sea Lion Field, 62 miles to the north of the islands. They have estimated that the field holds around 300 million barrels of oil, which would be worth in the region of £20 billion.

Administration of the islands
The Falkland Islands, as a British Overseas Territory under the 2009 Constitution, enjoys a large degree of internal self-government. The United Kingdom guarantees good government and takes responsibility for defence and foreign affairs. Executive authority is vested in Queen Elizabeth II, and is exercised by the Falkland Islands Governor on her behalf. The Governor is also responsible for the administration of South Georgia and the South Sandwich Islands but these are uninhabited. The governor acts on the advice of the Executive Council composed of himself as Chairman, the Chief Executive, the Director of Finance, and three elected Legislative Assembly Members. The Legislative Assembly consists of the Chief Executive, the

Director of Finance, and eight members elected for four-year terms by universal suffrage, of whom five are from Stanley and three are from Camp. There are no political parties or formal opposition, it is presided over by the Speaker. The first election under the current constitution took place on Thursday, November 5, 2009.

Justice is administered by a resident senior magistrate and a non-resident Chief Justice, who visits the islands at least once a year. The senior magistrate handles petty criminal cases, civil, commercial, admiralty, and family cases, and is also the Islands' coroner. The Chief Justice handles serious criminal cases and hears appeals. The constitution binds the judiciary to comply with decisions of the European Court of Human Rights when hearing cases related to human rights.

Population of the islands
In 2012, the population of the Falkland Islands (excluding British Ministry of Defence personnel and their families) was 2,841, 65 per cent of whom are of working age, plus 380 children between the ages of five and 16. The only city is Stanley on East Falkland, with a population of 2,121. About 70 per cent of the inhabitants today are British, mainly the descendants of Scottish and Welsh immigrants, and they wish the islands to remain British. Other ethnicities include French, Gibraltarian, Scandinavian, Saint Helena, Chile, and a few Argentineans.

British military garrison
A British military garrison is stationed on the Falkland Islands, and the islands also have a company-sized light infantry unit (FIDF), that is completely funded by the Falklands Government the cost of which, in 2009, was £400,000. The unit is trained under a secondment arrangement with the British Ministry Of Defence. Since 2010 the FIDF have employed a Royal Marine WO2 as a permanent staff instructor and a major as commanding officer, the rest of the force being made up of part-time staff. It is equipped with quad bikes, inflatable boats, and Land Rovers, and is armed with heavy machineguns, grenade launchers, and sniper rifles. In addition to defence duties, the force provides a mountain rescue service, and has been trained by the Royal Navy in mounting armed deterrence against illegal fishing activity.

Air transport on the islands
There are two airports on the islands, the main international airport RAF Mount Pleasant, and the smaller Port Stanley Airport on the outskirts of Stanley. Mount Pleasant is used for military purposes and for heavy aircraft that require long runways, whereas Stanley is used for internal flights and smaller aircraft.

The Royal Air Force operates flights from RAF Mount Pleasant to RAF Brize Norton in Oxfordshire, England, with a refuelling stop at RAF Ascension Island. RAF flights are via charter by the Portuguese Company, Hi Fly, who have modern Airbuses. Local military air support involving the moving of personnel, equipment, and supplies around the islands is carried out under contract by British International (BRINTEL) which operates two Sikorsky S61N helicopters. The principal civilian air operator at Mount Pleasant is LAN Airlines, which operates weekly flights to Santiago, Chile, via Punta Arenas.

The main operator at Port Stanley Airport is the Falkland Islands Government Air Service (FIGAS), which operates Islander aircraft that can use the grass airstrips at most settlements. Flight schedules, which are broadcast on the radio every evening, are planned on a daily basis according to passenger needs. Private operators from Stanley include the British Antarctic Survey, who operate an air link to the Rothera Research Station on the Antarctic Peninsula, and who also serve other British bases in the British Antarctic Territory using a de Havilland Canada Dash 7.

Prince Edward's visit to the Falkland Islands 2012

Continuing Prince Edward's visit to the Falkland Islands, by the following day, November 9, a tightly packed schedule of events was underway. At 09.10 am, Prince Edward met with the Government House staff, including the Government of South Georgia and South Sandwich Islands.

Prince Edward meets the residents

At 10.20 am, Prince Edward was flown on a British International Helicopter into San Carlos, where he was welcomed by Mrs Sharon Halford, MLA, to meet and greet the residents. In strong winds, freezing conditions, and occasional snow showers, Prince Edward walked on foot from Mrs Halford's house to the Cemetery. He then attended an open air Remembrance Memorial Service for veterans at Blue Beach Military Cemetery, which is a settlement in north-western East Falkland. San Carlos was the main British Army bridgehead during the Falklands War, when it was codenamed Blue Beach. There is also a museum that commemorates that period. The Band of the Royal Marines Scotland provided music. The names of all military and civilian personnel who died during the war were read out by members of the Falkland Islands community, and Prince Edward laid a wreath. Members of the public then attended a civic reception at the Town Hall.

Pebble Island

The remainder of the day was spent at Pebble Beach on Pebble Island, which Prince Edward reached, travelling on a British International Helicopter, accompanied by SAS veteran Mr Joe Niland. Arriving at the Island at 12.20 hours, they were met by Ms Jacqui Jennings and Mr Alan White, who run Pebble Island Lodge guesthouse. They had lunch at the guesthouse and changed in preparation for a later excursion of the area. Led by Mr White, they set out on a tour of the east end of Pebble Island. Prince Edward was shown round the site of the SAS raid that had taken place to recapture the airfield from Argentine forces in 1982.

That evening, joined by Mr and Mrs Raymond Evans, Prince Edward dined with the island's residents and guests, and remained for an overnight stay at Pebble Island Lodge. Mr Evans is the great nephew of Mr Johnny Evans, who introduced sheep farming to the island in 1846.

Wreath laying at Mount Tumbledown war graves

On the morning of November 10 Prince Edward visited HMS Coventry Memorial that is dedicated to those who lost their lives when, during the conflict on May 25,

1982, Argentine forces sunk the vessel.

Returning to Stanley at 10.45 am, accompanied by Mr Rob Ijssel and Mr John Smith, Prince Edward, in his capacity as President of the Commonwealth War Graves Commission, visited the graves at the Commonwealth War Graves Cemetery, Stanley. There are 33 graves, of whom 21 are veterans of the First World War, and 12 are veterans of the Second World War.

At 11.10 am, Prince Edward flew to Mount Pleasant harbour to visit the Royal Navy on board HMS Clyde. He met officers in the wardroom where there was a Presentation by Lieutenant Commander Mark Anderson. Officers then entertained him to lunch. Afterwards Prince Edward was taken on a tour of the ship, where he was shown a fire fighting demonstration.

Prince Edward flew on to Mount Tumbledown where, at 14.30 hours, in his role of Colonel of the Regiment, he laid a wreath at the Scots Guards Memorial. Mr Tony Smith accompanied him on a short tour of the area on foot. Mount Tumbledown was the scene of an important battle which formed part of a series of engagements during the British advance towards Stanley. On the night of June 13-14 1982, 2nd Battalion Scots Guards launched an assault on Argentine forces there, and succeeded in driving them from the mountain. The battalion was supported by the Mortar Troop 42 Commando Royal Marines, a troop of the Blues and Royals equipped with two Scorpion and two Scimitarlight armoured vehicles, a battery of 105-mm light guns from 4th Field Regiment Royal Artillery, and the 4.5-inch guns of two Type 21 Frigates (HMS Active and HMS Avenger).

In the evening, at 17.59 hours, Prince Edward attended a Liberation Service, and laid a wreath at the Liberation Monument, which is situated in front of the secretariat in Stanley. The Act of Remembrance took place with visiting 1982 veterans present. The monument was unveiled on Liberation Day, June 14, 1984, by The Honourable Harold Rowlands, OBE, Financial Secretary of the Falkland Islands Government. The 20 feet high, polished granite pillar, inscribed with the names of all the units which took part in the Campaign is surmounted by an eight feet high, bronze figure of Britannia, sculpted by Mr David Norris FRBS. There is a 10 feet high quartzite stone wall sculpted by Mrs Faith Winter ARBS, the stone having been taken from the battlefield areas, and in the centre of which is mounted a bronze relief depicting a scene showing many of the units that took part in the War. It is flanked by a bronze plaque, listing the names of those who died. The architect was Mr Harold Dixon a Falkland Islander. The monument was funded entirely by money raised by Falkland Islanders.

A dinner was given at 19.30 hours by the Governor, His Excellency Mr Nigel Haywood, for members of the Falkland Islands community, in the presence of Prince Edward. It was followed by an overnight stay for Prince Edward at Government House.

Remembrance Sunday 11th November

On Remembrance Sunday November 11, a Memorial Service was held in Christ Church Cathedral, Stanley, led by the Reverend Dr Richard Hines and other local ministers, in the presence of Prince Edward, who gave a bible reading. Also in attendance was Mr Nigel Haywood, Brigadier Bill Aldridge, members of the Falkland Islands Government (FIGs), invited guests, Mr Mark Lancaster MP, Mr Kevan Jones MP, Lieutenant Colonel (Retired) Mr Tony Davies OBE, Members of the Legislative Assembly, visiting and resident South Atlantic veterans, together with Senior Officers of the Armed Services.

The Cross of Sacrifice, Stanley Cemetery, and Memorial Wood, are all located at the eastern end of Stanley. Behind the Cross is the Cemetery and alongside it is Memorial Wood. A memorial service is held at the Cross of Sacrifice each year on Remembrance Sunday.

At 10.20 am, Guard Detachments representing the Royal Navy, the Army, the Royal Air Force, and a detachment from the Falkland Islands Defence Force, formed on Ross Road. The Band of Her Majesty's Royal Marines Scotland led the parade. They were joined by Veterans and Associations, and marched to the Cross of Sacrifice that commemorates the fallen of the two world wars, where youth organisations were already present. At 10.48 am, Prince Edward, Governor Haywood, a Member of the Legislative Assembly, and the Commander British Forces arrived. A short service was held and the Roll of Honour read out. At 11.00 am the two minutes silence for the fallen of two world wars and the Falklands conflict was observed, and was marked by the firing of the saluting guns on Victory Green. Wreaths were laid by Prince Edward, Mr Dick Sawle, Brigadier Bill Aldridge, and FIG official guests, followed by representatives of the Armed Services, Falkland Islands Defence Force, the Royal Fleet Auxiliary, and the Royal British Legion.

Prince Edward meets the Scouts

At 11.15 am, in his role of President of the Scout Association, Prince Edward met Scouts during a visit to Memorial Wood, Stanley. Prince Edward presented the Bar to the Medal of Merit to Mrs Jan Miller, Cub Scout Leader 1st Falkland Islands. Accompanied by Mr and Mrs Tim and Jan Miller and Mr Phil Middleton, along with the Scouts and Cubs, the party took a walk through the woods. An area has been set aside to commemorate members of the British Forces who served and died in the 1982 conflict. In his honour, a tree has been planted in memory of each British serviceman killed.

At 12.10 pm Prince Edward arrived at the Falkland Islands Defence Force (FIDF) Headquarters. He was met by Captain Andrew Brownlee and invited to ring the bell. There is a tradition that whoever rings the bell (made from a spent artillery case) buys the drinks. Usually at this juncture the Governor rings the bell. Prince Edward rang the bell on this occasion and then announced somewhat jovially that the Governor was still buying the drinks! There was then a relaxing opportunity for socialising with visiting veterans and parade detachments.

Volunteer Point nature reserve

At 14.15 hours, Prince Edward travelled on a British International Helicopters flight to Volunteer Point to visit the fine nature reserve, where he was met and shown around by the Warden, Mr Derek Pettersson. Accessed via the beautiful, white sandy Volunteer Beach, approximately two kilometres long, Volunteer Point is one of the most popular and important tourist destinations on the Islands. The site is a cornucopia of bird activity, and home to the largest King penguin colony, as well as Gentoo and Magellanic penguins, waterfowl, and other exotic birds.

Dinner and address by Prince Edward

In the evening of November 11, 2012, at 19.40 hours, a dinner was given in Prince Edward's honour, hosted by Members of the Legislative Assembly (MLAs) at the Café Carancho, Bluff Cove. In his address to the MLAs, where Mr Nigel Haywood and Brigadier Bill Aldridge were present, Prince Edward reassured them that residents would retain their British citizenship within the Falkland Islands:

> "Political progress has been achieved through your new constitution, with its new structures of government and its emphasis on the rights that are the bedrock of modern democracy. We all cherish those freedoms; they are the very essence of the liberty that our armed forces fought to deliver here in these Islands. And that is why, at this time of remembrance we salute the sacrifices of our armed forces and veterans; they are prepared to fight to protect fundamental rights and freedoms, which during times of peace can all too easily be taken for granted. But when hardship and threat have been experienced so recently, as has been the case here, those freedoms are all the more to be cherished. Hence I am particularly glad to be here this week to share your thanks for those who gave everything to secure the freedom of the Falkland Islands."

Then, bringing to Falkland islanders something of the flavour of the cheerful atmosphere of celebrations throughout the UK, Prince Edward concluded:

> "The Diamond Jubilee events, which took place in Britain earlier in the year, have contributed enormously to a thoroughly festive summer in the United Kingdom, together with the Olympic Games and the Paralympics. It has truly been a remarkable summer of celebration, which has demonstrated the best of Britain. Indeed, we have shown the world our history and heritage alongside our ability to achieve change, progress, and success."

At 9.30 on the morning of November 12, Prince Edward arrived on an official visit at the secretariat building of the Island Administration's Head Quarters, Stanley. In the Liberation Room, he received a briefing on current political and social issues with Mr Keith Padgett, Chief Executive, Mr Jamie Fotheringham, Head of Policy, Mr Stephen Luxton, Director of Mineral Resources, and all Members of the MLA.

Visit to hospital

Arriving on foot at 10.30 am, at King Edward VII Memorial Hospital, Prince Edward was met by Mr David Jenkins, Director of Health and Education, Dr Robert Queensborough, Chief Medical Officer, and Mr Michael Poole the Hospital Manager.

Entering the hospital's Day Centre, he met with Sheltered Housing residents, and was then taken on a tour of the hospital.

Visit to schools

At 11.15 am, Prince Edward visited the Falkland Islands schools. There are two schools in Stanley, the Infant and Junior School, which teaches ages four to 11year olds, and the Falkland Islands Community School. The Community School was opened in 1992, and caters for pupils of all abilities between the ages of 11 and 16. It also has a role of providing recreational and further education for the entire community. It incorporates a Leisure centre which includes a 25 metre swimming pool, a public library, a sports hall which has three badminton/short tennis courts, plus two squash courts, and an outside green for football, hockey, and athletics etc.

Prince Edward was met by Mr Tom Hall the Headteacher of Infants and Junior School, and the pupils, and Mr David Tongue, the Headteacher of the Community School. Much to the joy of the children, Prince Edward was taken on a tour of their schools.

Visit to Dockyard

At 13.35 hours, Prince Edward visited Stanley's historic Dockyard, where he was met by Museum Manager, Mrs Leona Roberts, and Chair, Mr Tim Blake OBE. Mrs Roberts' historic roots in the Falkland Islands goes back six generations on her mother's side. Her great-great-great-grandfather Mr James Biggs was one of 12 Royal Sappers and Miners who, with his wife and three children, arrived on the Islands in a boat from England in 1842, along with the first British civil administrator of the islands, Major General Richard Moody. Prince Edward also visited the Old Smithy to see the plans for the new museum, and he unveiled a plaque.

Visit to Environmental Research Institute

Arriving at 14.00 hours at the South Atlantic Environmental Research Institute (SAERI), Prince Edward was met by the Director, Dr Paul Brickle. A scientific research project begun in 2006 is underway by SAERI to promote marine research in the South Atlantic. The work is being undertaken by Shallow Marine Surveys Group, (SMSG), based in the Falkland Islands, who are discovering new species of plant and marine life. SAERI is an academic research organisation conducting environmental research from the tropics down to the ice in the South Atlantic, and its remit includes the physical and natural sciences. Prince Edward opened SAERI's new Head Quarters and unveiled a plaque.

Visit to oil yards

At Byron MacKay oil yards at 14.45 hours, Prince Edward received a briefing on the oil industry from local company representatives. Byron McKay Port Services Limited is a 50-50 joint venture company, owned equally by Byron Marine Limited and Neil McKay Limited. Byron McKay Port Services was created in 2005, specifically for holding a management service contract awarded by the Falkland Islands Government to manage a floating barge, berthing, and warehouse storage system (FIPASS), located at the eastern end of Port Stanley. The joint venture partners offer a range of port and related marine services to complement the activities of the Company.

Prince Edward's parting address

In the evening, at 6.00 pm, attending a reception at Government House for visiting veterans, FIGs, and guests, Prince Edward in his address, paid tribute to veterans past and present:

> "As always, I have much enjoyed the opportunity of meeting veterans from the conflict here. I know that the sacrifices made were great, but perhaps you are more fortunate than many veterans in that you can visit the place you served and liberated, and can see the legacy of the sacrifice that was made. That legacy is visible in the thriving community that you see around you, and it is evident in the successful economy and democracy that we find today in the Islands."

Prince Edward's parting words to the Assembly were most encouraging:

> "I know the people of the Falklands feel enormous gratitude for what was done here. In the end, all conflict, when it cannot be avoided, must be about the securing of liberty. That is what is enjoyed here today, and it is what people in many parts of the world enjoy, thanks to the efforts and sacrifices of our armed forces veterans. We salute you! And we wish the Falkland Islanders, the people you liberated, every success in their continuing effort to make the future bright for the generations to come."

At 8.00 pm, after a long and satisfying day, Prince Edward enjoyed a quiet dinner as the guest of Governor Mr Nigel Haywood and his wife Louise.

Visit to Mount Pleasant Complex

Rounding off the historic visit, on the morning of November 13, Prince Edward met with British Armed Forces servicemen and women at the Mount Pleasant Complex, also known as Mount Pleasant Airport or (MPA). RAF Mount Pleasant is a Royal Air Force station that is part of the British Forces South Atlantic Islands (BFSAI). Home to between 1,000 and 2,000 British military personnel, it is located about 30 miles (48 kilometres) southwest of Stanley on the island of East Falkland. The world's longest corridor, half a mile (800 metres) long, links the barracks, messes, and recreational and welfare areas of the base. Opened on May 12, 1985, the station was constructed as part of British efforts to strengthen the defence of the islands following the war with Argentina. The airbase goes by the motto 'Defend the right'.

Following the highly successful visit to the Falkland Islands, Prince Edward, later that morning, departed from Mount Pleasant Airport to return home to the United Kingdom.

As at April 2015, the British have sent reinforcements to the Falkland Islands.

Major General Julian Thompson who was a Brigade Commander during the 1982 war says:

> "One of the reasons the British were so keen on retaining the Islands pre-1914 (when the Panama Canal opened) was that the islands sat on the route to the Pacific via Cape Horn. Hence we established a coaling and wireless station there. If you hold the Falklands they can be used as a base to deny/guarantee access – provided you have a Navy of course.
> "I don't think that sending reinforcements to the Falklands is worrying. Rather the reverse, as it means that the Ministry Of Defence (or rather Ministers) have restored the garrison to the strength it should be."

Endnotes to Chapter 14 Part 2

[1] See also, Jonathan Walker, *Poland Alone: Britain SOE, And The Collapse of The Polish Resistance 1944*; and *Operation Unthinkable: The Third World War: British Plans To Attack The Soviet Empire 1945*, pub. The History Press Ltd. 2010 and 2013, respectively.

[2] By kind permission of the Office of HRH The Princess Alexandra, granted January 28, 2015.

[3] Sources have included online newspaper reports: *New Vision*: 3.10.12, articles by Hugo Vickers; 5.10.12, 8.10.12, 9.10.12. *Daily Monitor*, 5.10.2012. *News*, 5.10.12. *Africa Review*, 9.10.12. Article by royal historian Carolyn Harris, 7.10.12; *The Africa Report, 9/10/12; The New Times,* 10/10/12.

[4] Lieutenant Royal Navy (Retired) Guy Huntrods CBE, letter of February 15, 2015 to Celia Lee.

[5] Communications between Celia Lee and Major General Julian Thompson, dated April 8, 2015.

CHAPTER 15

WORSHIPFUL COMPANIES AND GUILDS

Introduction

The Livery Companies number 108 trade associations in the City of London, almost all of which are known by the prefix the "Worshipful Company of", followed by the name of the relevant trade, craft or profession. The medieval Companies developed originally as guilds, and were responsible for the regulation and protection of their trades and practitioners, controlling things like wages and labour conditions. Until the Protestant Reformation (1517), they were closely associated with religious activities, notably in support of chantry chapels and churches and the observance of ceremonies, and the mystery plays. The term Worshipful originates from the ancient religious charitable association with the companies.

Freedom of the City of London

One of the oldest surviving traditional ceremonies still in existence today is the granting of the Freedom of the City of London. It is believed that the first Freedom was presented in 1237. The medieval term freeman meant someone who was not the property of a feudal lord but enjoyed privileges such as the right to earn money and own land. Town dwellers who were protected by the charter of their town or city were often free, hence the term freedom of the City.

Today the Freedom is largely symbolic but it remains a part of London's history. From the time of the Middle Ages and through to the Victorian era the Freedom was the right to trade, enabling members of a Guild or Livery to carry out their trade or craft within the square mile of the City. A fee or fine would be charged and in return the Livery Companies would ensure that the goods and services provided would be of the highest possible standard. In 1835 the Freedom was widened to incorporate not just members of Livery Companies but also people living or working in the City or where there was a strong London connection. The Freedom of the City today is still closely associated with membership of the City Livery Companies. Prince Edward became a City of London Freeman on January 1, 1958.

Worshipful Companies and Guilds

Prince Edward was admitted as a Freeman And Liveryman of the Worshipful Company of Mercers (February 1, 1972); a Liveryman of the Worshipful Company of Salters (January 1, 1965); was admitted to the Freedom of the Clothworkers' Company by Patrimony, (April 2, 1958); became an Honorary Freeman of the Worshipful Society of Apothecaries (October 27, 1981); was clothed as a Liveryman of the Worshipful Company of Engineers (July 18, 1995); and was Patron of the British Menswear Guild from July 1, 1989 until 2010.

The companies are here treated in the order of the year in which they were set up.

WORSHIPFUL COMPANY OF MERCERS
Motto: *Honor Deo*
(Honour to God)

The Worshipful Company of Mercers is the premier Livery Company of the City of London and ranks first in order of precedence. It is the first of the Great Twelve City Livery Companies and was incorporated under a Royal Charter in 1394. Their aim was to act as a trade association for general merchants, and especially for exporters of wool and importers of velvet, silk, and other luxurious fabrics. By the 16th century many members of the company had lost any connection with the original trade. Today the company exists as a charitable institution, supporting a variety of causes. The word 'mercery' derives from the Latin *merx, mercis*, meaning merchandise from which root also derives the word merchant.

Schools and colleges

The company, and its associated charitable trusts, make substantial grants to support education, general welfare, church and faith, and arts and heritage. In terms of education the Company has administered St. Paul's School, London, since 1509, and St. Paul's Girls' School since 1904, and retains close links with Collyer's College, West Sussex, Dauntsey's School, Wiltshire, Abingdon School, Oxford, Peter Symonds College, Hampshire, and Gresham College, London, all of which were founded by Mercers. In recent times the Company has founded a City Technology College, Thomas Telford School in Shropshire, and two City Academies Walsall Academy, Bloxwich, and Sandwell Academy, West Bronwich. There was also a Mercers' School in the City of London that was granted its first charter in 1447, and closed in 1959, when pupil numbers fell. The school was most recently based in Barnard's Inn, Holborn, London, which is now the home of Gresham College. In 2011 the Mercers co-sponsored a new academy school, Hammersmith Academy, specialising in Creative & Digital Media and Information Technology, located in Hammersmith, west London. The school was established in a new building with support from the Mercers and the Worshipful Company of Information Technologists. The Company is closely involved with the running of seventeen schools across the country and supports them primarily through the appointment of governors.

A network of alms houses and other homes for the elderly are also managed by the charitable trusts associated with the Company.

The Mercers' Company is based at Mercers' Hall in Ironmonger Lane, off Poultry, London. Their previous accommodation that had existed since 1676, was destroyed by fire in 1941 during the London Blitz of the Second World War, and the present Mercer's Hall was opened in May 1958. The Mercers' Company is the only City Livery Company to have its own private chapel.

The company funds its activities from income derived from its investments, mainly property in London's West End and the City. They are also patron of a number of benefices in the Church of England, having the right to appoint the vicar or rector of a parish, and they maintain close links with its affiliated units in the United Kingdom's Armed Services.

The company is custodian of an archive stretching back to its earliest days, as well as historic buildings, art and other artefacts. In addition to maintaining this collection, the company keeps its history alive by continuing its own traditions and, as premier Livery Company, fully participating in the civic life of the City of London.

Membership

In the early days the route to membership was via apprenticeship. An apprentice would be "bound" to a Member for a term of about seven years and was virtually the Member's slave, but in exchange the member was required to teach the apprentice such that he was worthy of membership by the end of the term, when he became a Freeman, after which time he was no longer bound. Freemen of a Livery Company are also Freemen of the City of London, which used to carry certain privileges, such as the right to drive a flock of sheep without charge over London Bridge!

Right to become a Mercer

Today, children whose father or mother was a member of the Company at the time of their birth have an automatic right to become Mercers by Patrimony. Most other members have a family connection to the Company and obtain their Freedom by Redemption. This is a means of admission for someone who has neither been an apprentice, nor meets the criteria for admission by patrimony. Under this process applicants are recommended for membership after an interview and, if approved, they make a payment of a small sum of money referred to as a fine. Other people can also become Members by Redemption. Membership is sometimes granted because the Company wishes to honour the individual. One other route to membership is by apprenticeship, but this has not happened recently.

Amongst notable past Members who joined the Company by Redemption were Sir Thomas More, who was a councillor to King Henry VIII, and Lord Chancellor of England, October 1529 – May 1532, and Britain's wartime Prime Minister, Sir Winston Churchill. Prince Edward was admitted as a Freeman and Liveryman on February 1, 1972.

The Queen's Diamond Jubilee Luncheon

On Tuesday June 5, 2012, the Queen's Diamond Jubilee luncheon held at Westminster Hall in the Houses of Parliament and hosted by The Livery Companies and the City of London was the highlight of the year. Seven hundred guests dined, including members of the royal family and the armed forces. The National Children's Orchestra of Great Britain performed for the Queen as she arrived at Westminster Hall.

Master Mercer Thomas Sheldon gave the pre-luncheon address, welcoming the Queen and praising her "unstinting devotion to duty", and telling her "You embody the very best of our national values. You are our constant in a changing world."

The menu included delicious Cornish crab, Cambrian Mountain Lamb and a Sympathy of Desserts. The wines included Sancerre Jean-Paul Picard, Bue, Loire Valley France 2011, and Chateau Cap de Faugeres, Cotes de Castillion Bordeaux France 2007.

WORSHIPFUL COMPANY OF SALTERS
Motto: Sal Sapit Omnia
(for Salt Savours All)

The Worshipful Company of Salters was first licensed in 1394, and has its origins in the salt trade of medieval London. It is 9th in order of precedence as one of the Twelve Great Livery Companies of the City of London. Having originated as the Guild of *Corpus Christi*, a Royal Charter of 1607 re-incorporated the Company under its present name of the Master, Wardens and Commonality of the Art or Mistery of the Salters of London.

Originally the Salters' Company included individuals whose trades involved the usage of salts in the preparation and preservation (dry salting) of food. By the 14th century salt was an essential commodity in England, being used in the preservation of meat and fish and in medicines and ointments. Salt was also present in cleaning substances, used in bleaching, and in the dyeing of fabric, and softening of leather. Salters were trained in the drying and salting of fish and meat, and also dealt with flax, hemp, potashes and so on, and chemical preservations. Salters therefore grouped themselves together and lived in Bread Street, London, and also attended the same church the Parish Church of All Hallows.

Chemistry
In 1894 the company began giving to the sciences, and various Fellowships were offered support that included the Pharmaceutical Society's laboratory. After the First World War the company provided support to those chemistry students whose education had been interrupted due to their having served in the war. The Salters' Institute of Industrial Chemistry was founded in 1918. In 1975 the company launched the Graduate Prizes that are awarded annually to ten outstanding final year chemistry and chemical engineering students.

Today their main charity, the Salters' Institute, supports the teaching of science through the running of chemistry camps and festivals at universities and has its own A-level courses in Chemistry, Physics, and Biology, as well as a suite of science GCSEs.

The Company also operates two Almshouse charities and its grant-giving Salters' Charitable Foundation.

Salters' Hall

Over the years, the Salters have occupied several halls. In the 15th century The Church of All Hallows in Bread Street was the meeting place where Salters worshiped and conducted business and entertainment. Their later premises were systematically destroyed by fire, including Saltershalle which was rebuilt several times. A new hall was built at London Stone in the Parish of St. Swithin but that too was destroyed during the Great Fire of London (1666) and rebuilt in 1668 but, by 1810, was no longer suitable and a new hall was completed in 1827 named Salters' Hall. It was bombed during the Second World War on May 10-11, 1941. The Salters' Company were housed in temporary premises until 1976, when a modern hall was built that is today No.4 Fore Street, London EC2. Having for some years been obliged to use the halls of other Livery companies for their celebrations, the Salters now had their own ash-panelled Banqueting Hall.

Prince Edward was admitted as a Liveryman of The Worshipful Company of Salters on January 1, 1965, and was called upon to perform the official opening of the new hall.

WORSHIPFUL COMPANY OF CLOTHWORKERS

Mission statement:
"Through its grant-making, the Foundation seeks to improve the lives of people and communities, particularly those facing disadvantage."

The origins of the Worshipful Company of Clothworkers lie in the most ancient Livery Company of London, the Weavers' Company. From the Weavers' Company sprang two groups, known as the Fullers, who were incorporated by a Royal Charter in 1480, and the Shearmen, who were incorporated in 1508. The Fullers and Shearmen combined under a Royal Charter into the Clothworkers' Company in 1528. Their original purpose was to protect their members and promote the craft of cloth-finishing within the City of London.

The function of the Worshipful Company of Clothworkers has changed greatly since its inception. Their main role today is in the charitable sphere, through The Clothworkers' Foundation, which is an independent, registered charity. Their mission statement is: "Through its grant-making, the Foundation seeks to improve the lives of people and communities, particularly those facing disadvantage."

Both the company and the foundation operate from Clothworkers' Hall, in Dunster Court, off Mincing Lane, London EC3. The site was conveyed to a group of Shearmen in 1456, and the present building, completed as late as 1958, is the sixth on the site.

The original craft of the clothworkers was the finishing of woven woollen cloth, and a crucial part of the process involved in perfecting the cloth was termed fulling. It was carried out by female and male fullers who pounded the wet, soapy, cloth with their bare feet to cleanse it of grease and dirt. The exercise also matted the fibres and thickened the wool. It was then stretched onto great frames and held in place by tenterhooks to dry. The nap was raised with teasels and the cloth was sheared to a uniform finish. The terms fulling and walking or waulking, were used by Scottish workers in relation to the process. From the mediaeval period the fulling of cloth was undertaken in a watermill, known as a fulling mill, or a walk mill, or a tuck mill. In Wales the mill was called a pandy.

The Ordinances of The Clothworkers' Company was first issued in 1532, and signed by Sir Thomas More who, at the time of signing, was Lord Chancellor to Henry VIII, and it sought to regulate clothworking to maintain standards and to protect approved practices.

The first references to fulling mills were reported in Persia from the 10th century. By the time of the Crusades in the late 11th century, fulling mills were active throughout the mediaeval Islamic world, from Islamic Spain and North Africa in the west, to Central Asia in the east. Mechanical fulling was subsequently disseminated into Western Europe through Islamic Spain and Italy in the 11th and 12th centuries. The earliest known reference to a fulling mill in France, which dates from about 1086, was discovered in Normandy. The earliest reference in England occurs in the Winton Domesday of 1117-19, which was a document that recorded the landholdings in the city of Winchester in Hampshire. Other early references belonged to the Knights Templar in 1185. These mills became widespread during the 13th century and occur in most counties of England and Wales, but were largely absent in areas only engaged in making worsted cloth.

From the later Middle Ages, cloth production gradually moved away from London, a situation exacerbated by the Great Fire of London and the Industrial Revolution of the 18th and 19th centuries. The charitable role of The Clothworkers' Company has continued, supported by generous gifts of money and property donated by members and benefactors. Amongst its famous members are listed King James I of England, the London diarist, Samuel Pepys, Angela Burdett-Coutts, the 19th century philanthropist and the grand-daughter of the wealthy banker Thomas Coutts; and Sir Robert Menzies (1894-1978), a former Prime Minister of Australia.

Although few of their present members are involved in the textile industry in any direct way, they continue to promote textiles, principally through educational grants, fostering the development of technical textiles, and support for the nation's textile heritage. The assets of the company (based on property and investments) are used to support The Clothworkers' Foundation which is one of the largest grant-makers in Britain.

As one of the Great Twelve Livery Companies, The Worshipful Company of Clotherworkers enjoys a close bond of friendship and co-operation with other such companies, and the City of London Corporation. The company takes pride in performing its civic obligations and contributing to the living history of London. They foster fellowship amongst their members through events at Clothworkers' Hall.

Prince Edward was admitted to the Freedom of The Clothworkers' Company by Patrimony on the April 2, 1958. On the same date, he was also presented with the Honorary Livery of the Company. The Clothworkers' Company has, in fact, numbered several royals amongst its members in the past, their first being King James I of England and VI of Scotland, and has sought to continue this royal connection over time. It is particularly fitting that Prince Edward took up his Freedom of the company as both his parents were members. The Clothworkers was the first Company Prince Edward joined, and they consider themselves to be his parent or mother company. As such, their blessing was sought by the Mercers', Apothecaries', and Engineers' companies, who also admitted Prince Edward as a member.

Members of the Clothworkers have greatly valued Prince Edward's interest and, in particular, with regard to their shared connection in the field of mathematics. The Clothworkers' Company and Foundation has a long connection with the Royal Institution (RI), of which Prince Edward is President, and they have been a significant supporter of their maths master classes programme for many years. On July 2, 1990, Prince Edward unveiled a Clothworkers' Plaque at the Institution, acknowledging the company's endowment towards the programme. Their support in this field has grown in recent years, and on March 18, 2009, they held a Maths Soirée at Clothworkers' Hall, in order to make their Livery more aware of their work. They were particularly honoured to welcome Prince Edward to this event, almost twenty years on from their first support of the Royal Institution.

Prince Edward's attendance at the Hall in 2009 was also fitting, as it was in this year that they established an affiliation with the Scots Guards, and Prince Edward is Colonel of the Regiment. Several Court members and their wives were invited to dinner at the regiment's barracks by the regimental Colonel, which was held on February 24, 2009, at which the Prince was present. The company made a contribution of £50,000 to the Colonel's Fund, established to assist Guards wounded in Iraq and Afghanistan, and has since sent a number of buddy boxes to troops in Helmand. These were for front line troops and were filled with such items as toiletries, newspapers, Christmas cards, and Santa hats.

THE WORSHIPFUL SOCIETY
OF APOTHECARIES OF LONDON
Motto: Opiferque Per Orbem Dicor
(I am called a bringer of help throughout the world)

The Worshipful Society of Apothecaries of London is one of the largest of the Livery Companies and ranks 58th in the order of precedence. Its motto Opiferque Per Orbem Dicor meaning 'I am called a bringer of help throughout the world', is a reference to the Greek deity, Apollo, which appears on the society's arms overcoming the dragon of disease, and the society's crest is the rhinoceros.

Prior to the foundation of the society in 1617, London apothecaries were members of the Grocers' Company (founded 1345), and prior to that they were members of the Guild of Pepperers, founded before 1180. The Apothecaries separated from the Grocers in 1617, when they were granted a Royal Charter by King James I. During the rest of the 17th century its members challenged the monopoly of members of the College of Physicians to practice medicine. In 1704 the House of Lords overturned a ruling of the Queen's Bench in the Rose Case, finally giving apothecaries the right to practice medicine, and the apothecaries are forerunners of the today's general practitioners.

The Apothecaries Act 1815 granted the society the power to license and regulate practitioners of medicine throughout England and Wales. The regulation of medicine was taken over by the General Medical Council on its formation in 1855. More latterly, the society retained its licence to practice medicine between 1993 and 2001, operating as a member of the United Examining Board.

A number of people qualified in medicine as a Licentiate of the Society of Apothecaries (LSA), including Elizabeth Garrett Anderson (1865), who became the first known woman in the UK to gain a medical qualification.

The society has charitable status and is a member of the London Museums of Health & Medicine. Today the Apothecaries organise lectures and courses through two Faculties. They grant postgraduate diplomas in areas such as medical jurisprudence, history of medicine, philosophy of medicine, gorensic medical dciences, gorensic and clinical aspects of sexual assault, genito urinary medicine, HIV medicine, and medical care of catastrophes.

In 1673 the society founded the Chelsea Physic Garden in London and managed it until 1899. It is one of the oldest botanical gardens in Europe which grows 5,000 edible plants and is open to the public.

The society is located at Apothecaries' Hall, Blackfriars Lane, London EC4. In 1632 the Hall was originally part of the Dominican Priory of Black Friars but the building was destroyed in the Great Fire of London. It was replaced by a new hall in 1672 that included an Elaboratory for the first ever large-scale manufacture of drugs. Its late 18th century design has been retained and it is the oldest livery company hall in the City, with a Great Hall, Court Room, and Parlour.

The Court agreed to offer to admit Prince Edward as an Honorary Freeman on October 27, 1981, which offer was made by the Master on November 4, and Prince Edward accepted. The honour was conferred upon him at the Soiree on July 21, 1982.

Prince Edward attends Livery dinners at the Hall. He was present at a high profile Court and Yeomanry dinner at Apothecaries' Hall on Wednesday, October 26, 2011. It was typical of the tradition of the society in maintaining the standards of such ancient functions, celebrating the long established connections with the Armed Forces. Cadets from the Silver Bugles band of the Frome branch of the Somerset Cadet Battalion, The Rifles, played on the steps, welcoming Prince Edward as he walked up to the Court Room, accompanied by high ranking military officers and other dignitaries. The Battalion Medical Officer, Lieutenant Colonel Timothy Chambers OBE, had been appointed as the 396th Master of The Worshipful Society of Apothecaries of London that August. Commandant Colonel Paul Richardson said:

"This was a fantastic opportunity for our band to showcase their musical talents and a great honour for the Somerset Army Cadet Force. I am certain that all of the young people that played in the Apothecaries' Great Hall will remember it as one of the highlights of their time as cadets."

The society celebrated the 400th anniversary of their Appeal Fund in February 2013.

*108. Mr Rodney Croft, Liveryman of the Worshipful
Society of Apothecaries and a Freeman of the City of London,
opening Tower Bridge on January 25, 2015, to allow
MV Havengore to pass through during a re-enactment
on the 50th anniversary Sir Winston Churchill's state funeral.*

Sir Winston Churchill's 50th anniversary, 2015

Sir Winston Churchill died on January 25, 1965. At the 50th anniversary, January 30, 2015, of Churchill's historic state funeral that had partly taken place by barge on the River Thames, a re-enactment was carried out in his honour. Mr Rodney Croft, a doctor and vascular consultant from Essex, being a Liveryman of the Worshipful Society of Apothecaries and a Freeman of the City of London was asked by the Corporation of London to perform the duty of opening Tower Bridge to let the barge pass through. At 12.45 on January 30,

Mr Croft made the announcement to halt the traffic. He then pressed the buttons and pulled the levers, electronically raising Tower Bridge to a height of 90 degrees to allow MV Havengore that had carried Churchill's coffin, to travel along the same route. This time it was carrying members of the present day Churchill family. (See *Churchill's Final Farewell: The State and Private Funeral of Sir Winston Churchill* by Rodney J. Croft, (published. 2014).

WORSHIPFUL COMPANY OF ENGINEERS
Motto: Certare Ingenio
(Use Skills to the Best of One's Abilities)

The Worshipful Company of Engineers is for Chartered Engineers who are Fellows of the Royal Academy of Engineering or Fellows of the Professional Engineering Institutions. It was founded and became a Livery Company in 1983, was incorporated by Royal Charter in 2004, and ranks 94th in order of precedence for Livery Companies. Its motto Certare Ingenio is most fitting and means Use Skills to the Best of One's Abilities. Prince Edward was clothed as a Liveryman on July 18, 1995, and appointed as a Court Assistant from April 30, 1996.

The company works to promote the development and advancement of all aspects of the science, art, and practise of engineering, within the social and charitable ethos that is at the core of the Livery movement. To further these objectives the company organises an extensive programme of events, including lectures, technical visits, and social functions, working closely with and complementing the activities of the Royal Academy of Engineering, the Engineering Council, and the professional engineering institutions.

Through its charitable trust fund, the company gives awards, prizes, and grants to support and encourage excellence amongst professionally qualified engineers and those training to become so.

There are annual awards for excellence to civilian engineers, both student and graduate, as well as to members of the UK's Armed Forces. While the services' awards cover engineering training, operations in the field, and materiel support, the civilian prizes include: the Baroness Platt of Writtle Award of £1,000 to recognise an outstanding Incorporated Engineer amongst those registered during the previous year; the Cadzow Smith Award of £2,500 to recognise excellence on an accredited undergraduate engineering course at universities within London and the Home Counties; and the Fiona and Nicholas Hawley Award of £5,000 for the application of Engineering for a better Environment.

One-off grants are made for the relief of financial hardship prejudicing the completion of engineering degrees and to support other worthwhile charitable causes, especially those with a professional engineering character.

On April 27, 2004, Prince Edward presented the company with its Royal Charter on behalf of Her Majesty The Queen, and subsequently accepted the status of Honorary Liveryman and Court Assistant Emeritus from October 12, 2004. He takes a keen interest in the development of engineering and related subjects and, from time to time, attends Court and Livery dinners, including awards ceremonies.

BRITISH MENSWEAR GUILD

Savile Row, located in fashionable Mayfair in central London, has been synonymous with traditional bespoke tailoring for gentlemen since 1790, first in Cork Street and then in 1803, in Savile Row. The term bespoke, meaning a suit cut and made by hand, is believed to have originated in Savile Row. Famous early customers of

Savile Row suits have included Lord Nelson and Sir Winston Churchill. Following a ruling by the Advertising Standards Authority in 2008, bespoke suits may now be made by machine so long as they are made to measure. Hands with years of skill and a pride in their work can cut and stitch a suit in hand-woven British cloth in about 52 hours.

The 'Kent' cut, which is a double-breasted suit, has remained timeless in fashion since it was popularised by Prince Edward's father, Prince George. It possesses a longer lapel line that extends into the waist and is particularly suitable for tall gentleman with a slim waistline. Prince Edward is 6 feet 4 inches (195.072 centimetres).

The British Menswear Guild was launched in 1959, by such British brand names as Aquascutum, Church's English Shoes, and Daks. It is located at 5 Portland Place, London, W1. The 'Guild', as it is referred to, has always focused on high quality, design, and Britishness. Today the role of the guild is to promote the member brands through the strength of the group.

Prince Edward's personal appearance is very important in his role as a senior member of the royal family. He is constantly meeting important dignitaries and members of the public, both at home and overseas. Whether wearing lounge suit or black tie for formal occasions, or sports jacket and trousers for more relaxed occasions, Prince Edward is always immaculately dressed. He was Patron of the British Menswear Guild from July 1, 1989, until they amalgamated with the UK Fashion and Textile Association in 2010.

The guild's 50th anniversary took place in 2007, and was marked by a celebratory party at Kensington Palace, hosted by Prince Edward. Attended by 200 guests, the event was something of a networking opportunity for the Guild's Russian customers.

US retailer receives Warrant

In 1998 Mr Richard Carroll of Carroll & Co., who are centred in the United States, was the first retailer outside of Great Britain to receive a Warrant of Appointment for his services to the British textile industry. Dick, as he was known, had founded his own clothing company. He was Chairman of the Beverly Hills Planning Commission and spent more than thirty years on the Rodeo Drive Commission. President Ronald Reagan, Clark Gable, Cary Grant, and Fred Astaire were amongst Dick's famous name customers. The Carroll family travelled to London and joined 600 members of the British Menswear Guild where Prince Edward Presented Dick with the Guild's top honour.

CHAPTER 16

LONDON CLUBS

Introduction

London's gentlemen's clubland, first noted in the early 1700's, grew up and flourished from the 18th century onwards, around Pall Mall and St. James's. Admission was by membership only and these were places where gentlemen could be together. For many years no lady was allowed in through the door but women set up their own separate clubs. Luxuriously and comfortably furnished with leather sofas and armchairs, a bar and bedrooms for overnight stays, gentlemen club members were attended by servants. The term weekend, as we have been reminded by the Dowager Countess of Grantham (Maggie Smith) in the ITV television series Downton Abbey, was unknown in those days. Gentlemen of the aristocracy and landed gentry who did not work, but lived off the proceeds of unearned income from their vast country estates and investments, spent much time at their club. With the success of the industrial revolution and city business, they were joined in later years by those with new money, businessmen who were company proprietors and directors, and by stockbrokers and such like.

There was gambling, mostly card playing and horse racing. The finest food, wines, and spirits were served, hence the crop of wine and spirit merchants' businesses springing up close by. Some, like the Victorian Athenæum Club, were founded for more intellectual and serious-mined men with an emphasis on the arts and politics. Today the London club is where men and women with good jobs and incomes spend time when in town or attending social functions and conferences, or stay over-night rather than travelling to their homes in the country.

Prince Edward is a member of eight London clubs: The Travellers Club (1953); Boodle's Club (1955); Buck's Club (1955); the Polish Hearth Club (Ognisko Polskie) (late 1960s); The Cavalry and Guards Club, of which he became President (1974); The IN & OUT Naval and Military Club (1960); the Turf Club (1975); and The Army and Navy (the Rag) Club (1978); (For the British Racing Drivers Club, see Chapter 11: Sport).

THE TRAVELLERS CLUB

The Travellers Club is a gentlemen's only club at 106 Pall Mall, London, and is the oldest of the surviving Pall Mall clubs, having been established in 1819. It was the conception of Robert Stewart, 2nd Marquess of Londonderry (1769-1822), and others. Known as Lord Castlereagh, he was British Foreign Secretary from 1812, and was central to the management of the coalition that defeated Napoléon.

The architect of the club was Sir Charles Barry who, having completed the Grand Tour of Europe, was inspired by Raphael's Palazzo Pandolfini in Florence from which the front facade was copied, and the rear was influenced by the Palazzo Vendramini in Venice.

The club interior has a number of exquisite attributes; the vast library is decorated with a recreation of the Bassae Frieze marbles of the 5th century Greek temple of Apollo Epicurius at Bassae that was brought to the club by Charles Cockerell, who was another of its founder members. The original is in the British Museum and only one other copy exists at the Ashmolean Museum in Oxford. In recent years the club has developed further and there is a Map Room where modern travel literature, and a collection of maps of important journeys of exploration can be viewed.

Travellers

Part of the thinking behind the club was to assist travellers to and from foreign parts in providing them with a place to stay, and there are many past members of note. The Conservative Prime Ministers Arthur Balfour, Stanley Baldwin, and Sir Alec Douglas-Home were members, as was Lord Auckland, after whom Auckland, New Zealand was named.

The club attracted anyone involved in heroic travel, like Sir William Edward Parry, explorer of the Northwest Passage that is a sea route through the Arctic Ocean along the northern coast of North America, via waterways amidst the Canadian Arctic Archipelago, connecting the Atlantic and Pacific Oceans. There were literary men like French author Jules Verne (1828-1905), who wrote *Twenty Thousand Leagues Under The Sea,* and Graham Greene (1904-1991), author of the famous screenplay *The Third Man.* In more recent years, Terry Waite CBE, who was an envoy for the Church of England and travelled to Lebanon to try to secure the release of four hostages but was himself held captive between 1987 and 1991, is a member. Other members include the world's greatest living explorer, Sir Ranulph Fiennes, and Field Marshal Lord Bramall, who served as Chief of the General Staff of the British Army, (1979-1982), and as Chief of the Defence Staff (1982-1985).

Prince Edward was made an Honorary Member of the club on November 10, 1953, a month after his 18th birthday. It is the first record of his membership of any club or organisation.

On July 3, 2002, a number of clubs got together to form a joint summer party that was hosted by three clubs: The Athenæum, Travellers, and Reform Club, which was held at the Athenæum Club. Prince Edward was in attendance and the occasion was to celebrate the Golden Jubilee of Her Majesty Queen Elizabeth II.

BOODLE'S CLUB

Prince Edward was aged 19 years when, on January 1, 1955, he was granted Honorary Membership of Boodle's Club.

Now a private members' club, Boodle's was originally a proprietary club, formed in 1762, in premises occupied by Mr William Almack at Nos. 49-51 Pall Mall, London. Initially it seems that Edward Boodle, who was born in Oswestry, Shropshire, Wales, managed the club for Almack, eventually becoming its proprietor and giving it his name. Mr Almack had been a valet to James Douglas-Hamilton, the 5th Duke of Hamilton. Prior to the premises becoming Boodle's Club it had been Almack's Coffee House. The driving force behind its establishment was the Earl of Shelborne, William Petty-FitzMaurice, later the Marquess of Lansdowne (1737-1805), who was Whig Prime Minister (1782-1783) during the final months of the American War of Independence.

Boodle's is thought to be the second oldest club in the world, being outranked only by White's that was established in 1693. Boodle's moved from Pall Mall in 1782, taking over the premises of the defunct Savoir Vivre Club, designed by the architect John Crunden, (1775-1776), at No. 28 St. James's Street, and where the club remains today. After the death of the last proprietor, the club members acquired control in 1896.

Famous past members

Boodle's Club was never perhaps as politically partisan as other clubs, such as Brooks's. Boodle's Club came about when a group of gentlemen had been blackballed for membership of White's Club and, in 1762, they formed a private society at 50 Pall Mall. The society then split and some joined Brooks's Club, whilst others joined Boodle's Club.

In its early years Boodle's attracted a wide range of men that were leaders in public and literary life. In the later 19th century it was very much a club frequented by sporting and country gentlemen, with a generous sprinkling of military men. Famous past members are as politically diverse as the Scottish philosopher and pioneer of political economy, Adam Smith (1723-1790), his fellow Scot, David Hume, the philosopher and historian, and Edward Gibbon, author of the celebrated *Decline and Fall of the Roman Empire*. George "Beau" Bryan Brummell (1778–1840) was something of a 'dandy' and trendsetter in men's clothes. He was a friend of the Prince Regent, the future King George IV. Being a gambler, in 1816 he owed thousands of pounds in gambling debts. Before fleeing the country for France to escape the Debtors Prison, he is reputed to have placed his last bet at Boodle's. The last recorded entry for Brummell in the Boodle's betting book was 10 guineas on the Derby in May 1815.

One interesting late 19th-century member was Prince Victor Duleep Singh (July 10, 1866 – June 7, 1918), whose godparents were Queen Victoria and her husband Prince Albert the Prince Consort. Prince Victor was the eldest son of Maharani Bamba Müller and Maharaja Duleep Singh, the last Maharaja of Lahore, and of the Sikh Empire, and the grandson of Maharaja Ranjit Singh. The Prince was educated in England, where he met and married Lady Anne Coventry and they lived as English country gentry.

The club drew also to its ranks such men of action as Field Marshal Arthur Wellesley, 1st Duke of Wellington (1769-1852), hero of the Waterloo Campaign. The great Wellington is reputed to have said that he used Boodle's solely on account of its excellent lavatory facilities! World leader Sir Winston Spencer-Churchill (1874-1965), who carried the British people to victory in the Second World War, was one of the few people to be elected to honorary membership.

The London born, British award-winning actor and novelist Sir David Niven was a member. He was best known for his roles as Phileas Fogg in Around the World in 80 Days and as Sir Charles Lytton, a.k.a. the Phantom in the film The Pink Panther. Niven sponsored Ian Lancaster Fleming (1908–1964) for membership. Fleming was an English author and naval intelligence officer, famed as the creator of the fictional spy James Bond. A series of films were made of his novels dating from the 1960s. Fleming is said to have based the Blades Club which is featured in his film James Bond 007 on Boodle's Club, and Boodle's itself is referenced in his novel *Moonraker*.

For many years women were banned from gentlemen's clubs, and the playwright Oscar Wilde provided great fun for his audiences with this attitude. In 1895 *An Ideal Husband* was staged. After Lord Goring establishes that he is a bachelor, Sir Robert Chiltern says to Mrs Cheveley: "Lord Goring is the result of Boodle's Club, Mrs Cheveley". Mrs Cheveley responds coyly: "He reflects every credit on the institution." Just over 100 years later, in the 1998 American action spy film The Avengers, starring Ralph Fiennes and Uma Thurman, playing the parts of secret agents, Emma Peel (Uma Thurman) walks into Boodle's Club and is told: "No females have been in Boodle's since 1762."

The club celebrated its 250th anniversary in 2012. Boodle's Orange Fool, a fruit trifle smothered in cream, and seemingly as old as the club itself, has apparently been very popular over the years. It remains a traditional club dish and no doubt it was much in demand on the day!

BUCK'S CLUB

During the First World War (1914-18), Captain H.J. Buckmaster Royal Horse Guards, and some of his colleagues, agreed that after the war it would be good to establish a gentlemen's club to cater for their own tastes. They particularly wanted a club with an American Cocktail Bar, which at that time did not exist in traditional British gentlemen's clubs. Named after Buckmaster, Buck's Club was established in June 1919, and its American Bar was a focal point. American members were welcome, although treated separately from a constitutional standpoint. The club for many years kept its tradition of sourcing members from the British Household Cavalry regiments, although its membership is now drawn from many walks of life.

Situated at 18 Clifford Street, the club occupies a quiet corner in the heart of London's exclusive Mayfair. It is most conveniently located for clothing, being close to Bond Street, famous for its men's bespoke tailoring. Sir Winston Churchill, his secretary, Brendan Bracken, writer Guy Bolton, and actor Nigel Bruce are amongst its historic members. The writer, P G Wodehouse, mentions Buck's Club in some of his stories, and modelled his Drones Club mostly after Buck's, and in the Bachelors' Club, even naming the club barman McGarry.

Renowned for its exuberance, the club is perhaps best known for the drink Buck's Fizz, which was invented in 1921 by their barman, known alternatively as "Malachy" or "Pat" MacGarry, or more usually McGarry, who was bar tender there from 1919-41. Still as popular as ever, Buck's Fizz is made from champagne and orange juice, served widely at receptions, parties and weddings. Some old recipes also include grenadine which is a red syrup used in cocktails both for its flavour and because it gave a reddish/pink tinge to the mixed drinks, and ice could also be added. Grenadine was originally prepared from pomegranate juice or cherry juice and sugar, but it was later replaced by vodka. It was this type of unusual cocktail that may have endeared Buck's Club to the late Sir Winston Churchill, or even influenced the use of the ingredient in the drink.

Winston's mother, the famous American beauty Lady Randolph Spencer-Churchill, nee Jennie Jerome, invented a Manhattan cocktail at a banquet in New York in 1894, when on a world trip with her terminally ill husband Lord Randolph the second son of the 7th Duke and Duchess of Marlborough. Jennie had been born the second daughter of Leonard and Clarissa Jerome, Leonard being a flamboyant speculator who made millions on the New York stock exchange. Until 1867 the family had lived in a huge mansion on Madison Avenue, New York. Jennie's grandson, Peregrine Spencer-Churchill, told the authors that his grandmother's Manhattan Cocktail was influenced by his grandfather's, Lord Randolph Spencer-Churchill's cough medicine! Whatever the exotic mixture it remains popular today.

Prince Edward accepted Honorary Life Membership of Buck's Club in July 1955, just before his 20th birthday, during which time he was still in training as an officer in the British Army at the Royal Military Academy, Sandhurst. He became Patron of the Buck's Club on June 1, 1971. Prince Edward is a keen supporter of the club and a regular visitor, the latter as a private individual. He takes a keen interest in the club and his input and comments are highly valued. He makes regular visits both for special dinners and to attend long-serving staff retirement occasions. He is always interested in what is happening and, with his usual modesty, does a good deal behind the scenes to promote the success of the club.

CAVALRY AND GUARDS CLUB

The Cavalry and Guards Club is a gentlemen's club situated at 127 Piccadilly, London since 1890. The club is a merger of two clubs, the Guards Club founded 1810, and the Cavalry Club founded 1890. Prince Edward became a Member of the Cavalry Club in September 1956, qualifying as an Officer in the Royal Scots Greys. He became President of the Club on December 1, 1974, following the death of his uncle, His Royal Highness The Duke of Gloucester. In 1976, the two clubs came together with Prince Edward as President. Today there are approximately 800 members.

Since that time Prince Edward has been an active supporter of the club, having been involved in the amalgamation in 1976, and more particularly with the purchase of the freehold of the club, by the Members, in 1987.

Prince Edward regularly attends the club both in a private capacity and at regimental dinners and club events, and he attends the annual Chairman's Dinner on a regular basis. He was present at the Luncheon to celebrate the 200th anniversary of the founding of the Guards Club in 2010, along with His Royal Highness Prince Philip, The Duke of Edinburgh, who was representing Her Majesty The Queen. More recently he attended a Reception to celebrate 25 years since the purchase of the freehold.

THE 'IN & OUT' NAVAL AND MILITARY CLUB

Prince Edward was made an Honorary Life Member of The 'In & Out' Naval and Military Club on March 28, 1960. Lieutenant Colonel Christopher Hogan is Chief Executive and Secretary of the Club [1], and Miss Sarah Sinclair is Marketing & Events Manager.

The Naval and Military Club was founded in March 1862, to meet the demand of those who wished to join a Service Club. The founding officers were mostly members of the Royal East Kent Regiment, formerly the 3rd Regiment of Foot, and, until 1961, an infantry regiment of the British Army. Nicknamed the Buffs because they wore buff coloured coats made of soft leather, they were Major W. H. Cairnes, Captain W. Stewart, and Lieutenant F. T. Jones, plus Captain L. C. Barber, R. E. Barber Esq and H. H. Barber Esq, late of the 17th Lancers. Following a series of amalgamations since 1961, the Buffs lineage is today continued by the Princess of Wales's Royal Regiment.

The 'In & Out' Club

The In & Out Club, as it is referred to, began with 150 Members at an entrance fee of £15 and a home subscription fee of £5.5s, (today £5.25). It was housed in different buildings over the years and kept moving as its numbers increased. They moved into Cambridge House on Piccadilly, London, in April 1866, which building still stands today. In order to provide accommodation for Members, and facilities for the entertaining of ladies, the lease of an adjoining hotel, 42 Half Moon Street, was obtained in 1919. During that occupancy the club became known as the In & Out, on account of the prominent signs on the building's vehicle entrance and exit gates. These were displayed so that cars drove in on one side and out on the other.

The freehold of No. 4 St. James's Square in central London near St. James's Palace was purchased in 1998. One of its former residents was Nancy, Viscountess Astor who, in 1919 was the first woman who took her seat as a Member of Parliament. She was the wife of Waldorf, 2nd Viscount Astor of Hever. The club moved to the historic premises on February 1, 1999, which it occupies today.

Today the club offers its members and their guests a place of calm and sanctuary but it is also renowned for its vibrant socialising and entertainment. The clubhouse has two entrances. The front entrance in St. James's Square being formal, where a strict dress code is adhered to, and the Babmaes Street entrance, just off Jermyn Street, that allows direct access to the relaxed business centre, gym, swimming pool, and brasserie. There is a superb dining room and banqueting hall, bar facilities, lavish State rooms, a blissful courtyard, and 52 en-suite bedrooms.

An old-fashioned warm welcome greets Members and guests, and membership is open to non-Service Members. A varied programme of interesting events and activities takes place, including Fireside Chats that take the form of talks by guest speakers on a range of subjects from the arts, sport, naval and military history, and local interest. It is a place to relax and feel at home amongst historic statues and oil paintings in the heart of London.

Battles of Waterloo and Trafalgar celebrations

There are regular events that usually include the 'big three' formal dinners each year, celebrating the battles of Waterloo and Trafalgar, and the club's founding in March 1862. Speakers vary from event to event, but they include the great and the good who have a connection to or interest in the two great victories, all of whom relish the opportunity in sharing their knowledge with club Members and their guests.

The club admits women and Major Imogen Corrigan and Mr Paul Edward Strong, representing the Women in War group that began inside The British Commission For Military History, gave a talk titled: *Searchlights and Sniper-rifles, Women in Military Service in the Second World War (1939-45)*, based on chapters they wrote for a book *WOMEN IN WAR From Home Front to Front Line*, (pub. Pen & Sword, 2012). Their talk was introduced by Lieutenant Colonel Christopher Hogan and chaired by Professor Gary Sheffield.

A variety of other events organised by Miss Sarah Sinclair, Marketing & Events Manager, have included special occasion lunches and dinners, barbeques in the courtyard, celebratory balls, wine and champagne tastings, informal buffets such as the new members' supper, and club visits. There are also a number of societies for members with particular interest groups such as shooting, bridge, sailing, the under 35's group, and the Nancy Astor Society.

TURF CLUB

The Turf Club is a gentlemen's club that, since 1965, has been located at 5 Carlton House Terrace, London, overlooking the Mall. Established in 1861 as The Arlington Club, the original premises were in Bennett Street, Piccadilly. The Committee of the Arlington included such names as George Bentinck (1802 – 1848) and Sir Reginald Knightley, both Conservative Members of Parliament. Bentinck owned several successful racehorses, his stable being renowned for its quality. These included the famous Surplice (1845–1871), whose career lasted from July 1847 to October 1849. Surplice ran thirteen times and won nine races. He was the leading colt of his generation in England at both two and three years old. His wins included the Epsom Derby and the St. Leger in 1848, and he was the first horse for 48 years to win both Classics.

Bentinck was involved in eliminating fraud in the sport. It was at the Turf Club that the laws of the trick card game whist were drawn up and were then sanctioned officially by the Portland Club in 1864.

Carlton House Terrace was designed and built by the famous Regency architect John Nash, between 1827 and 1833. Over the years amongst the residents of No.5 were Lord Palmerston, (1784–1865), nicknamed The Mongoose, who served twice as Conservative Prime Minister in the mid-19th century, and the US Ambassador, John Hay (1838-1905). Possibly the most flamboyant incumbent was Harry Gordon Selfridge, (1864-1947), founder of Selfridges Store in London, and on whose life a television series shown on ITV has been broadcast since January 2013. Also living there was one of the most colourful women of her day, Maud, Lady Cunard, of Cunard Shipping fame (1872-1948), who gave herself the nickname, Emerald.

Prince Edward became an Honorary Member of the Turf Club on January 16, 1975. Amongst his numerous contemporaries are James Spencer-Churchill, Marquess of Blandford (1955), of Blenheim Palace; Michael Bowes Lyon, 18th Earl of Strathmore and Kinghorne (1957), great-nephew of the late Queen Elizabeth The Queen Mother and first cousin, once removed to Queen Elizabeth II; The Honourable Rupert Soames, OBE (1959), younger son of Christopher, Lord Soames and the late Mary, The Lady Soames LG DBE FRSL, (nee Spencer-Churchill). His elder brother, the Right Honourable Sir Nicholas Soames, is the well-known Conservative Member of Parliament for mid-Sussex.

Prince Edward admits however:

'I never took much to riding as a boy and only started seriously to enjoy it after I took an Army riding course at Aldershot in the 1950s. As a result I took up hunting in Yorkshire on regimental horses which I greatly enjoyed. But since that time my riding has been mainly confined to the annual Queen's Birthday Parade, when I ride as Colonel of the Scots Guards.' [2]

ARMY & NAVY CLUB
"The Rag"

Lieutenant-General Sir Edward Barnes GCB founded the Army & Navy Club in 1837. His proposal was to establish an Army Club, with all officers of Her Majesty's Army on full or half pay eligible for membership. However, when the Duke of Wellington was asked to be a patron, he refused to do so or even to have any association with the club unless membership was also offered to officers of the Royal Navy and the Royal Marines, so this was agreed. On August 28, 1837, the inaugural meeting took place to elect a Committee to settle the new club's Rules, with Sir Edward Barnes as the first President.

Shortly after opening the club acquired its nickname when Captain William (Billy) Higginson Duff became offended by the spartan nature of the fare offered to him upon returning from a spree. He described the club as a 'Rag and Famish affair' that was the name of a squalid gaming house. The Members were amused and formed a "Rag and Famish dining club". The name was gradually adopted as the club's nickname, eventually being reduced to "The Rag".

By 1851 the club was in a strong position with 1,102 members and a waiting list of 834. This pressure of popularity, not only of the Army & Navy Club, but also of the United Service and the Junior United Service, led to the founding of the separate and earlier mentioned 'In & Out' Naval & Military Club.

The Army & Navy Club's first home was at 18 St. James's Square, at the north corner with King Street, London. In 1843 the club began to search for a site to build a purpose-built clubhouse. In 1846 it moved to larger premises called Lichfield House, now 15 St. James's Square. Over the years there have been many alterations and additions, and the historic clubhouse was replaced by the present mid-20th century building, covering 80,000 square feet on eight floors, and including its own underground garage.

The club is now situated at 36-39 Pall Mall, south west London. It combines the comfort and facilities of an established London club together with the amenities of a modern hotel. It is very convenient for shopping on Bond Street, Regent Street or Jermyn Street, for West End theatre and shows, and also for the major traditional attractions that are an essential part of the London scene.

From 1962 Associate Membership was granted to women. Membership of the club is offered also to members of the Commonwealth armed services, to members' immediate families, and also to non-military members who appreciate the club ethos. Today membership numbers 5,000 men and women.

Prince Edward became President of the club on June 1, 1978, and he has been at the centre of some events in the club's history. In October 2001 he unveiled the club war memorial, a bronze statue of a Greek warrior at a re-dedication ceremony after it had been returned from an extended loan to the Ministry of Defence. The statue is now displayed in a strengthened glass case facing Pall Mall.

The club was the venue for a ceremony, in November 2007, in which Prince Edward presented the Torch Trophy Trust Award to Mr. Richard Bonehill, President of Truro Fencing Club, and an expert swordsman who has worked in the film industry for over thirty years. The award was in honour of Mr Bonehill's outstanding voluntary work for British Fencing.

When the history of the Army and Navy Club was published in 2009, in his foreword Prince Edward described the hard-earned success and stability of the club as it continues its future development. Eleven Members of the club were killed during the famous Charge of the Light Brigade on November 25, 1854, at the Battle of Balaclava, during the Crimean War. Members have been present at every British military and naval engagement since then, often serving with distinction. Past glory is recalled in pictures that adorn the corridors and rooms of the club, captured in battle scenes and portraits of famous military men. There are cases of medals and other historical memorabilia, including a mounted penguin that is a survivor from the first Antarctic Expedition of 1901–04, led by Captain Robert Falcon Scott (1868–1912).

109. HRH Prince George Duke of Kent with Princess Marina Duchess of Kent, performing the official opening of the Polish Hearth Club, South Kensington, London, July 16, 1940; His Eminence Cardinal Hinsley; and club director Mr Ronald Braden.

POLISH HEARTH CLUB (OGNISKO POLSKIE)

The Polish Hearth Club (Ognisko Polskie) as it exists today has, since 1945, been situated permanently on several floors of a former large, prestigious, Victorian town house, No.55 Prince's Gate, Exhibition Road, South Kensington, London. As this book is written in English and all official business at the club is required to be written and spoken in English, though the majority membership is either first or second generation Polish-speaking, the club will be referred to throughout as the Polish Hearth Club.

After his mother's death in 1968, Prince Edward took over his late father's role at the club, but the record of the exact date he became a life member and Patron has been lost but it certainly dates to the late 1960s.

Mr Andrzej Morawicz who has been a member of the Polish Hearth Club since 1975, and was Vice-Chairman (1988), and Chairman (1991-2012), has said:

"During the Duke of Kent's many years association with the Polish Hearth Club he visited often, coming sometimes at short notice as guest of honour to particular functions. The relationship between myself and His Royal Highness was cordial and he was extremely gracious to accept invitations to the club that were very much appreciated on behalf of the club members and the Polish Community, as both were equally represented. These included a series of visits he made throughout the 1990s and beyond, during my time as Chairman." [3]

50th Anniversary of the Polish Hearth Club

For the club's 50th anniversary in 1990, Prince Edward unveiled a plaque dedicated to the occasion which celebration actually took place in 1991. In his address, Prince Edward reaffirmed his friendship and loyalty to the Polish community:

"I can assure you that it does give me the most enormous pleasure to come to the Polish Hearth, this famous club which for a long time now has been a haven for the Polish community in London, and which gives me the chance to renew this family connection that goes back now rather more than fifty years to the day when my father inaugurated the Polish Hearth in 1940.

"You mentioned the Poles who fought in the Battle of Britain and they, I think, exemplify the spirit of those Poles who, exiled from their own country, in the dark days of the early part of the war, threw in their lot with Great Britain and fought alongside us at a time when we should otherwise have been facing our enemies alone.

"Last year, I had the great honour and the pleasure of unveiling the memorial to the Polish Forces in St. Paul's Cathedral and there were then, on that occasion, a great many Polish veterans. I don't know how many there may be here tonight but I know there are some.

"And so this evening, it gives me a very great pleasure indeed to unveil this plaque to commemorate the 50th anniversary of the Polish Hearth."

Margaret Thatcher, British Prime Minister (1979-90), visited the club and gave a formal address during which she told the audience of first and second generation Poles that the visa regime of administrative entry restrictions on those Poles trying to enter Britain had got to stay. Mrs Thatcher still received a rapturous welcome from a packed hall and was applauded throughout her speech. Robin Hamilton, Lord Belhaven & Stenton, who was present, says the audience were still applauding when she gave them this news and he assumed they didn't understand what she was saying. It then fell to him to take up the issue in the House of Lords and he initiated debates, eventually putting an end to the system of entry visas.

Statue to General Władyslaw Sikorski 2000

General Władyslaw Sikorski was a Polish military and political leader during both the First and Second World Wars. He was Polish Prime Minister from 1922-23, and Minister of Military Affairs 1923-24. Sikorski was killed in a 'plane crash at Gibraltar in July 1943, and speculation as to whether it was a tragic accident or murder has surrounded his death ever since.

Mr Morawicz in his role of Chairman of the British-Polish Council, hosted a Gala Dinner at the Polish Hearth Club on November 2, 1999, as part of the General Władyslaw Sikorski Appeal to raise funds to have a statue erected to him. At this event Prince Edward presented Certificates for donations from the Polish Air

Force Association Benevolent Fund, and to Colonel Andrzej Jeziorski, and Mr Julek Bogacki of the Allied Irish Bank, who were the bankers for the fund. General Sir Charles Gutherie GCB LVO OBE ADC, (later Lord Gutherie), was present as Patron of the General Sikorski Statue Appeal. Valeria, Viscountess Coke conducted a sale of Polish officers' military caps. Speeches were made by the Right Honourable Giles Radice MP, Chairman of the Appeal Committee, and General Gutherie.

The statue of General Sikorski was unveiled outside the Polish Embassy at Portland Place, London, W1, at 12 noon, on September 24, 2000. The event was followed by a luncheon at the Rubens At The Palace Hotel, hosted by Mr Stanisław Ciechanowski, Head of The Office for War Veterans and Victims of Oppression. In the afternoon Prince Edward and an official delegation with the Polish Ambassador Mr Witold Sobkòw, laid wreaths at the memorial. In company with the Ambassador, Prince Edward, wearing his Field Marshal's uniform and medals, did a walk about, speaking to veterans who were present. The day was completed with attendance at a Catholic mass at Westminster Cathedral.

Prince Edward wrote to Mr Morawicz the following day, September 25, 2000:

"I am well aware of the vast amount of trouble that you personally took to ensure the success of yesterday's proceeding and I am exceedingly grateful. I felt it a great honour to be involved in the ceremony, especially in view of my father's friendship with General Sikorski."

On July 4, 2013, Polish Minister, Jan Stanisław Ciechanowski led a delegation to Gibraltar to commemorate the 70th anniversary of the death of General Sikorsk, his entourage and the crew of the 'plane. The ceremonies held there were attended

110. British Prime Minister Margaret Thatcher's visit 1980s to the Polish Hearth Club, London, left to right: second person in, Lord Belhaven & Stanton; his wife Malgosia, The Lady Belhaven & Stenton; Mr Cichy; Mrs De Virion; standing at the back, the Rt. Hon. Cecil, Lord Parkinson; front centre Mrs Margaret Thatcher; Mr Racieski; Mr De Virion the Polish Ambassador.

attended by veterans who flew in from Poland and Britain. Arriving in London, Mr Ciechanowski along with His Excellency Mr Witold Sobkòw, hosted a Commemorative Gala Lunch at the Reubens at the Palace Hotel on July 15, where Prince Edward was Guest of Honour.

The Queen's Golden Jubilee year, 2002

Special significance was attached by the Anglo-Polish Community to Queen Elizabeth II's Golden Jubilee 2002, marking her accession to the throne. Mr Andrzej Morawicz, as President of the Federation of Poles in Great Britain and Chairman of the Polish Hearth Club, organised a Gala Dinner to celebrate the occasion. It was held on June 6, 2002, with Prince Edward as Guest of Honour. Present were His Excellency The Polish Ambassador, the former President of Poland Mr Ryszard Kaczorowski and Mrs Kaczorowski, and the former Commander-in-Chief of the Polish Air Force, General Mieczysław Walentynowicz and Mrs Walentynowicz. Her Majesty The Queen wrote to Mr Morawicz, February 6, 2002, saying: "I would like to think that your work will be particularly recognised during this Jubilee year."

Paying tribute to Prince Edward's work for the club, Mr Morawicz says:

"I hosted a party for His Royal Highness's 75th birthday in 2010. His brother Prince Michael of Kent was a guest. There was a supper and music and dancing. It was the Chairman's and the club's way of thanking His Royal Highness for the contribution he has made to the club's functions over the years."

Polish Hearth Club (Ognisko Polskie) today

The Polish Hearth Club today in 2015, is a modern Anglo/Polish club, and is non-party political. It is a place of culture for classical singers and musicians, traditional dancing, talks on art, literature, history and current events, modern musical events, drama, and book launches. Exquisite Polish cuisine is served in the restaurant including lunch, dinner, supper, buffet, and canapés, and modern bar services provide a variety of drinks.

During the autumn of 2012, a series of talks were arranged by the then Chairman, Mrs Barbara Kaczmarowska Hamilton (Basia) and the Events Organiser, The Lady Belhaven and Stenton (Malgosia), and the Club Committee. Their respective husbands, Mr Ian Hamilton, who is the great nephew of General Sir Ian Hamilton, and Robin, Lord Hamilton, courteously received guests in the front hall. There was a glass of punch or champagne waiting at the bar to warm guests on a chilly, autumn evening. Ian Hamilton is always easily distinguishable, wearing a maroon, velvet dinner jacket and the green tartan trews of the Gordon Highlanders regiment. The Hamiltons' two sons, Felix and Max, are also often much in evidence at the club, socialising with their friends. Mr Mirek Malevski of Fawley Court Old Boys most generously contributed the red and white wine served at such events.

There is generally about the club a feeling of warmth and a welcoming family atmosphere, generated by the Polish and Anglo/Polish members. Many of today's 500 members and patrons are second generation Poles who were born in London,

111. Portrait of HRH The Duke of Kent
1996, by artist Barbara Kaczmarowska Hamilton.

and who speak fluent English and Polish, and conversations in both languages can frequently be heard being conducted side by side.

Mrs Hamilton, known affectionately to all as Basia, painted an exquisite portrait of Prince Edward in 1996. Unveiled by the Prince, it hangs in the entrance hall to the club. Prince Edward's sister, Princess Alexandra, also visits the club as do other of his relatives. Basia's paintings of them grace the walls of the staircase leading to the original, chandelier-hung, Victorian ballroom, that today doubles as an events room: Her Royal Highness Princess Alexandra, who unveiled her own portrait in 1984; His Royal Highness Prince Michael of Kent (1998); Her late Majesty Queen Elizabeth The Queen Mother (2001); Prince Edward's daughter-in-law Paola, The Lady Nicholas Windsor (2007).

Cultural events at the club, 2012

Because a vast number of events take place at the club, it is only possible to highlight some of them here.

The autumn 2012 events were a dazzling success. Sir John Madejski OBE, Chairman of Reading Football Club gave a talk from his autobiography *The Story of My Life*, that was packed to capacity with football fans, and with fans of the author Sir Geoffrey Archer, who was there as a guest and who revealed his boyhood dream of becoming a Bristol Rovers Football Club Captain.

Chess Grandmaster Raymond Keene OBE, gave instant lessons in how to play

112.HRH The Duke of Kent at the unveiling of his portrait at the Polish Hearth Club, 1997, on his right: His Excellency the Polish Ambassador Ryszard Stemplowski; on his left Mr Andrezej Morawicz, then chairman of the club.

113. HRH The Duke of Kent enjoying a glass of wine with Mr Ian Hamilton, great nephew of General Sir Ian Hamilton, at the Polish Hearth Club, London.

chess, and after lunch the chessboards were set up on the white linen tablecloths in the restaurant. The youngest enthusiast was 10-year-old Stefan Brown, who was there with his parents and played a fine game of chess with the Master.

There was a literary lunch for the Women in War group who launched a book written by their members titled: *Women in War: From Home Front to Front Line.* Dr Halik Kochansi and Dr George Bailey OBE, presented the book, giving talks based on their chapters and re-telling the plight of their respective families when they were fleeing from both the Nazis and the Soviets during the Second World War.

The Lady Colin Campbell, known affectionately as Georgie, gave a riveting talk on her biography *The Queen Mother*, producing some startling revelations that held her packed audience spellbound.

Sir Winston Churchill's grand-daughter, the Honourable Celia Sandys, gave a pre-dinner talk titled *The Inspiring Leadership of Sir Winston Churchill, The Power of Words*, which was in fact so inspiring that afterwards a number of people thought the country today would be the better for some Churchillian-style leadership. Guests included Sir Richard Branson's mother Eve, and Mr Lee Pollock, Director of The Churchill Centre, who flew in especially for the talk from Chicago.

Writer and historian Count Nikolai Tolstoy brought a Russian name of fame into the club, as he is a descendant of the great novelist, Leo Tolstoy. His thought-provoking talk on those very ancestors The Tolstoys – Geniuses or Madmen, left the answer open-ended, for so often genius and mental fragility co-exist.

There was a swift move between past, present, and future, when Clare Mulley, author of The Spy Who Loved, flitted between the fantasy world of Ian Fleming's James Bond stories and the real life heroine of the world of spying the Polish Countess, Krystyna Skarbek, who was known in England as Christine Granville. In a twist of fate, Skarbek was murdered at a hotel that was within walking distance of the club. [4]

The year's series of events came to a climatic finale with a gala black tie dinner, held in the presence of Prince Edward, in celebration of the 90th anniversary of the passing of French novelist and essayist, Marcel Proust, who died in 1922, and whose series of novels, Remembrance of Things Past is a work of lyrical reminiscence and a portrait of French character and society. The programme opened with music by the string quartet of Trinity Laban Conservatoire of Music and Dance, of which it will be recalled (Chapter 9) Prince Edward is Patron. There followed A Homage to Marcel Proust. The opening address was given by former Times diarist, Mr Derwent May, author of Marcel Proust: Student Guide. Proust's immortal lines were spoken eloquently by the Honourable Tarquin Olivier, son of the famous actor and film star Laurence Olivier.

Events at the Polish Hearth Club, 2013

The year 2013 events at the club began in the early spring. There were evenings for ladies in floor length gowns and gentlemen wearing formal black tie dinner suits in the presence of Prince Edward.

Their Royal Highnesses The Prince Jean and Princess Diane of Luxembourg, and the Countess Christine Henckel, accompanied by Prince Edward, his elder son George, The Earl of St. Andrew's, and daughter-in-law the Countess Sylvana, were the special guests at a Chopin piano concert. The programme was introduced to the audience by Basia Hamilton and the new Chairman of the club, Colonel Nicholas Kelsey OBE TD. The concert was provided by Rose, The Lady Cholmondeley, whose performance on the new Steinway piano was of the highest professional standard, playing Chopin's Nocturne in C minor Op.48 No.1; Mazurka in C Op.24 No.2; Scherzo in C sharp minor Op.39 and other pieces.

There followed a dinner for 120 guests, carried out under the expert supervision of the new manager, Mr Jan Woroniecki, who is actually a Polish Prince, (and who is also owner of the well-known Baltic restaurant at Blackfriars Road, London). The exclusively Polish menu offered a selection of delicious delicacies and treats, served with top quality champagne and Polish wines, and the event went on well into the candle-lit night.

Artstur lectures and talks

The well-known art historian, Dr Rosa Maria Letts, Director of Artstur, Italian Art and Culture, Accademia Italiana Club, organised a lecture given by eminent historian and author Mr Ross King on Leonardo da Vinci's great 15th-century painting The

114. Miss Tatiana Roshupkina, translator from Siberia, being presented to HRH The Duke of Kent during a birthday celebration for Sir Winston Churchill at the Polish Hearth Club, London, 2009.

Last Supper, the mural on the refectory wall of the Convent of Santa Maria delle Grazie, Milan. Mr King's stirring talk kept the audience on the edge of their seats. It was like Dan Brown's dramatic description in his novel *The Da Vinci Code* sprung to life.

Polish Hearth Club reopens autumn, 2013

Prince Edward as a regular attendee at the Polish Hearth Club is on occasion accompanied by his sons George, The Earl of St. Andrew's and Lord Nicholas Windsor and their respective wives, the Countess Sylvana and Paola, Lady Nicholas Windsor and their friends. Paola's parents, Louis, Prince de Frankopan and Professor Emeritus Dr Ingrid Detter de Frankopan, also attend, making for a fine family evening outing.

In June 2014 Ingrid, who is a distinguished professor of International Law and former adviser on that subject for some 25 years to Pope John Paul II, gave a stirring talk from her book *The Law of War*. Ingrid explored the changing legal context of modern warfare in the light of events over the last decade. This development concerns, amongst other things, the new role of non-governmental organisations and the impact of terrorist groups.

Restaurant Manager Mr Jan Woroniecki invested a considerable sum of money in the club, having it refitted and upgraded during the late summer and early autumn of 2013. Reopening the club, he held a party in the splendid restaurant, upstairs events room, and gardens during September 18-19 with approximately 650 guests attending.

In early October the famous actress Rula Lenska launched her autobiography *My Colourful Life*. The audience sat in total silence savouring every word as Rula read a chapter that was both chilling and thrilling, of what it was like for her as a young aristocratic Polish girl, heiress to the title of Countess. Her parents had fled from Poland to England in 1946, due to the ravages of the Second World War, far away from their great castle and estate at Dzików. Rula was born in Cambridgeshire in 1947, but her mother still taught her to curtsey to the great ladies who visited their home.

Jonathan Walker, specialist in Polish history, gave a talk at the launch of his book *Operation Unthinkable*. Jonathan had been lucky enough to uncover the hitherto unknown secret plans that the British General Staff drew up in 1945, at the behest of Winston Churchill, for a possible attack on Russia, effectively starting a Third World War. This was meant to take place via the Baltic and was aimed at forcing the Soviet Union out of a large swathe of Eastern Europe. The talk was chaired by Major General Mungo Melvin, President of the British Commission for Military History who is himself one-quarter Polish. Between them Jonathan and Mungo set the debate alight, as Winston Churchill is not at all popular with many Poles, who believe he didn't fight hard enough for their independence at the Potsdam Conference of August 1945.

115. Guests at the Polish Hearth Club attending a piano concert by Rose, The Lady Cholmondeley, May, 2013; left to right: Mrs Barbara Kaczmarowska Hamilton, artist; The Countess Christine Henckel; HRH The Princess Diane of Luxembourg; and HRH Prince Jean of Luxembourg.

419

116. Mr Jan Woroniecki, Manager of the Polish Hearth Club's Ognisko Restaurant and Malgosia, The Lady Belhaven & Stenton, Events Organiser at the club's annual New Year's eve Party January 1, 2014.

The ultra-modern Polish Hearth Club

The present day Polish Hearth Club is a place of great beauty and culture, amidst displays of modern art, plush red carpets, and reinvigorated, ornate Victorian architecture. The staff really bring the place to life from the moment one enters the front door and is received with a smile and greeting, to the excellent bar and restaurant service. Everything is well done and to the highest professional standard. The traditional Polish cuisine, that is served with fine Polish wines, receives excellent reviews in both magazines and newspapers that have given the restaurant a top rating, and it is the ideal setting for conferences, weddings, birthdays, and other celebrations.

Musical soirées and drama, 2013/14

A programme of musical soirées and drama were held in the late autumn and early winter of 2013/14.

Trinity Laban Conservatoire of Music and Dance returned with a series of Musical Moments concerts that are performed at the club every first Monday of the month, the first of which featured the soprano, JuBa Weatlierfey, and Panaretos'l yiauitfu on piano. Later performances included the Palačinka trio playing clarinet,

117. Mr Mirek Milaveski, Fawley Court Old Boys, and Jola Pelczynska, enjoying a glass of wine in the garden of the Polish Hearth Club, London.

cello, and guitar.

The New Year of 2014 programme began with a Venetian masquerade ball, where the ladies wore traditional or modern ball gowns and the gentlemen were in a mixture of black tie suits or tails. The event was organised by members of the club's Ball Committee that was specially set up for the occasion. As in the Victorian era, the ballroom was adorned with masses of flower arrangements under sparkling chandeliers and coloured lights, provided by Basia Zarzycka, who also provided elaborate masks. Guests danced the hours away to the Vegas Underground swing band, who came highly recommended having played previously at Blenheim Palace.

Lady Gabriella Windsor, "Ella", makes her singing debut

A reggae band accompanied Lady Gabriella Windsor on the evening of Wednesday June 26, 2014, when she made her singing debut. Ella, as she is known to family and friends, sang two popular reggae numbers, 'Darling' and 'Here I Am'. Ella's appearance was in support of a function put on by the Earl and Countess of St Andrews, His Excellency Aloun Ndombet-Assamba the High Commissioner of Jamaica, and supported by Mr and Mrs Ian and Basia Hamilton and others, to raise funds for three charities: the Mary Obolensky Leukaemia Foundation, the Chain of Hope, and the Sir John Golding Centre. In attendance was Mr Anthony Underwood, who founded the charity in his wife Mary's name after she had died of leukaemia. Kirsten Rausing generously sponsored the band, The Allstars, formed by jazz

118. Lieutenant-Colonel (Retired.) Charles Messenger, Royal Tank Regiment and the actress Rula Lenska, attending a lunchtime function in the restaurant of the Polish Hearth Club, 2012.

musician Ciyo Brown especially for the event. They played Jamaican music from the 1950s, 60s, and 70s, with lead singer Matt Henry. Wearing a stunning, floor-length, pale green gown, Kirsten travelled from her stud farm in New Market, Suffolk to the event.

Lady Gabriella is the daughter of Prince and Princess Michael of Kent and there was a strong Windsor presence on the night. Ella was joined on the stage by stunning reggae artist, Alexis Mercedes. The Jamaican evening was titled Golden Eye, after the famous James Bond film, and was packed with 250 guests who danced away the hours to ska, rock steady, and early reggae.

Guests included the Jamaican High Commissioner, Her Excellency Aloun Assamba-Ndombet; the Governor General of the Bahamas, Sir Alfred Foulkes and Lady Foulkes; Mrs Dawne Bethel, the wife of the Bahamas High Commissioner to the UK, His Excellency Eldred E Bethel; Count Prince Miller; Count Nikolay Tolstoy; Georgie, The Lady Colin Campbell; and Mrs Heini Al Fayed the wife of Mohamed Al Fayed, the former Harrods owner.

The event was organised by the Chairman of the Polish Hearth Club, Colonel Nicholas Kelsey and the club committee. Much of the work, especially on the night, was undertaken by the Events Organiser, Lady Belhaven & Stenton, and club member Mrs Kristina Matson.

Colonel Kelsey took to the floor and proved that he can dance with the best of them. He takes on the role of MC at such events, entertaining guests with humour and wit that is no doubt a product of his days as an army officer.

The Misanthrope

During September six performances of the play *The Misanthrope* were put on by the Hamar Theatre group. Guests of Honour on the opening night were the Earl and Countess of St Andrews, the Mayor of Kensington and Chelsea, Maighread Condon-Simmonds, and former Polish actress Irena Delmar-Czarnecka, President of the Association of Polish Artists Abroad.

The fast-moving production of the comedy of manners by the French dramatist Molière, directed by Gigi Robarts, was refreshingly enacted by young actors and actresses. The scene opens in a colourful, modern salon that also embraces a sense of the 17th-century French drawing room, designed by scenographer Magdalena Rutkowska-Hunt. The main character, Alceste, rejects the social conventions of the 17th-century French salon and refuses to make himself a "nice" person, uttering in Act I: "Mankind has grown so base, I mean to break with the whole human race." The production of the play by Maja Lewis is so modern, it could have been written yesterday. Despite himself, Alceste is in love with the beautiful, witty, and flirtatious Célimène, who stands all of six feet tall, flaunting a scarlet, tantalisingly sexy, floor-length dress. Célimène sends Alceste a love letter, so despite his self-imposed alienation he has hopes of capturing her heart.

Maja Lewis's clothes design of modern casual, jackets, trousers, shirts and jeans brought the play into the every day lives of the audience. At one point Alceste sat in the vacant seat in the front row next Prince Edward, who was Guest of Honour on that particular evening, and began talking to His Royal Highness as though he were a character in the play. It was with some hilarity that Célimène's duplicated love-letter arrived as a series of mobile 'phone text messages, sent to each of the males in the play who, much to the amusement of the audience, read them aloud, in turn, in front of Alceste, making him a figure of fun.[5]

75th Anniversary of the Polish Hearth Club, 2015

The Executive Committee of the Polish Hearth Club is currently presenting a year of celebrations to mark the 75th anniversary of the club, July 2015, which year also marks Prince Edward's 80th birthday on October 9.

The celebrations began on New Year's Eve with a party, organised by Topaz, the Society of Polish Graduates and Professionals, and club member Bozena Karol. There was music and dancing, followed by a buffet supper with wine, from 8 pm until 2 o'clock on New Year's morning, the day being seen in with traditional Polish songs and ending with Auld Lang Syne.

In February, military historians Andrew Roberts and John Lee gave a talk on Andrew's brilliant new biography of Napoleon Bonaparte. It took the form of a discussion between Andrew and John about the rise to power as Emperor of the French and then walked the audience through Napoleon's campaign in Poland 1806-07, and his creation of the Grand Duchy of Warsaw.

The club is currently showcasing monthly screenings of the most intriguing

Polish films. These have included Ida by the Polish director Pawel Pawlikowski. The drama explores the complicated issue of Polish-Jewish relations in post-war Poland and has claimed five awards, including the best film of the year at the European Film Awards in Riga, Latvia, December 2013.

Then there was the more light-hearted film, 'The Lilpop Sisters and Their Passions', directed by Bozena Garus-Hockuba. Bozena received the Hollywood Eagle Documentary Award in 2007 for this film at the 8th Polish Film Festival in Los Angeles, and also the Audience Award at the 14th Ann Arbor Polish Film Festival.

In March 2015, Ronan Magill gave a piano concert. Of Irish descent, Ronan is a charming person and displays the native Irish innate perception of musical exposition that is known worldwide. His programme included Beethoven's Waldstein Sonata Op.53 that lasted a challenging 25 minutes and is a test for even the most experienced pianist. It was one of Beethoven's greatest and most complex piano sonatas from his 'Heroic' decade (1803-12), and Magill's enormous power on the keyboard did it justice, bringing the audience to their feet in a standing ovation.

In April Dr Chris Laoutaris of the Shakespeare Institute, Stratford-Upon-Avon, gave a talk on his book *Shakespeare And The Countess*, in which he unravelled the 400-year-old mystery of how William Shakespeare's newly built theatre at Blackfriars in south east London came to be shut down in 1596, before it had even been opened. The great playwright's demise came about when Lady Elizabeth Russell, who was an intimate of Queen Elizabeth I, decided she didn't want noisy, drunken Shakespearean audiences entering the road where she lived, and she got up a petition of powerful names against it. Near to bankruptcy, Shakespeare scraped together a group of followers and patrons who put up money and the now famous Globe Theatre was built in Southwark.

There was a welcome return of Hemar Theatre company in May, staging Noël Coward's most popular drama Private Lives. The 1930s comedy of manners in three acts ran for several evenings. The action focuses on a divorced couple who, whilst on honeymoon with their new spouses, discover they are staying in the same hotel in adjacent rooms. They recall the good times rather than the stormy relationship that drove them to divorce and now discover they still have feelings for each other.

The fast-moving action was brilliantly played by Hannah Keeley as Sibyl Chase, Martin South as Elyot Chase, Laurence Ward as Victor Prynne, and Lynne O'Sullivan as Amanda Prynne, with Nina Tolleret in the midst of it all in the role of Louise the maid.

Also during May Tina Santi Flaherty, who was named after the Polish Princess, Maria Clementina Sobieska, and who is a highly successful business woman living in New York, jetted into London, and gave a talk on her book What Jackie Taught Us, based on her observations on the life of Jacqueline Kennedy Onassis. Tina rented her downstairs apartment in 5th Avenue to Jackie for thirty years after the death of Onassis, and has written an intriguing book about this famous woman. Structuring the talk around 'Five Things You Did Not Know about Jacqueline Kennedy', Tina brought out inspirational aspects of a life where many choices had to be made, of happiness and heartache, of the price of fame, of self-awareness and acceptance of the most enormous tragedy.

119. Artist Barbara Kaczmarowska Hamilton (left) and the Honourable Celia Sandys, grand-daughter of the late Sir Winston Churchill, on the evening of Celia's talk about her grandfather, Polish Hearth Club, 2012.

Week of 75th anniversary celebrations

A week of celebrations took place to mark the 75th anniversary of the opening of the original club on July 16, 1940. On that day in 2015 a small reception was held in the club's nostalgic setting.

An exhibition spanned several days, highlighting the history of the club and the many aspects of its life throughout the years of its existence. A series of events were held starting on July 17, when a Concert was given by outstanding musicians and a quintet formed especially for the occasion by the very talented Michał Cwizewicz, featuring the Ćwiżewicz brothers and J.P. Ekins, playing Szymanowski's music. A piece that was composed especially for the occasion by Dr Krzysztof Ćwiżewicz titled String Quartet for Ognisko was world premiered. It was followed by an elegant banquet in the club restaurant.

On July 18, there was a 'Zakopiańskie ognisko', that is a Zakopanian roast barbeque in the club's gardens, with music as well as wonderful Polish Highland fare.

On July 19 Irena Delmar put on a theatrical extravaganza featuring items and music in English, Polish and Italian, followed by a cocktail party. Irena has been a part of the club since the earliest days and has created, or acted, in many of the performances held on the stage there. The evening closed with drinks and canapés for all thus marking an important milestone in the life of the Polish Hearth Club Ognisko Polskie.

Endnotes to Chapter 16

[1] Lieutenant Colonel C. Hogan held various aviation command and staff appointments. He was British Liaison Officer at the European Attack Helicopter Centre in the South of France. He then worked directly to the head of the Army, responsible for military interoperability with European Allies and the USA. His final role was in Paris as principal military interlocutor with French Defence Agencies.

[2] Correspondence between HRH The Duke of Kent and Celia Lee, October 15, 2012.

[3] Authors' interviews with Mr Andrzej Morawicz in the restaurant of the historic club on Friday, June 13, and Sunday, November 9, 2014.

[4] Claire Mulley, *The Spy Who Loved: The Secrets And Lives of Christine Granville* whose real name was Krysztyna Skarbek, who spied first for Poland and then for Britain during the Second World War. She was said to be Winston Churchill's favourite spy.

[5] The full caste included: *Alceste (*James Ducker); *Célimène* (Leonora Barton); *Philinte (*Mike Timney); *Eliante (*Pandora McCormack); *Ortonte* (Victor Klein); *Acaste (*Richard Armah); *Clitandre (*Michael Keene); *DuBois/Basque (*Michael Topolski); *Arsinoé* (Liz Mance).

CHAPTER 17

COUNTRY PURSUITS

Introduction

Prince Edward is a lover of the countryside and is a member of several clubs and like organisations with country settings. He is Patron of the Tree Council (February 1, 1985); joint Patron of the Sir Peter Scott Commemorative Expedition to the Pitcairn Islands (January 1, 1991); President of Anmer Social Club, Norfolk (March 1, 1974); Patron of Royal West Norfolk Golf Club (January 1, 1997); an Honorary Life Member of The Norfolk Club (March 28, 1986); an Honorary Member of The Royal and Ancient Golf Cub of St. Andrews in Scotland (September 1, 1979), and Patron of Keighley & Worth Valley Railways Preservation Society, West Yorkshire (June 1, 2009).

THE TREE COUNCIL
"Plant a Tree in '73"

Trees are often taken for granted until, suddenly, they aren't there any more. Remove the elms from a Constable landscape and it is fundamentally changed; take the London Planes from Parliament Square and a hard, urban terrain is revealed. It was the loss of millions of elm trees in the 1960s that precipitated the most significant replanting campaign of the last century: National Tree Planting Year, often known by its strapline, Plant a Tree in '73, out of which sprung the environmental charity The Tree Council. The UK's lead charity for trees in all settings, urban and rural, it was charged with promoting their importance in a changing environment and working in partnership with communities, organisations, and government to make trees matter to everyone.

Sir Sydney Chapman, whilst he was Member of Parliament for Birmingham Handsworth, was the primary parliamentary agitator for action in relation to the loss of elms due to Dutch Elm Disease. Sir Sydney became Director of the first and second National Tree Week. He was later Vice President of the Tree Council. Sadly, Sir Sydney passed away in October 2014, having not lived to see the coveted target of one million trees planted.

Now the coalition body for over 180 organisations working together for trees, The Tree Council focuses on getting more trees of the right kind in the right places; encouraging better care for all trees of all ages; and inspiring effective action for trees. It is responsible for an annual community programme that includes Seed Gathering Season, National Tree Week, and Walk in the Woods month, supporting the groups organising local events that are aimed at involving as many people as possible in planting, caring for and enjoying trees and woods.

The Tree Council is also active on particular issues of concern through initiatives such as Hedgerow Harvest, extending fruiting hedgerow networks; improving the numbers of Hedge Trees through the Hedge Tree Campaign, and making grants from its Hedge Fund; and the Tree Care Campaign for after-care to increase the survival rates of young trees. The Green Monument Campaign, a drive for proper recognition for heritage trees, was launched in 2003 to achieve effective safeguards, resources for custodians to promote their well-being and access to information on management best practice.

National volunteer Tree Warden Scheme

In 1990, The Tree Council founded and still co-ordinates the national volunteer Tree Warden Scheme. The 8,000 Tree Wardens form a national force of volunteers in local networks, dedicated to their neighbourhoods' trees. They organise activities, fundraise, research and advise on trees and related topics, and are a resource for their communities as well as participating in national campaigns in support of The Tree Council and its member organisations. For many years the organisation has also fundraised for income to operate a tree-planting grants programme for UK schools and communities to plant trees and create woodland habitats, as well as working on an agenda for change with its partner charities.

Prince Edward plants a tree

Prince Edward takes an eager interest in the environment, having become Patron of The Tree Council on February 1, 1985. One of his earliest duties was to participate in the launch of National Tree Week by planting a tree in Hyde Park, London, in November. To mark his patronage, The Tree Council made a gift of 10 Norway Maples and 15 small-leaved limes that were sited in a small plantation only a short distance from the Kent's then country home, Anmer Hall, in the grounds of the Queen's Sandringham estate in Norfolk. Prince Edward wrote to the Tree Council: "We shall thus be able to watch their future development very closely."

Although the trees continued to thrive, Prince Edward professed himself "devastated" when his household moved in 1990, and he had to leave them behind. In acknowledgement of Prince Edward's tireless representation of the interests of The Tree Council, the Council Chairmen with whom he had served, led by prominent landscape architect Professor Derek Lovejoy and Mr William Matthews OBE FArborA FIHort, tree surgeon by appointment to Her Majesty The Queen, were moved to arrange the planting of eight Liquidambar styraciflua and two Liroidendron tul Aureomarginata in the verge outside his new home, Crocker End House, Henley-on-Thames, a gift that he accepted with all good grace, observing in April 1993:

120. HRH The Duke of Kent with the late Lord Farnham and local children, planting trees in Norfolk for the Tree Council.

"I know the Liriodendron Tulipifera is going to be an important adornment of our driveway and an object of great interest, for many years to come." [1]

The Shakespeare Tree Garden

In May 1988 Prince Edward went on to formally open The Tree Council's Shakespeare Tree Garden, next door to Anne Hathaway's Cottage in the market town of Stratford-on-Avon, in the beautiful English county of Warwickshire. The trees were all specimens of the trees mentioned in Shakespeare's works, and were planted on a two-acre plot secured for the project by local writer, actor, and sometime academic, Mr Norman Painting, who played the part of Phil Archer in the BBC Radio 4 series The Archers, and was a Vice President of The Tree Council until he passed away in 2009.

Another very poignant activity later undertaken on the Tree Council's behalf was the planting of a copper beech *Fagus sylvatica 'Reversii'* tree at the National Memorial Arboretum on Monday, October 7, 2002, in tribute to the life of Norman's friend the late Lord Farnham, 12th Baron Farnham, who had been President of The Tree Council from 1992, and who had passed away in 2001.

Possibly the deed with the most significant continuing impact on the trees in both countryside and towns during Prince Edward's Patronage has been presiding over the formal launch of The Tree Council's successful national volunteering initiative, the Tree Warden Scheme, held at the Savoy Hotel, London, on September 19,

1990, with the then Secretary of State for the Environment, the Right Honourable Michael, Baron Heseltine and The Tree Council's first Tree Warden, Bob Arnold, who played the part of Tom Forrest, gamekeeper, in The Archers.

A reference to a conversation between Prince Edward and Tom Forrest was included in a subsequent Archers' script, much to the surprise of one listener who wrote to say:

"In an edition of 'The Archers', Tom Forrest was supposed to have spoken to His Royal Highness The Duke of Kent, is it fact or fiction please? I do not think they would be allowed to use Royal names in such a way [were it not true]." [2]

Prince Edward continues to be a consistent supporter of the work of this enthusiastic and committed community-based tree force in Ambridge, South Cambridge, and elsewhere. His formal position embraced a variety of responsibilities and included the launch of The Tree Council's Royal Anniversary Trees Schools Competition to celebrate the 40th anniversary of Her Majesty Queen Elizabeth's accession to the throne, at the Kensington Roof Gardens covering 6,000m² (1.5 acres) on top of the former Derry and Toms department store building in Kensington High Street, central London, on February 6, 1992. On March 5, 1992, Prince Edward presented certificates to the winners of the competition that was held over the 1991/92 planting season in which schools throughout England were invited to submit plans for tree planting schemes to enhance their school grounds, with the winning schools receiving £500 towards implementing those schemes. His commitment to seeing the campaign through culminated at noon on November 26, 1992, when he planted the first of 40 special trees at a ceremony in Hyde Park, London.

Prince Edward continues to play an active role and on November 25, 1993, he attended the launch of National Tree Week at the Islington Ecology Centre in north London. On April 20, 2010 he made it a proud day to remember for pupils, staff, and governors at Polehampton Church of England Infant School, when he visited the school and planted a Sweetgum tree named Liquidambar styraciflua 'Worplesdon'. The event had been arranged by the school's Trees and Landscape Team to celebrate the 120th anniversary of the school's opening.

Walk in the Woods Campaign
Support for the organisation was not confined to tree planting, however, and on May 24, 2000, Prince Edward launched The Tree Council's Walk In The Woods campaign at Wandlebury Ring in Cambridgeshire, taking the circular tour around the woods, stimulating public interest in opportunities for the enjoyment of trees and woodland. He has kept in regular touch with the activities of the organisation and remains a valued patron.

40th Anniversary of National Tree Week
The year 2015 will mark the 40th anniversary of National Tree Week which was first run in March 1975, to follow up and capitalise on the success of National Tree

Planting Year in 1973. National Tree Week has been celebrated every year since, though the launch date was quickly moved to the last full weekend in November, which is the start of the bare root tree planting season and has remained static ever since.

The Tree Council believes that every tree matters and each year, during National Tree Week, thousands more trees are planted. Everyone who cares for the environment is encouraged to plant at least one tree in the ground. Upward of half a million adults and children take part in around 2,000 events across the UK, organised by Tree Council member organisations, its 8,000 volunteer Tree Wardens, local community groups, and schools. Other ways of raising tree awareness are employed such as walks through woodlands, tree identification tours, tree surveys, tree workshops, wood fairs, informative talks, woodturning demonstrations, and storytelling. Many local authorities also give out free tree packs to those who wish to plant their own trees.

Positive effect of trees on our environment

The function of trees, as a carbon sequestration and storage tool and a regulator of the urban microclimate that takes up air pollution, is just one of the benefits of these green havens. They also ameliorate adverse effects of weather, reducing wind-speeds on blustery days, and giving shade on hot days. They cool the air, reducing heating and air conditioning costs, and saving energy. These measures also cut down air pollution caused by burning fossil fuels. Every tree has a role in moderating rainstorm impact as part of sustainable drainage systems and storm water management, lessening the likelihood of the damage done by flash floods. Trees also make a major contribution to the restoration of derelict and degraded land after the ravages of industrial development, waste disposal or other man-made blights. Trees create a more pleasant environment in which to live by bringing the delightful presence of nature to our own door.

Woodlands, animals, and birds

The UK's native trees individually and in woodlands, provide great habitats for wildlife. The sustainable cultivation of trees for renewable, low-energy construction materials, charcoal, food, and as an alternative energy source are significant ways in which every tree will matter, more and more, in years to come.

Heritage trees or green monuments

Heritage trees, sometimes called green monuments, may have started life centuries ago. They form historical links with the past, having for many years supported the existence of a wide range of other plants like mistletoe, and animals and birds, squirrels and woodpeckers, that might otherwise have become extinct. They are found in mature woodlands, parkland, estates and gardens of stately homes, village greens, public rights of way, grasslands, and old churchyards. For instance, heritage oaks can form part of hedgerows, and willow trees are often found growing by the edge of rivers.

In the summer of 1999 The Tree Council launched the Heritage Tree Record to record data and stories collected by its volunteer Tree Wardens as part of the local community millennium celebrations. The intention was to celebrate and record trees that are important as markers of history and keepers of a heritage legacy.

Strangely, whilst there are listed buildings and listed landscapes, there is no facility in this country for listing trees of heritage and cultural importance. In order to draw further attention to these important trees, Prince Edward wrote the foreword to The Tree Council's book *Great British Trees* on fifty of these trees, published to mark the 2002 Golden Jubilee of Her Majesty The Queen. In it he noted that:

"As we go about our daily lives, we sometimes take for granted the trees that shape and characterise our beautiful countryside, adorn our towns and villages, and enhance our public spaces and private gardens.

"By singling out these 50 Great British Trees, The Tree Council brings into fresh focus an important part of our heritage. The care of previous generations has ensured that these stirring reminders of notable events and people are still around for us to enjoy. It is particularly pleasing that The Tree Council has been able to make such an appropriate contribution to the Golden Jubilee celebrations of Her Majesty the Queen." [3]

A subsequent Green Paper (published 2003) by The Department of Culture, Media and Sport as a consultation paper on heritage listings and titled: "*Protecting our historic environment: making the system work better*", highlighted this omission and provided the impetus for The Tree Council to launch its Green Monuments campaign for change, supported by many of its member organisations. Both these and the Tree Warden volunteer networks across the country have been able to capitalise on the public interest generated to collect information about other important trees, both nationally and locally.

Related projects in support of the Green Monuments campaign include the Woodland Trust's 2004 Ancient Tree Hunt for which The Tree Council's volunteer Tree Wardens identified and recorded the majority of the trees, whilst others became verifiers: the Great Trees of East Devon; Epping Forest's Favourite Trees; the BTCV Ashford Veteran Tree project which was the template for the current Kent-wide Heritage Trees project, training Tree Wardens, and other volunteers to record local heritage trees. Despite some small concessions, however, there has been little overall improvement in the status of these trees, though the campaign continues.

Pauline Buchanan-Black, Director-General of the Tree Council has said:

"A tree planted close to where you live, work or study is good for you and for the nation's condition; trees have been proven to have positive effects on mental health and as an antidote to stressful lifestyles, even aiding recuperation from illness. Everyone should be able to see a tree from their window - and if you can't, then now is the time to set about changing the view."

There is a vast difference when you open the curtains on your window in the mornings and see birds flitting about. The commonest birds [4] are Blue Tits, tiny birds with blue and green feathers, Great Tits that are also blue and green but with yellow on their underside, and everyone's friend the robin, with its red breast.

The Big Tree Plant

The Big Tree Plant is a campaign to encourage people and communities to plant more trees in England's towns, cities and neighbourhoods. It is a partnership, under the Chairmanship of Pauline Buchanan-Black, bringing together national tree-planting organisations and local groups working with Defra and the Forestry Commission to facilitate opportunities to plant trees in towns. Defra is the UK government department responsible for policy and regulations on the environment, food and rural affairs. The target to plant one million trees by 2015 has been achieved this year, through the massive efforts of thousands of volunteers working in hundreds of community groups planting in 3,300 sites across England.

The offices of the Tree Council are located at 4 Dock Offices, London SE16 2XU.

SIR PETER SCOTT
COMMEMORATIVE EXPEDITION

Sir Peter Markham Scott, CH CBE DSC and Bar MID FRS FZS (September 14, 1909 – August 29, 1989), was a British ornithologist, conservationist, eminent artist, naturalist, naval officer, and sportsman. Born in London, Scott was the only child of Antarctic explorer Robert Falcon Scott CVO, and sculptor Kathleen nee Bruce. Peter was named after Sir Clements Markham, mentor of Scott's polar expeditions, and his godfather was J. M. Barrie, creator of the character, Peter Pan, the boy who never grows old.

Peter Scott was only two years old when his father died. Robert Scott, in a last letter to his wife, advised her to "... make the boy interested in natural history if you can; it is better than games." Peter was educated at Oundle School, Northamptonshire, and at Trinity College, Cambridge, initially reading Natural Sciences but graduating in the History of Art in 1931. Scott was knighted in 1973 for his contribution to the conservation of wild animals. He had been a founder of the World Wildlife Fund (WWF), a founder of several wetlands bird sanctuaries in Britain, and an influence on international conservation. He received the WWF Gold Medal and the John Paul Getty Prize for his work.

Henderson Island Scientific Expedition

In March 1989 the Governor of Pitcairn, Henderson, Ducie, and Oeno Islands, received from the Zoology Department of Cambridge University the first firm proposals for the Henderson Island Scientific Expedition. Henderson Island (formerly also known as San João Baptista and as Elizabeth Island) is an uninhabited, raised coral atoll in the south Pacific Ocean, that in 1902, was annexed to the Pitcairn Islands colony, a South Pacific Dependent Territory of the UK. Measuring 9.6 kilometres (6.0 miles) long and 5.1 kilometres (3.2 miles) wide, it has an area of 37.3 square kilometres (14.4 square miles), and is located 193 kilometres (120 miles) northeast of Pitcairn Island. The island was designated a World Heritage Site by the United Nations in 1988. It is unsuitable for agriculture and has little fresh water. There are three beaches on the northern end and the remaining coast that comprises steep, mostly undercut, cliffs up to 15 metres (49 feet) in height.

Sir Peter Scott, who had visited Pitcairn in 1973, agreed in July 1989 to act as Patron to the expedition. Following his untimely death later that year, the expedition organisers adopted the nomenclature The Sir Peter Scott Commemorative Expedition to the Pitcairn Islands. Prince Edward became its Joint Patron on January 1, 1991.

Conservation of the islands

With the primary intention of conducting a full geological, biological, and archaeological inventory of the UNESCO World Heritage site of Henderson Island, the expedition was also to provide a management plan for its future conservation. Additionally it encompassed specialist studies in ornithology, entomology, malacology, botany, oceanography, and marine biology throughout the Pitcairn Group.

Leader of the expedition, Dr Michael Brooke, with Mr Graham Wragg, expedition member and owner of the ketch luxury sailing craft Te Manu, made an initial brief visit to Pitcairn and Henderson in January 1990. After their return there followed months of planning and the first members of the expedition party reached Henderson in January 1991. The field phase, involving 18 scientists, three support staff, and seven field assistants, who participated in one or more of the five, three-month-long expedition modules, continued their work until March 31, 1992. Changeover of personnel was undertaken by charter yacht from 1,200 nautical miles distant Tahiti, while movements between the islands of the Pitcairn Group were co-ordinated by the Te Manu.

Rare bird and plant specimens found

Reports were compiled of the geological make up of Henderson Island and the rare specimens uncovered there. A few examples are here quoted with acknowledgement and thanks, courtesy of the Expedition members and Dr T. Spencer, Department of Geography, University of Cambridge, England.

Henderson Island is a coral atoll uplifted by approximately 30 metres, possibly compensating for the loading by the one-million-year-old volcano of Pitcairn, 200 kilometres to the West-South-West. This uplift has stranded a former lagoon in the island's interior with remarkably preserved, coral colonies and large areas of coral stick rubble. The great diversity of species and evidence of prodigious coral growth suggest an excellent interchange between lagoonal waters and the surrounding ocean. [5] Montastrea sp. with acropora spp. coral sticks have been formed there. Of the 68 higher plant species recorded on Henderson Island, eight are thought to occur nowhere else. One example is the Henderson Island Sandalwood, Santalum hendersonense.F.BR., which has an aromatic scent used in oils, perfumes, and incense.

122. Anmer Social Club end-of-season presentation
of prizes for the gentlemen's darts competition circa 1970s.

Petrel Pterodroma ultima, [6] a sturdy, long-winged, gull-sized grey seabird with a pale face, strong, hooked black beak, and webbed feet, was found on Henderson. Better known as Murphy's Petrel, it was named after Robert Cushman Murphy [7], an American seabird biologist and former Lamont curator of birds for the American Museum of Natural History in New York, as he first officially described the species in 1949. It feeds on squid caught far out to sea and only comes ashore to care for its single white egg, and then slow-growing downy chick, on the remotest coral islands along the southern edge of Polynesia.

In 1986 a single specimen of a new moth, or hawkmoth, Hippotion hateleyi, referred to also as Henderson Hawkmoth, was collected on Henderson Island. It was identified as a new species by Dr Jeremy Holloway at the Natural History Museum in London. Although the other hawkmoth species in the Pacific Ocean region are widely dispersed, this particular hawkmoth appears unique to Henderson. Several specimens were collected by the Expedition but even now little is known about the hawkmoth's habits.

Statue to Sir Peter Scott
The London Wetland Centre is a wetland reserve managed by the Wildfowl and Wetlands Trust (WWT) in the Barnes area of south west London. The site is formed of four disused Victorian reservoirs, tucked into a loop in the Thames. The centre first opened in 2000 and, in 2002 it was recognised as a Site of Special Scientific Interest as the Barn Elms Wetland Centre. It is here that a statue of Sir Peter Scott by Nicola Godden was erected outside the Centre, rather idyllically on a small island in a pool.

*123. Anmer Social Club end-of-season presentation of
prizes for the gentlemen's Darts competition circa 1970s.*

ANMER SOCIAL CLUB

Anmer Social Club is situated in a tiny village community of about 50 people, living on Her Majesty Queen Elizabeth II's royal Sandringham estate in Norfolk.

The word Anmer is thought to originate from the old English name for a duck pond, possibly referring to the still existing pond very near to the Church of St. Mary The Virgin. The main part of the church was built in the 14th century and the tower in the 15th century. The village is set in idyllic and picturesque English countryside and was in existence in Anglo-Saxon times (1066), when it was privately owned. In 1862 it formed part of the purchase by Queen Victoria of Sandringham House and estate as a wedding present for her eldest son and heir, Prince Albert Edward (Bertie) the Prince of Wales, later King Edward VII, (1841-1910), at the time of his marriage to Princess Alexandra. Sandringham House has been the private home of four generations of Sovereigns and the Queen and Prince Philip and other members of the Royal Family regularly spend Christmas there.

Norfolk lavender and lacemaking

Norfolk is well known as the home of Norfolk Lavender. The Lavender Lacemakers are a group of people of all ages local to the Anmer area and are so named because of the close proximity to the vicinity of the Lavender Mill at Heacham. The lacemakers are trying to keep a very old traditional craft, dating back to the middle of the 16th century, from dying out. There are several different types of lace, some very old and some very modern, and the type that the Norfolk Lavender Lacemakers use is called Bobbins Lace. It involves using a pillow and bobbins and the lace is made completely by hand. The group also attend craft fairs and various venues where they demonstrate the art of lacemaking.

Prince Edward at Anmer

Prince Edward's connection with Anmer dates from the early years of his marriage, from 1972 until 1990, when the Kent's country home was Anmer Hall, a late-Georgian country house. The house was built in the 18th century and has formed part of the Sandringham estate since 1898. The surrounding estate became a scheduled ancient monument in 2003, and includes earthworks marking the sites of buildings from the medieval village of Anmer. The village church of St. Mary lies close to the house.

The members of Anmer Social Club of which Prince Edward became President on March 1, 1974, met at the community hall nearby. Today they meet at a different, more modern community centre in the same location, named Anmer Community Hall Social Club.

During the winter months indoor darts and dominos team matches take place with the other estate clubs and social clubs in the vicinity, for both gentlemen and ladies. Prince Edward on some occasions presented the prize at the end of season presentation ceremony for the Men's Darts Competition.

Such activities as Christmas carol services, an Easter egg hunt, and Bonfire Night, along with other similar pursuits were, and still are, put on for the children in close cooperation with the Church. Community groups such as the Women's Institute, Lacemakers, and the Anmer Bowls Club, also enjoy the facilities that are available. The club has its own bowls team in the inter-estate-club league.

Prince Edward's wife, Katherine, took an active part in the life of the village during the time they lived at Anmer Hall and was a member of the Anmer Women's

124. Robert Burns supper 'haggis night' at Anmer Social Club.

126. Anmer Community Hall Social Club.

Institute, which still meets regularly at the club. The club is also the headquarters of the Anmer Mere Yacht Club, formed in 2010. The club puts on food nights, usually on a Saturday, one of which is an annual Robert Burns haggis night, Quiz Nights, and musical evenings, all of which provide an opportunity for the community to get together in their club.

New neighbours

The Anmer community have known for some time that they were to have new neighbours! It was announced by Buckingham Palace [8] that Anmer Hall was to again be occupied by members of the royal family. Their Royal Highnesses the Duke and Duchess of Cambridge, William and Catherine, and two-year old Prince George and his new baby sister Charlotte born in May 2015, took up residence there in the first week of May and it is now their country home. It is a beautiful and healthy setting in which to raise the next generation of royal children, and the house will once again ring with the sounds of laugher and children playing.

ROYAL WEST NORFOLK GOLF CLUB

Royal West Norfolk Golf Club is situated at Brancaster, King's Lynn, convenient to the Sandringham estate. It is one of the top 100 golf courses in the world and rated as one of the best in England. Surrounded by the North Sea and salt marshes, the walk across the beach from the clubhouse onto the golf course gives the golfer a pleasurable and relaxed feeling of anticipation.

The golf course was designed by Holcombe Ingleby (1854-1926), and was opened in 1892. Many of the holes he laid then remain still in play today. Ingleby was a solicitor and Mayor of the borough of King's Lynn in 1909, and again from 1919-22.

The club's royal status

The club's royal status was conferred when His Royial Higness The Prince of Wales, later King Edward VII, accepted the invitation to become the club's Patron. His Royal Highness The Duke of Gloucester and His Royal Highness The Prince of Wales (Later King Edward VIII) were Captains in 1928 and 1929 respectively. The Duke of Edinburgh was Patron until 1996. Prince Edward became Patron on January 1, 1997, having been elected Captain at Easter 1981, the fourth member of the Royal family to be Captain of the club. His father Prince George the 1st Duke of Kent had been Captain in 1937.

THE NORFOLK CLUB

The Norfolk Club was founded in June 1770, and moved to their existing premises at Upper King Street, Norwich in 1862. The first President of the club was Lord Suffield 1864-1870.

Situated in the professional centre of the City, between the Cathedral and the Castle, the club is conveniently only a short distance from the railway station. It offers the traditional service and atmosphere of a provincial county club, and is the ideal place to relax in an old world atmosphere.

Prince Edward became an Honorary Life Member of the club on March 28, 1986. Members are largely professional businessmen and women, and retired ladies and gentlemen of Norwich and the County of Norfolk.

The club is well provided with a library containing a comprehensive section on Norfolk. There is a welcoming bar, a large dining room serving lunches from Monday to Saturday, conference and meeting rooms, television room, billiard room, and a squash court.

There is no shortage of highlights at the club every year and a sample of these is taken from 2012. Being the year of the Olympic Games, there was a commemorative dinner for the arrival of the Olympic Torch. A champagne reception took place

127. A bowls match at Anmer Social Club.

whilst guests watched the arrival of the torch on a large television screen, followed by a three-course dinner.

The Battle of Trafalgar, (21 October 1805), in which Admiral Lord Nelson aboard HMS Victory led the British Royal Navy to defeat the French and Spanish navies, is an important date in the history of the Norfolk Club and it was celebrated with a dinner at which the special guests were Lord and Lady Walpole. Lord Walpole 10th Baron (who is a descendant of Sir Robert Walpole the first Prime Minister of Great Britain), shared with the guests his family stories of their connection with Lord Nelson.

There is an annual Christmas dinner presided over by the President of the club, who was then Mary Rudd. Their Carol service takes one to the heart of rural Norfolk, with mulled wine and mince pies being served afterwards.

The Justices Lunch was hosted at the club with the High Sheriff of Norfolk, Henry Cator and Her Majesty's Lord Lieutenant of Norfolk, Richard Jewson attending.

THE ROYAL AND ANCIENT
GOLF CLUB OF ST. ANDREWS

The golf club was founded in 1754 as the Society of St. Andrews Golfers, a local golf club playing at St. Andrews Links. There is no actual start date for the club but the defining moment in its history is May 14 of that year, when a competition started for a silver golf club presented by 22 noblemen and gentlemen of Fife. The game was played over the links of St. Andrews, and from this the society emerged. The Challenge was played annually, and the winner was named Captain of the Golf. Evidence that the Society of St Andrews Golfers had evolved from this competition can be seen in the regulations that were written in 1766, stipulating that members were to meet "once every fortnight by eleven of the clock ... and to play a round on the links. To dine together at Bailie Glass" and "to pay each a shilling for his dinner, the absent as well as the present."

Royal patronage
In 1834 King William IV (1765-1837) consented to a request from one of the society's members that it be re-named The Royal and Ancient Golf Club of St. Andrews (R&A). Following gentle persuasion, he also agreed to become the club's Patron. From that year on the club has always had a royal Patron, currently Her Majesty Queen Elizabeth II. It is therefore one of the oldest and most prestigious golf clubs in the world. From the late 19th century the club increasingly came to be regarded as a governing authority, both in the United Kingdom and abroad.

In 1897 in response to pressure from other clubs, the R&A agreed to take responsibility for the rules of the game. In 1920 responsibility for organising The Open and Amateur Championships shifted from the Delegates of the Associated Clubs to the R&A.

In 2004 a significant reorganisation saw these external activities being devolved to a new group of companies known collectively as The R&A, the name being derived from the earlier associations with the club. Mr Peter Dawson is the current Chief Executive of The R&A and is retiring after 16 years' service to be succeeded in October 2015 by Mr Martin Slumbers who will also become Secretary of St. Andrews. The R&A is based at St. Andrews and organises The Open Championship, major amateur events, and international matches. Together with the United States Golf Association, The R&A governs the game worldwide, jointly administering the Rules of Golf, Rules of Amateur Status, Equipment Standards, and World Amateur Golf Rankings.

That Scotland is regarded as the home of golf is legendary. The game is recorded as having been played there in the 15th-century. King James IV purchased a set of golf clubs in Perth in 1502. The modern game of golf was first developed and established in Scotland and the early rules were written there.

The Royal and Ancient Golf Club of St Andrews is today based at St. Andrews, Fife. The golf courses belong to the town of St. Andrews and are managed by the St. Andrews Links Trust. The iconic clubhouse, which overlooks the world-famous Old Course, is home to a worldwide membership of 2,400. Prince Edward was made an Honorary Member of the club on September 1, 1979.

The records of the procedures involved are an historical document in themselves. It is recorded that the club's General Committee met on December 12, 1979. Mr William (Bill) Miller who served on both the Championship Committee and the General Committee of the club was then Chairman.

"Mr Miller referred to Item 6 (a) in the Secretary's Report and after discussion, it was agreed that an approach be made to the Duke of Kent and that the Past Captains be given prior advice of this. It was also agreed that an approach be made to Lord Ballantrae. It was decided that if the Duke of Kent were to accept Honorary Membership the announcement of this would be made at the Spring Business Meeting …".

Lord Ballantrae was at that time Chancellor of St. Andrews University and also served as Governor General of New Zealand.

The record continues:

"Assuming the Duke and Lord Ballantrae accept the Committee's invitation, then the announcement for both would be made at the May Business Meeting."

It is further recorded that at the club's Business Meeting on May 7, 1980, Mr Stewart Lawson, who was also a member of the club and who served on the Rules of the Golf Committee and the General Committee, and was Captain from 1979-1980, made the announcement to the Business Meeting on May 7, 1980:

"… under Rule 7 (a) of the Rules of the club, the General Committee had invited His Royal Highness The Duke of Kent GCMG, GCVO, and Brigadier The Lord Ballantrae of Auchairne KT, GCMG, GCVO, DSO, OBE to become Honorary members of the club, and that both had been pleased to accept the invitation. The announcement was greeted with acclamation."

Since its inception the club has admitted gentlemen only. But on September 18, 2014 members voted to change the 260-year-old rules to admit women golfers by a convincing 85 per cent in favour. Mr Peter Dawson, the club secretary, said: "I am very pleased indeed to announce that the membership has voted overwhelmingly in favour of welcoming women members." Her Royal Highness Princess Anne The Princess Royal was among the first women to join the golf club. Other women golfers who accepted honorary member invitations were: Laura Davies, Renee Powell, Belle Robertson MBE, Lally Segard, Annika Sorenstam, and Louise Suggs. Captain of the Club, Mr George Macgregor OBE, said: "This is an historic day for the club and we could not be more proud, also to welcome women that have distinguished themselves in golf over many years and have been great players and champions."

Edward Guinness's story

Mr Edward Guinness CVO, who it will be remembered from Chapter 16, was a former Chairman of the Brewers Society, and Executive Director of Guinness, and 1956 Alumni, and later trustee of the Duke of Edinburgh's Study Conference. Mr Guinness tells a story of his visit to the club, when he tried to impress the other members of his study group with the merits of Scottish golf. Following a morning session with the dons of St. Andrew's University, the organisers of the conference hosted the participants to lunch at The Royal and Ancient Golf Cub of St. Andrews. Says Mr Guinness:

"It happened in the course of the first His Royal Highness the Duke of Edinburgh's Study Conference in 1956, when my Study Group went to Scotland and spent 20 hours at the University of St Andrews, and visited the town of St. Andrews, and Fife. ... There were about 18 of us, mainly in our thirties, from every part of the Commonwealth, and our Nigerian representative came in national dress.

"I told my colleagues that to lunch at The Royal and Ancient Golf Club of St Andrews was a privilege and honour, not often accorded to local people who had possibly lived in St. Andrews all their lives.

"I took them to a big window in the club, looking immediately out, onto the First Tee to where a foursome were teeing up for a round of golf. I expected balls to be hit away out into the distance – 150-200 yards – but I was chagrined when not one of the drives went above 50 yards. Up to that moment my colleagues had been impressed by my build-up but now looked at me askance while I weakly said that they were not typical of the R&A's high standards.

"I think they [the golfers] must have been tourists as they wore what

128. HRH The Duke of Kent being introduced to Oxenhope Parish Council by Dr. Ingrid Roscoe, Lord-Lieutenant for West Yorkshire, and Mr Paul Brown, past chairman, at Oxenhope Railway Station, Keighley & Worth Valley Railway, July 8, 2008.

in those days were known as co-respondent shoes." [9]

KEIGHLEY AND WORTH VALLEY
RAILWAY PRESERVATION SOCIETY

Mention of steam trains in Victorian and Edwardian times conjures up pictures of the characters in the children's storybook *The Railway Children*, published in 1906 by Edith Nesbit. Characters Bobbie, Peter, and Phillys, lived at Three Chimneys, the house near the railway and waved to the passengers on the passing trains. The scenes became more visual with the making of films, the most famous of which were made in 1967 for the BBC and the feature film in 1970 by EMI, both of which starred Jenny Agutter. Despite this romanticising of railways and trains, one does not however think of a real-life, royal duke today riding on the footplate on a moving locomotive!

Brief history

Our story is set at Keighley and Worth Valley Railway (KWVR), a 5-mile-long branch line that served woollen and worsted mills in the villages in the Worth Valley, and the people in its villages who worked in the mills. It is now a heritage railway line in West Yorkshire, England. Running from Keighley to Oxenhope, it connects to the national rail network line at Keighley railway station. It is the only complete preserved railway in its original form anywhere in the world. Adding to the period atmosphere, real ale is served on board most of its services.

Keighley and Worth Valley Railway came into being when, in 1861, a civil engineer, Mr John McLandsborough, visited Haworth to pay tribute to the famous

129. HRH The Duke of Kent speaking to Mr David Pearson, Deputy Lieutenant for West Yorkshire, and his late mother Mrs Olga Pearson, who was then First Treasurer, Keighley & Worth Valley Railway Trust, and Mr Pearson's aunt Jean Rothera, July 8, 2008.

Yorkshire writers Charlotte, Emily, and Anne Brontë, authoresses of *Jane Eyre and Shirley; Wuthering Heights; and Agnes Grey and The Tenant of Wildfell Hall* respectively. Most of the Brontë's stories are set locally. Mr McLandsborough found that Haworth was not served by a railway, so he put forward a proposal for a branch running from the main line at Keighley to Oxenhope via Haworth. The proposal for the new railway was incorporated by an Act of Parliament in 1862, and five years later, on Saturday April 13, 1867, the line opened, and was operated on a Victorian version of the modern railway franchise by the main line company, the Midland Railway. The new branch was highly profitable and served the mills, the valley people, quarrying, and agriculture.

Keighley railway in the modern age
Today the railway still serves the local people who use it to reach Keighley, in addition to the huge numbers of tourists who use it to reach the famous Brontë homeland in Haworth, plus many train enthusiasts and train spotters who travel on it out of personal interest.

The service continued for nearly 100 years, until it was closed in 1961. A preservation society was formed that bought the line from the then owner, British

Rail, and reopened it in 1968 as a heritage railway. The line is now a major tourist attraction operated by about 500 qualified volunteers and carrying more than 200,000 passengers a year.

On weekends and in particular on Saturday mornings, local residents who live in Oxenhope, Haworth, Oakworth, and Ingrow, can catch the early morning diesel service to Keighley, on their way to work or to shop, returning later on the steam hauled services.

As a privately owned heritage railway however, the line does not specifically serve commuters. Recent studies by the local authorities into the feasibility of a daily commuter service between Oxenhope and Keighley have shown that there is both a need and a demand for such services all year round. The cost would be considerable and currently research is under way to try to identify likely sources of funding.

Prince Edward rides footplate

On July 10, 2008 Prince Edward visited the Keighley and Worth Valley Railway, marking the 40th anniversary of its reopening. On arrival, he received a warm welcome, having been met at the station by local children. He then travelled on a specially prepared Royal Train, made up of locomotive 41241, LMS Class 2MT, pulling a single carriage named The Old Gentleman's Saloon, as featured in *The Railway Children*. The coach is in reality a former North Eastern Railway directors' Saloon, having been built at Crewe Works in 1949. Prince Edward travelled in the carriage and then, with the wind in his ears, stepped out and rode joyfully on the locomotive footplate.

Prince Edward became Patron of Keighley & Worth Valley Railway Preservation Society, marking the 60th anniversary of the construction of the 41241, on June

130. HRH The Duke of Kent being greeted during his visit of July 8, 2008, by pupils from Oakworth Primary School, at Oakworth which was the station where the Railway Children was filmed.

1, 2009. On that occasion, Dr Matt Stroh, KWVR chairman, said:

> "We know that His Royal Highness is a keen railway enthusiast and we are honoured that he graciously agreed to accept this role which we feel reflects the high standards that the railway sets itself. We are delighted that he helped us to mark our 50th anniversary and the carriage's centenary."

Prince Edward visited again on October 17, 2012 to mark the 50th anniversary of the founding of the preservation society. On this occasion, putting on a protective overall coat and white gloves, he rode on locomotive 1300, a goods locomotive of the former Lancashire & Yorkshire Railway pulling a train of matching coaches, including a mobile businessmen's Club Car that has been restored over the past 19 years, and which in 2012 was 100 years old. The car is used daily to carry businessmen from the Fylde coast to Manchester and may only be used by elected members of the club.

At the end of his journey, Prince Edward unveiled a plaque commemorating both anniversaries. Addressing the gathered members and civic dignitaries he said: "I came here four years ago and things have moved a long way since then. Many congratulations and all the best wishes for many more years."

The railway is looking forward to a period of development and expansion in the next few years. Having achieved charitable status in 2011, it seeks to improve its passenger, staff, and operational facilities into the future.

Endnotes to Chapter 17

[1] Quotation has been kindly provided by The Tree Council.

[2] Ibid.

[3] Ibid.

[4] See Andrew Verrall, *Highlights of the Birds at Brent Reservoir in 2010*, p.230, London Bird Report 2010, No.75, pub. London Natural History Society, 2013, ISBN 0 901009 33 4.

[5] Sir Peter Scott Commemorative postage stamps were issued in September 1992, illustrating some of the rare finds made in the Pitcairn Islands: 20c stamp, Montastrea sp. with acropora spp. (coral sticks); $1.00 stamp, Santalum hendersonense.F.BR. (Henderson Island Sandalwood); $1.50 stamp, Pterodroma ultima (Murphy's Petrel); $1.80 stamp, Hippotion hateleyi (Henderson Hawkmoth).

[6] Mr Andrew Verrall, professional bird watcher says: "Pterodroma ultima (Petrel) known as Murphy's Petrel – the first specimen was collected in 1922, and at that time was an unknown species with no name. One was found prior to that in the Cook

131. HRH The Duke of Kent enjoyed a ride, July 8, 2008, on LMS-designed 2-6-2 tank locomotive 41241 that was built at Crewe by British Railways in 1949.

Islands between c1899 and 1904. Petrel the English version after St Peter – Storm Petrel – and some of the other smaller petrels, actually flatter above the waves, with dangling feet touching the water, looking as if they are walking on water, even in rough seas."

[7] Mr Andrew Verrall says: "For 60 years Murphy travelled the world, searching for new and rare birds, his greatest interest being seabirds. In a quote from Murphy, October 28, 1912, on board the whaling brig *Daisy* in the South Atlantic, he said: ''I now belong to a higher cult of favoured mortals, for I have seen the albatross''. See R. C. Murphy, *Oceanic Birds of South America*, [2 volumes], pub. Macmillan, New York, circa 1936.

[8] Quoted in the *Sunday Telegraph*, January 6, 2013.

[9] Telephone conversation 20th January 2013, between Mr Edward Guinness CVO, and Celia Lee, and letters from Mr Edward Guinness to Celia Lee, dated 6th and 21st February 2013.

CHAPTER 18

ROYAL AIR FORCE
AND RELATED CHARITIES

"Never in the field of human conflict was so
much owed by so many to so few". (Winston Churchill, 1940)

Introduction

The Royal Air Force (RAF) is revered for its dramatic and colourful flypasts in Britain during important moments in the country's history. In 2012, during the Golden Jubilee of Her Majesty The Queen, 27 fighter jets formed the number 60 in a flypast above Windsor Castle. The Red Arrows also did a dramatic flypast over the Olympic Stadium in London during the 2012 Olympic Games.

Prince Edward's interest in and involvement with the Royal Air Force is considerable. He has, in the past, enjoyed flying, and held a private pilot's licence. He holds a number of positions in the Royal Air Force that date to the 1990s. He is Royal Honorary Air Chief Marshal (July 1, 1996); Honorary Air Commodore RAF Leuchars, (April 1, 1993); a Freeman/Liveryman of the Guild of Air Pilots and Air Navigators, (November 27, 1991); an Honorary Fellow of the Royal Aeronautical Society (May 7, 1993); and a Life Member of the Royal Air Force Club, (January 1, 2000). In addition, he is President of the RAF Benevolent Fund, (January 1, 1976), and Patron of the RAF Charitable Trust, (April 8, 2005).

The Royal Air Force is the aerial warfare branch of the British Armed Forces. It played a major role in Britain and her Allies winning the Second World War, and in more recent conflicts like the Falkland Islands War, Iraq, and Afghanistan. The RAF is the largest air force of a European Union country and the second largest in NATO (after the United States Air Force). The RAF's mission is to 'provide the capabilities needed: to ensure the security and defence of the United Kingdom and overseas territories, including [defence] against terrorism; and to support the Government's foreign policy objectives particularly in promoting international peace and security.'

Brief history

The RAF is the oldest independent air force in the world. The first Headquarters

(HQ) of the Royal Flying Corps (RFC) was set up in the former Hotel Cecil, on The Strand, London. After the amalgamation of the RFC and the Royal Naval Air Service (RNAS) in April 1918, this location became the HQ of the RAF. Today their Headquarters is at RAF High Wycombe, where HQ Air Command effectively carries out this role.

The Second World War (1939-45)

The RAF underwent rapid expansion prior to and during the Second World War. Under the British Commonwealth Air Training Plan of December 1939, the air forces of British Commonwealth countries trained and formed squadrons identified with their country of origin for service with RAF formations. Many individual personnel from these countries, and from the countries in German-occupied Europe, also served with RAF squadrons. In the Battle of Britain during the late summer of 1940, the RAF, supplemented by two Fleet Air Arm squadrons, and Commonwealth, Polish, and Czechoslovak squadrons, defended the skies over Britain against the German Luftwaffe, helping to foil Adolf Hitler's plans for an invasion of the United Kingdom. Wartime Prime Minister Winston Churchill made a speech in the House of Commons on August 20, 1940 when he famously said: "Never in the field of human conflict was so much owed by so many to so few". Churchill is believed to have first used these words upon his exit from the Battle of Britain Bunker at RAF Uxbridge, when visiting the No.11 Group RAF Operations Room, during a day of battle on August 16, 1940.

The RAF had developed a doctrine of strategic bombing which utilised the long-range bombers that had been under construction since the 1930s. It was this doctrine and the development of Bomber Command which assisted greatly in the destruction of the German war capability and the liberation of Europe. None of this could have happened in the time frame that it did, without the major part played by United States Land and Air forces.

Prince Edward's dedication to the RAF over the years includes much support to RAF related charitable causes.

RAF LEUCHARS

Prince Edward's position of Honorary Air Commodore of RAF Leuchars since 1993, has caused him to take a close and personal interest in this Station and its activities.

RAF Leuchars is the most northerly air defence station in the United Kingdom, located in Leuchars, Fife, on the east coast of Scotland, near to the university town of St. Andrews. It is primarily responsible for maintaining a Quick Reaction Alert capability, providing crews and aircraft at high states of readiness 24 hours a day, 365 days a year, to police Northern UK airspace and to intercept unidentified aircraft.

The other operational UK air defence base since June 2007, is RAF Coningsby in Lincolnshire, which is responsible for Southern UK airspace and works in harmony with RAF Leuchars.

The RAF Leuchars air defence role is primarily carried out by 6 Squadron RAF

132. At the International Air Tattoo 1979: HRH The Duke of Kent talks to the famous World War II fighter pilot Group Captain Sir Douglas Bader (right); Lady Spotswood and Air Marshal Spotswood, then Chief of Air Staff; and the Duke's younger son, Lord Nicholas Windsor, then aged 9 years.

which, since February 2011, has been operating the Eurofighter Typhoon FGR4 aircraft, as does RAF Coningsby.

The Station Commander of RAF Leuchars has under his command in addition to 6 Squadron, No.125 Expeditionary Air Wing, and No.6 Force Protection Wing. He is also responsible for a variety of other units on the station. The principal of these are 58 Squadron RAF Regiment and No.612 (County of Aberdeen) Squadron, Royal Auxilliary Air Force (an air-transportable surgical squadron). The station is also home to the East of Scotland Universities Air Squadron (ESUAS) and XII Air Experience Flight (12 AEF), who both use a fleet of seven Tutor T Mark 1 aircraft.

RAF Leuchars is also the parent station to the Universities of Glasgow and Strathclyde Air Squadron in addition to 661 and 662 Volunteer Gliding Squadrons. There is also an RAF Mountain Rescue Unit. Lodger units are 3 Flight Army Air Corps and 71 Engineer Regiment (Volunteers).

Presentation of Standard to 58 Squadron, RAF Regiment

In May 2012, in his role of Royal Honorary Air Commodore of RAF Leuchars, Prince Edward presented 58 Squadron, RAF Regiment with a new standard. The Squadron had completed a highly successful operational deployment to Afghanistan in 2011 as part of No.6 Force Protection Wing. The Squadron holds a distinguished operational record within the RAF Regiment, having seven battle honours, six of which are from the Second World War, and which are emblazoned on its standard. During the parade Prince Edward accepted the general salute from the Squadron as Typhoon aircraft from 6 Squadron flew overhead. This was in recognition of the critical role that the Gunners of the RAF Regiment accomplished in providing the protection on the ground that enables the UK Armed Forces and their allies to mount effective operations in the air. [1]

In his address Prince Edward said:

"The presentation of this Standard today underlines and encompasses everything that is important in terms of military ethos, and it provides due recognition of the service and sacrifice made by the Officers and Men of this fine and distinguished Squadron.

"I well recall meeting the initial few, who comprised the newly formed Squadron shortly after it stood up at RAF Leuchars back in 2010. It was therefore, a great privilege to meet with the fully formed Unit while they were deployed on operations in Afghanistan last summer, the transformation was quite remarkable.

"You have every right to parade this Standard with honour, knowing that you have taken forward the legacy set by your forbears in a manner that would make them justly proud."

Prince Edward made individual presentations to Sergeant Alan Bailey, aged 32, and Corporal James Hudson, aged 25, both of whom served with 58 Squadron in Afghanistan and were Mentioned in Despatches for their services in responding to casualty extraction emergencies, while providing Force Protection to Medical Emergency Response Team personnel. Each received an oak leaf for their Afghanistan campaign medal, and a certificate in recognition of their conspicuous gallantry.

The Officer Commanding 58 Sqn, Squadron Leader David Stellitano said:

"It is not every day that we celebrate the achievements of an operational Royal Air Force Regiment Squadron in such a way. The presentation of the Squadron Standard marks our return to the Order of Battle, recognises our proud history and reminds us of the actions and deeds of those before us.

"Our recent operational tour in Afghanistan was highly successful, the Squadron received commendations for its actions and I can only hope that the next chapter in our history is as glorious.

"I am immensely proud to have commanded the Squadron on operations, to have served alongside such outstanding Officers, Gunners and Airmen and to be here today in the presence of His Royal Highness the Duke of Kent to receive what is the most highly decorated Squadron Standard in the history of our Corps. All of this is down to the hard work and outstanding efforts of every man of the Squadron, they should all be very proud of what they have achieved."

During the parade the General Salute was marked with a flypast by four Typhoon aircraft of 6 Squadron.

GUILD OF AIR PILOTS AND AIR NAVIGATORS (GAPAN)

The Guild of Air Pilots and Air Navigators (GAPAN) was established in 1929. GAPAN was modelled on the lines of the City Guilds and Livery Companies. That it became a Livery Company of the City of London in 1956 is considered a proud mark of distinction. This factor increased the influence of the Guild, the 81st Livery Company to be formed in 800 years, and the profession of pilot and navigator in the United Kingdom and overseas.

Prince Edward was made a Freeman/Liveryman of GAPAN November 27, 1991. In an address to the Guild, Prince Edward described it thus:

"The Guild exists to bring all pilots and navigators together. It's more than a club because it has a more serious purpose. The Guild is concerned with every technical aspect of flying from safety to navigational aids, from airport facilities to training methods and in particular with new developments in aircraft and their handling. It's a unique organisation, as its upper membership is restricted to qualified pilots and navigators, and therefore it can truly claim to bring together the views and ideas of people who control aircraft in the air. Perhaps, the most important function of the Guild is to help set and maintain standards of conduct among flying people."

ROYAL AERONAUTICAL SOCIETY

The society was founded in January, 1866, with the name The Aeronautical Society of Great Britain. Today, as The Royal Aeronautical Society, it is well known throughout the world's aerospace community with 63 branches worldwide.

Its objectives include the support and maintenance of high professional stand-ards in aerospace disciplines; to provide a unique source of specialist information, and a local forum for the exchange of ideas, and to exert influence in the interests of aerospace in the public and industrial arenas. The embodiment of the society's purpose is to consider significant developments in their field and, in order to achieve this end, they hold conferences and lectures which stimulate debate and facilitate action on key issues of industry in order to respond to the ongoing innovation and progress in aviation.

In 2009 the society formed a group of experts to document how to better simulate aircraft upset conditions and thus improve training programmes. The Specialist Groups committees are: Aerodynamics; Aerospace Medicine; Air Law; Air Power; Air Transport; Airworthiness & Maintenance; Avionics & Systems; Environment; Flight Operations; Flight Simulation; Flight Test; General Aviation; Historical; Human Factors; Human Powered; Licensed Engineers; Management Studies; Propulsion; Rotorcraft; Space; Structures & Materials; UAV; Weapons Systems & Technologies.

Prince Edward opened the new aviation museum at Duxford, Cambridge, on Wednesday, July 11, 2007. Marshall of Cambridge is one of the major sponsors of this exciting new educational establishment. Chief Executive, Mr Michael Marshall and senior executives from Marshall Aerospace and the Group of Companies, including the Chairman, were present. The newly named Marshall Auditorium can seat 250 people.

RAF CLUB

The Royal Air Force Club (RAF Club) at No. 128 Piccadilly, London, was founded in 1918, as a place where serving and ex-serving RAF officers could meet. The club was opened officially on February 24, 1922, by HRH The Duke of York. On March 12 the club was visited by King George V and Queen Mary. Queen Elizabeth II is the club's Patron. Membership is open to men and women who hold or have held commissions in the RAF, PMRAFNS, Reserve Forces, and Commonwealth and friendly foreign air forces. The Chairman of the club is Air Vice-Marshal Matt Wiles RAF.

RAF BENEVOLENT FUND

In 1919, at the end of the First World War, Lord Trenchard founded the *Royal Air Force Memorial Fund.* The original intention was to raise a memorial to airmen who died in the war and to provide benevolence to the dependants of those lost during the War. Standing on the Victoria Embankment, London, and completed by 1923, it is a monument in Portland stone surmounted by a gilded eagle.

Once again Prince Edward has followed in the footsteps of both his parents. His father became Chairman of the Royal Air Force Benevolent Fund (its name since 1933) in April 1941. Following his untimely death in August 1942, his widow, Princess Marina, stepped forward in 1943 to become the President of the Fund for an unbroken service of twenty-five years until her death in 1968, during which she never once missed the annual meeting of the Council. Prince Edward would become President of the RAFBT on January 1, 1969. The Vanbrugh Castle School run by the Fund, for the children of deceased or disabled airmen, was re-named in 1976 The Duke of Kent School in his honour.

In the Fund's first year they spent £919 on welfare and the first assistance they gave was a shilling (12 pence then – 5p today) for a night's lodging in order that an unemployed person could seek work. Other assistance included money to provide a beneficiary with tools of their trade and the repair of a pair of working boots. By

133. HRH The Duke of Kent laying a wreath on the 70th anniversary (May 2001) of the Battle of Crete (May 1931), at Maleme RAF memorial to 30 and 33 Squadrons who died during the battle.

comparison, in 2011, the RAF Benevolent Fund spent over £21 million on welfare provision, which requires a great deal of hard work going into fundraising. This is all the more important as the RAF Benevolent Fund has assumed the duty of providing welfare support to the serving RAF, a responsibility previously undertaken by the Ministry of Defence.

Prince Edward visits Princess Marina House

On Thursday October 8, 2007, Prince Edward opened the new Garden Room at Princess Marina House, the RAF Benevolent Fund's Care and Respite Home, situated on the West Sussex coast at Rustington. On arrival, he was greeted by dignitaries including the Lord Lieutenant of West Sussex, Mr Hugh Wyatt, the High Sheriff of West Sussex, Mr Colin Field, and the Chairman and Controller of the RAF Benevolent Fund, Lord Trenchard, and Air Marshal Sir Rob Wright.

Prince Edward unveiled a commemorative plaque and was presented with a picture of Princess Marina House by centenarian and long-term resident at the home, Mr Victor Wells.

The new extension provides both residents and guests with a larger, more attractive area to enjoy visits from their families and friends, as well as a more comfortable space in which to rest and relax. The construction was made possible by the Princess Marina House Appeal which raised £300,000.

Prince Edward visits, 2009

On September 9, 2009, Prince Edward again visited Princess Marina House to attend the 90th anniversary celebrations. The official opening of Seacot House, which is a new respite facility for members of the serving RAF, took place the same day. The cost was met by a substantial grant from the RAF Charitable Trust. This new facility was designed to provide affordable breaks for serving personnel who find themselves facing difficulties over and above the usual stresses and strains of Service life.

Sir Rob Wright said: "I'm proud and delighted to welcome the RAF Benevolent Fund's President, His Royal Highness The Duke of Kent to the opening of these two outstanding respite facilities today." Mr Wright went on to say that the charity was founded originally "to help repay what Winston Churchill termed 'the Debt we Owe' to all those who have served in the RAF, by delivering the highest standard of care and support to members of the RAF family."

That commitment continues to this day.

RAF CHARITABLE TRUST

The Royal Air Force Charitable Trust (RAFCT), based at Fairford in Gloucestershire, came into being in January 2005. The RAFCT retained the objectives of the RAF Benevolent Fund Development Trust (RAFBFDT), although its scope was widened to include the RAF family of charities as potential beneficiaries.

The original trust had been established in the 1950s with a grant of £30,000, from the Air Council with the aim of reviving the legendary Air Pageants of the 1920s. In 1975 Air Marshal Sir Denis Crowley-Milling KCB, CBE, DSO, DFC and Bar, AE, Controller of the RAF Benevolent Fund, took a decision to re-establish military air shows as a way of raising money and awareness for the charity, and to aid recruitment to the Royal Air Force. The fledgling International Air Tattoo that had been founded in 1971 in support of the Royal Air Force Association (RAFA) was looking for new support. Another charity was required to take over the ownership of the world-famous Air Tattoo and its parent company. In January 2005 The Royal Air Force Charitable Trust was set up and Prince Edward extended his patronage of the Air Tattoo to include the charity. Today the Chairman of the RAF Charitable Trust and President of the Royal International Air Tattoo is Air Marshal Sir Kevin Leeson KCB, CBE, FREng.

Air Cadets

The RAFCT has been providing financial support to a wide variety of projects and initiatives. At the heart of the trust is its commitment to young people, to initiate and develop within them an enthusiasm for aviation in all its guises. In so doing, the trust aims to inspire the next generation of aerospace professionals, whether engineers, pilots or ground crew. To this end, RAFCT has forged strong links with the Air Cadet Organisation (ACO), supporting activities that directly enrich the young cadets' training experience. These include funding scholarships in flying, a trophy for Flying Excellence, and the purchase of equipment for Air Traffic Control (ATC) training.

RAFCT has also agreed to become a main sponsor of *Air Cadet* magazine, and has provided bursaries, through the Maritime Air Trust, to support ATC cadets through their education at college or university. The RAFCT is also keen to support Adventurous Training activities like the Ulysses Trust's Expedition Jubilee Eagle, which organised a successful trip to Ghana for twenty cadets from Middlesex Wing.

As part of the celebrations to recognise the 150 years that the cadet forces has been in existence, 60 cadets and 10 Cadet Force Adult Volunteers selected from the Combined Cadet Force, Sea Cadet Corps, Army Cadet Force, and Air Training Corps, were offered the opportunity of a lifetime. In July 2010 the party set off for a three-week expedition to the rugged and spectacular Kingdom of Lesotho. Their activities involved assisting in community projects in this isolated and impoverished country. Undertaking a number of challenging expeditions they traversed the unspoilt Drakensburg Mountains, visited some of the remote hillside villages, and enjoyed open canoeing around the stunning Katse Dam.

Fourteen members of the Kent Wing ATC went on a two-week expedition to Kenya in 2014, financed by the Ulysses Trust, RAF Charitable Trust, and the Singleton Trust. Activities included climbing the 4,985 metre peak of Mount Kenya via the Sirimon Route, and other climbing expeditions.

One of the Air Cadet initiatives to win the support of the Charitable Trust has been the provision of flight simulators and radio equipment to support Commandant Air Cadets' plans to create 12 Regional Activity Centres across the UK.

134. HRH The Duke of Kent talking to cadets at the Royal International Air Tattoo 2011.

RAFCT benefiting other charities

The success of the RAFCT is also benefiting other charities within the RAF family. RAFCT was quick to engage with the RAFA, the RAF Benevolent Fund, and the RAF Museum, to ensure that the aims and ambitions of the trustees complement, rather than duplicate the outstanding and enduring work of those long-established charities. Working with the Benevolent Fund, the RAFCT has helped refurbish some of their respite care facilities, whilst the RAF Museums at both Cosford and London (Hendon) have benefited from new interactive exhibits.

RAF stations have also been invited to apply for grants for projects that enhance the environment of service personnel and their families, particularly for projects benefiting those preparing for, or serving on, front-line deployments. RAF Odiham, RAF Honington, and RAF Brize Norton, were among the early beneficiaries but grants have now been made available to the majority of RAF stations.

The Freemasons' Grand Charity
grants £50,000 for youth projects

In June 2007 Prince Edward presented RAFCT with a cheque for £50,000 that was a gift from the Freemasons' Grand Charity. In acknowledgement, Chairman Air Chief Marshal Sir John Cheshire said:

> "The trust owes an enormous debt of gratitude to His Royal Highness, in particular. The money will be awarded to air-minded young people who, due to their financial circumstances, would not otherwise be able to participate in adventurous training and expeditions. These youngsters will now have the opportunity to develop their leadership and life skills."

The grant in its entirety has been used well, in supporting the underprivileged to obtain access to aviation activities.

Endnote to Chapter 18

[1] Source: RAF Leuchars press release in relation to the presentation of a Colour to No.58 Squadron RAF Regiment, by kind permission of the Ministry of Defence, Intellectual Property Rights Group, Defence Procurement Agency, Crown Copyright/MOD 2013.

135. HRH The Duke of Kent and his brother Prince Michael of Kent (right), attending at the Honourable Artillery Company, 1967.

CHAPTER 19

MILITARY AND RELATED ORGANISATIONS

Introduction

Prince Edward is Patron of The Gallantry Medallists' League, (May 27, 1965). He was enrolled as a Member of the Honourable Artillery Company, April 27, 1967. He is Patron of The Society for Army Historical Research, (February 1, 1966); the Combined Cavalry Old Comrades Association, (February 1, 1975); The Duke of York's Royal Military School, (October 1, 1975); the National Army Museum, (January 1, 1977); The Tank Museum, (July 1, 1983); and The Bletchley Park Trust, (April 1, 1996). He is President of Wellington College, (April 1, 1970); The Board of Trustees of the Imperial War Museums, (December 1, 1974); the Scout Association, (January 1, 1975); the Royal United Services Institute (RUSI) and RUSI International, (June 1, 1975). He is Royal Vice-Patron of The Chelsea Pensioners Appeal, The Royal Hospital Chelsea (February 3, 2004).

These organisations are here discussed according to the year in which they were set up.

459

HONOURABLE ARTILLERY COMPANY

The Honourable Artillery Company (HAC) was incorporated by Royal Charter in 1537, by King Henry VIII. Today it is a Registered Charity whose purpose is to attend to the 'better defence of the realm.' This purpose is primarily achieved by the support of the HAC Regiment and a detachment of Special Constabulary to the City of London Police. Regiments, battalions and batteries of the Company have fought with distinction in both the First and Second World Wars and its current Regiment, which forms part of the Territorial Army (TA) is the oldest surviving regiment in the British Army, and the second most senior regiment in the Territorial Army.

Known by several names in the past it was first referred to in Court Minutes as the Honourable Artillery Company in 1685, but only officially received the name from Queen Victoria in 1860.

The HAC Regiment's TA unit, based just north of the City of London, provides the British Army with its only dedicated Surveillance and Target Acquisition patrol regiment, operating small covert reconnaissance patrols that are gathering intelligence and target information. The regiment also has a dedicated long range communications capability and in recent years its role has expanded to cover liaison tasks.

The HAC also has a ceremonial role in providing guards of honour at the Guildhall in the City of London during state visits, and since 1924, (when the Royal Artillery ceased to be stationed at the Tower of London), has provided the saluting battery at the Tower of London for state occasions.

From April 3, 2012, the HAC came under the operational command of the General Officer Commanding Theatre Troops. Unlike most TA units, who are only required to train up to sub-unit (company or squadron) level, the HAC is required to train as a regiment.

An historic occasion 1967 – royal princes enrolled in HAC

Something of the flavour of the history of the HAC is conveyed in the enrolment of Prince Edward and his brother Prince Michael of Kent as members of the Company. In 1967 Prince Edward was a Major in the Royal Scots Greys. On Thursday, April 27, he visited Armoury House, the home of the HAC. He also attended the major annual event and the customary St. George's Dinner in the role of the Company's principal guest. A colourful occasion, the two royal princes, escorted by the Colonel Commandant, passed between the ranks of the Company of Pikemen and Musketeers in their bright red tunics to the Court Room to meet regimental and other VIPs. Prince Edward was greeted by Sir Frank Newson-Smith, the father of the regiment, who had completed 71 years of membership. Members took their seats in the Long Room to the strains of 'The Roast Beef of Old England' played by the regimental orchestra, which continued to provide appropriate musical accompaniment throughout the evening, including the Princes' Regimental Marches.

In his after-dinner address, Prince Edward proposed the toast of 'England' and made a short speech. Though the end of the Second World War (1939-45) was now over 20 years distant there were still jokes around that had been used to jolly the British people along during those bleak war years. Prince Edward began by alluding

136. HRH The Duke of Kent and Mr Bruce Clitherow, wearing Masonic regalia attending at the Honourable Artillery Company's Fitzroy Lodge, October 23, 2006.

to the rationing problems (which, due to food and clothes shortages, had continued into the late 1950s). He read a newspaper headline of around 1943, (obviously written by a naïve editor who had missed its double meaning): "Women's clothing to be held up until all the Services' needs have been satisfied." The gales of laughter that must have followed have not been recorded in the account in the HAC's journal. Prince Edward went on to congratulate the HAC on having survived the perils of reconstruction (so much of which was necessary in the post-war years). He suggested that such a long surviving body might even outlive the Regular Army itself.

Having been on this occasion accompanied by his younger brother Prince Michael of Kent, Prince Edward expressed his and his brother's deep appreciation of the offer of membership especially since it was the first time for over 300 years that two royal brothers had simultaneously joined the HAC. His speech received a standing ovation.

Prince Edward and Prince Michael, who was then a Lieutenant in the 11th Hussars, were enrolled in a short ceremony as members of the Company. Both signed the historic Vellum Book that had been specially illuminated with their armorial bearings. The last time two princely brothers had been admitted to the Company on the same day was on June 1, 1641, when Charles, Prince of Wales (later King Charles II), and his brother Prince James, Duke of York (later King James II), were enrolled together, aged eleven and eight years respectively. On this, their special day, Princes Edward and Michael were aged 31 and 24 respectively.

Since 1967 Prince Edward is toasted by members at HAC dinners with the company's traditional 'Regimental Fire'. [2]

A Masonic connection

The HAC's FitzRoy Lodge issued an invitation to Prince Edward to attend the Prestonian Lecture and dinner at the HAC on October 23, 2006. Every year the Grand Lodge sponsors the delivery of this memorial lecture to William Preston (1742-1818), the foremost Masonic educator of his age. Preston left a legacy to perpetuate his system of annual lectures. The topic for 2006 was 'The Victoria Cross: Freemasons' Band of Brothers', to commemorate the 150th anniversary of the Victoria Cross. The lecture was delivered by historian, Granville Stacey Angell. Afterwards 123 members dined in the beautiful Long Room at Armoury House. In his toast to Prince Edward, the newly-installed Master of the Lodge, Mr Bruce Clitherow, who joined the HAC in 1980, said that His Royal Highness was the first Grand Master to attend FitzRoy Lodge in the 157 years of its history. [1] They were photographed together in full Masonic regalia.

THE DUKE OF YORK'S ROYAL MILITARY SCHOOL

"I am always struck by the spirit, easy social graces,
and discipline of the pupils." (HRH The Duke of Kent)

The Duke of York's Royal Military School at Guston, Dover, is a distinguished, state boarding school for the 11 to 18 year old sons and daughters of pupils whose parents are serving or have served in any branch of the United Kingdom armed forces.

A Board of Commissioners appointed by Her Majesty The Queen governs the school. The Chairman and members are drawn up from top management positions in the services, education, civil service, industry, and the professions.

Brief history of the School

In 1801 His Royal Highness Frederick Duke of York laid the foundation stone in Chelsea of what was to become the Duke of York's Royal Military School. Originally it was an orphanage for children of soldiers killed in battle and was Britain's first coeducational, state funded, and state administered school.

Historic visits by Prince Edward

In his role of President, Prince Edward attended Grand Day on July 4, 2003, which was the school's bi-centenary, celebrating 200 years of high quality education. New School colours were presented by him at the Grand Day parade.

Changes and the future

Prince Edward became President of the school on October 1, 1975 and since that time the school has undergone many changes and is now an academy with military traditions. Prince Edward's title of President changed to Patron when the school became an Academy on September 10, 2010.

The real strengths of the Academy are its educational standards and pastoral

137. HRH The Duke of Kent attending Grand Day 1 of the Duke of York's Royal Military School, July 1, 2011.

care. It aims to develop each and every child, offering them life skills and leadership opportunities, developing them as citizens, and preparing them for adult life. The School offers outstanding pastoral care in a home from home environment to children, especially those of military families whose lives are so often disrupted by the demands of their parents' service in the Armed Forces. The full boarding provision plays a big part in this, making it a favourable option for those Service parents entitled to claim Continuity of Education Allowance. The Academy combines the unique and special ingredients of military and education.

Accommodation and life at the school
Every pupil is a full boarder. The School is therefore always active and busy, with a very full programme of sports activities and social events. These take place at weekends, with dances, film clubs, regular outings to the theatre, and the cinema, or ten pin bowling being offered. The pupils gain many friends, have plenty to do, and have lots of fun.

Curriculum
A broad and balanced curriculum is offered which leads to a high degree of success, both in public examinations and university placements and the world of work.

463

Academic work for 11 to 16 year olds follows the National Curriculum but at the same time, they are offered much more than the legal minimum requirements. Extracurricular activities include over 70 clubs and activities, such as the Military Band, Chapel Choir, fencing, horse riding, and trampolining, Duke of Edinburgh Awards Scheme, Combined Cadet Force, academic trips, and foreign language and sports exchanges with partner schools abroad. The School's GCSE provision is comprehensive and their success rate is significantly higher than that of the national average at GCSE A* C including Maths and English.

The introduction of BTEC Public Services has been very popular and the school are trialling BTEC Military Music. In the Sixth Form, a wide range of courses are available; currently sixteen at AS Level and seventeen at A2 Level. The curriculum is constantly under review and the school intends to include BTEC and Vocational courses in the future. They aim to academically stretch the high achievers. Their special needs department focuses on those pupils who, at any stage of their education are in need of additional help that includes intervention support during the examination years.

Sport
Sport provides a range of benefits, including promoting healthy lifestyles, encouraging leadership and teamwork, and developing self-confidence and talent. Pupils are encouraged to work towards coaching awards, physical education GCSE and A level. The School intends introducing the BTEC First Diploma in Sport, BTEC National Certificate in Sport (Performance and Excellence), BTEC Introductory Diploma in Sport and the Community Sports Leader Award. Sport will make a significant contribution to their aim of providing all pupils with the opportunity to excel and succeed.

Sporting facilities
The School has excellent sporting facilities and an enviable sporting reputation at local, county and national levels. In addition to extensive junior and senior playing fields there is a fully equipped gymnasium, a six-hole golf course, an indoor heated swimming pool, athletics track, tennis and badminton courts, squash courts, an all weather hockey pitch, indoor and outdoor shooting ranges, an indoor cricket facility, a multi gym and a multi purpose hard play area. The major sports are rugby, hockey, cricket, tennis and netball, with full opportunities for athletics, swimming, and rounders. The opportunity to participate in basketball, football, kayaking, climbing, cycling, karate, sailing, water-skiing, trampolining, shooting, fencing, and horse riding is open to all.

Music
Music is an underlying theme for the school and pervades much of pupils' everyday life. Junior years receive lessons in music and the subject is taught at GCSE and Advanced Level, while Music Technology is also offered at AS Level. The music department has its own music centre containing a concert room and a suite of individual practice rooms. It is particularly well resourced and pupils are offered

individual tuition in most orchestral instruments as well as guitar, piano and organ. There are regular public performances. The School's Military Band, one of the largest in the country, has regularly been asked to play at Twickenham for the Army/ Navy rugby matches and more recently at Test Matches at Lord's and The Oval cricket grounds. The School's Big Band also takes the stage with Jools Holland each year at the Army Benevolent Fund Concert.

Drama

The School is fortunate to have a spectacular assembly hall with modern stage and production facilities. There are regular drama productions of a high standard, including senior and junior plays, revues and musicals. Drama is taught at GCSE and Advanced Level. In addition, the school sets great store by providing many opportunities for pupils to attend professional plays, concerts and other cultural performances, both inside and outside the school.

Adventurous Activities and Overseas Trips

Through the Combined Cadet Force, Duke of Edinburgh's Award Scheme, camps, outward-bound courses, and School expeditions, pupils have many opportunities to experience water sports and other outdoor pursuits, such as mountaineering, hill walking, potholing, rock climbing, mountain biking, and skiing. There are also many sporting and cultural tours abroad. These include regular hockey tours to Germany and South Africa; annual ski trips and in the past a cricket tour to Australia; a technology trip to Italy; art trips to Paris and Amsterdam, and a netball trip to Grenada.

The school has an established gap pupil exchange programme with boarding schools in Australia and New Zealand. There are regular visits to France and Germany, including an annual trip to the French battlefields, and regular exchanges with schools in France, Germany and Spain.

Ethos

The Academy is open to those of any faith or none. The chapel services are non-denominational. The School also encourages pupils to belong to the chapel choir and choral society.

Military Heritage

The School's military heritage encourages a great sense of pride and self-discipline and enhances teamwork and leadership skills. There is a very active Tri-Service Combined Cadet Force, which amongst other things enables pupils to learn how to fly, to sail, to shoot, and to take part in adventurous training camps, and a wide variety of external courses.

The spectacular ceremonial side of the school involves parades throughout the year, culminating in Grand Day. This is a unique and spectacular event involving the Trooping of the school Colours. In line with its tradition over many years, the Academy continues to provide unwavering support to the children of parents who have died while serving their country.

Prize giving and 'Trooping of the Colour'

Every year the school celebrates the end of the school year with the Trooping of the Colour. The day includes prize giving in the morning, and then the whole school taking part in the formal parade in the afternoon. A guest of honour from one of the three Armed Forces is normally invited to present the prizes and to be the reviewing officer at the parade. In 2003 Prince Edward was invited.

Official Grand Day 2011

Prince Edward was invited by the Headmaster to attend the first Grand Day that took place after the school became an Academy on July 1, 2011. Prince Edward spent the morning as the guest of honour at the annual prize giving, and in the afternoon he was the inspecting officer for a full-scale trooping the colour parade in which the school's 450 pupils took part. Addressing parents, governors, and students at the event, Prince Edward said:

> "I am always struck by the spirit, easy social graces and discipline of the pupils. As you know, all pupils on parade wear over their hearts the cap badge of their serving parent. This is a highly poignant tradition and it is a great pleasure for me, with all my years' association with the Armed Forces, to work out all the cap badges of the different corps, regiments, and services which go to make up today's modern Armed Forces.
>
> "I am also struck by the magnificent site which the school enjoys with its 150 acres of tended parkland. There can be few schools in the land which can enjoy so enviable a setting."

Former student prefect and bandsman, Mr Mathew Prentice, aged 17, whose father is a Major in the Royal Engineers, said:

> "I felt very proud to wear my father's heart badge for Grand Day. It's a very special day and is our way of showing our gratitude to those who serve bravely in the Armed Forces. The parade lasts over two hours so it is a challenge, especially for the younger ones."

ROYAL UNITED SERVICES INSTITUTE
FOR DEFENCE AND SECURITY STUDIES
and
ROYAL UNITED SERVICES
INSTITUTE INTERNATIONAL

The Royal United Services Institute for Defence and Security Studies is colloquially still known by its old title, the Royal United Services Institution (RUSI), and is located in Whitehall, London. The oldest such institution in the world, it was founded in 1831 by The Duke of Wellington and, in 2011, celebrated its 180th anniversary. It is a British defence and security think tank engaged in cutting edge defence and security research and embodies nearly two centuries of forward thinking, free discussion, and careful reflection on defence and security matters. RUSI describes itself as 'the leading forum in the UK for national and international Defence and Security'. It won *Prospect Magazine*'s Think Tank of the Year Award 2008. In 2009 the same magazine named RUSI Foreign Policy Think Tank of the Year.

RUSI'S original mission was to study naval and military science, what the Prussian soldier and German military theorist Carl von Clausewitz called the 'art of war'. The Duke of Wellington spearheaded the establishment of RUSI in a letter to *Colbourn's United Service Journal*, arguing that 'a United Service Museum' should be formed, managed entirely by naval and military officers, and under the patronage of the monarch, then King George IV, and the commanders-in-chief of the armed forces. Such an institution would prove that the two professions have entered the lists of science, and are ready to contend for honours *tam Artibus quam Armis* [by Arts and Arms].

Subsequently Commander Henry Downes of the Royal Navy assembled a group with a view to forming a committee for action to which King George's First Aide-de-camp was commanded to convey 'His Majesty's gracious and high approbation of the undertaking and of the principles on which it is proposed to conduct it', which were stated to be suitable for 'a strictly scientific and professional society, and not a club'. The death of the King delayed matters, but The Duke of Clarence expressed his readiness to become a patron so, encouraged by the powerful support of the Duke of Wellington, the First Aide-de-camp, Sir Herbert Taylor, re-submitted the project to King William IV (the former Duke of Clarence), and was able to assure the committee that 'it could proceed under his Majesty's gracious auspices.'

On June 25, 1831 the committee met. The chair was taken by Major General Sir Howard Douglas, in his person a symbol of the 'United Service': a soldier who was the leading expert on naval gunnery. The resolution that the institution be established was put by the future Field Marshal Viscount Hardinge and seconded by the future Rear-Admiral Sir Francis Beaufort, the famous hydrographer. The first title adopted was 'the Naval and Military Museum', altered in 1839 to 'the United Service Institution', and to 'the Royal United Service Institution' by Royal Charter of Incorporation in 1860, retained until the present day. Today it is known as the Royal United Services Institute for Defence and Security Studies.

Although a British institution, RUSI operates with an international perspective. It promotes the study and discussion of developments in military doctrine, defence management, and defence procurement. It includes all issues of defence and security, including terrorism and the ideologies that foster it and the challenges which we face from other man-made or man-assisted threats and from natural disasters.

RUSI has a membership consisting of military officers, diplomats and the wider policy community, numbering over 2,000. There are also 50 Associate Fellows and 12 Fellows (FRUSI). They have access to a variety of activities. There are four categories of research activities: Military Sciences, International Security Studies, National Security and Resilience, and Defence, Industry and Procurement, plus such subjects as Climate Change and Conflict, and War and Culture.

RUSI experts are often called upon to provide analysis and commentary on the leading defence issues of the day. Content is drawn from its publications and briefings from its researchers. Their expertise has been utilised by governments, parliament, and other key stakeholders.

RUSI organises a number of lectures, seminars and conferences for its membership and the wider defence and international security community. Its location in Whitehall, conveniently situated next door to the Banqueting Hall, means that it is able to attract leading statesmen and policymakers. Its flagship publication is the *RUSI Journal* and it also publishes the RUSI Newsbrief and *RUSI Defence Systems*.

RUSI is governed by a Council. Prince Edward became President of RUSI on June 1, 1975. The Director is Professor Michael Clarke, and the Rt. Hon. The Lord Hutton is Chairman.

In his capacity as President, Prince Edward witnessed some of the most historic events in Britain's current military history. One of these was the first public meeting between the Commander-in-Chief of the Warsaw Pact and NATO's Supreme Allied Commander. The meeting took place in 1989 at RUSI in London, with the Russian officers nervously eyeing both their counterparts and the wine glasses at a time when then Russian President Mikhael Gorbachev imposed an anti-alcohol campaign on his country! Prince Edward not only had to handle a delicate meeting, but also had to preside over a rather sensitive round of drink-offering.

As President of RUSI, the Prince also opened the festivities of the 50th anniversary of the NATO Alliance, which took place at RUSI in 1999, just a few days before the outbreak of the Kosovo War. The Prince had to share his time between looking after the British Prime Minister Tony Blair, whose main concern was about the military operations then unfolding in the Balkans, and a bevy of other Alliance leaders who were much more concerned about highlighting NATO's achievements over half a century.

Traditionally, Prince Edward prefers to listen to debates, rather than ask questions, although when speakers attending RUSI conferences move away from the gaze of the crowds the Prince has been known to take an intense part in the security debates.

ROYAL UNITED SERVICES INSTITUTE INTERNATIONAL

Prince Edward has also been Honorary President of the Royal United Services Institute International since June 24, 2011.

RUSI International mirrors in its activities most of the research that is generated from London, with additional emphasis on events that may have a wider currency. RUSI International also monitors security and foreign policy developments in countries and regions throughout the world.

The work of the department is organised into five main programmes, which each have a geographical focus – Africa, Asia, the Middle East and North Africa, and the European Security and Transatlantic Security programmes.

138. Wellington College, Crowthorne, Berkshire – a British co-educational boarding and day independent school, built as a national monument to the Duke of Wellington (1769–1852).

WELLINGTON COLLEGE

Dr Patrick Mileham, author of *Wellington College: The First 150 Years* (2008), quoted Prince Edward's words in a foreword to the Great Wellington Callover, a pageant of drama, dance, music, and light that was staged at the Royal Albert Hall, London, in April 2012 to celebrate the 150 years of life at the College:

> "As President of Wellington College since 1970, it is a great pleasure to be here tonight. Every British monarch since my great-great grandmother Queen Victoria opened the College in 1859, has been the Royal Visitor to Wellington. Both she and Prince Albert, the first President, would have been delighted, I suspect, to see how the 'the Wellington College' of their imaginings has grown and flourished over the years.
> The success and high reputation which Wellington has achieved is a testament to the creative energy, talent, and vision of successive governors, Masters, teachers and pupils. I am sure we will see this energy and the powerful spirit and traditions of the College reflected in this evening's performance in the Royal Albert Hall."

Brief history of Wellington College

The plan for the College had been conceived as 'a living memorial' in a conversation at Windsor in 1852, after the death of Arthur, First Duke of Wellington, twice Prime Minister and victor of Assaye, the Peninsular campaign and Waterloo in 1815. In succession, King Edward VII (when Prince of Wales), his brother, Prince Arthur, Duke of Connaught (the Duke of Wellington's godson), and Prince Henry, Duke of

Gloucester, have all held the position as President of the College.

Co-educational School

Wellington College is a co-educational public school, located in the village of Crowthorne in Berkshire. It was built as a national monument to the Duke of Wellington. Wellington College was granted its royal charter in 1853 as the Royal and Religious Foundation of The Wellington College, and was opened in 1859. Its first master was the Reverend Edward White Benson, later Archbishop of Canterbury.

Leading English public school

Within twenty years of its foundation the College had established itself as a leading English public school in the tradition of Dr Thomas Arnold's Rugby. Orphaned sons of Army officers were its first pupils, joined later by sons of living Army officers and civilians. For a long period nearly half those at their leaving joined the Armed Services. They made a huge contribution to winning the First and Second World Wars, during which 1,208 Old Wellingtonians died. Wellingtonians won fifteen Victoria Crosses and one George Cross, four became Field Marshals, and one became a Marshal of the Royal Air Force.

Old Wellingtonians as professionals

Old Wellingtonians (referred to as OWs) have been represented in every sort of occupation over the past century and a half, including current members of the House of Lords and the House of Commons, and those serving as judges, ambassadors, senior academics (including Regius Professor, Sir Michael Howard), and in leading major international companies, financial services, science and the arts, the latter including President of the Royal Academy, Sir Nicholas Grimshaw, and celebrities such as novelist Sebastian Faulks, humourist Rory Bremner, and pop-star Will Young.[3]

Children of deceased officers

Originally the school supported children of deceased officers who had held commissions in the British Army, and in the Army of the East India Company. In 1952 a Supplementary Royal Charter extended the privilege of eligibility to the orphan children of deceased officers of the Royal Navy, Royal Marines, and Royal Air Force. A change in 2006 extended the privilege to the orphan children of deceased servicemen or servicewomen of Her Majesty's Armed Forces irrespective of rank, and to the orphan children of persons who, in the sole opinion of Governors, died in acts of selfless bravery. While for many years Wellington was a College for the sons of military families, only a minority of the children now have military connections. The first girls were admitted into the Sixth Form during the 1970's, and the school became fully co-educational in September 2006.

Wellington College today

The present Master of Wellington College is Dr Anthony Seldon and Mr Robin Dyer is Second Master. [4] Mr Julian Thomas will succeed to the position of Master in

September 2015, after he has trekked to the South Pole. There are currently just over 1,000 students aged between 13 and 18 years attending the college. Dr Seldon, has established the College more firmly than ever as a leading international institution in the private education sector. Wellington College International has been opened in Tianjiin in China, as well as a transformed secondary school in the state sector, the newly named Wellington Academy, near Tidworth in Hampshire.

Holistic education

The school is committed to an all-round or holistic education and the development in full, of each student's individual gifts. Students are required to engage with all eight of their aptitudes. The point of an eight aptitude focus, derived from the work of Professor Howard Gardner, an American Developmental Psychologist at Harvard University, is to delight in the various ways in which we experience the world around us and to develop as individuals. The aptitudes are reinforced by Wellington's five core values: kindness, courage, integrity, respect, and responsibility.

Eight aptitudes

The eight aptitudes explained here briefly are Linguistic: meaning the use of words, language, spoken and written, and interpretation and explanation of ideas; Logical: to mean logical thinking, scientific reasoning, analysing problems, performing mathematical calculations, and understanding the relationship between cause and effect; Cultural: covering the artistic ability and the appreciation and use of sound and vision, an appreciation of music, art and dramatic skill; Physical: taking in body movement control, physical agility, eye and body coordination, sporting, and dance prowess; Spiritual: involving awareness and appreciation of one's place in the world and thinking beyond materialism and the self; Moral: meaning awareness of personal responsibility, and understanding of right and wrong, openness and honesty, and establishing principles; Personal self-awareness: knowing one's self and understanding the need for reaction to change; and Social: the perception of other people's feelings and the ability to relate to others and get on with other people.

With justification the College can claim to be "the place where a fusion of originality, innovation and 150 years of tradition and history produces an education unlike any other."

Prince Edward visits – Speech Day 2013

Prince Edward visits Wellington College on a regular basis. He attended Speech Day on Saturday, May 25, 2013, in his role of President. For the first time ever, the whole Wellington College community of parents, pupils, and staff, congregated under one roof referred to as a Big Top that contained 3,500 people. It was in this exciting environment, amidst a celebration of the outstanding achievements of the College, that Prince Edward graced them with his presence. He spoke briefly, but warmly and supportively, and was enthusiastically welcomed by his audience. His Royal Highness then gave the most prestigious prizes to senior pupils, including the Queen's medals to the two Heads of College.

After the prize giving, Prince Edward was entertained at lunch by the Governors. He had played an important part in a great day, and departed leaving a lasting impression.[5]

THE SCOUT ASSOCIATION

The Scout Association is the World Organisation of the Scout Movement's recognised scouting association in the United Kingdom. Scouting began in 1907, through the efforts of Robert Baden-Powell, 1st Baron Baden-Powell, OM, GCMG, GCVO, KCB. The Scout Association was formed, under its previous name, The Boy Scout Association, in 1910. The Boy Scout Association was renamed as The Scout Association in 1967.

The Scout Association is divided into four mainland national groupings: England, Scotland, Wales, and Northern Ireland. Each of these divisions is further broken up into local Counties (England and Northern Ireland), Areas (Wales), or Regions (Scotland).

Promoting the development of young people

The stated aim of The Scout Association is to "promote the development of young people in achieving their full physical, intellectual, social and spiritual potential, as individuals, as responsible citizens and as members of their local, national and international communities". A programme is provided to help achieve this aim for young people from the age of six to twenty-five. Over 410,000 people in that age group are members of the association, with a further 33,000 people waiting to join.

Thanks to the work they have carried out, The Scout Association is a member of The National Council for Voluntary Youth Services (NCVYS). Girls were first admitted in 1976 to the Venture Scouts, and the rest of Sections on an optional basis in 1991. Since 2007 all Scout Groups in Britain must accept girls as well as boys, and religious preferences can be accommodated.

The Association's current Chief Executive is Matt Hyde and the Chief Scout is Bear Grylls. The roots of The Scout Association come from the fame of Robert Baden-Powell, following his exploits during the Second Anglo-Boer War in South Africa (October 1899 – May 1902). In 1907 "B-P", as he is known to members of the Movement, ran a camp on Brownsea Island for boys of varying backgrounds. These boys came from schools like Eton, Harrow, Parkstone, Hamworthy, and Bournemouth. This camp is now considered to be the start of the Movement. The following year, Baden-Powell wrote a series of magazine articles, *Scouting for Boys*, setting out activities and programmes which existing youth organisations could make use of. In a very short time, Scout Patrols were created up and down the country, all following the principles of Baden-Powell's book. By the time of the first census in 1910, there were over 100,000 members of the Movement. The Boy Scout Association was created in that year, in order to provide a national body that could organise and support the rapidly growing number of Scout Patrols. Many of the boys in the Scout Patrols had younger brothers who also wanted to participate, and there were many girls who also wanted the same thing. Baden-Powell came across a group of Girl Scouts at the Crystal Palace Scout Rally, London, in 1909. The solution for the

139. HRH The Duke of Kent with members of The Scout Association at the opening of the 21st World Scout Jamboree, July, 2007, Hylands Park, Chelmsford.

younger boys was simple, the Wolf Cubs Section was trialled from 1914 and formerly launched in 1916. However, Edwardian principles could not allow young girls to participate in the rough and tumble, wild activities of the Scouts, and so the Girl Guides were created by Baden-Powell's sister, Agnes, to provide a more "proper" programme of activities. Many of those who had grown out of Scouts still wanted to be a part of Scouting, so another section was created in 1918, the Rover Scouts.

Scouting was now a global phenomenon, with a Royal Charter granted by King George V on January 4, 1912, incorporating The Boy Scout Association throughout the British Empire, with "the purpose of instructing boys of all classes in the principles of discipline loyalty and good citizenship".

The first World Jamboree for Scouts was held in Olympia, London in 1920, and was a celebration and conference of the World Organization of the Scout Movement. Scouting in Britain went largely unchanged until it underwent a major review encompassed in The Chief Scouts' Advance Party Report in 1967. The name of the organisation was changed to The Scout Association. Major changes to the sections and their respective programmes were made. The youngest section were now named Cub Scouts, the Boy Scout section was renamed simply as the Scout section, Senior Scouts became Venture Scouts (for 16–20 year olds), and the Rover Scout section was disbanded. The Scout Uniform was also changed, most notably with the inclusion of long trousers for the Scouts (previously they had been wearing knee-length shorts). [6]

Several developments took place over the following years, including the intro-

140.   HRH The Duke of Kent with members of
The Scout Association at the opening of the 21st World
Scout Jamboree, July, 2007, Hylands Park, Chelmsford,
England.

duction of co-educational units of boys and girls. Parents involved in Scouting in Northern Ireland also began to organise activities for their children who were too young for Cub Scouts. This eventually led to the creation of the Beaver Scout section in 1986. Despite these changes, and many other minor ones, Scouting started to fall into a decline through the 1990s. This spurred a programme of change that took effect in 2003. In the late 1990s, a Muslim Scout Fellowship was formed in England and Wales. In addition to the main programme sections, a parallel Scouting programme, Scoutlink, provides support and involvement for young people and adults with developmental disabilities.

2001 onwards
Scouts had to balance the time they dedicated to scouting with school and homework. There was an attitude that the practice was old fashioned. The 2002 programme change overcame these challenges and the Venture Scouts was suspended and the senior section was replaced by the Explorer Scouts aged 14 to 18 year olds and the Scout Network for 15 to 18 year olds. New badges were also introduced for computing skills and skateboarding. New Scout uniforms for all sections and leaders were introduced in 2001, designed by Meg Andrews, more modern and appealing to young people. The 2010 figures show a total membership of just under half a

million.

Campsites
Across the country numerous campsites are owned by members of the Scout Association, usually Scout Districts and Counties, and are run by the individual Scout County or District councils. These campsites are also used by others outside the organisation, gaining additional income for the scout county or district.

Air and Sea Scouts
Some Scout Groups belong to separate branches called Air Scouts and Sea Scouts. Both branches follow the core programme in all Sections but can add more aeronautical or nautical emphasis depending on the branch, with some Group branches being recognised by the Royal Air Force or Royal Navy. In the United Kingdom there are approximately 400 Sea Scout Groups, of which about 25 per cent (101 Groups) are Royal Navy recognised, whilst of 117 Air Scout Groups, 43 are recognised by the RAF.

Scouting in Britain continues to promote the same Principles and Methods as written about by Baden-Powell in *Scouting for Boys* almost 100 years ago.

HRH Catherine The Duchess of Cambridge
In 2012 Her Royal Highness Catherine The Duchess of Cambridge (the former Miss Catherine Middleton) volunteered as a Scout Leader. The Duchess is a regular helper with junior Scout groups in London and north Wales. Well known for her hockey and rowing skills, Catherine will work with the six to ten year old Members of the Scout Movement i.e. Beaver Scouts and Cub Scouts, supervising games and other activities and going on weekend camps.

Progressive award scheme
An award scheme operates throughout all the sections in scouting, which forms a major part of the scout programme and promotes a consistent commitment to the programme. There are six awards, five of which are Chief Scout's awards and culminate in the Queen's Scout award. The first three awards, the Chief Scout's Bronze, Silver and Gold award, are the highest possible awards achievable in Beavers, Cubs, and Scouts respectively. To achieve these awards, a number of challenge badges must be obtained, demonstrating a wide range of skills, in addition to a personal challenge. The final three awards, The Chief Scout's Platinum, Diamond and the Queen's Scout award are all available in the Explorer Scout and Scout Network sections alone. The awards mirror the requirements of the Duke of Edinburgh's Award at Bronze, Silver, and Gold level respectively, consisting of a period of time volunteering in the local community, a prolonged physical activity, the advancement of a skill, and the partaking of an expedition. Achieving the Queen's Scout award is seen as a significant event on a national scale. Recipients of the award are invited to join the St George's Day service at Windsor Castle the year after completing the scheme and to parade before The Queen.

Fundraising and Community Impact

From the earliest days of the Movement Scouts have sought to have a positive impact on their communities, and fundraising has played an important part in this. During the First World War Cubs and Scouts raised money to purchase ambulances and to run "Scout Huts". These huts, which were located away from the trenches, provided a haven of peace and a taste of home comfort for thousands of soldiers recovering from front line duty. Similar fundraising schemes were run during the Second World War.

In 1949 Bob-a-job week was launched, Cubs and Scouts raised money for their groups by taking on tasks for neighbours or local organisations; this could vary from a bit of gardening to helping wash a local fire engine. Each helper would be paid a shilling, "a bob", for their help. In 2012 the scheme was re-launched as Scout Community Week. Projects are now more community focused than those taken on in the "bob-a-job" era, the premise being that the whole community rather than an individual will benefit from the work and the money raised will be invested back in Scouting. Innovation in this area continues and in 2015 "A Million Hands" was launched, working with national charities over half a million Scouts will take part in projects which over the course of three years will lead to genuine and lasting change for their communities.

Prince Edward's role

Prince Edward has been President of the Scout Association since January 1, 1975. He has a right to attend the AGM of the Scout Association, and he also takes the salute at the annual Queen's Scout parade at Windsor Castle when he is available. He has attended some of the highlight events of the Scout Association over the years. British Scouts played a major role in the centenary celebrations of Scouting in 2007. Events were organised on Brownsea Island, Poole, Dorset. The 21st World Scout Jamboree took place at Hylands Park in Essex on Saturday July 28. Prince Edward and His Royal Highness Prince William The Duke of Cambridge KG KT ADC(P) took part in the opening ceremony, which was attended by Scouts from over 160 countries around the world, marking the start of 12 days of celebrating 100 years since Scouting was founded.

Visit to scouts on the Isle of Wight

On Tuesday September 15, 2009, Prince Edward made a very special private visit to Osborne House in his role of President of the Scout Association. It was a most appropriate location, having been the favoured home of Queen Victoria. A Guard of Honour of the Island Scouts awaited him on his arrival by helicopter. It was in the middle of school term time and on a week day, when everyone would normally be in school, but twenty representatives from all five sections, from Beavers to Network and Leaders, formed up at midday at the main entrance to Osborne House under the direction of the County Commissioner, Mr Anthony Roberts. Prince Edward stopped and spoke to every person and was very impressed with his reception. The Scouts, in their immaculate uniforms, were a joy to behold. During the two-hour visit, scouts that did not have to return to school joined the hundreds of visitors, walking around the grounds. The great British weather did not fail, and there were several heavy showers during which the Scouts formed up in the shelter of the porch, from where they saw Prince Edward boarding his car for the short drive to his helicopter.

THE TANK MUSEUM

"And the Lord was with Judah, and he drove out
the inhabitants of the mountains: but he could not drive out
the inhabitants of the valley: because they had
Chariots of Iron." (Judges I: v19)

The Tank Museum, known previously as the Bovington Tank Museum, is the museum of the Royal Tank Regiment, Royal Armoured Corps, Bovington Camp, in Dorset, England. It houses a collection of armoured fighting vehicles that traces the history of the tank. With almost 300 vehicles on exhibition from 26 countries it is the second largest collection of tanks and armoured fighting vehicles in the world. It includes the only working example of a German Tiger I tank and a British First World War Mark I, the world's oldest surviving combat tank. The camp trains all sections of the British Army in tracked-vehicle driving, as well as repairing and maintaining the vehicles in its workshops.

Brief history
In 1916 the British War Office established the Bovington camp as a tank crew training facility. At that time the Army was introducing tanks into the First World War in an attempt to break the stagnation of trench warfare. In 1919 the tanks returned to Bovington from France. Many of them were fit only for scrap but a small number of the least damaged vehicles were put to one side so that tank crews and designers could have an idea of the tank's early heritage. In 1923 the writer Rudyard Kipling visited Bovington and recommended that a museum should be set up. The collection grew greatly after the Second World War, as many Allied and captured Axis tanks were added. In 1947 it was opened to the general public. The Tank Museum has continued to expand and today it is primarily seen as a means of educating and entertaining the general public. Many of the tanks are in complete working order and can be seen in action throughout summer months in special displays.

The Tank Exhibition
The Tank Exhibition is currently split into five sections: the World War I Hall, the Inter War Hall, the World War II Hall, the Tamiya Hall, and the British Steel Hall. The World War I Hall contains the whole British tank development from Little Willie to the Mark VIII "Liberty", plus an example of the British Mark V, one of the few World War I tanks still in working order. The Inter War Hall highlights the rapid progress made in tank design and vehicle armour during the period leading up to the Second World War. Also featured is Vickers A1E1 Independent, Peerless Armoured Car, Rolls-Royce Armoured Car, Lanchester 6x4 Armoured Car, Carden Loyd tankette, Tank Light MK IIA, and Cruiser Mk I. The World War II Hall is the biggest section, with tanks from most nations involved in the conflict. It includes

a German Tiger I tank, bearing turret number 131 that was captured in Tunisia in April 1943, and has been fully restored to running condition by the workshops at Bovington. It is the only Tiger I left that is capable of running under its own power. It also has the last surviving DD Tank with its canvas screen, and the only one still in working order. A further large display of tanks features post war Main Battle Tanks (MBT) such as the British Centurion, the American M60, and the Russian T-72. British Steel Hall holds the Chobham armour used in the Gulf War against Iraq and pays tribute to the Centurion tank which, during its 46 year career (1945–1991), proved to be one of the best British tanks ever produced. The Tamiya and British Steel Halls feature a further impressive display, including the Tortoise, Black Prince, Conqueror, Charioteer tank destroyer, Centurion, Chieftain, Challenger 1, Challenger 2, M41 Bulldog; Cold-War and Iraqi T-55's, T-62, T-72, and many others.

£1.5 million donation at Tankfest
Prince Edward has been Patron of The Tank Museum since July 1, 1983. In July 2010, during Tankfest, which is the museum's celebrated Armed Forces Day event, a most generous donation of £1.5 million was presented to Prince Edward by His Excellency Mr Khaled Al Duwaisan GCVO, Kuwaiti Ambassador to Britain, on behalf of the Kuwaiti Government. The money was donated to the Tank Museum in recognition of the Royal Armoured Corps' role in liberating the country in the 1991 Gulf War. Thousands had turned out in the sunshine to see the ceremony and enjoy the military armour festival with its host of action displays, historic armoured vehicles, and living history encampments. A unique demonstration from the British Army was the climax on both days of Tankfest as the Royal Armoured Corps (RAC) re-enacted counter insurgency operations, a drill that had never previously been seen outside of Afghanistan.

Prince Edward unveils a plaque
Joined by the ambassador, Prince Edward unveiled a commemorative plaque marking the generous donation from the Middle-Eastern nation. In recognition of the gift The Tank Museum has named its new purpose built outdoor Tank Action arena The Kuwait Arena. Home to some of the most important armoured vehicles to fight in the war to liberate Kuwait, The Tank Museum's collection includes the Challenger I, which was the very first tank to cross the Saudi Arabia-Kuwait border during the liberation in 1991. Major General Arthur Denaro, CBE, DL, who was the commander of that tank on the day of the invasion, was also present at the ceremony. Graciously accepting the donation, Prince Edward said:

> "There has long been a special bond between the people of Great Britain and those of Kuwait. It was a relationship that was close before 1991, but was shaped and strengthened by the sacrifices of the soldiers of both our countries as they fought side by side in the Liberation war. As Patron of The Tank Museum, I would like to thank His Excellency for the generosity of this gift which will enable future generations to learn about our Army, its people and the tools of its trade for years to come."

The Tank Museum's director Mr Richard Smith said:

"It was an extremely proud moment having the Kuwaiti Ambassador, The Duke and Major General Arthur Denaro, all here at the museum together. We are all extremely honoured by the generous donation from the Kuwaiti people which will go a long way in helping us to preserve our tanks and the remarkable stories of their servicemen for future generations."

Royal Armoured Corps War Memorial Benevolent Fund

The Royal Armoured Corps (RAC) was created from an association of armoured regiments, including the Royal Tank Regiment and the horse cavalry. Today it comprises 10 regular regiments and four Yeomanry regiments of the Territorial Army. It provides the armour capability of the British Army with vehicles such as the Challenger 2 Tank and the Scimitar Reconnaissance Vehicle.

The Royal Armoured Corps War Memorial Benevolent Fund was set up in 1974, and Prince Edward became Patron on July 1. It is a trust that promotes the efficiency of the Royal Armoured Corps in particular (but not exclusively), by encouraging esprit de corps i.e. the capacity of group members to maintain belief in an institution or goal, particularly in the face of opposition or hardship. The trust provides relief for persons in need, hardship or distress, who are either serving or former serving members of the Corps or their dependants, wives, and widows, whether remarried or not, and their children.

THE IMPERIAL WAR MUSEUMS
Mission statement:
'To enable people to have an informed understanding of
modern war and its impact on individuals and society'.

The Imperial War Museums (IWM) has branches at five locations in England, three of which are in London. The first museum was founded in 1917, during the First World War, and was intended as a record of the war effort and the sacrifice of Britain and her Empire. The museums gives its mission as 'to enable people to have an informed understanding of modern war and its impact on individuals and society'.

Housed originally in the Crystal Palace at Sydenham Hill, south east London, the museum opened to the public in 1920. In 1924 they moved to the premises of the Imperial Institute in South Kensington, and, in 1936, they acquired a permanent home that was previously the Bethlem Royal Hospital, Lambeth Road, in Southwark, London where they are today.

The outbreak of the Second World War saw the museum expand both its collections and its terms of reference, but in the post-war period, like many other large buildings the IWM experienced a period of decline. By the 1960s their Southwark building, now referred to as the Imperial War Museum London, had been re-developed and now serves as the organisation's corporate headquarters. During the 1970s the museum began to expand onto other sites. The first, in 1976, was the historic airfield in Cambridgeshire, now referred to as Imperial War Museum Duxford. In 1978 the Royal Navy cruiser HMS Belfast became a branch of the museum, having previously been preserved for the nation by a private trust. In 1984 Winston Churchill's Cabinet War Rooms, that had been his underground wartime command centre, was opened to the public. From the 1980s onwards the museum's Bethlem building underwent a series of multimillion-pound redevelopments that were completed in 2000. The fifth branch of the IWM, Museum North in Trafford, Greater Manchester, opened in 2002. The IWM has described itself as:

"Unique in its coverage of conflicts, especially those involving Britain and the Commonwealth, from the First World War to the present day. We seek to provide for, and to encourage, the study and understanding of the history of modern war and 'wartime experience'. We are proud to be regarded as essential sights of London, Cambridgeshire, and Greater Manchester."

Today the IWM is made up of a family of five museums: IWM London; IWM North in Trafford, Greater Manchester; IWM Duxford; the Churchill War Rooms in Whitehall, London; and the historic ship HMS Belfast, moored in the Pool of London on the River Thames.

The museum has extensive archives, and puts on permanent displays and special exhibitions, and education programmes. Their collections include archives of personal and official documents, photographs, film and video material, and oral history recordings; an extensive library, a large art collection, and examples of military vehicles and aircraft, equipment and other artefacts.

The IWM is funded by government grants, charitable donations, and revenue generated through commercial activity such as retailing, licensing, and publishing. Admission is free of charge to the IWM in London and Trafford, but an admission fee is levied at the other branches. [7]

Brief history

On February 27, 1917 Sir Alfred Mond, who was a Member of Parliament and First Commissioner of Works, wrote to the Liberal Prime Minister David Lloyd George to propose the establishment of a National War Museum. This proposal was accepted by the War Cabinet on March 5, 1917, and the decision was announced in *The Times* on March 26. A committee was established, chaired by Mond, to oversee the collection of material to be exhibited in the new museum.

The National War Museum Committee set about collecting material to illustrate Britain's war effort by dividing into subcommittees each of which examined such subjects as the Army, the Navy, the production of munitions, and women's war work. There was an early appreciation of the need for exhibits to reflect personal experience in order to prevent the collections becoming dead relics. Sir Martin Conway, the museum's first Director General said that exhibits must "be vitalised by contributions expressive of the action, the experiences, the valour and the endurance of individuals." The museum's first curator and secretary was Charles Ffoulkes, who had previously been curator of the Tower of London armouries. In July 1917 Mond made a visit to the Western Front in order to study how best to organise the museum's growing collection. While in France he met French government ministers, and Field Marshal Haig, who reportedly took great interest in his work. In December, following a resolution from the India and Dominions Committee, the name of the museum was changed to the Imperial War Museum.

The museum was opened by King George V at the Crystal Palace on June 9, 1920. During the opening ceremony, Sir Alfred Mond addressed the King on behalf of the committee, saying that "it was hoped to make the museum so complete that everyone who took part in the war however obscurely, would find therein an example or illustration of the sacrifice he or she made" and that the museum "was not a monument of military glory, but a record of toil and sacrifice." Shortly afterwards the Imperial War Museum Act 1920 was passed and established a Board of Trustees to oversee the governance of the museum. To reflect the museum's Imperial remit the board included appointees of the governments of India, South Africa, Canada, Australia and New Zealand. While the Act was being debated, some Parliamentarians felt that the museum would perpetuate an undesirable war spirit and Commander Joseph Kenworthy MP said that he would "refuse to vote a penny of public money to commemorate such suicidal madness of civilisation as that which was shown in the late War". The popularity of the museum is apparent, for by November 1921 it had received 2,290,719 visitors.

The building
The building, designed by James Lewis, was the former Bethlem Royal Hospital that had been vacated following the hospital's relocation to Beckenham in Kent. The site was owned by Lord Rothermere, who had originally intended to demolish the building entirely in order to provide a public park in what was a severely overcrowded area of London. Eventually the central portion of the hospital building was retained while its two extensive wings were removed. The museum was reopened by the Duke of York (later King George VI) in its new accommodation on July 7, 1936.

Second World War 1939-45
With the outbreak of the Second World War in 1939, the museum began to collect material documenting the conflict. The museum initially remained open but was closed in September 1940 for the duration of the war with the onset of the Blitz by the German Luftwaffe on London. On January 31, 1941, the museum was struck by a bomb that fell on the naval gallery. A number of ship models were damaged by the blast and a Short Seaplane that had flown at the Battle of Jutland was destroyed. While closed to the public the museum's building was used for a variety of purposes connected to the war effort, such as a repair garage for government motor vehicles, a centre for Air Raid Precautions civil defence lectures, and a fire fighting training school. In October 1945 the museum mounted a temporary exhibition, the first since the end of the war in August, which showcased technologies developed by the Petroleum Warfare Department. The museum reopened a portion of its galleries in November 1946. A third of the galleries were open by 1948, and a further wing opened in 1949.

In 1953, with Commonwealth forces engaged in Korea and Malaya the museum began its current policy of collecting material from all modern conflicts in which British or Commonwealth forces were involved. However, despite this expansion of remit, the early post-war period was a period of decline for the museum. Dr Noble Frankland, the museum's Director from 1960 to 1982, described the museum's galleries in 1955 as appearing "dingy and neglected" and in a "dismal state of decay", the museum's "numerous stunning exhibits" notwithstanding.

President of the Board of Trustees

Prince Edward was appointed by Her Majesty The Queen to be President of the Board of Trustees of the IWM on December 1, 1974, following the death of the previous President, HRH The Duke of Gloucester. (Today, Sir Francis Richards KCMG GVVO is Chairman of the trustees, and Diane Lees CBE, is Director-General). The Board of Trustees was encouraged by the appointment. The IWM's Director, Dr Noble Frankland, wrote on December 13, 1974 to a colleague, "It is after all a good many years since we had a fully fit President." On January 27, 1975 Sir Maurice Dorman wrote to Noble Frankland, "I have known the Duke of Kent quite well, partly from occasions when he has stayed with us in West Africa and we have met him several times subsequently. I have a high regard for him and think he will do us very well…I am sure the Duke will take a keen and knowledgeable interest in all our affairs." In his reply on January 29, Frankland said, "I have had the honour of being presented to him on a number of occasions and I must say that I found him a most extraordinarily agreeable guest when he came here for the preview of the Thames Television World at War series. … Over supper, the conversation ranged over a wide and fascinating field and reminded us all of what an intelligent and well-informed man the Duke of Kent is."

The first meeting of the Board of Trustees to be opened by the Duke on March 26, 1975 was well-attended, with 21 out of a possible 29 members present. Prince Edward expressed his great pleasure at the appointment, at the honour upon succeeding the late Duke of Gloucester, and of the interest he personally took in the work of the museum. They went on to discuss developing the site at Duxford and the potential to acquire HMS Belfast. After the meeting Noble Frankland wrote to Sir Richard Buckley, the Duke of Kent's private secretary saying that he had heard that Prince Edward enjoyed his first meeting and "we were much impressed by his interest and grip."

Illustrating how complex the life of a royal prince can be, Sir Richard wrote to Frankland on October 23, 1975 that the Duke

"… agrees that his Scots Guards bearskin which used to belong to the late Duke of Gloucester, should go on display in the museum [with the late Duke's uniforms]. He would like the bearskin returned to him three weeks before The Queen's Birthday Parade each year and it could be collected again as soon as convenient after the parade."

At his second meeting, on March 24, 1976, the Duke expressed sorrow upon reading of the death of Sir John Wheeler-Bennett and he led a silent tribute to that great historian before proceeding with business. The discussions included events for the Queen's Silver Jubilee in the following year, to include a Women at War exhibition, and a lively discussion on how to lead the museum out of its low point of interest and attendances in the 1960's.

At the meeting on November 30, 1977 the President invited the Director to read the text of a telegram to be sent to the Queen: "With their humble duty the trustees and staff of the Imperial War Museum submit to Your Majesty their heartfelt congratulations upon the Silver Jubilee and the completion of the joyful celebration of it at home and abroad." The Duke then went on to discuss in detail two important developments in the museum's outstations. The securing of a pre-production Concorde 01 for Duxford in the teeth of rival bids from many other sites was an achievement that reflected great credit upon the museum and its Corporate Friend, the Duxford Aviation Society: "It showed what the volunteer spirit could still achieve".

While it was not yet absolutely decided, the discussions about acquiring HMS Belfast, "the last surviving big-gun ship that had fought in the Second World War", were going well. "The addition of this unique vessel to the museum would, he stressed, greatly enhance the value of the IWM as a whole". The meeting recorded that visitors between November 1976 and October 1977 had exceeded one million for the first time. The pattern of including a tour of some of the museum's galleries and lunchtime conversations before the Board meeting was established. Sir Richard Buckley wrote to Noble Frankland that, "HRH finds this an excellent way of keeping in touch with your plans and problems". In his reply Frankland said that they were delighted to see his "keen interest ... he spends time talking to members of the staff, both senior and junior. This is the greatest possible encouragement to us all and leads everyone here eagerly to look forward to visits from our President".

In the same way, after a Royal visit to Duxford on July 21, 1978, the Chairman, Sir John Grandy, wrote to the Duke that it was "a real tonic to all concerned ... the time and trouble which Your Royal Highness was kind enough to spend in speaking to so many individuals was not only an honour to each of them, it was also a great service to the museum."

At the November 22, 1978 meeting, held on board HMS Belfast, the Duke reported on his recent visits to both Duxford and HMS Belfast. He warmly thanked Sir Peter Masefield on his retirement after "fourteen years of unstinting service" which oversaw the expansion of the museum's outstations. He was also able to welcome to his first meeting as a trustee Sir George Macfarlane CB, whom he knew as the former Controller of Research at the Ministry of Defence. Prince Edward would have reported to him when he was a General Staff Officer 1 in the early 1970s, working on the procurement of new tracked vehicles for the Army.

Sir John Grandy again wrote to the Duke:

"Your presence in our Museum ship, HMS Belfast, gave me and the Board a great boost ... It was also a tremendous encouragement, and particularly to the staff on the ship, to see your Royal Highness on board and everyone greatly appreciated the interest which you took in the machinery and the

483

exhibits. It was very good of you to speak to so many of the Yeomen and other members of staff on duty. This is such a great thing for morale."

In a personal letter of reply, Prince Edward saw HMS Belfast as "a uniquely valuable way of teaching history" and, taking his duties as a trustee seriously, he added "It does seem, though, that some way will have to be found of controlling the numbers of visitors at peak times." [8]

Shared Experience Art and War Exhibition, IWM, London

The Shared Experience Art and War Exhibition had begun its tour at the newly opened Canadian War Museum in Ottawa in 2005, to mark the 60th anniversary of the conclusion of the Second World War. That autumn it was at the Australian War Memorial in Canberra by which time it had been viewed by 200,000 people.

On March 23, 2006, the exhibition opened at the IWM, London. In this first ever exhibition of its kind, there were famous pictures and little known works from the three war museums, including views of war-hit London.

Paul Nash's Battle of Britain gave the viewer a sense of aerial battle over a wide area, with smoke trails in the air, and a winding river below, depicted in a huge painting which confronted the visitor at the exhibition entrance. Most striking was Duncan Grant's St. Paul's, which painting of St. Paul's Cathedral showed the distant dome from the vantage point of a heavily-bombed Queen Victoria Street, in front of St. Nicholas Cole Abbey. In 2006 the Church of England announced that a restored St. Nicholas Cole Abbey, which can be found near the north end of the Millennium Bridge, was to become a national centre for Religious Education. Grant had seen it in 1941 when, despite the blitz, its golden statue of St. Nicholas had survived above the gate. Flight from Reason, by the Australian artist Stella Bowen, who had left her home country almost thirty years earlier, depicted bomb damage opposite the Temple Church just south of Fleet Street. Before the end of the war she became an official war artist travelling with Australian crews of Bomber Command. Also from Australia, war artist Colin Colahan's Waterloo Station took the viewer into a foggy scene under the concourse clock, where a man in RAF uniform is saying farewell. Beautifully lit was Dame Laura Knight's Ruby Loftus screwing a Beech-ring. It was one of many pictures showing women at work. Canadian artist Mollie Lamb Bobak CM ONB, reminds us of the multi-racial involvement with a striking Private Roy, Canadian Women's Army Corps. During the Second World War, she was the first Canadian woman artist to be sent overseas to document Canada's war effort, and in particular, the work of the Canadian Women's Army Corps (CWAC). She sketched 'Private Roy' several times in a canteen in Halifax, Nova Scotia. The show offered to its audience a reminder of the huge Commonwealth commitment made to Britain during the desperate years of the Second World War.

In his opening address at the exhibition Prince Edward said:

"This Exhibition is about the past which forms an eloquent testament to the shared values and vision of Australia, Canada and the United Kingdom.
"By combining the rich resources of the three nations, we are privileged

to see a display of art that offers much more than any one institution could have achieved on its own. The combined insights of the curators enable us better to understand the differences as well as the similarities between our enterprises, and I trust that this will only be the first of many such collaborations.

"Our Commonwealth partners have given us invaluable co-operation in the past, most especially of course when our countries fought together side by side in both World Wars. What is more, the Imperial War Museum owes its own debt to those partners, because had it not been for their lobbying, we should only have been a National War Museum, without the broader remit to commemorate the contribution of the whole of Empire to the First World War, and we should have been much the poorer for it.

"I believe that visiting this Exhibition should renew our appreciation of the unquestioning of each nation's culture, whilst allowing us to share something of the experiences of the men, women, and children who lived through the war."

Imperial War Museum Duxford

The Imperial War Museum Duxford, in Cambridgeshire, is Britain's largest aviation museum. It houses the museum's large exhibits, including nearly 200 aircraft, military vehicles, artillery pieces, and minor naval vessels, in seven main exhibition buildings. The site also provides storage space for the museum's collections of film, photographs, documents, books and artefacts. The site accommodates a number of British Army regimental museums, including those of the Parachute Regiment and the Royal Anglian Regiment.

Based on the historic Duxford Aerodrome, the site was originally operated by the Royal Air Force (RAF) during the First World War. During the Second World War, Duxford played a prominent role during the Battle of Britain and was later used by the United States Army Air Force's fighter units in support of the daylight bombing of Germany. Duxford remained an active RAF airfield until 1961. Many of Duxford's original buildings, such as hangars used during the Battle of Britain, are still in use. A number of these buildings are of architectural or historic significance and over thirty have listed building status. The site also features a number of purpose-built exhibition buildings, such as the Stirling Prize-winning American Air Museum, designed by Sir Norman Foster. The airfield remains active and is used by a number of civilian flying companies and hosts regular air shows. The site is operated in partnership with Cambridgeshire County Council and the Duxford Aviation Society, a charity formed in 1975 to preserve civil aircraft and promote appreciation of British civil aviation history.

Prince Edward opens exhibitions at IWM Duxford

Hundreds of D-Day veterans from all over the world converged on the Imperial War Museum at Duxford on Sunday June 3, 2001, for the opening of two important new exhibitions titled The Normandy Experience and Monty, both of which were opened by Prince Edward.

The Normandy Experience focused on the role of the ordinary soldier during the 157,000-strong invasion of the Nazi-held French coast on June 6, 1944.

A second permanent exhibition titled Monty focuses on the life and achievements of Field Marshal Montgomery [9], commander of the Allied forces during the D-Day landings. Among the guests were Montgomery's son, Viscount Montgomery of Alamein CBE, and Sir Jock Stirrup.[10] Montgomery's father commanded the famous Eighth Army from August 1942 in the Western Desert (just before the decisive victory at El Alamein), through the final Allied victory in Tunisia and the invasions of Sicily and Italy in 1943. He was given responsibility for planning the D-Day invasion of Normandy. Montgomery was in command of all Allied ground forces during Operation Overlord from the initial landings until after the Battle of Normandy. 'Operation Overlord' was the code name for the Battle of Normandy, the operation that launched the invasion of German-occupied Western Europe. The operation commenced on June 6, 1944 with the Normandy landings (Operation Neptune, commonly known as D-Day).

Opening the exhibition on September 24, 2002, Prince Edward said:

"Sir Jock, my lords, ladies and gentleman. I was delighted to be asked to open this exhibition, which completes the Imperial War Museum's tribute to Britain's greatest battlefield commander since Wellington and to those who served under him, some of whom we are privileged to have with us today. It tells the remarkable story of Montgomery's life and career from his early years as a high-spirited schoolboy to his outstanding leadership during major action in the Second World War and his post-war work with NATO. [11]

"Out of the great treasure-trove of Montgomery material in the possession of the museum, many fascinating exhibits – in addition to those mentioned by Sir Jock – have been assembled: a less than favourable school report, in which Monty's form master at St. Paul's writes: "To have a serious chance for Sandhurst he must give more time to work;" a telegram sent to his parents in 1914, reporting that he was missing on the Western Front; extracts from his personal diary, written during the evacuation from Dunkirk in 1940; notes for a series of briefings which he gave to senior officers of the Eighth Army before the Battle of El Alamein; top secret planning documents drawn up by him for the D-Day landings; a message from the War Office warning him that his conspicuous appearance made him an obvious target for the enemy; his unique autograph album containing the signatures of many of the most famous politicians and soldiers of his time; and an astrakhan hat given to him on his visit to China in 1961.

"All this material is drawn from what is without question the most important personal collection held by the museum, which will be an essential source for future generations of students and academics.

"The exhibition reveals a man who was totally dedicated to his profession, especially after the tragic death of his wife in 1937; was meticulous in his planning and in his attention to detail; possessed the ability to reduce complex military problems to essentials; was a skilful tactician with a flair for assessing changing situations; was totally unflappable; and above all who had the knack of instilling his own boundless self-belief into the troops under his command – in short a General who was truly 'master of the battlefield'."

Duxford celebrates its birthday

The Duxford Imperial War Museum celebrated its 89th birthday in 2007. It is home to more than 70 flying warplanes, which can regularly be seen in the skies. It also stages many airshows yearly, attracting around 80,000 people who travel from all over the world to watch the displays. It is home to more than 30 iconic British and Commonwealth aircraft, including the Supermarine Spitfire, Avro Lancaster, English Electric Lightning and BAC Aerospatiale Concorde.

Prince Edward opens an exhibition

In July 2007 Prince Edward officially launched a multi-million-pound exhibition, AirSpace, at Duxford, that charts the history of civil and military aviation. Much of the thinking behind the new exhibition is to give visitors a new insight into the country's rich aviation heritage. The display occupies over three acres and will provide a formal learning environment and inspire future generations to realise the potential of careers in aerospace engineering.

Air Chief Marshal Sir Peter Squire, Chairman of the museum's Board of Trustees, said:

> "AirSpace underlines the relevance of Duxford and the contribution it makes at the heart of the east of England. This remarkable building celebrates not just Britain's extraordinary achievements in the field of aviation, but also the opportunities available to future generations of pilots, engineers and designers."

AirSpace, which cost £25 million to build, includes an area devoted to conservation, a range of supporting exhibition and gallery spaces, a suite of classrooms and education workshops, a conference facility, and a 200-seat lecture theatre.

Prince Edward spoke of his pleasure at opening the exhibition, which he described as one of the "most ambitious projects of its kind" ever to be undertaken. Continuing he said:

> "With a footprint exceeding 15,000 square metres, and over three times as long as the distance covered during the Wright Brothers' first flight, AirSpace is one of the largest, most spectacular spaces for the interpretation of aviation heritage anywhere in the world.
>
> "In completing AirSpace, the Imperial War Museum brings to conclusion 10 years of development and build that has, from every perspective, delivered a museum of national significance and international standing."

The Cabinet War Rooms, London

The Cabinet War Rooms is an underground complex that served as a British government command centre throughout the Second World War. It is a bunker that sheltered wartime Prime Minister Winston Churchill and his government, particularly during the London Blitz. Located beneath the Treasury building in the Whitehall area of Westminster, the facilities became operational in 1939 and were in constant use until their abandonment in August 1945, after the surrender of Japan.

Their historical value was recognised early on in the modern era and the public were able to visit by appointment. However, the practicalities of allowing public access to a site beneath a working government office meant that only 4,500 of 30-40,000 annual applicants to visit the War Rooms could be admitted. The IWM agreed to take over the administration of the site in 1982, a development keenly supported by the then Prime Minister Margaret Thatcher, who was a great admirer of Winston Churchill. Affectionately referred to as 'Churchill's bunker', Mrs Thatcher opened the Cabinet War Rooms in April 1984. In 2003 a further suite of rooms, used as accommodation by Churchill, his wife Clementine, and close associates, including his brother Major John (Jack) Spencer Churchill, were added to the museum.

In 2005 the accommodation and offices were re-branded as the Churchill Museum and Cabinet War Rooms, with 850 m^2 of the site redeveloped as a biographical museum exploring Churchill's life. The centrepiece is a fifteen metre interactive table which enables visitors to access digitised material particularly from the Churchill Archives Centre, via an 'electronic filing cabinet'. The museum was renamed the Churchill War Rooms in 2010.

The work of the Imperial War Museum remains one of the chief delights of Prince Edward's public duties. In the 40 years he has been President of the Board of Trustees he has opened 22 exhibitions at the London branches of the IWM, besides some 17 visits to see how the museum and its galleries were progressing, attended 13 events at Duxford, and three at IWM North. He attended eight meetings with senior members of the staff, besides the numerous full board meetings, and on four separate occasions combined visits to America with special fund-raising events for the new American air museum at Duxford. His interest in the full workings of the Imperial War Museum is a constant source of encouragement to the staff and volunteers working there and these duties combine his interest in military history, veterans' affairs, aviation, technology, and education in a most satisfactory way.

THE SOCIETY FOR ARMY HISTORICAL RESEARCH

Established in 1921, to encourage the study of the history and the traditions of the British Army, The Society for Army Historical Research is one of the nation's oldest military history societies. Since its early days, the society has expanded its interests which now include non-regular and auxiliary British military formations such as Militia, Yeomanry, and the Territorial Army, as well as the crown offices and civil institutions that maintained them. The society also aims to encourage the scholarly study of the land forces of the Commonwealth and the Empire, including forces maintained by non-Crown bodies, such as the Honourable East India Company, or forces allied to and forming an integral part of the land forces operating on behalf of the Crown.

Chronologically, the society's interests range from the late Middle Ages to the 1980s, having advanced their coverage of the availability of primary material of more recent date in line with the Thirty Year rule on the release of documents in accordance with Britain's National Archives system, Kew, Richmond, South West London.

The main activity of the society is the publication of a quarterly peer-reviewed journal reflecting its members' interests that are also catered for by a programme of special events and lectures. The society is also interested in the study of military artefacts and pictures, uniforms, badges and medals, arms, and equipment.

To encourage the study of British military history among the younger generation, the society recently instituted an annual essay prize for students at universities and schools. Some modest research grants for graduate students are also available. The essay competition is open to all university undergraduates and sixth-form students, to encourage interest in military research.

Prince Edward was made Patron of The Society for Army Historical Research on February 1, 1966.

The Army Historical Research national essay prize 2010

In 2010 the essay prize was won by Mr Christopher Choy, a War Studies student from the University of Kent. The prize giving ceremony took place at the Cavalry and Guards Club in London, on Wednesday, April 21, with Prince Edward making the presentation. Mr Choy received first prize for his winning entry titled: '*Last Stand on the Imjin River: Could the loss of the 1st Battalion, Gloucestershire Regiment have been averted?*' Mr Choy said: "I am delighted that my essay was chosen. It was a tremendous honour to have been presented with the prize by the Duke of Kent and I would like to thank both Professor Mark Connelly and Mr George Hay from the University of Kent for their support." Mark Connelly, Professor of Modern British History at the University's School of History, said: "Chris' entry shows his determination and enthusiasm to produce high quality work, and the degree of engagement our War Studies programme inspires in our students."

2011 prize

Mr Scott Ansel, an undergraduate student at New College, Oxford, was awarded the 2011 Essay Prize, presented by Prince Edward as part of the annual Templer Award Ceremony held in the Special Forces Club, London. Mr Ansel's essay titled, '*Trench Raiding in the First World War: a misunderstood practice*', came out on top of a very competitive field which featured a record number of entries from Schools and Universities across the country. A first Runner up prize was also awarded to Mr James O'Riordan for his fascinating essay "*Has the threat to British soldiers increased since World War II?*"

The Templer Medal

The Templer Medal was established by The Society for Army Historical Research in 1981 to commemorate the life and achievements of Field Marshal Sir Gerald Templer KG (1898-1979), and to mark his presidency of the society between 1965 and 1979.

The society's interests embrace the political, social, and cultural aspects of army and regimental history, as well as the study of individual campaigns and commanders. To recognize outstanding original research the society awards the Templer Medal to the author of the best book published in the preceding year on the history of the British Army.

Professor Richard Holmes awarded the Templer Medal

The Society for Army Historical Research took much delight in announcing that Professor Richard Holmes had been awarded the Templer Medal in 2011 for his outstanding work: '*Soldiers: Army Lives and Loyalties from Redcoats to Dusty Warriors*'. *Pro*fessor Holmes' social history of the British army, which takes its reader from the English Civil War through to the present day, makes an important contribution to questions of military continuity and change, whilst always maintaining a focus on the individual soldier, as well as producing a grand narrative.

The presentation of the Templer Medal always takes place at the Annual General Meeting in the year following. Sadly, Professor Holmes who was President of The British Commission for Military History, died on April 30, 2011, aged 65, after suffering from cancer. Prince Edward therefore presented the prize to Richard's wife, Katharine Saxton, and their two daughters.

COMBINED CAVALRY OLD COMRADES ASSOCIATION

The Combined Cavalry Old Comrades Association (CCOCA) is the title for all British Army Cavalry, modern and antecedent, and Yeomanry Regiments, and their Regimental Associations. It also includes Cavalry Regiments of the Commonwealth, although today representation is limited to the Indian Cavalry.

Each year on a Sunday in May, a Parade and Service is held and each Regimental Association takes its place in the Parade in order of seniority, with the regimental association banner carried at the head of its contingent. The Salute is taken by a selected personage and the parade is usually commanded by a senior officer of the same association. It is customary for the Service to be conducted by the Chaplain General to the Army, assisted by the Senior Chaplain from the Royal Garrison Church of All Saints from Aldershot, and the Verger and Choir also take part.

Today up to a total of five Cavalry Bands (in 1992 there were ten) play the music for the whole service and, prior to the actual Parade, they march from Hyde Park Barracks to the forming up area in Hyde Park, London, and on the conclusion of the service they march from the Memorial of Saint George, back to Hyde Park Barracks.

The Processional Cross used at the Annual Service was presented early in 1932 by Colonel G.E.N. Brooker of the 5th Princess Charlotte of Wales' Dragoon Guards, and was consecrated on June 12, 1932 in the Royal Garrison Church at Aldershot,

490

where it is kept for safe custody.

Over recent years the Parade and Service has attracted up to 2,000 marching participants and a congregation of at least 500. The tradition for officers to wear bowler hats for the annual parade dates back to the first such event 88 years ago, when the outfit was considered correct dress for walking out.

When the parade began it was held at the beginning of May so that people could go to the regimental cup final on the Saturday morning, the FA Cup final in the afternoon, the regimental dinner in the evening, and then to the parade on Sunday.

Traditionally, serving Cavalry officers were expected to wear their City gentlemen's attire whenever they are in London on duty. This has been relaxed and, as an example, the Household Cavalry officers' standing orders state that: "Bowler Hats and stiff collars are no longer required to be worn by Officers in London, Officers visiting HQ Household Cavalry or Household Cavalry Mounted Regiment are not to wear extravagantly tailored or coloured clothing". The dress for Household Cavalry, adopted by most Cavalry Regiments for the Cavalry Memorial Sunday, is Bowler Hat, Dark Suit, stiff white collar, Household Division (or Regimental) Tie, Medals, Umbrella and Black lace-up Shoes.

Prince Edward became Patron of the Combined Cavalry Old Comrades Association on February 1, 1975. He has taken the salute several times on Cavalry Sunday, both as Colonel of the Royal Scots Dragoon Guards (Carabiniers and Greys), and for the Yeomanry.

Memorial to Saint George

Part of the CCOCA Committee's proud responsibilities is to monitor the condition and repair of the Cavalry Memorial erected to Saint George, which is part of their history.

The memorial, near the bandstand in Hyde Park, is unique in that it is the only example in London of a statue in complete armour, the main features being drawn from the effigy of the Earl of Warwick dated 1454. The statue was cast from metal obtained from enemy guns taken by the Cavalry and it was sculpted by Captain Adrian Jones, himself an ex-Life Guardsman. The statue portrays Saint George, the Patron Saint of Cavalry, who, at the moment when having broken his Lance in the dragon and given the coup-de-grace with his sword, reins in his charger and raises his sword high in token of victory. On a bronze panel are inscribed the titles of every Cavalry Regiment of the British Empire that took part in the First World War. Between the columns into which these titles are divided appear four Field Marshals' batons, thus recording the fact that the cavalry arm gained four such honours during the War.

The unveiling was carried out on May 21, 1924, and was attended by Field-Marshal The Earl of Ypres, Earl Haig, Sir William Robertson, their Royal Highnesses Prince Albert, the Prince of Wales, Colonel of the 12th Royal Lancers, and the Duke of Connaught.

Thirty-one Regiments of regular Cavalry, Gunners of RFA batteries, armoured car mechanics, signallers, etc., borrowed swords and again marched proudly forth as Yeomen of the old County Regiments for the unveiling of the Memorial. The Parade moved off headed by the band of the Royal Horse Guards to Stanhope Gate. Here a hollow square was formed. On one side was the Memorial; opposite was the enclosure for ticket holders, the two remaining sides being occupied by officers and other ranks of the parade and the Military Attaches of the Allied Nations. After singing the hymn "O God our help in ages past", the Memorial was unveiled by the Earl of Ypres, who in a brief address touched on the work of the Cavalry during the Great War, especially on the saving of the Channel Ports early in the war, and the rolling up of the Turkish Armies in Palestine in 1918.

There then followed the dedication of the memorial by the Right Reverend Bishop J. Taylor Smith, Chaplain-General to the Forces. The trumpets of The Blues rang out the Cavalry Reveille with its glorious message of hope. The ceremony was completed by the singing of the National Anthem and the laying of wreaths. The first of these, a tribute from the Cavalry of the empire to their fallen comrades, was placed in position by an exceedingly smart, though diminutive, trumpeter of The Blues, followed by HRH the Prince of Wales.

At the conclusion of the Second World War in 1945, it was agreed that the wording on the Memorial Stone should be added to in order to include that war. In 1975 the words "And on Active Service thereafter" were added, in order to commemorate those cavalrymen who have made the supreme sacrifice in the service of their country since the conclusion of the Second World War.

With the widening of Park Lane in 1961, the memorial had to be moved from Stanhope Gate to its presenet location.

THE GALLANTRY MEDALLISTS' LEAGUE
Motto:
"United we stand"

The Distinguished Conduct Medal League was founded in 1931. Prince Edward became its Patron on May 27, 1965. Following the Government review of honours and awards in 1993, the DCM League opened its membership to include all Level 2 awards and became The Gallantry Medallists' League.

Brief history
During the Crimean War the British Government came under pressure from the House of Commons and the Press to recognise the individual acts of gallantry being performed by soldiers of the British Army. While the Order of the Bath had been used to recognise acts of gallantry by officers of field rank or above, no official awards for gallantry existed until the introduction of the Distinguished Conduct Medal (DCM) in 1854.

Today the UK Honours and Awards system recognises distinguished acts of bravery or gallantry of the highest order by members of the civil community and the uniformed services. Recipients will have selflessly placed themselves in jeopardy to protect or save lives and property, often with little concern for their own safety. Decorations and medals for gallantry are not freely given and the importance of the gallantry awards can scarcely be overstated; they are the ultimate public recognition an individual can receive. Gallantry medal recipients, at any level, stand as an example to us all and provide an inspiration to everyone.

Membership

Membership of The Gallantry Medallists' League is now open to all recipients of a Level 2 or Level 3 gallantry award from the UK or Commonwealth; other classes of membership are open to recipient's families as well. These awards have gone to men and women for unselfish acts of great bravery in the UK, the Commonwealth and overseas; they have been made in times of peace and war, and war-like situations. Awards are also made posthumously to those who died whilst showing remarkable courage and placing the interests of others before themselves. The League also recognises that there are many others, both military and civilian, whose selfless acts of courage and heroism are not recorded.

The aims of the League

The main objective of the League is to create, cherish and maintain "esprit de corps" and comradeship amongst League members through the frequent exchange of information and regular meetings on both a formal and social basis. The league is established for the following charitable objects for the public benefit:

> To grant assistance where possible to relieve the need of any Life Member in need or distress by the provision of resources, including care, support, advice and information, which would otherwise have been unavailable to them.
> To advance the education of the public, throughout the UK and Commonwealth, as to the deeds and sacrifices of gallantry medal recipients from the UK and Commonwealth including by recording and making information and relevant materials available for the benefit of this and future generations.

In pursuit of the above objects the League may:

> Organise or assist with the organisation of Parades, Services, Musters and other events for the League members as and when applicable.
> Provide through the medium of a Newsletter and a website, information concerning the deeds and sacrifices of recipients of gallantry medals and the history and activities of the League and a means whereby members can maintain contact with others in the League.

BLETCHLEY PARK TRUST

'The goose that laid the golden eggs and never cackled'.
(Sir Winston Churchill)

In the aftermath of the end of the Second World War in 1945, Britain was dependent upon the United States for a huge loan that had to be repaid in full. There was a chronic shortage of housing, and many children evacuated from the East End of London were still living in the homes of strangers in the countryside, who were taking care of them as their homes had been destroyed in the bombing. There was a food shortage, and rationing was introduced during the war that continued until July 4, 1954. Rationing meant that certain items, be it food, clothing or furniture, were only available by exchanging coupons from a ration book. During the war years, industry and farming had been run mainly by women, who had driven tractors on the farms, gathered potatoes in the fields, and harvested what crops they could manage. In the factories, women had taken the places of men, filling bombs and shells with high explosives, and helping keep other essential services going. The UK economy was bankrupt and would take some years to rebuild. The Government and the people were preoccupied with the long, hard task ahead of getting the country back to normal, which would take many years.

Bletchley Park

It is understandable, therefore, that neither the time nor the money existed to preserve many of our buildings and institutions, which should have been historic landmarks and were left as crumbling ruins or torn down to build blocks of flats and houses. Bletchley Park, near Milton Keynes, Buckinghamshire, which had been established as a code breaking centre in 1938, and referred to only as "Station X", had been one of the most important nerve centres of the war. Here, in total secrecy, existed the United Kingdom's main decryption establishment, the Government Code and Cypher School, (GCCS), having been originally established after the First World War and by which name it was known until 1946. [12]

In a series of code breaking huts, ciphers and codes of several Axis countries were decrypted, and the most important of these were ciphers generated by the Germans. When the Germans were in communication with each other in the army, the navy, and civilian life by radio, the personnel at Bletchley Park intercepted these messages from the German Enigma and Lorenz machines, recorded the information, and put it through Allied code breaking machines, in order to transcribe it into understandable English. Military, economic and diplomatic codes were deciphered. The high-level intelligence produced at Bletchley Park, and codenamed Ultra, provided crucial assistance to the Allied war effort, and is credited with having shortened the war by about two years, thereby saving many thousands of lives. The men and women at "Station X" worked in secrecy to the extent that their own families did not know they were there or what their work involved, and this secrecy continued long after the war's end. A number of 'covers' were invented to explain why someone went out to work in the morning to a job and returned in the evening or worked night shifts. Employees were sworn to secrecy, and if asked about their job they had a story ready, they said their department at Bletchley Park was responsible for awarding medals.

Even before the outbreak of war, Admiral Sir Hugh Sinclair, Director of Naval Intelligence and Head of British Intelligence, MI6, tried to persuade the Government to take over the site for intelligence purposes, but they would not agree. It is believed (though it is not entirely clear) that Sir Hugh purchased the building with his own money for £7,500 or it may have come from a government 'slush fund'. Here, he founded the Government Code and Cypher School. Young men and women were introduced to code breaking and how to carry it out, and this programme of work increased and expanded and became more accurate as the war progressed. Those turning up to work there referred to themselves as 'Captain Ridley's shooting party' as the inhabitants of old country houses were seen regularly out shooting grouse on their estates, and it was an ideal cover. The location was chosen because of its close proximity to the universities of Oxford and Cambridge, that would supply many of the young academics who became code-breakers, and it was also convenient to railways services that would transport them to and from work.

The decoding computer *Colossus* had been designed by engineer Dr Tommy Flowers, with input from Mr Harry Fensom, Mr Allen Coombs, Mr Sid Broadhurst, and Mr Bill Chandler.

Crucial role of Alan Turing

A crucial role was played at Bletchley Park by Mr Alan Mathison Turing, OBE, FRS, (23 June 1912–7 June 1954). Mr Turing was an English mathematician, logician, cryptanalyst, and computer scientist, who had graduated from King's College, Cambridge in 1934, with a first-class honours degree in Mathematics. He was highly influential in the development of computer science. On September 4, 1939, the day after the UK declared war on Germany, Turing had reported to Bletchley Park. He worked there throughout the Second World War, and was initially responsible for German naval cryptanalysis, and he devised a number of techniques for breaking German ciphers. Turing was a genius and a determined and leading participant in the breaking of German ciphers. He concentrated on Cryptanalysis of the Enigma machine along with Mr Alfred Dillwyn 'Dilly' Knox, another senior code breaker. At a meeting in Warsaw in July 1939, the Polish Cipher Bureau had provided the British and French with the details of the wiring of an Enigma machine's rotors and their method of decrypting Enigma messages. (See also Chapter 14) The approach of Alan Turing and Dilly Knox was more general, and they used a straightforward, crib-based decryption for which Turing produced the initial functional specification of the *Bombe,* which was an electromechanical machine that could find settings for the *Enigma* machine. Specifying the Bombe was the first of five major cryptanalytical advances that he made during the war, others would follow. The Bombe was an invaluable electromechanical device used by British cryptologists to help decipher German Enigma-machine-encrypted signals [13] throughout the war.

After the war, Turing received no particular acknowledgement for the work he had carried out nor did others who had worked at Bletchley Park, due to the work being covered by the Official Secrets Act.

In early January 1952 Turing's life took a tragic turn. Following a burglary at the place where he was staying, he admitted to the police that he was homosexual, which in those days was illegal. He was prosecuted and made to undergo severe medical treatment, his homosexuality being diagnosed as a hormonal defect. The drugs interfered with his brilliant brain, and he was in mental turmoil. On June 8, 1954, he committed suicide. The name of Alan Turing remained secret for over thirty years, until it was almost forgotten.

Bletchley Park becomes a conservation area

It was not until the wartime information was declassified in the 1970s that the best-kept British secret began to gradually enter into the public domain.

There are several versions as to how the process to conserve the Bletchley Park site came into being.

Mr Peter Wescombe said that in 1991, he and his wife Rowena went to tea with Dr Peter Jarvis and his wife Sue at their home in Milton Keynes. Dr Jarvis, a local general practitioner, was a member of the Bletchley Archaeological and Historical Society. The possibility of saving Bletchley Park was discussed over tea but at that stage no progress was being made on the matter by Milton Keynes Council. Mr Wescombe suggested a big farewell party at Bletchley Park, to which all the Second World War Codebreakers would be invited. Arriving to arrange it at Bletchley Park Mansion ('The House'), Mr Wescombe was, at his first attempt, escorted off the premises by security. He went back in immediately by climbing through a hole in the fence and entered the house, where he managed to be taken seriously and arranged the party which was to take place in Block E.

In May 1991 Bletchley Archaeological and Historical Society had been formed and their small Committee traced 400 Bletchley Park veterans who attended the party on October 21. Many astonishing stories were told of the wartime code breaking work and other experiences that had taken place there. Veterans were asked if they would support the idea of saving the Park and a consensus was reached. The party was deemed a great success and the Committee continued to meet with a view to the preservation of Bletchley Park for future generations. Plans began to take shape but there was a long, hard road ahead for all who would take part. [14] An enormous peace-time battle ensued to preserve "Station X".

Over the next few years, several steps were taken which proved crucial to the survival of the Park, including a set of protection orders on the trees, which had been planted during the 1880s. The downside, however, was that the interlocking roots of the trees underground meant the planners could not put any road through or put in any infrastructure, and the development was held up. [15]

Bletchley Park Trust is formed

In 1992, a young Milton Keynes Councillor, Mr Sam Crooks, persuaded the Council to declare the house and grounds at Bletchely Park a conservation area. The Bletchley Park Trust was formed immediately in February of that year. "Station X" was now a project to be preserved for historical purposes and, in particular, for those studying and interested in intelligence, and for the population in general, and as a tourist attraction. There was a great deal of work still to be done and, most importantly, funding to be raised.

Mr Tony Sale spearheaded the campaign for the preservation of Bletchley Park, along with Professor Brian Randell of Newcastle University. Dr Tommy Flowers and some design engineers produced academic papers describing the main code-cracking machine, Colossus. Tony was at that time working at the Science Museum in

London, restoring early British computers. He gathered together all the information available, which consisted of eight 1945 wartime photographs taken of Colossus, along with some fragments of circuit diagrams that some engineers had kept. Dr Arnold Lynch, who, in 1942, had originally designed the reader system in Colossus, was still alive. Though now well into his 80s, he went to Tony's house and together they re-engineered the reader system to his original specifications. Tony Sale was then able to get on with the re-build of Colossus.

The Bletchley Park Mansion (again known as "The House", as it had been in wartime) and the huts were gradually becoming a series of museums, run by the Bletchley Park Trust. In 1994 the framework of the museum was in place and it was opened to the public with a selection of codebreaking machines on loan from Government Communications Headquarters (GCHQ). That winter, Mrs Jarvis and Mrs Wescombe helped run the office in one room of "The Bungalow", Park Gardens, assisted by volunteers. Peter Jarvis recalled: 'It was blooming cold in there. We all crammed in there together. We had one small Amstrad computer.' Mrs Jarvis and Mrs Wescombe made sandwiches at home to sell to visitors in the Park, and another lady baked cakes. The volunteers were as enthusiastic as if they were on a crusade. [16]

Bletchley Park reopened by Prince Edward

On Monday July 18, 1994, Prince Edward carried out the re-opening of Bletchley Park. Addressing the Chairman, Lord Lieutenant, and His Excellency Mr Mayor and the assembled guests Prince Edward said:

"I am delighted to be with you today to mark yet another milestone in the fascinating history of Bletchley Park. You, Chairman, as a member, are aware that I am Patron of the British Computer Society, and therefore have a particular interest in both the *Colossus* rebuild project being undertaken here by the computer Conservation Society, and the various exhibitions commemorating the other vital work carried out during the Second World War here at "Station X".

"I have been greatly impressed by all the exhibitions presented by the organisations that are working with the trust in this endeavour. I would normally mention each but the widespread and enthusiastic support for the trust is no better illustrated than by the range of organisations involved here today.

"As General Eisenhowever, Commander-in-Chief Allied Forces Northern Europe, said in a letter to General Menzies in 1945:

'The intelligence which has emanated from you before and during this campaign has been of priceless value to me. It has simplified my task as a commander enormously. It has saved thousands of British and American lives and, in no small way, contributed to the speed with which the enemy was routed and eventually forced to surrender.'

"This sentiment was echoed by President Truman, awarding on behalf of the American nation for the very first time to a non-American citizen, the Order of Merit to Sir Edward Travis for the work undertaken by his staff at Bletchley Park during the Second World War and which is normally awarded to someone who has aided the US during wartime. Having been appointed CBE in 1936, Travis received a knighthood in June 1944.

"There is no doubt that Winston Churchill fully appreciated the value of Bletchley Park's work and the vital contribution it made to the overall war effort when he described it as his 'The goose that laid the golden eggs and never cackled.' I am sure that he, too, would have been fully supportive of the aims and objectives of the trust.

"I congratulate the trust on its beginning and, like you, Mr Chairman, look forward to the creation of the permanent memorial here. I hope that the negotiations between the trust and the current owners rapidly reach a successful conclusion and that you meet your target of a full opening of the Park by the 50th anniversary of VE Day.

"It is with great pleasure that I now unveil this Plaque and announce the opening of the Bletchley Park exhibitions and the start of the Colossus rebuild project."

Prince Edward visits Bletchley Park 1996

On April 1, 1996, Prince Edward, who has a special interest in intelligence gathering efforts, became Patron of the Bletchley Park Trust, and carried out the official opening, although it had already been open to the public at weekends. Tony Sale was still working on Colossus, and some Post Office engineers and others came to assist him. The team of volunteers and helpers had grown in numbers over the years as word got around about the historic significance of "Station X". Tony had Colossus up and running as it had been in wartime. Prince Edward returned on June 6, that year, and personally switched it on.

In 2004 Bletchley Park as a museum was open to the public every day. In 2006 Mr Simon Greenish was appointed the new Director of the Bletchley Park Trust. On June 19, 2007 a statue, specially-commissioned by philanthropist Mr Sidney E. Frank in commemoration of Alan Turing, was unveiled in the grounds. Finally, the great genius who had helped Britain and Sir Winston Churchill win the war was properly recognised.

Prince Edward visits in 2007

In July, 2007 Colossus was finally complete, and Prince Edward visited again. He was joined by such veterans as Jean Valentine, who had worked as an operator on the *Bombe* decryption device in Hut 11, breaking large numbers of Enigma messages, and Ruth Bourne, who received Honorary Membership of the Bombe Rebuilt Team from Mr John Harper. Jean was a member of the Women's Royal Naval Service (WRNS). During the time she worked at Bletchley Park, she lived in Steeple Claydon, Buckinghamshire. She says she started working for pay of fifteen shillings (75 pence) a week. After the war Ruth became manageress of a laundrette, which she preferred as she met more people. She had found the Park rather a lonely, isolated place. Also present were other members of the WRNS, who had worked at "Station X". Dr Tommy Flowers and Mr John Harper were present when Prince Edward officially opened the Bombe Rebuild, which project had taken twelve years to complete, having been led by John Harper. On July 17, 2007, Prince Edward again addressed the assembled crowd at Bletchley Park:

"Today we are celebrating the successful culmination of the British Computer Society Bombe rebuild project. It is exciting to think that John Harper in his riveting account of the rebuild project, told us it has taken 10 years to complete in the hands of a group of enthusiastic and dedicated BCS Conservation Group volunteers under his leadership.

"As is now well-known, although it was one of the most closely-guarded secrets for many years, cracking the Enigma code was crucial to securing victory for the Allies in World War II.

"History rightly acknowledges the role of the famous code breakers and engineers who achieved so much here at Bletchley Park, but they were the tip of the iceberg. Today, we have also been reminded of the contribution of thousands of ordinary servicemen and, especially, the servicewomen, who worked day and night to help decode the Enigma intercepts which flowed into Bletchley. Not only did their commitment save many Allied lives in the North Atlantic convoys and probably the country from starvation, on the D-Day beaches as well, in many other theatres of war but it is reckoned that the intelligence provided as a result may have shortened the war perhaps by as much as two years. Without exaggeration we can say that this work amounted to one of the decisive weapons of World War II.

"The Bombe Rebuild, whose switch-on we mark today, provides a lasting memorial to all those, known and unknown, who worked tirelessly to sustain the flow of essential intelligence to the Allied commanders. Our thanks and congratulations go out to both Bletchley Park and the BCS for ensuring that this vital part of our computer heritage is now preserved for posterity."

Today visitors can see the Bombe in operation at Bletchley Park, exactly as it was during wartime.

Restoring the buildings

There was, however, much still to be done. Little in the way of maintenance had been carried out from the war years, and the actual buildings which had housed the machines and the staff who operated them were dilapidated and in a desperate state of disrepair. The code breaking huts were rotting and the iconic Bletchley Park (Mansion) House was leaking through the roof.

Dr Sue Black a Senior Research Associate in the Software Systems Engineering group in the Department of Computer Science at University College London, who was a winner of the John Invinson Award, paid the museum a visit. From July 2008

Sue joined in the campaign to save Bletchley Park. That November, English Heritage came to the rescue and stepped in with investment of £330,000 to carry out the repairs. They would provide a further £100,000 per year for three years to carry out a backlog of maintenance work. In 2009 Milton Keynes Council put it to a public vote as to whether the Council should provide the required funding and the result was an overwhelming 'Yes'.

Bletchley Park, thanks to the Bletchley Park Trust set up in 1992, has been saved for the nation. The high profile afforded to the Bletchley Park story by the awarding of GCHQ commemorative badges in 2009, and an ever-increasing media profile thanks to programmes including the Antiques Roadshow, Timewatch, and The Bletchley Circle, has all helped to bolster wider interest from both visitors and investors. [17]

In 2011 the trust was successful in securing £4.6 million in Heritage Lottery Funding, along with £2.4 million in match funding from other sources. This money will be spent transforming Bletchley Park into a world-class heritage site and education centre, and allow the trust to restore some of the iconic wartime Huts and Blocks which have fallen into dereliction. The trust is no longer focused on day-to-day survival of the Park but is looking forward to a bright and exciting future. [18]

Women employed at Bletchley Park
Women working at Bletchley Park constituted over 80 per cent of the staff, outnumbering men by around 3 to 1 during the war years. Women were employed in all areas of operations, a progressive step in the UK of the 1940s. Some were code breakers working in cryptography. Others were in the WRNS, working in radio communications and in the secret listening service, and as clerical workers. Members of the Women's Auxiliary Air Force, (WAAF), were working as cooks and cleaners.

Commemorative Badge for veterans
On July 9 2009 Mr David Miliband, the then Labour Government's Foreign Secretary, announced that all surviving military and civilian veterans, who had served at Bletchley Park and its outstations, were eligible for a commemorative badge. In an ironic twist, the staff that had used as a cover for their secret work during the war that they awarded medals were now themselves to be honoured. The award of a badge is a fitting recognition of the vital role played by the Government Code and Cypher School during the war years. It is thought that up to 12,000 people worked at Bletchley Park, and many more in the outstations across the country. When the war ended, records were destroyed to preserve secrecy. Now a request was put out for those who worked there to come forward and the surviving 5,000 former employees qualified for a badge.

Prince Edward visits 2009
On July 16, 2009 a Veterans Commemorative Badge Launch Ceremony was held at Bletchley Park, where Prince Edward met some of the veterans. He also unveiled a painting, which featured some of the men and women who worked there. He visited

the National Museum of Computing [19], where he presented long-service awards to volunteers, and Tony Sale received two awards. The museum is located in the grounds and is dedicated to collecting and restoring historic computer systems. Having been opened in 2007, the actual building Block H was the first purpose-built computer centre in the world, hosting six Colossus computers by the end of the Second World War. The museum houses a rebuilt Colossus Mark 2 computer, an exhibition of the most complex code cracking activities performed during the war, and examples of machines continuing the history of the development of computing from the 1940s to the present day. Also on display are many famous early computing era machines, the Colossus rebuild project and related machines, and the museum is open to visitors seven days a week.

The Queen unveils a memorial

Bletchley Park has also been delighted to welcome several high profile visitors in recent years, including Her Majesty Queen Elizabeth II, His Royal Highness The Prince of Wales, and Mr Roger Moore, the star of the James Bond spy thriller movies, which has helped visitor numbers to soar, contributing to the trust's financial security. [20]

On July 15, 2011 the Queen unveiled a memorial at Bletchley Park. It consists of two eight feet high slabs of Caithness stone interlinked at the top. It signifies the mutual reliance of those that worked at Bletchley Park and those that intercepted enemy transmissions at the 'Outstations'. One block displays the wording: 'We also served', and the other contains a sculpted list of some of the 300 plus outstations that existed across the world. There is also a Morse code message engraved on the back of the memorial, which says: 'My Most Secret Source'. This was one of Churchill's famous expressions wherein he described the value of 'Ultra' intelligence, obtained from the decryption of Enigma intercepts. A stone on which Sir Winston Churchill stood to address a gathering there is preserved on the lawn opposite the front door of the Mansion.

On February 23, 2012 Bletchley Park Post Office issued four limited edition first day cover stamps to celebrate Alan Turing's centenary year. The Alan Turing Year, 2012, marks the celebration of the life and scientific influence of Alan Turing on the occasion of the centenary of his birth on 23 June 1912. Turing's important contribution to code-breaking, and the development of computing, was officially recognised at last.

Miss Katherine Lynch, Media Manager, says:

"The Bletchley Park Trust, is hugely grateful to the thousands of supporters who, over the last 20 years, have given their time, faith, energy, and enthusiasm to the cause of saving Bletchley Park and transforming it into the vibrant tourist attraction with an extremely bright future that it is today. The Trust, having celebrated its 21st birthday in 2012, endeavours to recognise the enormous collaborative effort that spanned nearly two decades." [21]

Today, the aim is to turn the Bletchley Park complex into a world-class heritage site and education centre.

NATIONAL ARMY MUSEUM

The National Army Museum (NAM) is the British Army's central museum. It is located in Chelsea, London, adjacent to the Royal Hospital Chelsea, the home of the Chelsea Pensioners. The current Chairman of Council (2014) is General Sir Richard Shirreff KCB CBE, formerly the British Army's Deputy Supreme Allied Commander, Europe.

The National Army Museum relates the overall history of the British Army, British colonial, imperial and commonwealth forces, and the British Indian Army as a whole, from 1066 to the present day and its effects on national and international history.

The Museum was first conceived in the late 1950s, and owes its existence to the persistent hard work of Field Marshal Sir Gerald Walter Robert Templer who was its first director and after whom the museum's study centre is named. It was established by Royal Charter in 1960, with the intention of preserving and exhibiting items related to the history of the forces of the British Army and to Commonwealth nations prior to their independence. Its displays having been originally housed at the Royal Military Academy, Sandhurst, were moved into the present building in 1971.

Prince Edward became Patron of the National Army Museum on January 1, 1977. He has made a number of visits to the museum over the years, meeting with staff and stakeholders alike. On Thursday October 16, 2003, he officially opened the Crimean War (1854-56) Special Exhibition; a function he carries out at every opportunity.

In addition, he is also very supportive of the museum's future plans as part of its Building for the Future project. The Museum closed in April 2014, whilst a major refurbishment project was being undertaken and it is due to reopen in 2016.

Prior to the temporary closure, the museum's main exhibition space on the ground floor housed displays on a variety of subjects. These have included Helmand: The Soldiers' Story, held from August 2007 to August 2009, on soldiers' current experiences in Helmand province during the conflict in Afghanistan; War Boy: The Michael Foreman Exhibition, was held from September 2009 to August 2010, showing original artwork by Michael Foreman on themes from the First and Second World Wars, alongside medals won by Foreman's family, and objects from the museum's own collection; the 2010-2011 exhibition titled The Road to Kabul: British Armies in Afghanistan, 1838 – 1919, focused on the First, Second, and Third Afghan Wars, as well as a display of watercolours of the conflict in Afghanistan by Matthew Cook. These were followed, from October 2011 to April 2013, by an exhibition entitled War Horse: Fact & Fiction, exploring the Michael Morpurgo novel of that name, alongside real-life stories of horses involved in war and the men who depended on them, and drawing also on the play and film adaptations of the novel.

Prince Edward visits in 2011

On November 16, 2011 Prince Edward visited the museum. In his address to the museum's then Chairman of Council, General Sir Jack Deverell KCB OBE, Miss Janice Murray, Director General, and guests, he said:

"Let me first of all say what a great pleasure it is once again to be able to come to the wonderful National Army Museum. I have been lucky enough to have been its Patron ever since it was first established in the 1960's by the indefatigable Field Marshal Gerald Templer, whose brain child this truly was and it is an organisation in which I have taken a great interest and have much admired ever since.

"I hope you all enjoyed looking at the exhibition entitled War Horse. I have found it fascinating and I particularly enjoyed seeing the painting contributed by The Duchess of Cornwall of Sefton, who you may remember was the Household Cavalry horse which made an almost miraculous recovery, having been very seriously injured by an IRA bomb in 1982.

"The museum of course means more than exhibitions. First of all, it has an enormous collection of well over one million items going back to 1415, and as well as that it is dedicated to education and research projects. All that it does with great passion and great academic vigour, and as you have been hearing it also has very bold plans for the future. I think it is actually rather astonishing if one reflects that there was no museum dedicated exclusively to the Army until this one started in the 1960's and therefore we should all value it the more highly for the way it recognises and describes the history of the British Army which has played such a crucial and central role in the history of this country, helping to shape the world and the society that we live in today. So as you have heard there are ambitious plans for the future which have been outlined by General Deverell and the Director.

"The important thing is the history presented by the museum and this project, which you have heard outlined, is going to bring considerable new life to this story, and is intended to transform the existing facilities into a museum truly fit for the 21st century.

"But, needless to say, and there always is a 'but' on these occasions, we can't do this alone. The National Army Museum will need the support of all of you and so we hope that you will read the literature that you will be handed at the end of the evening and perhaps speak to members of the staff, and if you feel that you are able to help in any way, then that will be immensely appreciated because it is only with your time and whole-hearted support that we can fully realise our goals.

"Thank you all very much indeed and I am most grateful to you for coming here this evening."

Prince Edward visits in 2012

On November 28, 2012 Prince Edward attended an NAM fundraising event and dinner hosted by the Chief of the General Staff of the British Army, Sir Peter Wall. Addressing the assembly Prince Edward welcomed everyone and said:

"...As Janice [Murray] has so clearly explained this is an organisation which is so constantly striving for excellence and I believe that its ambitious plans for the future will create a Museum which is fit for the 21st century.

"The National Army Museum ... maintains a huge collection of more than one million items from the time of the Battle of Agincourt to the present day and is dedicated to education and research projects. The Museum carries out its task with great resolve and vigour, but it is also determined to remain fully in step with developments in the Army world, and hence its bold plans for the future. I don't think any of us would argue with the thought that we need to recognise the unique role which the British Army has played in the history of this country and indeed in helping to shape the society in which we live today. This new development project is going to extend the scope of the museum's coverage right up to the present day, and is going to transform the existing facilities, I believe, in a very exciting way.

"But in order to carry out these ambitious plans the museum needs your support. I am grateful to you for sparing the time to come to this evening's event, but I hope that you will now either speak to Jack Deverell or to Janice and perhaps read the literature which you will be given at the end of the evening. If you feel you can help in any way, then would you please contact our Development Manager after the event, because it is only through your time and wholehearted support that we shall be able to realise these essential goals.

"I have no doubt that the redevelopment museum is going to be a fitting home for this remarkable collection and I entirely endorse the plans which have been presented today."

THE CHELSEA PENSIONERS' APPEAL
THE ROYAL HOSPITAL CHELSEA

The historical land mark of the Royal Hospital, Chelsea, London, which houses the Chelsea pensioners, is set on the north bank of the River Thames, and comprises Grade I listed buildings designed by Sir Christopher Wren and Sir John Soane.

A Chelsea pensioner

A Chelsea pensioner is an in-pensioner, living at the Royal Hospital, Chelsea, London, which is a retirement home and nursing home for former members of the British Army. Admission is subject to the applicant being free from the obligation to support a wife, partner, or family. The phrase in-pensioner originally applied to two types of pensioner: those living in the hospital and those living in their own home, known later as out-pensioners.

Brief history and status of the Royal Hospital

During the reign of King Charles II, the Royal Hospital was still under construction, so in 1689 the King introduced a system for the distribution of army pensions. The pension

141. HRH The Duke of Kent with Chelsea Pensioners at the Imperial War Museum, London, opening the exhibition titled 'Monty: Master of the Battlefield', September 25, 2002.

was to be made available to all former soldiers who had been injured in service, or who had served for more than twenty years. By the time the hospital was completed, there were more pensioners than places available. Eligible ex-soldiers who could not be housed in the hospital were termed 'out-pensioners', receiving their pension from the Royal Hospital. In-pensioners, by contrast, surrendered their army pension, and lived within the Royal Hospital, and so it continues today. In return, they receive board, lodging, clothing, and full medical care. Upon arrival at the Royal Hospital, each in-pensioner is given a berth, which is a small room, 9 feet x 9 feet, (3 metres by 3 metres) in a ward, and is allocated to a company. The size of the hospital berths has increased over time and there are now 18 berths to a ward.

In 1703 there were only 51 out-pensioners but, by 1815, this figure had risen to 36,757. The Royal Hospital remained responsible for distributing army pensions until 1955, following which the term out-pensioner became less common, and the term 'Chelsea pensioner' was used, largely to refer to an in-pensioner.

The Royal Hospital today

Today the Royal Hospital can accommodate up to 280 former soldiers as pensioners living in, who have decided to surrender their military pension to the Treasury in return for accommodation, food, uniform clothing, professional care, and medical attention when they need it.

In-pensioners may wear civilian clothes outside of the hospital but within, they are encouraged to wear a blue uniform. If they travel further from the hospital or appear at a special event they should wear the traditional scarlet coats for which they are now quite famous. On ceremonial occasions a tricorne hat is added to the apparel. When in uniform, they wear their medal ribbons and the insignia of the rank they reached while serving in the military and other insignia, and some wear parachute jump wings or SAS jump wings. Chelsea Football Club has for many years been affiliated with the Pensioners.

Admission of women

In 2007 the policy allowing only male candidates into the hospital was changed, and it was announced that female ex-service personnel would be admitted. In order to accommodate them modernisation of some wards was required. The first woman, Dorothy Hughes, aged 85, was admitted in March 2009, as an in-pensioner. On arrival, Dorothy told the press that she felt like Cinderella at the ball. She was soon followed by Winifred Phillips, aged 82. Dorothy had joined the army in 1941, and eventually worked as part of 450 Heavy Anti-Aircraft Battery in the London Division. In 1945 the Battery was deployed near Dover to defend against VI rocket attacks. Winifred had trained as a nurse, and, in 1948, joined the Auxiliary Territorial Service. She later served in Egypt, and enlisted in the Women's Royal Army Corps in 1949. Following 22 years service, Winifred retired with the rank of Warrant Officer Class 2.

The Royal Hospital Chelsea launched the Chelsea Pensioners' Appeal in 2004 to fund the biggest development campaign in the Hospital's history. Prince Edward became their Royal Vice-Patron on February 3 that year. The Hospital received a major donation of £50,000 from the Freemason's Grand Charity to commemorate Prince Edward's 40th anniversary (2007) as Grand Master. On behalf of the Royal Hospital, Chelsea Pensioners Gordon 'Sandy' Sanders and Arthur Barrow made a joint speech of thanks to Prince Edward and the assembly. The money was used to help in the completion costs of the new Margaret Thatcher Infirmary, within the main Hospital grounds. In September 2013, Lady Thatcher's ashes were interred in the hospital grounds.

The architects of the new building retained the design of the original, late 17th-century design of the Hospital by Sir Christopher Wren, including the Doric portico. Opened in January 2009, the Infirmary can accommodate 125 people. It has produced high-specification healthcare capabilities, and provided an effective, modern healing environment. The sense of community and shared experience that had continued with the residents throughout their history with the Army are enshrined in its design.

For the pensioners the communal areas are the focal points of day-to-day life, with corridors designed as streetscapes. This familiarity of design, retained from the original Hospital building, helps maintain a smooth transition for In-Pensioners, moving into the Infirmary. Each In-Pensioner has a bedroom with an en suite bathroom, which was crucial to allowing ladies to be admitted for the first time in the Hospital's history. There are lots of communal areas for pensioners to meet with visitors, and all rooms are spacious. There is a medical centre on the ground floor that all pensioners have access to with two medical General Practitioners available and a team of multi-disciplined professionals. There are four units: Paget, Nicholson,

Campbell and Jones, two of which are used for nursing care, and two for residential use.

Outdoors, there is a lawn and beautiful gardens, famed for their profusion of spring daffodils. The Royal Hospital is an idyllic and interesting retirement place for those who served their country well.

But there is always more work to be done to meet the costs of further improvements to the pensioners' living accommodation. With this in mind, seven gallant Pensioners released an album on November 8, 2010, to raise funds through the Chelsea Pensioners' Appeal. Featuring the wartime forces favourite, Dame Vera Lynn DBE, the album is full of well-known wartime songs, including the soldiers' traditional march, The Old Brigade. Also featured along with the soldiers is the famous Welsh classical singer, Katherine Jenkins OBE, and the 80-year-old Glaswegian grandmother, and darling of Britain's Got Talent, Janey Cutler, who stunned the audience with her rendition of Edith Pief's iconic ballad, No Regrets.

Endnotes to Chapter 19

[1] *HAC Journal*, Vol. 84, No. 472 (Spring 2007). The journal of the Honourable Artillery Company.

[2] *HAC Journal*, Vol.44, No.364 (June 1967).

[3] Dr Patrick Mileham (OW), author of *Wellington College: The First 150 Years*; pub. 2008.

[4] Mr Robin Dyer Second Master of Wellington College has provided the material on the College for the authors.

[5] Ibid.

[6] The Advance Party Report was not welcomed by all members and a rival report, *The Black Report*, was produced in 1970 by The Scout Action Group. This provided alternative proposals for the development of the Movement and asked for Groups that wished to continue to follow Baden-Powell's original scheme to be permitted to do so. The rejection of these proposals resulted in the formation of the Baden-Powell Scouts' Association.

[7] The museum is an exempt charity under the Charities Act 1993 and a non-departmental public body under the Department for Culture, Media and Sport.

[8] Quotations by kind permission of the IWM, London.

[9] Field Marshal Bernard Law Montgomery, 1st Viscount Montgomery of Alamein, KG, GCB, DSO, PC (17 November 1887 – 24 March 1976), nicknamed "Monty"

was a British Army officer. On May 4, 1945, Montgomery took the German surrender at Luneburg Heath in northern Germany.

[10] Sir Chief Marshal Graham Eric "Jock" Stirrup, Baron Stirrup, GCB, AFC, FRAeS, FCMI (born 4 December 1949), is a former senior Royal Air Force commander, who was the Chief of the Defence Staff from 2006 until his retirement in late 2010. He is now a Crossbench member of the House of Lords.

[11] North Atlantic Treaty Organisation.

[12] After that time the name became Government Communications Headquarters (GCHQ), a British intelligence agency, responsible for providing signals intelligence (SIGINT) and information assurance to the UK government and armed forces. Today, based in Cheltenham, it operates under the guidance of the Joint Intelligence Committee.

[13] The US Navy and US Army later produced machines to the same functional specification, but engineered differently.

[14] Bletchley Park news, *21 Years of The Bletchley Park Trust*, published December 3rd 2012.

[15] Ibid.

[16] Ibid.

[17] Material provided by Miss Katherine Lynch, Media Manager, Bletchley Park Trust, March 7, 2013.

[18] Ibid.

[19] Despite being on the same site at Bletchley Park, The National Museum of Computing is an entirely separate charity with its own fund raising. TNMOC receives no lottery funding and relies on the generosity of donors and supporters. The museum also includes a number of machines from the 1960s, 1980s, and up to 2009.

[20] Miss Katherine Lynch Op cit.

[21] Ibid.

CHAPTER 20

COMMONWEALTH WAR GRAVES COMMISSION

"At the going down of the sun and in the
morning we will remember them." (Laurence Binyon)

In 1915 a Graves Registration Commission, under Fabian Ware, began its grim work in France and Flanders. The desire for a permanent record of the sacrifices being made by so many led to a Royal Charter on May 20, 1917, establishing The Imperial War Graves Commission (IWGC). (The name was modernised in 1960 to the Commonwealth War Graves Commission (CWGC).

There was early controversy over the decision to commemorate the war dead in situ but in a memorable House of Commons debate the Commission's new Chairman, Winston Churchill, made a powerful speech calling for cemeteries that would endure "in periods as remote from our own as we ourselves are from the Tudors" and he established the important principle of equality of remembrance of the sacrifice of all ranks and social classes. King George V set out the guiding message of the Commission's work in a speech in 1922:

"We remember, and must charge our children to remember, that, as our dead were equal in sacrifice, so they were equal in honour, for the greatest and the least of them have proved that sacrifice and honour are no vain things, but truths by which the world lives".

Quite quickly the beautiful and serene nature of the cemeteries and memorials established itself and the pattern spread throughout the world.

The IWGC was just completing its work relating to the First World War (with over a million commemorations) when the Second World War broke out, adding over 600,000 new names to the lists of the war dead. Today the Commonwealth War Graves Commission administers to some 1.7 million dead (from the Crimean War to the most recent conflicts) in 23,237 burial grounds and memorials in 148 countries. The cost is borne in proportion to their casualty lists by the governments of the

142. HRH The Duke of Kent talking to a Crete veteran onthe 60th anniversary of the Battle of Crete, May 2001.

United Kingdom, India, Canada, Australia, New Zealand, and South Africa, and so on through the smaller Commonwealth states. Their primary task is to mark the graves of known war dead, to build memorials to those known to have died who have no known graves, and to keep records and registers of the dead. The work is one of constant care and maintenance that goes on, quite literally, in perpetuity. The responsibility ranges from the 304,437 dead remembered in 12,367 sites in the United Kingdom, the 574,887 at 2,914 sites in France, and the 204,810 at 614 sites in Belgium, to the single graves tended in the Canary Islands, Costa Rica, Guatemala, Honduras, Martinique, Nepal, Puerto Rico, Saudi Arabia, Togo and Venezuela. The heavy presence of the war dead in Egypt, Germany, India, Iraq, Italy, Kenya, Myanmar (Burma), The Netherlands, Pakistan, Singapore, Tanzania, and Turkey reads like a gazeteer of the Commonwealth's military history.

It is a proud boast of the Commission that it has been served as its President by an unbroken line of Royal Princes. The Prince of Wales (later King Edward VIII, and Duke of Windsor), himself a staff officer during the war and influential in its creation, served the IWGC from 1917 to 1936. The Duke of York (King George VI) served briefly in 1936/37, and was followed by the Duke of Gloucester from 1937 to 1970. Prince Edward The Duke of Kent has been the serving President since February 27, 1970.

Prince Edward's army career and flair for languages equipped him well for the role of President of the Commonwealth War Graves Commission, which post he has now held for over 45 years. In 1976 he became Vice-Chairman of the British Overseas Trade Board (BOTB) later British Trade International (BTI), (see Chapter 3). As an important adviser to the government of the day on the promotion of overseas trade and export he travelled widely which was to also play a major role in his work for the Commonwealth War Graves Commission.

143. HRH The Duke of Kent with Admiral Sir Michael Boyce, attending at Crete on the 60th anniversary of the Battle of Crete, May 2001.

In 1999 Prince Edward had this to say about his approach to his CWGC work:

"In the course of my travels as President of the Commonwealth War Graves Commission, I have often had cause to reflect on the scale of loss suffered during the two World Wars. The Commission cares for war cemeteries and memorial in no less than 145 countries, where one and three quarter million Commonwealth servicemen and women lie buried or are commemorated on memorials to the missing.

"But although such appalling large numbers are involved, it is always the individual we remember; each one by name. the names, the ages, the personal inscriptions chosen by relatives all go to make each cemetery a poignant and eloquent testimonial to the human cost of war; the loss of husbands, wives, parents and children.

"In our task of commemorating those who gave their lives we strive to make the war cemeteries oases where visitors may pause to recollect. And looking to the future, these memorials will remind generations yet to come not only of the suffering of war, of the striving together against a multitude of hardships, but also of the need to work tirelessly for a free and peaceful world."

Prince Edward has undertaken 21 major tours of several days duration for the Commission – to France in 1976, 1991 and 2006, Italy in 1980 and 2009, Turkey and Egypt in 1983, Germany, the Netherlands and Belgium in 1985, Greece and

Cyprus in 1987, Belgium in 1988, Tunisia and Sicily in 1990, Hong Kong in 1991, Ethiopia, Kenya and Tanzania in 1993, India, Sri Lanka and Pakistan in 1995, Russia in 2002, Egypt for the 60th anniversary of El Alamein in 2002, Libya in 2004 Cyprus in 2007, Turkey in 2009, Ireland in 2013 and 2014, and Australia in 2015. In addition he has represented the Commission or the Royal Family at a further 40 memorial events between 1984 and 2015, often marking important anniversaries in both world wars. But wherever he was in the world, usually on travels relating to his work for the BOTB/BTI, he would always try to see the nearest CWGC site or office, engendering a further 26 visits between 1971 and 2000, in places as far apart as Denmark and Poland, and Japan and Malaysia, and many more since then.

The major tours were organised with a military precision that would have been entirely familiar to Prince Edward. Months before the trip the planning covered the itinerary, timed to the minute, details of the occupants of each car, of all the places to be visited (with special notes provided of each cemetery or memorial, with particular reference to the several regiments with which the Duke was personally associated), and of the people to be met, including ambassadors, military attaché's, local dignitaries and CWGC staff. The planning for the extended business and official CWGC trip to India, Sri Lanka and Pakistan in March – April 1995, began in March 1994! These could be punishing schedules: the 1976 visit to France has him landing at Carpiquet Airport, Caen at 2.15 pm, visiting five British and Canadian cemeteries in the next three hours before an evening reception in Caen. The next day sees a further five visits, including American and German cemeteries, before flying on to the Pas de Calais. The third day sees eight visits to offices, cemeteries and memorials in the Arras, Somme and Amiens areas, meeting the New Zealand, South African and Australian Ambassadors and Indian military figures at places of significant importance to each of those nations, before flying home at 6 pm. The five-day visit to Italy in 1980 would include 19 visits to cemeteries and one to the CWGC Area office, two official receptions, six connecting flights within Italy (between Salerno in the south and the Asiago plateau in the north) and one day's rest! As part of the Turkey and Egypt tour in 1983, he would visit 18 Gallipoli sites in the space of 24 hours. The long trip in 1993 to East Africa remembered the fallen in the protracted 1914-18 campaigns to conquer the German colonies, and the expulsion of the Italians from Abyssinia in 1941. Prince Edward commented favourably on the remarkable job done by the gardeners in areas where the water supply could never be taken for granted.

His long military career, and a deep interest in military history, makes him a particularly fine representative at the many ceremonies and visits he attends. He fully appreciates the importance of anniversaries for stimulating interest in the work of the CWGC – he was at the Thiepval Memorial to the Missing for the 70th (1986) and 75th (1991) anniversaries of the Somme.

At the latter service he paid special attention to the 35 veterans able to attend, and showed special concern for those feeling unwell on the day. He was at the Menin Gate, Ypres, for the 70th anniversary of the end of the Great War (1988), "a very special day" in his own words, where he would attend long ceremonies in the morning,

*144. HRH The Duke of Kent attending the
anniversary of D Day at Normandy, June 2004.*

including planting a new tree at St. George's Church, and insist on seeing three cemeteries after lunch before flying home. Other visits to mark significant anniversaries included Singapore 1985, Crete 1991, El Alamein 1992 and 2002, and Monte Cassino and Normandy 1994. The military history of the location was always of interest and, with his wide knowledge of the subject, Prince Edward would set high standards to be followed. Some anxious military officers had to 'mug up' on Montgomery's Tunisian campaign to do a battlefield presentation to him between a visit to Enfidaville Cemetery and a meeting with the President of Tunisia at Carthage!

Especially poignant are some of the smaller ceremonies, where Prince Edward represents both the Commission and one of the regiments with which he is associated. When 27 bodies were discovered near Monchy-le-Preux in 1996, he, as Colonel-in-Chief of the Royal Regiment of Fusiliers, with family members and serving soldiers of the regiment, was able to attend the burial of two Royal Fusiliers "in an extremely moving funeral". Again as the Colonel-in-Chief, he attended the burial of Fusilier Harry Wilkinson on November 1, 2001 at Prowse Point Cemetery, near Ypres. Wilkinson had been killed on November 10, 1914 and hastily buried by his comrades near the edge of Ploegsteert Wood ('Plug Street' to the British Tommies) in Belgium. He was found there, with his ID tags, 87 years later by a local man. It is fitting and proper that these men are honoured as if they had died but yesterday; the CWGC exists to remember them forever and they will never be forgotten.

*145. HRH The Duke of Kent attending
the dedication of Zehrensdorf Indian Cemetery,
Germany, October 29, 2005.*

Any lengthy tour on behalf of the British Overseas Trade Board (now British Trade International) would incorporate as many visits to local CWGC sites as possible. This aspect of Prince Edward's work is so important to him that it is often made without any direct involvement of the CWGC and they are, of course, deeply grateful for the extent to which he goes out of his way to carry out these duties.

A visit to Norway in February 1989 illustrates how he maximises his time during a business trip. It is also to be remembered that the important functions Prince Edward carried out for the British Overseas Trade Board and the Commonwealth War Graves Commission were entirely unsalaried. Everything is planned to keep expenses to a minimum and multi-tasking on each visit helps towards that goal, as well as contributing to the modern concept of reducing one's carbon footprint. After a scheduled visit to one of his regiments, 2nd Battalion Royal Regiment of Fusiliers, on their winter training grounds at Voss in Norway, he flew to Oslo on February 8, 1989. On February 9 he laid a wreath at the Vestre Gravlund cemetery, on behalf of the CWGC but without any prior knowledge by them, and then went into an intensive series of meetings all day with Norwegian business men, while still finding time to lunch with King Olav and other members of the Norwegian royal family and meet the Oslo (St. George's) Scout Group in the afternoon. After a black tie dinner for the Norwegian business community that evening, he prepared for another busy day of museum visits and business meetings on February 10 before returning to the UK. (A purely BOTB visit to Budapest in May 1988 also saw an 'unscheduled' visit to the Solymar CWGC cemetery where Prince Edward congratulated the local gardeners on the huge improvements they had made to the site).

In October 1993 an appointment to open a new Fisons plant in Singapore could be timed to allow a visit to Kranji Cemetery first; a meeting with the Federation of Malaysian Manufacturers in Kuala Lumpur would permit the Cheras Road Cemetery to be seen. This unceasing concern to pay his respects to the fallen and to the untiring and dedicated local staff caring for them makes Prince Edward such a valued ambassador for the Commission. At the end of a busy four days of trade and royal functions in Thailand in October 1994, he took a memorable afternoon to visit two cemeteries associated with the notorious 'Death Railway', Kanchanaburi and Chungkai, where over 8,500 Commonwealth and Dutch prisoners are buried. At Chungkai, after a short service of remembrance, he spoke personally to the five gardeners working there, who must have heard with special pride that this highly travelled President thought it "the most beautiful cemetery I have ever visited."

Prince Edward's visits could have important diplomatic consequences for the work of the Commission. The lengthy preparations for a busy trip to Tunisia in 1990 stimulated the successful conclusion of protracted negotiations over a War Graves Agreement. While planning a trade mission to Moscow and Leningrad in 1991, Prince Edward immediately thought to include a visit to the lonely cemeteries at Archangel and Murmansk. Though the trip had to be cancelled, the preparations for it led to a good deal of restoration at, and a renewed local interest in, these hard to visit places.

In July 2002 an official visit to Russia allowed Prince Edward and Mr Richard Kellaway, Director-General of the CWGC, to honour the work done at Murmansk and Archangel. The Foreign and Commonwealth Office briefing written for this tour reminds us what an optimistic time that was in Anglo-Russian relations. It remarked on the high popularity of the 'reforming' President, Vladimir Putin, and the keen approach of Russia to bilateral activity with the UK. A Naval Co-operation Programme had already seen exchange visits between warships. There was a brief history of the military operations against the Bolsheviks in 1918-19, and Prince Edward was even told that the governor of Murmansk "liked fishing, football and volleyball". The two sites, remembering 606 British war dead, had improved enormously over the last few years. Attention was drawn to the 58 Royal Fusiliers, including the Victoria Cross winner, Sergeant S. G. Pearse, remembered there, and five men of the Devonshire Regiment.

146. HRH The Duke of Kent laying a wreath at
Lembet Road military cemetery, Salonika, Greece, July 13, 2012.

147. HRH The Duke of Kent at Benghazi cemetery, November, 2004.

A business trip to the three Baltic states in 1993 also brought back onto the agenda the fate of small First World War cemeteries that had been impossible to maintain during the Soviet era and were not covered by War Graves Agreements with the new Russian Federation. New work is going on in Latvia, Lithuania, and Estonia to remember the fallen there.

The work of the Commission is beset with difficulties in many ways and their task of eternal vigilance can never relax. During the terrible civil wars in the Lebanon the war cemeteries there were almost completely destroyed. But as soon as the fighting ended the Commission began its work again and, during the 1990s, Beirut War Cemetery has been completely restored. For obvious reasons the care and maintenance of graves in Iraq has been impossible for some time but we can be sure that plans already exist so that the moment relations are normalised, the work of restoration will begin. During all the frequent troubles in Israel and Gaza, the dedicated staff of the Commission continue their noble tradition of care and attention to the memorials to the fallen.

In this respect the visit to Libya in November 2004 was significant. Although verbal assurances were given by the Libyan Prime Minister in January 1954, "that the cemeteries are regarded as sacred", there had never been any formal documentation regarding the protection of the four important sites in that country, holding some 8,500 Commonwealth war dead. Once again a political 'rapprochement' with Libya in the early 2000's led to a revival of interest in these sites and much improved work on their care and maintenance. All four cemeteries were visited between November 8 and 12, as were the British School, and the Jamahariya Museum in Tripoli.

As well as this careful attention to overseas sites, Prince Edward carries out numerous duties in the United Kingdom associated with the moving international

Brookwood Military Cemetery in Surrey, the Air Forces memorial at Runnymede, the National Arboretum at Cannock Chase, Staffordshire, and with the annual services conducted by the Commission. He attends every Remembrance Sunday service at the Cenotaph as President of the Commission. In March 1972 he was able to inaugurate the fine new headquarters of the Commission in Maidenhead, and he is a frequent visitor there, encouraging the work as it moves into the electronic communication age in its constant quest to keep alive the interest of the nation in the last resting places of its war dead. The launch of the Debt of Honour Register on the Internet has been an astounding world-wide success; it currently receives 250,000 'visits' a week.

CWGC's 85th Anniversary 2002

The year 2002 marked the 85th anniversary of the work of the Commonwealth War Graves Commission. The granting of the Royal Charter was celebrated on May 21, at a reception at St. James's Palace, where Prince Edward was in attendance. Besides the important visit to Russia in July, there was a special ceremony at Ieper (Ypres) in Belgium to mark the 75th anniversary of the unveiling of the Menin Gate Memorial to the Missing.

Prince Edward possesses that happy and royal ability to make whomsoever he meets in conversation feel both at ease and to be engaged with someone with a deep and abiding interest in the work of remembrance. To serving soldiers, veterans of past conflict, families of the fallen, and to the staff of the Commonwealth War Graves Commission he is a constant source of good-natured inspiration. With all his heart he believes in the importance of Laurence Binyon's immortal lines: "At the going down of the sun, and in the morning, we will remember them".

148. HRH The Duke of Kent wearing
Field Marshal's uniform during a visit to El Alamein, 2002.

517

*149. HRH The Duke of Kent attending an iterment at
the new CWGC cemetery at Fromelles, France, July 19 2010.*

A major project of the CWGC that received the enthusiastic support of Prince
Edward was the appeal to build a new Visitor Centre at Thiepval, in Picardy, and he
was prominent in the official opening of the completed centre in September 2004.

The Thiepval Memorial is a major war memorial to the missing who died in
the Battles of the Somme between 1915 and1918, and for whom there is no known
grave. Designed by Sir Edwin Lutyens, the memorial was built between 1928 and
1932, and is the largest British battle memorial in the world. It has 16 piers of red
Accrington brick, faced with Portland stone, and is 46 metres (150 feet) high, with
foundations 6 metres (19 feet) thick which was required due to extensive wartime
tunnelling beneath the structure. Edward, Prince of Wales (later King Edward VIII),
carried out the inauguration in the presence of Albert Lebrun, President of France,
on August 1, 1932.

The missing
The names of the missing are engraved on the memorial. A large inscription on an
internal surface of the memorial reads:

> 'Here are recorded names of officers and men of the British Armies who
> fell on the Somme battlefields between July 1915 and March 1918 but to
> whom the fortune of war denied the known and honoured burial given to
> their comrades in death.'

On the Portland stone piers are engraved the names of over 73,000 men who were lost in the principal Somme battles between July 1916 and March 1918. The Commonwealth War Graves Commission states that over 90% of these soldiers died in the first Battle of the Somme between July 1 and November 18, 1916.[1]

Over the years bodies of soldiers have been discovered on former battlefields and, where possible, they are identified. In these instances a proper funeral is arranged with full military honours, and the name is removed from the memorial. On the top of the archway, a French inscription reads: Aux armées Française et Britannique l'Empire Britannique reconnaissant (To the French and British Armies, from the grateful British Empire) and underneath is carved 1914 and 1918.

The Thiepval Memorial also serves as an Anglo-French battle memorial, commemorating the joint offensive of 1916. There is a cemetery containing 300 British Commonwealth and 300 French graves located at the foot of the memorial. Many of the soldiers buried there are unknown. On the British headstones is the inscription "A Soldier of the Great War/ Known unto God". The French crosses bear the single word Inconnu (unknown). The cemetery's Cross of Sacrifice bears an inscription that acknowledges the joint British and French contributions.

Each year on July 1, which is the anniversary of the first day of the commencement of the Somme battles, a major ceremony is held at the memorial. There is also a ceremony on November 11, commemorating the end of the war at the 11th hour of the 11th day of the 11th month.

150. HRH The Duke of Kent and
HRH The Prince of Wales at Fromelles, France, July 19 2010.

151. HRH The Duke of Kent speaking at the House of Commons exhibition, November 10, 2008. On his right Admiral Sir Ian Garnett KCB, Vice-Chairman of the CWGC 2008-11; on his left is the then Labour Government Defence Secretary the Rt. Hon. Mr John Hutton.

Thiepval Project

A visitors' centre was very much needed to explain to tourists the purpose of the memorial, and why such battles had been fought during the First World War. The memorial is very popular with those who lost loved ones during the war and is visited each year by coach trips of tourists and school children. In 1999 Prince Edward became Patron of the Thiepval Project and, working with Sir Michael Jay, the then British Ambassador to France, a small group of people came together to promote such a centre. The group consisted of Sir Frank Sanderson OBE (a Royal British Legion branch chairman), Colonel Piers Storie-Pugh (Royal British Legion) Madame Geneviève Potié MBE (the Mayor of Thiepval), Brigadier Andrew Gadsby (then Military Attaché at the British Embassy in Paris) and Sénateur Fernand Demilly, then Président of the Conseil Général of the Département of the Somme.

The centre was built with aid from the Conseil General de la Somme and public contributions. The French volunteered to match the British contribution, with a target of £1.85 million to build the Centre, jointly achieved with substantial European Union funding.

As Patron of the Thiepval Project, Prince Edward gave an address:

"I strongly support the creation of an educational centre at Thiepval.

"During the course of my many visits to Thiepval, the scale of the sacrifice made by so many of our countrymen has been doubly impressed upon me by the grandeur of Lutyens's architecture. The task of designing a monument to contain the names of over 73,000 men would have daunted most architects, but Lutyens rose to the challenge magnificently and it is not surprising that the Imperial War Graves Commission chose his design to crown the great hill of Thiepval.

"This centre will help to ensure that the many thousands of visitors to Thiepval will have a clearer understanding of the Somme battles and of the background to them. I most heartily congratulate all those responsible, from the Conseil Général of the Somme in France and from the Thiepval Project Charitable Fund in the United Kingdom. Above all our thanks have to go to all the generous Donors, without whom none of this would have been possible.

"The Missing of Thiepval and the casualties of the Great War will not be forgotten."

Prince Edward opens new Visitor Centre 2004

On September 27, 2004, some 88 years after Thiepval was captured by the 12th Battalion Middlesex Regiment, the Visitors' Centre at Thiepval was officially opened by Prince Edward, with a large number of important French dignitaries present. Prince Edward opened his address in French:

'J'espère que vous me permettiez de continuer ma parler en anglais. [I hope that you will permit me to continue my talk in English.]

"It is now three years since I came here on a very wet afternoon and met you M. le Sénateur, Madame le Maire and Sir Frank Sanderson at the birth of the plan to create this Franco-British educational visitor centre.

153. HRH The Duke of Kent attending at Pembroke Military Cemetery, Malta, March 1, 2011, talking to Ms Louise Stanton, the previous British High Commissioner for Malta.

154. HRH The Duke of Kent St. James's Palace, May 23, 2014, presenting the CWGC's President's Commendation award to Mr Steve Rogers, Co-ordinator of the War Graves Photographic Project; present also is Mrs Sandra Rogers.

"Since that time, an enormous amount of work has gone into the funding and construction of this most impressive building. The French architects and British designers and historians are to be congratulated, but it is the people of the Somme and the Donors of the Thiepval Project who have made it possible.

"The number of Donors here today shows the depth of feeling that the events of almost 90 years ago still arouse in the hearts of the British nation.

"This centenary year of the Entente Cordiale [2] is being celebrated in grand style in our capital cities, but perhaps the true and natural testing of the entente is best seen at local level. Here we have a project where the Conseil Géneral has not only found half of the funding for the building but has also managed all the construction. On the British side an equal amount of money has been raised and an educational exhibition has been designed, constructed and installed. There has been a complete and natural blending of talents and total co-operation. It is the natural and seemingly automatic way in which this co-operation has flowered in this locality that our nations should now celebrate.

"The exhibition explains the events of that terrible war and of the battle of the Somme; it does not try to draw conclusions – that task is left to the visitor. However, the subsequent European Union funding for this project and the presence here today of His Royal Highness The Duke of Württemberg whose forebears, the 26th Reserve Division, held this stronghold of Thiepval from 1914 to 1916, gives us proof that the peaceful Europe which was so hoped for by all who fought here, is now a reality. However, the events of the past are an essential guide to the future and if we ever forget them we will be doing so at our own peril.

"Today, we remember all those who fell in this battle; and at the opening ceremony in a few minutes time we will symbolically have as our first official visitors, descendants of two of their number and inheritors of the hard-won peace. They will represent: Jean-Baptiste Pasquier a 35-year-old reservist in the 137 Regiment d'Infantrie, who was Killed in Action on the slopes below this village in 1914; he is buried in the large French national cemetery in Albert, and Charles Skey, a volunteer Royal Fusilier who rose through the ranks and was a Captain in the Black Watch when he was Killed in Action near High Wood in August 1916. He was 24 years old and his name is on the Memorial to the Missing. These two soldiers will be represented by a great niece Emilie Poupard and a great nephew Jonty Leggett. These young children represent the future of our nations and of Europe and we have a duty to help them create the new, peaceful and free world that all these soldiers fought and died for.

"Let us hope that the education available in this centre will help to make it certain no such war ever happens again in these lands of ours."

Inside the entrance there is a model of the memorial and a panel of 600 photographs representing the 73,000 men whose names are commemorated on the Memorial.

155. HRH The Duke of Kent at St James's Square,
London, at the start of a charity tank run, May 25, 2007.

The rest of the interior contains panels describing the war in general as well as others explaining the battle of the Somme. Maps and a screen with an animated Front Line, highlights the battles of the war, giving the detail in English, French, and German. There is a video room where three films each lasting about 10 minutes are shown, covering Thiepval, The Somme in the Great War, and Memory. Computers are available allowing visitors to search the database for information on these men.

Another minutely planned visit to France of great importance took place in July 2006. After travelling from London to Lille by Eurostar, Prince Edward's party visited six cemeteries and memorials on the afternoon of July 24, starting in Armetières and ending, via Bailleul and Fromelles, at the beautiful memorial to the Indian Army at Neuve Chappelle. (In 2005, during a business meeting to old East Germany, Prince Edward had made a point of going to the rarely-visited Zehrendorf Indian cemetery, where 210 Indian prisoners-of-war had died in captivity between 1915 and 1918). On July 25, he saw four CWGC cemeteries in the morning and, after a lunchtime reception in Arras, visited the great French National Cemetery at Notre Dame de Lorette, before speaking to many CWGC staff at the large Cabaret Rouge cemetery. One remarkable grave there is that of Lieutenant-Colonel E. G. Bowden, Queen's Royal West Surreys, killed on July 22, 1918, aged just 24 – the youngest colonel in the British Army. The trip ended on July 26 with a tour of the 1914-1918 tunnels in Arras known as the Carrières Wellington and a visit to the CWGC area office at Beaurains and two more cemeteries in the area before returning to London by Eurostar. The trip drew extensive press coverage in France and was a great success. In a follow up letter the very next day Mr Nicholas Adamson, Private Secretary to HRH The Duke of Kent, wrote to Richard Kellaway (CWGC), "His Royal Highness was very struck by the high morale and professionalism of those he met in France from the Commission, and he was very struck by the good state of all the cemeteries, in spite of the exceedingly high temperatures". Mr Adamson added a note to Mr Kellaway to say how much they had all enjoyed the trip, and saying how grateful he was for his help and his "excellent company".

In April 2009 Prince Edward made a return visit to Turkey for the renowned dawn service at Gallipoli. His first visit to the peninsula had been in May 1983 when, in just two days, he visited eight sites at Cape Helles and ten in the Anzac Cove area before departing for Egypt to complete the CWGC programme of visits. The Duke's party stayed 'under canvas' at the CWGC site near Anzac Cove on that occasion. In 2009 he flew to Ankara on April 23 and had meetings at the British Embassy that afternoon. Next day the party flew down to Cannakale and crossed to the Gallipoli peninsula by ferry. There were services at the main Turkish Memorial on the peninsula, at the relatively little known French Memorial near Morto Bay and at the principal CWGC Memorial at Cape Helles, before returning to Cannakale for a Governor's Reception. He was up at 3 am on April 25 to be at the dawn service at Anzac Cove which takes place at 5.30 am every year. After laying a wreath there for the CWGC he went on to services of remembrance at the Lone Pine Memorial, the Turkish 57th Regiment Memorial and the New Zealand Memorial high up on Chunuk Bair. He then flew back from Cannakale to Istanbul for the flight home to London.

June 2009 saw a return visit to Italy where Prince Edward was anxious to visit lesser known sites that he had not seen before. On May 8 he flew into Bologna airport to meet Mr Richard Kellaway, who introduced him to staff from the CWGC Western Mediterranean Area Office. After visiting Bologna War Cemetery, a bus ride to Argenta included a sandwich lunch eaten on board. Visits to Argenta and Ravenna War Cemeteries completed the afternoon programme with an overnight stop in Rimini. June 9 saw visits to those cemeteries associated with the hard fighting in 1944 up the east coast of Italy – Faenza, Forli, Forli (Indian), Coriano Ridge and Gradara. There was a large scale meeting of the CWGC at the Grand Hotel, Rimini on June 10, followed by a visit to the Rimini Gurkha War Cemetery before the return flight from Bologna to Gatwick airport.

A very busy 'working visit' to Malta early in 2011 was interrupted by a major political crisis. It was Prince Edward's first visit to the 'George Cross Island'. In a press release he said:

"For me, this trip represented a wonderful opportunity to see first-hand how the Commission works in partnership with local people all over the world, to ensure the memory of those who died in the World Wars is never forgotten. On Malta, our staff – both Maltese and from further afield – do a superb job in caring for the cemeteries and memorials which mark the sacrifice of so many".

Arriving on February 28, 2011 Prince Edward visited the Malta Memorial that afternoon. Next day he was at five cemeteries, three military and two civilian, but, regrettably, the final visits to Jewish and Turkish memorials had to be cancelled.

156. HRH The Duke of Kent speakaing to staff at Tyne Cot
Cemetery, Belgium, during the unveiling of new visitor information panels.

The German ferry Express Santorini arrived in Valletta harbour carrying civilians, including many British, evacuated from Libya because of the dangerous situation to see and encourage the work of the BHC and Foreign and Commonwealth Office (FCO) staff working through the crisis.

In November 2012 Prince Edward was on an official visit to Ascension Island in the South Atlantic when bad weather delayed his departure for the Falkland Islands by some six hours. It is entirely in character that, after lunch, he made use of this valuable extra time and made an unscheduled detour to visit the few Commonwealth war graves in the Island's New Cemetery on the coast. It contains just six Common-wealth burials of the First World War, two of which cannot now be traced and are represented by special memorials, and one burial of the Second World War.

Prince Edward's visit to Ireland, May 2013

The great success of the four-day State Visit to Ireland by Her Majesty The Queen and His Royal Highness Prince Phillip in May 2011 (the first such in a hundred years) has led to closer ties between the two countries at a number of different levels. Prince Edward was already very familiar with, and well-known in, Ireland through his work with the Royal National Lifeboat Institution (RNLI). During May 1-2, 2013, he made his first visit as Patron of the CWGC. Flying into Dublin from London in the morning, he was taken to Glasnevin (Prospect) Cemetery. He made a full tour of the cemetery, which contains the graves of some of the most famous figures in recent Irish history – Daniel O'Connell, Michael Collins, Charles Stewart Parnell, Arthur Griffiths, Countess Markiewicz, Sir Roger Casement and Eamonn de Valera – as well as 208 scattered war graves maintained by the CWGC. Prince Edward went on to lay wreaths at the Front Screen Wall and at the Sigerson Memorial to the fallen Irish volunteers of 1916. The magnificent memorial that stands at the entrance to the cemetery was designed by Dublin-born Mrs Dora Sigerson Shorter (1866-1918), poet, painter, and sculptress, and who was renowned as one of the most important figures of the Irish literary revival of the 19th and 20th centuries.

That afternoon Prince Edward met the President of Ireland, Mr Michael D. Hig-gins, and also saw Kilmainham (St. James) Church of Ireland with its small plot of nine CWGC graves. On May 2 he visited Dean's Grange Cemetery, County Dublin, where the first ever CWGC sign, the green and white markers so familiar to visitors all over the world, has been erected in Ireland showing the way to where 102 CWGC graves are kept, (75 from the First World War; 25 from the Second). He moved on to Grangegorman Military Cemetery, the largest in Ireland, containing 622 graves from both world wars. The final CWGC visit of the day was to the Curragh Military Cemetery, County Kildare, marking the final resting place of 103 men who died in this most iconic of British military camps. There he met members of the RNLI and accompanied them on a visit to Dunmore east Lifeboat Station, in another example of his multi-tasking to get the most out of each of these visits.

Prince Edward visits Glasnevin Cemetery, Dublin, July 2014

Arising from the great interest shown from the visit in 2013, it was proposed that the

157. HRH The Duke of Kent and Mr Michael D. Higgins, President of Ireland, during the Dedication of the Cross of Sacrifice, Glasnevin Cemetery, Dublin, July, 2014.

first Cross of Sacrifice be raised at Glasnevin Cemetery. The Dedication of the Cross of Sacrifice – an Irish Limestone cruciform structure – took place on July 31, 2014. Leading the dedication were Ireland's President Michael D. Higgins, and Prince Edward, in his role of President of the Commonwealth Graves Commission, and together they carried out the unveiling of the cross in honour of Irish war dead.

Over the last four years the CWGC has worked with the Glasnevin Trust to erect headstones and mark 208 graves in the cemetery of Irish men and women who served in the British armed forces. On arrival at the cemetery, Prince Edward was greeted by Mr George McCullough and Mr John Webster, Political Secretary, the British Embassy, and escorted to the Cross of Sacrifice in the cemetery by Defence Attaché Colonel Sean English. Traditional Irish music was played by the military band.

Marking this most historic occasion of the co-operation and friendship between Ireland and Britain, President Higgins laid a laurel wreath at the commemorative walls in memory of the Irish rebels, while Prince Edward laid a poppy wreath to commemorate those who died in the First and Second World wars.

Mr John Green, Chairman of the Glasnevin Trust in his opening address emphasised that the work done on remembering the Irish war dead was cementing relations with Britain. Said Mr Green:

'The Commonwealth War Graves Commission ... has been a wonderful partner without whom most of the 208 graves of people who fought in the First and Second World Wars would still be unmarked despite their great sacrifice. ... It has been a wonderful collaboration and we believe one that is playing its part in further strengthening the bonds between our two great nations in this modern era.'

Prince Edward toured the site, led by cemetery historian Mr Shane Mac Thomais, who highlighted some of the more significant plots. He also saw the graves of Sergeant Patrick Dunne and Volunteer Edward Ennis, two young men aged 19 years, who died within months of each other in 1916, one fighting for Ireland and the other Britain during the First World War. Mr Mac Thomais said: "The Duke was very impressed with the site and the nature of the historical importance and mindful of the amount of work that it would take to keep the place as well as we do." Prince Edward was joined on his visit by Mr Jimmy Deenihan, Minister for the Arts, Heritage and the Gaeltacht, Junior Minister Mr Brian Hayes, the British Ambassador Mr Dominick Chilcott, and Northern Ireland's Democratic Unionist Member of Parliament for Lagan Valley, Mr Jeffrey Donaldson.

In his Presidential address, extracts of which are here reproduced, Mr Higgins said:

"It is important that the First World War, and those whose lives it claimed, be not left as a blank space in Irish history. Today therefore is a significant day, as we dedicate this Cross of Sacrifice – the first such Cross to be erected in the Republic of Ireland.

"On an occasion such as this we eliminate all the barriers that have stood between those Irish soldiers whose lives were taken in the war, whose remains for which we have responsibility, and whose memories we have a duty to respect.'

Speaking in Irish the President continued:

"San iliomad uaigheanna ar fud na hEorpa, tá glúil de fhir óga curtha taobh le taobh, agus is sna huaigheanna sin ar fad ina n-iomláine atá íospartach an chogaidh sin.'

[Translation: In so many graves across Europe, the flower of a generation lies together, and all of their graves taken together hold the victims of that war.]

"We cannot give back their lives to the dead, nor whole bodies to those who were wounded, or repair the grief, undo the disrespect that was sometimes shown to those who fought or their families.

"In recent years, an increasing number of writers and scholars, religious and political leaders have redirected our gaze to the complexity of the Irish engagement with World War I, allowing for a more inclusive remembering at public level.

"This is facilitated by easier access to, and a renewal of interest in, the writings of Irish soldiers – their diaries, notebooks, letters and poems. The line "not for flag, nor King, nor Emperor" in the sonnet Thomas Kettle dedicated to his three-year old daughter, Betty, four days before his death during the battle of the Somme, or the poem Francis Ledwidge wrote in honour of his close friend Thomas McDonagh, while recovering from his wounds in Manchester in 1916, lend us a better sense of those men's multi-layered senses of belonging.

"Such writings throw light on the complex motives and circumstances that led so many Irishmen to volunteer to join the British Army."

In his address, Prince Edward said:

"The Cross of Sacrifice we dedicate today is an important step in the continuing process of recognising and remembering those Irishmen and women who died in the two world wars. It represents a lasting tribute to their sacrifice and it is my hope, in the years to come, that memorials such as these continue to inspire successive generations to remember."

Deirdre Mills, the CWGC's Director of UK Operations, said:

"In the year that marks the Centenary of the First World War, the Commonwealth War Graves Commission is delighted that our joint initiative to erect a Cross of Sacrifice in Glasnevin Cemetery has reached fruition. The Cross is an important feature of our work worldwide, commemorating those from both Ireland and throughout the Commonwealth who gave their lives during both World Wars. We are extremely grateful to the Irish Government, public, and the Glasnevin Trust, all of whom have done so much to support our work of commemoration and remembrance in Ireland."

Designed for the CWGC after the First World War by renowned architect Sir Reginald Blomfield, the Cross of Sacrifice represents the faith of the majority and the human sacrifice of all Commonwealth war dead, and can be found in CWGC cemeteries across the globe, wherever Commonwealth servicemen were laid to rest during and after the two world wars. Hundreds of thousands of Irishmen and women served with the British and Commonwealth armed forces during the First and Second World Wars and as many as 60,000 are believed to have died.

Gallipoli Centenary April 2015
Despite suffering a dislocated hip on April 6, while staying at Balmoral Castle in Scotland, Prince Edward remained fully committed to the important visit to Australia to commemorate the centenary of the Gallipoli landings. The party left London Heathrow at 1.30 pm on Sunday April 19, for a flight of 22 hours 25 minutes (including a stopover in Dubai) to land at Melbourne, Victoria at 8.55 pm Monday April 20. The very next morning Prince Edward visited the brand new Australian-Turkish Friendship Memorial sculpture on Birdwood Avenue, which had only been opened on April 13. From there he went to the Shrine of Remembrance to lay a

wreath. Here the state of Victoria remembers 114,000 of its citizens who enlisted in the First World War, 89,100 of whom served overseas and 19,000 of whom did not return home.

In a style so well established, Prince Edward combined this visit in the service of the Commonwealth War Graves Commission with other functions that reflect his range of interests. These activities related to musical education for under privileged schools, fund raising dinners and speeches to RiAus – the Royal Institution of Australia, a visit to the only particle linear accelerator in the southern hemisphere (the Synchrotron), and an event at the Monash University science school to meet 200 final year science students. In a speech delivered to RiAus on April 22 in Melbourne, addressing issues of leadership and innovation and the importance of the STEM subjects (Science, Technology, Engineering and Mathematics), Prince Edward drew heavily on his abiding interest in military history, illustrating his points from the career of Australia's greatest soldier, John Monash.

Having relocated to Adelaide, South Australia, on April 24, Prince Edward met more young scientists and the 'first responders' who battled the extensive bush fires in that region in January 2015. He visited the Centennial Park Cemetery, the Garden of Remembrance and the West Terrace Cemetery, where four Victoria Cross winners lie amongst the 275 Australian war graves there.

From Adelaide he flew to Canberra to prepare for the major commemorations on Australia's National Day. On April 25, he left Government House at 4.15 am to attend the traditional dawn service that marks the moment when troops of the Australian and New Zealand Army Corps (ANZAC) first landed in Anzac Cove on the Gallipoli peninsula on April 25, 1915. The service was at 5.30 am; (the instructions warned that 'the temperature could be freezing'.) After a short rest, he attended the main event at 10.15 am, the National Anzac Day service at Australia's National War Memorial. He laid a wreath on behalf of the CWGC. The crowd was estimated at between 100,000 and 120,000 people – more than double the expected number. Prince Edward then toured some of the museum galleries, including those devoted to the First World War, the Victoria Cross, and Afghanistan. The Anzac Day dinner at Government House saw the end of a long and memorable day.

The trip ended with a visit to the National Arboretum on April 26, before the flight home via Sydney and Dubai, arriving at London Heathrow at 6.55 am on April 27.

Prince Edward has said of his hopes and aspirations for the future continuance of the work of the CWGC:

"In 1926, the Commission's founder, Fabian Ware, said that the cemeteries and memorials built and maintained by the Commonwealth War Graves Commission "will bear a message to the future generations as long as the stone of which they are constructed endures." On Remembrance Sunday in November, when I stand before the Cenotaph as President of the Commission, as I do every year, I will pray that the work of the Commission continues steadfast, as in the past, so that the stone, the gardens, the records, the memory and the message endure."

Endnotes to Chapter 20

[1] Also included on this memorial are 16 stone laurel wreaths, inscribed with the names of sub-battles that made up the Battle of the Somme in which the men commemorated at Thiepval fell. The battles so-named are Ancre Heights, Ancre, Albert, High Wood, Delville Wood, Morval, Flers-Courcelette, Pozieres Wood, Bazentin Ridge, Thiepval Ridge, Transloy Ridges, Ginchy, Guillemont.

[2] The *Entente Cordiale* was a series of Agreements signed on April 8, 1904, between the United Kingdom and the French Third Republic, ending almost a millennium of intermittent conflict between the two nations.

CHAPTER 21

PRINCE EDWARD'S MILITARY CAREER

In 1953 the 18-year-old Prince Edward began his officer training at the Royal Military Academy, Sandhurst. He gained the Sir James Moncrieff Grierson language prize in French there, thanks to his time at school in Switzerland from 1951 to 1953. He qualified as an interpreter of French and 'passed out' as a Second Lieutenant on July 29, 1955, joining the distinguished cavalry regiment, the Royal Scots Greys at their barracks at Catterick Camp, Yorkshire. He joined C Squadron at a time when the Army decided that all its soldiers should have a trade qualification of some sort. As a mechanised unit, the Royal Scots Greys tended towards automotive skills and the subalterns were all involved in developing this aspect of training. Prince Edward was instrumental in devising a useful training aid which introduced young men, with far less experience of motor vehicles than we have today, to the mysteries of the driver's cab. A number of 'static training aids' were built, a wooden reconstruction of the cab with steering wheel, clutch pedal, brakes and accelerator, where the basics of driving and signalling of intent could be explained at a fraction of the cost and none of the inherent dangers of putting learners behind the wheel of actual vehicles.

Being posted to the regiment as 2nd Lieutenant HRH The Duke of Kent, Prince Edward broke a long tradition of royal princes going into the Royal Navy, and the Army life suited him very well. While it might be unusual for a new subaltern to be the guest of honour at the regiment's Waterloo Dinner in 1956 (the Royal Scots Greys had captured the eagle of the French 45th Line Infantry Regiment at the battle of Waterloo, June 18, 1815), the Prince played a full part in the exercises and training of the regiment. His brother officers remember how he completely entered into the daily life of the regiment, in its social and sporting life as well as its dedication to professional excellence. When Her Majesty The Queen paid an 'informal' visit to the regiment at Catterick on July 10, 1957 (one of three visits she made on that day) she was formally introduced to C Squadron's new subaltern. There is a delightful photograph of the two cousins shaking hands, barely concealing their mirth at the situation. Prince Edward then spent some time showing The Queen the new static training aids and explaining their working.

In 1957 2nd Lieutenant Charles Ramsay joined the regiment and began a life-long friendship with the Duke. In a poignant coincidence, both had lost their fathers to wartime air crashes; Prince George of Kent in August 1942; Admiral Ramsay in January 1945. In an interview with the authors, Charles Ramsay recalled their shared love of sports cars, with Ramsay favouring Jaguars and the Duke preferring Aston Martins. Young subalterns have plenty of excess energy to 'burn off', to which good colonels turn a blind eye if it does not interfere with the work of the regiment, and it was quite 'normal' for Prince Edward and Charles to race down the A1 to London (with far less traffic in the way in those days) to attend a smart party and be back in Catterick in plenty of time for the morning parades. Aston Martin were apparently delighted that Prince Edward drove one of their metallic green DB series cars. This love of cars was inherited from his father who loved driving so much that he would take the wheel, with his wife beside him in the passenger seat and their chauffeur, Field, reclining on the back seat until his services were required! [1] Prince Edward was a very good driver, having passed his Advanced Driver's Test and owned a variety of cars including a Mini shooting brake and a Mini Cooper, both with 'souped up' engines. His keen interest in car racing and motoring organisations developed from this.

This excellent officer was very popular with his men and progressed steadily in his chosen career. He was promoted to Lieutenant in 1958 and was a troop leader in C Squadron for his first posting to the British Army of the Rhine in October. In 1960

158. Battle of Balaclava, Brilliant charge of
the Scots Greys, October 25, 1854, by Augustus Butler.

he was a captain and second-in-command of C Squadron. 1962 saw a brief spell of duty on the staff of the Chief of the Imperial General Staff at the War Office, before returning to regimental duty. Skiing became very popular in the regiment, with both Prince Edward and Charles Ramsay forming part of the Downhill Team and taking part in the army championships at St. Moritz, sometimes under the watchful gaze of the Duke's mother, Princess Marina. The Duke disarmingly admits that he was not the best skier in the world and, in 1961, he had a bad fall, losing both skies, and in 1962 and 1963, he competed in the individual racing, climbing from 43rd to 31st place out of a contest usually involving about 120 racers. The regiment competed for the Princess Marina Cup for army skiing in 1962, finishing in fifth place. They would be too busy to compete the following year, but he was keenly engaged in 1964, 1965, and 1966. (Later, as Patron of the British Army Ski Association, he would get to the January British Army ski championships as often as he could). Aside from the odd sprained ankle, Prince Edward remains annoyed with himself for losing time on the Giant Slalom at St. Moritz by missing one of the gates. He reconnoitred the Cresta Run for the regimental team but was not able to take part in the run itself, in which the team sadly did not perform well.

In 1963 the Royal Scots Greys deployed to Aden, all except C Squadron that went to Hong Kong (in November 1962) to form part of 48 Gurkha Infantry Brigade. In December he was joined by his wife and six month old son, George, The Earl of St. Andrews. After some 20 months the regiment re-united in Germany in late 1964.

During a flight back from Hong Kong for a Christmas break, Prince Edward demonstrated the regular soldier's useful ability to snatch some sleep wherever and whenever the opportunity arose. This led to an amusing episode on their return journey on December 5, 1963, when the pilot commander of the BOAC army charter flight, a long-range prop-jet, was John Brooks from Maidenhead, Berkshire. His widow Mrs Joan Brooks who was for many years a Voluntary Steward in St. George's Chapel, Windsor Castle, where she pointed out to tourists the Duke of Kent's Garter Knight banner, takes up the story:

"My late husband was a fighter pilot in the Second World War, flying Hurricanes and Spitfires. Most BOAC pilots [after the war] were former bomber or flying boat pilots. He had survived being shot down three times, and then the dangerous times of flying the world's first jet airliner, the ill-fated Comet One. His last aircraft was the VC10.

"John was in command of a BOAC army charter flight for the sector Karachi – Istanbul – London [Heathrow Airport]. His flying logbook shows that their Royal Highnesses the Duke and Duchess of Kent and their child boarded the 'plane at Hong Kong. Apparently, the Duke slept for most of the night sector and the Chief Steward told my husband that the Duchess was awake, so John said to invite her up to the flight deck. After a little while the Duchess arrived and sat for some time, about two hours, on the seat between the two pilots, chatting away to the flight crew about how

159. HRH The Duke of Kent wearing the uniform of the Deputy Colonel in Chief of the Royal Scots Dragoon Guards.

they were "going home to see the folks for Christmas." She asked the crew were they married, what their wives and families made of their continual absences from home, how long they had been doing the job etc. They explained the pre-flight and pre-landing check lists to her, and John, in his usual leg-pulling fashion, told her that there was one item missing at the end of the landing checks – "wedding rings on", which amused the Duchess.

"When she finally returned to her seat in the cabin, the flight engineer spread a clean handkerchief on the seat before he resumed his position, saying that no way should his rear end besmirch where the Duchess had sat!

"On landing at Heathrow, my husband saw that various dignitaries were waiting in the rain to welcome their Royal Highnesses and he and his crew formed up under a wing of the aircraft. On reaching the bottom of the aircraft steps, the Duchess led the way across to the crew where she and the Duke thanked each one of them. Meantime the dignitaries got wetter!"

The regiment served in Germany until September 1965. It must have been a poignant moment for the regiment for Prince Edward and his wife Katherine to attend the 150th anniversary of the Duchess of Richmond's Ball on June 15, 1965 at the British Embassy in Brussels. (In 1815 the officers attending the ball had to slip away at about midnight to rush south to meet the invading French army). In 1966, newly appointed as a Personal Aide-de-Camp to The Queen, the Duke successfully passed the course at the Staff College, Camberley. (From December 1, 1974 he would be Patron of the Army Staff College Club.) The following year he was promoted to Major, at which point he was the commander designate of C Squadron. (That year he and his brother, Prince Michael, were enrolled as members of the Honourable Artillery Company – see Chapter 19.) Prince Edward first served as General Staff Officer II, Eastern Command from February 16, 1967 to May 22, 1968. His duties would have covered operational planning and the deployment of troops from Eastern Command overseas. He then served a year as a Company Instructor at the Royal Military Academy Sandhurst. During this time he was appointed Colonel-in-Chief of the Royal Regiment of Fusiliers. From 1970 he was commander of C Squadron and, after large scale exercises at Otterburn in Scotland, took them to the British Sovereign Base Area, Cyprus where they wore the blue helmet of the United Nations on peace-keeping duties. He retained the post of squadron commander when the Royal Scots Greys merged with the 3rd Dragoons (Carbiniers) on July 2, 1971 to form the Royal Scots Dragoon Guards, an armoured car reconnaissance regiment. Her Majesty The Queen presented a standard to the new regiment at Edinburgh in July.

From October 26, 1971 to July 28, 1972 he carried out important work for the General Staff, Operational Requirements Department of the Ministry of Defence (MOD) in the role of General Staff Officer (Weapons) and Assistant Project Manager, CVRT (Combat Vehicle, Reconnaissance, Tracked). He was the 'interface' between the MOD Defence and Alvis, the manufacturers of the new Scorpion and Scimitar armoured vehicles then entering service. His work woud include inspection visits to the factories manufacturing armoured vehicles for the Army and writing reports on the work. A subsequent holder of this appointment, Lieutenant-colonel Charles Messenger, Royal Tank Regiment, remarked on how well kept the files were relating to this work, and on the perfect legibility of Prince Edward's handwriting. From October 31, 1972, as an acting lieutenant-colonel, the Prince was General Staff Officer I working on the International and Industrial Policy committee of the MOD's Procurement Executive. He served in that role until the end of 1974, at a time when his royal duties were increasing considerably. This interest in new technology was apparent from his earliest days in the army and is a major factor in the organisations he subsequently became involved with as royal patron.

Back in Scotland C squadron was assigned as the 'spearhead' unit and was ordered at short notice to Northern Ireland, where it was attached to 17th/21st Lancers at Omagh in County Tyrone. However, the deployment was only for three weeks and they were then withdrawn for operational reasons.

From June 30, 1973 he was a substantive lieutenant-colonel. Since 1966 his increasing royal duties had taken up much of his time and so, in 1976, he decided to retire from the Army after an unbroken service of twenty-one years. His first duty in March was to visit a number of regiments of the British Army of the Rhine in Germany, which he did again in 1977 and 1978. In 1976 he became a very active Vice-Chairman of the British Overseas Trade Board and combined this work with his role as President of the Commonwealth War Graves Commission. He retained the closest possible links with his old regiment, where he was permanently enrolled as a 'supernumerary' lieutenant-colonel. He is enormously proud to be the Deputy Colonel-in-Chief of the regiment since December 1993. (The Colonel-in-Chief is HM The Queen). He lends his name to the medal for 'meritorious service' to the regiment, and to the trophy awarded annually to the best tank crew on the ranges. He was made a Major-General in 1982 but, in 1993, he was at first minded to turn down the offer of the honorary rank of Field-Marshal in the British Army. On being told that this was probably the last such appointment ever to be made he graciously accepted the proposal in June 1993, and is now seen in November of every year in the uniform of that rank at the Remembrance Day service in London.

THE ROYAL SCOTS GREYS

A Brief History

The Royal Scots Greys was a cavalry regiment of the British Army from 1707 until 1971, when they amalgamated with the 3rd Carabiniers (Prince of Wales's Dragoon Guards) to form The Royal Scots Dragoon Guards (Carabiniers and Greys).

The regiment's history began in 1678, when three independent troops of Scots Dragoons were raised. In 1681 these troops were combined to form The Royal Regiment of Scots Dragoons, numbered the 4th Dragoons in 1694. They were mounted

160. London Scottish Regiment presenting a silver Pipe Tune Holder to the Scots Guards at St. James's Palace, London, December 16, 2008. Pictured are Hamish Barne, Nicholas Adamson, David Rankin-Hunt LVO MBE TD, Regimental Colonel; George Robertson, Honorary Regimental Colonel; James Hughes, Stuart Young, Regimental Secretary; Adam Guthrie, Julian Lawrie, David Carter, Officer Commanding; HRH The Duke Of Kent, Alastair Mathewson, and Hamish MacKay-Lewis.

on grey horses and were soon being referred to as the Grey Dragoons. In 1707 they were renamed The Royal North British Dragoons (North Britain then being a common name for Scotland), but were popularly referred to as the Scots Greys. In 1713 they were renumbered the 2nd Dragoons, as part of a deal between the establishments of the English Army and Scottish Army, when they were being unified into the British Army. In 1877 their nickname was finally made official when they became the 2nd Dragoons (Royal Scots Greys), which was inverted in 1921, to The Royal Scots Greys (2nd Dragoons). They kept this title until July 2, 1971, when they amalgamated with the 3rd Carabiniers. The regimental badge combines the eagle of the Greys with the crossed rifles of the Carabiniers.

They are famous for taking a French eagle at Waterloo and, soon after Prince Edward joined the regiment, that trophy was returned from the Royal Hospital, Chelsea, to Scotland. On July 7, 1956 the eagle was 'laid up' in Edinburgh Castle along with a regimental guidon that had served for fifty years before being replaced by a new one, handed over by The Queen just two days before at a ceremony at Holyrood House where the regiment provided the Guard of Honour. (Both would take pride of place in the new regimental museum opened in the Castle in July 1995). 1978 saw another great round of celebrations as the regiment marked the tercentenary of the creation of the first troops of Scots Dragoons. The Queen often used Royal Week in Scotland to renew her contacts with the regiment and HRH The Duke of Kent always plays a part in these events. It was at a regimental dinner at St. James's Palace in December 1993 to mark her fortieth anniversary as Colonel-in-Chief that The Queen announced the newly created Field Marshal HRH The Duke of Kent was now the deputy Colonel-in-Chief of the regiment.

He was Patron of the Royal Scots Dragoon Guards Museum Trust Project and Appeal that existed between 2004 and 2009, and he attended the opening of the museum in July 2006 together with Her Majesty Queen Elizabeth II. An eyewitness to The Queen's first visit to the museum recalls her finding the picture referred to above when she was introduced to a new subaltern, her cousin Edward. "Oh, Eddie! Eddie! Look, here's a picture of you and me!"

THE SCOTS GUARDS

Prince Edward has been Colonel of the Scots Guards since September 9, 1974 and always plays a particularly close role in the life of the regiment. He presented new colours to the 2nd Battalion during a visit to Germany in April 1978.

The Scots Guards (SG) is a regiment of the Guards Division of the British Army, whose origins lie in the personal bodyguard of King Charles I of England and Scotland. Its lineage can be traced as far back as 1642, although it was only placed on the English Establishment (thus becoming part of what is now the British Army) in 1686.

The Scots Guards is ranked as the third regiment in the Guards Division; as such, Scots Guardsmen can be recognised by having the buttons on their tunics spaced in threes. The regiment consists of a single operational battalion, which has been based in Catterick since 2008, in the armoured infantry role. However, since

161. Operation Apollo. Warrant Officer
Mike Kase on patrol in Kabul, Afghanistan, October 2006.

1993, the regiment has also maintained an independent company, F Company, permanently based in Wellington Barracks, London on public duties. It is the custodian of the colours and traditions of the 2nd Battalion, which was placed in permanent suspended animation in 1993 as a result of Options for Change.

Brief history

The Scots Guards regiment is rich in history dating back to the Irish Wars of 1641.

During war with France the 1st Battalion was involved in the Low Countries for the first time. Under John Churchill the 1st Duke of Marlborough it distinguished itself at Walcourt, and in 1691, was joined in Belgium by the 2nd Battalion. Together they took part in the Battles of Steenkirk, 1692, and Landen, 1693, hard fighting which established the credit of the British soldier on the Continent. It was during this campaign that King William granted to Captains in the regiment the double rank of Lieutenant-Colonel and to Lieutenants the double rank of Captain, thus giving them precedence within the Army.

The Scots Guards served in the War of The Austrian Succession in 1743; the Seven Years War in 1758; the French Revolution 1789; The Peninsula War 1809; the Waterloo Campaign, Sevastopol and Egypt, 1882, and the Anglo-Boer War in South Africa 1899-1902. [2]

They served throughout the First World War, having been heavily involved on the Western Front, including the Battle of the Marne 1914, Ypres 1914, Neuve

Chapelle and Loos 1915, the Somme 1916, and several battles during 1917and 1918. [3]

During the Second World War they served in North-West Europe in many battles between 1944-45, in North Africa between 1941-43, and Italy from 1943-45. [4]

The Falkland Islands Conflict began on Friday April 2, 1982, when Argentina invaded and occupied these islands in the South Atlantic. The British Government dispatched a naval task force to engage the Argentine Navy and Air Force and retake the islands by a modern amphibious assault. The conflict lasted 74 days, ending with the surrender of the Argentines on June 14, 1982. The Scots Guards served at Tumbeldown Mountain in 1982, and were in the Gulf in 1991.

In December 2008 Prince Edward hosted a dinner at St. James's Palace for officers of the Scots Guards and their sister regiment, the London Scottish (TA). The 'London Jocks' presented the Scots Guards with a fine silver pipe programme holder to cement the special relationship between the two regiments. Prince Edward expressed great interest in the London Scottish and visited the regimental headquarters at Horseferry Road, London, on March 24th, 2009. For the past 120 years the London Scottish have had an active lodge of the Freemasons in their ranks, part of a long tradition of regimental lodges in the British Army. As Grand Master of the Freemasons Prince Edward would have found this an added interest in their work.

Prince Edward Visits Afghanistan

On July 15, 2010, Prince Edward made a two-day visit to the 1st Battalion, The Scots Guards Battlegroup, front line troops who were serving in Afghanistan. They had been deployed there since April, where they had been working with the Afghan National Police and Army. Prince Edward toured the main British military base of Camp Bastion, visited Lashkar Gah, and inspected a remote check point.

Lieutenant Colonel Lincoln Jopp, Commanding Officer of the 1st Battalion Scots Guards, spoke of the tremendous boost to morale by the Duke's visit:

> "He is such a huge supporter of the regiment and has recently visited our families back in Catterick and our casualties in Selly Oak, so to get him out here to see the Guardsmen is fantastic.
>
> "Nothing was going to stand in his way of seeing his men on operations.
>
> "The Scots Guards have been deployed to Afghanistan since April, where they have been working with the Afghan National Police and Army."

Scots Guards Granted Freedom of Wantage

On May 21, 2011 the Scots Guards, having been granted the Freedom of the town of Wantage, were admitted as Honorary Freemen. The town's association with the regiment is through Robert James Loyd-Lindsay VC KCB, 1st Baron Wantage of Lockinge, a most distinguished soldier in the Scots Fusilier Guards. They marched through the town 'with bayonets fixed, swords drawn, drums beating, bands playing and Colours flying' [5], in the presence of His Royal Highness The Duke of Kent, the Lord Lieutenant of Oxfordshire, Mr Tim Stevenson, High Sheriff Penelope Glen, and Mr James Sibbald, the Town Mayor. The Mayor of Wantage Councillor

Mrs Charlotte Dickson presented the Freedom Scroll to His Royal Highness Prince Edward The Duke of Kent, as Regimental Colonel of the Scots Guards. On this historic occasion the Scots Guards were honoured with a message from Queen Elizabeth II and which was spoken by Prince Edward. The Queen wished to:

> "Convey my warm thanks to the town councillors and citizens of Wantage for their message of loyal greetings, sent on the occasion of Her Majesty's Scots Guards being admitted as Honorary Freemen of Wantage.
>
> "As Colonel-in-Chief of the Scots Guards, I much appreciate your kind words and, in return, send my best wishes to all concerned for a most memorable and enjoyable event." [6]

The Scots Guards then presented arms to their Regimental Colonel, the Duke of Kent. Charlotte Dickson said: "It was a fantastic day for Wantage. It was a great way to show our appreciation for all our servicemen and women. There was a lot of goodwill behind them." High Sheriff Penelope Glen said: "There are so many tragic things happening in the world so it's lovely to have a day like this."

The crowds were then treated to a Royal Air Force flypast and a military freefall parachute display.

SCOTS GUARDS COLONEL'S FUND

The Scots Guards Colonel's Fund was set up to make provision by continuing to raise funds especially for soldiers injured in Iraq and Afghanistan.

As patron of the fund, Prince Edward said:

> "The Scots Guards are among the Army's first soldiers of choice on operations. They have already seen active service in Iraq and Afghanistan, and will be called upon again. We need to be prepared as a regiment to shoulder responsibility for a larger number of long-term casualties than we have experienced for a very long time.
>
> "We need to make provision now by continuing to raise funds.
>
> "That some of us no longer serve with the colours does not matter. What does matter is that we are all of us Scots Guardsmen, bound together in the Queen's service until we die by a chain, the links of which are invisible but which are as strong as steel."

Injured Guardsman David Watson had a proud moment when he carried the Olympic Torch in Lancashire on Friday, June 22, 2012, during the Olympic Games in Britain.

SCOTS GUARDS REGIMENTAL ASSOCIATION

The Scots Guards Regimental Association was founded in 1903.
Prince Edward has been Patron of the association since September 9, 1974.

Colonel G.H.F.S. (Harry) Nickerson is the current President, and Major M.M. Davidson MVO MBE BEM is Secretary.

Scots Guardsmen and their families remain a part of the regiment for life and the association helps serving and retired members to stay in touch, while coordinating support to their troops in the front line or members of the regimental family in time of need. They take great care in looking after their old soldiers and their families, which costs are met from their charitable fund. [7]

There is considered to be a bond between the Scots Guardsmen regardless of length of service or rank. Major Davidson says: "It is always good to meet up with those whom you have served with or even those who were in before you. There is a common bond between us and that is that we are all SCOTS GUARDSMEN." [8]

Objectives

The objectives of the association are to maintain the connections between past and present members of the regiment and to promote friendship and association amongst those in civil life who worthily maintained when in the regiment, and continue to uphold in civil life, the high character of the regiment.

To foster *Esprit de Corps* and promote the best interests of the regiment.

To bring to the notice of Regimental Headquarters any case deserving of assistance from Regimental Funds, and to give particular assistance to any member, wife, widow or children who may be in distressed circumstances.

Branches hold Annual General Meetings, Re-union Dinners, Monthly Meetings, Picnics and Outings. A Bi-annual Gathering, a Gathering Week End, is organised where the regimental family come together, at agreed venues.

On the regimental Remembrance Sunday (Black Sunday) the Service of Remembrance is held in the Guards Chapel, Wellington Barracks, London, and during the service a wreath is laid in the regimental Cloister by an Association Member. The Association, together with serving members, then march to Horse Guards where a second wreath is laid at the Guards Division Memorial by an Association Member from a second branch. On return to barracks there is a family lunch.

Prince Edward's close association with the Guards and his belief in museums as centres of education was continued through his work as Patron of the Society of Friends of the Guards Museum from April 2007 to April 2012.

THE ROYAL REGIMENT OF FUSILIERS

The Royal Regiment of Fusiliers (RRF) is an infantry regiment of the British Army, and part of the Queen's Division.

The regiment was formed on April 23, 1968, as part of the reforms of the army that saw the creation of the first 'large infantry regiments', by the amalgamation of the four English fusilier regiments – The Royal Northumberland Fusiliers; The Royal Warwickshire Fusiliers; The Royal Fusiliers (City of London Regiment); and The Lancashire Fusiliers – some of the proudest regiments in the British Army.

The Royal Northumberland Fusiliers were raised in 1674 and became the 5th Regiment of Foot. The Northumberland link began in 1782 and they were designanated Fusiliers in 1836. In 1935 the Northumberland Fusiliers received their royal prefix. They fought at the Boyne 1690, in Spain from 1707 to 1713, in Germany 1755-1762, America 1775-1780, Spain and Portugal 1807-1814, in the Indian Mutiny 1857-8, Afghanistan 1878-80, and South Africa 1899-1902. They raised 52 battalions in the First World War and the 34th Division had two entire brigades of Northumberland Fusiliers (the Tyneside Irish and Tyneside Scottish) that suffered so terribly at La Boisselle on July 1, 1916, the disastrous first day of the battle of the Somme. They served in all theatres of war 1939-1945, and in Korea.

The Warwickshire Regiment was raised in 1685 as the 6th Regiment of Foot, and would not become a fusilier regiment until 1963. They were at the Boyne in 1690, and served in Spain and America in the 18th century. They were named the Warwickshire Regiment in 1782, and served in the West Indies during the French Revolutionary wars, before going to Spain, Portugal and Canada. They were the Royal Warwickshire Regiment from 1832, and served in all the great imperial wars – on the North-West frontier of India, in the Sudan and in South Africa. They raised thirty battalions 1914-18, and were in all the main theatres of both world wars. In 1963 they were taken into the Royal Regiment of Fusiliers as the Royal Warwickshire Fusiliers.

The Royal Fusiliers (City of London Regiment) was raised in 1685 from companies of troops at the Tower of London armed with the fusil, a type of flintlock musket when most of the army still carried matchlocks. In 1751 they were designated the 7th Regiment of Foot (Royal Fusiliers). They fought in Canada 1775-6, America 1776-80, Spain and Portugal 1809-1814 (being particularly distinguished at the battle of Albuera 1811, where the Fusilier Brigade was described as "that astonishing infantry"), and the Crimean War 1854-56. They wore the fusilier bearskin and were popularly known as the 'Baby Guards' or 'The Shiny Seventh'. They raised no less than 76 battalions during the First World War, winning the first two Victoria Crosses of the war at the battle of Mons, August 1914. They served in all theatres in both world wars, and in Korea.

The Lancashire Fusiliers were raised in 1688 as Preston's Regiment of Foot and were designated the 20th Regiment of Foot in 1751. They were at the great battles of Dettingen 1743, Fontenoy 1745, Culloden 1746, Minden 1759 (one of six British infantry regiments that attacked and overthrew the French cavalry on that extraordinary day), and at Saratoga in 1776. From 1782 to 1881 they were designated the East Devonshire Regiment and served in the Peninsula War (1807-1814) and in the Crimea. In 1881 they became the Lancashire Fusiliers. They raised thirty battalions in the First World War and are famous for winning 'six VCs before breakfast' in the assault landings at Gallipoli on April 25, 1915. They served in all theatres in both world wars.

Prince Edward became Colonel in Chief of the regiment on July 1, 1969. He visited the regiment in Germany in May 1981, Cyprus in May 1987, Norway in February 1989, and Germany again in November of that year.

On formation, the regiment consisted of four Regular battalions, one Volunteer battalion covering the four Regimental areas and the Depot. Due to a series of Gornment defence reviews, 'Options for Change' and a 'Strategic Defence Review' the regiment now comprises just two Regular battalions and a number of Territorial Army companies located in the four Regimental Areas.

As an outcome of the reforms of the infantry that were announced in December 2004, the only change was that the regiment received the 5th Territorial Army Battalion RRF, through the re-designation of the Tyne-Tees Regiment, on April 1, 2006. The TA battalion will retain a multi-badged identity, preserving links with Fusilier units and Rifle units with associations with Durham and Yorkshire. Since 2009 the regular battalions have remained in fixed locations. The 1st Battalion is stationed at Tidworth, and the 2nd Battalion is serving in London. The 2nd Battalion rotates this posting with a resident posting to Cyprus with two other light infantry battalions.

The regiment's mascot is an Indian Blackbuck Antelope and is a tradition inherited from the Royal Warwickshire Fusiliers. The current mascot's name is Bobby and he holds the rank of Corporal. Bobby attends all major parades held by the regiment.

The new battle honours are the combined battle honours of The Royal Northumberland Fusiliers, The Royal Warwickshire Fusiliers, The Royal Fusiliers (City of London Regiment) and The Lancashire Fusiliers, to which have been added Wadi al Batin, Gulf 1991, and Al Basrah, Iraq 2003.

The 1st Battalion is equipped with the WARRIOR Armoured Infantry Fighting Vehicle and skilled in the complex demands of fast-moving armoured warfare, while the 2nd Battalion is a Light Role battalion with the ability to deploy quickly and adapt to any operational scenario.

Whether keeping the peace in the Balkans or engaged in close combat in Iraq and Afghanistan the Fusiliers have proved capable of meeting every challenge with courage, determination and a will to win.

The Territorial Army Fusiliers serve with their regular comrades on operations and on exercise, fitting seamlessly into the tough demands of modern soldiering.

The Regimental Creed

The Regiment is justifiably proud of its achievements over these past 40 years, with distinguished service in Cyprus (at the start of the Turkish invasion), Germany, Northern Ireland, the Balkans, Kosovo, Iraq and Afghanistan. The Colonel of the Regiment directed that they should adopt and publish a Regimental Creed. It is noteworthy that this creed has emanated not from the top down, but from serving Fusiliers and their officers, and was presented to the regimental Council as the way all Fusiliers should conduct themselves professionally, and go about their daily business. This in itself says much about the Royal Regiment of Fusiliers.

I am a Fusilier, trained and ready to deploy.
I will defend my country's freedoms with respect and integrity.
I will always maintain my arms, my equipment and myself.
I will place the mission and the team first.
I will never accept defeat nor let down my mates or my Regiment.
I will always be one of England's finest, a Fusilier.

*162. A number of Lorne Scots just prior to a deployment
to Bosnia in Canadian Forces Base Petawawa, Ontario, 2003.*

THE DEVONSHIRE AND DORSET REGIMENT

Visits by a royal commander-in-chief are an occasion of great pride for any regiment but there was one sad moment when Prince Edward attended the ceremony that marked the disbanding of a popular regiment.

The Devonshire and Dorset Regiment, usually just known as "the Devon and Dorsets", was an infantry regiment of the British Army, formed on May 17, 1958, in Minden, Germany, by the amalgamation of two old county regiments. The new 1st Battalion, Devonshire and Dorset Regiment was commanded by Lieutenant Colonel Guy Young, formerly commanding officer of the 1st Devonshires, while the colonel of the regiment was Major-General George Neville Wood, formerly of the Dorsets.

Having served in Northern Ireland, the battalion in more recent years had performed public duties in London and Windsor. These included providing the Queen's Guard at Buckingham Palace, and in April 2002, attending the State Funeral of Queen Elizabeth, the Queen Mother.

In 2003 a defence white paper, *Delivering Security in a Changing World*, was published. Among the changes proposed was the amalgamation of all single-battalion infantry regiments into multi-battalion large regiments. In December 2004 details of the amalgamations were announced, and the "Devon and Dorsets" would be amalgamated with the Royal Gloucestershire, Berkshire and Wiltshire Regiment to form a new battalion of The Light Infantry. As part of the preparation for the change, the regiment moved from the Prince of Wales' Division to the Light Division and, on July 22, 2005, was renamed the Devonshire and Dorset Light Infantry. On Novem-

545

ber 24, the Ministry of Defence announced yet further changes. The merger would also involve joining a new larger regiment created by the amalgamation of The Light Infantry and the Royal Green Jackets. This newly formed regiment was to be called "The Rifles" from February 2007. The battalion that resulted from the merger of the "Devon and Dorsets" and the Royal Gloucestershire, Berkshire and Wiltshire Regiment was designated "1st Battalion, The Rifles".

The sad outcome was that on becoming part of a large rifle regiment, the "Devon and Dorsets" no longer carried their own colours. A solemn ceremony took place in Exeter Cathedral on January 27, 2007, conducted by the Rt. Revd. Bishop Michael Langrish, and attended by Prince Edward to mark the laying up of the Colours.

As a rifle regiment, a private soldier in The Rifles is known as a Rifleman and Serjeant is spelt in the archaic fashion; the regiment wears a Rifle Green beret.

The new regiment's "Double Past" march (the music used when marching past at the double) is an amalgam of the Light Infantry's (Keel Row) and the Royal Green Jackets' (Road to the Isles).

THE LORNE SCOTS (PEEL, DUFFERIN AND HALTON) REGIMENT

The Lorne Scots (Peel, Dufferin and Halton) Regiment, is a Primary Reserve infantry regiment of the Canadian Army. It is part of 32 Canadian Brigade Group, 4th Canadian Division. Prince Edward became Colonel-in-Chief of the regiment, on June 11, 1977.

Brief history

On September 14, 1866, the 36th Peel Battalion of Infantry was authorised, and on September 28, the 20th Halton Battalion of Infantry was formed. These two regiments, some 70 years later, were to be reorganised to form The Lorne Scots (Peel, Dufferin and Halton Regiment). The first Scottish connection was made on September 27, 1879, when the Halton Rifles were reviewed by His Excellency The Marquess of Lorne, 4th Governor General of Canada 1878-83, later 9th Duke of Argyll. Permission was received in 1881, to re-designate the 20th Halton Rifles as the 20th Halton Battalion Lorne Rifles. In addition, the wearing of tartan trews and the diced Glengarry were authorised and a Pipe Band was formed.

During the Anglo/Boer Wars in South Africa (1880-81 and 1899-1902), the regiment, as a unit, did not go to war. However, many officers and men from both regiments served there.

First World War (1914-18)

During the First World War (1914-18), regiments as such were not mobilised but drafts from various units were called up and formed into numbered battalions. The 36th Peel Battalion and the 20th Regiment Halton Rifles provided 16 officers and 404 other ranks to the 4th Battalion of the 1st Canadian Division. Subsequently, many more men from the two regiments were allotted to the 20th, 36th, 58th, 74th, 76th and 81st Battalions. The 126th, 164th and 234th Battalions were raised

*163. A number of Lorne Scots just prior to a deployment
to Bosnia in Canadian Forces Base Petawawa, Ontario, 2003.*

exclusively in Peel, Dufferin, and Halton Counties.

After the war, the 36th Peel Regiment was reorganised, becoming in 1923, the Peel and Dufferin Regiment. The regimental badge adopted was the Demi Lion, which was the personal crest of Sir Robert Peel (Prime Minister of the UK from December 10, 1834 to April 8, 1835, and again from August 30, 1841 to June 29, 1846). The Halton Rifles was reorganized as the Lorne Rifles (Scottish) in 1931, and permission was received from His Grace the Duke of Argyll, the senior Duke of Scotland, to use his personal crest, the Boar's Head, and his personal tartan, the Ordinary Campbell.

On December 15, 1936, following a general reorganisation of the Militia, the Lorne Rifles and the Peel and Dufferin Regiment were amalgamated to form the present regiment, The Lorne Scots (Peel, Dufferin and Halton Regiment).

The Second World War (1939-45)

The Lorne Scots was one of the first units in Canada to be mobilised at the outbreak of the Second World War in 1939, proceeding overseas in January 1940. It was organised into defence companies and platoons at Brigade, Division, Corps, and Army Headquarters, and served in every theatre of war in which Canadian soldiers fought except Hong Kong. They were in France with elements of the 1st Division early in 1940. A platoon of the Lornes served with The Queen's Own Rifles of Canada at the capture of Boulogne in 1944, where some of the platoon was killed or wounded. Elements of the platoons with 4 and 6 Brigades took part in the raid on Dieppe in August 1942. The 1st Division and 1st, 2nd and 3rd Brigade platoons landed on the beaches of Sicily on July 13, 1943. The 3rd Division Platoons (3rd Div HQ and 7, 8 and 9 Brigades) landed on Juno Beach, Normandy as part of the D-Day operation.

Since the war, the regiment has been well represented at all military functions, and in 1955, had the largest attendance at summer camp of any infantry regiment in Canada. In autumn of 1963, in a ceremony at Caledon the regiment was presented with its colours by the Lieutenant-Governor of Ontario, The Honourable W. Earl Rowe. An upsurge of interest and prowess in marksmanship in the unit followed, and it began immediately to dominate competition shooting at all levels from local to national. This domination has continued to the present time, with the unit being represented at various World Championships, Olympics, Pan-American Games, and the Bisley Competition in England.

In the late 1960s, the Lancashire Fusiliers, the allied regiment in England since May 9, 1929, was subject to amalgamation, and in the process bestowed its revered primrose hackle on the Lorne Scots for custodianship. It is now worn proudly on the headdress of all Lorne Scots infantry personnel.

With the coming of the late 1960s & 1970s, the role of the Militia expanded, resulting in some Lorne Scots members serving in Germany. (Many served with the British Army of the Rhine).

Prince Edward visits

The Regiment's first ever Colonel-in-Chief, Field Marshal His Royal Highness Prince Edward The Duke of Kent, visited the regiment in 1979 and 1983. Prince Edward presented the unit with a new Regimental and Queen's colour on September 14, 1991, in Brampton on the occasion of the regiment's 125th birthday.

164, Lorne Scots march on the Remembrance Day Parade in Brampton, Ontario, November 11, 2012.

165. Lorne Scots conducting urban operations in winter climates on Exercise Aggressive Viper 2 at 4th Division Training Centre in Meaford, Ontario, March 23, 2014.

His Royal Highness again visited the regiment in October 2001, where he participated in a Trooping of the Colours which he had presented in 1999 (270 soldiers were on parade), attended a fund raising dinner, a Gala Ball for the regiment and dedicated a memorial park in Georgetown Ontario.

The regiment has provided troops to many of the United Nations Peacekeeping Forces to which Canada has contributed. These include the Golan Heights, Namibia, Cambodia, Cyprus and the Former Republic of Yugoslavia. (Over 50 Lorne Scots served in Yugoslavia). A number of troops participated in the clean-up activities during the Ice Storm of 1998 in Eastern Ontario, and Sovereignty Operation NANO-OK in the Canadian Arctic throughout 2007-2010. Soldiers from the regiment also participated in the Security Perimeter for the 2010 G20 Toronto Leaders Summit when, under the Royal Canadian Mounted Police, they led the Integrated Security Unit. They did not, however, interact with protests or protestors during the Summit.

The unit has also participated in a number of international training exercises in the US and the UK.

Afghanistan

The Regiment deployed over 40 soldiers to Afghanistan as part of the International Security Assistance Force throughout 2001-2012. They participated in mentoring the Afghan National Army and the Afghan National Police, Humanitarian Operations, Security Operations, and Combat Operations. This marked the first time that soldiers from the Lorne Scots Regiment became directly engaged in combat operations since the Korean War of 1950-53. The campaign honour "AFGHANISTAN" was awarded to the regiment in 2014.

The Lorne Scots Band of Pipes and Drums

The Lorne Scots Band of Pipes and Drums was formed in 1881, and is one of the oldest Pipe Bands in Canada. It is a first rate military band and has been active locally and internationally since its inception. They are currently under the direction of Drum Major Iain McGibbon CD and Pipe Major Doug Wickham. The Band plays at street parades, military tattoos, indoor and outdoor concerts, art festivals, ethnic celebrations, royal visits, civic receptions, and public entertainment. They possess a substantial repertoire of music for both Pipe Band and Combined Military Bands. They were the first Canadian Reserve Pipe Band to play at the Edinburgh Tattoo, Scotland, in 1960, and again in 1970. They have performed in the presence of Her Majesty Queen Elizabeth II, HRH The Duke of Kent, The Duke of Argyll, Governors General, Lieutenant Governors, The Prime Minister, and various Premiers. The Band has toured the United Kingdom, playing at the Tower of London, in Bury at several Gallipoli Day Memorial Services including the 100th anniversary of the Gallipoli landings in April 2015, The London Guildhall, and also at various engagements in the United States and Southern Ontario.

It is the intent of HRH the Duke of Kent to officiate at the presentation of new colours in September 2016, where "Afghanistan" will be added to the regiment's battle honours. He will also dedicate at least three memorial monoliths/columns in honour of the regiment's 150 years of service to the nation. At present they will be located in the cities of Brampton & Oakville and the town of Georgetown.

Endnotes to Chapter 21

[1] Vincent Poklewski Koziell *The Ape Has Stabbed Me* V.P. Koziell 2014 p. 13.

[2] Pre-First World War battle honours: Namur 1695, Dettingen, Lincelles, Egypt, Talavera, Barrosa, Fuentes d'Onoro, Salamanca, Nive, Peninsula, Waterloo, Alma, Inkerman, Sevastopol, Tel-er-Kebir, Egypt 1882, Suakin 1885, Modder River, South Africa 1899–1902.

[3] First World War 1914-18 battle honours: Western Front: Retreat from Mons, Marne 1914, Aisne 1914, Ypres 1914 1917, Langemarck 1914, Gheluvelt, Nonne Bosschen, Givenchy 1914, Neuve Chapelle, Aubers, Festubert 1915, Loos, Somme 1916 1918, Flers Courcelette, Morval, Pilckem, Poelcapelle, Cambrai 1917 1918, St. Quentin, Albert 1918, Bapaume 1918, Arras 1918, Drocourt-Quéant, Hindenburg Line, Havrincourt, Canal du Nord, Selle, Sambre, France and Flanders 1914–18.

[4] Second World War battle honours: North-West Europe: Stien, Norway 1940, Quarry Hill, Estry, Venlo Pocket, Rhineland, Reichswald, Kleve, Moyland, Hochwald, Rhine, Lingen, Uelzen, North-West Europe 1944–45.
North Africa: Halfaya 1941, Sidi Suleiman, Tobruk 1941, Gazala, Knightsbridge, Defence of Alamein Line, Medenine, Tadjera Khir, Medjez Plain, Grich el Oued, Djebel Bou Aoukaz 1943 I, North Africa 1941–43.

Italy: Salerno, Battipaglia, Volturno Crossing, Rocchetta e Croce, Monte Camino, Campoleone, Carroceto, Trasimene Line, Advance to Florence, Monte San Michele, Catarelto Ridge, Argenta Gap, Italy 1943–45.

[5] Source: Mr James Sibbald, the Town Mayor of Wantage.

[6] Communication from Queen Elizabeth II sent from Buckingham Palace signed Elizabeth R.

[7] Source: Colonel G.H.F.S. (Harry) Nickerson is the current President.

[8] Source: Major M.M. Davidson MVO MBE BEM is Secretary.

Notes on Sources

Except where otherwise stated, original sources are from the papers of His Royal Highness Prince Edward The Duke of Kent, located at the offices of St. James's Palace, London, including quotations from the Duke of Kent's speeches and formal addresses.

The Head Office of the Commonwealth War Graves Commission at Maidenhead, Berkshire, England, provided the research material for Chapter 20.

ACKNOWLEDGEMENTS

Lieutenant Commander (retired) Sir Richard Buckley KCVO, former Private Secretary to HRH The Duke of Kent 1961-1989, provided invaluable assistance in relation to Prince Edward's duties as Patron and President of many charities and his overseas visits, and gave a real insight into the character of his employer.

Mr Nicolas Adamson LVO, OBE, former Private Secretary to HRH The Duke of Kent from 1993-2011, provided every possible assistance.

Mr Nicholas Marden, Private Secretary to HRH The Duke of Kent since 2011, has provided every possible assistance.

Miss Patricia Lawrence MVO, former Personal Assistant to HRH The Duke of Kent 1998-2015, provided Celia Lee with every possible assistance over the lengthy period of her research, including copies of the Duke of Kent's papers.

Mrs Suzanne Casey, Personal Assistant to HRH The Duke of Kent, provided Celia Lee with every possible assistance.

Mr Damon de Laszlo DL, Chairman, Harwin plc., kindly provided the Foreword to the book.

Dione, The Lady Digby, DBE whose opinion on the chapter titled Prince Edward's Music Patronages And His Taste In Music, and her proof reading of the chapter, has been invaluable and much appreciated.

Mr John Barrett, author of *Wimbledon - The Official History*, pub. Vision Sports Publishing, 2014, 4th edition, for his most generous assistance and guidance, and proof reading of Chapter 10, Wimbledon Tennis Championships.

Mr C. Edward Guinness CVO, formerly Chairman of the Brewers Society and an Executive Director of Guinness and author of *A Brewer's Tale*, spent many hours in painstaking guidance and gave help that is much appreciated.

Mr Vincent Poklewski Koziell, author of THE APE HAS STABBED ME: A cocktail of Reminiscences, pub. 2014.

Major General (Retired) Charles Ramsay and his wife Mrs Mary Ramsay. Charles Ramsay served with Prince Edward in his regiment and they have been lifelong friends ever since. A visit to the Ramsay's home in Coldstream, Scotland, was essential to an understanding of the strength of the regimental bond.

Lieutenant Colonel (Retired) Charles Messenger, Royal Tank Regiment, later fulfilled one of the staff appointments held by Prince Edward and provided a valuable insight to the work.

Major General Julian Thompson CB OBE, provided guidance on the Falklands conflict, having commanded a brigade there during the war of 1982.

Professor Peter Simkins MBE FRHistS, formerly Senior Historian and Head of Research and Information Office, Imperial War Museum, London.

Mr Andrew Lownie, Life President of the Biographers' Club, 36 Great Smith Street, London, SW1P 3BU, literary agent for Celia Lee and John Lee, has provided insight and assistance that has been invaluable over a number of years.

The following very generously contributed professional photographs free of copyright charges and/or assisted with the photographic production:

The Honourable Mrs Sandra de Laszlo, Director and Executive Editor, The de László Catalogue Raisonné, by Philip de László 1869-1937, The de Laszlo Archive Trust: Mr Damon de Laszlo DL; Mr McKenna Forrest, Photographic Editor.

Mr Christopher Malski, member of many years of the Polish Hearth Club, South Kensington, very generously donated photographs of historic events that took place there.

Mr Andrew Hannath, member of the Polish Hearth Club, most generously provided photographic services free of charge.

Mr Hampar Narguizian provided photographs taken at an Anglo Jordanian Society event.

Miss Sarah Frandsen, provided photographs of the prize giving at Wimbledon Lawn Tennis Championship finals.

Mr Paul Strong and Ms Tatiana Roshupkina provided photographic enhancements.

A vast number of people provided professional guidance and assistance with the material contained in this book. Thanks are extended to those who so caringly and painstakingly corrected and edited draft manuscripts on each specialist subject. An enormous debt of gratitude is owed to the following charities, organisations, clubs, and individuals:

Aidis Trust: Mr Richard Bull, Fundraiser; Mr Michael Kenny, Trustee.

Anglo Jordanian Society: Miss Emma Bodossian, Honorary Secretary of the Anglo Jordanian Society.

Anmer Social Club: Mr Peter Harris, Honorary Secretary; Mr Roger Haverson, former Chairman; Mr Michael Williamson, Club Member.

Army and Navy Club (The): Major P.N. Skelton-Stroud.

Army Winter Sports Association: Lieutenant Colonel (Retired) M.K. Allen, Secretary.

Ascension Island Visit 2012: Thanks are due to Mr Nicholas Adamson, former Private Secretary to HRH The Duke of Kent for his help.

Association of Men of Kent & Kentish Men (The): Mrs Tess Robinson, Association Secretary.

BCS, The Chartered Institute for IT: Miss Lynda Feeley, Head of Press and PR. Ms Amanda Matheson, Press Officer.

Band of Brothers Cricket Club "BB": Mr St. John Brown, Honorary Secretary; Mr James Ryeland.

Bletchley Park Trust: The Lady Trumpington; Miss Katherine Lynch, Media Manager; Mr Richard Lewis, Senior Archivist.

Boodle's Club: Mr Richard Samways, former consultant archivist to Boodle's Club.

Borough Council of King's Lynn And West Norfolk: Honorary Alderman Dr Paul Richards, FSA, FRSA, Mayor of King's Lynn, 1998-2000.

British-German Association (The): Mr John Sewel Faulder, a permanent Vice-

President, who kindly provided the history of the BGA; Mr John Hobley, a Vice-Chairman; Mrs Susan Austin, Executive Secretary.

British Overseas Trade Board later British Trade International and UK Trade International: Sir Richard Buckley KCVO, former Private Secretary to HRH The Duke Kent. Mr Nicholas Adamson, former Private Secretary to HRH The Duke of Kent. Mr Nicholas Marden, Private Secretary to HRH The Duke of Kent. Miss Tricia Lawrence MVO, former Personal Assistant to HRH The Duke of Kent; Mr Michael D. Lawley, (retired) formerly an executive of Kuehne & Nagel, London and Middle Eastern specialist in shipping and forwarding.

British Racing Drivers Club (The): Mr Stuart Pringle, Secretary BRDC.

Buck's Club: Major Rupert Lendrum, Secretary.

Cambridge University Scientific Society: Mr Filip Szczypiński, President, (2012-2013).

Canterbury Cathedral: the Receiver General, and Mrs Pauline Smith, Personal Assistant to the Receiver General.

Cavalry and Guards Club: Mr David J. Cowdery, Club Secretary.

Chelsea Pensioners Appeal, Royal Hospital Chelsea: Mr John Blake, Commercial Director.

Chest Heart & Stroke Scotland: Mrs Fiona Swann-Skimming, PA to Chief Executive.

Civil Service Motoring Association: Mr Michael Tambini MA, General Manager and Curator; Mr Bradley D. McCreary, CSMA Club Archivist. Mr Peter Jones, Vice President (Former Chairman) and Club Historian.

Commonwealth War Graves Commission: Victoria Wallace, Director General; Mr Andrew Fetherston, Archivist and Records Manager; Miss Maria Choules; Records Administrator, and the staff of the CWGC, Maidenhead, Berks.

Communications And Public Service Lifeboat Fund (CISPOTEL): Ms Angela Saunders, HROD and Honorary Secretary.

Combined Cavalry Old Comrades Association: Major Paul Stretton, (retired) (former Chairman), Household Cavalry Regimental Secretary.

Cranfield University: Diane Dalgarno, External Communications Executive, The Vice-Chancellor's Office; Michèle Astley, PA to the Vice Chancellor and the Group Director of Finance and Resources.

Dresden Trust (The): Dr Alan Russell, Chairman.

Duke of Edinburgh's Commonwealth Study Conference: Mr C. Edward Guinness CVO, formerly Chairman of the Brewers Society and an Executive Director of Guinness. Mr David Ward, Trustee of the UK Fund. Mrs Libby Gawith Trustee of the UK Fund. Mr Dhruv M. Sawhney, Chairman, Triveni Engineering & Industries Ltd. Mrs Kavita Sharma, Senior Executive Secretary to the Chairman & Managing Director, Triveni Engineering & Industries Ltd.

Duke of York's Royal Military School: Mrs Amanda Baker, Marketing Director; Miss Tiffany Sausby, Marketing Assistant.

Edge Foundation: Thanks are extended to the staff for their help.

Endeavour Training Disadvantaged Kids: Mr Les Roberts, Chief Executive; and Joe Malia.

Engineering Council (The): Mr Andrew Ramsay, former Chief Executive Officer; Professor Kel Fidler, former Chairman; Richard Shearman, Director of Formation and Deputy Chief Executive Officer; Mrs Sue Brough MCIM, Marketing and Communications Director.

Falkland Islands, official visit by Prince Edward: Mr Nicholas Marden, Private Secretary to HRH The Duke of Kent. Major General Julian Thompson CB, OBE, acted as adviser on the Falklands and his guidance has been invaluable.

Freemasons' Charities (The): Miss Laura Chapman, Chief Executive and the staff of the Grand Charity for providing material; Mr Aitkenhead, Librarian for a tour and explanation of the beauty and architecture of Freemasons' Hall, Great Queen Street, London; Professor Ian Beckett for academic guidance.

Friends of the Guards Museum: see Society of Friends of the Guards Museum

Gallantry Medallists League: Lieutenant Colonel (Retired) J.R.T. Balding MBE GM.

Henley Society (The): Miss Nora Scanlon, Honorary Secretary; Mr Errol Facy, Committee Member; Mr Paul Clayden, former Chairman; Mr David Whitehead, present Chairman of the Planning Committee; Mrs Sandra Moon, Treasurer.

Honourable Artillery Company (The): Miss Justine Taylor, Archivist.

Honourable Society of Lincoln's Inn (The): Mr Guy Holborn, Librarian MA, LLB, MCLIP. Mrs Wiebke, Member Services Manager, Treasury Office.

Imperial War Museums: Suzanne Bardgett, Head of Research and Academic Partnerships; Mrs Sarah Henning, Museum Archivist; Mr Ian Carter, Senior Curator – Photographs; Mr Alan Wakefield, Head of Photographs.

Institute of Advanced Motorists Motoring Trust (The) and The Automobile Association Motoring Trust: Mr Ben Schofield Communications Manager; Miss Tanvir Nandra Communications Officer.

Institute of Export (IOE) International Trade: Ms Lesley Batchelor, Director General of Institute of Export and International Trade.

Institute of Occupational And Environmental Medicine, University of Birmingham: Professor Malcolm Harrington; Professor Johnathan Ayres OBE; Jayne Grainger PA to Prof. Jon Ayres.

Kandahar Ski Club: Mr Nick Morgan, Chairman.

Keighley & Worth Valley Railway Preservation Society: Mr David Pearson, JP MA (York) FRSA, being an expert on trains, provided both material and expert guidance.

Kent County Agricultural Society: see Association of Men of Kent

King Edward VII's Hospital Sister Agnes: former Chief Executive, Mr John Lofthouse; present Chief Executive, Mr Andrew Robertson; Matron Miss Caroline Cassels; Mr Joe Vincent, Marketing Manager.

Last Night of the Proms Krakow: Malgosia, The Lady Belhaven & Stenton.

Leukaemia & Lymphoma Research: Miss Cathy Gilman.

London Metropolitan University: Mr Peter Fisher B.Sc. (Jt.Hons), Archivist.

Lorne Scots (Peel, Dufferin and Halton) Regiment (The): Sargent (retired) Daryl Porter MBA, Regimental Association President; MCpl Chris Banks, CD Training NCO, E Coy 4th Canadian Division Training Centre, Department of National Defence, Government of Canada.

Music Chapter: Proof read by Dione, The Lady Digby, DBE, DArts(hc) D.L., Founder Chairman and Artistic Director Summer Music Society of Dorset 1963-2002; Chairman, Bath Festival, 1975-1981; Member Arts Council of Great Britain 1982-1986; Member, Music Panel; Vice Chairman: Dance Panel and Chairman of Training Committee; South Bank Board; Founder member, 1986-1990. Trinity Laban Conservatoire of Music And Dance – Edited by Ms Sarah Lebrecht, Communications Department; Adviser, Ms Susie Haywood, Media Manager; Heather Stephenson, Music Performance, Marketing, Media and PR. Royal Opera

House (The): Elizabeth Bell, Head of Press and Communications. Wigmore Hall: Mr John Gilhooly OBE, Director of the Wigmore Hall and Chairman of the Royal Philharmonic Society. Mr Jonathan Carvell, Executive Assistant to the Director.

Myalgic Encephalomyelitis Association (ME): Dr Charles Shepherd Honorary Medical Adviser to the ME Association.

National Army Museum (The): Miss Rebecca Hubbard, Head of Marketing and Communications; Anna Smith, Picture Librarian;

Naval & Military Club (The) "In and Out": Miss Sarah Sinclair, Marketing & Events Manager.

Noël Coward Society (The): Mrs Barbara Longford, Chairman.

Norfolk Club (The): the Club Committee; Mr George A. Wortley, General Manager; Mrs Janie Coppen-Gardner, Club Chairman.

P G Wodehouse Society: Mrs Hilary Bruce, Chairman, provided material and academic advice and guidance for the piece, as did Mr Tony Ring, former President of the Wodehouse Society, editor of *The Wit and Wisdom of P G Wodehouse,* Special publications and events. Thanks are extended to Mr Barry Day, author of *The Complete Lyrics of P G Wodehouse*; Sir Edward Cazalet, Committee member, step grandson of PG Wodehouse and his Literary Executer; Mr Mike Swaddling, Website editor; Miss Ellie King; Sir Terry Wogan, President of the Society; and Miss Victoria Pakenham, Sir Terry Wogan's Manager; and Mrs Virginia (Ginni) Beard for photographs.

Polish Hearth Club (Ognisko Polskie) and The Special Relationship With Poland: Mr Andrzej Morawicz, former Chairman of the Polish Hearth Club. Colonel Nicholas Kelsey OBE TD, present Chairman. Mrs Barbara Kaczmarowski Hamilton, former Chairman. The Lady Belhaven & Stenton, Club Events Organiser and Committee Member Cracow Industrial Society. Mr Juliusz E. Bogacki, present Director, Ognisko Polskie, (Polish Hearth Club) Ltd. Mr Mirek Malevski, Fawley Court Old Boys. Mr Jan Woroniecki, Club Restaurant Manager.

Restore Burn And Wound Research (formerly Stoke Mandevile): Mr Jonathon Pleat MA DPhil FRCS(Plast), Consultant Plastic Surgeon and Director of Research, Restore Burn and Wound Research. Michael Constant, Chairman, Restore Burn and Wound Research.

Royal Air Force (The): Mr Stuart Hadaway; Mrs Nicola Hunt, MOD Crown Copyright Administrator, Defence Intellectual Property Rights. Major Christopher Halsall. Mrs Christine Halsall.

Royal Air Force Benevolent Fund (The): Group Captain (Retired) Mike Neville CBE, Chief of Staff.

Royal Air Force Charitable Trust (The): Air Commodore (Retired), Tim Winstanley, former Director, RAFCT. Miss Amanda Butcher, Director, Royal Air Force Charitable Trust.

Royal And Ancient Golf Club of St. Andrews (The): Mrs Angela Howe, Director, Museum & Heritage, British Golf Museum.

Royal Armoured Corps War Memorial Benevolent Fund: see The Tank Museum.

Royal College of Surgeons of England (The): Mr Jonathan Fountain, Development Director, Development Office.

Royal Geographical Society: Mr Alasdair Macleod, Head of Enterprise and Resources.

Royal Institution of Great Britain (The); Ri Australia: Miss Kristen Dodd, Marketing and Communications Manager; Susan, Baroness Professor Greenfield CBE; Miss Emily Smith, Personal Assistant to Baroness Greenfield CBE.

Royal National Lifeboat Institution (RNLI): Mr Andrew Freemantle CBE, former Chief Executive of the RNLI. Mr Michael Vlasto OBE FRIN FNI, Operations Director. Mr Freemantle and Mr Vlasto were very helpful to the authors when they visited the RNLI Headquarters, Poole Dorset. Sir Richard Buckley KCVO. Draft checking was carried out by Mr Barry Cox, RNLI Honorary Librarian, Heritage Department volunteer. The chapter benefited greatly from the advice of Mrs Bethany Hope, Editor, RNLI, and the professional guidance provided by Mrs Tamsin Herbert, Marketing Services Account Executive, Mrs Carol Waterkeyn Editor/Review Editor, Creative Services and Miss Claire Siddons, Manager, Chief Executive's Office. Portaferry Lifeboats Branch: Mrs Eveleigh Brownlow MBE, President; Captain Edward Magee, Honorary Treasurer; Mrs Marie McGee. The detail relating to RNLI Republic of Ireland Lifeboats was proof read and edited by colleagues in Operations, Heritage and Media Team, Ireland and at HO Poole.

Royal Photographic Society of Great Britain: Mr Michael Pritchard, Director General; Mr Roy Robertson Hon.FRPS President.

Royal United Services Institute (The) and RUSI International: Dr Jonathan Eyal.

Royal West Norfolk Golf Club: Mr Ian Symington, Club Secretary.

Royal Scots Dragoon Guards Museum Trust – Project and Appeal: Major Robin W.B. Maclean TD, Curator, The Royal Scots Dragoon Guards Museum, The Castle,

Edinburgh, Scotland.

Scout Association (The): Mr Simon Carter, Interim Director of Communications; Claire Woodforde, Archives/Heritage Assistant and the Media Team; Caroline Pantling, Archive and Heritage Manager.

Sir Peter Scott Commemorative Expedition: Mr Andrew Verrall, professional birdwatcher. Mr Allen Packwood, Director, The Churchill Archives, The University of Cambridge; Miss Chelsea Carney, Archives Trainee; Miss Emily Dezurick-Badran, Superintendent, Manuscripts.

Ski Club of Great Britain (The): Beth Begg, PR/Partnership Manager.

Society For Army Historical Research: Mr Andrew Cormack FSA, military historian, Keeper of Medals, Uniforms and Visual Arts, Royal Air Force Museum London.

Society of Friends of the Guards Museum (The).

Stoke Mandeville: (see Restore).

Stroke Association (The): Mr Anil Ranchod, Assistant Director of Communications (media and special projects); Mr John Harvey, Head of Major Gifts. The authors attended an interview with Mr Ranchod and Mr Harvey on 8th October 2012, which was most helpful and informative in bringing the great work of The Stroke Association to life. The Association paid tribute to Mr Nicholas Adamson, former Private Secretary to HRH The Duke of Kent, in regard to his tremendous help.

The Tank Museum: Major Colin Hepburn (Retired), Regimental Secretary.

Travellers Club (The): Mr David Broadhead, Secretary.

Tree Council (The): The detail owes much to the literary skills of Ms Pauline Buchanan Black, Director-General and Chair of The Big Tree Plant Partnership Board, Defra Civil Society Advisory Board lead, Plant Health.

Turf Club (The): Colonel A.J.E. (Sandy) Malcolm OBE, Secretary.

Uganda visit 2012: Captain Charles Pearson, the Scots Guards, Equerry to HRH The Duke of Kent.

University of Surrey and Post Graduate Medical School University of Surrey: Ms Sam Jones, Executive Officer to the President and Vice-Chancellor, Professor Sir Christopher Snowden.

Watlington Hospital Charitable Trust: Mr Tom Holden, Chairman.

Wellington College: Dr Patrick Mileham (OW). Mr Robin Dyer, who at the time of writing 2013, was Acting Master and has done much in the way of shaping and editing the presentation of the piece on the College, and is now Second Master of the College; Mr Joshua Moses, Marketing & Design Executive.

Wimbledon Lawn Tennis: Audrey Snell, Assistant Librarian, AELTC (Championships) Ltd. Mr J.E. (John) Barrett MBE, author of *Wimbledon The Official History Of The Championships*. Mr B.N.A. (Barry) Weatherill CBE, former Chairman of the IC Council and current President of the IC of Great Britain. Mr Boyd Cuthbertson, Honorary Secretary, International Lawn Tennis Club of Great Britain. Mr Dave Malia, British Tennis Services. Mr John James, formerly LTA Secretary.

Worshipful Company of Clothworkers (The): Jessica Collins, Archivist.

Worshipful Company of Engineers (The): Mr A.G. Willenbruch, Clerk of the Worshipful Company of Engineers.

Worshipful Company of Mercers (The): Ms Jane Ruddell, Archivist, Curator, Records Manager.

Worshipful Company of Salters (The): Mr David Morris, Clerk, The Salters' Company, Salters Hall.

Worshipful Society of Apothecaries of London (The): Mr Andrew Wallington-Smith, Clerk, Worshipful Society of Apothecaries.

About the authors

Celia Lee is a military historian and biographer and is an Honours graduate of the Open University, where she studied the 19th-century novel and social and military history. She is an Honorary Research Fellow of the Centre for First World War Studies, University of Birmingham.

Celia published Jean, Lady Hamilton (1861- 1941) A Soldier's Wife, in 2001, that is the story of the wife of General Sir Ian Hamilton who led the failed attacked at Gallipoli in 1915, during the First World War, Foreword by Professor Ian Beckett. She is the main author of *Winston & Jack: The Churchill Brothers*, published privately, and *The Churchills: A Family Portrait*, published by Palgrave Macmillan New York, 2010. This book, already translated into Hungarian, is due to be published again in the Russian language by AST Publishing, Moscow, in hardback, paperback and as an ebook. The authors were invited to both New York and Budapest to give talks based on this edition of their Churchill book.

Celia has undertaken a study of work carried out by women in the Second World War and, with Mr Paul Edward Strong, runs a Women in War group. She has contributed a chapter on the work of HRH Princess Marina The Duchess of Kent as Commandant of the Women's Royal Naval Service (WRNS), to a book titled: *Women in War: From Home Front to Front Line*, published by Pen & Sword, 2012, and of which she is joint editor with Mr Paul Edward Strong.

Celia is a member of the British Commission for Military History, the Gallipoli Association, the Western Front Association, the Douglas Haig Fellowship, the Biographers Club, the International Churchill Society (UK), and the Polish Hearth Club (Ognisko Polskie), South Kensington, London, of which she is the English speaking press executive. She gives a joint talk with her husband, John Lee, titled 'A General, His Lady and The First World War'.

John Lee is well-known in military history circles as a writer, lecturer and battlefield tour guide. He has an honours degree in Modern History from Birkbeck College, London, an MA in Social and Economic History from Birkbeck, and an MA in War Studies from King's College London. He is an Honorary Research Associate of the Centre for First Word War Studies at Birmingham University.

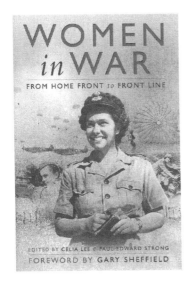

He is a member of the British Commission for Military History, the Western Front Association, the Gallipoli Association, the Army Records Society, the Douglas Haig Fellowship, the Napoleonic History Society, the American Civil war Round table (UK) and the International Churchill Society (UK).

John Lee is the author of *A Soldier's Life: General Sir Ian Hamilton 1853-1947* (Macmillan 2000; Pan paperback 2001 – described as "a model of military biography" by *The Spectator*); *The Warlords: Hindenburg and Ludendorff* (Weidenfeld & Nicolson 2005), and *Gas Attacks: Ypres 1915* (Pen & Sword 2009). He has contributed many chapters to collections of essays on the First World War. With Celia Lee, he is the joint author of *Winston and Jack: the Churchill Brothers* and *The Churchills: A Family Portrait*.

As a tour guide for more than twenty-five years, he has visited large numbers of battlefields relating to the Napoleonic Wars, the American Civil War, both World Wars, and many others besides.

16329808R00321

Printed in Great Britain
by Amazon